LEO TOLSTOY in Conversation with FOUR PEASANT SECTARIAN WRITERS

LEO TOLSTOY in Conversation with FOUR PEASANT SECTARIAN WRITERS

Edited by
Andrew Donskov

Letters compiled by
Liudmila Gladkova

Correspondence translated from the Russian by
John Woodsworth

UNIVERSITY OF OTTAWA PRESS
2019

The University of Ottawa Press (UOP) is proud to be the oldest of the francophone university presses in Canada and the only bilingual university publisher in North America. Since 1936, UOP has been "enriching intellectual and cultural discourse" by producing peer-reviewed and award-winning books in the humanities and social sciences, in French or in English.

Library and Archives Canada Cataloguing in Publication

Title: Leo Tolstoy in conversation with four peasant sectarian writers / edited by Andrew Donskov; letters compiled by Liudmila Gladkova; correspondence translated from the Russian by John Woodsworth.
Names: Donskov, Andrew, 1939- editor. | Gladkova, L. V., 1955- compiler. | Woodsworth, John, 1944- translator. | Container of (work): Tolstoy, Leo, graf, 1828-1910. Correspondence. Selections.
Description: Includes bibliographical references and index. Identifiers: Canadiana (print) 20190079738 | Canadiana (ebook) 20190079789 | ISBN 9780776627793 (softcover) | ISBN 9780776627809 (PDF) | ISBN 9780776627816 (EPUB) | ISBN 9780776627823 (Kindle)
Subjects: LCSH: Tolstoy, Leo, graf, 1828-1910—Correspondence. | LCSH: Authors, Russian—19th century—Correspondence. | LCSH: Peasants—Russia—Correspondence. | LCGFT: Personal correspondence.Classification: LCC PG3379.A2 E5 2019 | DDC 891.73/3—dc23

Legal Deposit: Second Quarter 2019
Library and Archives Canada

Copy editing	Robbie McCaw
Proofreading	Robert Ferguson
Typesetting	Édiscript enr.
Cover design	John van der Woude and Elizabeth Schwaiger

The University of Ottawa Press gratefully acknowledges the support extended to its publishing list by Canadian Heritage through the Canada Book Fund, by the Canada Council for the Arts, by the Ontario Arts Council, by the Federation for the Humanities and Social Sciences through the Awards to Scholarly Publications Program, and by the University of Ottawa.

Canada Council for the Arts   Conseil des arts du Canada

To Natalia, my beautiful wife,
the love of my life,
for her constant counsel,
unconditional support and patience

Lev Nikolaevich Tolstoy

TABLE OF CONTENTS

PREFACE

The present volume of Leo Tolstoy's correspondence with four major peasant sectarian writers constitutes an expanded edition of a volume published in 2008 under my editorship by the Slavic Research Group at the University of Ottawa. Before that, many of these letters, as well as some other pertinent materials, had appeared in a variety of publications (in either their Russian original or Woodsworth's translation) in Russia, Canada and Germany. This new edition includes an additional forty-four letters, published here for the first time in any language — twenty-two by Bondarev and twenty-two by Novikov — all newly translated by John Woodsworth, who also translated the correspondence in the earlier edition. Moreover, previously published letters and their annotations have been updated for accuracy.

Not only is such a publication historically important and useful to religious groups such as the Molokans in America and the Doukhobors in Canada, but it fills a lacuna in an area of Tolstoy studies which remains under-investigated in both Russia and the West.

As the prominent American anthropologist Ethel Dunn (2001) states in her preface to the English translation of the Tolstoy-Zheltov correspondence (and equally applicable to the other letters in this volume), "In our more secular times it is hard to realize the importance of religion in the lives of Russian peasants and even the Russian educated classes at the end of the nineteenth and beginning of the twentieth century."

The juxtaposition of Tolstoy's letters with those of his four sectarian[1] correspondents — **Timofej Mikhajlovich Bondarev** (1820–1898), **Fëdor**

1 While some groups (the Doukhobors, for example) reject the label of *sect* or *sectarians*, believing themselves to be true Christians (as Tolstoy described them), these terms are used here

Alekseevich Zheltov (1859–1938), **Pëtr Vasil'evich Verigin** (1859–1924) and **Mikhail Petrovich Novikov** (1871–1939)[2] — makes them even more significant by showing them in their original context of a dialogue, or conversation.

For many years Tolstoy sought the meaning of life, particularly in the peasantry, and learnt a great deal from his 'conversation' with them through these exchanges — not only superficial traits of their culture but, more importantly, how they thought and reflected, as members of their class, presenting what may be seen as an 'inside view' on important questions of life, death and turn-of-the-century Russian society.

The integrated correspondence presented here offers a unique insight into the minds of five spiritual thinkers as they engage in an earnest discussion on a wide spectrum of religious, philosophical and social questions, and thus should prove of significance to scholars and general readers interested in a wide variety of disciplines — Slavic studies (especially Tolstoy studies), European history, philosophy, sociology and religious studies, to name but a few.

To present the conversation in an even broader context, I briefly discuss Tolstoy's relationship with peasants in general, as well as with each of the four individual writers. In addition, I have provided a background sketch of the two major religious groups represented (which Verigin and Zheltov respectively identified with), the Doukhobors and Molokans, both of which still claim sizeable populations of followers in North America today. Members of these groups may be particularly interested in exploring a fascinating aspect of their heritage through studying the materials presented. Bondarev's Sabbatarian connection, on the other hand, did not last long and was tenuous at best. And while Novikov experimented with various sects, he remained largely without any kind of group affiliation.

All the Russian texts translated in this collection have been verified against the original manuscripts — a process that has helped fill in a multitude of lacunæ (including simple oversights by proofreaders and what could be deliberate omissions by censors) as well as correct earlier misreadings.

Note that the name *Leo Tolstoy* is the anglicized variant of the author's Russian name *Lev Nikolaevich Tolstoy* [Лев Николаевич Толстой]. Both the 'Lev' and 'Leo' variants are used interchangeably throughout the text.

Titles of Tolstoy's works (both books *and* articles) are cited throughout the text in *italics,* and in English only. See "Index of Tolstoy titles" for their original Russian titles.

in their historical sense, designating minority groups who protested against and separated themselves from the official Russian Orthodox Church.

2 The dates of correspondence with Tolstoy for each of these writers is as follows: *Bondarev:* 1885–1898; *Zheltov:* 1887–1909; *Verigin:* 1895–1910; *Novikov:* 1896–1910. It is these dates that have determined the order in which the four correspondents and their letters are presented in this volume.

I should like to express my appreciation to the L.N. Tolstoy State Museum, in Moscow; to its former director, Vitalij Borisovich Remizov, for his unwavering support; to its current director, Sergej Aleksandrovich Arkhangelov and to Vladimir Il'ich Tolstoy, director of the Tolstoy Museum Estate at Yasnaya Polyana, for providing valuable materials; to the staff of the Bogorodsk District Museum for supplying me with a number of important documents on the life of Fëdor Zheltov.

My heartfelt gratitude goes out to Liudmila Viktorovna Gladkova, who is both senior researcher at the Russian Academy of Sciences' Institute of World Literature (Moscow) and associate director of the L.N. Tolstoy State Museum, for compiling Zheltov's and Novikov's letters in their original Russian, as well as for a number of commentaries. And to Dr. Marina Shcherbakova, head of Russian Classical Literature at the same institute of the Russian Academy of Sciences, for sharing her extensive knowledge on Russian sectarianism.

I should also express my thanks to Arkadi Klioutchanski, a member of our Slavic Research Group, for his participation in the work (including his assistance in the translation of the newly published letters); and a special note of gratitude to my colleague, John Woodsworth, for consenting to render what amounts to a number of very challenging examples of Russian text into contemporary English, as well as for his assistance in preparing this volume for publication. I am also thankful to my daughter, Tatiana Donskov-Carter, for her contribution to the editing process.

Finally, I am grateful to Lara Mainville, director of the University of Ottawa Press, along with her team members, Elizabeth Schwaiger, Sonia Rheault, Veronica Omana and Mireille Piché, for suggesting and facilitating this second, enhanced edition of what should prove to be an important twenty-first-century contribution not only to Tolstoy scholarship but to the ever-growing fascination with this great writer — and the hitherto unknown peasant writers he so courageously brought to the world's attention — on the part of the English-reading public.

Ottawa, Canada
November 2018

Andrew Donskov, F. R. S. C.
Distinguished University Professor
University of Ottawa

A NOTE ON CALENDAR DATES AND MEASURES

AREA. Land area in nineteenth-century Russia was commonly measured by a unit known as the *desjatina*, equal to 1.09 hectare. This term has been retained in the text.

DATES. Before February 1918, Russia operated on the 'old-style' *Julian calendar*; by that time most Western countries had adopted the 'new-style' *Gregorian calendar*, proclaimed by Pope Gregory XIII in 1582 as a reform of the Julian one, designed to reflect more accurately the actual solar year by abolishing the date of 29 February for those centenary years not exactly divisible by 400. As a result, by the nineteenth century, the old-style calendar was twelve days behind the new style (thirteen days in the twentieth century).

For example, Christmas Day (25 December) 1898 in the old-style calendar came on 6 January 1899 according to Western calendars, while on New Year's Day (1 January) 1899 in Russia, it was already 13 January in the West.

In the year 1900, however, another day's discrepancy was added, since the day of 29 February, omitted that year from the Western calendar, continued to be observed in Russia, according to the old Julian calendar. Hence New Year's Day 1901 old style fell on 14 January new style.

The Bolshevik 'October Revolution' was named from its old-style date of 25 October 1917, now celebrated (new style) on 7 November. A few months later, at the beginning of 1918, the new Bolshevik government brought Russia into line with the rest of the world by officially switching the country to the Gregorian calendar. The old Julian calendar, however, continues to be used in the Russian Orthodox Church to this day.

The date and place of writing is shown (according to the old-style calendar, unless otherwise noted) in the heading to each letter. Any other appearance of a date, either at the beginning or the end of a letter, reflects the original writer's own indication.

DISTANCE. The most common unit of distance measurement in Imperial Russia was the *verstà*, known in English as the verst, roughly the equivalent of 1.07 km. Smaller units of measurement were the *sazhen'*, equal to 2.1 m, and the *arshin*, equal to 0.71 m.

WEIGHT. A standard unit of measurement for foodstuffs in Imperial Russia was the *funt*, which at 409.5 g was slightly less than a pound (453.6 g). Larger quantities were measured in a unit known as a *pood*; 1 *pood* = 40 Russian *funts*, or 16.38 kg.

INTRODUCTION

Leo Tolstoy, peasants, and sectarianism in the second half of nineteenth-century Russia

ANDREW DONSKOV

Russia in the nineteenth century was a largely peasant country. Demographics at the close of the eighteenth century put the population at 96.4 per cent rural and 3.6 per cent urban. A century later, according to the census of 1897, peasants still constituted 87.4 per cent of the population of the Russian Empire (Riasanovsky 1968: 263).

At the beginning of the century, the peasants were separated from the educated social classes by a deep gulf. However, the second half of the nineteenth century was characterized by feverish attempts on the part of both the intelligentsia and repentant noblemen to understand why the peasantry had been oppressed for so long, and to draw closer to them.

Some two decades before the start of the 'going to the people' [*khozhdenie v narod*] movement in 1874, Russia witnessed an explosion of literary interest in its peasantry,[1] not only on the part of so-called secondary writers, but from such notables as Ivan Turgenev, Fëdor Dostoevsky and Leo Tolstoy. Perhaps, in Tolstoy's case, this was conditioned by a general aspiration to make amends for his privileged position, as well as by a personal need to seek out a higher meaning for his own literary activity. It was Tolstoy who went on to explore the peasant theme in his works more than any other Russian writer of his day.

1 A. N. Pypin (1890–1892) notes in his *Istorija russkoj ètnografii* [History of Russian ethnography] that from 1858 to 1878 more than four thousand different works devoted to the Russian peasantry saw the light of day.

My study of this theme yielded results which have been published in a number of articles,[2] as well as in the book *The Changing Image of the Peasant in Nineteenth Century Russian Drama* (Donskov 1972), and led to the concept of a gradual evolution from mainly comic situations in the works of the classical period, through the depiction of tense landlord/peasant relations (A. N. Radishchev), to the description of the concerns faced by both peasants and all other people (N. M. Karamzin) and, finally, to the affirmation of their personal rights as human beings and Russian citizens (I. S. Turgenev, A. F. Pisemskij), which preceded the 1861 emancipation [*Raskreposhchenie*] act and the abolition of serfdom [*otmena krepostnogo prava*].

Even though the next two decades saw an idealization of the peasants in a multitude of both fiction and critical writing, in time it was 'discovered' that the peasantry were not ready to benefit from, for example, the education being offered them, and in the 1880s there appeared a series of negatively oriented works emphasizing the peasants' crudity and ignorance. This trend reached its apogee in 1897 with Chekhov's *Muzhiki* [*The Muzhiks*], which supposed that just as there was nothing to be learnt from the peasants, it was also impossible to teach them in any practical sense of the word. Tolstoy rejected Chekhov's evaluation as too limited (or, at least, applicable only to Moscow and its environs).

Tolstoy's approach, by contrast, was marked by a sense of deep respect for the peasants, combined with serious efforts to improve their lot through education, which he considered vitally important for their individual and social development. One day, however, as he attended a rural festival, he noticed how unhappy these working people actually were and promised to himself that he would assist them (*PSS* 49:81–82).[3]

And Tolstoy made valiant efforts to keep that promise. He began by easing the peasants' lot on his own estate of Yasnaya Polyana. He established personal contact with them, and ended up organizing a school for peasant children, which ran from 1859 to 1863. This pedagogical experiment led him to found the educational journal *Yasnaya Polyana*, twelve issues of which were published in 1862–1863. However, the radical and progressive ideas in Tolstoy's writings attracted the notice of the authorities, resulting in a police raid on the estate in 1863 and a confiscation of a great many of his writings and personal letters.

Over his whole lifetime Tolstoy showed a lively interest in education and considered it essential to make it available to all social classes. This thought was clearly behind the establishment (with the help of Vladimir Grigor'evich

2 For example, "The peasant in Tolstoi's thought and writings" (Donskov 1979); "L. N. Tolstoi as an editor of literature by peasant writers" (Donskov 1983).

3 *PSS* = *Polnoe sobranie sochinenij* [Complete collected works] (90 vols., known as the 'Jubilee Edition') — see L. N. Tolstoj 1928–58 in the Bibliography.

Chertkov) of the Posrednik publishing house, in 1885.[4] Over the course of at least the next ten years, he directed the firm's activity, published both narratives about the peasants and works by the peasants themselves on a wide variety of themes — from discussions on morals and ethics to economic treatises on agriculture.

By 1892, two hundred and sixty-five titles had been published 'for the people,' forty-four of them written by Tolstoy.[5] By 1905 the total output had reached six hundred titles.[6] Sales volumes, too, rose dramatically: 400,000 copies sold during the first nine months of operation, twelve million after four years.[7] The government censor sadly noted how impatient the peasants were to buy up books — not just one at a time, or from time to time, but by the cartful.[8]

The founders of Posrednik endeavoured to offer their readers something more meaningful than the commonplace examples in what was mockingly referred to as 'cheap popular' literature. Tolstoy established as his publishing goal the putting out of works which were useful, intelligent and affordable to everyone, not just to a narrow circle of the elite. Their moral content was to be in accordance with Christ's teachings.

There is no doubt that works based directly or indirectly on such principles would provoke the wrath of the state censors. In the first place, the authorities were concerned (especially after the assassination of Tsar Alexander II in 1881) about the "possible damage" that could arise from certain religious and social views presented in some of Tolstoy's works, such as *A Confession* (1879–80) and *What I Believe* (1884; banned upon publication). Secondly, by the mid-1880s, it was clear that what Tolstoy presented in his works as "useful to everyone" and "full of morality" was synonymous with his own concepts of usefulness and morality. Paradoxical though it may seem, even as he accused the intelligentsia of wilful ignorance of the peasants, as well as for using the peasant question as an excuse for abstract discussions, Tolstoy constantly used his own works as a vehicle for affirming his own moral and ethical credo as a measure of good and evil, of what was and what was not acceptable.

In his educational activity Tolstoy felt an impelling need to seek out new forms of literary creativity. First, he turned to drama, creating new plays as well as adapting his earlier works for the stage. In a single year (1886) he

4 Vols. 85 and 86 of *PSS* contain approx. two hundred letters between Tolstoy and Chertkov on problems connected with Posrednik. Some of the better-known works concerning Posrednik include Bank 1969 [Study of readers in nineteenth-century Russia]; Bljum 1979 ["Posrednik and its readers"]; Ishchuk 1958 ["L. N. Tolstoy and the beginning of Posrednik"]; Ishchuk 1975 ["On the struggle for the folk reader," Chap. 3 in *Problema chitatelja v tvorcheskom soznanii L. N. Tolstogo* [The problem of the reader in L. N. Tolstoy's creative consciousness]]; Fodor 1989.

5 See Otto 1987: 135.

6 See Lindstrom 1957: 194.

7 Ibid., 193.

8 See the 1887 report by government censor Pëtr Evgen'evich Astaf'ev (Donskov 1995b: 223–36).

published *The Power of Darkness, The First Distiller, Haggai* and *Peter the Publican.*[9] That same year Posrednik published two of his 'stories for the people' [*narodnye rasskazy*]: *God Sees the Truth, But Waits* and *What Men Live By.* This genre turned out to be handy for propagating his moral convictions.[10] These narratives, like his narrative dramas (often tailored to suit their author's moral convictions) would sometimes touch upon and try to solve a series of contemporary socio-ethical problems. Tolstoy considered the traditional dramatic form too awkward and ill-suited for didactic purposes, not to mention foreign to the kind of audience he was aiming at. His dramatic legends were filled with wise elders, recluses and pilgrims who understood humanity's failings and had compassion for human weaknesses.

These images were basically designed to show the way to attaining inner freedom and spiritual peace. The narrative dramas vividly profiled such ideas as the rejection of personal interests, contemplation of God as love, the polemic of good versus evil, selfless service to one's neighbour, the horrors of war and, above all, the rejection of resisting evil through violence.

As Posrednik's popularity grew, along with its success in spreading Tolstoy's ideas, so too grew the censors' alarm and displeasure,[11] which began to manifest itself especially at the beginning of 1886. Weekly issues of the Russian Orthodox Church's *Moskovskie tserkovnye vedomosti* [Moscow Church News] warned of the disastrous consequences of what the church considered impermissible departures from traditional interpretations of the New Testament in Tolstoy's narrative dramas — which could only lead to the spread of sectarianism. Typical of the time was a brochure published in Voronezh, in southwestern Russia, by a priest named A. Ivanov, entitled *O knizhkakh dlja naroda, izdavaemykh firmoju «Posrednik».*[12] Ivanov lambasted Tolstoy's "distortion" of religious texts and the "socialist tendencies" concealed in his apparently innocent children's fables.

Subsequent official criticism was even harsher. In February 1886 the St. Petersburg Censorship Committee banned the forthcoming publication of Tolstoy's story *The Three Elders* on the grounds that it could provoke false representations of prayer — as well as interpretations inimical to the teachings of the Orthodox Church — among the common people, for whom it was intended. The censorship board's direct attack on Posrednik also became evident at this time: L. E. Obolenskij's *Strannik* [The wanderer] was banned, and shortly thereafter the board's appraisal procedure for Tolstoy's *The Godson* dragged on for seven months, ending in a rejection in November 1886.

9 See Donskov 1988: 1–13.

10 It is curious to note that Tolstoy's efforts at morality preaching, especially through folk tales aimed at peasant readers, increased proportionately to the growing attacks on his 'tendentiousness.'

11 See Lebedev 1968 ["The Posrednik publishing house and censorship"].

12 Ivanov 1886 [On books for the people, published by the firm Posrednik]. For more on A. Ivanov, see Bazanov 1973 ["On the folk tales of L. N. Tolstoy"].

It is interesting to note that while the report of the Moscow Censorship Committee on Tolstoy's works, presented to the government at a special sitting in the summer of 1886 (see Donskov 1995b: 223–36), adhered strictly to the official position held by the church, it still demonstrated a refined and penetrating insight into the nature of the writer's fundamental religious and moral-ethical views. What was especially important, however, was that while both Tolstoy and the censors argued about what was 'useful for the people,' the people themselves were left with the role of passive observers of this polemic.

My analysis of the role of the peasantry in Tolstoy's philosophy (see my previous publications in the Bibliography) led to the conclusion that his pre-1880 writings looked at the peasants in terms of certain stereotypes: they were symbols of honesty, simplicity, naturalness. After his so-called religious crisis in 1880, more and more of his works began showing peasants learning from each other and becoming imbued with ideas corresponding to those of the author. One could say that the image of the peasant grew from merely illustrating a lesson aimed at aristocrats (and, later, peasants themselves) into a vehicle or device through which Tolstoy intended to enlighten all mankind.

In sum, Tolstoy's contribution to the portrayal of the peasant in nineteenth-century Russian literature could be viewed as an extreme expression of Russian populism, linked (by association) not only with the ideas of Christian doctrine but also with a belief in the Russian peasantry and their way of life.

It was probably most distasteful for Tolstoy to see the peasant, to whom he had devoted a significant part of his life and literary output, being embodied in such negative images in the prose and drama during the last two decades of the nineteenth century and the opening years of the twentieth. But that is what happened. Peasants were no longer uniquely endowed with the same positive qualities as before. They were denied their accustomed aura of greatness and they began to be portrayed as incapable of even approaching such a standard. The basic theme in pertinent literature was now the *unenlightened reality of the countryside* apparently deprived of any common sense and characterized by the utterly ridiculous. The peasants were being described as a drunken, lazy, ignorant mass, without any hope for a better future.

A few works appeared, however — enlightened treatises, descriptions, articles and narratives — which had been written by the peasants themselves, and which were all the more deserving of study since their authors were in one way or another connected with Tolstoy. Not only did they write under his influence, but they in turn exerted a major influence on Tolstoy's own thought.

These were the so-called *samouchki*, or self-taught writers. Tolstoy published a good many of them — either through Posrednik or through various journals he recommended them to. He was in contact with a long list of peasant authors, either as a publisher or a consultant, including F. A. Zheltov, I. G.

Zhuravov, V. F. Krasnov, V. D. Ljapunov, T. M. Bondarev, V. S. Morozov, N. A. Polushin, F. F. Tishchenko, S. T. Semënov and M. P. Novikov.

Tolstoy attracted peasant authors for a variety of reasons. First and foremost, the majority of them came from extremely poor families,[13] experiencing first-hand the challenges Tolstoy was describing in some of his works. Their often crudely crafted works touched upon many common themes: peasants being encouraged to avoid cities and their corrupting effects, since the meaning of life itself was founded on nothing if not the hard labour of the land-tiller; the vices of alcoholism and debauchery; the destructive influence of money; the evils of militarism; the meaning of repentance and obeying the old commandments, along with a number of other moral themes.

It was only natural that these writers turned to Tolstoy, an acknowledged master who had put forward all these questions himself, someone who shared their views and was always ready to hear them out, especially after he had decided to devote almost all his efforts to the peasant question. An equal influence on the peasant writers proved to be Posrednik's publications, written in a clear, simple language.[14]

Tolstoy had a warm-hearted attitude toward the peasants, supporting and encouraging them in every possible way, as confirmed by a series of reminiscences left by these writers.[15] This is brought out even more vividly in Tolstoy's diaries,[16] where he enthusiastically talks about the increasing number of peasant works coming from the people. No doubt the opportunity to get to know the peasantry better and attain a deeper understanding of them was another important factor in Tolstoy's interest in this growing group of writers since, as mentioned, peasant themes became increasingly more significant in his later works.

Tolstoy took a particular interest in writers who shared his view of the peasantry, and sharply broke off communication with those who did not maintain their erstwhile loyalty to his ideals (see Donskov 1972: 157–58). Further, Tolstoy loved to see other writers express his views. However, his artistic taste suggested to him that, often, novice writers were simply superficially imitating his works. The situation became even more complex when

13 For biographical details on these writers, see Belousov 1926 [Literary Moscow: Writers from the people], Bol'shakov 1978 [Your friend Leo Tolstoy] and Zajdenshnur 1965 [Tolstoy as editor].

14 Semënov 1912 [Reminiscences of Tolstoy] describes the impression he received from Posrednik's publications as "tremendous," and how other writers he knew experienced similar feelings. Such works spawned an unconquerable desire to write — a new phenomenon at that time. And people started writing.

15 See, e.g., Tishchenko 1903 [How Tolstoy teaches writing] and Morozov 1917 [Reminiscences of Tolstoy by a pupil of the Yasnaya Polyana School, Vasilij Stepanovich Morozov].

16 On Tolstoy's relations with various peasant authors see the following excerpts in *PSS:* On Tishchenko, 63:325–26, 425; 64:35–36. On Zhuravov, 50:145; 51:30–31; 65:233; 65:206. On Zheltov, 64:40. On Krasnov, 81:26–27. Tolstoy also corresponded with Polushin and Semënov (see Rozanova 1978: 2:609–48).

he realized that some peasant writers were pursuing selfish ends, demanding immediate compensation for their publications. Tolstoy was particularly disenchanted with authors who, having received an honorarium for their works (through Tolstoy's own intervention), quickly abandoned their land-tilling and became professional writers.

In dealing with beginning writers, Tolstoy first tried to discover not so much the talent (or 'capacity') for seeing, observing and giving literary expression to what he thought as paramount as the presence of an inner need on the part of the writer to share his thoughts with others. According to Tolstoy, an individual's thought should mature to such a degree that it begins to disturb him, to make him have doubts and regrets, to give him no peace so that he cannot help writing.[17] Whenever Tolstoy detected the absence of such a feeling, he would communicate this directly to the writer. When he did this in one particular instance, he asked the writer's forgiveness if his words gave offence, on the assumption that for an old man to lie was just as unworthy and shameful as for a rich man to steal (*PSS* 61:113). He once advised Semënov (a writer he had often assisted) to destroy a manuscript since, even though the idea contained within was good, its artistic embodiment had turned out to be poor (*PSS* 64:281).

The more Tolstoy liked a work, the more demanding he became. He paid particular attention to details, as well as to originality. He once read a manuscript by N. N. Ivanov, who described a man walking along a road in springtime, exhausted by the sun's heat, while the rooks flew contentedly overhead or sat on the edge of the road, their long beaks glistening in the sun — a detail which greatly appealed to Tolstoy. He believed that such 'trivia' revealed a writer's true talent, that all was lost without them.[18] He did not attempt to correct Tishchenko's linguistic faults, noting that he found such "inaccuracies" pleasing and contributing to an original characteristic style.[19]

In sum, what benefit actually accrued to beginning peasant writers from their contact with Tolstoy as a publisher? For one thing, they received a unique and far-reaching lesson in the creative process. A great many remarks found in a multitude of manuscripts, similar to "and further, as we mentioned before," indicate the content of the long hours of conversation spent with the great master. Even more telling are the reminiscences and notes left by the peasant authors, some of whom did go on to become professional literary writers.

Fëdor Fëdorovich Tishchenko (1858–after 1916), who was friends with Tolstoy for many years and received from him a great deal of helpful advice, notes that under Lev Nikolaevich's influence he decided not to write about

17 See Zajdenshnur 1939 ["Meetings with Tolstoy. From the diary of A. V. Zhirkevich"]: 426.

18 See Ivanov 1928: 194; Zajdenshnur 1965: 14–15.

19 See Tishchenko 1903: 11; Gladkova 2000 ["On true art (according to Tolstoy's correspondence with the peasant writer F. F. Tishchenko)"].

unusual and improbable events but, rather, to select ordinary personages and occurrences from everyday life, comprehensible to anyone. He realized that in order to maintain the reader's interest when describing commonplace events, the writer required greater skill and talent than was needed for the description of something extraordinary. Tishchenko observes that he was quite impressed by Tolstoy's remarks on his writing. All the awkward words and phrases were thrown out. In many places Tolstoy made the narrative more concise without changing its essence. The narrative became livelier, the description more three-dimensional. It reached the point where it was beyond criticism, where nothing more could be done to improve it. Tishchenko was only left wondering how he could have missed making the improvements himself (Tishchenko 1903: 11).

Much is learnt about Tolstoy's relationship with these writers through the correspondence. His letters to and from peasant sectarian writers is of particular interest, being far more extensive and complex than his exchanges with members of his own class. Like his treatises, these letters, while open to accusations of self-centredness and an attempt at self-cleansing, reveal a humanitarian willing and ready to help, expecting no reward or recognition for the efforts expended. Moreover, the correspondence is far from being a one-sided pæan of praise for the peasants; he did not agree with them on all issues, and his position on some shows change over time.

It is also noteworthy that Tolstoy's sectarian correspondents were Russians, in contrast to those of many of his contemporaries, who were more attracted to the depiction of foreign evangelists (e.g., Lord Radstock of England, or of his Russian disciples, such as Vasilij Pashkov).[20] Tolstoy was attracted, though, by certain ideals of non-Russian sects — for example, the innovative nature of the Shakers, their communal farms, their strong adherence to the doctrine of chastity, their rejection of church authority, their belief in the moral benefit of physical labour.[21]

The reforms initiated in the early 1650s in the Russian Orthodox Church by the patriarch Nikon[22] provoked major resistance among believers, ending in

20 On Tolstoy's negative opinion of foreign evangelists proselytizing in Russia, see Heier 1970, esp. Chap. 3 ("Tolstoj," 82–102); also, Heier 1971: 46–47. Such evangelists are treated in a hostile manner in *Resurrection,* for example, where Nekhljudov (decidedly, Tolstoy's mouthpiece) turns into a defender and spokesperson for the peasants and sectarians.

21 On other points he disagreed with the Shakers — e.g., the claim that one of their number, Ann Lee, was the incarnation of Christ in female form. It might be noted that some of the early Doukhobor leaders considered themselves to be an embodiment of Christ (see, e.g., Document #1895-11-01c in Woodsworth 1999a: 22–23). For more on Tolstoy and the Shakers, see Haugh 1978 and Fersen 1979 ["Tolstoy and the Shakers"]. On Tolstoy and the English Quakers, see Greenwood 1975.

22 These reforms resulted from internal divisions within the church as well as external pressure from both State and Western religious institutions. One salient example was Nikon's decree that the sign of the cross should henceforth be made with three fingers instead of two. Other examples involved modifications to sacred texts and liturgy. The Old Believers (or Old Ritualists) — i.e.,

the schism [*raskol*] which even today reverberates through Russian religious life. Over time, it led to a profusion of dissident sects,[23] in whom Tolstoy grew increasingly interested, especially following the publication of his *Confession*. The truths he discovered after *Confession* not only saved Tolstoy himself from despair but infused his whole writing activity with considerable new meaning. His sharp criticism of the anti-Christian structure of society led to a confrontation with authority and the power of the state, with the church and with his own family. The latter conflict was aroused by his outline for the autobiographical drama *And the Light Shineth in Darkness* (begun in the 1890s but not published until 1911) — which Tolstoy repeatedly called 'my drama' — and resulted in his final departure from his Yasnaya Polyana estate. As to his argument with the official church, his 'falling away' from it led in part to a rupture with many of his beloved Russian peasants, who traditionally adhered to Orthodoxy.

The critical pathos evident in Tolstoy's works strengthened the protestant, disuniting mood in the country, which was marching irrevocably toward revolution, in spite of the postulate of 'non-violent resistance to evil' and the conviction that evil could be conquered not through violence but simply through refusal to participate in evil actions. Hence his ardent support of all sorts of sectarian movements, even while realizing the limitations and disuniting influences inherent in each of them.

The text of Tolstoy's treatise *What Then Must Be Done?* (1886) includes a powerful call for moral regeneration. He wrote:

> Over my whole lifetime two Russian thinking people had a profound moral influence on me; they enriched my thought and clarified my world-view. These people were not Russian poets, scholars or preachers — they were two remarkable men who are still alive today, having lived their whole lives by the sweat of their brow — the peasants Sjutaev and Bondarev.[24]

those who did not accept Patriarch Nikon's reforms — were later divided into the *popovtsy* [priestists], who were willing to accept repentant Nikonian priests, and the *bespopovtsy* [priestless], who conducted their services and performed sacraments without clergy, holding that the reforms and the deaths of Old-Believer bishops and priests made any further ordination impossible.

23 Official statistics of 1863 indicate that the Russian nonconformists numbered 8,220,000, not including the Old Believers, who, historically, ought not to be considered 'sectarians.' See Bolshakoff 1950: 15–16; Miljukov 1972: 114–16; Heier 1970: 16–21; *Missionerskoe Obozrenie* 1896: 1 (January): 31–44.

24 *PSS* 25:386. Vasilij Konstantinovich Sjutaev (1820–1892) was a peasant thinker who shared Tolstoy's views and exercised a fairly strong influence on the writer. See Prugavin 1881a [Thirsters after righteousness]; Prutskov 1976 [The Siberian Utopia of T. M. Bondarev's Triumph of the land-tiller]; Kosovanov 1958 [Timothy Bondarev and Leo Tolstoy]. In 1882, the artist Il'ja Repin painted a portrait of Sjutaev, bearing the title *Étude*. On Tolstoy's insistence, the famous Russian art collector Pavel Mikhajlovich Tret'jakov acquired the portrait, which for a long time bore the title *A Sectarian*.

This particular passage reveals several important features in Tolstoy's thought. It begins with a reference to his lifelong preoccupation with moral questions. It suggests the exclusion of any contribution from his own class or from the clergy to his *Weltanschauung*. Tolstoy's world view drew upon the solid moral fibre of ordinary Russian peasants, whose life derived its meaning from working by the sweat of their brow. They had not only enriched, but actually *clarified* (*ujasnili*) his thought for him. This was an extremely important point for him in his so-called post-conversion period (following the completion of *Anna Karenina*, in the late 1870s) and is of utmost importance in any discussion of Tolstoy and the peasantry. It is also significant that the two peasants mentioned were both sectarians: Sjutaev was well known to Tolstoy and contemporary writers, as was Timofej Mikhajlovich Bondarev, who carried on an extensive correspondence with Tolstoy from 1885 until his death in 1898.

The word *ujasnit'* [to clarify, make more comprehensible] may be seen here as a key to understanding the development of Tolstoy's thought. It suggests the confirmation of an idea — in this case, the writer's moral stance. Elsewhere in the same treatise he writes (*PSS* 25:226):

> *The moral laws already exist*, mankind has only to clarify them for itself.... This *clarification* [*ujasnenie*] of the moral law is not only the most important, but is the only cause for all mankind [to espouse]. (Italics added)

In this connection, the image and function of the sectarians is similar to that of other peasants, both in his life and in his works, taking the form of a catalyst in the regeneration of his aristocratic heroes — see, by way of comparison, the function of the peasant Karataev in the regeneration of Pierre in *War and Peace*,[25] Levin and the peasant Platon in *Anna Karenina*, Nekhljudov and the peasant sectarian in *Resurrection*. Levin was transformed by the story he heard from one peasant about the just and meaningful life of another peasant, and he comes around full circle to the 'truth' that already lies within him. He says at the end of *Anna Karenina*: "I've discovered nothing. I've simply learned about what I knew already."

It is significant, however, that his mentor was a peasant, free of the burdensome layers of civilization. Tolstoy realized that the question of 'how

25 Like the peasant Gerasim in *The Death of Ivan Il'ich* (1886), in *War and peace* the peasant Karataev also serves as an embodiment of peasant 'collectivist thinking' in contrast to Pierre's individualism; calmness and steadfastness in contrast to moral perplexity; rural simplicity and sincerity in contrast to the artificiality and decorum of the aristocracy. In order to find any kind of solid foundation, Pierre must be complemented by someone who reflects the spirit of all people and not just one of its individual components. Pierre, whose very name represents the foreign-influenced nobility, must become *Pëtr* (pron. *Piotr*) — free, as much as possible, from the layers of 'civilization.' For him, Karataev signifies the whole of which Pierre seeks to become a part. He is especially attracted to Karataev's *roundness* (Tolstoy uses this term and its many derivatives to describe him) — an image which, like the circle, from ancient times symbolized completeness and was often used in reference to *Bozhestvo* [Deity] and *Bogojavlenie* [Epiphany].

to live' (and die)[26] which tantalized his characters of station (and himself) could not be answered through moral-intellectual discourse; the questions are 'answered,' however, on a deeper, more organic level — through the 'truth' as perceived both by himself and by his characters of nobility (which are the almost exclusive focus of his major works) through their association with peasants.

Tolstoy's interest in the sectarians, and his support of them, met with a mixed reception. Some contemporaries took his attitude to be that of a 'repentant nobleman,' seeking to atone for past wrongs toward the peasantry on the part of the upper classes (to which Count Lev Nikolaevich Tolstoy belonged by birth), while ecclesiastical critics judged Tolstoy's actions to be undermining the foundations of the Russian Orthodox Church, which excommunicated him in 1901. Others detected in them traces of anarchism, a threat to the foundations of the Russian state.

The reaction of the authorities was entirely predictable: reports, investigations, police surveillance. Nevertheless, in the 1870s and 1880s, some of Russia's intelligentsia supported Tolstoy's interest in the Russian sectarian movement; others thought that sectarian opposition to the official church could also be successfully used to form an opposition to the tsarist government. As Nikolaj Gusev noted, "many journals, such as *Otechestvennye zapiski, Delo, Slovo* and *Russkaja mysl'*, willingly published articles about the sectarians."[27]

As early as 1880, partly as a result of publications by Posrednik and other presses, and Tolstoy's personal contacts with Russian peasants and "novice writers from the people," word quickly spread that Tolstoy was sympathetic to Russian sectarians.

His affinity for and financial assistance to the sectarians notwithstanding, however, Tolstoy persistently rejected one of their principal tenets — namely the importance of group identity (i.e., the sense of belonging *to their own faith*), which inherently signified disunity and separation from those of other faiths.[28] He himself insisted (both in his correspondence and his works) on subjugating such identity to the overarching concept of the *unity of people*, which alone could provide a true motive power for the moral and spiritual uplifting of mankind.

26 See Silbajoris 1996.

27 Gusev 1970 [Lev Nikolaevich Tolstoy. Materials 1881–1885]: 53. In his diary, Tolstoy mentions the publication in *Otechestvennye zapiski* in 1881 (N°N° 4 and 5) of an article by Fedoseevets entitled "Programma voprosov dlja sobranija svedenij o russkom sektantstve" [Questionnaire for collecting information on Russian sectariansim]. On Tolstoy's interest in the Pavlovtsy sect (lit. 'Paulites'), see, e.g., Camfield 1990.

28 It should be noted that Tolstoy frequently used the term *sectarian* with a negative connotation. In his letter (N° 3) to Pëtr Vasil'evich Verigin of 14 October 1896, for example, Tolstoy criticizes Verigin's condemnation of books as follows: "To tell you the truth, your stubborn resistance to books seemed merely a sectarian habit of defending a position once it has been declared."

The Orthodox journal *Missionerskoe Obozrenie* (Missionary Review; hereafter cited as *MR*)[29] was founded in 1896, at least in part for the purpose of counteracting both the sectarian activities of Tolstoy and his followers and the widespread popularity enjoyed by the writer's teachings. It was also designed to deal with questions relating to the church's internal, anti-sectarian mission, its struggle against 'rationalistic' and 'mystic' sects[30] existing among the Orthodox population.

By the mid-1890s the church had taken upon itself the mission of active opposition to the sectarian movement, which it considered a spurious heresy and "a sad and painful phenomenon in the life of the church and society," one as dangerous to the state as to the church itself.[31]

As a result of the analysis and classification of the sectarian movement, as approved by the Second Missionary Conference, held in Moscow in 1891, under the direction of V. K. Sabler, head of the synod's chancellery, the most dangerous sects were determined to be the Doukhobors, Molokans, Stundobaptists and Pashkovites. "This is also the category where *Tolstoyism* belongs; it was not discussed by the Conference as it was only later that it was determined to be a sect all on its own with clearly expressed anti-ecclesiastical atheistic and socialistic characteristics" (January 1896: 5).

The 1860s and 1870s, in the view of many *MR* writers, had seen the culmination of the Russian intelligentsia's estrangement from the Russian people and their turning to the West for inspiration, spurred on by Alexander II's reforms.[32]

Noting that the common people were now more susceptible to influence by 'rationalist' sects than ever before, Archbishop Ambrosius of Khar'kov

29 I have selected these first five years of *MR* as the most representative example of the stand of the Russian Orthodox Church vis-à-vis not only Tolstoy, but also his followers and, indeed, the Doukhobor and other sectarian movements in Russia in the period of their most fervent activity.

30 These included both old established sects such as the Jews, the Doukhobors and the Molokans, along with newly formed groups — e.g., the Baptists and their offshoot, the Stundists (an evangelical movement of German Baptists in Ukraine, named for the *Bibelstunden* [Bible hours] they organized); the Pashkovites (named after its founder, a retired colonel, Vasilij Pashkov in St. Petersburg, uncle to V. G. Chertkov, who had become enamoured with the ideas of Lord Radstock); and the Tolstoyans. Still other groups — e.g., Khlysts (a group practising self-flagellation, otherwise known as the 'Khrists'), the Shaloputians (lit. 'ne'er-do-wells'), Mormons and Skoptsy (lit. 'castrators') — were classified as 'secret sects.'

31 *MR* January 1896: vi–vii. Witness the following paragraph from that very first issue of *MR* (viii): "History and contemporary observations show that forms of religious vacillation and freethinking conceal and sometimes deliberately serve as a cover for social freethinking, while religious belief and profession today are so closely connected with political sympathies, that there is no way politically one can close one's eyes to the religious sectarianism and ecclesiastical anarchy popular in society." (Note: references to *MR* will henceforth be designated by date and page alone.)

32 See the article by Father I. Fudel', "The basis for the struggle with sectarianism" (January 1896: 18–19): "These [reforms] resulted on the one hand in a great mental turbulence, on the other in a turbulence in the nation's economic well-being, social structure, in its religious and moral attitudes...[The people] had to come face to face with principles practised by the intelligentsia that were contrary to their own world view."

denounced what he saw as the "spirit of rejection in respect to Christian doctrines and the practical institutions of the Orthodox Church," which was inevitably fostering a general desire for "independence from all authority, including the church's." He was particularly concerned about the susceptibility of the young.

The journal expressed a specific concern in regard to the alleged attempt of *educated* sectarians (i.e., members of the intelligentsia) to control sectarianism in the public at large (*narodnoe sektantstvo*) — not just in religious matters but on the political and societal level under the guise of religion.[33] In this category the Tolstoyans were frequently the targets of specific condemnation:

> Stundobaptist propaganda has been going on among the Molokans for many years now, and in recent times Doukhoborism has been driven crazy by Tolstoyism, which has found in this sect compatible ground and is enjoying considerable success. (January 1896: 73)

The "News and Notes" column in the October 1898 issue of *MR* reported on a Tolstoyan colony in England, reproducing (in Russian translation) a description by Maurice Muret published in the *Journal des débats* of 14 August 1898. Similar reports were published on other Tolstoyan colonies, especially those that suffered a demise.[34]

The following May, *MR* featured an opinion piece by K. Popov, a priest of the Penza diocese, entitled "Plody uchenija grafa Tolstogo" [The fruits of Count Tolstoy's teachings], in which he describes his encounter with the elderly father of a young Tolstoyan at the gates of the Nikol'skij Monastery in Moscow:

> For a long time I thought about this hapless old fellow, abandoned by his son in old age without anything to live on. For a long time I could not forget about my meeting with him, his tears, his mental anguish, for which Count Tolstoy and his teachings were to blame. And what if this old man is not alone, but one of many left hapless and penniless by Count Tolstoy? I thought. How will Tolstoy answer before the Lord God for troubling the souls of inexperienced people with his anti-Gospel teachings, leading them astray from "the true path" and ruining the happiness of so many families? (May 1899: 571)

The essence of Russian sectarianism was described in *MR* by F. Titov as "*an independent attempt* — granted, a false one and occasionally even downright ugly — *an attempt on the part of our people to find the path to salvation apart from the guidance of the Orthodox Church,* independently of its teachings and

33 For one thing, the church saw as its mission a struggle not just against "popular darkness" [*t'ma narodnaja*] but against "the darkness of the evil spirits of the educated sectarians" [*t'my dukhov zloby intelligentskogo sektantstva*] (January 1897: 49–50).

34 For a thorough discussion of Tolstoyan activities in England, see Holman 1978, as well as Holman 1988 for Chertkov's Tolstoyan activities after his exile in England. On the demise of Tolstoyan colonies in Russia, England, the Netherlands and America, see Buyniak 1969.

traditions" (January 1896: 31). The 'rationalistic' sects, influenced by the liberalism of the 1860s–1880s, were considered especially dangerous. These specifically included the Doukhobors, Molokans and, above all, the Tolstoyans.[35] The Tolstoyans were described as the "chief instigators of this movement, so unfortunate for the Doukhobors," as they were "luring a peaceful population into criminal anarchy" (January 1900: 131).

By the summer of 1897 the sectarian question had become a topic of some prominence in the Russian and foreign press (even in the 'heavy' literary journals such as *Vestnik Evropy* [Herald of Europe] and newspaper giants like *The Times* of London), especially in regard to their coverage of the Third All-Russian Missionary Conference held in Kazan' that August. *MR*'s editor, V. M. Skvortsov,[36] himself parodied their tone:

> And indeed: here was a conference of some kind of priests and parish schoolteachers daring to pronounce their condemnation "on the religious--philosophical views" of Count L. N. Tolstoy, consigning this idol of liberal society to the slums of dissident sectarianism, casting a shadow on the tinsel glint of Tolstoy-worship and its cult which have blinded the false wise men of the close of our century! (September 1897: 738–39)

MR contributors were of varying opinions regarding the degree to which the origin and development of Russian sectarianism could be attributed to external causes. Titov, for example, considered them less significant than the

35 According to the Khar'kov diocesan conference, "Tolstoyan sectarianism…has the potential to become the dominant form [of sectarianism], bringing our unstable, diversified, rationalistic sects together. And this is understandable: in comparison with the others, the teachings of this sect include a lot of things of actual practical interest, tempting to the errant masses; in regard to questions of faith, the Tolstoy doctrine rouses devout people's religious feelings and offers a solution to issues of a particular community life. In doing so it unleashes and feeds the beast of political passion dormant in every crowd — passion which over the past millennium has been controlled and held in check by the benevolent power of Orthodoxy, which has fostered in the Russian people their inherent feelings of ideal citizenship, a world-renowned sense of selfless loyalty and obedience to authority" (January 1897: 47). And on the following page: "Tolstoy's numerous agents began applying particular zeal and energy to *merging all the various teachings of rational sectarianism with those of its own heretical teacher.… Sectarian heresies are gradually losing their uniqueness and originality as they unite with Tolstoy's heresy.…* Sectarians are cooling to purely religious issues *and are approaching socialist and nihilist grounds.…* Molokans, Khlysts and ne'er-do-wells have recently been lured by various itinerants into Tolstoyism and, *forsaking religion, are giving themselves over to more societal ambitions.*" It should be pointed out, however, that not all scholars include the Tolstoyans in the category of 'rationalistic sects' — see Inikova 2002 ["The teachings of L. N. Tolstoy and the Sons of Freedom in Canada"]. Note: Unless otherwise noted, italics as per the original text.

36 According to his biographer, I. S. Prokhanov, Skvortsov was "one of the most zealous missionaries" of the Orthodox Church of the time, and notorious in the foreign press as comparable to the Spanish Grand Inquisitor, though foreign sectarian publications dared not say a word against him (see November 1898: 1499). The name *Skvortsov* is derived from the Russian word for *starling*, and this was the codename sectarians used to designate Skvortsov's agents in their correspondence (see Prokhanov 1933: 84).

Russian people's own fundamental ignorance of their own faith, an ignorance which made them susceptible to harmful religious influences (see January 1896: 41–42).

That Tolstoyan ideas had been observed among south Russian Stundists suggested that Tolstoyism had built strong nests among the Orthodox peasant population of Khar'kov Gubernia, and was here displaying its socialist--communist tendencies — a consequence of what *MR* saw as its evident 'anti-Christian' character.[37]

Toward the end of the decade *MR* was once more taking notice of a tremendous well of support for Tolstoyan and sectarian ideas on the part of the press, both at home and abroad — resulting from "agitation on behalf of supposedly repressed sectarians by the liberal-progressive sector of our society, including all the devotees and followers of the sectarian teacher of Yasnaya Polyana" (January 1899: 137).[38]

The church's fears were strongly expressed in Skvortsov's report to the opening of the Tauride Missionary Conference in May 1899: "On old events and new phenomena in the sphere of sectarianism and the missionary cause":[39]

> Intelligentsia apostates…are attempting to join themselves to popular sectarianism with the aim of becoming their leaders — or, as they see it, the front line of the popular forces on the road to progress both in their religious and especially in their societal views… The societal and anti-Christian religious views of the Tolstoyans have been more accepted by the hearts and minds of both old and new sectarians than Pashkovism. Tolstoyism is beginning to penetrate more and more into the populace. The Tolstoyans' destructive influence on the Doukhobors is already known. It has also found its way both into the new Stundism and into the old Molokanism. (October 1899: 307–08)

Skvortsov went on to depict Tolstoy's humanizing of the Christ figure as undermining the only 'restraining wall' keeping sectarians from falling into outright socialism — namely, "faith in the divine inspiration of the Scriptures and in Christ as the Redeemer and Saviour" (October 1899: 310). Citing the "Rules of the Society of Educated Molokans,"[40] Skvortsov warned that such

37 This designation was evidently based on the Tolstoyan (and general sectarian) perception of Christ not as a god-figure but "a mere mortal, albeit a great philosopher and moralist (Tolstoy, however, rated higher in the eyes of the Tolstoyans!)" (February 1897: 178).

38 Singled out for particular criticism were a handful of Tolstoyans in Britain: Vladimir Chertkov, Dmitrij Khilkov, Pavel Birjukov and Ivan Tregubov — who had started their own publishing firm (Svobonoe Slovo) and were putting out their own modest periodical *Bratskij listok* [The Brotherhood Page] to slander, as *MR* put it, "both the Orthodox Church and government authority" (January 1899: 137).

39 Not the same document as Skvortsov 1899 in the Bibliography.

40 These included the following tenets:

- *Unification* of educated sectarianism on the basis of a worldview that would exclude any contradiction between religion and science, and would lead to a state of mutual harmony between them.

heresy was the fruit of a union between popular sectarianism and the "secto-phile intelligentsia," which was already leading to a state of popular nihilism and godlessness in Russia. In other words, what the church hierarchy had predicted several years earlier was now coming to pass.[41]

At the Third All-Russian Missionary Conference in Kazan', in 1897, it was determined that Tolstoyism as a sect had begun developing and promoting its teachings among the Orthodox populace and mystic sectarianism around the end of the 1880s. Its branding by the church as the "deceitful enemy not only of Orthodoxy, but also of Christianity as a whole" was based on the teaching's practical application to the ideas and the life of ordinary people.

Tolstoy himself was accused by the *MR* of creating "his own made-up Christianity…with his own gospel, commandments and other blasphemous caprices of a wild religious fantasy, unrestrained by the laws of the Divine mind or by obedience to the authority of the church" (January 1896: 60). Tolstoy's mistaken view of God (in the church's eyes) as 'people-dependent' is elaborated in an article by S. Kokhomskij in the second January 1896 issue of *MR*, entitled "The made-up teachings of Count L. Tolstoy and his arbitrary interpretation of the beginning of the Gospel of John" (in Russian).

Two years later, Kokhomskij followed up with a scathing attack on Tolstoy's *Catechism*, pointing out what he saw as inexplicable contradictions

- *Transformation of traditional* (i.e., popular) *sectarianism* through the help of such a world view.
- Membership in the society is open to *all people* sympathetic to its goals and wishing to act according to its spirit (Skvortsov asks: "And just how many sectarianism sympathizers are there among the intelligentsia or even among people in public and government jobs?!").
- In order to promote the ideas of the sect (religious, scientific, moral, economic), each member of the society must be in the closest possible contact with the sectarians — go to their meetings, hold discussions, organize local self-educational circles, set up lectures and courses on various subjects, establish libraries, etc.
- Moral and financial encouragement and support for any tendency among sectarians for primary, secondary or higher education.
- Preparation and distribution among sectarians of various mimeographed educational brochures.
- An accumulation of capital by the society on the basis of membership fees and voluntary contributions to offer financial aid to novice sectarians and for various other expenses. (See October 1899: 310–11.)

41 For example, the Doukhobors' successful emigration to Canada (beginning in 1899) prompted a group of Stundobaptists in the Pavlovka region of Khar'kov Gubernia to apply for exit permits, this time to the United States. However, according to *MR*, reports on the hardships experienced by the Canadian Doukhobors caused them to have second thoughts, fearing conditions in America might be equally difficult. Just as the Tolstoyans had taken control of the Doukhobors in the Caucasus, the Stundobaptists, in the journal's view, were continuing to win over their cousins the Molokans in southern Russia. This new attraction was considered especially dangerous: even though the Molokans had departed further from the letter and spirit of Gospel teachings than the Stundobaptists, they were still perceived as constituting a lesser threat to the established socio-political order and to the dominance of the Orthodox Church.

in the writer's philosophy of a man-based God (May 1898: 738),[42] although he admits that "Tolstoy himself in certain places, out of necessity, leans toward the true concept of God as the Supreme Being, the Creator, and the Lawgiver of mankind."

Tolstoy's socialist tendencies were further analysed by N. I. Ivanovskij, a respected theologian and distinguished professor of the Kazan' Seminary, who went so far as to say "Count Tolstoy is by no means a theologian and no interpreter of the Holy Scriptures, but an outright socialist" aiming to "reconstruct the social order" (February 1896: 8–9).[43]

Ivanovskij noted further that even though not an organized sect, Tolstoy's followers were to be found everywhere, and observed that "the same spirit of socialism has permeated other sects of the Molokan-Doukhobor type" and that "exposing all this will be a service not only to the church but to society as well" (February 1896: 11).

Well aware of the attacks on his literary and social activities (especially in the mid-1890s) on the part of both the government and Orthodox Church hierarchies, Tolstoy continued to intercede on behalf of persecuted sectarians as well as to keep in 'brotherly touch' with them through extensive correspondence.

The correspondence presented in this volume will be better appreciated in the light of brief biographical outlines of each of the four sectarian writers in turn, including the religious movements strongly associated with two of them.

42 Kokhomskij specifically accused Tolstoy of confusing love for God with love for one's fellow man, thereby limiting God to whatever love one can find in man — a confusion he saw most strongly in the treatise *What Men Live By* and confirmed in *Where Love Is, There Too Is God* — see July–August 1896: 9). The critic had a more favourable opinion of a third Tolstoy treatise, *Two Elders* (ibid., 13), but even here, he still took the writer to task for focusing too much attention on God's love and not enough on His wrath.

43 His accusations against "the most typical representative of modern socialism" (February 1896: 11) went further: "[Tolstoy], therefore, only used the Gospel texts as means of applying his personal ideal of a moral Christian life to the conditions of societal life; he wished to incarnate the kingdom not of this world in an earthly kingdom.... This has led to a confusion between personal moral, Christian ideals and the demands of the public state.... To counter Tolstoy,...one need only point out and thoroughly explain that it is impossible to apply [Gospel commandments] to the conditions of an earthly kingdom, until we have come unto the perfect man, unto the measure of the stature of the fulness of Christ (Eph. 4:13)" (ibid., 8–9).

PART I

Lev Nikolaevich Tolstoy
and
Timofej Mikhajlovich Bondarev

Timofej Mikhajlovich Bondarev

LEO TOLSTOY AND TIMOFEJ BONDAREV

> *In the Bible it is given as a law of man: "In the sweat of thy face shalt thou eat bread" and "In sorrow shalt bring forth children."*[1] *In his article on this, the peasant Bondarev illuminated the wisdom of this saying for me.*

This rather categorical declaration is taken from Tolstoy's treatise *What Then Must Be Done?* (1886).[2] The reference is to the work of the Russian peasant writer Timofej Mikhajlovich Bondarev's *Torzhestvo zemledel'tsa ili trudoljubie i tunejadstvo* [The triumph of the land-tiller, or industriousness and idleness].[3] The basic theme of this work, completed in the early 1880s, was taken from the passage in the Book of Genesis (3:19): "In the sweat of thy face shalt thou eat bread, till thou return unto the ground; for out of it wast thou taken."

This volume of Bondarev's, on which he worked for more than five years, consists of 250 questions and answers, passionately defending the thesis of honest labour as something everyone should experience. Bondarev was convinced that people sin because they do not observe this Genesitic edict, which he understood in its literal sense. His work includes no poeticization of the peasant's hard work, nor of the land he is supposed to till, nor of Nature, with which he ostensibly should live in harmony — that is, none of the themes normally associated with the idea of the land in 'populist' writers. Nor is there any indication of moral self-perfection, which Tolstoy insisted on to such an extent. All he seems to want to do is to restore the 'original law' as stated in Genesis.

Bondarev's book begins with a description of the hardships of his life. He then goes on to paint a rather hopeless picture of the oppressive state of life in the country, which, he believes, has contributed to the plight of the peasants. Still, he ranks his own world, oppressed by the higher classes, on a much higher level than these. Bondarev remarks that the welfare of the 'noble class' increases proportionately to the poverty of the 'debased class.' Two fundamental questions are raised at the beginning of his treatise (Bondarev 1906: 9):

1 Gen. 3:16, 19.

2 The statement is immediately followed by Tolstoy's admission of the 'moral influence' he felt from Sjutaev and Bondarev.

3 We are aware of abbreviated versions of Bondarev's works from publications in the weekly *Russkoe delo* (1888, N° 12–24), which included the Afterword by Tolstoy. In 1890, with Tolstoy's co-operation, a French translation appeared under the title *Léon Tolstoï et Timothée Bondareff. Le travail.*, translated from the Russian by B. Tseytline and A. Pagès (Paris 1890). It is noteworthy that an English translation [*Labour: The Divine Command*, trans. Mary Cruger] appeared in the same year, rendered not from the Russian original but from Tseytline and Pagès' French version (see Bondarev 1890). More than once Bondarev complained to both Tolstoy and Gleb Uspenskij about the poor translation of his work (he had a reverse translation done by a local translator), which included many omissions. In his final letter to Bondarev (18 September 1898), however, Tolstoy dismisses his concerns as groundless. The 200-page manuscript was also published in an abbreviated Russian version by Posrednik in 1906.

> My whole story consists in two words: first, why do you [members of the higher class] not earn your bread with your hands according to the original commandment, but instead swallow up other people's labours? Second, why do you not approve of land-tilling and land-tillers in any of your writings — religious, secular or any other — but utterly debase them?

It is impossible to achieve any kind of equality, Bondarev supposes, as long as everyone does not earn their daily bread with their own hands. If they did, he says, all religious differences would disappear of their own accord and there would be only one religion on the Earth, uniting people in an indestructible brotherhood.

He realizes, of course, that not everyone can be a peasant under existing circumstances. Still, he insists that social conditions, as well as social morality, would be significantly improved if every member of the higher class spent at least forty days a year working on the land, "earning his own bread."

In an appendix to his main 'sermon,' he proceeds to devote thirty-two mini-chapters to developing his fundamental ideas and introduces the notion (which later becomes the subject of several of the letters he exchanges with Tolstoy) that the commandment on labour is higher than the commandment on love — that is, that "love without labour is dead." The extended quotation which follows is typical of Bondarev's arguments (Bondarev 1906: 52–53):

> Here is proof of this: I have encountered the celebrating of love for one's neighbour at every step, in all sorts of writings. Love is exalted in all faiths and peoples, even among savages. Love is praised in all languages and dialects, and celebrated in a host of proverbs and sayings. Preachers' tongues are already growing weary of praising love.
>
> Now I ask you: are there any fruits and results in the world from all these praises and sermons about love for one's neighbour? None at all. They will not feed the hungry, nor give drink to the thirsty, nor clothe the naked, nor help the poor, nor show mercy to the widow, nor do good for the orphan, etc., etc.
>
> Why is this love not respected? The answer is simple: because it is a great but one-sided virtue. While labour has taken love into itself, love has not accepted labour as a part of itself. Love without labour is like a person without a head — indeed, it is dead. This is why love is a one-sided virtue.
>
> I offer the following example as even more convincing proof of what I have said: delete and erase all the places in Scripture that focus on love for one's neighbour, and in place of those insert an explanation of this law, that is, "In the sweat of thy face shalt thou eat bread." Don't say a word about love, but bring this to the attention of everyone. And you will find that in just a short time, a single day even, every person will find themselves drawn willy-nilly to loving their neighbour, because the root of its teaching is in in bread and in the grain farmer. By contrast, idleness and luxury are the chief foes and detractors of this love for one's neighbour.

And so, I would ask you, my readers, to fix this word in your memory and write it on the tablets of your heart,[4] that labour which involves honouring this law is the head of love. This labour is strong enough without love — that is, without any preaching about love — it is strong enough to put the Universe on the highest level of worthiness before God, while love without labour is not strong enough to do that, as we already indicated earlier, because true and genuine love is hidden in labour, while love without labour is dead (people may love and respect their neighbour, while idleness is still the fruit of their labour). I said it earlier and will say it again, that preachers are weary of wailing, their throats have gone dry, their tongues have become ill in preaching love, and what is the use of it? There is no use at all, anywhere in the world.

If there were love in the world, would twenty-four million people be handed over to the unrestricted power of the landowner, as recently happened with us? If there were love, would all the fertile lands be handed over to those same landowners — landowners who wear kid gloves — as a possession in perpetuity, while the people (and even more insultingly, young children) are virtually one step from death by starvation for lack of land? In the meantime, these landowners sell their own land (which they supposedly created themselves, along with heaven and earth, without God, and so claim it as their own property) to those poor people at a costly price, and then go lose their money playing cards or waste it in some other fashion. See how great the love for one's neighbour is out there?!

Behold, I have given you," said God, on the sixth day of His creation, "Behold, I have given you every herb bearing seed."[5] The whole universe, it seems, is not obeying His command. It doesn't want to sow seed but has dumped the whole burden on the shoulders of a poor soul who is not able to defend himself. And it has taken the fertile lands away from him and handed it in perpetuity to kid-gloved landowners, and named it their property — that is, the landowner who never works a day in his life. See how great your love for your neighbour is, which you preach to us, and not to yourselves!

Do not my arguments ring true — namely, that love without labour is dead, while labour performed in honour of this law is alive even without love? Because love is hidden in labour — that is its home, its place of residence. Love without labour is like a body without a soul. Only this law is alive, but not for everyone, only for those who do its will, as well as for those who, with all their hearts, desire to do its will — that is, to work, but who have no opportunity to work.... As for love for one's neighbour, there's nothing to say here, either.

Some of Bondarev's still unpublished works are housed in the L.N. Tolstoy State Museum in Moscow. For example, *Pervorodnoe pokajanie* [Original repentance], *Gordiev uzel* [The Gordian knot], *O ljubvi k blizhnemu ot nachala veka na svete nebyvaloj i ne budet* [On love for one's neighbour, which has been unknown on earth since time immemorial and will remain unknown], *Spasenie ot tjazhkoj nishchety* [Salvation from burdensome

4 See 2 Cor. 3:3.

5 Gen. 1:29.

poverty], *Pamjatnik* [The monument] — all of these involve the same questions as are presented in *Triumph of the land-tiller*, but they cannot be considered as significant as his basic work.

Bondarev's treatise has evoked many controversial questions among the post-reformist Russian intelligentsia. These questions, and their solutions, need to be investigated on the basis of this 'original law,' going back to its original formulation. This means the restoration of justice and morality and the achievement of both personal happiness and happiness for all people.

As a member of the Sabbatarian sect[6] (which he later turned away from, maintaining his customary sectarian intransigence), in 1867 Bondarev was exiled to a remote Siberian village in the southern part of Minusinsk region of the Bejskaja Volost.[7] Upon arriving there with his wife and children, he began promulgating his ideas on the necessity of tilling the land, and zealously worked on his 'sermon.' Life was doubly complicated for him. Some peasants deemed him obsessed with an *idée fixe,* while educated people saw him as a 'renegade of the dark milieu.' He himself, in trying to come to terms with such a state of affairs, supposed himself to be a 'great martyr.'[8] The authorities' refusal to allow the publication of his life's magnum opus, along with the appearance in the press (thanks to the collusion of such well-wishers as Gleb Uspenskij and Leo Tolstoy) of abbreviated excerpts of his essays, increased the feeling of loneliness and disappointment on the part of this man who was already being torn apart — both physically and morally. The full text of *Triumph of the land-tiller* is still awaiting its publication.

Tolstoy showed interest in Bondarev's works, and, quite uncharacteristically, took the initiative in establishing their acquaintanceship. Their correspondence, which lasted thirteen years, began with Tolstoy's first letter to Bondarev, in 1885. Tolstoy had taken a special interest in Bondarev the previous year, following the publication of Uspenskij's (1884) article "Trudami ruk svoikh" [By the works of their hands] (see Prutskov 1976: 136–37) in *Russkaja mysl'*, which was written in part under the influence of Bondarev's treatise, and requested the Minusinsk Museum to send him a copy of the manuscript.

6 Bondarev was a Sabbatarian [*Subbotnik*], not a Molokan as Tolstoy and some other critics had supposed. In a letter to Gleb Uspenskij in the early 1890s Bondarev wrote: "How come you've taken to calling me a Molokan? Did you get that from my manuscripts? No way!… I never have been one and never shall be!" (Institut russkoj literatury, n. d., G. I. Uspenskij archive).

In the nineteenth century the Molokans split into the *Subbotniki* (who observed Saturday as the sabbath) and the *Voskresniki* (who worshipped on Sunday — the name is derived from the Russian word for 'Sunday'). Many Sabbatarians considered themselves to be "the New Israel" and rejected the divinity of Jesus Christ. Bondarev was a member of the sect during his military service, before his exile to Siberia in 1867. He went through the Jewish rite of circumcision and adopted the name of David Abramovich.

7 *Bejskaja Volost* — is now part of the Bejskij Rajon of Khakassia in south-central Siberia. For biographical dates, see Belokonskij 1905, Shokhor-Trotskij 1913 and Gusev 1970: 428–50.

8 For additional details on Bondarev's life, see Litvinova 2004 ["The triumph of the land-tiller: The Siberian peasant Timofej Bondarev and Count Leo Tolstoy"].

After receiving it from a certain V. S. Lebedev, Tolstoy, in a return letter, noted (*PSS* 90:257):

> Yesterday I read this manuscript to our family circle. After the reading, everybody got up silently and left in embarrassment. It seems all too familiar, but it has never been so simply and clearly expressed, without the superfluity which tends involuntarily to creep into our intelligent discussions.
>
> I am very, very grateful to you for sending me this manuscript. It has made a huge impression on me and will have a huge influence on my work.... I want to write [Bondarev], but if I don't get around to it, tell him that there is someone, namely me, who is in complete agreement with his teachings, without reservation, and desirous of devoting the remainder of my life to persuading people of it in both word and deed.

That same day, Tolstoy wrote to L. D. Urusov about his impressions of Bondarev's work: "Surprisingly forceful. There hasn't been anything like it said by the whole science of economics" (*PSS* 63:275). And in a letter to V. G. Chertkov he briefly referred to it as "Surprisingly true and forceful" (*PSS* 85:242). From that moment on, Tolstoy made every effort he could to get Bondarev's essay published,[9] assist in its distribution and refer to it in his own works, along with his correspondence with Bondarev, which lasted right up until the latter's death in 1898. While some of both correspondents' letters have been lost, we still know of eleven of Tolstoy's letters to Bondarev, and twenty-three from Bondarev to Tolstoy.

The whole thirteen-year correspondence is permeated with feelings of mutual love and respect. Here are several examples (from Bondarev):

- "The one and only sincere friend I have in the whole world is Lev Nikolaevich" (1 December 1885).
- "The only friend of my heart and soul in the whole world is Lev Nikolaevich" (9 September 1891).
- "...soul of my soul, Lev Nikolaevich" (31 August 1891).
- "Your[10] letter — among us old folk, it is simpler and more decent to write to each other using the familiar rather than the formal form" (25 August 1895).

9 Tolstoy made considerable efforts to distribute and publish Bondarev's works. In a letter to Bondarev (see Letter N° 4 herein), he wrote: "I made copies of your sermon for many of my friends. I am sending it by today's post to St. Petersburg, to the journal *Russkoe bogatstvo*, and am making every effort to have it printed the way you want, without any additions or deletions" (*PSS* 63: 332). On 26 March of the same year he wrote: "I often read your manuscript to my acquaintances." In another preserved letter of Tolstoy's from August 1887 (published in *Jasnopoljanskij sbornik* 1968: 176–77), it is evident that Tolstoy edited (or rearranged passages in) "Triumph of the land-tiller" before forwarding it to a wealthy benefactor by the name of K. M. Sibirjakov, who had provided funding for its publication abroad.

10 *Your* — in Russian, Bondarev here uses the familiar form *tvoe* (instead of *Vashe*), similar to *ton* (as opposed to *votre*) in French.

And examples from Tolstoy's letters:

- "Esteemed friend and brother, Timofej Mikhajlovich" (1–20 [?] March 1886).
- "Dear friend, Timofej Mikhajlovich" (19–26 August 1895).
- "I embrace you as a brother, [signed] Lev Tolstoy" (12 November 1896).

Tolstoy dedicated two articles to Bondarev: "Industriousness, or the triumph of the land-tiller" (*PSS* 25:463–75) and variations (ibid., 656–58); and "On T. M. Bondarev. For S. A. Vengerov's Dictionary" (*PSS* 31:69–71). A whole series of notes in Tolstoy's diary, frequent references to Bondarev's writings in his correspondence with Russian writers and, finally, his many requests to government officials on Bondarev's behalf — all testify to Tolstoy's serious and ongoing interest in this peasant 'kindred spirit.'

Here are some excerpts from Tolstoy's diary and letters:

- "After our departure yesterday I decided to have Bondarev's article translated into English.... Ask Semevskij to send me a corrected copy of Bondarev for translation." (Letter to P. I. Birjukov, 2 February 1888)
- "Bondarev originally wanted to publish in *Russkoe delo*, but now he is hesitating." (Letter to P. I. Birjukov, 29 February 1888)
- "I am very glad...that you understood the idea behind Bondarev's article so accurately, and have so taken it to heart." (Letter to S. T. Semënov, 2 June 1888)
- "The other day I received from Paris a translation of Bondarev's article with my Foreword and the translator's Foreword, under the title "Le Travail." The book came out very well, and I think it will be helpful to people." (Letter to G. A. Rusanov, 30 June 1890)
- "Bondarev's 'Le Travail' is a marvellous book." (Diary, 29 June 1890)
- "...there is a society in America which protests land ownership and favours the organization of labour, with questions and expressions in sympathy with Bondarev's book." (Letter to N. N. Ge Jr., 22 February 1891)
- "Votre appréciation de Bondareff est tout à fait juste." (Letter to Charles Gide, 3 March 1892)

Tolstoy's letters, of course, have already been published in their original (in *PSS*), but with many glaring inaccuracies, which have here been corrected. Also, by being integrated in this volume with Bondarev's letters to Tolstoy, they acquire even greater significance, enhancing the continuity and immediacy of their dialogue.

The basic theme underlying their correspondence is a discussion of Bondarev's treatise, along with the possibility of its publication. In addition to this, there is a discussion of a wide range of burning social problems and religious questions of the day.

Tolstoy is in basic agreement with Bondarev's point of view on the corruption of government officials. Both are extremely critical of the upper classes. Both condemn the narrow-mindedness and intolerance of the church authorities. Both openly declare their opposition to militarism.

Tolstoy and Bondarev are also linked by their common concern for the problem of landless peasants. As a writer, Tolstoy had long been interested in this question, and continued his involvement until the end of his life. Observe the importance he attached to it throughout his play *The Fruits of Enlightenment* (1890–91) — for example, in the pleading of the third peasant (*PSS* 27:118–19):

> Have mercy, father. Our land is small. Without land we're lost! How can we live without land? There's not even enough room for a chicken, let alone cattle, you know, and there's nowhere for them to run loose. (Bows.) Do not sin, father! (Bows.)

Tolstoy speaks further about this "Do not sin," as well as the importance of land for the peasants, in his letter to Bondarev of 23 June 1894, in which he outlines the gist of American political economist Henry George's plan to liberate the land "from its devourers, or, rather, to liberate the workers from slavery due to ownership of the land by those who do not till it…"

In his letters, Tolstoy repeats time and again that the labour of land-tilling is a prerequisite for a moral, happy and joy-filled life on the earth. Bondarev, in turn, frequently promotes the idea that working for one's daily bread is the fundamental *religious* law of life. In his letters to Tolstoy, Bondarev comes across as a most colourful figure. This Russian peasant is unshakeable in his convictions, yet at the same time foreign to his own milieu by virtue of his unusually sharp and penetrating analytical mind and the logic of his arguments.

Having been deprived by his birth of a right to education, Bondarev's letters show a passionate aspiration toward learning. Like other independent sectarian thinkers, he was persistently persecuted, yet he was armed with an unquestionable knowledge of the Bible. All this made Bondarev a subject of lively interest among writers and thinking people in Russia concerned about the situation of the Russian peasantry.[11]

11 It was not only Uspenskij who showed interest in Timofej Bondarev's writings — see Kosovanov 1958: 18. In a letter to Tolstoy of 7 May 1886, the novelist N. N. Zlatovratskij (who conveyed Bondarev's manuscript to Tolstoy through M. A. Shmidt) wrote (Rozanova 1978: 1:198):

> Much esteemed Lev Nikolaevich,
> I received the manuscript from Mrs. Shmidt, and thank you for it with all my heart. Its impression still lingers with me to this day. In my opinion, this is an extremely important document. In any case, forgive me for being so bold as to tell you this. You have long given it a thousand-times better appraisal than I ever could. *[continued on next page]*

The Russian populist writer Nikolaj Nikolaevich Zlatovratskij, for example, shared Tolstoy's attraction to Bondarev's ideas, especially since they expressed in a convincing and timely manner the 'inner point of view' — that is, the point of view of the peasants themselves. However, they had each come to a similar conclusion independently of Bondarev. Hence, Tolstoy found himself obliged to defend himself against accusations of plagiarism from Bondarev in a letter to Feliks Shrëder, dated 21 May 1893 (*PSS* 66:335–36):[12]

> ...in "What Then Must Be Done?", in my eagerness to cite a striking example of the insignificance of any influence on me by scientific literature, I mentioned somewhere that all my life not a single piece of writing exerted as much influence on me as the thoughts of two barely literate peasants. This expression was not only interpreted literally, but people took it as a confession that I had borrowed from Sjutaev and Bondarev.... It's not that I would be reluctant to consider myself the follower of a peasant — I have nothing against that, and I would much prefer to be considered the follower of a peasant than any school touting itself as 'scientific' — but it would seem strange, to say the very least, to borrow thoughts from a pupil when one has before one the teachings of the master [i.e., Christ].

This same thought was expressed in a somewhat different form by Zlatovratskij in his letter to Tolstoy of 24 August 1886, where he mentions the influence of Bondarev's work on his world view (Rozanova 1978: 2:199–200):

> Much esteemed Lev Nikolaevich,
>
> With all my heart I thank you for your dear, kind letter. I am immeasurably glad that our common aspirations are becoming more and more evident. And what should cheer and impress me the most about Bondarev, but the way he reflects, with such impressive force, the mighty growth of the consciousness of the common people, and in the very direction my own consciousness and my vague, instinctual impulses — erroneously, perhaps, but irrevocably in their fundamental aspects — have been leading me. I was cheered, too, by how Bondarev has confirmed for me much of what I myself saw and felt before — again, perhaps not with the requisite level of confidence — when I encountered the 'soul of the people,' expressed either in the languor of the proletariat or the 'foundations' of the land tiller/commoner.
>
> But what increased my energy and lifted my spirits even more was the premonition of that exalted 'creative' moment when all that sincerely feel and think in Russia are joined together by a feeling of united common sympathies and a united fundamental solution to all the problems that perplex and alarm us.

I shall allow myself to simply remind you of your intention to write a Foreword. Would you please be so kind as to advise me whether you are still thinking of acting on this and how soon — or have you had second thoughts?

I shall probably be here until 15 May.

Please do not forget about our Sbornik [Collection], or us.

I wish you the very best.

12 Cf. the quotation from Tolstoy's *What Then Must Be Done?* above.

> And what can better and more compellingly confirm this than the fact of a simultaneous and alarming state affecting all our social levels and classes on the one hand, and at the same time the impulse of consciousness tending in a single direction — with either you ('standing on high') or Bondarev ('standing on the threshold'), or with us, *raznochintsy*, tortured by pangs of despair in that horrid 'mediastinum' between the higher and the lower.

The full extent of the impact of Bondarev's ideas on Tolstoy still awaits objective analysis. Tolstoy's interest in this thinker, who was for him an inexhaustible font of inspiration and self-affirmation, could undoubtedly serve as a point of departure. There is probably no point in examining their correspondence for signs of one influentially dominating the other.[13] It would be more worthwhile concentrating our attention not on the similarities, but rather on the differences in their ideas, as well as on the human qualities which attracted them to each other — that is, on all that mutually enriched and stimulated their thought.

Again and again Tolstoy comes back to Bondarev's ideas. In 1904, while working on *A Cycle of Readings,* Tolstoy includes in one of his "Monthly Readings" sections an excerpt from Bondarev's work, accompanied by an article Tolstoy wrote about him in 1895. In 1906, he once more mentions Bondarev's name in a diary entry (*PSS* 55:212):

> It has recently become abundantly clear that the lifestyle led by the land-tiller is not just one of various lifestyles, but is life itself, just as the Bible is life itself — the only life of humanity which is capable of bringing out the full range of the highest human qualities. The main mistake in the structure of human societies — one which eliminates the opportunity for any kind of intelligent structure of life — is that people want to set up their society without a land-tilling life, or in such a way that the land-tilling lifestyle is only one (and the lowest) form of life. How right Bondarev is!

All this attests to the correctness of the assumption that the two thinkers 'complemented each other,' as confirmed in Tolstoy's letter to Bondarev of 26 March 1886:

> I read your lengthy manuscript and addendum. Both are very good and completely true…I am in agreement with everything written therein, and I myself am writing only on this subject, albeit from a different point of view.… I agree with you that the first law is "In the sweat of thy face shalt thou eat bread," but to prevent this law from being broken, a second law must also be observed: "Resist not evil."

And Tolstoy goes on to say:

13 See Kosovanov 1958: 26–28.

> In you I have found a strong helper in my cause. I hope you will also find a helper in me. We have a common cause.

It should be noted that Bondarev's work proved very timely for Tolstoy. It appeared in print just at the time when the writer was especially troubled by questions concerning the peasantry, hard labour, injustice, simplification of one's lifestyle and the problems associated therewith. All these questions arose out of a sense of deep dissatisfaction which the writer experienced in regard to his social class, even more in regard to himself.

The land question, of course, was something that interested Tolstoy throughout his lifetime. He constantly approved of the many publications on this question put out at an affordable price by both the Posrednik and Derevenskoe Khozjajstvo publishing houses, under the editorship of Ivan Gorbunov-Posadov. For example, the following 'catalogue' appeared on the cover of Bondarev's *Triumph of the land-tiller* (published by Posrednik in 1906, as noted, in an abbreviated version):

1. Prof. P. Kostychev. Obshchedostupnoe rukovodstvo k zemledeliju [Easy--step guide to land-tilling]. 3rd ed. Price: 50 kopeks.
2. ——. O bor'be s zasukhami [On coping with drought]. Price: 20 k.
3. A. Zubrilin. Kak poluchit' bol'shie urozhai khlebov pri nedostatke navoza [How to reap big harvests with an insufficient quantity of manure]. Price: 6 k.
4. ——. Kak uluchshili svoe khozjajstvo krest'jane [How the peasants have improved their living standard]. 2nd ed. Price: 2 k.
5. ——. Kakuju pol'zu prinosit travosejanie i kak ono ustraivaetsja na krest'janskikh zemljakh [Benefits of fodder-grass cultivation and how to establish it on peasant lands]. 3rd ed. Price: 4 k.
6. ——. Lën i ego obrabotka na volokno [Flax and its processing into fibre]. With illustrations. Price: 4 k.
7. Prof. Timirjazev. Nauka i zemledelie [Science and land-tilling]. Price: 10 k.

BOOKS ON THE LAND QUESTION

L. N. Tolstoy. Velikij grekh [A great sin]. (On people's need for land.) Price: 3 k.

——. Letter to a peasant on land. Leaflet. Price: 1/2 k.

Henry George. Selected speeches and articles. (On the land question and the raising of people's living standards.) Trans. from English by S. D. Nikolaev. 3rd ed. Price: 75 k.

S. D. Nikolaev. Velikij borets za osvobozhdenie zemli [A great fighter for liberation of the land]. (The life and teachings of Henry George.) Price: 10 k.

P. A. Kropotkin. Zemledelie, fabrichno-zavodskaja promyshlennost' i kustarnye remesla i promysly [Land-tilling, factory industries and cottage handicrafts and trade]. With an English translation by A. N. Konshin. 2nd ed. With tables and illustrations. Moscow, 1904. Price: 80 k.

STORIES AND VERSE ON LAND-TILLING

L. Tolstoy. Skazka ob Ivane-durake [The Tale of Ivan the Fool]. Price 1 1/2 k.

——. Zerno s kurinoe jajtso [Chicken-Egg-Size Grain]. Price: 1 1/2 k.

Postupaev. U zemli i u kotla [On the land and at the cauldron]. Poetry. Price: 25 k.

Indeed, Tolstoy's world view was considerably enriched by Bondarev's ideas on land and on the absolute necessity of physical labour in the life of every individual. It imbued his approach to the question with an almost religious fervour.

TOLSTOY AND BONDAREV: LETTERS 1885–1898

N° 1. L. N. TOLSTOY ❧ T. M. BONDAREV
15–20 July 1885. Yasnaya Polyana.[14]

Timofej Mikhajlovich!

Your manuscript was delivered to me the other day — an abbreviated outline of your teachings. I had read some excerpts earlier and was quite struck by the impression that all this is right and well set forth, but reading your manuscript gave me an even greater delight. What you say is sacred truth and what you have set forth will not be for naught; it will expose people's falsity. I shall try to publish your article and I myself am trying and shall continue to try to clarify the same things. It is the duty of people who have recognized the truth to share it with others and put it into practice; as to whether they will see the fruits of their labours, God only knows. Moses never managed to enter the Promised Land, but he led the people to it, and didn't leave [to chance] anything that was necessary to get the people there.

Nothing can be done through either the Minister of Internal Affairs or the Tsar, even if he were to listen to you; in any case, there's no use trying. The government compels people by force to do what it deems necessary; but people should fulfil God's primal law not through force, but by their own free will. We need to expose people and call them to repentance, as did Christ, and then they themselves will come to the truth. This is not the work of a moment — it takes ages, but neither do trees grow overnight, and yet we plant and nurture them, while others (not us) will expect to reap their fruits.

In my opinion, man cannot put his mind, or his word, to greater use than to learn God's law and to explain it to himself and others and put it into practice, and help others, too. Matthew 9:37.[15] The harvest is great, but the workers are few. Ask the Lord to send (i.e., multiply) workers. The harvest is large and can't be reaped by one person alone, but [one person can] work his own small plot and not leave behind any 'goat' (i.e., *prozhnivo*), as they say here in Tula.

14 This letter was originally published in *PSS* 63:276–77. Two variants have been preserved: N° 23 (draft) and N° 34 (fair copy); the latter is considered the original. In 1894, a copy machine was installed at Yasnaya Polyana (see Gladkova 1994: 153–66), which Vladimir Chertkov had brought from England. Before sending, the letter was copied onto moist, thin paper, which produced an imprint, as with several other letters. Tolstoy's first letters published in the Jubilee Edition (*PSS*) were from the Chertkov archives, but these copies were incomplete, without salutation or date, sometimes with gross errors and gaps. In 1989, the L.N Tolstoy State Museum received *full* and *more correct* copies from the Minusinsk archive, made at some point from original copies, in beautiful scribal handwriting by someone in Bondarev's circle of acquaintances on large sheets of paper compiled into a notebook with sewn binding. This necessitated major corrections in Tolstoy's first letters in *PSS*. ❡ Annotation on the copy: "Received 10 August [18]85."

15 Matth. 9:37 — "Then saith he [Jesus] unto his disciples, The harvest truly is plenteous, but the labourers are few" (English Authorized Version, also known as the King James Version).

If [only] everyone did his own work, the Lord's harvest would be reaped, and He would leave no good worker behind. Only one shouldn't bury one's *talent* in the earth, but do the will of Him that sent us. And the will of Him that sent us is this: that everyone should first and foremost earn his bread by the sweat of his brow, and this should be explained to people, and they will and do understand it, because they are exposed by their conscience.

I wish you success in your endeavour, which is my endeavour, too, and thank you for your writings. I find them very useful and joyful.

Lev Tolstoy

Nº 2. T. M. BONDAREV ❧ L. N. TOLSTOY

October 1885. Village of Iudino.

Esteemed Lev Nikolaevich.

It is with a great feeling of gratitude together with joy that I received your letter of 8 September, which you sent me in mid-August 1885.[16] With my very limited intellect I don't know where or how to begin or finish expressing my gratitude for your most respectful reception of my sermon. But as long as my eyes are closed by an everlasting gloom, I shall implore the judgement of heaven to vouchsafe to you blessings both temporal and eternal.

Now I would ask and implore you, Lev Nikolaevich, to kindly send my sermon to an editorial office for publication. Please put my full name and residential address and send me two copies. I need to send one home to Russia, and I shall pay you whatever it costs. And another thing — publish my articles without any additions or omissions. However, if you find it appropriate to add anything, place it above or below my text with reference to my articles.

Lev Nikolaevich, you are in possession of the abridged version of my manuscript.[17] I know that that contains only one fifteenth (or less) of my proofs. Besides, it has no beginning or ending. I began this discussion of mine with the fall of Adam, but I was not silent either about Eve's crime, and introduced there some persuasive arguments to the effect that before their crime in Paradise, before Cain, many people were born, from which descendants Cain took himself a wife and with these people Cain built the first city on the Earth. And all this is justly and convincingly proven, and no one has the right to contradict it. I have many, many such proofs of this original law, which none before have heard. I wrote 250 articles[18] in the course of six months, whereby

16 Reply to Tolstoy's letter of 15–20 July (*PSS* 63:276–77; see Letter Nº 1).

17 After completing his work, Bondarev sent the manuscript to the Minusinsk Museum, from where, in all probability, it was forwarded to Gleb Uspenskij (1884), author of the above-mentioned "Trudami ruk svoikh" [By the works of their hands], published in *Russkaja mysl'*. Apparently, Tolstoy had received the manuscript in an already abbreviated form.

18 As indicated in the Introduction, Bondarev wrote his composition (or 'Sermon,' as he himself called it) in the form of questions and answers — about 250 questions and corresponding

my 'little house' received a significant boost, as I worked not without a touch of guile. And all these arguments I took exclusively from the Antediluvian period, not going into later texts. But there is nothing said of that in the abbreviated version you have.

As for sending you my complete manuscript, I cannot do that, or I shall be left with nothing. Neither do I have the strength to write a new one for you, since my family consists of but four workers — my wife and I, who are 65 years — what kind of workers can we be? — and our son and his wife, along with their three small children. I am a slow writer, I would need two solid months to work on it. Besides, our cattle all across Siberia have become infected. Where the infection takes hold, only five or six animals out of every hundred are still clean, and so I live with my cattle in the mountains and forests, about 15 versts[19] from our village.

I imagine you get many visitors to your place in Tula — people who, like you, respect the original law of God with their whole heart. I ask and implore you to advise me on what to do in such a tight situation: how do I get everything to you for publication and distribution?

If God had not been able right from the start to find another way to produce bread — here it is undoubtedly evident how indispensable this thing, i.e., bread, is to everyone, and even to the Tsar himself, He would have undoubtedly included therein a penance for all our sins — as though leading us willy-nilly to repentance, or, more properly speaking, to His own embraces. Back since the beginning of time, people concealed this law from the whole world's eyes, just like the lazy slave in the Gospels hid his talent in the earth.[20] It was a loss we land-tillers didn't miss for thousands of years, and now we've decided to investigate it and track it down — but who to turn to for help? It's quite a climb up to God, but it's a long way to the Tsar.

On 18 July 1883, I put in a request (N° 1933) through the Minusinsk Post Office in Enisej Gubernia to the Minister of Internal Affairs. Having received no reply over a ten-month period, on 30 March 1884 I put in a repeat request (N° 938), to which I have had no reply to date, and it is now October [1885]. Has the Minister simply given up on this? I cannot think so. Perhaps these requests got lost somewhere else.

It should be understood that this original commandment was given by God himself not to the kid-gloved elite [beloruchki], but just to us land-tillers, but highly placed people boldly took it away from us, or stole it secretly, or underhandedly seized it for themselves — that is, they never made reference to it any writings. What do you think, Lev Nikolaevich, if I have paraded all this before the intelligent eyes of my soul, will not the two-edged sword

answers. Subsequently he deleted some of the questions and added others, complicating the definition of the actual canonical text.

19 *verst* = 1.07 km (see note on measurements following the Preface).

20 See Matth. 25:25.

pierce my heart and kill my insufferable soul with sorrow? And so, I repeat my request once more to you, Lev Nikolaevich, give me your advice as to how to proceed in such a tight situation — that is, how to convey my complete work to you for distribution, and quickly at that, since I am 65 years old. And I am standing with but one foot on the ground, the other already in the grave, and what will happen without me, since this living commandment was laid in the grave from the beginning of time, and there it will remain until the end of time. And as poor people have suffered in terrible destitution, so they will have to go on suffering for ever and ever.

And so, Lev Nikolaevich, if something is to be done, it must be done — there's no point in fooling around with just the abbreviated version.[21] I have a lot written down, and better writers than I will increase this tenfold more and out of this will come a tremendous book entitled "Industriousness, or the joy of the land-tiller." Then many thousands of people will fight to buy copies of these books, which will reward all your labours and expenses tenfold. And then the reward you will receive for this from God is something that cannot be appreciated by our minds.

Just as everything is visible in a mirror, so the Heaven of righteous judgement has entrusted you, Lev Nikolaevich, with the task of bringing the original law out of the darkness of ignorance into the light of knowledge. And so, Lev Nikolaevich, harness all your efforts to bring this into an order that is pleasing to God and useful to people.

Your letter was like a thunderbolt to me. All the privileged people here, both in Minusinsk and in the surrounding villages, are gritting their teeth like a mad dog at a stone thrown at it, since they have nothing but hate and scorn for my sermon. Why? Because I am poor and do not belong to the elite. I thought it would be the same everywhere, but now your letter has shown me quite the contrary. In the Scriptures it is said that a prophet is not without honour[22] — it is only in his own country and his own house that he receives not honour, but only dishonour.

The principal virus in our land-tilling class, leading us willy-nilly into poverty and destitution, is the division of our brethren into different families and loneliness. Can this harm be expressed in just a few words? It cannot. And it all has one and the same cause. If this law were explained to people, then they would live a hundred souls together, they would not constantly try to get ahead of each other. Instead they would compete to make way for each other,

21 Bondarev was apparently annoyed that Tolstoy had only the abbreviated version of his manuscript. This does seem strange, since L. N. Zhebunëv (a political exile living in Minusinsk) wrote to Tolstoy on 13 January 1886: "I carefully read your letter to Bondarev, and noted that you were informing him of the receipt of the 'abbreviated outline' of his teachings, since in May 1885 I sent you, through the editors of *Russkaja mysl'*, the complete outline of Bondarev's teachings" (*PSS* 63:278).

22 See Matth. 13:57.

and the one who commands would not feel pride in his position, and the one who obeys would not feel shame.

If a husband or wife should die among them and leave as many as ten small children behind, in a group of people so unified in heart and soul, this would not constitute a significant blow, for these orphans would have a whole lot of fathers and mothers, a whole lot of brothers and sisters, a whole lot of sponsors and saviours. And the women — every last one of them is merciful — would not show to their own children as much favour as to orphans, but seeing as people are divided, then even the hundredth part of that desire will not remain with them.

But if in the dividing of people there are so many orphans left with a single father or a mother, then what happens?

Indeed, if one were to describe all the harm that comes from divisions, and all the interest that flows from everything together, it would easily fill more than ten pages. In a word, this law would gather all virtues unto itself and eliminate all vices. And this is no empty saying: God sees what is good. But you have taken this good and hid it from the eyes of the whole world.

Oh! Ah! Why have you taken all the highest places? Are you in fact worthy of them?

Oh, how stupid can I be! What am I doing sowing the good seed in stony and unfruitful soil, where there are few labours and many losses, and in place of benefit I receive only harm? And yet I still say of myself that I am a good land-tiller, but to determine where the good soil is and where the useless, is beyond my ability. This is what I am saying about the request I put in to the Ministry of Internal Affairs.

When you publish my abbreviated version, could you possibly bring this to the attention of the great Ministry or the Tsar?[23] Am I looking for praise for myself? No, what would that mean to me at the very end of my life? You will be erecting a monument to yourself, which will carry over even into your life beyond the grave. It is dearer than all the precious things of this world, because it is original.

In December I intend to submit this request to the Tsar, only from a different address — this time from Tomsk Gubernia. If I sent a hundred petitions from my own Enisej Gubernia, they would all come to naught.

T. M. Bondarev

23 Bondarev made many copies of his manuscript and sent them to many highly placed people, including the Ministry of Internal Affairs and the tsar himself. Naturally, he did not receive any replies. Tolstoy repeatedly advised him not to turn to high offices and not to count on any support for publishing his composition, warning him that this would lead nowhere. Tolstoy added: "God's original law is not something people ought to be forced to carry out; they must want to."

N° 3. T. M. BONDAREV ❧ L. N. TOLSTOY
1 December 1885.

My one and only true friend in the whole world, Lev Nikolaevich!

I received one letter from you on the 17th of March, and another on the 8th of September of this year, for which I most humbly thank you.[24] I am also grateful to you for re-ordering my articles according to their worth and their content so that the sense of one article carries over to the next. I myself have spotted discrepancies among my articles, but have been unable to correct for them. First because I haven't the time and secondly because I am not accustomed to it nor have I an instinct for it. I hope you were able to do a great job of correcting — beyond just re-arranging.

And so I would ask you, if possible, to send me your corrected and enhanced manuscript — rather a copy of same.

No sooner had I begun to write it than I was already hoping that it would not be published or promoted, wondering whether there would be even one person in the whole wide world who would willingly agree to take this burden — this vice of vices, this parasitism — upon himself. You said that they would publish it abroad uncensored. No, I dare say, not even there will it be published, unless Heaven's Justice should somehow intervene; I am not despairing about this.

Remember how I said right at the beginning of my work that this commandment will never be resurrected for you, O elite class, nor you for it, as long as ages last. Not only that, labour is engaged in a dispute with idleness and breadwinning with parasitism and, in the judgement of high government, idleness and parasitism will flourish and gain the upper hand, while labour and breadwinning will fade and fall. You, Lev Nikolaevich, please don't think I am so overwhelmed day after day, or that I'm unable to write or read or speak fine words — still, my prophecies will not fail to come to pass. According to the proverb, thunder comes not just from a black cloud in the sky, but from below as well.

As to the censorship board of *Russkoe bogatstvo*, to which you were going to send [my work] for publication, what did they reply to you and why did they reject it? Write to me [about it].[25]

For our part, you and I, Lev Nikolaevich, have done as much as we could to promote this law; after that, the project is more problematic.

Earlier I was not allowed to venture outside my region, while now I am permitted to visit any corner of Russia. It seems you know many people who wholeheartedly respect my sermon, and respect me along with it. Then ask them in my name whether they might be willing to help me come and meet

24 These letters have not been preserved.

25 Bondarev's article was not published in *Russkoe bogatstvo*.

with you while we are still alive; I am unable to afford this on my own. I'm not a decrepit old man, and I shall spare no effort, no matter how difficult the obstacles I encounter along the way, and no matter how great the financial hardship.

You call me a friend and brother, and I consider you the same, but these are only words between us. No, the Scripture says show me your faith by works, not words — but not works from this fascinating [earthly] world, but works more akin to that original source you are familiar with. Can it be that just because of our attachment to this world we shall die without ever having seen each other's face? That is a big mystery to me.

You and I have become acquainted not over some insignificant cause, but over a cause that embraces the very love of humanity which we have already investigated. And if it embraces that very love, might there remain some other virtues which this labour, which is being carried out in respect to this law, would not include? Are there any vices left in the world which this labour would not exclude or destroy? There are none. In a word, this labour was created along with the creation of the world, and it is not within the capacity even of an Angelic mind to fathom its entire value. That is why we became acquainted. And if all that is true, what considerations or obstacles could prevent us from meeting in person? There are none.

And now farewell, my highly respected (in words) Lev Nikolaevich. Farewell until a pleasant meeting in person.

T. Bondarev

Send me back the latest 50 articles of mine which I sent to you, as I do not have a draft copy of them.

Nº 4. L. N. TOLSTOY ➧ T. M. BONDAREV[26]

9 February 1886.[27] *Moscow.*

Timofej Mikhajlovich!

I received your letter last year, which I haven't got around to answering to date, but yesterday I received a letter from Leonid Nikolaevich[28] about you, and now I am replying to both at once. I copied your sermon for many of my friends, but have not yet submitted it for publication. I am now forwarding it to St. Petersburg, to the journal *Russkoe bogatstvo,* and am trying my best to have it published just the way you wanted it, without any additions or deletions. If it is published, you will be sent a copy of the booklet.

26 Letter published in *PSS* 63:332–34.

27 A copy of this letter includes the notation: "Received approx. 20 March 86." The exact date of 9 March can be ascertained from Bondarev's reply (Letter Nº 7).

28 *Leonid Nikolaevich Zhebunëv* — who helped facilitate the conveyance of Bondarev's manuscript to Tolstoy.

Your article contains a good deal of helpful material, and in the book I am now writing on this subject,[29] I am mentioning that I learnt this not from scholars or from the wise of this world, but from the peasant T. M. Bondarev. I would like very much to send you a copy, but, you know, all these past five years that I have been writing on this — about how we are all failing to live in accordance with God's law — everything has been forbidden by the government and my books have been banned and burnt.

This is why I wrote you in particular that it is no use trying to submit a petition to the Minister of Internal Affairs and the Tsar.[30] Both the Tsar and the ministers refuse to let us even talk about it. I'm especially concerned that they won't let your sermon be published in full, but only in abbreviated form. I would very much like to read your larger work, but if there are so many obstacles in the way, what can we do?

I think that if an individual has understood God's truth and expressed it either orally or in writing, it will not get lost. Moses never got to see the Promised Land, and yet it was he who led his people to it. That's the way it is with all of God's servants. It's a poor ploughman who looks back to see how much he's ploughed. I'll tell you about myself: while I was writing books about trivial things, which rubbed people the right way, all my books were praised and published. Even the Tsar read and heaped praise on them; but as soon as I had the desire to serve God and show people how they weren't living according to the law, everyone rejected me. They don't let my books pass, they burn them, and the government considers me its foe.

But I tell you, this not only does not upset me, it even gladdens me, for I know that they hate my writing not because of me but because it exposes them; they hate me for what I say about God's law, which they have overturned. And I know that God's law cannot be hid, it can't be burnt with fire or drowned in the sea. And persecution only makes it more visible to people who are striving for God.

So don't you go grumbling that your petitions aren't accepted and you don't get any response. You yourself say that you are petitioning the very people you are complaining about. And don't go grumbling that those close to you don't understand or appreciate you. What is that to you? You are not, and have not been, working for human praise. You are working, rather, for God, and God who sees in secret will reward you openly.[31]

Just so long as you know that you are serving God's cause. And your cause is God's. It has brought forth and is continuing to bring forth fruit, only we don't happen to be able to see or taste it. I know both from my own experience and from others' that your writings have helped a great many people, and will

29 Tolstoy is referring to his treatise *What Then Must Be Done?* See *PSS* 25:386, 469.

30 In his first letter to Bondarev, Tolstoy wrote that there was no point in petitioning either the ministers or the tsar to allow publication of his works.

31 See Matth. 6:6.

continue to help many. But you cannot and should not expect everything to work out all at once.

You can't force everybody to work, because all power is in the hands of those who are unwilling to work. People must come to understand themselves that life is work, according to the law of God, and that work is more blessed than idleness.

And there are people who understand this and abandon idleness all on their own, and enthusiastically take up work on the land. But those who have gone astray don't understand this and cling on to their idleness with all their might, and will not give up their error any time soon. As long as they refuse to understand, there is nothing you can do with them. And to make them understand, you need to explain the law of God to them.

Indeed, this is exactly what you are doing — you are thereby serving God and so you know that you, and not they, will triumph. How soon will that happen? That is up to God. That is how I see it.

Farewell, my respected friend and brother, Timofej Mikhajlovich. May God help you. If they won't publish your manuscript, I shall send it back to you.

Lev Tolstoy

N° 5. T. M. BONDAREV ❧ L. N. TOLSTOY
First half of February 1886.

My greatly esteemed Lev Nikolaevich!

I received the package from you — my manuscript. Only without any [covering] letter: I looked through all the papers to see whether there were any pencil marks in the margins, and there were none.

I suppose I might have offended you with the wordiness in my letters to you; they might have included some words too pointed for your taste.

Perhaps it didn't occur to you to do me the favour of allowing for the deficiencies or excesses in my letters to you. What I wrote to you was not out of any devilish or evil motives, but out of a pure heart.

If some vitriolic word unwittingly crept into my letters, I would ask and beg of you, Lev Nikolaevich, in the name of God, to forget any inappropriate occurrences.

This past January I sent you an additional 50 articles, in addition to my manuscript, through Zhebunëv. Also without a [covering] letter.

There is still a lot I need to tell you, but I am afraid, as before, of not expressing myself appropriately.

Yours, T. Bondarev

First half of February. I have no idea when Zhebunëv will post [this letter to you].

N° 6. L. N. TOLSTOY ❧ T. M. BONDAREV[32]

26 March 1886. Moscow.

Timofej Mikhajlovich!

I read your large manuscript and the supplement.[33] Both are very good and completely true. I shall try and keep the manuscript and share it in copies or in the press, as much as I am able. There are a few articles that in my opinion could be omitted so as not to weaken the force of the book as a whole. I could place the omitted articles in the notes at the end. What do you think?

As to whether or not the minister received your manuscript,[34] I haven't been able to find out anything, but I don't see much use in trying, since in all probability he didn't even look at it, but tossed it somewhere in the general office. Even if he did read it, he would have only made fun of it.

I often read your manuscript to my acquaintances. Most of them, with the rare exception, tend to get up and leave. When I am surrounded by boring people, I start reading the manuscript and I am rid of them at once, although there are those who actually enjoy reading it. I am in agreement with everything written therein, and I myself am writing only on this subject, albeit from a different point of view.

I often ask myself: How can people close their eyes (and others' eyes) to the original law? What makes them think they can escape fulfilling this law? And to this I reply: this has happened because a few people who have usurped power over others (Saul's appointment as king[35]) have equipped others with weapons and brought them into subjection. It is these people — commanders and soldiers — who were the first to depart from the original law. First they took food by force, and then money, and so could get by without working the land themselves. And then they began handing out food and money to their families. And a kid-gloved elite was born.

That makes me think that there are just two causes of all evil: first, that the original law ("In the sweat of thy face shalt thou eat bread"[36]) is hid, and second, that the other law is hid too: "Ye have heard that it hath been said, An eye for an eye, and a tooth for a tooth: But I say unto you, that ye resist not evil."[37] This law applies to everybody, and nobody, no matter what title he has taken upon himself, has a right to break it.

32 Published in *PSS* 63:337–38.

33 On the manuscript copy is the notation: "Received 16 May 86." The first manuscript was sent to Tolstoy by L. N. Zhebunëv, the second by V. S. Lebedev. See *PSS* 63:339.

34 See Letter N° 4.

35 See 1 Samuel 11:15; 13:13–14.

36 Gen. 3:19.

37 Matth. 5:38–39.

And when violence is done away with, nobody will be able to go against the law of working for one's own food, for whoever will not work will either have to beg or die of hunger.

I agree with you that the first law is "In the sweat of thy face shalt thou eat bread," but to prevent this law from being broken, one must also obey the other law: "Resist not evil."

Well, good-bye for now, and may God grant you all good. In you I have found a strong helper in my cause. I hope you will also find a helper in me. We have a common cause.

I shall soon turn sixty and have had agonies running into the hundreds of thousands, but in past years I have cut hay and ploughed, and hope to do so again this year. And the joy and health and spiritual peace that this work gives me I find to be greater than anything else.

Lev Tolstoy
26 March 1886

N° 7. T. M. BONDAREV ❧ L. N. TOLSTOY
April [?] 1886. Village of Iudino.[38]

Lev Nikolaevich.

The letter you sent me on 9 February this year[39] to Minusinsk arrived on 4 March. But I live 160 kilometres from Minusinsk, and so I had the fortune to receive it on 15 March, and for certain reasons was not able to answer you right away. I got delayed several days after that.

On 9 January of this year I sent you, through L. N. Zhebunëv[40] (my closest friend) a series of fifteen important questions I would like to add as an appendix to my sermon, along with a letter. But it appears that my parcel did not reach you in time for your most recent letter.

In early March I sent you a brief sketch of my life, along with a portrait of me,[41] also through Zhebunëv. And I would ask you, Lev Nikolaevich, to include both of these along with my sermon, so that future generations will not simply put all of this down to some kind of criticism, saying that all this was written by a white-gloved elitist who has no right to be talking about industriousness and idleness and so laid everything on the shoulders of some unknown peasant. My portrait and biographical sketch will remove any lingering doubt on the part of future generations.

38 *Iudino* — the name (from 1850 to 1958) of a village in Voronezh Gubernia, now known as Bondarevo, renamed such in 1958 in honour of its most famous resident, Timofej Bondarev.

39 Letter N° 4.

40 See Note 28 to Letter N° 4 above.

41 The photo of Bondarev taken with a group of other Minusinsk exiles has been lost. His portrait, however, executed by the artist Ivan Alekseevich Volguzhev (1860–1899), is still to be found in the Tolstoy Museum in Moscow. See Kosovanov 1958: 17.

Zhebunëv paid for the portrait and shipment of papers out of his own pocket, not mine.

I thank you, Lev Nikolaevich, for sending copies of my sermon to your acquaintances. And so, even if not in print, it will be circulated in writing, and sooner or later we'll find a way to persuade even the Tsar to accept it.

Both the newspaper *Sibirskaja gazeta* (N° 27 of 1884), in an article entitled "Derevenskaja filosofija" [Rural philosophy],[42] and the journal *Russkaja mysl'* (1884, Vol. 5, Book 11, p. 301), published brief excerpts from my abbreviated manuscript which came down unbearably hard on idlers, and these excerpts passed the censors. So I hope that they will let my whole book pass. They can't fail to let it pass, since there is and can be — either in heaven or on the earth — nothing truer than this truth which flows from the original law.

Now I solemnly assure you, Lev Nikolaevich, that if this sermon of mine were presented to the Tsar, he would indeed clasp it to his heart — 1) because he has never ever heard or imagined the like; 2) this commandment is founded and grounded in the very bread he eats; 3) it all stems from the original law given to man when the heavens and the earth were created; 4) it contains a universal salvation from difficult poverty and unbearable hardship; 5) it involves restraining one's self from evil deeds; 6) it is an inescapable encouragement to virtue; 7) it is sufficiently strong to unite all faiths, peoples and earthly tribes into a single faith, a single church and a single love.

This commandment recognizes no righteous or sinful, no rich or poor, clever or stupid, elite or common folk, and it recognizes no discrimination by faith — it doesn't descend into our stupidities and petty quarrels. It has taken the whole universe into its embrace and if all peoples knew of it, they would clasp it to their heart, and God would not speak in vain of his creation of the world when he said "It is good."

If there should be an opportunity to present my original manuscript to the Tsar, then he would have a clear picture of it all. As for my brief petitions — has he seen them? Unlikely. But even if he did, could it be possible that a peasant might in fact write something useful — just as in the biblical saying: "Can there any good thing come out of Nazareth?"[43] — or only out of Jerusalem? Yet it was in Nazareth, the curse of the world, that Christ was born, while the universally celebrated Jerusalem was where he was crucified.

I heard in passing that you, Lev Nikolaevich, are the same age as me, 66 years old.[44] I would therefore ask you (in case of your death), to acquaint me by letter with one or two of your close acquaintances. In the case of my own

42 Bondarev is here referring to the article "Rural philosophy" which was published in *Sibirskaja gazeta* (Tomsk, 1 July 1884, N° 27) under the sub-heading: "Letter from Minusinsk," mentioning "originality of thought, style and language." This article, signed with the initials "A. Sh.," appeared before Gleb Uspenskij's article in *Russkaja mysl'* (see Note 17 in Letter N° 2).

43 John 1:46.

44 At this time, in April 1886, Tolstoy was, in fact, fifty-seven.

death there is nobody to acquaint you with. We have a saying here: throw a stone at a dog and you'll hit a literate man — but what is the point? After all, literate men are just animals, no better and no worse.

Make a copy of my manuscript and send it to me, as well as of the condensed version. But keep the original for yourself: in case the government should complain about your activities, you can point out the spot and thereby justify yourself. They have no right to come after me, since to them I am like a father and mother to small children — a provider. Only send me a clear and accurate copy, and not just any old haphazard thing.

In the above-mentioned newspaper and journal, my articles have been so altered, distorted and garbled that the Devil himself couldn't make sense of them. It jumps from one idea to another, it's all turned upside down, and there's no beginning or end. In a word, endless, disgusting chaos. There's a lot I could say, but I'll simply point out two examples. Here they are:

I had: "take a hundred-*pood*[45] rock and *nosi* [carry]." But in the journal this last phrase was altered to *kosi* [cut, mow down] (I even smiled wryly at that one). Yes, indeed! Do people use rocks to mow? Another instance: "I hear Jacob's voice, but I feel the hands — the hands of Esau."[46] That's the way it is in the [Russian] Bible, and that's the way I had it, but in the newspaper and the journal they both wrote (as though they had conspired between themselves): "I hear Jacob's voice, but I feel Esau." It's difficult enough talking about all these mockeries, not just mistakes, with one's tongue, let alone describe them in writing.

And now the whole universe will be justified in heaping criticism on such mockery, but they won't blame the copyists — they'll blame me. No wonder, people will say — no wonder he's called a *muzhik*[47] (which is pretty much the same as a fool). He'll die a *muzhik*. Do you see what nonsense he is uttering? God forbid. In your case, too, Lev Nikolaevich, the same sort of nonsense might result, and then where could I hide from such an unmerited rebuke? You see, Lev Nikolaevich, no matter what we hope for and where we expect it from, we only get sorrow in return.

A brief abridgement, but they've cut it down three times beyond that. One might have supposed those copyists to be extraordinarily clever people and simply skip over articles utterly against the law. But no: they let through things many times more vitriolic than that, while they skipped gentler things worthy of great respect. All this simply cannot be described in detail.

I sincerely hoped and was really counting on good writers affording this law an ever more brilliant development. But now my hopes are dashed; what I was counting on has disappeared.

45 *pood* = 40 *funts* or 16.38 kg (see note on measurements following the Preface).

46 Gen. 27:22. In the Authorized Version: "The voice is Jacob's voice, but the hands are the hands of Esau."

47 *muzhik* — a colloquial word for a peasant or an uneducated man.

And there's really no point in my complaining about the copyists. Not only the residents of the earth but, indeed, all those in heaven know that this law was not given to the kid-gloved elite, but specifically to us, the land-tillers, back when God created the heavens and the earth. Who will look after a stranger's property, if not its owner?

As to the relationship between the white-gloved elite and this law, or rather between them and food — it can be said that they are each other's mortal enemy, for ever irreconcilable. And here I am starting again to complain that my articles have been distorted beyond recognition. For this reason I asked the Ministry of Internal Affairs to summon me in person. I knew in advance that it would be this way and that they would be making all sorts of alterations. And that with time even the memory of my sermon would vanish from the face of the earth. And this law has been locked away since time immemorial, and will remain that way until the end of time.

I would ask you, Lev Nikolaevich, if my book should go to publication, to include in future editions my biographical sketch and portrait, and send me five copies of this booklet. I'll reimburse you for the cost.

I'm not sure how my articles appear on the copies you have, but it seems to me they should read something like this: my first question should be followed by an evaluation of its truth or falsity. Then should follow another question, with an appraisal of whether it is precious or cheap, useful or harmful, etc. If I ask you something face to face, you are obliged, after all, to respond. Why should it be any different on paper?

I remain in good health and with a deep respect for you.

T. Bondarev

It used to be that they would not give us any documents or even permission to travel, but now they will let us go on leave anywhere in Russia. Therefore I would ask and implore you, Lev Nikolaevich, couldn't you possibly put in a petition for me with the government to require my presence with you in Russia for a brief time? It will not cost the state treasury very much. I would go on my own, but I don't have the strength for that, and there are a lot of things I urgently need to talk about with you face to face.

You can make the case to anyone in authority that I am working not for my own benefit, but for the benefit of the whole world. And in conjunction with this, I desire to visit my homeland, from which I have been exiled for thirty-two years now. If I should think of anything to add to the promotion of this law, should I send it to you or not? Could it be accommodated in future editions of this law or not? Is it permissible to sow good seed on stony or infertile ground or not?[48] I would think not, but what would you say?

48 See Jesus' parable of the sower, in Luke 8:5–8.

I asked you earlier to send me five booklets — that is, only if my sermon is published all by itself in the form of a little inexpensive booklet. If, however, it appears as part of a larger book costing as much as five roubles, then just send me one copy. I shall read it silently to myself and then send it back to my homeland. Here in our village, it is best not to even mention this law by name. As it is said, don't cast pearls before swine, etc.[49] Then, depending on circumstances, if necessary, I shall send you the money and you send me the books.

I am complaining *to* the very person I am complaining *about*, and launched a lawsuit against the very person I am counting on for a hearing and even a decision. To this end I have also subjoined the Tsar to my class of land-tillers. In other words, I have likened Him to a queen bee, while others may attribute this to my cowardice or superstitious aberrations.

N° 8. T. M. BONDAREV ❧ L. N. TOLSTOY
23 July 1886.

My greatly esteemed Lev Nikolaevich!

I received your letter on 20 March, as well as another on 16 May,[50] both of which I answered right off. In the last days of February of this year 1886 I sent you a letter with my picture. Since I live 160 versts from Minusinsk,[51] all this correspondence goes through Zhebunëv's hands and I pay for the postage. I don't know whether you received these letters. I have absolute confidence in Zhebunëv's trustworthiness.

And you are putting all your efforts into promoting this primal law. By what means, when and how can I thank you? In fact, I have no means, and I cannot flatter you with words. Only one choice remains, and that is to ask God that He might, for His part, send you all the best. You call me a friend and brother. Do I really deserve that honour? I think not. Right this moment send me all my original manuscripts, and if you should still have need of them, when I no longer have a use for them I shall soon offer them to you again. If my sermon is published, send me one copy, and I shall send you the money [for it]. If a person who eats the fruit of his own works and feeds others and saves them from starvation, and is still branded by the whole universe and at every turn as someone base and insignificant and unworthy of respect — if that person, i.e., a tiller of the land, calls all these humiliating insults upon himself, he ought not to fret about it, since it is all true.

How shall we now call that person who not only refuses to feed others but himself feeds off others' labours — what shall we call him? It should be

49 See Matth. 7:6.
50 See Letter N° 4, dated 9 February 1886, and Letter N° 6, dated 26 March 1886, respectively.
51 *Minusinsk* — an historical town located in Krasnoyarsk Territory in central Siberia.

remembered that the land-tiller brought all those humiliating judgements upon himself. I myself have [never] been in this worthy group, and it was only last year that you excluded yourself from the company of spongers (you were working last year), so you would know better what term to use, and in your next letter tell me how you would call a man drowning in luxuries. It seems to me that it is not a lie nor an empty dream.

Moreover, all the commandments and laws of both the Old and New Testaments left the stamp of their truth in human blood and tears, while for the truth of this commandment, which is the mother and engenderer of all laws and commandments, nobody has ever shed even a drop of blood or a single tear, which might make one think, perforce, that it is less significant than those that followed.

Did Christ stamp it with his blood? No, He said: "Behold the fowls of the air: for they sow not, neither do they reap, nor gather into barns; yet your heavenly Father feedeth them."[52] It is evident from this that he rejected it — that is, he did not shed blood over it. Despite the fact that since the beginning of time and to this day it is still alive, even though buried in the earth — do you think it is easy for someone to lie in a grave alive?! — there has been no tribute to it in proverbs or writings, nor even any requiem for the peace of its soul. But now I am assured by a kind of premonition, that the judgement of Heaven predetermined me to witness and stamp this truth in my blood and tears. But that doesn't fluster me: I shan't have two deaths and, even so, I can't escape the one.

Leonid Nikolaevich [Zhebunëv] got a bit annoyed with me, in a friendly way, and [I know] you agree with him that I should not present a petition about this to the Tsar. But the above-mentioned fact is strongly pushing me in this direction, and it seems I shan't be able to hold out, but will write a petition at some point. I ask and beg you, Lev Nikolaevich, to bless me in this quest; after all, people have been suffering and even dying for the truth, and who are we? But it could turn out that I shan't suffer after all — the heart of the Tsar is in the hand of God. The Tsar will deal with me as it pleases God.

Again I repeat my request: this very day and this very hour send all my papers to the post office.

Farewell, my friend, soul of my soul. With my deepest respect,

T. Bondarev
23 July 1886

52 Matth. 6:26.

Nº 9. T. M. BONDAREV ❧ L. N. TOLSTOY
1886.

Greatly, greatly esteemed friend and brother, my Lev Nikolaevich!

The letter you sent me in the first days of June[53] I only received during the last days of September, Popov hung on to it for so long in Minusinsk; along with it I received 7 booklets and another letter urging me to abstain from drunkenness. Whatever God knows, there's nothing that can be hidden from you — you are a man, like everyone else. Until recently, I was by no means the least among boozers. After receiving your advice to abstain from drunkenness, I, along with many around me here, made a mutual pact not to drink wine or to entertain with wine. If anyone else had written that to us, we might not have listened to him, but since it was Tolstoy writing, his advice could not be disregarded; that's what everyone says.

As to [the copies of] my published articles which you sent me, I have not received them. But why not? [Perhaps] I didn't receive them because you [packaged] them the way they do newspapers, bound together with a single clip, but newspapers, as you know, don't contain anything of interest, and that is why they arrive. But as soon as people see my articles, they're passed around from hand to hand, and so they go astray — or it could be they stayed in Minusinsk. That would be my guess.

In view of everything I wrote above, I would humbly ask you, Lev Nikolaevich, as soon as you receive this to send me at once two copies of the said articles. One of them I shall keep for myself, and the other I shall send home to my brother. And do seal them in an envelope, otherwise they won't get here. And don't address it to Popov, but directly to me, Bondarev.

If possible, could you send me more copies, and whatever they cost, I'll send you the money. I need them to pass along to people I know. I'm very surprised that in spite of these clear and true proofs you are still unwilling to admit that Cain was a righteous man, but instead you call him bitter, and 'bitter' is the same as 'cursed.'

Even if we should call [others] from the Old and New Testaments 'cursed,' for example, Abraham, Isaac, Jacob, Moses, John the Baptist, Peter and Paul — we would [certainly never] see him [Cain] in this crowd. No, but we would consider the first man born into the world cursed. I always shudder when I think of this, but my Lev Nikolaevich doesn't agree with me. I get the impression that you do not recognize him as a saint because [in that case] they would consider you a rebel — that is, it's out of fear that you reject his sainthood, since the whole world would accept your word as law.

What difference does it make to us whether Cain is cursed or not? No, no, I do not subscribe to that. It's easy to call a sinner a saint, but to consider a

53 The whereabouts of this letter are unknown.

righteous man as cursed — that's something to think about. Always before God I even pronounce Cain's confession, this is MY GREATEST FAULT.

I've lived so many years in the world, as you already know, and I'm always talking with people about God and His law [and], regardless of any differences of opinion we might have, there has not been any conflict or hatred. Indeed, quite the opposite: more and more, friendship and love have taken root. And you're afraid that conflict and hatred might arise from this. Never!

And so, Lev Nikolaevich, again I repeat what I said before — send me the above-mentioned treat which is dearest to me in the whole world.

T. Bondarev

N° 10. L. N. TOLSTOY ❧ T. M. BONDAREV
12 February 1887. Moscow.[54]

Timofej Mikhajlovich!

I received and read your manuscript.[55] I agree with you that love without labour is a mere deception and lifeless, but one cannot argue that labour includes love in itself. Animals labour in their quest for food, but without love they savage each other and tear each other apart. The same with man.

I am endeavouring to promote and publish your first essay,[56] but nothing has been accomplished to date. As soon as it is published — and I don't doubt that it will be — I shall send it to you. Since mid-summer I have been ill and only recently recovered, and that is why I have not been writing to you.

It will do you no good to get upset, Timofej Mikhajlovich, over your writings not being published, or the government not taking any action on your proposals. Human thought is holy by the very reason that it acts on people freely and not through force, and nobody can force people to think this way or that, and, by the same token, nobody can stop or delay human thinking, if it is true, and originates with God. Truth will claim its own, and sooner or later everyone will recognize it. Only just as it was not given to Moses to enter the Promised Land, it is not given to everyone to see the results of their labours. But we must sow and rejoice that God has called us to be sowers of the good seed, which will grow to come to people's aid, if it is good seed. The same is true of your thoughts. They have already benefited many, exposed falsity to them and pointed out the truth. They will continue to ignite, like a flame passed from one candle to another. Worrying that my thoughts are not being recognized now, this moment, and not brought to fruition — such worries can be entertained

54 This letter is published in *PSS* 64:12–13. Notation on the copy: "Received 17 March."

55 This manuscript is unknown. It is possible Tolstoy had in mind one of the 'addenda' to Bondarev's major article. Bondarev made frequent additions to his *Triumph* (see also Letter N° 14 below).

56 *Torzhestvo zemledel'tsa ili trudoljubie i tunejadstvo* [The triumph of the land-tiller, or industriousness and idleness].

only by someone who doesn't believe in the truth of his thoughts, whereas if I believe that my thoughts originate with God, there's nothing to worry about. God will claim His own and find Himself servants, and knows His own time, and I can only rejoice that I have been led to be a servant in God's work.

I wish you all the best from God, and peace and joy in your thoughts.

Lev Tolstoy

N° 11. L. N. TOLSTOY ❧ T. M. BONDAREV
4 August 1887. Yasnaya Polyana.[57]

Dear friend Timofej Mikhajlovich!

At the beginning of last winter your articles were given to a person who wanted to publish them uncensored, but evidently this was not possible and so he returned them. I was partly glad at this, for [some people] could have suffered, but I was sad that useful thoughts were being prevented from spreading. In the spring, though, I met a very good, clever and rich man, who does not consider it lawful to own an estate and live off others' labours, and wants to put the estate belonging to him to good use, so as not to be owning it himself. He read your articles, copied them, and wants to publish them abroad in Russian. Then they can be easily imported from abroad and many will come to know them. I have not seen him for some time, but I know that he is a trustworthy fellow — he does what he says — and so I think he has either published them or is publishing them. He will probably send me several copies and I'll forward [some of them] to you right away. I have changed the order of some of your articles to enhance the impact of your thoughts. Everything that could not be disputed or evaded I lumped together, while what I thought, based on my knowledge of most readers' thoughts, might be argued against, I put at the end. The main thing is that there are no rough spots and that nobody can excuse their guilt. Otherwise, if there is anything they could find fault with, those under accusation will be happy to argue over some [trivial] mistake, just so that the really important questions are forgotten.

I shan't say that I feel sorry about your illness, for I suggest that disease and carnal death itself are just as much a benefit as health and carnal life, as long as they don't interfere with the peace of the spirit or faith in God. And this is something I wish you whether you are healthy or ill or even on your deathbed. "Having accepted good, shall we [not] accept evil?"[58]

With love and respect,

Lev Tolstoy
4 August.

57 This letter was published in *Jasnopoljanskij sbornik* 1968: 176–77. Notation on copy: "Received 8 Sept. '87."

58 Cf. Job 2:10, where Job is questioned by his wife: "Shall we receive good at the hand of God, and shall we not receive evil?"

Nº 12. T. M. BONDAREV ❧ L. N. TOLSTOY
End of June 1888.

Lev Nikolaevich.

At the beginning of June I sent you a letter, and on the 22nd of this month from the Head of the High Command of the Chancellery for receiving petitions to His Majesty I received the following answer (among all the other communications that are useless for us):

"There has been no positive response to Bondarev's petition to publish his essay on industriousness and idleness. In view of its groundlessness Bondarev is required to acknowledge our decision in writing." This is what he [wrote] to the Governor of Krasnoyarsk, and [says] ["]this Your Excellency will keep on file awaiting our further instructions.["] This is how [the matter] ended.

On the "groundlessness" of the petition. What, exactly, does this mean? Is it because I have phrased my petition not in the way I ought to, or did I send it to the wrong place and the wrong person? How do I correct this deficiency? It's a puzzle the Devil himself cannot solve.

This makes me think that they will soon be demanding I send them my essay, and so I would most humbly ask you, Lev Nikolaevich, to send me immediately, as soon as possible, your edited version which you prepared for publication. Otherwise they won't even begin to read my work.

In another two months I am thinking of writing another petition to the Tsar, i.e., reminding him of this matter. May I do that?

I still have one other goal: when they demand of me just to send the materials, I won't give it to them, but I'll tell them: command me [to come] along with them, for the simple reason that I am the very first exponent of this unprecedented law which has existed from the beginning of time, and this is why I must be present when it is published, and I shall be happy to be there, and so forth. How does this goal of mine seem to you — useful or harmful?

And so once again I repeat and humbly ask you, Lev Nikolaevich, to send me immediately, as soon as possible, your edited version.

Bondarev

Nº 13. T. M. BONDAREV ❧ L. N. TOLSTOY
1888–1889.

It seems to me I have lost my presence of mind in the promotion of the primal law, my dear Lev Nikolaevich, whom I esteem from the bottom of my heart.

And I can't help losing it — since it is not a solid wall but an impassable mountain that stands in the way of introducing this law to the world. Is God Himself, let alone a man, able to bring this law to light through some hidden passage, quiet footsteps, or an unknown road? No, He can't, since God does not have the right to drag someone along the path of virtue; human desire and God's grace are both needed, as much as a bird needs two wings to fly.

There's only one thing that doesn't cause me to despair, and that is God, and that He will carve out a passage to bring this law to light, as He did during the time of the Flood,[59] [and] with Moses in Egypt at the Red Sea, the desert, over Jordan and in the Promised Land.[60] This is the only thing I do not despair over. And will God do the same [again]? He will, He will, and I repeat once more: He will. My prophecy shall not fail, He will do it, but it is impossible to do it quietly and calmly, without compulsion, through good advice alone. You yourself know whom this chief among vices — the vice of idleness — is first aimed at.

I have no idea here as to whether they themselves do not accept this law, or whether the law itself rejects them as outcasts. But I'm more inclined towards the latter [conclusion]. Imagine, Lev Nikolaevich, in the understanding eyes of your soul, the most important virtue in the world is to produce bread in the world, and God Himself has entrusted this [task] to the least people in the world, and many are crossing over from our class to theirs, and not one from them to us,[61] i.e., our class is like wheat stalks fluttering in the wind.

I have submitted two petitions about this to the Minister of Internal Affairs, with no reply, and two to the Tsar — the latest this past February — putting "Confidential" on the "Address" side of the envelope. No answer to these either. Now I intend to write this coming December, once more to the Tsar Himself, in which I shall set forth for him the unbearable bitter truth. I cannot die twice; even so, I can't escape one death. In all my 68 years I have not seen any bright days, only gloomy ones, but what are they to me now? Let my soul drink my cup of suffering to the last drop!

Do send me, Lev Nikolaevich, a copy of your revised version, in the form in which you submitted it for publication. And also send me back the package I recently sent to you — 50 articles on love for one's neighbour. Tell me what answer you were given by the censorship board as to why they could not pass my articles. And why have they not been published abroad without censorship? [I mention this as] you wrote me about a respected gentleman [willing to facilitate this].[62] I sent you a letter last autumn — did you receive it?

I have another favour to ask of you, Lev Nikolaevich: could you look in Moscow bookshops for [copies of] the Psalms in Russian translation? But only [editions] with a preface signed by the translators: Serafim Metropolitan of Novgorod, Filaret Archbishop of Moscow and Semion Archbishop of Yaroslavl. And send me at least 3 copies, and I'll send you the money, and

59 See Gen., Chap. 6–8.

60 See Exodus, Chap. 13–15.

61 "With the sole exception of L. N. Tolstoy, who has joined us. In your letters you tell me that you are working, as I am assured by many eye-witnesses" — Note by T. M. Bondarev.

62 See Letter N° 11 above.

with that write out the address of the shop and how much they cost. I'll start a subscription, since we need them very much here, preferably in a hard cover.

Can you tell me how, why and wherefore all fertile lands, meadows, forests, fish-inhabited rivers and lakes throughout Russia are private property? Did the landowners earn them or did they buy them? Or just boldly seize them? Or acquire them through stealth? Who, when and under what regulations handed them over? The whole world is standing with one foot in the grave of starvation for want of land, and here they are still selling it to millionaires. You know all about this; in God's name I am asking for the truth and I beg you to write to me clearly about it. And to what extent has the government hated and despised our lower class that they would even hide the sun from us if they could and redirect its radiance [exclusively] to themselves, and dry up all our waters — in a word, order the Earth to devour all of us living on it. No doubt this is all evident from the land that has been taken from us under the cloak of the above-mentioned law.

It is with a fervent desire that I ask for death, to save me from this torment — in other words, so that my eyes may be spared from seeing and my ears from hearing this tremendous and unmitigated injustice and the lawlessness of this world. But for some reason death is taking its time.

Your familiar [friend],

T. Bondarev

Again I ask, write me about my query; I shall await with firm hope all your explanations.

Nº 14. T. M. BONDAREV ❧ L. N. TOLSTOY
1889.

Greatly esteemed Lev Nikolaevich.

At the beginning of August of this year [18]89 I received a letter from you,[63] for which I do not know, in my limited mind, where to begin or finish expressing my gratitude. Apart from my one desire to wish you all the best in the world from God.

You said in your letter that you are trying and will keep trying to publish my articles, and now it has come to my attention that they have not been accepted, — and that's no surprise, since the primal law, so sweet and pleasant for the lower class of people, is so bitter and repulsive to the upper class. In a word, it has brought to people not peace, but a sword.[64] And of these two classes, which one is more powerful? Because here not only earthly but even heavenly powers will exhaust themselves in their attempts to bring this law to light.

63 The whereabouts of this letter are unknown.
64 See Matth. 10:34.

Earlier I stated and even wrote in my petition to the Minister, that laziness and idleness will flourish and increase right in the face of the highest government, while labour and breadwinning will fade away and be denigrated, and this prophecy of mine has not failed and will not fail to come to pass.

In the name of God I beg you, Lev Nikolaevich, to make every effort you can and take all measures to bring my sermon to the attention of the High Ministry or of the Tsar himself. Let them [try to] overthrow this primal law: In the sweat of thy face shalt thou eat bread.[65] Then you will stay true to God, and He will not leave you unrewarded.

Because of my poor level of literacy I was not able to understand from your letter whether you received my whole manuscript or only an abbreviated version, since in my letter which I sent to you back then I ended up saying a lot of extra things, for which I ask your forgiveness.

For certain valid reasons I have not been to Minusinsk for two years, and just the other day I received a letter in which he[66] urges me to come to Minusinsk to discuss something essential with me, but I can't come until mid-March.

I have submitted to the Minister of Internal Affairs two petitions about this. The first was on 18 June 1883 under N° 4933, and the second on 30 March 1884 under N° 938; I have had no reply to either of these to date. And now I intend to submit one to the Tsar, but it won't be before mid-April.

I am taking the opportunity of sending you, through Lebedev, 12 additions to my manuscript, which I would ask you to insert at the appropriate places.

I would humbly ask you, Lev Nikolaevich, to write to me everything about the consequences of this undertaking. Might you not have the opportunity to find out whether the Minister received my petitions and what his decision [regarding them] was? He could at least give me an answer yes or no. I would be content with that.

I remain your ever deeply respectful Timofej Mikhajlovich Bondarev. I am healthy and wish you the same for many years to come.

I live 160 versts from Minusinsk.

I serve as a teacher in my village, I have 60 pupils. The children who can read eagerly devour your books. Someone, somewhere sent them their own copies on your behalf to sell for almost nothing (1½ kopeks each), and everyone sends you their gratitude in return.

Lev Nikolaevich, I would ask you not to blame me or treat it as an insult if I don't praise you enough [in my letters]. I don't think there's any point in it.

Again I repeat, write me soon, immediately, about all the consequences of this undertaking, and as clearly as you can.

65 See Gen. 3:19.
66 "Doctor Lebedev" — Note by T. M. Bondarev.

N° 15. T. M. BONDAREV ❧ L. N. TOLSTOY
20 November 1889. Village of Iudino.

Lev Nikolaevich.

In our village, which consists of 120 households, there is a man named Gavrila Petrovich Fedjanin, and he has three sons between thirty and forty years of age. He isn't wealthy by any means, but he's fairly well off. He is the only one who, along with his whole family, does not drink and does not even bring wine into his house. He will not serve it to any guest and will not accept it from anyone. A lot of people complain about him, but he pays no attention.

And when I read to him the books you sent about drunkenness,[67] assuring him that you had authored and published these books, he at once got up from the chair he was sitting on, raised his hands to heaven and began praying to God to send you everything you desire. Then he made a deep bow to you, turned in your direction, extended his hand and vigorously 'shook your hand' and wished you the very best.

Then he began asking me and kept pleading with me to write you a thank-you letter on his (Fedjanin's) behalf. He was going to give me a silver rouble, but I accepted only 10 kopeks for the stamp. And all this happened in my house in a special room where only the two of us were present. He asked me to express his great gratitude to you in my letter. But I don't think I need add anything more — enough has been said already.

And I would ask you, Lev Nikolaevich, to write him (Fedjanin) a letter, saying something like this: "I have heard about your strict sobriety through a certain gentleman in Minusinsk (no need to mention my name here), about how you do not drink and do not bring wine into your house." And do everything you can to thank him (Fedjanin) for this, and then tell him:

"O, cruel Viper (that is, wine), that seven-headed serpent with its seven-headed brood! The first head is dishonour, which blackens a man's good name. The second is disease. The third is abject poverty and unbearable destitution. The fourth is sorrow and sighing for one's wife and children, father and mother. The fifth is joy to one's enemies. The sixth tramps down the path to prison and turns one's wife into a widow, one's children into orphans, and in the end devastates one's home. The seventh and last serpent head is premature death, which has been thoroughly investigated by doctors. Even its name is like a frightening serpent. Any crime involves guilt, and wine is guilt.[68]

"When we go and say to one another: 'Let's go down to the pub and have a drink of wine,' we're not talking about simply taking it into our hands or

67 It is not clear which of Tolstoy's works Bondarev was specifically referring to. We know that Tolstoy wrote a good deal about the harm caused by drunkenness in both his fiction and non-fiction.

68 The Russian word for 'wine' is *vino,* while the word for 'guilt' is *vina* (both stressed on the last syllable).

putting it in our pocket, but we're pouring this wine into our very insides, into our very heart. If we use the Ukrainian term *gorilka,* right away we have *sorrow* or *something inflammable* — which means *fire.*[69] Oh, what frightening behaviour! Man becomes his own mortal enemy. Even senseless beasts have enough sense to run from evil. But man, God's intelligent creation, cannot be restrained from running *into* evil. If I take a drink of wine, that is a crime. I write this and smile wryly to myself as I think about human folly. If I take a drink of wine, well, 'one little jigger is no sin and won't hurt' — that is what people always say. But my response is: a jigger, a glass, a half-pint or a pint — they're so much alike they always want to go together. Whenever you ask for just a jigger, a full glass won't be far behind, and this is inevitably tied to a half-pint, and then a full pint, which means that from a single jigger comes such a fire that even the biggest barrel of water won't put it out.

"In the meantime the drunkard just staggers around and enjoys himself; he finds any old place to sleep it off. His morning hangover brings him no cheer and people start throwing him queer looks. It is not clear who beat him last night when he was drunk. His face is all swollen and his food has rotted in his belly, and if anyone's around to mind, they'll get a stink worse than what's given off by swine. 'Oh, what a good time I had yesterday for sure, and now my head aches and I've got a hangover with no cure. I'd better at least pawn a shirt, at least that way I shan't lose it. So I'll put on this old one, torn and grey, the one that came with my wife's dowry on our wedding day.' With hangovers it's like that for everyone — they sell or pawn their last thing they own.

"Even if I had not just one tongue but many in which my words might be sung, even then I still could not recount all these sorrows in detail, and there would still not be enough time to tell of all the afflictions that flow from the fount of wine. Anyone's lips will fail to outline all the harmful consequences it entails. Oh, what a cruel viper it is to be sure — sooner or later it will only lead to doom!

"And so, you who read or hear what I write, I ask you to bring your respect and esteem to the most blessed of all men. And who might he be? Gavrila Petrovich Fedjanin. Imitate his noble way of life. He wishes to save and deliver you from all the above-mentioned afflictions. But are you listening to him? It seems to me that you are not. And is it permissible to be an enemy to one's self? If you are an enemy to yourself, then to whom are you a friend?"

I would ask you, Lev Nikolaevich, to write this — write everything I have said and add your own convictions if you can. And then I would ask you further, Lev Nikolaevich, not to attach shame or vice to me for giving you

69 *gorilka* (pron. *ho-RIL-ka* in Ukrainian) — a word designating whisky or a strong drink; this reminds Bondarev of the Russian words *gore* (pron. *GOR-yeh*) — 'sorrow' and *gorjuchij* (inflammable).

instructions on how to write, as though the hen were being taught by its eggs. This is something to think about.

And again, I would ask you not mention at all my name, the name of Bondarev, in your letter to Fedjanin, or even hint at it. I have sent you my own letter in a special envelope by the same post, but I would ask you to send us your letters separately a week apart.

If people should find out that you are writing to Fedjanin at my request, that will not bring us good, but only harm. You know the law of the whole world: "People don't listen to what's being said, they watch to see who's speaking."

Since Fedjanin is not too literate, you should write very distinctly, so that each letter will be clear in and of itself. Then he himself will be able to read it to others.

While the white-gloved elite may have the right to admonish and warn us about drunkenness, when it comes to manual labour, there will be less sin if the deaf keep their tongues in and not utter a peep.

I have not received any of my articles which you sent me.

After writing this letter I read it to Fedjanin. He is very, very happy with it.

Nº 16. T. M. BONDAREV ❧ L. N. TOLSTOY
1890.

Lev Nikolaevich,

In Minusinsk we have a local doctor, Mikhail Prokop'evich Popov [*sic*],[70] a man I have a heartfelt respect for, and he cannot bring himself to agree with me that Cain was embraced by God. And so he and I find ourselves in a serious debate on this question. We jointly agreed to ask Lev Nikolaevich Tolstoy what he thinks of Cain, so that subsequently, i.e., after hearing your decision, we would no longer argue with each other. And so I ask you to decide this question as you see fit and let us know of your decision as soon as possible, so as not to torment us. And send it to Popov's address, which he will indicate below, and after he reads your decision, he will send it to me. This is what we have agreed.

T. Bondarev

What Popov is more inclined to accept — the industriousness you are so familiar with, or idleness — I still have no idea. In England[71] they've worked

70 A reference to Prokopij Mikhajlovich Popov.

71 Postscript by P. M. Popov: "A misunderstanding on the part of the writer here. What I actually told Bondarev was that in the French middle, and especially upper classes (I read this somewhere, in Taine, I think), there are many women who don't want to bear children at all yet be married at the same time, or want to have only one or two, and to achieve these results without any kind of infanticide, without resorting to any known means of contraception which might forever damage the woman's health, killing the fetus in embryo. The latter — i.e., poisoning the fetus — is,

it out this way: if a woman wants to, she can have a lot of children, or she may decide not to have any, or to have just two or three, as she likes. I consider this [abortion] infanticide, while Popov sees no murder in it. [Please] resolve this disagreement, too.

Write Popov a good, long letter, and just a short one to me, Bondarev, even just one word as to which of us is right.

If you are still of the opinion that it is Prokopij Mikhajlovich, [please] explain why.

N° 17. T. M. BONDAREV ❧ L. N. TOLSTOY
9 May 1891. Minusinsk, Village of Iudino.

Lev Nikolaevich.

How many years have passed between us in silence,[72] and now I am breaking this silence with the following request to you.

I have reworked my book (which you know about) in a different vein. I deleted significant parts of the text, and kept adding to it so that is now about twice the size of the old version, and it has improved in quality by the same ratio.

Last summer I happened to see Volume 2 of Gleb Ivanovich Uspenskij's 1889 work, which includes an article on page 8014 [?] entitled "Trudami ruk svoikh" [By the works of their own hands].[73] But it is not modelled after my complete book, but after a small excerpt, and he praises my work in every way possible.

Then, when I went to Minusinsk to send it [my new manuscript] by post to Uspenskij, I met there a socialist, a political [exile] named Captain Bubnovskij (I don't know his first name or patronymic),[74] who had been granted permission to go to the homeland, to St. Petersburg. He assured me that he is personally acquainted with Uspenskij. So, he says, 'entrust this to me and I'll make sure it gets to Uspenskij.' And at that time I was quite naïve and trusted his unproven words, and gave it to him. And now nine months have passed and I have received no word about it. But you, Lev Nikolaevich, know what they

of course, infanticide and should be punishable as a crime." The reference is most probably to French critic and historian Hippolyte Adolphe Taine (1828–1893).

72 The last extant letter of Tolstoy's is dated 4 August 1887 (see Letter N° 11). There was one further letter which Bondarev received from Tolstoy, in August 1889, but its whereabouts are unknown.

73 A three-volume edition of the works of Gleb Ivanovich Uspenskij was published in 1889–1891, with a foreword by N. K. Mikhajlovskij; it included an article entitled "Skuchajushchaja publika" [A bored public]. In Chap. 4, as indicated above, he discusses the essence of Bondarev's teachings, and in the next chapter, "Mechtanija" [Reveries], he speaks about several attempts on the part of the intelligentsia toward 'simplification' (*oprostit'sja*) and to 'work the land,' 'growing their own food.'

74 No information is available about this person.

say: "where your treasure is, there will your heart be also."[75] Since then I have written Uspenskij two letters,[76] but have received no reply.

I have the impression that you, Lev Nikolaevich, often visit Petersburg,[77] and so I would shake your hand *in absentia* and ask and implore you, in the name of the God of truth, to do this favour for me: see if you can find the above-mentioned Bubnovskij and Uspenskij, find out about my package and write me about it. Bubnovskij was to spend a month in the homeland, in Petersburg, and whatever step was to follow that would have been included in his orders. You could ask his relatives whether they might know about my package, and write to me.

I have a feeling that after reading it himself Bubnovskij handed it over to someone else, and then it got passed to a third party, and so forth, and so he can't find it and won't bother looking for it.

If I had discovered a means to become rich without working, then everybody would pay attention to it, and then what foolishness would they find in my writings?! "In the sweat of thy face thou shalt eat bread."[78] Just imagine, Lev Nikolaevich, who among our kid-gloved elite would go along with that? Not one in a thousand, and so the most appropriate place for it is the one indicated above.

And so, Lev Nikolaevich, if you should find the manuscript, I would ask you to take it and send it to me. If they need confirmation that I am the one asking for it, show them this letter and the envelope written in the same hand, as well as the postmarks.

This is so that I can collect all these draft papers together and bind them into a single bundle. Then I shall ask my son: When I die and you bury me, put these papers in with me.[79] As for the petition which I have already written and affixed a 60-kopek stamp to, put it in my right hand and bury me for the ages I cannot cross.

This petition was written on four sheets of cheap paper. Where is it addressed, and to whom? To the Head Office of the celestial Ministry of Internal Affairs. What is the main content of the above-mentioned petition?

75 Matth. 6:21.

76 On Bondarev's two letters to Uspenskij (the first was his reaction to G. Uspenskij's article (1884 [By the works of their own hands]), the second about the publication of his sermon), see Prutskov 1976: 132–34. These letters were published for the first time in Donskov 1996b: 133–39.

77 In fact, in contrast to his wife, Sofia Andreevna, Leo Tolstoy rarely went to St. Petersburg during the latter part of his life.

78 Gen. 3:19.

79 Bondarev gave instructions for his son to bury him and put a desk containing his manuscripts atop the grave, so that any passerby might read them and become acquainted with his teachings. These instructions were carried out, but, as indicated by Kosovanov (1958: 16), those who truly appreciated Bondarev's work brought the manuscripts to the Minusinsk Museum. Bondarev was buried in the Iudino cemetery. In 1958, the village of Iudino was renamed Bondarevo and a monument was erected on Bondarev's grave.

A complaint against those people who read it and pay no attention. Why [did they pay no attention]? Because of my family's low social class. And more and more because of the chief Ministry of this world.

I've sent them so many petitions, and they have not deigned to reply to even one of them. I sent a letter to the very highest name[80] (need I say more?), and I got this answer back: "Because there is no justification for this petition, it has not been acted upon." And so I ask and implore the celestial government to summon all the opponents I have named to deal personally with me before the celestial court.

What can I say to entreat and persuade you, Lev Nikolaevich? It's a pity I cannot express myself with beautiful turns of phrase the way you can, to enlist your efforts in my above request. But of equal import is the petition I have written to the original commandment and to the ground whence comes our food, which, contrary to the original decree, languishes unbearably in the hands of the white-gloved elite — that is, of the man who is unworthy to set his foot upon it. One can only contemplate and tremble at the thought.

The day you receive this, that very same day write me a reply, or I shall be extremely wrought. Ask Uspenskij why he chose to publish so little of the great amount of interesting material. I would say it is because insofar as it is just, it is vitriolic for freeloaders, and therefore it must not be published.

I think you will find the above-mentioned volume of Uspenskij's in your bookshops. Send it to me, only tell me how much it is and I shall then send you the money.

Don't send me letters by ordinary mail, have them registered, or they will not go through. I am faced with such a serious foe that as soon as he sees my name on an envelope, he will tear it up at once into bits and throw it under foot. And the letter will not escape his hands.

Nº 18. T. M. BONDAREV ❧ L. N. TOLSTOY
9 September 1891. Minusinsk, Village of Iudino.

The only friend to my heart and soul in the whole world Lev Nikolaevich, and why the "only" one? We shall soon see. I wrote two petitions to the Minister of Internal Affairs and one to the Minister of Petitions, and one to the Tsar, [marked] confidential, to which I received the following answer: "In view of the groundlessness of this petition, no favourable response ensued." What constituted its "groundlessness"? Not a word [about that].

A gentleman came to see us from Irkutsk. At his request I gave him the manuscript which you had, on condition that he return it to me very soon, and it is almost two years now and he hasn't sent it to me. I wrote him two letters, no response. Don't you see, Lev Nikolaevich, is this not a bloody insult

80 *the very highest name* — i.e., the tsar.

to me? They — all the above-mentioned people, can see that I am not working for my own benefit, but for the benefit of the whole world, including them. They are all people educated in advanced science, not like me; is it permissible to return evil for good and hate for love?

I had a sermon along this line newly written out, in which I deleted a lot of things, and kept adding new [ideas] to what was there before. I went to Minusinsk to send it off at the post office to Uspenskij for publication. There I happened to run into a political socialist [named] Captain Bubnovskij, a resident of Petersburg, who had just received an order to return to his home base, and he persuaded me to entrust this parcel to him, as he knows Uspenskij personally and where he lives. "I'll be very sure to take it to him," he said. And, innocent chap that I was at the time, I trusted his dishonest word, gave it to him and urged him to write to me about how it turned out. It's been a year and two months now and not a word in reply. I've written him two letters — but no answer.

I believe, Lev Nikolaevich, that you often go to Petersburg. Could you look up this Bubnovskij and find out about this? I suspect he (Bubnovskij) recognized that they won't print this in Russia, and that [even asking] could land him in trouble, and so he secretly sent it abroad. That could be why he hasn't written — he's afraid that I might discover this secret. If you find him, show him this letter for authenticity — he knows my handwriting.

In Minusinsk it appears that many have respect for my sermon, but it is somehow half-hearted, cold and insipid, and more and more [on the part of] those who find any way they can to topple, reject and contradict. And there's the rub: if by some chance I figured out a way to become rich without working or have others do it for me — but no: [I prefer] living off my own [labour] instead — who would agree with me?

For my enemies there is but one victory and one plague — the fact that so great a personage as Count Tolstoy is engaged in correspondence with me, plain and simple man that I am. Many would like not to believe this, but there is no denying it — [your] letter and the address is written in a single hand and the postal imprint on the envelope — all that is a plague to them.

Stick it to them, Lev Nikolaevich, stick a plague like this to theirs: it is not something I wish — God is my witness that it is not something I wish. Still, keep writing me all sorts of praise and gratitude and in your genuine hand so that anybody can recognize it. Name someone else who has respect for my whole article. Then not as an enemy but as a friend will I fling this in their pug-nosed faces and their evil tongues will be silenced.

Wasn't I right when I referred to you at the beginning of this [letter] as my only friend in the whole world? And what have I offered you for this — either before people or before God, my celebrated Lev Nikolaevich? Send you money? I don't have any. Express my gratitude on paper (as many do) with eloquence and flattery? That I am not able to do. And so I remain in your debt.

Do you believe in a life for our future age beyond the grave? I don't know about it, but I firmly and undoubtedly believe in it. And since we're both old men, in our seventies, I would think it might not be long before we both find ourselves in the next world, and so it will be then and there I give you the gratitude you deserve.

I wrote on two sheets of paper (i.e., on four pages) a complaining petition with as much expression as I could muster, and to whom? [A complaint] against whom and what for? To the Tsar of tsars and the God of gods, Who holds Heaven and the Earth in His hands. Against whom? Naturally, not against the tail, but the head — this is the great Ministry (metaphorically). For what? For taking land away from poor land-tillers all across Russia, for hiding the above-mentioned [biblical] law from them — and for the former serf law of slavery, which, even though it has been repealed, still leaves a bitter taste in the mouth. And I put a 60-kopek stamp on this petition and gave an order to my son, that when I die and you put me in the grave, stick this petition in my right hand, and place my manuscript and all my drafts in the grave with me for untold centuries. And I shall ask the above-mentioned Tsar that after my death he promptly and immediately summon to court — for a face-to-face interrogation — a collection of all the opponents and enemies of the primal commandment. Do you approve this goal of mine? When I die, I shall let you know through my son, and don't keep mum about your own death so that we don't waste time in [unnecessary] letter-writing.

Your letter and parcel took 20 days [to get] from Moscow to Minusinsk, and I received them intact. [Please] send me the French book you mentioned; there's a chap here who can read it and interpret it in Russian.

Write and tell me who or what Ministry prohibited the publishing of my articles. I shall write a petition to it, without mentioning who told me about the prohibition. Why does the whole universe accept the power and value of the primal law, and Russia alone [tries to] denounce and destroy it? This dream of hers is neither empty nor unimportant, since it is clearly evident, just as in a mirror, that Russia will not escape the righteous judgement of Heaven. Not only has she left the current millions of land-tillers — those who feed her — naked and impoverished, but she has done the same to all future generations 'til the end of time, along with their children (including their littlest ones). And for what cause? For the sake of Russia's laziness and luxury.

Once again I repeat what I said before: look up that Bubnovskij I mentioned; also find [another] two or three people, who would join in approving my [work].

Farewell, Lev Nikolaevich, until our [next] pleasant meeting.

In sending off this letter, even though I am well in my [spiritual] life — my whole body and head are aching, and food doesn't go down, as with a fever, though [my body] isn't trembling.

I'm very much afraid that just a small excerpt from my manuscript has been published abroad, just as here. [People may say:] If only he had spared us his pungent articles, but no: he passed over the soft and friendly ones, sweet and pleasant for the whole world, while the provocative ones he selected for publication. Why is that?

Nº 19. T. M. BONDAREV ❧ L. N. TOLSTOY

28 February 1892. Minusinsk.

Lev Nikolaevich,

In September of 1891 I received a letter[81] from you along with a package [containing] the newspaper *Svet*. I wrote you right away that I had received it. I still don't know whether you received my letter or not.

Where should I begin, and where and how should I stop offering you my gratitude? In those minutes I stretched out my hand to you and firmly, firmly shook your hand with all my strength. Even though this is the only gratitude I can muster, with such a humble mind as mine, had I started trying to express more gratitude in words, would it have been appropriate?

I most humbly ask you, Lev Nikolaevich, to send me the book in French that you mentioned in your letter. We have here a chap who is able to read it and translate it into Russian, and I know him quite well; besides, I can get to Minusinsk. And emphasize in your letter that this book contains my (Bondarev's) essay. Without your confirmation, people will not believe me and consider me a braggart.

While I haven't seen this with my own eyes, I have heard a rumour that in Minusinsk there is a book of your writings, Volume 13, which includes my article on drunkenness, tobacco and extra-marital relations and is being passed from hand to hand all around the town [so many people are dying to read it].

I most humbly beg you, Lev Nikolaevich, to send me this book, too.

In my essay, which you are familiar with and used to have in your possession, only a tenth or less has actually been published, consequently the government doesn't know anything about it. Even with this intolerable blow I have not lost presence of mind; quite the opposite, I ignited this whole thing, and fervently hope it will not be snuffed out. I destroyed many articles from my previous manuscript, and added more and more, polishing them in the process and making them flattering to everyone. How this turns out I shall let you know then. I shan't stop talking about this until my eyes close in eternal gloom. Otherwise I shall continue to appeal to them, just like the Gospel widow to the unjust judge who feared not God nor people's shame.[82]

81 The whereabouts of the letter are unknown.

82 See Luke 18:1–6.

What compelled me to write another manuscript and take such a tremendous labour upon myself? Here is the reason. Of my former manuscript only a tenth part has been published, while the other 9 parts have been lost. It would be all right if it had been the intolerably pungent and bitter parts that were lost. But no, the lost ones were those that were sweeter than honey and most useful of all for all levels of society — more precious than all the treasures of this world. They were all consigned to destruction, while the bitter and intolerably pungent parts were published — and who did that, I have no idea.

And just how did this tangle come about? I know of no other explanation but the following: as I already said, a great gulf opened up between the above-mentioned commandment and the 'kid gloves' — with no passing from it to them, nor from them to it[83] — they became enemies and mutual malevolents, which turned them into momentary lunatics without them even realizing it.

God forbid this same kind of pettiness be sent abroad — what would happen? According to everything I've heard, neither the government nor anyone else in the world knows what I said or how I said it. And now the whole world will clearly see the treasured reaches of my heart. This is the reason that compelled me to take upon myself this huge task amidst all my daily activities and cares.

And so, Lev Nikolaevich, again I repeat: send me the above-mentioned books. I wish you all the best, with my heartfelt respect,

T. Bondarev

Nº 20. T. M. BONDAREV ❧ L. N. TOLSTOY

1 October 1893. Village of Iudino.

Lev Nikolaevich. As I am now already 74 and you are probably somewhat close to that,[84] you can see we both have one foot in the grave already. Thus in continuation of this letter I shall tell you a radiant truth. You, Lev Nikolaevich, are the only close friend I have in all the world. There has been and cannot be any friend as close to me as you are. God is my witness that I am telling you the truth.

Why a close friend? Because you have taken every possible measure on your part to promote my sermon which is now familiar to you, and if the whole universe has not accepted it but bitterly rejected it, you are certainly not to blame.

Lev Nikolaevich, I detect in myself some kind of emotional imbalance, and a serious one at that, which I am either ashamed or afraid to tell you about. What kind imbalance am I speaking of? It goes like this.

I am of a Judaic-based faith, otherwise known as a Sabbatarian, grounded on the Old Testament alone (though I by no means accept the Talmudic

83 See Luke 16:27.
84 In October 1893, Tolstoy would have been sixty-five years old.

traditions — in fact, I despise them) — that is, I am following in Christ's footsteps. What does that mean? It means this!

Christ recognized only one God. He had no gods made by human hands, nor worshipped any. Neither do I. Christ was circumcised, observed the Sabbath, and ate according to Passover law. So do I, etc. etc. Christ says: "Think not that I came to destroy the law — not to destroy but to fulfil until heaven and earth pass, not one jot or tittle shall pass from the law."[85] And I am fulfilling what is lawful, insofar as I am able.

We have here 130 Sabbatarian households and in all of them there is a hatred of Christ. If you ask someone "Why do you hate Christ?" he will answer: "I don't know. I can't find anything wrong with him, and yet I hate him." As for the Jews, they have a supernatural and immeasurable hatred for him.

I have persistently enquired of learned Jews why they have so much hatred for Jesus the son of Mary and where did it come from? "He was an illegitimate child; besides, he was a sorcerer and a wizard," they reply. "Weren't there a lot of illegitimate sorcerers and wizards?" I respond. "Do you hate him?" I ask. "No," they say, "no. He called himself God," they offer as an excuse, accusing Him. "Then what's all the fuss about?" I ask. "It's only that you don't believe him, and there's no motive cause for evil. Now tell me the honest truth, as a fellow-believer," I say, pretending to be a zealous follower of the Talmudic traditions, "tell me, or rather, show me the source where it gives the reason why you should hate him so much." "We've already said it," they reply. But there is no truth in those sayings of yours, they're nothing but lies and slander.

Your ancestors had some illustrious enemies: the pharaoh Nebuchadnezzar,[86] Antiochus Epiphanes,[87] Artaxerxes,[88] and Haman,[89] who had the intention of expelling the whole Jewish nation, which they did, though they did not succeed completely. "Do you hate them?" I ask. "No," they reply, "no, we don't." Yet hatred was evident at the time of the crucifixion: they demanded the release of Barabbas, a thief who had killed living people, while Christ, who had raised the dead, was condemned to death.[90]

85 Matth. 5:17, 18 (according to the Church Slavonic Bible quoted by Bondarev). The Authorized Version reads: "Think not that I am come to destroy the law, or the prophets: I am not come to destroy, but to fulfil. For verily I say unto you, Till heaven and earth pass, one jot or one tittle shall in no wise pass from the law, till all be fulfilled."

86 *Nebuchadnezzar II* (630–552 BCE) — ruler of Babylon in the Chaldean Dynasty, known in particular for his conquests of Judah and Jerusalem. He figures prominently in a number of books of the Old Testament, notably 2 Kings, 2 Chronicles, Jeremiah and Daniel.

87 *Antiochus IV Epiphanes* (215?–164 BCE) — ruler of the Seleucid Empire 175–164 BCE.

88 *Artaxerxes* — King of Persia 465–424 BCE. See the Book of Ezra, Chap. 7.

89 *Haman* — a Persian nobleman and vizier to the Persian King Ahasuerus (Xerxes I), father of Artaxerxes. Rabbinical tradition portrays Haman as an archetype of evil and a persecutor of the Jews. See the Book of Esther, Chap. 3–8.

90 See Matth. 27:16–23.

Christians will say that their hatred was inflamed by His blood which they had on their hands. "His blood be on us, and on our children."[91] No, no, Lev Nikolaevich, this argument is unfair, since even before then they were angry at Him. After all, even the sun was ashamed to look upon their mockery of Him; at noon it hid its rays, and the earth trembled and shook for fear, the mountains shook, rocks fell apart and the veil of the temple was rent from the top to the bottom,[92] and even the heart of Pilate, as cruel as he was, was softened by His sorry sight and he brought Him before the public to see if they might have had any change of heart. But upon seeing Him, they cried in unison to Pilate: "Take Him, take Him and crucify Him."[93] All this happened before the people said, "His blood be on us."

Pilate called Jesus a righteous man, and then proceeded to have him crucified. What for? Because of just one word: "Not Cæsar's friend"[94] — in other words, "we'll report you as a traitor."

Two high priests served as Jesus's judges: one was Annas, the other Caiaphas.[95] When Christ spoke, Annas didn't like it: "Do you dare annoy God's high priest?"[96] And when He refused to speak, this upset Caiaphas, and He got spat in the face.[97] When He spoke, they considered Him guilty, and when He would not speak, they took this as a sign of insanity. And all of this was before the remark about blood.

All those torments — beatings, cursings, insults of every kind, the purple robe, the crown of thorns, the slaps in the face, the nailing to the cross, the piercing of His ribs with a spear[98] — all these He suffered as he kept his silence. But when the servant of the high priest struck Him on the right cheek — a light blow, after all, and insignificant in comparison with the other torments mentioned above, for some reason He didn't restrain himself, but said: "Why

91 Matth. 27:25.

92 See Matth. 27:45–54.

93 Cf. John 19:6: "When the chief priests therefore and officers saw him, they cried out, saying, Crucify him, crucify him. Pilate saith unto them, Take ye him, and crucify him: for I find no fault in him."

94 Cf. John 19:12: "And from thenceforth Pilate sought to release him: but the Jews cried out, saying, If thou let this man go, thou art not Cæsar's friend: whosoever maketh himself a king speaketh against Cæsar."

95 See Luke 3:2.

96 Cf. John 18:19–22: "The high priest then asked Jesus of his disciples, and of his doctrine. Jesus answered him, I spake openly to the world; I ever taught in the synagogue, and in the temple, whither the Jews always resort; and in secret have I said nothing. Why askest thou me? ask them which heard me, what I have said unto them: behold, they know what I said. And when he had thus spoken, one of the officers which stood by struck Jesus with the palm of his hand, saying, Answerest thou the high priest so?"

97 Cf. Mark 14:60–65: "And the high priest stood up in the midst, and asked Jesus, saying, Answerest thou nothing? what is it which these witness against thee?… And some began to spit on him, and to cover his face…"

98 See, e.g., Mark 15:17, Matth. 26:67, Matth. 27:35, John 19:34.

smitest thou me? If I have spoken evil, bear witness of the evil: but if well, why smitest thou me?"[99]

It seems to me, Lev Nikolaevich, that this was because all the above-mentioned torments happened in secular places: on the streets of Jerusalem, in Pilate's court, on the hill of Golgotha, but here He was struck in the face right in the high priest's house, before the high priest himself — that is, iniquity was happening in the very place where truth should be flourishing. And all of this came before the above-mentioned reference to blood.

In other words, anger at Him boiled in their hearts right from the time of his birth, when this anger caused the killing of fourteen thousand infants just so they could kill Him. And did they say back then: "His blood be on us, and on our children"? No, they did not.

It is evident that He, Christ, did no miracles before the governors. Note that when the Governor summoned Him to see whether He might perform some sort of miracle for them, He did not deign to answer.[100] Hence the government saw nothing with their own eyes, and there was a question as to whether the folk tales could be believed or no.

Did the government of the day summon for questioning all those He had healed or raised from the dead? It did, but they all answered out of fear: "We know not this person." This assumption of mine is attested by the Apostle Peter. As you know, he might have been forced into such a denial under threat, by someone like the high priest or Pilate or Herod. But no, he was simply afraid of one lowly damsel, the high priest's servant, when she asked him: "Weren't you with Jesus of Nazareth?" And here he felt obliged to deny this with an oath.[101]

I kept asking myself, Lev Nikolaevich, what would have happened if the Jews had embraced Christ and not done the things that they did — what would have happened then? All the prophecies concerning Him would then have been given the lie, because He would not have suffered and died, not have risen and ascended, and there would be no Orthodoxy as we know it

99 John 18:23.

100 The reference here is to Herod, governor of Galilee, to whom Pontius Pilate, the Roman governor of Jerusalem, had sent Jesus for questioning. Cf. Luke 23:6–9: "When Pilate heard of Galilee, he asked whether the man were a Galilæan. And as soon as he knew that he belonged unto Herod's jurisdiction, he sent him to Herod, who himself also was at Jerusalem at that time. And when Herod saw Jesus, he was exceeding glad: for he was desirous to see him of a long season, because he had heard many things of him; and he hoped to have seen some miracle done by him. Then he questioned with him in many words; but he answered him nothing."

101 Cf. Matth. 26:69–74: "Now Peter sat without in the palace: and a damsel came unto him, saying, Thou also wast with Jesus of Galilee. But he denied before them all, saying, I know not what thou sayest. And when he was gone out into the porch, another maid saw him, and said unto them that were there, This fellow was also with Jesus of Nazareth. And again he denied with an oath, I do not know the man. And after a while came unto him they that stood by, and said to Peter, Surely thou also art one of them; for thy speech bewrayeth thee. Then began he to curse and to swear, saying, I know not the man."

today, and practically the whole world would have remained in the darkness of its own ancient superstition. This is what I kept asking myself, but did not come to any satisfactory answer. Only I came to the following conclusion as best as I could:

Since God knows no time, neither past nor future, but everything is in the present — that is, a thousand years have gone by for us, but for Him they simply *are,* or the next thousand years have not gone by for us, but for Him they simply *are.*[102] Hence His unsearchable plan — a plan incomprehensible even to the Angels — had determined from time immemorial at what time and in what place, and by whose hand and by what means He, Christ, was to suffer and die.

And even if we had been there in that very place, and it had been determined that He should suffer and die on account of us, would we be in a position to avoid or get around His timeline? Impossible. And if all that has been said has been determined by God, then the Jews' present hatred of Him is also unavoidable for them. And if everything has been determined by God, consequently, there is no question of the Jews being to blame for their being inflamed to hatred of Him, as I mentioned earlier.

On the basis of all that I have said, I would ask and implore you, Lev Nikolaevich, to collect together all your scattered thoughts concerning worldly cares, consult with them and write to me as to how and by what means to heal this plague on our souls, namely, hatred of Christ. Can we be converted to Orthodoxy? No, that is unthinkable. Here the first and second commandments stand on the path leading us to Orthodoxy as an insurmountable barrier. Am I the only one whose heart pains because of this? No, there are many of us. It is they who have compelled me to turn to you, Lev Nikolaevich, for relief from this frightful mental illness.

T. Bondarev

Lev Nikolaevich, you have a book in French containing my work.[103] Send it to me. There is someone here who can read it and translate it into Russian.

I may be the brightest of all or the stupidest of all. It's just that I do not have a single soul here that can advise me, and I am suffering from extreme restlessness.

In a month you will receive a letter from me on a completely different subject.

1 October 1893. Village of Iudino.

102 Cf. II Peter 3:8: "...one day is with the Lord as a thousand years, and a thousand years as one day."

103 Bondarev is here referring to the French translation of his *Torzhestvo zemledel'tsa ili trudoljubie i tunejadstvo,* made with Tolstoy's collaboration and published in Paris (see Note 3; see Bondarev and Tolstoj 1890)

N° 21. L. N. TOLSTOY ❧ T. M. BONDAREV[104]

3 December 1893. Moscow.

Timofej Mikhajlovich!

I was very glad to receive your letter — first, because I see from it that you are alive and healthy and remember me, and secondly, because you are asking yourself what is to my mind the most important question of all. I shall try as best I can to give you my answer.

I would answer as follows:

The Jews and the Sabbatarians hate Christ out of a misconception, because people have gone astray and replaced the one eternal God by another God in the form of Christ, and this has overshadowed the true God and even hid Him from people. I say that they hate Christ out of a misconception, because they need not blame Christ, who never claimed himself to be God, but called himself — as he did everyone else — the son of God. They ought to blame those who made him into a God. This is how I would explain the Jews' hatred of Christ.

As I see it, Christ is not God and never claimed to be God, but he was the great, last Hebrew prophet, teaching not only Jews but all people on earth how to serve the one true God, calling himself and everybody else His son.

Consequently, Jews and Sabbatarians ought not only to refrain from hating Christ, but ought to honour him and follow the Divine law which he revealed to them. The law of Christ is consistent with law of Moses and with the prophets — not in all details, but in essence, in the idea of love for God and one's neighbour. It is just that Christ stated this law more clearly and accurately. More importantly, Christ was the only one of the Hebrew prophets to give this law not only to the Jews but to the whole world and thereby put an end to the Jews' isolation from other peoples. Since the time of Christ, God's law has become common to all peoples, as the prophets said. (This is indicated in John 12:20, when he declared the truth directly to Greeks.) It was not the Jews as a whole, but the high priests, Pharisees and Sadducees who tortured and crucified Christ. On the contrary, the Jews were his disciples and spread his teaching throughout the world. And if some godless people had not called Christ God, all the Jews would not only have not hated Christ, but long ago would have honoured and loved him as the last great prophet, revealing the truth to them. This was prevented by the blasphemy of the godless in calling Christ God, but in any case the Jews will come, and are already coming, to this recognition. A Jew cannot be converted to Orthodoxy, but the Jews, just like those of the Orthodox faith, ought to recognize Christ as

104 This letter is published in *PSS* 66:437–39. It was written in response to Bondarev's letter of 1 October 1893 (Letter N° 20).

a *man* (see 1 Timothy 2:5),[105] as a prophet of God, and then both sides will join together.

I shall send your French book in a few days. It is back in the country.[106] And I am now in Moscow. I shall be very glad to receive your next letter, as you promised.

May God grant you all good.

Lev Tolstoy
3 December.

Write to me in Moscow at: 15, Khamovnicheskij Pereulok.

N° 22. T. M. BONDAREV ❧ L. N. TOLSTOY
30 April 1894. Village of Iudino.[107]

Lev Nikolaevich,

Even the most vindictive of Christ's enemies have taken your advice and softened [their tone]: they have recognized Christ in the way you recommended, and turned the anger they previously had for Him against those who forced practically the whole world to consider Him the Maker and Creator of heaven and the Earth and everything therein, and who are not ashamed but say outright in their accounts: "We have no other God but Thee."[108] And everyone has been giving you gratitude in whatever way he can express it. And the Jews who were at your reading — it was at a large gathering in the synagogue around Passover — were being shamed and cursed. Only a small part of our population are practising Jews — there are more Sabbatarians, Karaims, who are founded just on the Mosaic law and the prophets, and do not accept the Talmud traditions at all. Of the thousands of vain traditions they hold to I'll name just one — here's one: when God created Eve, she was a beauty, and when he put some sort of crown on her [head], she became even more beautiful. Then God did some sort of dance with her (i.e., he crawled up on her like a human being). And there's another point: if God doesn't understand something, he asks the rabbis, and whatever the rabbi says God should automatically fulfil, and whatever God says, the rabbi is not obliged to fulfil His words. It's all the same: just as with Orthodox Christians, Christ ranks higher than God, with the Jews the rabbi is superior to God, and with the Mohammedans Mohammed is above God.

105 Tolstoy's own reference. This verse reads in the Authorized Version: "For there is one God, and one mediator between God and men, the man Christ Jesus."
106 *in the country* — i.e., at Yasnaya Polyana.
107 On the envelope in Tolstoy's handwriting: "Answered. Attach to the reply a letter about Henry George and concluding remarks" (cited in *PSS* 67:160).
108 Cf. Hosea 13:4: "Yet I am the Lord thy God from the land of Egypt, and thou shalt know no god but me:..."

Tell me, Lev Nikolaevich, who called the Orthodox faith "Orthodox"?[109] Did it name itself that? People here say that it's as though they wanted to establish one faith in God for the whole world — have you heard that? That is something I would desire with all my heart, only not under any current denomination, but under a brand new one.

Tell us, Lev Nikolaevich, in your opinion, is it permissible to worship icons, to treat them as holy, to place one's hope and trust in them, and with that to inevitably idolise them? Is it permissible to pour out all one's heartfelt and emotional feelings before them? The sacred icons, the Kiev-Pechersky relics — is all that genuine?

Oh, my one and only friend in the whole world, Lev Nikolaevich, it used to be that the mere mention of death would cause me to shudder in horror, but now, having seen the injustice of this world, I have such a strong desire for death, just as someone hungers for bread or thirsts for water!

That sermon on idleness that you had, is that the only one I've written? No. In spite of the fact that my works are forbidden to be published, I have written three more [even] longer, which I kept perfecting all along, and have now sent them off into the hands of the highest levels of government, but why and to what end? You yourself will be able to guess right as to why. Have I got any answer back from them? It's like I've been throwing stones into a whirlpool.

In connection with this great and terrible insult, I have written two petitions to the celestial and inaccessible (to our [mind]) court — one a page long and the other of equal length; on each one I put 60 kopeks worth of stamps and told my son: When I die and you put me in the grave, place these packets in my right hand so that they lie on my heart, and bury me with them for centuries untold. To our sight they will be in the ground, but to God they will be in the world, for us they will decay, but for God — never. This is why I wrote them, to hand them personally to God in the next life. Does that mean I picture God as a person, a human being? No, such a picture would not be God, but some kind of dead abstraction of God. I picture God as infinite Spirit and inaccessible to the Angelic mind.

In my latest manuscript it is said: Astronomers tell us that there are multitudes of these dark planets, such as our Earth — they move through the air above our heads, and without the aid of telescopes we are unable to see them with the naked eye. (My eyes see poorly under candlelight, hence the crossings-out — don't hold that against me.) And these planets are inhabited — what kind of inhabitants is unknown. Of course we can think with some degree of confidence that they are people like us. Let's imagine [the following scenario]. Here from one of those planets a person possessing unlimited power has come down to the Earth, and I am the first one he questions: "How

109 The Russian term *pravoslavie* literally means 'right praising'; its traditional, Greek-derived English equivalent (orthodoxy) means 'right teaching.'

are things going with you on the Earth? Is everything going fine, pleasing to God and useful to people? Tell me the truth." "We have some stupid people on the Earth;" I answer, "they feed smart people with bread and save them from starvation." He fixed his curious eyes on me and cross-questioned: "What are you saying?" [I rephrased:] "Here stupid people treat the smart ones like little children or invalids and provide them with bread." "Hey, brother," [he replied,] "are you in your right mind? Who would believe that a smart person for no logical or inevitable reason would agree to eat the poor out of house and home, ride on their backs and put bridle-bits in their mouths? But if that's true, then you've made a miscalculation in how you name them: you should call the feeders the smart ones and those who are fed, stupid, or even crazy. In any case, I'll find out myself over time. Anyway, are there any other evil-doings like that?" the celestial visitor enquired.

"There's more," I responded. "For well-nigh three hundred years these feeders have been tortured in feudal slavery, a fate worse than death." "What do you mean, slavery?" asked the celestial visitor. And here I gave him the whole account of the cruelty — cruelty which I didn't just hear about from others, or guessed at, but actually experienced myself. And the more I talked, the more his eyes sparked with the fire of anger and revenge. And once more, in a voice trembling with rage, he asked: "Is there still yet another case of evil-doing comparable to this?" "There is," I replied. "It is this: On the Earth we recognize breadwinning as a primal law given by God Himself at the creation of the world: 'In the sweat of thy face shalt thou eat bread'[110] — that is, except in legitimate and unavoidable circumstances one should earn his own bread by his labours, and not ride on the backs of the poor.

"This law has never been given a proper explanation anywhere in the world, and all across our land it is acknowledged to be a living corpse. In the whole world there has been found just a single representative (that's me) of the above-mentioned martyrs — the serfs — who has afforded this law or commandment a brilliant development for its power and value. Here it's turned out that this law contains only bliss for people of the lower classes and, by contrast, for them [the upper classes] nothing but humiliation and vice. This is why our main government has consigned all this to destruction." "Now," said the celestial visitor, "now I understand the whole importance of the commandment you cited, along with all the vain subterfuges of your government. And what else is there? Are there no other barbarities in this land of yours?" "There are. Here's one: All the arable land near waters, all the meadows, forests, fish-rich rivers and lakes have been taken away from the feeders in perpetuity, and sold to landowners and millionaires. Landlords and merchants have fenced off the countryside and people are confined like prisoners behind a stockade. And when will this imprisonment cease? Never. People can only be saved from it by death."

110 Gen. 3:19.

At the mention of such a heinous deed never seen nor heard of under the sun, he covered his face with sorrow and grief, lowered his misty eyes to the ground and talked softly with himself, barely audibly, saying: "Who indeed has the right to take public land away from someone who, like those hungering for bread or thirsting for water, gives himself unstintingly to his labour, and, moreover, to give thousands of *desjatinas* of land in perpetuity to someone who avoids labour like deathly poison or a poisonous snake and hides himself away from it anywhere he can? And who has the right to hide from people the law of industriousness given by God Himself, and who has the right to consign to slavery — under the unlimited power of a landlord — people who feed the whole world and save others from death by starvation? That is unnatural and excessive impudence or, rather, highway robbery! I have travelled," said the celestial visitor, "through the whole celestial cycle, and have visited a multitude of such planets and multitudes of such people, and nowhere have I seen such evil-doing or barbarity practised as on this world. Among all the creatures either on land or in water," said the celestial visitor, "none do so much evil as here. The very devils in hell live on friendly terms with each other, without offending each other.

"Ach! Alas, alack, such woe is felt by the people living under the control of such a godless government! Is it really possible, is it permissible to take away land from the land-tiller and give it to kid-gloved idlers and spongers?! How is it that God will not strike these highway robbers on the Earth with His inscrutable punishing sword of justice?!

"Such an evil-doing is unheard of anywhere in the universe. I shall bring it in writing to the attention of the whole celestial circle, all the planets, so that as they read about this they will throw up their hands in horror. And the whole celestial circle will pray God that He send upon these tyrants the measure of punishment they deserve."

After this celestial ruler learnt from me not only what I have described here, but all the insolent details besides, he went on to ask me whether our government had any virtues that might compensate for the crimes and insults against its poor. "When it comes to virtues, there are indeed many," [I said,] "especially over these past thirty-five years." "What kind of virtues?" "Well, there's this and that," and I named all that I could [think of]. "Yes," he responded, "those are truly great virtues, but by comparison with the offences you mentioned, which transgress the bounds of any evil-doings, they are of lesser importance and even insignificant; not only are they not enough to compensate for or soften the offences committed against the poor, but they are even more heartbreaking when it comes to the little children. It is our duty to do good to others. Is it also a duty to offend them? People should be shown examples of love for humanity, while they, by contrast, have shown examples of all sorts of offences among human beings, as we mentioned earlier."

After all that is said and done, [he] through his unlimited power, summoned our highest-level Russian government [officials] (among them my

Lev Nikolaevich — this thought provokes me to laughter — it was not mentioned in the manuscript), who stand before him with fear and trembling at the threshold, and [he] asks them, or rather [all of] you: "Do you know who I am, whose I am and whence I came?" "We do not," you reply. "If only you knew who I am and whence I came!"[111] At this point he explained to you all the details about himself and the reason for his coming to the Earth, and the power that had been given him, and how he can travel to planet after planet in a short space of time — all this he explained.

At this point I shall finish the excerpt from my essay. What happened next between them, how the condemnation or justification of our government ended up — that I'll tell you about in my next letter, only if you wish to know. Or you may well dismiss all this as empty chatter. In that case I need not bother [writing it out]. But what do you think, Lev Nikolaevich, will their eloquence and trickery serve to justify them before that terrible and unrelenting Judge? Here I see four kinds of crime: 1) sponging, 2) slavery, 3) hiding behind the law and 4) taking land brazenly away from people.

Where I come from, we have a hayfield 8 versts long and 2 versts wide, which is overrun by water in the spring. There are thousands and thousands of haystacks there, all belonging to a landlord, and not even one armload of hay for people to harvest anywhere. Back on 1 January 1893 my brother had one cow and she died of starvation. There were no cattle, or sheep, or horses, or pigs, or chickens — nothing, and no wages to be had. Six lakes and a river full of fish. "Nobody can or will dare go near the lake or the river," says the merchant who bought the land from the landowner, "that's my property in perpetuity." From this it is evident that the same is happening all over Russia. But you, Lev Nikolaevich, living in Moscow, can't imagine any of that, you have enough to eat; the landowners and millionaires are happy, and that's that, and let the people have nothing. Do I not speak the truth? It's the truth and nothing but.

Allow me to give you a friendly reproach. You publish large volumes. You need to use two whole bales of paper and you have enough time for that. But when it comes to me, you write just a single sheet of paper, and that's it — nothing more to say to me — which means, you consider me of lower value.

Did you ever write me a letter through Dr. Popov at Minusinsk which I did not receive? Yet he maintains that he sent me your letter from Minusinsk.

Why did I not answer your letter for a long time? That is because you promised to send me my book within a few days, and I kept waiting for it, but even now I haven't received it. Now farewell, Lev Nikolaevich, farewell, my only friend in this world, I wish you all the best. I remain healthy.

T. Bondarev

111 Cf. John 8:14: "Jesus answered...I know whence I came and whither I go; but ye cannot tell whence I come, and whither I go."

N° 23. L. N. TOLSTOY ❧ T. M. BONDAREV
23 June 1894. Yasnaya Polyana.[112]

I am writing to tell you that Henry George[113] has come up with a plan to free land from its encroachers, or, rather, for freeing workers from slavery as the result of land being owned by people who do not till it, but [I] didn't write you the details of his plan. I shall try to do this [now].

Henry George's plan consists in the following:

The profitability and conveniences of land use are not the same everywhere. Since there will always be a great demand for more fertile, convenient lands close to the more populated zones, and the better and more profitable the land, the larger the demand, all such lands need to be valued according to their profitability: the more profitable lands will cost more, the less profitable [will cost] less, and the even less profitable — even less. Any land for which there is hardly any demand should not be included in the evaluation, and can be given away free of charge to whoever is willing to work it personally. —

Under such an evaluation system, here in Tula Gubernia, for example, useful arable land will be assessed at 5 or 6 roubles per *desjatina* [per year], vegetable gardens in settlements around 10, water meadowlands around 15, etc. In cities, by contrast, land would be valued at 100 to 500 roubles per *desjatina*, while in Moscow and St. Petersburg, and in prominent locations and harbours on navigable rivers — several thousand, or even tens of thousands of roubles per *desjatina*. All land throughout the country would be assessed this way. Henry George proposes passing a law that starting from a given date all land would cease being the possession of any individual, but would belong to the whole state, the people as a whole, and so anyone holding land would be obliged to pay [rent] for it to the state — that is, to all the people, whatever it has been assessed. Payments would be used for all public, state projects, and so should replace all other duties and taxes, including both external and internal customs duties. According to this plan, it would mean that a landowner now holding 2,000 *desjatinas* could continue to hold them, but would have to pay the state for them — here in Tula [it would be] 12,000–15,000 per *desjatina*, since we have both meadow and estate lands, and not a single landowner could come up with that amount and would abandon his land. On the other hand, our Tula peasants in the same location would pay two roubles less per *desjatina* than they are paying now, and they would always have free land around them, which they can rent for 5 or 6 roubles [per *desjatina* per year]. Besides, not only will they not have to pay any duties, but they will have all the goods they need, both Russian and foreign, without customs duties.

112 Letter published in *PSS* 67:158–59.

113 As is well known, Tolstoy greatly respected Henry George's ideas on the land question. See W. Smirniw's article "Discovering the brotherhood of the destitute: Tolstoy's insight into the causes of urban poverty" (Donskov and Woodsworth 1996: 194–204).

In the cities, owners of houses and factories would be able to hold on to their properties, but would pay the amount assessed for the land they occupied into the general treasury.

The advantages of such a system would consist in the following:

1) There won't be anyone deprived of the opportunity to use land.

2) There won't be any idlers, owning land and making others work for them for the right to use their land.

3) Land will be in the hands of those who work the land and not in the hands of those who don't.

4) People who have the opportunity to work their own land will not enslave themselves in factories or domestic servitude in cities but will disperse among villages.

5) There won't be any more supervisors or collectors of duties in factories, institutions or customs houses, but only collectors of rent for land which cannot be stolen — rent being the easiest of all to collect, and

6) Most importantly, people who don't work will be delivered from the sin of exploiting others' labour, which often they are not actually guilty of, as they have been educated into idleness from childhood and don't know how to work, as well as from the even greater sin of all the lies and deceits they use to justify themselves in sin; and people who do work will be delivered from temptation and the sin of envy, condemnation and showing anger towards those who don't work, and this will mean the elimination of one of the factors which divide people from each other.

Nº 24. T. M. BONDAREV ❧ L. N. TOLSTOY

31 August 1894. Minusinsk (postmark).

My only friend in the whole world, soul of my soul Lev Nikolaevich! God is my witness that [you are] the only one. Our whole country has given me a ferocious look and sharpened their claws against me. I received your letter of 23 June, which I found helpful in many respects.

You advise me to follow the example of the Gospel widow, but you should know, Lev Nikolaevich, that I do not feel dejected, and am not losing my spirit of cheerfulness, as long as I have enough mental strength, though in my gubernia I am still presenting the same thing to the authorities, only in various ways.

I have a desire to write a letter to the Supreme Ministry describing their idleness and the land which they have brashly taken away from people, and burn them hotter than fire and freeze them colder than frost. But not to burn them with insolence and brashness, but with the bright truth which has always come to their mind. I have recognized that while they wear a lot of gold [jewellery], in fact they are nothing but [stupid] rams. They only know how to wag their tongues like a dog wags his tail, but this is not the time or place to go into that in any detail. Besides, you yourself know — even better than I do — how empty-headed they are.

Tell me, Lev Nikolaevich, where and what Ministry I should write to, and how to write the address? And not just for one, but addresses for the second and third as well. I am well aware that they will not listen to me or give me an answer, but that doesn't bother me. To tell them or write them — that's my job, but whether they respect or reject me, that's up to them. But to say which one of us is right and who's to blame — that will become clear [eventually].

They will keep silent, but their conscience will not keep silent; after all, it, they say, is some kind of 'God's fool Agatha.'[114] You can't buy it off with money, you won't escape from it through eloquence, and you won't trick yourself out of it. It's just that, to our misfortune, it is immersed in an undisturbable sleep, and will waken only at the end of one's mortal life. Is this a correct picture?

And I shall ask the authorities to put these letters of mine into their permanent archives for the benefit of future generations. Sixty years ago what silliness there was both in our social class and in the government — simply horrible! So you can imagine how in another sixty years our grandchildren and great-grandchildren will think back on our current 1890s. They, our grandchildren and great-grandchildren, will be a hundred times better than us. It won't be until then that they publish my final and complete sermon; it will be so much better than the one you saw, the one our Krasnoyarsk Governor put away in the archive where important state documents are stored in perpetuity (I asked the Governor to do this); this is what I heard through a rumour, I don't know it for certain. Krasnoyarsk is 500 versts from here. I am fully confident that at that time they will publish my sermon in full.

I have asked you, Lev Nikolaevich, and continue to ask that our followers write me letters of support for our victory over our enemies or opponents, only in special envelopes with the address written in their own hand; otherwise I shan't be believed. I shall then stuff these letters right in their mutton faces. Just picture it: here I am alone, and there are thousands of them; Am I able to fight with them [all by myself]? But then there will be many [more] on our side. In reference to you they say to me: "Tolstoy writes you letters of friendship at your request, and not because you deserve them."

If they had any sense, would they hand people over to slavery and consign the law of industriousness to oblivion, and take away land from the land-tillers and give it to idlers in perpetuity? Isn't it obvious that they have not a single crumb of sense in them? To sentence millions and millions of poor people to death by starvation — what kind of sense is that? [...]

There's an article about that in my latest manuscript — here it is.

114 Possibly taken from a book by early-nineteenth-century novelist Vasilij Potapov, *Marfa Vasil'evna: tainstvennaja jurodivaja, Kievskaja ved'ma* [Martha Vasilievna, mysterious God's fool, Witch of Kiev], which includes several references to *jurodivaja Agaf'ja* [God's fool Agatha].

When launching on an important project or starting out on a journey, if an accident occurs within the first few steps, it means that your undertaking will turn out to be no good. The whole world unquestioningly believes in this law and it seems to me that even my Lev Nikolaevich will not deny it.

When starting out on its endless journey, the human race met with an accident at its very first step: the birth of Cain. He was the first one to plant his feet on the Earth, the first to claim sovereignty and seniority in the world. Then was born the righteous Abel, whom he killed. The Scriptures do not represent a strictly logical truth. It could be that this never happened, though if the whole world says it happened, no matter how fantastical [it seems], it must have happened. The voice of the people is the voice of God. This is what the God-inspired man Sirach[115] says. Did not an inner 'Cain' reign for generations, and did he not [keep] killing Abel metaphorically, and so on until the end of time? Were Cain and his descendants unhappy people? No, they flourished. Cain built the first city on the Earth and named it after his son Enoch.[116] This shows that he was the first tsar or lord on the Earth at the time. His descendant Tubalcain was the first blacksmith to work with iron and copper.[117] And from his line came the best livestock-breeders on the Earth — that is, they kept a multitude of cattle, and they were the first to produce singers and harps. This shows that they had constant revellings, dances and merry-making, along with public orgies. The Scripture says: "...the sons of God, the tribe of Seth, having seen the daughters of the tribe of Cain as being fair — princesses of supernatural beauty — went in unto them, and bare them children, and they were giants of their age, men of renown"[118] (heroes, strongmen). It was from here, it seems to me, that feudal slavery began, which Moses confirmed in his ten commandments: "...thou shalt not covet thy neighbour's [...] manservant, nor his maidservant."[119] Nor did Christ forbid this greatest example of all lawlessness. Why did they not forbid it? Because [even] they were close friends with wealthy people, while poor people were treated the way they are treated by our authorities today — like dogs.

So can you see, Lev Nikolaevich, how the tribe of the cursed Cain exalted itself? And if we start tracing the descendants of Seth, we don't see anything of significance there, but when the Flood came, everyone perished together; and here we see that the tribe of the blessed Seth wholly submitted to the charms of the tribe of Cain — it couldn't help but submit — you see, that's the whole significance [of Cain].

115 A reference to the book of Ecclesiastes.

116 See Gen. 4:17 (not to be confused with Noah's ancestor Enoch).

117 See Gen. 4:22.

118 Cf. Gen. 6:2, 4: "...the sons of God saw the daughters of men that they were fair, and they took them wives of all which they chose.... There were giants in the earth in those days; and also after that, when the sons of God came in unto the daughters of men, and they bare children to them, the same became mighty men which were of old, men of renown."

119 Ex. 20:17.

If we examine the times after the Flood, we see how strong the balance of power was weighted in favour of the tribe of the cursed Ham over the tribes of [his brothers,] the blessed Shem and Japheth, and the same [situation] is still continuing today and will continue until the end of time, since from the first step of the human race into the world it was destined to be this way. But why? To solve this riddle one must be above God or at least equal to Him, but God has no time for the past or the future; everything is in the present.

People were freed from feudal slavery, but instead of that they found something else to oppress them with, namely, land. Even if they go ahead and divide the land according to Henry George, they'll still find the means to keep them under, otherwise how would these famous people find millions to spend on their pleasures and luxuries? The first step into the world (as mentioned above) never stays in a lie; it [can] stay in a lie only until the full strength and merit of the primal law is presented to the eyes of the whole world in all its strength and merit. But will that come to pass? What do you think? They write to us from [western] Russia that there's no firewood there; earlier they used manure for fuel, but now there are no cattle or manure to stoke the stoves with over the winter — evidently, death by starvation. Where's the cattle? A third of the cattle died from infection, two thirds from starvation — all the hayfields are in the possession of landowners and rich men. Have you heard anything to the effect that the tsar is taking land away from landowners and giving it to the people, since it falls within his unlimited power to do so? Write to me [about it]. He could put that into force with a single word or decree, a single stroke of the pen.

Did I write you about my latest manuscript — my article about the celestial visitor, who asks me about how things are coming along on the Earth?

Did I write you about the monument I am making for myself at the cemetery? I've forgotten whether I wrote you about this or not. Let me know.

I have not received from you my book in French. Your latest letter I am not showing to anyone and not to everyone, but only to those who are trustworthy. Might not there be anything else of a secret nature? Be sure to write me and send it by registered mail.

Have you written a letter to Dr. Popov at Minusinsk to forward to me? But I am reluctant to believe that. He asked me: "Did you receive Tolstoy's letter which I sent you from Minusinsk?" But I didn't receive it. He boasts about supposedly being acquainted with Tolstoy, too.

N° 25. L. N. TOLSTOY ❧ T. M. BONDAREV
25 August 1895. Yasnaya Polyana.[120]

Dear Friend Timofej Mikhajlovich.

I received your letter (it is simpler and more suited to us oldsters to use *ty* to each other rather than *vy*)[121] to my daughters of 15 July, and nothing to date has prevented me from answering you. Evidently I have not yet deserved to suffer for doing God's work, but up to now [the authorities] prefer to beat the carriage but miss the horse, or do not dare to hit it.[122]

I received [your story about] the celestial visitor and when the occasion arises, i.e., I shall append it to your long composition when the time comes to publish it.

I very much regret that the French translation of your essay which my daughter sent to Minusinsk got lost, but to date we have not obtained a new copy. When I have a chance, I shall try to get one and send it to you. In other countries, wherever [so-called] *enlightened* people live, land is taken away from the land-tillers and is owned by people who do not work on it. It is only among [so-called] savage, *unenlightened* people that land is considered God's property, and is owned by those who actually work on it. From this it follows that people need to be convinced that what they consider enlightenment is really not enlightenment but obfuscation and that even now, as long as they own land or buy and sell it, they are worse than any savage idol-worshippers or robbers. This is what I want to show to people in as clear as possible a way before I die. And it's what I am writing about at the moment.

I would like to send you my book *The Kingdom of God is Within You*, but I'm afraid it might be intercepted or get lost. Write to me an address to which I can safely send it. As to what you wrote about judgement being internal rather than external, I agree, and I think so, too. Please write me anything important you have to say. We don't have that long to live, and so what we have to say must be said as soon and as faithfully as possible, while we are still alive. I wish you the closest possible at-one-ment with God.

Your loving brother,
Lev Tolstoy

120 This letter was published in *PSS* 68:143. In the copy book (sheets 99 and 100) the date of 25 August is noted. See a very interesting article by Liudmila Gladkova (1994c) [L. N. Tolstoy's letters in copy books].

121 In Russian (as in French) there are two sets of pronouns corresponding to *you, your,* etc. — the formal (*vy/vash*, etc., like French *vous/votre*, etc.) and the informal (*ty/tvoj*, etc., like French *tu/ton*, etc.). Up until now, Tolstoy and Bondarev have used the formal variant in their correspondence, but here Tolstoy proposes switching to the informal alternative.

122 A metaphor for the authorities' frequent persecution of Tolstoy's followers, even while refraining from going after Tolstoy himself.

Nº 26. T. M. BONDAREV ❧ L. N. TOLSTOY
30 March 1896. Iudino, Beya District (postmark).[123]

Lev Nikolaevich,

Your whole upper social class has rejected my sermon on industriousness and idleness and cast it away with loathing. In light of everything I said, you are the one and only sincere friend and brother who is close to my heart. The word *brother* I utter with a firm handshake at a distance.

In the opening lines of your letter to me,[124] you say that we oldsters should address each other as *ty* rather than *vy*. This tells me that you, Lev Nikolaevich, are disdainful of your vain superiority.

You also say that you will add [my story of] the celestial visitor to my writings when the time comes for them to be published. Do you really hope that they will in fact be published? I have heard a rumour that they will never be published in Russia and people are not allowed to order them from abroad, and that the name Bondarev cannot be mentioned in any publication. Whether this is true, I have no idea. I ask and beg of you, Lev Nikolaevich, if at all possible, to send me the book with my writings in French.

I had hoped earlier that Russia would be ashamed of [its comparison with] foreign countries, and then start to give land to the people, but now, after seeing from your letter that all land there is not only taken away from people but given to idlers as well, now I am quite convinced that they will never give the people land, and that within a century they will force people back into feudal slavery over land. Will the then Tsar feel sorry for his people? No, he will delight in their misery.

I was unable to gather from your letter whose address I should provide you with, to send me a copy of the book *The Kingdom of God is Within You* (of course, hellish torment is within us, too).

Last year, in 1895 [in Letter Nº 25] you, Lev Nikolaevich, asked me to write something important, but here's how I would answer your request. The land-tiller who sows his seed in barren soil and obtains no fruit is worthy not simply of regret, but of real lamentation. Also, do not cast your pearls before swine,[125] and so forth. I wrote them so many times, and what [is the result]? They took [my letters] to the toilet with them [for use as toilet paper] — and only that. Shall I continue to work? If so, I would be committing a sin before God. Now I went over your whole letter, and answered everything that I need to as best I could. Now I have questions for you.

123 Bondarev's original handwritten letter has not been preserved. In the manuscript division of the L.N. Tolstoy State Museum, in Moscow, there are two typewritten copies thereof. Only the original envelope has been preserved, with the notation, in Tolstoy's handwriting, "Answered."
124 In reply to Tolstoy's letter of 25 August 1895 (Letter Nº 25).
125 See Matth. 7:6.

Do you, Lev Nikolaevich, hope for life beyond the grave in the next century? Do you accept Jesus, Mary's son, as the true God, or as a human being? Did God truly command Moses thus: If you acquire a servant, he shall serve thee 6 years without payment, and in the 7th you shall let him go with nothing?[126] And thou shalt give him only the food and clothing [he needs] for his journey — that is, some old rags — clothing and shoes and a stale crust of bread, the kind fit for a dog. That will be his whole reward for six years of service. And in another place God says to Moses: Pierce thy servant's ear with an awl, and he shall be thy servant for ever.[127] Do you accept, Lev Nikolaevich, that this is what God commanded Moses? We have some true examples of this, as can be seen from the following:

When Hagar quarrelled over something with her mistress Sarah, did Abraham take his servant Hagar (or have someone take her) to other people? No, he put some clothing on her shoulders, gave her some bread and a bottle of water, put the child in her arms (the child he himself had fathered) and chased her away like a dog into an inhospitable, terribly hot, waterless desert.[128] Evidently, so that she and her child would be torn apart by bloodthirsty beasts. Their water ran out, the child cried out from thirst, she put him under a tree and withdrew from him, so as not to hear him crying. One can only imagine how that mother must have felt in her heart. It is evident from this that he — that is, Abraham — treated all his servants in the same way. When one of his workers either became a cripple or grew old, he would be whipped out of the house with a block of wood, just as Hagar was cast out. If Abraham was a righteous man who talked with God as an equal, and this was the way he treated people, how should we think about the simple landowners of all the centuries past? But why should we refer to [events] we have never witnessed ourselves? People worked for landowners for close to three hundred years, and how did [the landowners] reward them when they let them go? They cast them out of their house and land like dogs, with a block of wood, as they did Hagar — and that was it. I went around [the whole] village — even a chicken cannot cross property lines. And people sit as though incarcerated in a mighty fortress. And when will this incarceration end? Never.

Oh, you and I must be the stupidest of all people! If only we hadn't known — but no, we do know — that from the beginning of time (if time had a beginning — I think not), that evil has taken root in the world, and now we want to root it out. In view of everything above, I wish for death as one who is starved for bread and thirsting for water. If I should die first, I shall ask my son (he is now a village clerk) to let you know. If you should die first, please have [someone] let me know. Today [you] have received my letter; write me a reply

126 Cf. Exodus 21:2: "If thou buy an Hebrew servant, six years he shall serve: and in the seventh he shall go out free for nothing."

127 See Deut. 15:17.

128 See Gen. 21.

tomorrow. I have no time to slow down, I'm in my 76th year. I am not ill, and I eat as I should, but my strength is extremely weak. From this it is evident that I am standing with one foot in the grave already. And you, Lev Nikolaevich, are not far from that yourself. You're just a bit younger than I am.

I have never had, have not now, and never shall have so sincere a friend as you, Lev Nikolaevich. You are such a highly celebrated person, and who am I? A landowner's feudal serf, than which there is nothing worse or more repulsive in the world, yet despite all that, you keep calling me your dear friend and brother. What have I to bring or give to you in return for everything [you've] said? Nothing. I have no money, and even if I had, you wouldn't take it. I'm sorry that I cannot speak smoothly or eloquently. I shall tell you what I'll bring to you, if you only agree with me. Since we are both close to the grave, let us agree to the following: If you find yourself in a blessed place in the next world, and I in a poorer place, [please] take whatever steps you can to get me out of there. And if it is the other way round, I shall pray God to grant you a blissful life with me. If that is not possible, then I shall go to you at the poorer spot — that is, so that we can live and die together, face God's judgement together and go together wherever we are sent. I am confidently and fully counting on the hope that what we have agreed to here will come to pass. And that there we shan't be looking at any guilt or vices we may have, but only at our virtues and good deeds. Are you in agreement with all this, Lev Nikolaevich? If you are in agreement, then give me your hand on this, at least virtually, and I shall shake it vigorously as a sign that our terms as agreed to above shall remain unchanged, both in this life and the next. This is what I bring to you, Lev Nikolaevich, in return for your recognition of me. Are you content with this? Around Moscow you are surrounded by clever people, who know how to talk on an elevated level, and so I think you must have many friends who are close to your heart, and so life is not boring for you. By contrast, here am I alone, all by myself, either because I'm more clever than anyone else, or more stupid than anyone else. There's no one here I can ask or tell anything to.

My latest manuscript, which is much improved in comparison to the one you had, I gave to the Krasnoyarsk governor[129] to read back in 1890, which he still hasn't returned to me. Despite the number of times I wrote to him asking him to send it to me, there has been no reply. Last year, in 1895, in mid-October, when he passed through our village, I went to ask him about it, and what happened? He didn't let me get in a single word, and chased me out of his sight. It seems to me he wasn't aware of who I was or why I came. Would it be possible for you, Lev Nikolaevich, to ask him to send it to you to read?

129 Cf. *PSS* 69:101: "Krasnoyarsk was an administrative centre in Yenisei Gubernia, and was ruled not by a governor, but by a chief of police, which in 1896 was Aleksandr Adol'fovich Greve; the Yenisei governor was Leonid Konstantinovich Teljakovskij."

Everyone trembles and shakes at the mere [mention of] your name. He will send it to you along with the 22-page addition, written separately. This addition is more valuable than the main essay. And you will return it to me. And you'll tell him that "Bondarev wrote such and such to me" and then remind him how he chased me out of his sight. I have no back-up copy of it. I wrote out 5 copies and they've all got lost. I didn't consider it worth telling you about all this here. In my next letter I'll jot down something nice for you — something that the world has never seen and never heard of anywhere on the globe. Lev Nikolaevich, don't pay any attention to [...][130]

I shall expect a letter from you in the first half of May.

I did ask you and plead with you in [an earlier] letter to send [my] "Celestial visitor" abroad, so that it could be added to my essay, but it seems you have not sent it.

Our agreement mentioned above and what [you will find] written below has led me to a state of considerable discomfiture in that among people of your social class you continually meet those who not only refuse to acknowledge life in a future world and even deny the existence of God, but go so far as to ascribe the creations of the whole universe to blind chance. Are not you one [of them], Lev Nikolaevich? If you are, you belittle me as never before. In any event, [go ahead and] belittle me — as you know, that's your decision, but to wish you all the very best — that is mine.

Beyond all that, I shall reveal the bottom of my heart to you, Lev Nikolaevich, as my true and sincere friend. This is it: [concerning] the above-mentioned primal commandment — fertile land and food — I picture them as not dead, but living beings, though by no means sacred; I hold nothing sacred apart from the one and only God. The same applies to the celestial visitor and the residents of the whole celestial circle, since for me they are old acquaintances — not just through words, but through deeds, I recognize, and, at prayer times, picture them as individuals similar and equal to myself — since it is the same [power] that created both them and me, and so I call them my brethren. Just who is of greater or lesser value in God's eyes is not our concern. There are a total of ten people in this society. I made an agreement with them — not the same one I made with you, but somewhat similar — which I wrote out on four sheets of paper, put into an envelope and sealed it, giving instructions that, when I die and am placed into a coffin, this packet be placed in my hand so that it rests upon my heart, on the faith that though the paper may decay to our sight, it will not decay in God's sight, even after untold centuries. If you should give me your agreement in a subsequent letter, I'll include your name as well, Lev Nikolaevich, in this society, as I indicated above, so that we might live and die together.

130 There is a gap at this point in the text from which this letter was copied. The whereabouts of the original handwritten letter are unknown.

Will I recognize kindred spirits on this Earth — those saints mentioned in the Old and New Testaments as well as in the legends — as Holy Fathers? No, I shall not. 1) Because they established feudal slavery, whose cup of sorrow, disease, sadness and bitter sighs I, Bondarev, have drunk to the dregs. 2) They allowed themselves to possess their own land. 3) Out of countless millions of land-tillers, not a single one has been included in the ranks of saints, or if any-one has, it is only when they left this work to go somewhere else, and so forth and so forth. These are the reasons for which Heaven and the Earth groan and do not allow me to recognize them as kindred spirits. Now comes the question: the celestial visitors — could it be that they are worse than us? To this I reply: whether they are worse than us, nobody knows. Are they better? We don't know that either. So if we don't know the answer to either question, it is more proper to retain our conviction that they are better than us. It could be that they have a few vices, but feudal slavery — taking land away from those who feed them or hiding the most important law from people — that they do not have. Because Heaven and the Earth groan under the weight of these three iniquities. Now farewell, Lev Nikolaevich, farewell, my precious friend. Farewell until our pleasant meeting — if not in this life, then in the next, whereby we shall soon see each other.

T. Bondarev

This next summer, that is, in the summer of 1896, the railway line will reach Krasnoyarsk. If I had the money and the strength, I would definitely come to see you, as it's cheap and quick. This winter I am living seven versts from the village on a homestead with livestock. Even though my health is extremely weak, I still earn my bread. Tell me the address of the Ministry of Agriculture and how should I write to them — through a letter or a petition? I shall listen to their confession and take communion for them. Of course it won't bring any result, but it will soundly resonate in the ears of their conscience. I have heard that foreign tsars forced our Tsar to free people from slavery, otherwise he never would have freed them. Is this true?

You can see for yourself what part of my letter this relates to. The commandment regarding Land, Bread and so forth. Why did I accept them into my society and they (as I imagine them) me into theirs? It is because I, as well as they, have been bitterly cast out by the whole world with its circle into the boondocks, where mankind has left its waste in the ground and dumped all sorts of rubbish besides. And so, all ten of us, like outcasts, we have got together, paying no attention to our sins and vices. All the rest of it you, Lev Nikolaevich, can figure out for yourself. I have heard some [rumours] that you, too, like us, have been cast out of your circle? If so, then, Lev Nikolaevich, please do join our society, if you only have hope in the life of the next world. And if not, then you are no friend to us.

N° 27. L. N. TOLSTOY ❧ T. M. BONDAREV[131]

23 May 1896. Yasnaya Polyana.

My dear friend Timofej Mikhajlovich. I do apologize. I received your letter[132] some time ago, and have not answered it until now. Either I was busy, or in ill health, but I did not want to give just any old answer.

My concerns at the moment lie only in explaining to people as clearly and as understandably as possible the truth of life which I know and which benefits me, and which people do not know but, instead, believe in a lie taught them by deceivers. There is no need to despair, but simply say what you know insofar as you are able. It may not be in our lifetime, but afterward they will recognize and believe whatever is right in our sayings. Truth does not burn up and does not drown. What you have written has done, is doing and will continue to do its work, removing people's coverings and opening their eyes. I am very sorry that I have not been able to send again to you the French translation of your work (I sent it once before, but it got lost). Now have I asked for another copy and I shall send it to you directly I receive it.

As to your questions, here are my answers: it would be pointless for me to write to the Governor of Krasnoyarsk: if he did not return it to you, he will not send it to me, and I shan't write. But if an opportunity presents itself, I shall try to obtain the manuscript through an acquaintance. I am very sorry it got lost.[133]

As to your question on whether I accept that God gave the commandments to Moses, I would respond that I do not accept it. I know that just as today our government puts foward all kinds of wretched human schemes with the blessing of the church, as though they were God's will, so also with the Jews: whatever they needed to prescribe for the people they presented as God's words spoken by Moses. The books of Moses were not written by Moses, witness the fact that they also describe Moses' death.[134] What is sacred is the spirit of

131 Published in *PSS* 69:99–100. This was written in response to Bondarev's letter of 30 March 1896 (Letter N° 26).

132 Tolstoy uses the familiar form of address. In a previous letter to Bondarev dated 25 August 1895 (Letter N° 25) Tolstoy had written: "it is simpler and more suited to us oldsters to use *ty* to each other rather than *vy*." This distinction is similar to that between *tu* and *vous* in French.

133 Tolstoy is probably referring to a new manuscript of Bondarev's: "Pol'za truda i vred prazdnosti" [The benefit of labour and the danger of idleness] — *PSS* 69:101, reprinted (as part of Letter N° 28) in Donskov 1996b: 103–10. In his letter of 30 March (Letter N° 26), Bondarev describes how he had sent the manuscript to the Krasnoyarsk governor in 1890, but the governor had not returned it in spite of many requests. He also mentions going to see the governor as he passed through a nearby town, only to be given a rude brush-off. Bondarev asks Tolstoy to write to the governor, requesting the manuscript for himself (which he would in turn pass on to Bondarev), and reminding the governor of Bondarev's failed attempt to talk with him.

134 The 'five books of Moses' are the first five books of the Bible (Genesis, Exodus, Leviticus, Numbers, Deuteronomy) — otherwise known as the Torah or the Pentateuch. Moses' death is mentioned in the last chapter of Deuteronomy (34:7).

God, which lives in people, not in books. The books which are called sacred contain a lot of lies.

As to your second question as to whether or not Jesus the son of Mary was God, I would answer that Jesus the son of Mary was a man and not God. To consider him God is a great sacrilege, as I keep telling all the priests I meet.

As for the life to come, I think there are two 'halves' in us: the Divine and the animal. And if in this life we acknowledge our Divine half and live by it, we shall go on with it to God, whereas if we live according to our animal half and treat this half as ourselves, we shall die with it. Therefore I would say that whoever lives in God will never die, but will continue to live in God. What the life to come will be like, we cannot know, but we know that it exists and that I shall not die. I know only that I came from God and shall come to him, and that it will be well for me with God.

I think, too, that the truth and the good that I have recognized and desired and applied in life here, that truth and that good I shall find already prepared in my life to come, and that in this life to come there will be new truths and new good which I shall strive to attain, and with success, and so I shall keep getting ever closer to God. And just as I serve Him here, so shall I serve Him there, and continue to serve eternally. This is what I think.

And consequently I think that no one can help another — there is no point in it — since each can find God within himself, and join with Him and live according to Him, and then he will no longer need anyone or anything. These are my thoughts concerning God and the life to come.

There is a lot more I should like to discuss with you on this subject, but it is impossible to say it all in a letter. I am now busy compiling a formulation of my faith. If God leads me to complete it, and we are still alive, I shall send it to you. I am sending you a few articles. Then farewell, and write to me.

I embrace you as a brother.

Lev Tolstoy
23 May 1896.

Nº 28. T. M. BONDAREV ✱ L. N. TOLSTOY
12 August 1896. Village of Iudino.[135]

Lev Nikolaevich.

[As to] the letter and package you sent to me, I had the great pleasure of receiving both of them on 31 July. The package was very pleasant for me, and

135 On the third recto page there is a notation by Bondarev: "Because of constant interruptions from my work, and secondly, not having a firmly established habit, I mixed up the sheets of paper. [Please] don't hold this against me. I imagine the same thing often happens with you." On the reverse there is a notation by P. V. Velikanov: "Dear Lev Nikolaevich! I am sending you my greetings. P. Velikanov, 12 August." On the envelope is a notation in Tolstoy's hand: "Answered." Tolstoy replied to this letter on 12 November 1896 (Letter Nº 29 below).

the letter was sweet, sweeter than honey. You explained in your letter just what I am in agreement with — that is, concerning the books of Moses, [while] at every step in the New Testament and in all the traditional [writings] one meets such nonsense, and I can't even get my tongue around it — and all this in the name of God. People are tempted at night by the Devil in the dark, and by each other during the day. That means that people are worse than any devil. And is there a devil or an Angel? I don't think so, otherwise God would be like a human being who cannot control everything by himself but needs servants [for support]. Wouldn't that be a frightful blasphemy against God? That's the question.

Sixty years ago — we well remember those times, what madness there was in those times! And if we go back hundreds or thousands of years, well, what were [people like] then? Outright savages they were! And now they say that such people were writing and speaking in the name of God. So what can I say of people 25 years ago when I myself was a [stupid] ram? It was only my correspondence with you, Lev Nikolaevich, that took away the murky veil from my eyes which was preventing me from seeing the light of truth; but for that, I would still find myself today in the abyss of madness, while today I myself am benefiting from it, and inspiring other people as much as I can, and they are accepting it.

How sorry I am that you, Lev Nikolaevich, did not accept my proposed agreement — that is, about you and me living together in the next world. Of course, one can present a lot of evidence that it is helpful or unhelpful, and that one alternative or another is possible. As they say, everyone goes out of their mind in their own way. Just think: just as we are surprised at the madness of people before us, in three or four hundred years people will also be surprised at our current madness, which we are unable to see in hindsight. We are like three-year-olds: they mutter a few words, often quite inappropriate, and their parents are thrilled. This is how we are in God's sight: we mumble something, we grasp truth as much as our mind allows, and are often displeasing to God. He doesn't pay any attention to our ignorance, but is just thrilled with everything [we do]. That's how it is with my agreement with you — after all, it was proposed for a good, not an evil, purpose. And yet you took it and cast it off.

You should not keep silent, but you need to tell people this truth that you know in the most rational way possible. This is what you, Lev Nikolaevich, advise me to do. I thank you ever so much, and so I do the same. I wrote a message to the supreme government c/o my Archbishop for Yenisei and Irkutsk.[136]

Since you, Lev Nikolaevich, aren't the least 'big cheese' in your elite class, burn their [hearts] with these writings of mine, light a fire under them. How

136 This message is not included in the current translation. For the Russian text, see Donskov 1996b: 103–10.

to burn their [hearts] and light such a fire — *that* I don't have to teach you. If they had been written by some person of great stature, they would not have as much force as these, which are written by a landowner's feudal serf — a lackey whose owner has sucked the blood out of his veins and devoured his mind to boot, and still keeps preaching. Do share, Lev Nikolaevich, do share copies with all your acquaintances. And they in turn will send them to theirs, and theirs [will send them] to their own, and so forth. By this am I seeking my own glory? No, you yourself know who I am, so what use would I have now for glory?

It seems to me that [my] "Celestial visitor" is resting dormant in your hands, no shoots coming out of it, and so this one, too, will remain dormant — much to my sorrow, much to my sorrow.

I plan to present this essay to the Governor-General of Irkutsk.[137] I shall not keep silent until the day my eyes are covered by eternal gloom. My purpose is to write and share, while if you take it to the toilet with you — that is not my concern.

Nº 29. L. N. TOLSTOY ❧ T. M. BONDAREV
12 November 1896. Yasnaya Polyana.[138]

12 November 1896.

Timofej Mikhajlovich.

I received and read your letter some time ago now. [Your manuscript] "The benefits of labour and the harm of idleness"[139] I have read to myself and am still reading to my friends. You say the same thing in this piece as in your main essay, although from a different angle, it's always helpful to read it. There's no way it can be published in Russia at the moment. But the time will come when all your thoughts will be shared and make their way into people's hearts. Moses never saw the promised land, and it is not given to every worker in God's field to enjoy the fruits of his labours or even to see them. If only we knew for certain that whatever we do, it is not our work, but God's! Our work never comes to a close, and any project we undertake ends in death; it is only God's projects that are unceasingly carried out, grow and come to fruition, and they have no end. That is why it is such a joy to participate in them. And I think the work you have been doing, explaining to people the law of labour and the sin of idleness, is indeed God's work. And so you can rest assured and rejoice that your work will not fail to bear fruit. If not in your lifetime,

137 Most probably a reference to Aleksandr Dmitrievich Goremykin (1832–1904), who was governor-general of Irkutsk and Eastern Siberia from 1889 to 1900. But note there was also under him a governor of Irkutsk proper, from 1889 to 1897, named Konstantin Nikolaevich Svetlitskij (1842–?); evidently, the two did not always get along.

138 This letter was published in *PSS* 69:203–04.

139 This manuscript was enclosed with Bondarev's letter (Nº 28) of 12 August 1896.

then after your passing, they will celebrate you and repeat your thoughts and words. As to your plan to write and share [your latest piece] with the Irkutsk governor[-general], I approve. Just as the unjust judge got worn down by the widow's questioning,[140] so we must wear them down by repeating the same thing over and over. The cause you are espousing is one of great importance, but there is a matter even more important — the root cause underlying the evils of stealing land and of idleness you are struggling against — this [cause] is militarism — the fact that these same people who have been robbed are conscripted into the army and, under the pretext of defending the fatherland against its enemies, end up defending those very rulers who took their land away and are now depriving them of their work. This is the cause that concerns and torments me. Once people understand this deception and refuse to become soldiers when they are recruited, the government feels threatened and starts fearfully persecuting them. These refusals are happening everywhere today: in Austria, too, dozens, even hundreds of Slavs and Hungarians — called Nazarenes — refuse [military service] every year on the basis of their Christian faith, and they are imprisoned for up to ten years; there was recently a case in Holland (I am sending you an article about this) and he was put in prison. But what is most frightening is what is happening here in the Caucasus.[141] Two hundred men have been imprisoned for their refusal to serve, thirty in a disciplinary battalion. One was beaten to death, their families have been exiled from their villages and impoverished, and more than two thousand souls have been left poor and rotting away in the [various] Tatar villages they were exiled to. Two others, *Ol'khovik* and *Sereda*, peasants from the Khar'kov region, are now in the Irkutsk disciplinary battalion for their refusal to join the army. This is a *struggle* between a few dozen weak people and millions of strongmen, but God is on the side of the weak ones, and so I know that they will win. Still, it is frightening and painful that they are the ones who are suffering, and not I. Now farewell.

I embrace you as a brother.

Lev Tolstoy

I am also sending you an article on the Doukhobors.[142]

140 See Luke 18:1–6, also Letter Nº 19 above.

141 Tolstoy is referring to the persecution of the Doukhobors. When conscription was introduced in the Caucasus in 1887, the Doukhobors refused to swear an oath of loyalty to Tsar Alexander III on the basis of their peace-loving principles. Tensions reached their peak in 1895, when mass demonstrations erupted, accompanied by the Doukhobors' burning of their firearms in three different regions of the Caucasus. As might be expected, all this led to the hardening of police surveillance, corporal punishment and imprisonment.

142 This is most probably a reference to Pavel Birjukov's article "Persecution of Christians in Russia in 1895" with a foreword by L. N. Tolstoy (Geneva, 1896).

Nº 30. T. M. BONDAREV ❧ L. N. TOLSTOY[143]

28 December 1896. Village of Iudino.

Lev Nikolaevich.

I bring to your attention[144] the fact that I had the great fortune to receive the letter you sent me on 12 November on 2 December 1896. I also received the book containing my work in French, which you sent me.

I very much regret that I am unable to speak delicately and beautifully and with fancy turns of phrase, and so I don't know how and where to begin or stop expressing my thanks for your recognition of me.

I ask and implore you, Lev Nikolaevich, to tell me frankly why you have such a fervent respect for me? After all, before you, a man famous throughout the world, I am nothing, a 'nought.' Many serious bigwigs would love to have correspondence with Tolstoy, but do not. Tolstoy tells them: "Stay away from me" and responds to their recognition of him with a pungent silence. But what do you respect me for? Even my portrait shows me from all four sides, from above and below, inside and outside, as unkempt on workdays. I might add that your own portrait presents no sense of lordliness, but shows you in the great labours of a weary man, one hand on your waist, a cloth or canvas-type shirt, your unkempt hair on your head and beard, and somewhat bent over. When I talk with you *in absentia* at night in my special isolated room, while looking at your portrait, it seems that my words have been resounding all over the globe and thundered throughout the very circle of heaven.

Collect your scattered thoughts on worldly cares together and consult with them as to what answer to give to these following questions I have:

Question 1. In the Gospels it is written somewhere: "I beheld Satan as lightning fall from heaven."[145] How so? God has cleansed His house from such a plague, and chased it into our house, and left it here, and the celestial dwellers now move about the circle of heaven, their hands in their pockets, and sing and whistle — no temptations there.

2. If we were all once as smart as all those white-gloved elite, what did we eat back then? A smart man would agree that it is better to die of starvation than to take one crumb of bread into his hands. So what did we eat back then?

3. It seems to me that the Jews are not to blame for Christ's crucifixion, since God determined aforetime, before time and the world began, at what time, in what place, by what death and by whose hands he was to die. If God had determined that he was to die at the hands of you and me, would we be in a position to avoid His decree? If everything is pre-determined, then today it is by pre-destination that they do not accept Christ.

143 On the envelope is Tolstoy's notation: "Unanswered."

144 Bondarev reciprocates with the familiar form of address (see Note 132 in Letter Nº 27).

145 Luke 10:18.

4. If the Jews did accept Christ, that would give the lie to all the prophecy about him, since He would not have suffered and died, not have risen nor ascended, and there would be no Orthodoxy in the world.

5. If God is in every place, where is the Devil? Where does he live?

6. Every person works for God for a selfish purpose, to give Him little and get much from Him, but such work does not lead to salvation, but into great sin. What would you, Lev Nikolaevich, say to that?

7. Why in the Old and New Testaments is everyone a Jew, and even God Himself, that is Christ, is a Jew, and there is not a single mention of other peoples? Why is that so?

8. Heaven and earth testify to God's existence, but what proof is there of Christ's Divinity, apart from ink and paper, which is the work of human hands? This is a serious question.

9. There are many people like this in the Scriptures, but I shall point to just two: both Lot's wife and Joza[146] died for a single little and trivial sin. The question is, of all the many and great virtuous people, why has not one of them risen from the dead? It is clearly evident from this, as in a mirror, that sin is alive while virtue is dead. Lev Nikolaevich, untie this Gordian knot which weighs upon my chest.

10. I am imagining you, Lev Nikolaevich, for a moment in the place of the Chairman of the State Council, and you have just condemned to oblivion my sermon (which you are familiar with), to punish me — for what? 1. because I am of lowly birth; 2. a *muzhik*, a former serf, a bondman; 3. insufficiency of eloquence and artifice; 4. my poor handwriting; 5. some sort of incorrect faith in God, etc. For all of this you punish me by destroying my sermon on industriousness and idleness. How is it possible, Mr. Chairman, that you cannot imagine that by this destruction you are punishing not me, but millions upon millions of poor people, who, upon hearing everything I've said, in just a short time could start to live an upright and happy life, while now they are obliged to remain as living corpses from generation to generation? If I have so incriminated myself before you, as outlined above, then I would ask you to find other means by which to punish me, whereas this strike at me, this destruction, is something I myself am insensitive to, while it will be a near-deadly blow to millions of poor people. How have they incriminated themselves in your eyes? What wrong have they done to you? Why do you punish them so viciously?

Write me the appropriate address [of the State Council]. I shall write them a letter like this. It is with fervent hope that I await a written reply from you, Lev Nikolaevich, to all these ten questions that I have put to you.

I seem to remember writing an article to you like this before, I don't know, but even if I did, I do not consider it a waste of time to repeat it.

146 Lot's wife was turned into a pillar of salt for turning to look back at the destruction of Sodom and Gomorrah (see Gen. 19:23–26); the identity of Joza is unknown.

In getting any important venture underway, or in setting out upon a grand highway, if some sort of accident befalls one's first steps, that means that no good will come from the direction taken. The whole world undoubtedly believes in this law.

In setting out on an endless highway, mankind met with an accident at the very first step — Cain was born, who was cursed by God Himself.[147] He was the first to set foot upon the ground, the first to claim dominion and seniority in the world (Adam and Eve, after all, were not *born*), and afterward was born his pious brother Abel, whom he slew. And doesn't Cain as a concept continue to dominate even today, from generation to generation, and continue to kill the pious allegorical Abel until the end of time? In the complete version of my work, it is clearly proved how the seed of the cursed Cain flourished right up to the Flood, and how the seed of the blessed Seth withered and dried up, and how after the Flood the seed of the cursed Ham was exalted, while the seed of the blessed Shem and Japheth was demeaned.[148] What am I explaining this for, anyway? After all, you've seen it yourself.

There are eighty feast-days in the Orthodox calendar and all in honour of Christ. Why is there not one day in honour of God? Why is this so? Say something to me about this.

I have a multitude of enemies (no fewer than you, I believe), who criticize me on every possible level for my correspondence with you and heap scorn on my work. Hence I would ask and implore you, my good friend Lev Nikolaevich, to write a piece in full praise of my work. I'll chuck it into their mutton-faces. As for how to write it, I shall not tutor you in that. Only one thing I would ask, that you write your accolade on a separate sheet of paper, separate from your letter to me. Do I need this accolade? No, I'm now 77 years old. If not today, Death will come along tomorrow with its scythe and cut me down.

I have the impression that I have annoyed you with my letter-writing. If that is so, then write me a letter of refusal or don't answer me at all. It is a good thing for me to be acquainted with a distinguished man, but what am I to him — just a *muzhik*, eh? That could be humiliating for him.

I thought that you accepted an afterlife beyond the grave. I wrote you something about that, but not a word from you in reply.[149] It is clear from this that you do not accept any afterlife. That is not good.

Either I know more than anyone else or less than anyone else. Here in our village we have 200 households, but there is no one I can talk with. In a word, they are animals on all fours.

Lev Nikolaevich, I am daring to pour all this out to you not as an enemy, but as a friend. You publish books of seven hundred pages — how many sheets

147 See Gen. 4:9–16.

148 *Seth* — Adam's third son (see Gen. 5:3); *Ham, Shem, Japheth* — the three sons of Noah (see Gen. 6:10); *the Flood* — see Gen. 7:6.

149 Tolstoy responded to Bondarev on this point in his letter of 23 May 1896 (see Letter Nº 27).

or sheaves of paper must be written by hand? Even that, I fear I am underestimating. But how much do you write me? Just one small letter sheet and that's it. And why? I don't like this little puzzle. In that case either refuse to write to me or stop writing, so that I too will stop writing.

They have put through the railway line to us in Siberia, and the train goes to Krasnoyarsk. It could go on to Irkutsk, another 800 km, but they haven't put a bridge across the Yenisei yet, and how they are going to do it is a major mystery. The river is terribly wide, deep and rocky, and besides, it is fast-flowing. How to build a bridge here? It's quite a mystery. The *krigy* will come in the spring — those are large and thick ice-floes. What to do about them?

Today you have received this letter, and write me a reply tomorrow or never. If I don't receive an answer, I shall not write to you again.

Farewell, my friend Lev Nikolaevich. I wish you all the best in the world. Wish me the same. I remain in good health.

T. Bondarev
28 December 1896.

N° 31. T. M. BONDAREV ❧ L. N. TOLSTOY
Beginning of July 1897.

First days of July, '97[150]

Lev Nikolaevich,

In the last days of December '96 I sent you a letter, to which I have had no reply to date. Where it got to or got lost, I have no idea.[151]

I did receive [the copy of] my book in French which you sent me. I really don't know where or how to begin to thank you, Lev Nikolaevich, for your appreciation of me; after all, compared to you I am nothing but a nought minus one. Many serious bigwigs would like to have a close acquaintanceship with you — that is not to be. Even if he doesn't say it, Lev Nikolaevich is thinking: "Go to the Devil, [you] charlatan." If I have written or wrought something there, then that work, by comparison with good writers, is the 'thousand and second night.' Now I shall pose some questions of a serious nature.

1. It is written somewhere in the Gospels: "I beheld Satan as lightning fall from heaven."[152] And Milton, the author of "Paradise lost," says so. And now I ask: Have the residents of Heaven cleansed their house from this plague, which was actually born in their house, and chased it into our house, and left it here? And then they prescribe for us thousands of commandments and laws for resisting this plague. If the Scriptures are to be believed with confidence, this is a bad thing — cleansing one's own house of serpents,

150 This is the date assigned by the writer. The envelope bears a notation by Tolstoy: "Unanswered."
151 Bondarev evidently considered lost the letter he sent to Tolstoy on 28 December 1896 (Letter N° 30), as he repeats the same questions in the present letter.
152 Luke 10:18.

chasing them into a neighbour's house and leaving them there — is that permissible?

2. It seems to me that the Jews were in no way responsible for Christ's crucifixion. And why [do I think so]? Because it was foreordained by God from time immemorial. For God there is neither past nor future time, but all is present; for us a thousand years have gone by, but for Him they are [a present fact], or for us a thousand years have not yet come, while for Him they already are [a present fact]. And so, before time and the world was, it was already established by God at what time, in what place and by whom He was to be born, and by whom and what means He was to suffer, and what death He was to die. If God had decided that He would die at our hands (yours and mine), would we be able to avoid this decree of His? That would be impossible. Were Joseph's brethren to blame for selling him into Egypt, if this was ordained by God, and so forth? God does not allow us to remember offences, but He Himself remembers them. He does not allow us to avenge, but He Himself avenges. Why? It is evident from this that we leave a lot of sins in our wake which we have done according to decree, along with many virtues which we practise not of our own free will, but by decree.

3. If the Jews had embraced Christ, this would have given the lie to all the prophecy about Him, and there would have been no [Christian] Orthodoxy in the world.

4. I firmly believe that there is nothing either in Heaven or on the Earth that was not in God and God in it — not to mention man. Also, there is no spot where the face of God is not. And where is the Devil's place or domain? It seems to me that the Devil is a non-entity, but that if there is an evil spirit, he was created that way by God, and therefore he is in God, and God in him.

5. We work for God for selfish purposes, to give Him or do for Him as little [as we can], and to get from Him as much [as we can], but such work is not sweet for Him, but annoying. But what can we do to be saved from this malicious purpose? I do not have either the physical or mental strength to answer. But what would you say?

6. Why in the Old and New Testaments is everyone a Jew, and not a single representative of another people? Some sort of great mystery lies concealed here, and even God Himself — that is, Jesus — is a Jew. Explain this mystery to me, if you can. Besides you, whom would I ask? No one.

7. Heaven and the Earth testify to God's existence, but what proof is there of Jesus' Divinity? The Scriptures? These are ink and paper, the work of human hands. What do you think?

8. I think I may have written to you about this before, but in any case I'll ask again. There are a lot of such people in the Scriptures, but I shall mention just two: Lot's wife and Joza, that [were punished] for one small sin — the

first, for looking back, and was turned into a pillar of salt,[153] the second for touching the ark which seemed to him that it was falling, and died at once. I ask [you] why it is that so many people died over one small sin, and why was not a single person raised from the dead for their many great virtues? This is one step [leading] to the conviction that sin is alive and virtue is dead, sin is powerful while virtue is weak in God's eyes.

9. I would put you, Lev Nikolaevich, in the place of the Chairman of the State Council. No, you are above him; the whole universe proclaims your virtue with all its bells and one can imagine this sound resonating throughout the celestial circle. And who is he? His value is the same as mine. You are now the chairman and you have consigned my sermon to oblivion to punish me — for what? Because I am of lowly birth, and I [dare to] submit petitions on such an important matter. How is it you did not consider that you through this consignment have punished not me, but millions of poor people? What are these people guilty of in your sight? Why do you punish them so viciously? For me this consignment is a barely audible push, but for them it is a near-fatal blow. If I am to blame for something in your eyes, then look for other ways to punish me. It is clearly evident from everything I have said, as in a mirror, that all of you recognize God only in words, so as to maintain your high esteem, while in reality there is no God for you at all. As it says [in the Bible], I hear the voice of Jacob, but I feel the hands of Esau.[154]

10. On what grounds and by what calculation did you, Mr. Chairman, 'thank' the person that feeds you with bread and saves you from death by starvation, by taking away arable land [from him] and giving it to idlers and spongers? I know your answer to this in advance, that you are inclined to justify Tamar rather than me.[155]

11. The wonders God hath wrought in Heaven and on the Earth, we see with our eyes and hear with our ears and feel with our hands, which means: truly, truly there is no deception or mist here — truly, truly. The wonders wrought by the Holy Fathers of the Old and New Testaments — where are they? Let us say these were people, and Christ is the true God, and where are His wonders? That is a question.

12. From the creation of the world (but was there a beginning to the world? No. And will there be an end? No) there have been countless millions of bread-tillers. Why are there not any of them among the saints, and if there are, it is only those who somehow hid themselves from this work and concealed themselves from it in some corner, and then joined the holy saints — why is that so? Here is but one step to despair; the only reason people don't despair is that they do not consider this to be so.

153 See Gen. 19:23–26.
154 See Gen. 27:22.
155 See Gen. 38.

13. In my last letter I told you that we need to cease our correspondence, and you are [evidently] glad about that, as you have not written for six months now. No, do not stop. In any case I shall be silenced for centuries untold, and you will not be far behind me. You see, then we shall cease our correspondence [for good], and I shall no longer bother you, and you will stop serving me, but now do answer all these thirteen questions, and I shall greedily anticipate [receiving your answer] around the end of August. I respect you for everything, Lev Nikolaevich, as I said earlier, but there is one thing I do not honour you for — and what might that be? For the fact that you have no concern for life in the next world. I haven't heard about that from anyone, and you have not written me about it, but I did see a hint of it in one of your letters. Destruction of one's soul has to begin with the head, and not with the tail — that is, one would first have to destroy God's being, and only then to destroy it [one's soul] in the next life. Farewell, Lev Nikolaevich, good-bye, we'll see each other in the next world.

T. Bondarev

Don't you have any new and interesting rumours? Tell me. What do you think — will land be given to the people or will it remain for ever in the hands of landowners and merchants?

The railway has come to us. The Yenisei River is terribly wide, deep and rocky. They're putting a bridge across it. Rumour has it that the railway will go to Vladivostok, five thousand versts from us to where the sun sets in the summer [*sic*].

There's a man close to 35 years old with a son of 13 years from Chernigov Gubernia, whose name is Pavel Vasil'evich Velikanov;[156] he's bald with a pale face. He lived in our village for eight months as a teacher. He left in early May. On 28 June he sent me a brief letter, saying he was now in Moscow, but didn't have a position yet. But when he obtained a position, he said in his letter, he would write me a detailed letter. If you have the opportunity to see him, Lev Nikolaevich, accept him as a man of the best possible character and embrace him warmly with your heart. What are his virtues? He is a man of poor financial means, but in terms of an honest and enlightened mind he is a millionaire; this is not the place to describe him in detail. I seem to think he has already been to see you. He and I have been very close to each other, like two bodies with one heart and one soul. I don't know how he looks on me, but he is to me as I have described. We know prominent — that is, rich — people, and what does he see in them? If you ask him, he will tell you: a hot, dry and waterless desert.

156 *Pavel Vasil'evich Velikanov* (1860–1945) — initially a follower of Tolstoy, he met with Tolstoy in the summer of 1891; however, he subsequently turned critical and hostile in his articles and letters. See S. A. Tolstaya, *My Life,* Part V, Section 116.
In the following letter (N° 32), Bondarev describes him as being from Nizhegorodskaja Gubernia.

Now I have two friends: Tolstoy and Velikanov. Who of them is ahead and who is behind, I shall know very soon, and shall say then.

N° 32. T. M. BONDAREV ❧ L. N. TOLSTOY
23 November 1897 (postmark).[157]

Lev Nikolaevich,

In early July of this year I sent you a letter, to which I have had no reply to date; it has got lost somewhere. Earlier I had imagined that there must be some aspect of my letters which you found annoying and boring, but now I picture a different scenario, as follows: If we lived close to each other and talked with one another about something twice a year for a half-hour, would we annoy each other in this? No, such a rare meeting would be a real treat for us — isn't that what we can deduce from our letters?

I asked you, Lev Nikolaevich: Who called the Orthodox faith "orthodox," and you replied to me in a lawful and appropriate fashion, for which I sincerely thank you. From these words I could clearly see, as in a glass, the bottom of your heart.

As much as my ideas of life, Lev Nikolaevich, are not bad ones, yours are much worse than mine — in what respect? In this: It is good if you consider an icon as a great sacred object, if you bow down to it and honour it with all your heart, that is good for you. But if you despise it, what then? It was painted by some kind of charlatan, wretch, drunkard or outcast, and you are supposed to give it all divine honours, and to bow down to it and kiss it. What kind of song will your conscience sing then? That is a question! She [your conscience], say the writers, is some kind of 'God's fool Agatha'; eloquence and trickery will not save you from her; she has one answer to everything: "Aha!" and "Ach!"

The same with Jesus, Mary's son, if you consider Him higher than God, as it is said, He sat down at the right hand of the Father,[158] meaning above God in worth, and again: the Father judgeth no man, but hath committed all judgement unto the Son,[159] and He Himself would not be concerned, in view of [His] decrepit old age.

If you have such confidence, then that's good, your conscience is clear. And [what] if you picture God as all the great minds picture Him, as a limitless spirit — [which is] unfathomable, not only to the human intellect, but also to the Angelic mind — and that's how [you actually] should picture it in a hypocritical view, as mentioned above[?] There are seventy feast-days a year and they are all in honour of Jesus and the icons, but not a single day or a single

157 The envelope bears Tolstoy's notation: "Answered." The whereabouts of Tolstoy's reply are unknown.

158 See Hebr. 1:3; Hebr. 10:12.

159 See John 5:22.

hour is devoted to honouring God. Feast-days don't matter a thing, but the attitude of the heart matters a great deal.

Other famous people are not followed, but everyone stares at Tolstoy to see whether he considers our sacred objects as sacred or not, and *how* he considers them.

And what can be done? How to escape this hypocrisy? There are no solutions for it. It is absolutely necessary to show one's self to be a zealous icon-worshipper, and so forth.

If I have disassociated myself from all this rubbish, that is unimportant, only they carted me from one place to another on government wagons, from a worse place to a better one; I live here like the Russian letter F[160] in clover. And if you reject [it], too, what of it? They'll shut you up secretly in an asylum, and feed you black bread and water. And they'll tell the whole world that Tolstoy's gone mad, and your name will disappear and the memory of you will vanish from off the face of the whole earth. In that case you should bow down and pay homage to all and everything, at least hypocritically. I ask and plead with you, Lev Nikolaevich, I ask and plead with you not to shame or disgrace me over this. Who am I in comparison to you? A nought minus one, and yet despite such insignificance I have made so bold as to offer you advice and give you direction.

I praise, indulge and exalt you for everything except one, Lev Nikolaevich, and what is that? It is that you do not accept life in the next world beyond the grave; this I noticed in one of your letters. This conviction of yours I strongly disapprove of, it seems that to destroy the soul one must begin with the head and not with the tail — that is, one must first declare that there is no God, and then say that there is no afterlife.

Pavel Vasil'evich Velikanov from Nizhegorodskaja Gubernia[161] lived eight months with us. He is pale, not a hair on his hand, about 35 years of age, and has a son about 13. He was teaching children literacy, and his flat was across the street from my house, and he would come see me once a day, sometimes twice. He took a great disliking to our upper-class people; I don't know whether he saw good or bad in me. When he left here he said he would employ any means he could to see Tolstoy in person.

If you have met with him, whatever he said about me, good or bad, believe him without a doubt. He is a man of highest worth, he will not lie. Whatever he told you about me, write it down for me. I shall not take offence even if he said something bad about me, for all that is the honest truth. Towards the end of August he sent me a brief letter saying he was in Moscow, and had not yet found a position, but that when he obtained one, he would write me a detailed letter. But [I have heard] nothing further to date. If you know where he is, I

160 The Russian letter F (Ф) is treated as symbolizing a posture of confidence and self-satisfaction.
161 In Bondarev's previous letter (N° 31), Velikanov is described as being from Chernigov Gubernia.

would ask you, Lev Nikolaevich, to write him a letter, telling him what I am saying here about him, and pass along my regards and a virtual handshake. I have one son — what did Velikanov tell you about him? If it was favourable, spell it out for me. If it was negative, just put an ellipsis and I will understand that it was negative. As a village scribe, he will get to see the letter first, he will read it and destroy it.

There's a certain I. M. Chernjaev, a gardener who is personally acquainted with you. He requested in a letter that I describe for him life in Siberia. But unfortunately I have lost his letter, and without his address, where would I write to? Right now he's extremely upset with me. I would ask you, Lev Nikolaevich, to tell or write to him about my situation; my heart aches over this something awful. He says that I get no rest from the priests.

I have lived quite a long time in the world, and have been learning and learning and learning, and have [finally] learnt, and truly learnt — [but] what have I learnt? I have learnt that I don't know anything — that's not just a metaphor — I literally don't know anything. Forty years ago I knew everything, I saw no deficiency in myself, and now I am left with nothing, I'm good for nothing. And this is why, like [a person] starving for bread and thirsting for water, I'm waiting with such desire for death, but for some reason it's slow in coming.

Tell me — I ask and plead with you, Lev Nikolaevich — tell me why my sermon is banned from being published in Russia. If it is harmful in Russia, it should be harmful abroad as well, but what is happening here: it's useful abroad but harmful in Russia? Why is that? It seems to me it is because, if it had been written by a follower of Orthodoxy, then it would be exalted to the heavens and expanded to fill a thousand pages. But since it was written by someone who has rejected the Orthodox faith, that is why it was banned. But what would you say? I have heard a rumour that [even] ordering a copy from abroad is prohibited. Is this true or not?

Man always works for God out of selfish motives — to give Him little but receive a lot from Him, only work like that is not salvation, but a great sin. But what to do, how to escape this motivation? For my part I find no way of doing so, but what do you say? And another thing: man is always flattering before God, only under the pressure of fear does he crawl before Him on his knees, but he doesn't feel any love for Him.

With man this is impossible, but with God all things are possible.[162] If you take a man who has lived to a ripe old age, and put all his bad deeds, words and thoughts into one pan of the scales and his good deeds, words and thoughts into the other pan, which way do you think the scales will tip, Lev Nikolaevich? What your answer will be, I have no idea. I myself remain fully confident that it will be on the side of good; moreover, on the former side you will have to

162 See Matth. 19:26.

deduct [three parts:] his misunderstandings, his innate incapacity for good, and the temptations of this world he was not able to withstand without shaking, and the last little part of his bad deeds will be covered by His infinite mercy. In sum, the whole human race will be embraced by God. But what would you say?

How is it, Lev Nikolaevich, that countless millions of people came before us, and now the universe is all full of people? Why has not even one of them been assigned to develop the primal law? But it has been given to a cast-off, a landowner's serf, a slave — and, besides, one who has turned away from the Orthodox faith. Herein is concealed some huge big secret, which I cannot begin to fathom with my near-sighted mind. And the fact that they banned publication, and that not by blind chance. God forbids us to remember offences, and even the sun will not go down on your wrath, but He will remember it Himself for centuries untold. He orders us not to avenge, but He Himself will avenge. Why is that? That is a question.

If you or someone else had written me everything I have written [to you] here, I would have used all my powers of reason to answer each of their questions to the best of my ability. Yet my Lev Nikolaevich is so miserly in his answers to me, and that gives me cause for considerable complaint. We have a certain Fedjanin here (Velikanov knows him); he is a real windbag. [Fedjanin] confidently assured me that "your Tolstoy" is now dethroned and is consigned to the ranks of scoundrels. "For what?" I asked. For carrying on a correspondence with a cast-off, that is, with Bondarev. And many 'prominent' people say the same. But I respond to them all simply with a bitter silence, without any indication of being offended.

Since you, Lev Nikolaevich, have no trouble finding the words you need, in the name of God I ask and plead with you, write me a letter that I could stuff into their idiotic faces and tie their sly tongues with cords of muteness.

I am now 77 years of age, and by nature I am physically weak, this is why my strength is extremely exhausted. I am not ill with anything, but I can barely walk, eating gives me no pleasure, and everything in this world is unpleasant and loathsome, and it seems to me that I myself have become unpleasant and loathsome. It is quite clear that I am one step away from the grave, and so I have written you a letter, put a stamp on it, and left instructions for it to be sent to you after my death. What I wrote in that letter you will find out then.

With a firm virtual handshake, Lev Nikolaevich, with a deep bow and with a flaming kiss on your sweet fiery mellifluent lips, I say: Farewell, farewell, farewell, my only friend in the whole world! Farewell, farewell, [you who are the] first and last delight of my heart! Farewell until our next meeting! I am firmly hoping and very much counting on seeing each other in the world beyond the grave.

God is witness between me and you, Lev Nikolaevich, that I love you fervently, not just with ink and paper,

T. Bondarev

See what great (my arms are wide open) gratitude [I owe] you, Lev Nikolaevich, for the Primer which you have compiled for the instruction of children. And for showing yourself in a picture in working clothes and immersed in labour, my gratitude to you goes well beyond my poor little mind, beyond even an Angelic mind.

Nº 33. T. M. BONDAREV ❧ L. N. TOLSTOY[163]

15 August 1898. Village of Iudino.

15 August 98.

Lev Nikolaevich.

At the beginning of July 1897 I wrote you a very interesting letter,[164] to which I have received no reply. Why not? This question, too, remains unanswered.

The book containing my work which you sent me in a French translation, has now been retranslated into Russian in handwritten form,[165] and what did I see there? Oh, so many of the best changes are missing, but, instead, the worst changes are there, how much darkness and confusion! My idea was to bring enlightenment to the present world as a whole, as well as to all future generations, but it came out quite the opposite and turned inside out.

In the name of the God of truth I ask and implore you, Lev Nikolaevich, to do all you can on your part to help me; I am drowning in this abyss of evils. What help am I asking for? This:

I have this manuscript which, in comparison to the one you had, has been cut to half the size and now includes many of the best sayings.

I have a great desire to send it to you so that you can pass it on to the same publisher — I mean the one abroad, where this [French] book was published. This is all I pray and ask of you.

I would send it myself, but there are reasons for not doing so: 1) I don't know the address, and the second, more importantly, since your good name, Lev Nikolaevich, has flown around the whole globe, it is clear (as in a mirror) that it has thundered through the whole circle of heaven, and so they, the ones abroad, will unquestioningly do everything you tell them to — that is true without a doubt.

And so, Lev Nikolaevich, today you have received this letter, and tomorrow write me a reply as to whether you will send my manuscript abroad or not.

In mid-October I shall await a reply from you with unfailing hope.

163 On the envelope is Tolstoy's notation: "Answered."

164 See Letter Nº 31.

165 See Note 103 to Letter Nº 103. After reading the retranslation of his book from French into Russian, Bondarev complained bitterly to Dushan Makovitskij (Tolstoy's personal physician) about the inaccuracies in the French edition. The abbreviated translation was done by V. I. Kuz'min (who later wrote under the pseudonym V. A. Sagajskij). See Kosovanov 1958: 31. See also Tolstoy's reply in Letter Nº 34.

There are a lot more interesting things I could say on this subject, Lev Nikolaevich, but I feel such a tremendous spiritual disorder that my pen is falling out of my hand. I remain in good health, which I also wish you, Lev Nikolaevich, with all my heart.

T. Bondarev

Once again I repeat what I said above: you have received this letter today. Tomorrow write me a reply.

N° 34. L. N. TOLSTOY ❧ T. M. BONDAREV[166]
11 September 1898. Yasnaya Polyana.

Timofej Mikhajlovich,

There's no reason for you to think that your book has been distorted in translation. It's probably that those who translated it for you [from French back into Russian] did a poor job. All the essentials have been translated there, and if there is anything missing, it is only something that might only repulse (instead of attract) the reader.

It has been superbly translated into French and reads very well.

They will not print it again or add to it. There would be no point. In the form it is in right now, the book is doing and will continue to do its work — that is, it will make people aware of their sin and point out the means by how they can atone for it.

From my heart I wish you peace in your soul and in your life and in meeting death, which is already approaching us — that is, the destruction of our body and the transition of our spirit into another state.

Your loving brother,

Lev Tolstoy
11 Sept. 98

166 Published in *PSS* 71:438. Bondarev's signed notation: "Received 27 September 98." In acknowledging receipt of the letter, Bondarev's son informed Tolstoy that his father had passed away 3 November of the same year.

PART II

The Molokans and Fëdor Zheltov

Fëdor Zheltov

A BRIEF OUTLINE OF THE MOLOKANS

In the early 1880s, Tolstoy made the acquaintance of Fëdor Alekseevich Zheltov, a Molokan from the village of Bogorodskoe in Gorbatov Uezd of Nizhegorod Gubernia. Tolstoy had made his first contact with the Molokans back in 1871 in Samara,[1] where his family owned an estate. Tolstoy often met with representatives of the local population, whom he treated with deep respect.

The Molokans, who called themselves 'Spiritual Christians,' were a group of Russian peasants who (like most other sects) broke with the official Russian church about three hundred years ago. They were subjected to cruel persecutions and were sent en masse to the Transcaucasus, where they managed to live out several generations in relative security. The persecutions resumed, however, with the outbreak of the Russo-Japanese War. As committed pacifists, they refused to bear arms or even to perform non-combatant army service. In anticipation of further persecutions, about 5,000 Molokans emigrated to America (principally California) in 1905–1907, seeking freedom of conscience.[2]

In contrast to the Doukhobors, from whom they separated approximately at the end of the eighteenth century, the Molokans acknowledge the Scriptures as a source of knowledge of the truth, although they interpret them rather freely. They reject the doctrine of the Trinity and of the saints' perseverance; their concept of church amounts to accepting a society of believers in which all are equal; they reject an ordained, paid clergy, along with icons and the sacraments, and, in accordance with the Ten Commandments, refuse to swear oaths, of allegiance or to bear arms (their mystic and ascetic tendencies are evident in their belief that the Holy Spirit descends upon them and reveals the Lord's power to them). With a few exceptions, their ideas correspond to the tenets which Tolstoy postulated, following his so-called religious conversion, as the most significant. While the topic "Tolstoy and the Molokans" is not as extensive as "Tolstoy and the Doukhobors," its importance derives

1 In her article "Spiritual and Economic Renewal among Molokans and Doukhobors," Ethel Dunn (1995: 166) presents a statistical table compiled by I. Morozov for 1925, showing the Molokans as a percentage of the overall sectarian population.

The outskirts of Samara (on the Middle Volga) had a general population of 19,500 sectarians, of which 2,967 (i.e., 15.22 per cent) were Molokans. According to Dunn, these figures were deliberately represented as lower than in actual fact. Dunn rightly points out that "the virtue of Morozov's table is that it suggests that every region of the Soviet Union had Molokans" (ibid.).

2 At the present time — early in the twenty-first century — good relations prevail between the Molokans and the Doukhobors. While the Doukhobors emigrated to Canada rather than America, the two groups still celebrate holidays together and maintain a good working relationship.

Even in the Caucasus, the Molokans and Doukhobors enjoyed completely friendly relations. For an example of how the Molokans helped the Doukhobors in an extremely difficult situation, see the Slavjanka Doukhobors' letter to Ivan Mikhajlovich Tregubov, Document #1896-02-27c in Woodsworth 1999a: 76–77.

from both the writer's active involvement in the Molokans' destiny and their considerable usefulness to him in working out his philosophy in the 1880s and, especially, in the 1890s.

Various questions relating to aspects of the Molokans' life, character and beliefs are noticeably reflected in Tolstoy's letters, diaries, articles and involvement in civic affairs, as well as (to a lesser extent) in his literary works — notably his novel *Resurrection* and his writings in the memoir genre.

Let us briefly examine a number of documents in which Tolstoy's overall favourable attitude toward the Molokans is clear. Tolstoy respected them (as he did sectarians in general) for their freedom of thought, their disagreement with the official church, their boldness in confronting the authorities, their inner purity and simplicity. In a letter to his wife, Sofia Andreevna, written 19 July 1881 from Patrovka (Samara Gubernia), where he was undergoing a programme of *kumys* [fermented mare's milk] treatments, Tolstoy wrote (*PSS* 83:293–94):

> I have just...spent a whole day in Patrovka, attending a Molokan meeting and dinner, as well as a district court session where an innocent Molokan was on trial, and later another Molokan meeting.... The meeting included a discussion of the Gospels. They are clever people and remarkably bold.

He continues the description of these people a few days later in another letter to his wife, of 22–23 July (ibid., 296):

> They are shy about their poverty, being scarcely aware of it. The Molokans are extremely interesting people. I attended their prayer service, observed their interpretation of the Gospels, and participated, and then they came to me and asked me to interpret them from my own understanding; and I read to them excerpts from my outline [of the Gospels]. The seriousness, interest and clear common sense of these semi-literate people is astonishing.

In a letter to Velikanov, dated 17 December 1896, Tolstoy emphasizes the intensity of their faith (*PSS* 69:222):

> The impression you received from the Siberian Molokans is the same one I remember receiving from the Samara Molokans upon my first acquaintance with them. I was expecting too much of them, and I gather you did too. But upon becoming more closely acquainted with them, I discovered among these protesters, both young and old, an active movement and a growing religious feeling.

After being informed that certain Molokan children had been taken from their parents and sent to various monasteries and nunneries, with the aim of breaking the Molokans' will and punishing them for confessing their faith, Tolstoy wrote two letters of concern to Tsar Nicholas II, condemning such actions. At the same time, these letters served as a passionate call for freedom of religion (10 May 1887, *PSS* 70:74):

> You have only to send an impartial, righteous person to the places where those persecuted for their faith have been exiled — to Siberia, or the Caucasus, or the Olonets region, and to the places where they have been imprisoned, and you would see from this person's report the frightful deeds that are being committed in your name.[3]

On 18 September 1897, an announcement sent "to the English papers" informed readers of the violence being committed against the Molokans, with special emphasis on the fact that the Molokan children abducted from their parents had been languishing in monasteries and nunneries for four months (see ibid., 138).

It is known that Tolstoy frequently helped famine victims in poor harvest years. His letter "To the editor of *Russkie vedomosti*" of 28 February 1898 (*PSS* 72:79–80) testifies to his ongoing interest in the Molokans and his assistance to them.

He offered moral and financial help to those Molokans who wanted to leave Russia and join the Doukhobors in Canada, this after learning that they would not take his advice and stay in Russia and being persuaded that they would not go back on their decision to flee persecution — see his letter to Aleksandr Nikiforovich Dunaev of 9–11 September 1900 (*PSS* 72:450), as well his reply to Aleksandr Bodjanskij of 2 October 1900 (ibid., 465–66), who had written from Canada on 21 August 1900, describing the arrival of three Molokans who had come to enquire into the possibility of resettling their brethren there.

A. S. Prugavin's account "Lev Tolstoy and the Samara Molokans" gives an impression of the warm human relations between Tolstoy and the Molokans without any hint of criticism. Prugavin met with Tolstoy in the summer

3 In 1897 there was a report circulating through the Nikolaev and Buzuluk Uezds that local police superintendents and officers were abducting children from their homes at night. It turned out that these children were being sent to various monasteries and nunneries throughout Samara Gubernia. In spite of verbal and written protests by lawyers and other well-wishers, the authorities relented only when Tolstoy, with his characteristic resourcefulness and power of persuasion, succeeded in attracting the attention of both the Russian and foreign press, which condemned such actions. The children were returned to their parents, but not until February 1898. Tolstoy's daughter Tat'jana L'vovna also petitioned on their behalf before the procurator of the Holy Synod, Konstantin Petrovich Pobedonostsev. Such ill-conceived actions on the part of the authorities were to some degree facilitated by the proposals adopted at the Kazan' missionary conference that took place in August 1897 (*see PSS* 70:17–20). Along with other measures to counteract dissident sects, it was decided to petition for the adoption of a law allowing children to be removed from parents and sent to diocesan shelters. It was not long before this measure was applied to the Molokan children. After reading an account of the conference in the newspaper *Russkie vedomosti*, Tolstoy noted in his diary: "A disturbing account of the missionary conference in Kazan" (*PSS* 53:150).

of 1881 "in the wilds of the Samara steppes" (as he put it), in the village of Patrovka, Buzuluk Uezd, at a Molokan meeting. Prugavin emphasizes in his article that following the Samara famine of 1873–1874, when Lev Nikolaevich did so much for the Samara peasantry, Tolstoy began to enjoy an exceptional popularity and trust, not only among the population of Patrovka but also in the neighbouring regions. Prugavin speaks about the warm, close relations between Tolstoy and the Molokans, who, even if not followers of his teachings, considered him a kindred spirit, a true friend and patron.[4]

Indeed, Tolstoy maintained contact with the Molokans, Doukhobors and other sectarians right up to the end of his life. He was sympathetic to their plight, shared their dismay at the authorities' cruel treatment of nonconformists, but still insisted that these persecutions would have a positive outcome. In a revealing letter to Prince Dmitrij Aleksandrovich Khilkov (written July–August 1896), he offers encouragement to the Molokans and other sectarians (*PSS* 69:140–41):

> ...persecution is not only an inescapable condition of establishing truth, but it is a compulsory condition thereof. Don't be concerned about the friction — if there is no friction, I can tell you right from the start that there will be no progress.

But when certain sectarian rituals contradicted the laws of nature (or, frequently, his own concepts), Tolstoy was by no means a model of patience. Thus, in a reply to the Skopets[5] sectarian G. P. Men'shin (31 Dec. 1897, *PSS* 70:225), offering his opinion on the Skoptsy sect and the foundations of their teachings, he wrote: "Forcible or even voluntary castration is counter to the whole spirit of Christian teachings," and reminded him about the interpretation of Matthew 19:12 regarding castration: "...even if the interpretation of the letter should seem unconvincing to you, one must remember that it is the spirit alone that quickeneth."

Perhaps the following treatise of Zheltov's (who wrote a great deal about the sect and was their spokesperson) will serve as a basic summary of the Molokans' beliefs. It was written 10 May 1888 and sent to Tolstoy along with a letter dated 12 May 1888. It is reproduced here in full.

> On life as faith in Christ
>
> I often wonder about the meaning of life. — What is this meaning of life?... I understand that if reason is the basis of righteousness, then on this basis I can also comprehend the meaning and purpose of my being. The righteousness of life means that within myself my personal selfhood must serve this righteousness; it means that what we call the righteousness of life must be, first

4 See Prugavin 1911a.

5 *Skopets* — a male member of the Skoptsy sect, which practised asceticism, including castration of both men and women.

and foremost, I myself, and what I need to do is to bring righteousness into the world and create good for mankind, since, before creating happiness for myself, I must create happiness for others, at least by not doing them wrong. What I thereby gain for myself will be good for me as well as good for others, and this is what we call love. My spiritual self is not called upon to serve falsehood, and the point is to love this self equally in myself and my neighbour, to love as though it were something common to both of us.

I understand why Christ suffered. He suffered for the Word he gave to the world, and this Word was reason, and to show the triumph of reason and that man's life is not made up of flesh and that what people wanted to kill will go on living — this was the Word he suffered for, and what he was went on living, it did not die and will not die. His Word was His own life, His flesh, and I must see that it becomes my flesh too, just as it was the flesh of Christ. The outward, self-indulgent service to Mammon which brings temptation into my life must fall away from me just as worldly temptations fell away from Christ, because I live not to serve Mammon but to serve what constitutes the eternal law of righteousness, because I myself originate therein and must exist therein.

I see God in the work of righteousness and love as the work of intellect, and God to me is the eternal, universal intellect and the creative power of life, and therefore He is life, and what we call death is not death in relation to this life. False life with its false demands is in fact death, and since it cannot be eternal, death for it represents the fact that the personage is destroyed, since the personage, departing from the eternal law of life, dwelling wholly apart from it and considering its life restricted to false gratifications, cannot unite with immortality. In order for it to approach immortality, it must undergo resurrection to a new life, whose majesty must consist in serving itself as eternal good, the universal will and liberty of mankind.

Departure from the unifying law of life is sin, leading to death, and hence he who thinks that he lives to serve the flesh is not a person of intelligence as life, but a person devoted to falsehood, whose actions lead life itself to annihilation. He who lives for God lives for the fulfillment of the will of Him who gave him life and hence he lives to serve this eternal life, as by introducing into the life of society as a whole the law and righteousness he has been given, and therefore he must strive to hold on to it; his life is the equivalent of intelligence, and this is not temporal but eternal — that upon which rests the foundation of the world — and hence for this life there is no death.

There was no death for Christ since his life was the life of the spirit, and he wanted to give this life to the world, and He did this by rejecting service to the flesh, by living only to serve intelligence as the spirit of the Father; he held on to this right up until the last moment of his life, and his death marked a new life and the salvation of the world. He was crucified, put to death and buried, but this did not destroy Him — He went on living because He held himself to be what He taught, and for this teaching of His, He had to endure suffering, and by these sufferings He redeemed what was necessary for salvation, and He proved faith in this salvation as a disregard of false and temporal life.

Accepting faith in Christ does not mean I accept that which speaks of the supernatural and miraculous, but that which speaks of my salvation as my true life. I can recognize His divine origin by His service to the Father, because His service, His strength of spirit, is rebirth to truth as principle, and intelligent life.

What can give me faith in Him is simply my recognition of the power of service to the true life; this power, once I accept it, makes me free, it removes me from subjugation to unrighteousness, it helps me in my struggle against evil by its own inherent and true means. This faith cannot be contained in any strictly defined forms apart from one's own life and in people's relationships to each other; this faith itself, as a source of living water, can serve me and others as a means of satisfying one's life, because it is the true good, and therefore it is service to and worship of God, taking the place of dead rites and formalities which neither give life nor merge with it; moreover, it is prayer to Him, since true religion should be none other than my whole life, hence religion is not a form, religion is intellect.

My prayer must be a true, living dialogue with God, it must be expressed in actions according to my calling, since my true spiritual self is the ability to understand this calling, while the outer self is the work of life, the work of love and righteousness, and thus my work is true service to the Father of life. My service to the Father should not be expressed in perceiving Him as something apart from me but as joined together with me by the only unbreakable bonds of eternal life-creating love and righteousness, and so I must let this righteousness pass through my spiritual self, as gold is passed through a crucible to be purified.

If I can be of service to others, then I must serve them with what God has given me, and thus before purifying others I must purify myself, and if I start with myself, then I shall be the yeast, and they the dough. My life must be not only my personal life, but also the life of others, the life of all people, and I must sacrifice everything for it, for I do this for the sake of the principle which unifies people's lives, and what this gives to me will be good not only for me alone but good for all. Therefore one must resist everything false not by destroying it but by that which must be introduced into life through the meaning and the intelligence of the law of life itself.

This is the question: how to bring to the true faith those who believe in Christ only for His miracles? — This is what I think: if someone believes in Christ only on account of the miraculous, he is still in a state of unbelief, as he cannot apply one iota of all the miracles to his own salvation. To obtain it, he must gain an understanding of the truth of the Saviour's teachings, to learn to know Him as He really is and then he will come to faith in Him as the true law of life, and his faith will be expressed in applying what he holds to be good to his life, and this will quicken his faith.

We often ask ourselves immaterial questions and try to work out the question of the future before that of the present, thinking sometimes that it will give us a solution for the present, but why do we even think about the question of the future when we have not yet worked out the question of the present? The point is to gain an understanding of that which is real and material prior to that which that is in the future and abstract.

The questions about God, revelation, Christ, faith, etc., as I see them, all boil down to a single question, namely the question of truth, of that universal truth which, forever unchanging as the creative power of love and righteousness, brings well-being into one's life, and all I need to know about it is simply to gain an understanding of my place in the order of creation, as a point of departure for an intelligent life, which gives me the true view of everything else.

There are people who deny Christ merely because they perceive the truth about Christ as it has been distorted by His false disciples, hence they themselves stand outside the truth. There are people who believe in Christ only according to outward characteristics which they take to be divine, and expect healing from Him, when He has already given this healing in His teachings on how to obtain salvation. Both are equally in a state of unbelief; to bring them to the faith, they have to emerge from that circle where they cannot see anything and stand where what was hidden from them will become visible to them. Their understanding of Christ is incomplete — in the former case because they have been thrown off balance by fanaticism substituting itself for Christ's teachings which consequently emits no light, in the latter case because they have not recognized Christ for what He was and what He was here for and why He was the Saviour of the world and the son of God.

Only one thing is necessary for both these groups: to show the truth as it is, and once they understand it, that which darkened the light will fall away from them all by itself, and what they believed in superficially will take on a completely different meaning and significance in their eyes. Consequently, I do not need to deny what they believed in superficially just because they gave it the wrong interpretation; I need only try to impart to them an understanding of the true significance of the object of their faith.

Let us suppose that someone believes in Christ by the miracles he attributes exclusively to His divine power. All right. For me His divine power has a special significance and meaning, for me it is comprised in His teachings, in His life, and the miracles too have a special significance and explanation, again related to His teachings as a sermon of truth. I can explain all the miracles not as something miraculous, but only because I cannot confuse the life of the son of the flesh with the sphere of life of the son of the spirit; the actions of these two are different, inasmuch as the one serves the power of darkness while the other serves the Father of light.

The Son of man is not the son of God if he does not serve the Father of life; if he serves the will of the Father, then he is the Son of God in the flesh, as Christ was the Son of God, and thus His birth as the Son of God must be spiritual (John 1:12–13). And so what was betrayed into the hands of men was not the Son of God, but the Son of man, even though in vilifying and slaying the Son of man they actually wanted to vilify and slay the Son of God (Luke 22:48, Mark 14:41). But God glorified Himself in Him and glorified Him (John 13:31–32). And in the death of the Son of man everyone glimpsed the glory of the Son of God, who was resurrected into eternity. He gave His life for the good of all mankind, to do the will of the Father-God.

One cannot understand man simply as a false man — one should understand him as he must be according to God's will. The Son of man is flesh. The Son of God is spirit. For the one, life means the life of the flesh, for the other this life is the life of the spirit. It is impossible to serve both; one can only serve the one — that is, intellect, the son of the Spirit. What is perceptible to intellect as the spirit in the flesh, what is perceptible to one's understanding, is that which also serves to attain well-being in life, because everything needed for this is given to him by the Father in terms he can comprehend, and anything beyond this is no longer mine, it is above and beyond the limits of the intelligence granted to me; I cannot go beyond those limits, it is not for me to know — the servant cannot know more than his master, his task is to know his own work.

God did not create people incapable of understanding what is necessary for good; He created them in such a way that they can understand what they need to understand of the Father's will. What is beyond that is beyond life itself — it is eternity and the life of God Himself, who is all; my task is to be close to Him and to be in Him; my task is to be faithful to Him in the little things, in order to partake of greater things.

What would I gain if I tried to work out the question of what the future will be when I myself am not around? This question is vain — vain because it does not comprise my real life, and false because it cannot give me the meaning of my life.

If I tell someone not to believe in the resurrection and think I am giving him the truth by this denial of a tenet of faith, I am engaging in a lie, because I myself believe in spiritual resurrection to a new life, and consequently am using the wrong approach to point out the truth, when a proper and true approach is required. By uttering such a denial I am not speaking the truth, and may alienate people from the truth, since I take things one way while somebody else sees it differently, and therefore my denial is not a denial of the tenet itself, but a denial of the false perception of my brother.

To cleanse this false perception of his, I have to take him directly to the goal, I have to make him see *for himself* the truth as truth and the lie as a lie — that is the only way to purify false perceptions. If we identify a lie simply as a lie before explaining the basic truth as a reliable source of support, we shall start pushing ahead without being consistent, and thus all we want to convey as truth, and must convey as pure truth — the truth itself will expose and denounce the lie, and then the truth itself, once it becomes the basis of faith (and only then), will be a lamp of righteousness, an explanation of the unexplainable, an understanding of that which was before inaccessible to the understanding, as an understanding of righteousness. Therefore what is needed for enlightenment also needs to be offered as a pure fount of living water, restoring to life all that is dead.

The foundation of faith in Christ must lie in what constituted Christ's mission, and then what is needful to me as the truth of faith is an understanding of this foundation. It is all the same to me whether Jesus walked on the water or not; I only know that this is not the foundation of faith, nor of its increase. I must learn to know that law of life which He imparted to us by his life and his teachings. No one who has learnt this will build the foundation of his faith on miracles, and hence his healing is the understanding of the salvation given by Christ. Through this understanding of the present as basic, everything that is not included in this circle will fall away of itself — this is the entrance to the true path, where a person is convinced that he has entered upon the road that will take him to his destination.

Christ did not destroy false faith by what people believed in; he destroyed it by the might of his teachings about truth. He said: You think that the bread which your fathers ate in the desert and were satisfied, that this bread came from heaven — they ate it and died, whereas the bread from heaven is such that he who eats it does not die; this bread is my teachings;[6] labour not for bodily sustenance, but for that sustenance which leads to eternal life.[7] He was not talking about something that had not happened, but talking directly about how things must be. — He gave people true sustenance directly, letting them understand righteousness; He practised faith in heavenly bread as the true spiritual bread, the word of His teachings.

Faith in miracles will no longer be faith when a person recognizes true faith — false faith will fall away of its own accord, as one who has come to know true faith will himself find out how to free himself from the false. Until the true faith is recognized, all my attempts to free a person from false perceptions will be in vain, because this comes about through the will of God and not my will, and thus my task of teaching is not to be above the master, above this truth, but to call people to the truth, to set them on the path that leads to this truth.

A person's regeneration does not depend on me — my task is to sow the pure seed, and God will cause it to grow. A premature attempt to take the plank out from under the feet of someone walking on it is dangerous. I know that the person will come walking to me along this plank and he himself will see what I want to impart to them. Perhaps his path is dangerous, perhaps the plank is rotten — I only know that this plank has been thrown across from the path of ruin, where the person could utterly disappear, to the path of salvation, and my task is not to take the plank out from under his feet, but to hasten the transition, so he doesn't fall into the abyss.

Along with this we must always take into consideration that not everyone finds himself at an equal distance from truth, and not everyone is able to take in solid food. Those who have already understood the mysteries of the kingdom of God may be given perfect sustenance and spoken with as being able to comprehend, while those who are still heading toward it need a different kind of sustenance; one must treat them like an invalid and hence with love, and not expect much of them, but intelligently give them sustenance for regeneration; one must not fill their soul with unnecessary discord and dissension as suffering; one must only do for them what could illuminate the path itself. Vain questions are very dangerous for them, as they are premature, and I am in a hurry to bring about that which will come about of its own accord, and they themselves will see the work for what it is. I have only one thing to do: through my own life and works bring others to the thought and understanding of how to distinguish righteousness from unrighteousness, of how to avoid mistaking a lie for truth and serving it, thereby falling into temptation.

Christ's service to the Father meant that by this service people would be shown that true life is in doing the will of the Father as the law of life, and this understanding is attained through union of the person's flesh and blood with the Saviour's own teachings. What power bestows this? The majesty of this power is manifest in intelligence and joins with the flesh to serve the spirit of life, and therefore the increase of faith is in learning and doing righteousness.

6 See John 6:31–35.
7 Cf. John 6:27.

This is the most important, and hence the fundamental thing, and I hold this to be the most important thing only when it is understood what faith in the teachings of truth must consist in and what the teachings and redemption of Christ amount to, and consequently everything else that merely serves to exalt these teachings to the divine, none of it adds or subtracts one iota for me. I have taken these teachings to be divine by virtue of their true characteristics, by their eternal righteousness which before was hidden from my eyes, and now I have a different view of a great many things that I used to see the wrong way because of my insufficient faith, and it is easily explained to me.

None of the actions and events accompanying Christ's sermon are a stumbling-block for me — I do not rely upon them as a basis for understanding truth, and it makes no difference to me whether they happened or did not happen, or how they happened, whether they were imaginary or real, whether the Gospels were written by the apostles or by someone else — none of that makes a difference nor is it dear to me. What is dear to me is only the truth which Christ imparted — it in itself is a precious jewel and my task is to know its price and to know why it is so precious.

To wonder whether things actually happened the way they were written is useless, in my opinion — it does not contribute anything new to our souls, it remains the same as before, and I can understand it this way or that way; whether I talk about it or not makes no difference — it is not what shows the way to truth. Once I have recognized what constitutes salvation, everything unrelated to salvation remains outside my sphere of convictions and consequently is no longer an object of my faith or my sermons.

If these things (unrelated to salvation) are mixed with grains of true faith and if by their brightness they serve to attract others, there is no need for me to toss them away as tares;[8] they will remain tares in any case for those who know how matters stand; because the seed which can give growth is precious, it will grow, and the fruitless [tares] will remain fruitless, even though it is possible that they have attracted many workers to the cause. I need only know that for false believers it is fruitless to tell them that their faith is dead; I have to see to it that this faith of its own accord is driven out by truth, and therefore I need only impart the essence of the truth itself, and set people on the true path with such conviction that they themselves believe this path to be the true one that will lead them to their destination and where they cannot go astray, and there is no cause that can dissuade them [and make them] believe that they are on the wrong path. One armed with such a conviction will know that to reach his destination he has to move forward and not stand still, he must work for himself and draw himself nearer to the desired goal of which he is convinced and find good for himself.

Fëdor Zheltov

1888, May 10th
Village of Bogorodskoe
Nizh. Gub.

8 See Matth. 13:24–30.

LEO TOLSTOY AND FËDOR ZHELTOV

Tolstoy's correspondence with Zheltov began in 1887. It was in April of that year, according to some sources, that he first met Zheltov, in Moscow. In his letter to V. G. Chertkov of 24–25 April 1887, Tolstoy commented on a meeting with two peasant writers: "One was a young Molokan, the other was a factory worker named Kassirov.... The meeting was a very happy one" (*PSS* 85:49). Zheltov met with Tolstoy again on more than one occasion. His visit to Tolstoy with his mother is especially interesting. Prugavin,[9] who was also invited, recorded his impressions of this visit, which are here reproduced in full, as they shed light on several characteristic traits of the Molokan writer:

> Zheltov told me in person that Lev Nikolaevich had asked me, if I was free, to go to see him that same evening, that he (Zheltov) would be there, along with his mother Marija Ivanovna, also a Molokan. After talking with Zheltov, I became convinced that here was a well-developed and well-read peasant who had deep convictions about the absolute rightness of the teachings of the 'Spiritual Christians.'
>
> When I came to see Tolstoy that evening, I found him hard at work: he had rolled up his sleeves to the elbows and was busy sewing a pair of boots.
>
> Zheltov and his mother arrived, and a conversation on religious themes ensued, in which Tolstoy became most actively involved. Zheltov's mother turned out to be a clever and serious-thinking woman, who spoke with a marvellous, pure folk accent of the Volga region. She acted in a simple, calm and dignified manner. She made a most favourable impression on Lev Nikolaevich, as he himself later said.
>
> The Zheltovs still reside in the village of Bogorodskoe, on the River Oka,[10] where they are engaged mainly in saddle- and harness-making. They have their own stall at the Nizhnij Novgorod Fair, which every Molokan who comes to the fair considers it his duty to patronize. At present Fëdor Alekseevich Zheltov is on the staff of the Molokan journal *Dukhovnyj Khristianin* [The Spiritual Christian]; in addition, he is in the process of compiling collections of stories for popular reading and takes an active role in local educational organizations.[11]

Checking T. P. Bondarenko's (1992) biographical dictionary of Russian writers, one notices that there are few biographical details on Zheltov. Fortunately, Zheltov's brief autobiography (to 1913) has been preserved in the S. A. Vengerov archive. It is presented in full below:[12]

9 *Aleksandr Stepanovich Prugavin* (1850–1920) — Russian historian and ethnographer, specializing in the historical schism in the Russian Orthodox Church, including Old Believers and other dissident sects.

10 *Oka* — a Volga tributary which the Moscow River flows into; it joins the Volga just south of Nizhnij Novgorod, (then capital of Nizhegorod Gubernia).

11 Prugavin 1911a: 105–07.

12 F. A. Zheltov, letter to S. A. Vengerov. *On the envelope:* To: Semën Afanas'evich Vengerov / Zagorodnyj 210 / St. Petersburg (Institut russkoj literatury, n. d., S. A. Vengerov archive). For the

To Professor Semën Afanas'evich Vengerov[13]
Zagorodnyj 21, St. Petersburg
Dear Sir,

Here is some information about myself.

Fëdor Alekseevich Zheltov was born 12 March 1859 in the village of Bogorodskoe, in the Gorbatov Uezd of Nizhegorod Gubernia, into a peasant family, to local peasants Aleksej Grigor'evich and Mar'ja Ivanovna Zheltov, who were of the Spiritual Christian (Molokan) denomination. The Zheltovs are long-time residents of the village of Bogorodskoe and even the founders of several settlements in Nizhegorod Gubernia, traces of which remain in the neighbouring Balakhna Uezd, where there are several settlements which still bear the name 'Zheltovka.'

During the period of serfdom[14] several Zheltov families were exiled for their Molokan faith to the village of Rasskazovo in Tambov Gubernia, where the name 'Zheltov' is firmly established. They became involved there in industry and agriculture and acquired a good deal of farmland. The Zheltov family included many prominent people who were elected to public office both during the period of serfdom and afterward.

Fëdor Zheltov's father, Aleksej Grigor'evich Zheltov, was elected by his community to petition for the protection of the peasants of the village of Bogorodskoe against the abuse of power by landowner S. V. Sheremet'ev back in 1858, some time before the abolition of serfdom. Thanks to the Nizhegorod governor — the well-known Decembrist[15] Aleksandr Nikolaevich Murav'ëv — and several other officials, he managed to have the petition delivered in person to Tsar Alexander II, who upon investigation placed the whole Sheremet'ev estate in trusteeship and exiled the landowner abroad without right of return to Russia. With the abolition of serfdom, Aleksej Grigor'evich was unanimously elected by the whole village community as the first district administrative elder of the village of Bogorodskoe.

Fëdor Alekseevich studied nowhere except the village primary school and received only home upbringing and education. He took to book-reading early, and during his youth spent all his free time reading. His curiosity and inquisitiveness constantly provoked in him serious thoughts and aspirations. His father had a relatively large library for that time, which was very soon unable to satisfy the inquisitive mind of the curious lad.

With his acquaintances and connections, Fëdor Alekseevich's father obtained books from the private libraries of people he knew, in particular

opportunity of using this particular document, I am grateful to the late Dr. Galina Jakovlevna Galagan of the Institute of Russian Literature, in the St. Petersburg branch of the Russian Academy of Sciences. This and the following extensive quotations are presented here in the hope that this extraordinarily interesting and important person, with many of his works still unpublished, will eventually be the focus of a sustained critical study.

13 *Semën Afanas'evich Vengerov* (1855–1920) — Russian historian, collector of archival materials on L. N. Tolstoy and other writers.

14 *serfdom* [*Krepostnoe pravo*] — the right of landowners to buy and own serfs, feudal labourers, officially abolished in 1861.

15 *Decembrist* — a participant in the unsuccessful uprising of army officers against the tsarist regime (and serfdom in particular) that took place following the death of Alexander I, in December 1825.

from the vast collection of the well-known explorer of the Nizhegorod region Aleksandr Serafimovich Gatsisskij (1838–1893), who, as a researcher on sectarianism, along with the Nizhegorod writer P. I. Mel'nikov,[16] was a frequent visitor to the Zheltovs' home. Even after his father's death in 1876, Fëdor Alekseevich maintained his ties with Gatsisskij, to whom he was much indebted for the latter's guidance in his reading, paying visits to him in Nizhnij Novgorod. The relationship continued uninterrupted until Gatsisskij's death.

In the circle of Gatsisskij's acquaintances, Fëdor Alekseevich had the opportunity to meet many social activists and writers, even some fairly prominent ones. His thought patterns and aspirations were greatly influenced by his contacts with such people, and his thirst for reading caused him to gradually acquire various books recommended to him. It was not long before he had a considerable library of his own, which later served as a free lending library for people in the community who shared his passion for reading.

His first timid steps toward a literary career began with simple exchanges of correspondence, then light short stories, published first in the Nizhegorod provincial newssheets and the Nizhegorod paper *Volgar'*, and subsequently in the Moscow papers *Russkij kur'er* [Russian Courier] and *Sovremennye izvestija* [Current News]. All these were timid initial attempts touching on topics of local interest, and the stories reflected scenes of peasant life. Encouraged by the publication of his stories, Fëdor Alekseevich set about writing them in earnest, and gave more careful thought to observing what was going on around him.

At this time the Posrednik publishing house appeared, which printed inexpensive books for popular consumption, headed by no less a major personage than Lev Nikolaevich Tolstoy. Fëdor Alekseevich wrote his story *Na Volge* [On the Volga], and entered into correspondence — and eventually into personal acquaintanceship — with L. N. Tolstoy. This story was approved by Lev Nikolaevich and sent with very few changes to Posrednik. It was soon followed by other stories: *Pered ljud'mi* [In People's Sight], *Na skhodke* [At the Village Meeting], *Vdova* [The Widow]. Later his stories *Trjasina* [The Quagmire] and *Kost' i Zoloto* [The Bone and the Gold] were taken up by other publishers.

At the same time Posrednik published his anti-drinking leaflet entitled *Perestanem pit' vino i ugoshchat' im* [Let us stop drinking wine and entertaining with it].

Questions of raising children in a sectarian family and his unique understanding of the meaning of religion also left their characteristic religious-philosophical imprint on the writings of Fëdor Alekseevich — the imprint of free thought which deeply penetrated into the issues of life. This, along with a fascination for Tolstoy, kept him in a constant, close relationship with Lev Nikolaevich, who discussed many issues with him in correspondence and

16 *Pavel Ivanovich Mel'nikov* (pseud., Andrej Pecherskij) (1818–1883) — a historian, ethnographer and writer, author of *V lesakh* [In the forests] (1871–1874) and *Na gorakh* [On the mountains] (1875–1881). The former deals with Old Believers, and the latter with sectarians. The Molokan prophet Maksim Rudomëtkin appears as a minor character. Mel'nikov also gathered materials on sectarian groups as part of his duties as an official collecting statistical data for the Russian Ministry of Internal Affairs.

personal conversations. There were instances in which Lev Nikolaevich sent to Bogorodskoe (with the recommendation that they contact Fëdor Alekseevich) those who were attracted by a one-sided understanding of the truths he expressed and were striving, in confusing conditions, to gain *everything* through tilling the soil in colonies which were then frequently forming only to collapse soon afterward. Perhaps it was simply a desire to offer the opportunity to have contact with people of a different way of life and thinking without overtones of personal superiority, but whatever it was, it served its purpose as a means of mutual enrichment of man's spiritual nature through intelligent communication.

There are probably not many still living who remember these moments of communication, or the embarrassment of the young, well-read but modest person that Fëdor Alekseevich was before these educated people who were restlessly seeking and thirsting for the truth. Such a fact, no matter how insignificant in life, actually had a deep psychological significance and one can only marvel at the spiritual strength and genius of Lev Nikolaevich Tolstoy, at the deep insight he had into the needs of the human spirit and how he was able to perceive the most delicate movements of the human heart, and as a genius and an artist galvanize these movements into creative acts through communication with people.

All this could not help but enrich a person's spiritual world with its forces of inner light, which were capable of precisely defining the vague impulses arising in the soul, refining them into clear, intelligent concepts about the purpose and meaning of life and imparting an understanding of the true means for their attainment.

Fëdor Alekseevich's particular world view and religious bent soon led him into a different genre of literature, that of the religious-philosophical treatise. This genre reflected the freedom of the liberated thought residing in sectarianism which is capable of penetrating remarkably deeply into the essence and meaning of what religion is all about, as individually understood — religion not as an abstract concept but as the practical business of life, the business of the welfare of all mankind.

Beginning in 1895, religious-philosophical articles began appearing in the newly founded Molokan journal *Dukhovnyj Khristianin* [The Spiritual Christian]; some of these articles were published separately by the editors of this journal, produced in St. Petersburg by A. S. Prokhanov.

A whole series of brochures was published which attracted attention not only from the sectarian world, but also from foreign theologians, and the editor of *The Spiritual Christian* received many requests for these brochures from abroad.

To date, the following articles by Fëdor Alekseevich have been published in this journal, in thousands of copies:

1) *Sleduj za mnoj* [Follow me], 2nd ed., 1910, St. Petersburg, 32 pp.

2) *Poklonenie Gospodu v dukhe i istine* [Worship the Lord in spirit and in truth], 2nd ed., 1912, Tiflis, 16 pp.

3) *Dukh i obrjadnost'* [The spirit and ritual], 1st ed., St. Petersburg, 1909, 18 pp. & 2nd ed., Tiflis, 1912, 16 pp.

4) *Razumnoe sluzhenie* [Reasonable service], 1909, St. Petersburg, 8 pp.

5) *Dva puti* [Two paths], 1909, St. Petersburg, 24 pp.

6) *Dukh i voda* [Spirit and water], 1910, St. Petersburg, 12 pp.

7) *Kreshchenie vodoj* [Baptism by water], 1910, St. Petersburg, 20 pp.

8) *Svidetel'stva dukha* [Testimonies of the spirit], 1910, St. Petersburg, 15 pp.

9) *Chto est' istina?* [What is truth?], 1911, St. Petersburg, 16 pp.

10) *Plody i list'ja* [The fruit and the leaves], 1911, St. Petersburg, 31 pp.

11) *O zelënoj palochke* [On the green twig], 1911, St. Petersburg, 23 pp.

12) *Na Volge* [On the Volga], 9th ed., Posrednik, 1911, Moscow, 48 pp. First published 1888.

13) *Pered ljud'mi* [In people's sight], 1st ed., 1892, Posrednik, Moscow, 54 pp. & 2nd ed., 1906, 48 pp.

14) *Vdova* [The widow], 2nd ed., Posrednik, 1911, Moscow, 47 pp.

15) *Kost' i Zoloto* [The bone and the gold], Zhirkova Publ., Moscow, 1895, 30 pp.

16) *Kost' i Zoloto* [The bone and the gold], Zhirkova Publ., Moscow, 1899, 30 pp.

17) *Trjasina* [The quagmire], 1893, Moscow, 31 pp.

18) *Perestanem pit' vino i ugoshchat' im* [Let us stop drinking wine and entertaining with it]. Leaflet, Posrednik, Moscow.

The following are some of the stories published in newspapers:

1) "Fedosij Ivanovich Kocheryzhkin" — *Russkij kur'er*, N° 282, 1886.

2) "Ablakat" — *Russkij kur'er*, N° 325, 1886.

3) "Derevenskij prazdnik" [Village holiday] — *Russkij kur'er*, N° 30, 1887.

4) "Krest'janskij nedug" [A peasant ailment] — *Nizhegorodskie Gubernskie vedomosti*, N° 43, 1886.

5) "Chto u nas chitaet narod" [What our people are reading] — *Nizhegorodskie Gubernskie Vedomosti*, nos. 45–46, 1887.

6) "Zatmenie" [The blackout] — *Nizhegorodskie Gubernskie Vedomosti*, N°N° 45–46, 1887.

7) "Legenda o dushe monastyrja" [The legend of the monastery's soul] — *Nizhegorodskie Gubernskie Vedomosti*, N° 8, 1887.

8) "Arkheologicheskij interes Gorbatovskogo uezda" [Points of archæological interest in Gorbatov Uezd] — *Nizhegorodskie Gubernskie Vedomosti*, N°N° 44–45, 1888.

9) "Utro literatora" [A literary person's morning] — *Russkij kur'er*, N° 40, 1887.

10) "Trjasina" [The quagmire] — *Russkij kur'er*, N° 101, 1888.

11) "Na skhodke" [At the village meeting] — *Russkij kur'er*, N°N° 103–104, 1888.

12) "Kost' i Zoloto" [The bone and the gold] — *Russkij kur'er*, N°N° 72–73, 1889.

13) "Sorvalsja" [Broken off] — *Russkij kur'er*, N°N° 102–106, 1889.

14) "Zvonar'" [The bell ringer] — *Russkij kur'er*, N° 241, 1889.

15) "19-e fevralja 1886 g. v s. Bogorodskom" [19 February 1886 in the Village of Bogorodskoe] — *Sovremennye izvestija*, N° 62, 1886.

16) "Molokane v s. Bogorodskom" [Molokans in the Village of Bogorodskoe] — *Sovremennye izvestija*, N° 168, 1886.

17) "Golos iz derevni" [A voice from the countryside] — *Russkij kur'er*, N° 145, 1885.

18) "O tserkovno-prikhodskikh shkolakh i religiozno-nravstvennykh sobesedovanijakh" [On parochial schools and religious-moral discussions] (Letter to the editor) — *Russkij kur'er,* N° 177, 1885.
19) "Golos krest'janina" [Voice of the peasant] — *Russkij kur'er,* N° 21, 1889.
20) "Na rabote" [At work] — *Volgar',* N° 236, 1900.
21) "Rozhok i Vilejka" — *Volgar',* 1900.
22) "Trofim sudejshchik" [Trofim the judge] — *Volgar',* 1900.

Besides these articles, a number of minor announcements, articles and letters were published in these periodicals, describing current events.

In the critical literature, Fëdor Alekseevich's popular stories are noted in articles by Rubakin, Alchevskaja and others; the articles published in *The Spiritual Christian* are noted in issue N° 1 of *Narodnaja molva* (Khar'kov), in an article by Tjazhelov, and in other provincial publications.

Fëdor Alekseevich Zheltov is mentioned in a listing of people of the Middle Volga region by A. S. Gatsisskij in his publication *Nizhegorodka,* in A. S. Prugavin's reminiscences about L. N. Tolstoy, and in Tolstoy's published letters to L. E. Obolenskij [see *PSS* 64:282–83].

At the present time, Fëdor Alekseevich is still continuing his literary work, which takes up all his free time, and continues to humbly work for the development of moral-religious thought on the basis of pure Gospel teachings.
F. Zheltov
Address: Village of Bogorodskoe,
Nizhegorod Gubernia.
19 May 1913.

In his biographical sketch Zheltov does not mention his correspondence with V. D. Bonch-Bruevich, V. G. Korolenko,[17] and other writers and government officials (which was especially lively during the Multan trial[18]), that he was a member of the Peasant Union, a delegate to the Peasant Congress of 1906, and subsequently arrested. During the First World War he served as a member of the Bogorodskoe Military-Industrial Committee.[19]

There are practically no materials relating to F. A. Zheltov's life or career as a writer in the Soviet period. One thing that has been preserved is a "Copy of questionnaire included in the letters of L. N. Tolstoy" [*Kopija ankety pri pis'makh L. N. Tolstogo*], handwritten by F. A. Zheltov and sent to V. S. Mishin (commentator for *PSS*) on 28 May 1929. It is reproduced here in full, as it offers a unique glimpse into the relationship between these two thinkers:

17 *Vladimir Dmitrievich Bonch-Bruevich* (1873–1955) — social activist and communist, a major collector of materials on sectarians, later personal secretary to V. I. Lenin; *Vladimir Galaktionovich Korolenko* (1853–1921) — writer and publicist, attracted by democratic and humanitarian ideals.

18 *Multan trial* (1892–1896) — a trial of Udmurt peasants from the village of Old Multan, Vjatskaja Gubernia, accused of ritual murder. Defended by Korolenko and the prominent jurist Anatolij Fëdorovich Koni (1844–1927), the accused were eventually acquitted.

19 See Bondarenko 1992: 264.

Copy of questionnaire included in the letters of L. N. Tolstoy, sent to the Editorial Commission[20] *28 May 1929*

1. F. A. Zheltov, peasant by birth, a Molokan sectarian by religious conviction. Brought up from birth in a Molokan family.

2. *Date of birth:* 1859, 12 February[21] [24 February new style].

3. Studied at the primary school in the Village of Bogorodskoe, Nizhegorod Gubernia, and later home-schooled. Read and studied a lot.

4. Lived in Bogorodskoe right from birth.

5. Worked in the family business. His father had a saddlery business in Nizhnij Novgorod; died in 1876. His mother expanded the operation, had a leather manufacturing concern. I [Fëdor Alekseevich] looked after the office.

6. Married to the daughter of a peasant factory owner, E. I. Kukina, 9 October 1878 [21 October new style]. Children: sons Aleksej, Aleksandr, Anatolij and Ivan; daughters Nadezhda and Lidija.

7. *History of relations with L. N. Tolstoy:* After reading *Ispoved'* [Confession], *V chëm moja vera?* [What I Believe] and other writings, I was led to write my first letter to L. N. in 1887, after which our first meeting took place in Moscow; [this was followed by] further correspondence.

8. *When and where did you become acquainted with L. N.?* — In Moscow, in L. N.'s home, in March 1888.

9. *Were you ever at Yasnaya Polyana?* — I was there once, on 13 February 1890, on a journey with my wife, sister and brother-in-law.

10. *Where and when did you meet* [with Tolstoy] *apart from Yasnaya Polyana?* — During all his remaining years, when L. N. lived in Moscow, I visited him at least once a year at his home in Khamovniki.[22]

11. *Were you in correspondence with L. N.?* — Constantly, even if not all that frequently. Occasionally his daughter Marija L'vovna would write at L. N.'s request, but most of the letters were written by Lev Nikolaevich himself.

12. *How many letters did L. N. write you and in what years?* — In 1887 — 3 or 4 letters; in 1888 — 5; in 1889 — 3; in 1890 — 3; in 1891 — 2; in 1892 — 2; in 1893 — 2; in 1894 — 3; in 1895 — 2; in 1896 — 2 letters, up until 1909.

13. *Have they ever been published?* — No, they have never been published.

14. *Where are the originals of these letters now?* — Some of these letters are in my possession, but the letters from the early years of our correspondence were lost in a fire.

15. *How many letters did you write L. N. and when?* — In 1887 — 3 letters; in 1888 — 4; in 1889 — 4; in 1890 — 3; in 1891 — 2; in 1892 — 2; in 1893 — 2; in 1894 — 3; 1895–1899 — 4; 1909 — 5; 1897 — 3; 1898 — 2; other writings have not been preserved (my last letter was written 17 September 1909).

16. *Have they been published anywhere?* — No, nowhere. Some of them have survived in copy form.

20 *Editorial Commission* — a commission responsible for gathering documents for inclusion in *PSS*.

21 In 1913, Zheltov had given his birthdate as 12 March 1859 (see above), here (in 1929) he identified it as 12 February.

22 In 1882, Lev Nikolaevich purchased a house in Khamovniki Lane in Moscow, which he and members of his family used as an urban residence until 1901.

17. *Do you have any copies of your letters to L. N.?* — I have the ones that have been preserved.

18. *Have you written any reminiscences about L. N.?* — I have, in draft form. Some excerpts from a conversation were sent by A. K. Chertkova.

[signature]
25 May 1929

Addendum: Besides the nine [original] letters, the rest are in copies.
Letters whose originals have not survived:

1 letter of 20 April 1887
1 " " 10 July 1887
1 " " ? February 1887

These letters were written in response to my letters. I reported on them to Vladimir Grigor'evich Chertkov on 20 and 29 August 1927 through V. S. Mishin's secretary.

Note: I am enclosing *Nine* originals of L. N. Tolstoy's letters, along with several of the envelopes. I would ask you to take good care of the letters and envelopes and return them to me when you have finished with them, *sending me advance notice of this.*

In case any questions arise about any of the letters, it is sufficient, in writing me, to indicate the number inscribed in blue pencil in the corner of the given letter, as I have made copies with the same numerical identification.

F. Zheltov [signature]
25 May 1929

In Bondarenko's biographical dictionary, mentioned above, the date of Zheltov's death is indicated as "after 1938." Not very long ago, I should note, I received a copy of the newspaper *Bogorodskaja gazeta* of 19 June 1997, clarifying and supplementing some of the details of Zheltov's life and work; the date and cause of his death are also indicated. In his article "He used to meet with Tolstoy," V. Bashkirov (1997), drawing upon materials preserved in the local museum as well as the regional archives, gives a biography of Zheltov, mentions his contacts with several Russian cultural figures, and takes special note of the meetings and the correspondence between Zheltov and Tolstoy. This article is worth reproducing in full, from the *Bogorodskaja gazeta* of 19 June 1997:

HE USED TO MEET WITH TOLSTOY

As is known, our Bogorodsk region has a rich history, as is evident from old street names and the reminiscences of our long-time residents about prominent citizens of the area. Unfortunately, we do not always take good care of our historical legacy. The face of the old part of town is changing, old buildings are disappearing, but it is good to see that over the past years in the centre of Bogorodsk they have started constructing, instead of box-like apartment blocks, buildings whose external appearance fits in with our historical traditions.

At the same time, little is known about the life of our area's prominent citizens, including, for one, Fëdor Alekseevich ZHELTOV.

I went looking through the material in our city museum about this talented individual. We know that he was of peasant stock and belonged to the Molokan sectarian faith. He was the owner of a leather-goods factory (renamed the Venetskij Factory after the revolution, now known as the Bokoz Company). This was a highly cultured person, a great book lover with a rich library which townspeople could use free of charge.

Unfortunately, in the late 1930s Fëdor Alekseevich fell victim to the wave of political repression.

This is basically all that has been known up to now.

In studying documents at the regional archives on the past history of the leather-manufacturing concern, with the help of the archival staff, I learnt quite a few new things about the life of F. A. Zheltov.

He was born in 1859 (12 February, old style [24 February new style]) to a Molokan family. He went to primary school, and then received education at home, where he did a lot of reading. His father had a small saddlery concern. After his death in 1876 the business was run by Fëdor's mother, who expanded the business at the expense of the leather factory. Fëdor at this time looked after the office.

In 1878 he married the daughter of a local peasant factory owner named E. I. Kukina. We can assume the marriage was a happy one, since his family grew in size along with his financial status. Fëdor Alekseevich had four sons — Aleksej, Aleksandr, Anatolij and Ivan — and two daughters — Nadezhda and Lidija. This was the status of his household at the end of the nineteenth century.

Along with his business, which by then he was running all by himself, F. A. Zheltov was also active in the Molokan community, which in the 1870s and 1880s was exposed to Western preachers of Lutheran, Baptist and Evangelical persuasions.

He writes about this in his recollections about the sectarians of the village of Bogorodskoe.

Being very outgoing and curious by nature, he had friendly contacts with the self-taught astronomer K. I. Kaplin-Tezikov and other members of the local intelligentsia.

Beginning in 1894 Zheltov was in constant contact with two of the future statesmen and political leaders of our country, V. D. Bonch-Bruevich and E. D. Stasova (as noted in the documents, "...he was in contact [with them] for the purpose of delivering materials for both legal and illegal publications").

At this time, in the late 1880s and early 1890s, Fëdor Alekseevich was known as a local writer. In the Nizhegorod Archival Commission catalogue, in a long list of works I found the titles of two of Zheltov's stories: *Kost' i Zoloto* [The bone and the gold], an ancient tale (Moscow, 1891) and *Pered ljud'mi* [In people's sight], a peasant's story (Moscow, 1892).

Here is how Bonch-Bruevich described him in 1928:

I have known F. A. Zheltov since 1894. I got to know him when he was still a young peasant writer, and since then I have kept up correspondence with this interesting and gifted ethnographer, who has written some very good descriptions of the lives of peasants and workers; these, by the way, were wholly suppressed by tsarist censors, who tried to persecute their author for anti-government remarks in the stories. I was even called in for questioning on this, as I was then an editor with a publishing house of popular books and wanted to publish these stories there.

A special place in Zheltov's life is devoted to meetings and correspondence with the great Russian writer L. N. Tolstoy.

Zheltov was motivated to write to Lev Nikolaevich in 1887 after Tolstoy published his *Confession* and *What I Believe*. This was followed by their meeting in Moscow and subsequent correspondence.

On 13 February 1890, Fëdor Alekseevich, his wife, sister and brother-in-law visited Lev Nikolaevich at Yasnaya Polyana. They continued to meet thereafter, in Moscow. Their correspondence was not all that frequent. Occasionally Tolstoy's daughter Marija L'vovna answered Zheltov's letters at her father's request. The last letter is dated 1909.

Unfortunately, Tolstoy's early letters were lost to fire, and nine of his letters were sent to the Editorial Commission in 1929, when preparations were underway to publish a complete collection of his works in honour of the hundredth anniversary of Lev Nikolaevich's birth [1928].

In the meantime, the leather factory grew and developed. By 1917, fifty hired employees worked there. Apparently, all production decisions were taken by one of Fëdor Alekseevich's sons — Ivan Fëdorovich. The factory's annual output was 84,000 small-scale production units of sheep and goat skins. For those times, it was considered a major concern. And then, in 1918, it was nationalized by the Soviet authorities. All major entrepreneurs, including F. A. Zheltov, were deprived of voting rights.

In an attempt to prove his loyalty to the new authorities and also to have his civic rights restored, Fëdor Alekseevich actively worked in various government and social organizations.

Thus, beginning in June 1918, he was a member of the Nizhegorod Scholarly Archival Commission, which exercised control over the execution of the decrees of the Council of People's Commissars on the destruction of archival documents by institutional personnel.

In 1919–1922 F. A. Zheltov was one of the organizers of the *Trudovoe sodruzhestvo* [Labour Commonwealth] agricultural artel. He was directly involved in the organization of the *Pakhar'* [Ploughman] and *Trudovik* [Labourer] co-operative agricultural artels.

Here is a memo from the former supervisor of the Kud'ma–Pavlovo Railway construction site, B. Troitskij:

I received from F. A. Zheltov the following which he helped prepare:

1. Material compiled for determining the route of the Kud'ma–Pavlovo Railway line.

2. An outline of the route.
3. Statistical materials needed for mapping out the projected railway route.

Recently, Nikandr Vasil'evich Migunov, a long-time resident of the city who knew Zheltov, told me the following story. One day, when he was a young man, Nikandr Vasil'evich met a friend on the street, and they lit up their cigarettes. Zheltov walked by and said:

"I wouldn't smoke if I were you, it's very harmful."

Along this line, there is a copy of a letter from the People's Commissar of Health, Nikolaj Aleksandrovich Semashko, addressed to Fëdor Alekseevich:

I received your letter. I completely agree with your views on smoking. I shall use it if I happen to be writing again on this subject.

3 May 1923 N. Semashko

On 10 May 1932, Fëdor Alekseevich's voting rights were restored. Now along in years, he worked with the city's Museum of Regional Studies and became a member of the Russo-German Culture and Technology Society, and actively defended the rights of the Molokan community. He carried on correspondence with Baptist sects in Germany, America, Estonia and Latvia.

All this played a crucial role in his fate.

On 15 October 1937, Zheltov was accused of counter-revolutionary propaganda in association with sectarian organizations in other countries. On 22 December 1937 he was sentenced to capital punishment. In spite of petitions by Bonch-Bruevich and Stasova, he was executed by firing squad on 14 January 1938.

He was rehabilitated by the presidium of the Gor'kij Oblast Court on 12 August 1959.

Fëdor Alekseevich left us a rich legacy in the form of descriptive material on the settlement of the Bogorodsk area and on the growth of various handicraft industries in its territory. Unfortunately these documents have been lost, but the search for them cannot be considered hopeless.

A second point: The museum has no photograph of F. A. Zheltov or his children, although it does have old group photographs of Bogorodsk residents. Given Fëdor Alekseevich's outgoing nature, it is likely that he is present in some of them. But we need help from those who knew him.

If any of F. A. Zheltov's relatives are still living in Bogorodsk, we hope they respond to this article and come to the city museum.

V. BASHKIROV
City Museum staff

The correspondence between Zheltov and Tolstoy began in 1887 and continued until 1909. Some of the letters of both correspondents have been lost. As Zheltov has indicated, for example, many originals of Tolstoy's letters to him were lost to fire. Zheltov's letters to Tolstoy are kept in the L.N. Tolstoy State Museum, in Moscow. All letters known to date are included (with annotations) in a previously published volume under my editorship (Donskov 2001).

Tolstoy's correspondence with Zheltov is permeated with a feeling of mutual respect on the part of these two remarkable people. The closing expressions speak for themselves: "With brotherly love," "Your loyal brother," "With sincere love and faithfulness with all my heart." However, in spite of this closeness and close spiritual kinship between two (one may say) preachers, since their written dialogue was one *among equals,* there are a few letters where notes of disagreement may be heard, where the authors stand by their own views.

The fundamental content of the letters published below is the discussion of religious questions, along with a wide array of burning social problems. Zheltov's religious beliefs, which in many respects coincided with the views of Tolstoy, are discussed in some detail in a letter (N° 15 below) dated 15 October 1889, along with the tenets of the Molokan faith. The content of this letter, as well as of several other of Zheltov's letters, which are so extensive as to approximate detailed critical articles or treatises, give a picture of their author as an extremely intelligent person and, at the same time, a rather colourful figure. On the one hand, this Russian peasant sectarian remains unshaken in his convictions as a thinker, while on the other, like Bondarev, Verigin and Novikov, he stands out as a stranger to his own milieu by virtue of his sharply penetrating analytical mind, the breadth of his reading experience and the logic of his arguments.

Zheltov's letters to Tolstoy are fraught with a multitude of interwoven themes. These include educational issues (especially relating to child-raising), the true meaning of literature, marriage, prayer (should it be in a group or in solitude? — "only in solitude," replies Tolstoy), the person of Jesus Christ, famine, drunkenness and useful books for the people to read.

In most cases Tolstoy agrees with Zheltov's point of view. In a number of his letters he offers advice, as a veteran to a novice; in some he gently criticizes the inflexibility common to the majority of sectarians. Both correspondents decry the corruption of government agencies, both are critical of the upper classes, they condemn the limited and intolerant attitudes of the ecclesiastical authorities, and take a strong stand against militarism.

Tolstoy and Zheltov are also linked by their common concern about the problems of the landless peasants.[23] The letters, like those of the other peasant sectarian writers discussed in this volume, frequently mention the need for physical labour on the land as one of the conditions for a moral, happy and joyous life on earth.

23 Russian peasants were freed from serfdom according to the decree by Alexander II in 1861 but were not given sufficient land of their own, which meant that most peasants continued to be at the mercy of landowners.

TOLSTOY AND ZHELTOV: LETTERS 1887–1909

N° 1. F. A. ZHELTOV ☛ L. N. TOLSTOY

18 April 1887. Village of Bogorodskoe.

"Sir, give me this water,
that I thirst not…"
(John 4:15)

My deeply respected Lev Nikolaevich!

Forgive me if my letter distracts you for a few minutes. Please believe that it is written by someone who *sincerely* respects you, who fully shares your views and is sensitive to your aspirations and ideas, all the more so since these aspirations and ideas are in complete agreement with his own worldview, as well as the religious views and convictions of those people with whom he has the honour to associate. The people of whom I am speaking are the sectarians — the 'Spiritual Christians,' or simply *Molokans.*

We are simple people, simple peasants — literate, but not well-educated; we still have a lot to learn, to understand, yet at the same time we realize that these great truths for which mankind has been striving either consciously or unconsciously for æons, which it has expressed and still is expressing by various means and which it is searching for either directly or by roundabout ways, are to be found only in the unchanging, eternal moral law, which summarizes their totality in just a few words: love for one's neighbour, love for one's enemy, love for God, hence in knowledge of God, in an understanding of good and truth… How can a person say that he has known God, i.e., love Him whom he has not seen, if he does not love his brother whom he has seen?... How can God's love dwell therein? (1 John 4:16, 20–21; 1 John 5:1, 3; Titus 1:16).

What is life?... For a man to live without the *true* life within him, without putting his name to deeds of righteousness, without registering his name in the Eternal Book — the 'Book of Life' — is to dwell in death, to exist in darkness!... Where is the light?... Where is life?... The light is in truth, life is in God, in Christ!... The true life is God; the light of truth is His unchanging, eternal law of spirit, liberty and love.

To live in the light one must live in love, for someone that says he is in the light but hates his brother is still in darkness. He who loves his brother dwells in the light and there is no temptation in it. But he who hates his brother is in darkness, and walks in darkness, and does not know where he is going, because the darkness has blinded his eyes (1 John 2:9–11). The point is that light must not be made darkness (Luke 11:35). For if the light be darkness, how great is that darkness!... (Matth. 6:23). If one has the light burning within him, let him be a light for others (Mark 4:21). A candle is not lit to be hidden under a bushel (Matth. 5:14–16).

What shall we do then?! (John 6:28; Luke 3:10). Master, tell us, what shall we do then?... To give people the knowledge of salvation? (Luke 1:77).

Yes, we must do something — and not just for the sake of doing *something*, but to make the truth, and this is why I am permitting myself to write to you for advice.

Christ says that he that hath is to give to him that hath not, that one who is wealthy should share his wealth with those who lack it. He says there is wealth that is right, and wealth that is not right, there is the true and the false, there is one's own and there is another's (Luke 6:2–12). And that in this wealth there are faithful stewards, but there are also unfaithful stewards. He says there are treasures that are right, higher than anything in the world — those are the true, spiritual treasures (Matth. 6:19–20). Everyone should share what he has: one can have a lot and share a lot; one can have little and share little. If I have this wealth, then consequently I should not hide it away, but put it into circulation (Luke 19:20–23) and share it with the impoverished, just as a light burns to provide light for everyone in the house. And even though what I have is not sufficient for me to share a lot, even so, sometimes a 'mite' is equal to a large contribution; remember the poor widow who threw her two mites into the treasury (Mark 12:42–43). And even if I give away all my goods, but have not love, then will I reap no benefit but evil (1 Cor. 13:3).

And so, to do something myself, to do the best I can to serve what mankind should be serving, I have chosen the way of literature; I chose it because I feel called in that direction; I do not want the light, if it is within me, to go out; I want it to burn brightly, even if it flickers, for that is what is good. But I have a question: what is the true bread, what are the *true* tasks of literature?... As one who is weak in this line I need guidance, but I believe that this is needed by many literary people. I want to know which way I am to go at this stage of my life. Point it out to me. Set my youthful energies to the task. Set me to work, not to fruitless labour, but to useful, fruitful, life-creating labour. I am writing a few things, I am getting my stories and sketches published in the papers,[24] but something tells me that is not what I should be serving. I am tormented by this question and I ask you, implore you, to answer it for me and to point out where I can best be of service, and I await your reply with faith. I hope that you will share your light with a weak brother and will set him on the true path. *I wait as one that thirsteth — for the fount of water.*

In deep respect and with a heart grateful for your writings, which have now begun to reach the ear of the common people[25] and are serving to awaken the spirit,

24 Zheltov's first publications appeared in the newspapers *Nizhegorodskie gubernskie vedomosti* [Nizhegorod Gubernia News] and *Volgar'*; from 1885, he began to be published in the Moscow paper *Russkij kur'er* [Russian Courier].

25 The reference is to the publications of Posrednik, the publishing house established in Moscow in 1884, with Tolstoy's blessing, by one of Tolstoy's followers, Vladimir Grigor'evich Chertkov.

I remain your loyal

Fëdor Zheltov

P.S. I am enclosing several of my shorter articles. Would it be possible for you to send me a copy of *V chëm moja vera?* [*What I Believe*] and *Evangelie* [*The Gospels*]? I should like to become acquainted with them.

1887, April 18th
Address: Fëdor Alekseev[ich] Zheltov
Village of Bogorodskoe
Nizhegorod Gubernia

Nº 2. L. N. TOLSTOY ❧ F. A. ZHELTOV
21 April? 1887. Moscow.

Fëdor Alekseevich![26]

I was so happy to receive your letter; happy to see your development... I believe the writer has but one task: to convey to others the thoughts and beliefs which have made his life a joy. Life is made joyful, truly joyful, only by understanding the Gospel truths and applying them to one's self, to the various facets of one's life.

Only this can and ought to be written about in all possible ways: as discourse, as parables, as stories. There is just one danger, and that is [the temptation] to write only from the point of view of logic, instead of from that feeling which would encompass a person's whole being. The main thing is, not to be in a hurry to write, not to get tired of going over and over and correcting the same thing ten or even twenty times, not to write too much, and, by the mercy of God, not to make writing one's means of living or showing off to others. In my judgement it is just as foolish and harmful to write immoral things as to write educational essays with a cold heart, without believing in what you are teaching and without the passionate desire to give people that which gives you happiness.

I am unable to put into a few words what I consider essential for a writer, other than point you in the direction of my latest stories for the people and the preface to *Tsvetnik* [The Flowerbed], in which I have attempted to express what constitutes the essence of poetic writing.[27] I am extremely glad that you want to write — first, because you are a peasant, and second, because you are free from false ecclesiastical dogma which closes people's eyes to the meaning of Christ's teachings.

26 The salutation and the first sentence of the letter, which were not preserved in the copy, were taken from the original manuscript — see *PSS* 90:268).

27 Tolstoy's preface to the *Tsvetnik* [Flowerbed] collection, compiled by the staff of Posrednik, appeared in the Kiev edition of 1886. See *PSS* 26:307–09.

I read your articles. The best in terms of content are the ones about travel and the dream;[28] but the latter seems to me to have an unsavoury literary flavour, more like a satirical piece, and not much content. The dream could have been an episode in a much longer work, but it has little to say all by itself. The article about the festival is cold and is likewise too literary in its style. By 'literary style' I mean that it is aimed at newspaper readers, intellectuals. I would suggest that something else might be desirable: the imagined reader you are writing for should not be a literary person, an editor, a government official, a student, etc., but rather a fairly literate 50-year-old peasant. That is the reader I always have in mind for myself and recommend to you. For a reader like that you won't use fancy words and expressions, you will refrain from empty and excessive talk, but express yourself clearly, concisely and meaningfully. Read the story "Razdel" [The partition], written by a peasant,[29] and "Ded Sofron" [Grandpa Sofron].[30] People are moved by both these stories, since they speak to people's vital interests, and their interests are more important than those of authors.

If you want to send me something you write for publication by Posrednik, send it to Tula.

Your loving brother

I think you can write, not only because of your mastery of language, but, more importantly, because from your early years you have imbibed Christ's teachings and their moral significance, as is evident from your letter.

N° 3. F. A. ZHELTOV ❧ L. N. TOLSTOY
6 July 1887. Village of Bogorodskoe.

My deeply respected Lev Nikolaevich!

Taking advantage of your kind offer to send something I have written for Posrednik, I am enclosing herewith my manuscript entitled *Na Volge, ili Zlom gorju ne pomozhesh'* [On the Volga, or You Won't Help Sorrow By Evil]. I have no idea whether this corresponds to something worthy of publication, especially by such a beneficent organization as Posrednik; however, I think whatever speaks of righteousness deserves publication, even though it is not expressed in such a literary style.

In the fervent desire to affirm some kind of Gospel truth which would by inescapable logic prove what is the actual righteousness of life, I have written, to the best of my ability, what I wanted to say in affirmation of this truth. I do hope you will be indulgent toward me, a beginner, and therefore I most

28 The reference is to Zheltov's articles "Derevenskij prazdnik" [Village festival] and "Trjasina" [The quagmire] in *Russkij kur'er,* 31 January and 15 April 1887, respectively.
29 This story by I. G. Zhuravov was published anonymously by Posrednik in 1887.
30 A story by V. I. Savikhin, also released by Posrednik.

humbly ask you, after reading the manuscript, to point out its deficiencies to me which you have noticed in my brief work — this will stand me in good stead for the future.

If you find my manuscript worthy of publication, I shall place it at your *complete* disposal; if, however, you find it unsuitable for publication, or if you find it not yet sufficiently worked out, I would humbly ask you to return it to me, for which I am enclosing the necessary stamps.

In awaiting your reply, I remain, with deepest respect,

Your brother F. Zheltov

1887, July 6th
Village of Bogorodskoe
Nizhegorod Gubernia

Address:
Fëdor Alekseevich Zheltov
Village of Bogorodskoe
Nizhegorod Gubernia

N° 4. L. N. TOLSTOY ❧ F. A. ZHELTOV[31]
20 July 1887. Yasnaya Polyana.

Fëdor Alekseevich!

I received your story. In terms of both spirit and content, it is very good…[32]

I am delighted on the whole to communicate with you. The point is not so much to write, but to live a Christian life; that is the highest creative achievement available to mankind. Let us strive to bring it about, and in proportion to our achievement of it, both our words and our writings will be good, and useful to others.

I am sending your story to Vladimir Grigor'evich Chertkov at Rossosha Station in Voroznezh Gubernia. He's in charge, he's the founder of Posrednik. He will either edit the story, if he agrees with me that it deserves to be published, or he will be in touch with you and send it back to you for reworking.

With brotherly affection,

Lev Tolstoy

31 Note on copy: "Rec[eived] 24 July 1887."

32 An omission in the copy. In a letter to V. S. Mishin (the *PSS* commentator, as noted) dated 26 August 1927, Zheltov filled in the missing words from memory about "the want of a more literary presentation of the beginning of the story:" "why not outline the events and experiences described by the mother to her son in her retelling of her whole experience." Zheltov's story *Na Volge* [On the Volga] was published by Posrednik in 1888; its ninth edition appeared in 1911. In forwarding the manuscript to Chertkov, on 21 July 1887, Tolstoy remarked about its author: "This is a Molokan whose letters are full of the Christian spirit. No literary talent, but once the story is edited and shortened, I think it can be published" (*PSS* 86:68).

N° 5. F. A. ZHELTOV ❧ L. N. TOLSTOY
27 January 1888. Village of Bogorodskoe.

Village of Bogorodskoe,
Nizhegorod Gubernia

My much respected Lev Nikolaevich!

I take the liberty of bothering you again, and enclose a letter which, if you don't find it a burden, please read and, if you can, answer.[33]

In a few days I hope to send you a manuscript for Posrednik.

My earlier manuscript (On the Volga) has probably already gone to press, since Vladimir Grigor'evich Chertkov informed me of editorial changes back in November.

With respect and brotherly love toward you I remain

F. Zheltov

1888, January 27th
Address: Fëdor Alekseevich Zheltov
Village of Bogorodskoe, Nizhegorod Gub.

N° 6. L. N. TOLSTOY ❧ F. A. ZHELTOV
1–2 February 1888. Moscow.

Dear brother Fëdor Alekseevich! The questions you put to me touch upon such serious subjects that I cannot hope to give you a satisfactory answer, even in writing.

Your two questions — about the upbringing of children and relationships with others really boil down to one question for me, namely the latter: how to relate to others not just in words but in deeds: do I have the right to possess any kind of property and defend it against my brothers, do I have the right to divide my brothers into those who live a bad life and those who live a good life? If this question is answered and a father's life is shaped by one answer or the other, that father's life will include the whole upbringing of his children. And if he decides correctly, the father will not introduce temptation into his children's lives; if not, however, things will turn out differently. The knowledge which the children acquire or do not acquire is of secondary concern and not in any way important. Whatever the child's abilities are, that is what he will learn, even if he lives in some remote place. What is traditionally called education is more than half made up of evil and deceit, and so the farther removed he is from that kind of education (given in all our institutions), the better for the child. The whole question, it turns out, is how the father will answer the question of practical living for himself.

33 This letter remains unknown.

My dear brother, be careful how you answer this question in your own consciousness. Anyone can sin and everyone does sin, but the difficulty is that when someone judges falsely, he looks away. "If … the light that is in thee be darkness, how great is that darkness!"[34] "Ye cannot serve God and mammon."[35] The question of relating to others was answered by Christ long ago, and was answered not only abstractly, but in a practical sense as well. "A rich man cannot enter the kingdom of God."[36] "Woe unto you that are rich!"[37] "Give to him that asketh thee."[38] "Sell that thou hast, and give to the poor"[39] and so on. — A Christian cannot countenance private property, and therefore he should not have any surplus, and hence there can be no question about how to share it. If I have a surplus, then first of all I have a great deal of thinking to do about the worthiness of the person I am to share it with, I am obliged to judge myself, and judge myself severely for having a surplus, and admit that I am sinful and guilty. For the Christian there can be no question about how to do good with a surplus, but only the one question: how to be delivered from the sin that caused me to gather and keep that surplus.

This is my opinion, but I understand your thought completely: it pains you to see people living a heathen life — so far from good. Your feeling is most legitimate and good, but it is useless for you to confuse it with private property — the desire to share a surplus under certain conditions. Act to influence others with all the powers God has given you, chief among which is not your private property, but the degree of rejection of personal life and private property you have already reached. If you were to simply get rid of your property without giving it to anyone (i.e., not tempting others by destroying it to no purpose), and were to show that you were not only just as joyful, but even more joyful, calm, kind and happy without property than with it, you would make a much stronger impression on others and would do them a greater good than if you were to entice them with dividing up your surplus among them.

Do not think, dear friend, that I am condemning you — far from it — since I myself experienced, with a painful heart, those same thoughts and feelings which you yourself are now experiencing. I thought a lot about it, and came to the conclusions I expressed in *Chto zh nam delat'?* [*What Then Must Be Done?*]. Some of them, those that were not prohibited by the censor, were published in Volume XII of my works.[40]

34 Matth. 6:23.
35 Matth. 6:24.
36 See Mark 10:23–24.
37 Luke 6:24.
38 Matth. 5:42.
39 Matth. 19:21.
40 *Sochinenija grafa L. N. Tolstogo* [Works of Count L. N. Tolstoy], Part XII (Works of recent years [in Russian]), 1886. Excerpts from the book *Tak chto zhe nam delat'?* [*What Then Must Be Done?*], which was banned in Russia, were included in this volume under the title "*Mysli, vyzvannye perepis'ju*" [Thoughts arising from the census].

I do not say one should not influence or assist others; on the contrary, I think this is what life is all about, but one must help with something pure, and not with something impure, like private property; and to be in a position to help, the main thing is, as long as we ourselves are not yet pure, to purify ourselves.

Forgive me if I have said anything that is unclear or unfriendly. I wanted to respond to your good letter as best I could.

Lovingly,

At the end of last year we began a campaign against drunkenness. Many people of all different walks and classes of life have joined us. I am sure you, too, will join us and so am sending you our leaflet.[41] This evil is so frightful and so special and goes to such lengths that one must fight against it in a special way, and support our brethren hand in hand, so that everyone knows he is not alone.

N° 7. F. A. ZHELTOV ➧ L. N. TOLSTOY

2 May 1888. Village of Bogorodskoe.

My dearest Lev Nikolaevich!

Forgive me for keeping your manuscript longer than I should; I was so delighted with it that I am copying it out for myself; I hope you have no objection.[42] In any case I shall not keep it much longer but shall send it to you at the first opportunity. The bearer of this letter, my friend Fëdor Alekseevich Serjakov, is also a peasant; I am recommending him to you in the hope that you will be helpful to him. In a few days I shall send you a manuscript outlining some thoughts that came to me upon reading your manuscript.

I am enclosing the names of those who support the campaign against drunkenness; I have some other people in mind and am very happy to see the moral influence against this evil being exerted on others.

Your deeply loyal brother,

F. Zheltov

1888, May 2nd
Village of Bogorodskoe
Nizhegorod Gub.

41 The text of this "leaflet" was composed by Tolstoy. See *PSS* 90:132.

42 *Kratkoe izlozhenie Evangelija* [*Brief Synopsis of the Gospels*] was banned in Russia but circulated by manuscript and lithograph. It was printed in Geneva by M. Èlpidin in 1890, and in St. Petersburg in 1906. See *PSS* 24:801–938. Zheltov obtained a manuscript copy while visiting Tolstoy in Moscow in March of 1888. Tolstoy wrote of him in a letter to Vladimir Chertkov at the time: "This young man is very intelligent and religious. Their teachings are most rational and free from dogmatism and superstition" (*PSS* 86:138). The reference here is presumably to the Molokans.

P.S. Can you send me some popular books against drunkenness?
Enrol as members in the campaign against drunkenness:
Pëtr Privalov, peasant, village of Bogorodskoe, 41 years old.
Ivan Ivanov Balakin, peasant, village of Bogorodskoe, 36 years old.

Nº 8. F. A. ZHELTOV ❧ L. N. TOLSTOY
12 May 1888. Village of Bogorodskoe.

My dearest brother Lev Nikolaevich!

How grateful I am for your granting me the pleasure of reading your brief outline of the Gospels. It is very good, since it presents the most vital elements in a brief statement that is easy to comprehend and gives a more comprehensive picture of the essence of the Gospel teachings.

I can honestly say that, having read it, I have more resources to answer several questions that did not seem clear to me before. I have become aware of just how great this energy is which summons our spirit to serve the law eternal. I have become aware of how much power it has to triumph over everything false and burdensome introduced into life, but not by reason — such as illegitimate functions which destroy people's happiness and well-being. This is the law — the divine law, the law of righteousness and love, the law of the majesty of life. We cannot deny the divinity of Christ's teachings; they are divine because they speak of the eternal law of life, of the law which leads the way to the achievement of good and through which is brought about the unification of flesh and spirit in the service of life itself as life, and for the destruction of evil through good as the will of God Himself. We can reject faith in the divinity of Christ's teachings only as false indicators of why people want to consider them divine, and the task is to convey those true indicators which show them to be really divine. They themselves are evidence of their own divinity, and this testimony is true by virtue of the power which, when applied to our lives, serves as a strong support for our understanding of what we are and why we are, and wherein our well-being consists.

In respect to the filth of life, to its perversion, these teachings are a light — a light containing within itself that which can quicken life itself and give it true well-being and joy.

There is nothing worse than not being able to do what is needed to make my life a genuine life, and not being aware of the power I have to provide this life with joy and happy conditions both for myself and for others. There is nothing worse than walking down the road blind and not even knowing where it is taking you or where you will end up — we are all in this position when we are far from applying that law which tells us directly how to proceed and where we will end up and why we need this road. Ignorance of what we have been provided with to eliminate evil from our lives is itself a procreator of evil, and people suffer because they have cast aside the natural law of life and will not accept it as their own, but unconsciously wait for something to fill that void they have been left with, and which they cannot fill with anything themselves. Their life goes by in just trying to fill this bottomless barrel with water, completely unaware of the futility of their actions and their labours. Hence the struggle of evil against evil, and enmity between one another, and the craving for material security, all the while hoping to create, out of this external condition of well-being, the true well-being and joy of life.

The knowledge of how to create good for ourselves and others was given to us by Christ as the law of God's love to mankind, as the law which produced life itself, and which is, therefore, the principle of life. The personage of Christ was united with this law, so that He did not consider himself to be beyond this law, did not consider his personage as such, but as the law itself, and He was committed to this law throughout His life, throughout His service, and therefore His life was not restricted to His temporary, personal well-being but was the attainment of that life which according to the law of God is common to all mankind as the law eternal, creating a new world for life, a world full of bliss and joy, a world full of life, beyond the temporal, beyond death. This law entered into His flesh and blood, and His flesh and blood as life served to manifest this law in the world, hence people's lives have a single purpose — the manifestation of the law eternal as the manifestation of love; this manifestation gives Him true life and only therein does He find His well-being and liberation from evil.

Forgive me for such an outpouring of feelings and thoughts. There is much, perhaps, that I am judging too carelessly and without sufficient accuracy. There is a lot about which I talk a lot and excessively, but there is a lot that I cannot, that I am simply powerless to convey in words — it is in my heart, in my thoughts, in my consciousness, it is just the way I feel, and I see how joyful the path is — the joy, the calm, the happiness and the sense of strength that it pours into the soul in proportion as one gains within one's self the supremacy of the spirit, the triumph of the truth…

I am enclosing a brief manuscript[43] in the hope that you will not deny me a reply. I shall be sending your manuscript back in a day or so.

With sincere love and faithfulness with my whole soul,

Your brother, F. Zheltov

P.S. Please let me know your address where I should write to and send your book.

12 May 1888
Village of Bogorodskoe
Nizh. Gub

43 "On life as faith in Christ" — reproduced at the end of "Brief outline of the Molokans" above.

N° 9. F. A. ZHELTOV ❧ L. N. TOLSTOY
16 July 1888. Village of Bogorodskoe.

My dear brother Lev Nikolaevich!

Forgive me for only now replying to your last letter.[44] In today's post I am sending you your manuscript which I borrowed to read. I have already written to you about how delighted I was with it. The explanation of the Saviour's teachings is so brief and concise, yet at the same time complete, speaking only to the essential points, thereby conveying all the more clearly the truth itself and leading people directly into that world of righteousness that was Christ's.

We read your article as well as Bondarev's article in *Russkoe delo.*[45] These articles have given rise to many stirrings in society. Along with your manuscript I am sending you an article to look at (and I apologize in advance for bothering you with it) about the significance of labour for mankind and on the distinction between physical labour essential to life and mere physical exercise. I would like to send this article either to *Russkoe bogatstvo* or to the weeklies, but so far I have not dared to do it, as I am not sure that I have said anything new in this article, and am therefore offering it to you for your appraisal. If you approve of it, either send it to the editors of some paper or journal for publication, or return it to me with your comments. The question of labour is a most significant one for people's lives, so I thought that if such issues were raised more often, they would be more quickly developed and understood.

I await your reply and assure you of my sincere brotherly love for you.

Your loyal brother

F. Zheltov

16 June 88
Village of Bogorodskoe, Nizhegor. Gub.

P.S. Please enrol as a member of the temperance society: Vasilij Ivanovich Khokhlov, a peasant from the village of Bogorodskoe, age 20.

N° 10. F. A. ZHELTOV ❧ L. N. TOLSTOY
4 July 1888. Village of Bogorodskoe.

Dear brother Lev Nikolaevich!

My sincerest thanks for the brotherly compassion you showed me by reviewing my article.[46] I am doubly grateful for your advice. I have long wanted

44 The whereabouts of the letter are unknown.

45 T. M. Bondarev's article "Trudoljubie, ili Torzhestvo zemledel'tsa" [Industriousness, or the triumph of the land-tiller], together with a foreword by Tolstoy, was published in issues N°N° 12 and 13 of the weekly *Russkoe delo* (19 and 27 March 1888, respectively).

46 The whereabouts of Tolstoy's letter are unknown.

to clarify for myself as much as possible this question of the true significance of literature. I often ask myself the question: what good is it to describe any given facet of life in photographic detail? What kind of renewing element am I contributing simply by writing for the entertainment of idle readers?... Now I am convinced that I need to write, as you put it, not just about what people are doing or have done, but what they should be doing according to the will of God. I am now convinced that in literature, as in life, there must be life-renewing streams, and that every *pure* idea introduced into a work of literature is not just a subjective addition but an actual stream of renewal, which, when manifest in life, must act as a motive force on life itself, as a living cause, leading to the attainment of mankind's universal well-being.

Thank you for the anti-drinking leaflet you sent. I am ordering a hundred copies of it today. Mama sends her respects and thanks you for your greeting.

Your ever faithful and loving brother,

F. Zheltov

1888, July 4th
Village of Bogorodskoe.

Please enrol as a member of the temperance society:
Mikhail Ivanovich Frolov, a peasant from the village of Bogorodskoe, age 55.
And, in case I forgot to mention it in my last letter, Vasilij Ivanovich Khokhlov, a peasant from the village of Bogorodskoe, age 20.

Nº 11. F. A. ZHELTOV ❧ L. N. TOLSTOY
31 January 1889. Village of Bogorodskoe.

Dear brother Lev Nikolaevich,

I hasten to send you the article I have written on drunkenness. How I wish it could be published more quickly! I wish it could be printed right away in brochure form, which I think is more convenient for the public — booklets in people's hands last longer; indeed, it would be good to have it printed as both a booklet and a leaflet. I don't know whether or not it is suitable for printing in the form in which I am presenting it to you, though it seems to me that this makes it more convincing for the ordinary public. If you find it necessary to edit anything, I shall be most grateful [for your editing]. If you approve of it, go ahead and publish it wherever you like. I am not averse to publishing it myself, though I think it could have the imprint of a Posrednik publication. I await your decision.

I have not written to you for some time, as I did not want to disturb you. But I had to write… How is your Temperance Society doing?... I am comforted here by the fact that it has borne some fruit, even though not much. I don't have any new reports for the moment, beyond what I have already given you, but I am thinking about them and could get them even now if I wanted to — concerning people especially addicted to the vice of drunkenness, who have been influenced in any case by some of the convictions [expressed by the Society]. I know one man who was a frequent drinker of vodka, who gave it up completely, praise God, eight months ago now and does not drink. I am very happy about this — I hope he will persist in his good behaviour. There are people whose passion for wine has noticeably diminished, and that is fine — in time they can be brought to the [higher] good. I am not in a hurry to enrol them, but I allow them freedom and support their courage.

I find that Posrednik does not have very many booklets aimed at counteracting drunkenness, but they are so very much needed — they can have a tremendous influence, especially *your* words; your words carry considerable weight with the public.

Don't you feel that the resources the Temperance Society has available at the moment may not be enough for people who have joined arm in arm, as you put it, in the struggle against drunkenness, to bring all their energies together and do more than is possible at the moment? What I am saying is that the unifying idea of the Society could be made more tangible. For example, I was reading in the papers that the peasants of the Zolotnikovskaja[47] Volost of Saratov Gubernia came to a unanimous agreement to close all the pubs and taverns in their district, but for some reason the decision did not go through, even though the locality where this took place was not in contravention of any regulations of the new drinking laws; they say it failed because of the machinations and pressure by the pub owners on their [political] friends. Then the peasants drew up another agreement, setting forth terms by which strict sobriety was to be observed, and no peasant was allowed to visit pubs or taverns or drink vodka at home or anywhere else for fear of a fine. I think you will agree that this is a worthy step in the right direction. But even this agreement was judged to be illegal by the Volost Council and no support was forthcoming, at least according to the papers. And this is no isolated example — I have encountered many. The peasants' efforts to set up desirable temperance conditions for their lives always fail — they don't know where to turn for help or what they can count on to root out the temptation that afflicts them.

The temptation has been successfully spread by the pub-owners in various forms, and is so destructive to those who are weak. Could not the Temperance Society offer some help here? If only it had better resources for this, if only it had a whole [structure] in place… Granted, it is a kind of a complete [structure] even now, but it seems rather intangible, fragmented. But if people are joined in the struggle arm in arm, they should be stronger. I am sure that if

47 I try, wherever possible, to put the town for which the volost is named, rather than simply adding the Russian adjectival ending (in this case, feminine). *Zolotnikovskaja* is almost certainly a misprint, assuming that Zheltov really meant Saratov Gubernia. The volost town may be Zolotoe — see Minkh 1990 2:323–32.

peasants knew that there was such a Society that could support them in their efforts to reach their temperance goal and offer them help and advice on how to escape from the pubs, they would ask for help directly from the Society.

Don't you feel it would be a good idea to work out a constitution for the Society and officially incorporate it, mainly to give the Society the fullest possible opportunity to co-ordinate its actions and unite its fragmented forces by reporting on the results, by offering help to peasant societies desiring to free themselves from the pub-owners, by holding public lectures on the dangers of drunkenness, by publishing books, pictures and brochures on this subject, by working out all sorts of measures to combat drunkenness, by setting up reasonable forms of entertainment in various villages, settlements and other locations to attract people away from spending wasteful hours in taverns, and by petitioning local authorities to take steps to further the goals of this society? I think it wouldn't hurt the cause to create more opportunities than now exist. I eagerly look forward to your reply.

Please send me your articles published in *Nedelja.*[48]

Your article *Day of Enlightenment* made a big impression on me.[49]

I sent my best regards to your whole family and embrace you in brotherhood. Your loyal and loving

F. Zheltov

1889, January 31st
Village of Bogorodskoe
Nizhegor. Gub.

Nº 12. F. A. ZHELTOV ❧ L. N. TOLSTOY

7 February 1889. Village of Bogorodskoe.

My most kind and dear brother Lev Nikolaevich!

I hasten to reply to your letter[50] and give you my full permission to edit the article I sent you — I have absolutely no objection and can only count myself grateful and much indebted to you. Please, if it is not too much trouble, could you send me a copy after editing for me to look at, but don't bother doing this if it is only going to be a waste of time in view of getting it published more quickly. I shall wait to hear from you.[51]

48 Chap. 22–25 and the Conclusion of the book *O zhizni* [*On Life*] were published in the St. Petersburg paper *Nedelja*, NºNº 1–3, 4 and 6, 1 January–11 February 1889.

49 Tolstoy's article *Prazdnik prosveshchenija* [*Day of Enlightenment*] appeared 12 January 1889 (St. Tat'jana's Day) in the paper *Russkie vedomosti.*

50 The whereabouts of this letter are unknown. It is mentioned by Tolstoy in his diary entry of 5 February 1889 (*PSS* 50:33).

51 The reference is to Zheltov's leaflet *Perestanem pit' vino i ugoshchat' im* [Let us stop drinking wine and entertaining with it]. In a letter to Pavel Birjukov of 5 February 1889, Tolstoy called it "very good." It was published by Posrednik in 1890.

I am thinking of going to Moscow in early March, and I would like very, very much to see you.[52]

I thank you with my heart for your brotherly love and kind support. Your ardently loyal and loving brother,

F. Zheltov
1889, Febr. 7th

Nº 13. F. A. ZHELTOV ❧ L. N. TOLSTOY
12 June 1889. Village of Bogorodskoe.

Address:
Fëdor Alekseevich Zheltov
Village of Bogorodskoe
Nizhegorod Gubernia

My kindest brother Lev Nikolaevich!

Having returned from my trip,[53] I set about finishing the manuscript on drunkenness I promised you. I hasten to send you by today's post not only the promised manuscript but also two others like it. The latter I would like to publish as well, with your approval: one of them in an abbreviated form as a leaflet, and the other in a booklet. I cannot expect that I have revised the manuscript to the extent that you would wish — I would be most obliged if you would take upon yourself the task of reviewing it and the final polishing of the manuscript, which would strengthen the article even further and make it more useful; or at least to jot down a number of notes and instructions and return it to me so that I can work on it again. I hope you will not decline to participate in this common cause. We must work as much as we can to publish anti-drinking booklets with a particularly moral and religious basis for their arguments against the sin which drives people into the custom of drinking or entertaining at every occasion in life with all kinds of intoxicating drugs.

Such principles may be more convincing for ordinary people, which is easily noticeable when one is obliged to refer to religious and moral grounds in discussing drunkenness.

I should very much like to know your opinion on the manuscripts I am sending you and whether I might count on their publication. You may do

52 According to Tolstoy's diary, Zheltov came with his mother, Marija Ivanovna, on 3 March 1889. But even earlier, on 22 February, a diary entry reads: "Zheltov arrived, and we went through the bookshelves.... What a pure man Zheltov is!" And later, on 11 March: "After dinner Zheltov arrived. We talked about their [the Molokans'] rituals. I spoke of the danger in this, [and] about the meaning of the Lord's Prayer" (*PSS* 50:40, 49).

53 Tolstoy noted in his diary for 26 April 1889: "Had a good conversation here with Zheltov. A very serious fellow. He is on his way to Tambov, Saratov and Samara Provinces for meetings with the Molokans" (*PSS* 50:74).

with them as you see fit. I shall await your reply and count on your help and support for my weak work, which I want with all my heart to prove useful.[54]

I shall write you again upon receipt of your reply, as I do not fully know your present correct address, and I should like to share with you some thoughts that have come to me, partly as a result of my trip. Please let me know where to write you.

My respects to your whole family and to all the people I know. I wish you every success in your good work. Yours lovingly and faithfully with brotherly sincerity,

Fëdor Zheltov

P.S. Please tell me whether the journal *Sotrudnik* you were talking about is for sale.[55]

1889, July 12th
Village of Bogorodskoe
Nizh. Gub.

N° 14. F. A. ZHELTOV ✉ L. N. TOLSTOY

Beginning of October 1889. Village of Bogorodskoe.

My most kind and dear brother Lev Nikolaevich!

My sincere thanks for your two messages,[56] which I received, and my apologies for not sending you the promised reports about my trip with this letter. I can only say I am very happy to have met with my distant brethren, who are so close to me in spirit, and with whom I may now even correspond.

I have hitherto been prevented by certain circumstances from writing you in more detail about this, but I shall avail myself of the first opportunity to share with you everything I consider worthwhile reporting. Forgive me for writing so briefly now.

Sincerely loyal to you in brotherhood, lovingly,

F. Zheltov

54 On 19 June 1889 Tolstoy edited the anti-drinking manuscripts he received from Zheltov, noting in his diary: "One of them is fine. I have edited the second, and the third is no good." And on 23 June: "I did more editing on Zheltov's papers" (*PSS* 50:97–98). A copy of the manuscript (On the sin of drunkenness [in Russian]), with Tolstoy's corrections, is housed in the collection of the L. N. Tolstoy State Museum, in Moscow.

55 In December 1888, I. D. Sytin decided to publish a journal called *Sotrudnik* for popular consumption. Tolstoy prepared a plan and gathered materials for the first issues. The publication never materialized.

56 Zheltov's letters of 18 and 23 June 1889 have not been preserved.

Nº 15. F. A. ZHELTOV ❧ L. N. TOLSTOY
15 October 1889. Village of Bogorodskoe.

Dear brother Lev Nikolaevich!

I apologize for not being able to keep my promises up to now to share my recollections of my trip. This past spring I became closely acquainted for the first time with several Molokan communities, and this has given me a new perspective on the level of spiritual growth where the greater part of the Molokans find themselves today. Up until now I knew only my own community, and since I have belonged to it from birth, I have assimilated as much as possible the spirit of the teachings it has expressed. I cannot say that I am entirely satisfied — there is much that is still not clear to me, much that has seemed to be deficient, much that still needs to be thought about — such is the lot of anyone who attempts to summon within himself the full consciousness of the truth that alone can constitute the sum total of his life.

You are already well acquainted with the Molokan teachings, but its basic tenets and views cannot escape being subjected to those living currents which act as a refiner's fire on the underlying spirit of all things — the truth that must become a living, integral part of a person's life. In observing my community, I have been noticing certain stumbling-blocks which are capable of hindering the flow of the fount of living water into eternity, but these stumbling-blocks, thank God, have not yet reached the point where they can be considered man's flesh and blood, or where they have become fully-fledged starting-points for a false faith, giving the illusion of slaking man's spiritual thirst.

The point at which a person passes from one stage of his outlook on the world to the next cannot yet be regarded as the completion of his spiritual growth, but it is difficult when his spiritual progress is beset with all sorts of obstacles, which may either ruin the natural course of events, or ultimately kill the living force which is to promote this course in a particular case. This latter has been of some concern to me. Are not the communities experiencing similar delays, which can be a serious hindrance to the introduction of the living stream which refreshes one's conscious relationship to truth? Are not mankind's religious strivings being poured out into a deadened soulless form whose cold attitude is only lulling man's spiritual energies and easing his conscience? Do not such attitudes lead to a darkening of man's intelligent relationship to God, thereby preventing people from facing the truth and turning them back to the confusion of false doctrine? All this and much more has given me cause to probe deeper into the lives of those who have expressed a certain degree of understanding of truth. How do such people express their faith?... To find true faith is not as easy as it seems. Its elusive signs are not so easily perceptible to the eyes. It is a different story with the false teachings — despite their considerable numbers, they are dead, there is no life in them, they offer nothing that the soul can absorb.

One cannot consider a faith complete which has decided to reject anything that does not measure up to the mark of a healthy mind and of the true law of God. Such a faith cannot be completed, since its substance is reflected in actions which bring mankind closer to God and is thereby endowed with new foundations of life which constitute the true kingdom of peace on earth. The completeness of religion is always poured out into a dead form, which may be properly called the death of religion, but true religion must live, since faith is life and its living current constitutes the true happiness which all mankind is seeking. People may indeed experience imperfections and deficiencies along the way, all the more so with people who express themselves with varying degrees of understanding. Let there be insufficient understanding of eternal truth, but no stumbling-blocks where people stand with chained hands and foaming at the mouth at the prospect of the [next] individual steps in their spiritual growth.

It is not these individual steps that matter so much as the overall progress which is taking place. Phases of regeneration are only signs of that remarkable process underway both in individual lives and in the community as a whole as a result of certain irrepressible mental convictions. Only that which fits tightly together, forming an integral whole — like different components of a mechanism manufactured piece by piece in different places — can survive as truth. Just as a single error cannot be tolerated lest it ruin the whole, so all lies and falsehoods must crumble by their own weight and fall away from the action of the intelligence which is guiding one's life to the truth. True faith, if you like, is brought to completion, but it is completed *in God,* and is completed so that it can *go forth,* and thus it is living and eternal.

It was from this point of view that I watched and observed those communities with which I had the opportunity to establish a close association. In the majority of them I did not perceive among the Molokans ardent defenders of any arbitrary outpourings of formal, soulless relationships to God, but chiefly the substitution of something 'thought up' for that living faith which ought to flow from man into life eternal. I am not saying that the latter does not exist at all among Molokans, I am simply talking about that freedom under which access to nourishment by truths is still a comforting sign of that good soil for the growth of the seed of true life.

Can faith be described dogmatically? I doubt it. In true faith the indisputable starting-point is God alone. The true understanding of life is that reflection of the eternal God as expressed in man's soul, hence there can be no question here of *conditional indisputability*, there can only be that truth which has passed through understanding. This closed, eternal circle, where nothing false or harmful can enter in, constitutes the true kingdom of God, and this is the only thing we can understand by the word *truth.* Once we step outside this circle, each one of us is already setting up our own thing, and on such a basis we can never come together and reconcile ourselves to each other, since each one's lie, inasmuch as it is something not born of God, cannot bear any of the hallmarks of our unity with God, and hence the spirit of truth does not recognize these children as its own, and each one denies his own child by denying the legitimacy of another's.

Man's strivings should be focused on the circle where God's kingdom is to be found. There is no dispute there. By entering that circle and not venturing beyond its boundaries, all may join together in faith. But once someone descends from that milieu, he has already entered upon that false and fatal path which leads to the eternal kingdom of darkness and unrighteousness. The latter path is always dangerous. The true believer has no need to step outside this circle, but must strive to enter the circle of salvation, and lead others there as well.

When I had the opportunity to chat with people who had a high regard for their shaky underpinnings of false faith, I always noticed how these people initially took offence at the frank manner in which I, as an unskilled operator, touched upon their most painful nerve, and with which I hoped to undertake the desired operation at once; but this did not bring anything to the person except needless pain and only complicated even further the task I hoped to accomplish. It was a different matter when I drew someone's attention directly to what was on a level higher than the one on which he was seeking truth; the level of his understanding increased imperceptibly, and he was able to cut off without pain the decaying incrustation which he had so cherished — somehow it retreated and fell away all by itself, and the spirit was thus uplifted by a natural process which transcends the vain struggle with the incrustations of false faith, and immediately unmasks this faith. The unmasking of false faith frees man, and true faith must be sought only through man's free and rational approach to everything. When I had the opportunity to speak of faith in Christ as the son of God, I would ask:

"What true signs should we look for in those who would show us Christ's sonship with God?"

The question was evidently new, at least in the form in which I stated it. People believed in Christ without sorting out the fine points of their faith. The divinity of Christ was accepted, but accepted as the authority for the teachings He brought to mankind. What was I to do? Disabuse these people of their crude outward signs of Christ's elevation, which the majority of people are content to accept as the main tenet of their belief? But after all, the people I am talking with are in the process of broadening their horizons, and even though outward things remain within the scope of their understanding, they cannot be completely considered the starting-point for a chain of dogmatic formulas which are fruitless in terms of life. They have already left such things behind as of no value. Their attention is absorbed by the moral aspect and by the high level of that spiritual unity with God which was expressed so forcefully in Christ as the true son of God.

We must dwell on these signs. We must dwell on them in order to strengthen our faith in the one and only will of the eternal Father of life, and we must express this faith in ourselves, in our life, in the same sense in which it was poured forth in full force in Christ. The purely rational question will always be the same: "Where does my salvation lie?" — hence only that which constitutes my salvation is the vessel into which my faith ought to be poured. This question implies only one corollary — the application of my energies to the means of my salvation… *"Every single effort leads to the kingdom of heaven."* This effort does not mean deciding in advance what the door through which I must pass will look like — is it made of pine or linden? That doesn't make any difference to me, as long as I know that this door will lead me to salvation. I picture it as follows:

You and I are in a room. The room is suddenly in flames and is burning. We dash to the windows and doors to get out, but both the windows and doors have been so engulfed by flames that there is no escape. I notice one door through which we can go and save ourselves, and point to it. And suddenly you imagine that this door is a miraculous image, that is sent from heaven. Instead of moving quickly to save ourselves, I stop you and try to persuade you that your supposition is groundless, and we begin arguing. I say the door is just an ordinary door, like any other…. Why do I need to bother about that?... Just so long as that is indeed the door of our salvation!... So too in life such needless questions crop up all too often, questions that can never be the true means by which people can be led to the light of pure reason. It is best to avoid these needless questions, otherwise they will interfere with the current which is doing its work in mysterious ways through the spiritual regeneration of man.

I know that whatever there is of incontrovertible truth in man, it will always respond exclusively to that eternal truth which is at one with the intelligence of life; it is drawn in and merges with that immaculate quality of soul known only to God and with man's spiritual enlightenment, which is the reflection of eternal light and life.

People's regeneration, just as their entire lives, can be compared with a pure grain of wheat which is sifted through the sieve together with the weeds. The sifting action purifies only the grain, and it remains to be held on to, while the weeds and the rubbish fall away. Now we need simply to shake the weeds and rubbish out of human consciousness, and I know that the same sieve that lets the weeds fall to the ground will hold back the wheat, which is the real valuable.

I very much liked the answer given by an elderly Molokan (V. N. Sopin of Rasskazovo), who said during our discussion of Christ:

How did the son of God come into the world? I might ask, whether the son of God was in Abel?... in Enoch?... in Noah?... and other people who led righteous lives?... Well, was he?... So, the son of God who came down from heaven into people, He is the one who has risen into eternity; therefore, it is said: He led captivity captive, and gave gifts unto men (Ephesians 4:8). The coming of Christ into the world of old, He is the same from the beginning to the end. And what is said about the second coming, that it will come to pass, that we must wait for it, here is how I understand it: the coming of the second Christ is not to be recognized physically, literally, at some other time, as some people believe, but as spiritually already happening, not something to be waited for, but to be always ready for, each moment, each hour. Christ Himself said that His Kingdom would come not with observation, not in any specific time and place — if they say so, don't follow them or chase after them. Where is His Kingdom?... His Kingdom is within you — it has been said.

I asked him how they understand the 24th chapter of Matthew.

What is said in this chapter very simply relates to the fall of Jerusalem and its kingdom, and all that happened, and all that is happening still today — Christ saw people's destinies and saw that his followers would withstand the snares of the enemy. Christ is not to be found where there is unrighteousness, He must be sought within, life is full of deceptions and these deceptions seduce people away from the truth, and these deceptions at some point in life will become visible, so always watch lest such a moment come upon you, and that is your judgement, there will be no other judgement for man, it is carried out, there is nothing to wait for beyond the grave, you will receive according to your deeds. Once someone has died, he has already received judgement and goes on either to life or to death. (V. N. Sopin)

Like two grains between millstones, one of which is taken and the other left, and like two in the field, one of which is taken and the other left, so it is with man's life: one is swept away, while the other enters in and preserves life. Or one could liken it to this: the two millstones in man are the spirit and the flesh, their task is life itself, and just as a millstone causes wheat to bring forth flour, so man brings forth light from his intellect. At last only one millstone remains — that is the spirit; it is eternal, while flesh receives its lot as flesh, and is left behind. Thus in life, make the transformation within yourself with the two millstones which have been given to you, and watch and know what you do — for this task God has given you understanding. He that soweth to his flesh shall of the flesh reap corruption, but he that soweth to the spirit shall of the spirit reap life everlasting.[57] How are we to live our lives according to God?... Neither a drunkard, nor a slanderer, nor a murderer, nor a usurer, nor an adulterer, no one with his sins can partake of God's reward. All of this is to be feared. One must have light, so that your life is not like that of the heathen — this is what must be worked out. (See Ephesians, Ch. 4.) (M. M. Zheltov, *Rasskazy*)

57 Gal. 6:8.

Re: faith. By faith Enoch obtained righteousness, by faith Abraham received the promise. Faith without works is dead; works which do not proceed from faith are not works of God's will, and in the world there is only one will in which people find salvation — that is the will of our Father of life, the Lord God; if we live in His will, we are fulfilling the law which is appointed to us. What that law consists of is something we must understand, and not only understand but carry out, and herein lies my whole faith, because I believe in this according to my understanding, I cannot help but believe, if I have understood my salvation. Living faith must be in our works…

For one who believes in Christ's teachings, life must be in the renewing of the spirit (Eph. 4:21–25), and for this person there is no disease, nor death, nor poverty, nor nakedness — nothing shall separate us from the love of God….[58] There is no need to fear death, since in Christ there is no death, in Him there is only life…. When you turn to God in prayer, at that same moment you enter into yourself, the same as examining yourself before God, but you should *always* examine yourself this way, if you want your spiritual worship of God to be genuine. (V. N. Sopin)

Why do we gather to talk? (Molokans gather together every Sunday — in some places just for a morning meeting, in others for both morning and evening meetings — where they read the Old and New Testaments, sing psalms and talk — this is called either a "meeting" or a "talk" — such meetings are sometimes held on other days of the week as well.) To confirm ourselves in the faith, to strengthen the spirit of truth. Such communion is pleasing unto God, and we don't talk about anything else, we talk with God; if I read the Scriptures, I do so for the enlightenment both of myself and of those that hear me, and I must read with understanding — explain rationally, discuss so that it will be comprehensible to anyone what the reading is about, and what the whole matter is about, without interpreting, that is, without commentary, not everyone can grasp right away how God assigns His tasks and to whom. We should read not only the letter, but also understand and retain the spirit.

Our singing?... Well, singing is not a ritual, everything is for enlightenment, for comfort, and sometimes just for relaxation… we understand that.

What is the essential element of our salvation?... Nobody will say it is simply going to meetings; everyone knows that we go there only for sharing with others; that is not bad; there is nothing bad here. When we come to talk, we strengthen ourselves with the words of the Scriptures, and if we come out after talking and do not hold on to the good in our soul, that is not a service [to others]. (M. M. Zheltov)

I was twice present at the Rasskazovo Molokans' general "talks." I liked these talks very much; they were characterized by a complete freedom of thought

58 See Romans 8:35–39.

and that simplicity in which clarity of understanding is obtained more quickly than in all the subtleties of 'thought out' interpretations and sharpening one's wits on seeking out hidden meanings where they don't exist. The direct approach in such talks is felt more keenly by one's soul and one can grasp the degree of consciousness people express. A free and critical discussion of subjects, which we would not consciously express to such an extent in other faith situations, is the mark of the liberation of thought from the chains that fetter any natural forward movement toward the understanding of power and law, eternity and God.

I think it is worth mentioning that in Rasskazovo, as well as several other communities, I came across the same critical approach to the translation of the Scriptures — naturally, at a level within their grasp — specifically, on the comparison of the Slavonic and Russian texts. But this only confirms the absence of the pedantry which has been so crudely expressed in certain false doctrines to the utter detriment of any common sense and understanding.

I shall not go into all the details regarding the talks we had, I shall not speak about other communities with which I am acquainted. I shall say only this, that the communities more or less resemble each other in their following of a single path, and if there are imperfections or deviations, they, as private interpretations, cannot form part of that unity of the true church, which alone can express the spirit of Christ's teachings. Certain differences (minor ones at that) that I noticed in the Rasskazovo, Saratov and Samara communities, are no more and no less than the result of human thinking. Where are those external forces that could repel such a movement?... It is like self-fermenting dough. I now have a better understanding of these words of Christ: "But be not ye called teachers, for one is your teacher, even Christ; and all ye are brethren."[59]

I must mention another good talk I had with the brethren of the Samara community, especially the words of the elder Fedosej Ivanovich Chernyshëv, which I recollected from memories of my conversation with the brethren as well as from a letter I subsequently received as a continuation and repetition of that same exchange of ideas:

> It is good, brethren, that we find ourselves in such a strong sense of unity that we can say that our views and our visible rituals form a single whole from among our geographically divided communities, but that is not [saying] very much — it can be found in many places. But God looks within us, nothing can be hidden from His all-encompassing eye, the Lord knows our secret sins and secret thoughts. He gave us the moral law, by which the righteous govern themselves as by the law of truth — this is the spiritual fruit on which our spiritual Temple is built, an holy priesthood, attached to the body of Christ.

59 Matth. 23:8 (according to the Russian Synodal Bible).

Let us look thoroughly at our earthly life, and the teachings and sufferings of Christ and his true followers — the chosen servants or workers of the invisible kingdom of God. The Cross is the token of God's love, it is our heavenly Father's rod of love, the conqueror of passions, which awakens us to love and regenerates true meekness and humility.

Look and see where those great men, the heralds and keepers of Christ's church — Joseph, Moses, Daniel, Paul, Peter, John and the others received their education. In the school of the Cross. When did the church grow more complete and flourish and bring forth the fruits of holiness? Only when the whole field of the Lord was constantly being torn apart by the Cross and watered by the blood of martyrs for truth. These continue to serve day and night in the true temple of God.

What shall we say then to these things?... Let us hear what the supreme, heavenly lawgiver says: "The pupil is not greater than his teacher and the servant than his lord."[60] In our faintheartedness we often complain; nevertheless: our enemies offend us, but have not yet taken our life; they heap ridicule upon us, but have not smitten us on the cheek; they wish us to perish, but have not yet nailed us to the cross — this is an unending source of comfort in all our tribulations. I look at myself: my face has not been spat upon for the sake of Christ's name and teachings, my body has not a single wound, my head is unharmed, my arms and legs have not been broken, I am not yet all covered in blood — I have not yet been bloodied in the battle against sin.[61] We deserve to be beaten and tortured as sinners, while He had not a single fault or evil and He commanded us to forgive those who offended and smote us. But we despise such an action. He himself did as He commanded us, and we refuse to look to His example. The Saviour's love rises to the heavenly Father and comes down to the world. Love for God is filled with the passion of God; love for man is compassionate toward man; love for God requires that God's law of righteousness be fulfilled; love for man does not let the violator of the law perish in his unrighteousness; love for God strives to vanquish God's enemy. This is the Christian duty of Christ's followers. Do we have within ourselves this strength of will shown by the Saviour?... Are we following him?... Are we submitting to His direction?... But we by our works are not yet worthy of such a high appellation as we attribute to ourselves. We call ourselves Spiritual Christians, hence we should also have spiritual fruits within us. The fruit of the Spirit is love for God, and love for our neighbour. He who loses love loses all; he who is angry with his neighbour cannot at the same time be a friend of Christ.

The Spirit of God teaches us through the Apostle, saying: "He that hateth his brother is in darkness, and walketh in darkness, and knoweth not whither

60 John 13:15.
61 See 2 Cor. 4:8–9.

he goeth, because that darkness hath blinded his eyes,"[62] but darkness has blinded the eyes of the hating brother's heart, darkness has completely engulfed him, and he that hateth his brother is in a state of spiritual death.

Such stumblings happen in our life and in our views on the Scriptures and in our hypocrisy, and in the words of our Saviour, hypocrites will know only sorrow, so let us be careful and not flatter our hearts nor lie to our conscience; in any case, we shall never deceive God. Whatsoever a man soweth, that shall he also reap.[63] When the Lord comes, He will illumine all that is hidden in the gloom, the intents of the heart will be revealed; eternity is inescapable.

We are pilgrims and wanderers upon the earth; has not every one of us neglected his own soul? Has he not left it unattended? Does not our inner self sit like a blind man at the crossroads, does it not sit in darkness and in the shadow of death where it cannot see or feel God's light on the path of truth? But God in His omniscient wisdom and infinite mercy does not fail to come to each one of us, He stands over us, knocks at the door of our hearts and appears to those who do not seek Him or ask about Him. He always stands before each one of us with saving help at hand, but we in our thoughtlessness do not recognize His goodness and His closeness to us, or we neglect Him, or we do not accept His help, or we do not hold on to the help we have accepted. How we neglect the life example of the Saviour and His saints!... As though it were possible for us to find another way of salvation than the one laid down by Christ?!...

The voice of God is always crying out and saying: do not forsake each other day by day, while you can speak, because now is the accepted time, only now is the day of salvation and you will not bring back lost time later by any amount of tears.[64] God, who teaches us what is useful by various means, leads us along the path in which we must walk and meticulously follow His commandments of love. These commandments are a mirror for our soul, in which we can always see our own faults, as well as the fulness of others; this is our true humility, and may it be our cornerstone in everything, since the founder of our faith is Christ, who is all meekness and humility, and we must be His followers, that is, in His likeness. We must willingly, even joyfully, bear the cross of suffering, and pray for our enemies — this is the new life of regeneration, which will make us joyous and good in the Lord's cause. Our life must serve as a preparation from the action of the spirit for eternity in the power of grace. We should taste the heavenly gift even in this present world, and accept in this world the spirit which is from God. We must ask God to give us the strength to walk this path according to His will and to be the sons of light.

I am a fleshly, mortal man; my understanding and insight are very small and insignificant — all this is in God, and I am hardly in a position to examine

62 1 John 2:11.

63 Gal. 6:7.

64 2 Cor. 6:2.

myself. Our lives do not correspond to that knowledge which we have accepted, and if we hide our faults and increase our insignificance, can a person correct himself? If God's image is lost in us, then our life is the only period in which we must seek and restore Him, for if we do not do this, the Lord will not recognize us as his servants, and does not this compel us to enter into ourselves and see whether we have been regenerated by the Holy Spirit, whether we are close to the kingdom of God which must be within us, in our souls, to see what kind of works we are doing, what are our thoughts and desires? Have our hearts been the Temple of God or the den of sin? This is all that each of us must do for ourselves, and he who has been called and adopted must be an eye for the blind, a leg for the lame, a physician for the sick, a father for the orphaned…

(from remarks and a letter by F. I. Chernyshëv)

I can only rejoice in that light that is burning brighter and brighter in human consciousness; he is not far from the kingdom of God who embodies his faith directly in the practical aspects of his life — herein is his well-being and the well-being of others. There are deficiencies in the lives of believers, but this lack of complete faith is not yet "blasphemy against the Holy Ghost"[65] and has not yet become a principle of life fixed in the mind; it is a temporary condition which does not rule out the possibility of moving forward; once people have given themselves over to the free relationship of intelligence to life, their intelligence will lead them to the kingdom of heaven.

Truth will prevail. Intelligence is eternal. The light of the sun will gradually extinguish the light of the stars and the eternal light will triumphantly light up the world with the day of joy, full of life and liberty!

I embrace you as a brother and am spiritually with you, sincerely, lovingly,

yours, Fëdor Zheltov

1889, October 15.

Nº 16. F. A. ZHELTOV • L. N. TOLSTOY

16 October 1889. Village of Bogorodskoe.

Address:
Fëdor Alekseev[ich] Zheltov
Village of Bogorodskoe
Nizhegorod Gubernia

Dear Lev Nikolaevich!

Forgive me for not having fulfilled until now my promise to share with you some of my recollections of my trip. Today I sent you a detailed letter on this

65 Matth. 12:31.

through Aleksandr Nikifor[ovich] Dunaev,[66] as I do not know your current correct address, nor whether you are in the country or in Moscow. Aleksandr Nikiforovich will probably deliver this letter to you before long, and I should like to know, once you have read it, what you think about everything I stated there. I trust that you will not deny me a brotherly response, which imparts even greater strength and courage to my soul, especially when I am feeling in poor spirits, as sometimes happens.

How happy I am to have made the acquaintance of Aleksandr Nikiforovich. And how happy I am to have spent the duration of the Nizhegorod Fair in good conversations with him; we saw each other there almost every day. These conversations have clarified a great deal for me.

The other day I received a message from V[ladimir] G. Chertkov to the effect that of my two manuscripts which you sent to him, he will publish the one which he likes. I remember that you did not approve the third manuscript — a rather large one; if you still have it intact, could you possibly send it back to me so I can rework it? If possible and not too much trouble, please send it.

I await your reply after you have received my detailed letter from Aleksandr Nikiforovich.

My regards to your whole family.

Sincerely and lovingly,
F. Zheltov

1889, 16 October
Village of Bogorodskoe.

N° 17. F. A. ZHELTOV ❧ L. N. TOLSTOY
23 November 1889. Bogorodskoe.

Dear, kind brother Lev Nikolaevich!

In my letter to you of 15 October, which I sent to you through A. N. Dunaev, I described to you some of the spiritual aspects of the Molokans' way of life, along with my own views on the religious convictions which are supposed to make up the substance of our faith. As I am interested in anything you might have to say in this regard, I would ask for your brotherly response — ask you to share the light of life which burns within you, and thereby give me that firm support which is vital to the weak in spirit, who are constantly wearied under their weight of doubts, their searchings for truth and the insufficiency of their faith. There is nothing more tormenting than the state of mind of a person who expends all his energies in striving to break through the gloom around

66 *Aleksandr N. Dunaev* (1850–1920) — a close acquaintance of the Tolstoy family's, director of the Moscow Commercial Bank.

him, which surrounds all people like the Egyptian darkness, and when he is seeking the light which would show him the way leading to salvation.

Fulness of faith constitutes mankind's entire happiness, but this fulness will only appear when the light of true understanding shows me the whole length of the path I must take to the kingdom of life, and the pathway is so narrow, so strictly defined, that we are compelled to stop at every step, lest by some thoughtless step we find ourselves straying off onto the path of doom and temptation, which leads people to death. And our life is so tangled up that the whole length of the path is beset with snares, representing the temptations of the world, and we often find ourselves falling into those snares and struggling with those obstacles which distract people from the true path of life. We often find ourselves falling and sinning, and our weakness of spirit involuntarily causes us to doubt ourselves and our efforts. What is that?... Where, indeed, is perfection?... Might not my struggling efforts be in vain if I am incapable of reaching those heights of understanding which would lead me steadfastly along the path of life? If I walk along this pathway of life with the conviction that it is leading me to eternity, then where do I find the faith that it is in fact salvation and eternal life that await me at the end of the path? Is it really at the end of the path, this eternal life, rather than right within myself? Might not the struggle to overcome obstacles be a struggle simply to preserve this life and is not my complete perfection, too, to be found through the struggle?...

If the fulness of faith were to implant itself in my heart, I would then feel my life to be inseparable from that eternal truth toward which I am headed, I should feel that the goal set before people's minds was close to me and, my failings notwithstanding, I would see it as a brightly shining beacon amid the waves and hidden rocks of life's sea, I would have a foretaste of the blissful spiritual state which serves as immortality's crown. Life!... How complex it is, how much unrighteousness lies therein, how many trodden paths it has — but which is the path that leads people to life and not to doom? The true definition of this path both confuses my spirit sometimes and depletes my strength. I struggle and I become weary, I go forward and I doubt. The sin I have done in conscious violation of the law lies in wait for my soul and makes me doubt my ability; the thought that I can sin knowingly makes me close my eyes to others' sins and prevents me from rebuking their sins, their evident and sometimes deliberate deception and not only their blasphemy against the son of man, but, I'm afraid to say, their blasphemy against the Holy Spirit…

What about myself?... What am I proud of?... What makes me any better than those people?... Am I not being a hypocrite when, thinking that I'm standing on the true path, and still I fall and sin, just like them, and consider myself superior to others, what makes me any different from that band of hypocrites who stole the keys to the kingdom of God?... Is it perhaps the fact that I have rejected only those external forms which have been put into circulation as a sedative by the enemy of the world — the Devil — to fetter man's free understanding and spiritual life?... And my own personal weaknesses?... And my misdeeds, my sins?... They say something about me — do not they identify me with those very same hypocrites and put me on the same path as them, only from the other end?..

These are the thoughts and doubts which sometimes arise in my soul and trouble my spirit. What about the difference between sin leading to death and sin not leading to death — do not both have the same root, and is not the struggle with evil all that constitutes life? Where then is the complete rejection of evil, where is complete perfection? Is man never to come once and for all out of that circle, that hell of torment for his soul, and enter into the full bliss of eternal joy and triumph over death, ascend into the life of paradise of Christ's kingdom of intelligence?...

I await your healing word for my sick soul, I await the strengthening of my energies for the fight, I await the light — so that I can understand the light!...

In loyal brotherhood, and lovingly,

F. Zheltov

1889, November 23
Village of Bogorodskoe

Address:
Fëdor Alekseevich Zheltov
Village of Bogorodskoe
Nizhegorod Gubernia

Nº 18. F. A. ZHELTOV ❧ L. N. TOLSTOY
11 February 1890. Rasskazovo.

Dear brother, Lev Nikolaevich!

I am writing you this letter as I wish you to become acquainted with one of the Spiritual Christian brethren — Pëtr Vasil'evich Popov.

Please show him your brotherly attention and treat him as a brother who is thirsting to know the truth and to strengthen the understanding of life in his consciousness.

I am saying this to you, not because you might deny him a brotherly response, but only out of my desire to acquaint you with Pëtr Vasil'evich, as this acquaintance will be extremely beneficial for his spiritual growth. Forgive me and accept my brotherly love.

Lovingly,
F. Zheltov

Rasskazovo,
11 February 1890

On the reverse:
To Lev Nikolaevich Tolstoy
Yasenki Postal Station
Tula Gubernia

N° 19. F. A. ZHELTOV ❧ L. N. TOLSTOY
16 March 1890. Village of Bogorodskoe.

Dear brother, Lev Nikolaevich!

I have just returned from my trip and find myself still under the influence of the lively impression of brotherly hospitality which you and your whole family showed us during our visit to you at Yasnaya Polyana.[67] I cannot refrain from writing you this letter to express my gratitude for your love, whose light all by itself inspired us to come and see you, and to say thank you for those radiant works through which you have not only poured into people's lives the pure stream of living Christian teachings but also shed light on the dark aspects of that unrighteousness which under the guise of Christ's truth, would, as the son of perdition, take Christ's place (see 2 Thess. 2:3–4; John 17:12). Your works have given many a true understanding of life according to Christ's teachings, and have broken down the age-old barriers by which the spirit of falsehood has hidden the true light of understanding which shone so brightly in the great Teacher of life. We see how the great work you have done is already bearing fruit, and we believe that it will continue to grow and give strength and multiply, establishing in people's lives an intelligent basis for their relationships. — I can't help thinking of the words: "Whosoever shall do one of these least commandments, and shall teach men so, he shall be called great in the kingdom of heaven..."[68] Forgive me, Lev Nikolaevich, for beginning my letter this way; I cannot at this moment do any differently after what I experienced during my trip and my contacts with the many people I had the opportunity to see — with the many close to me in the spirit of understanding.

Your words along with those of others which burned with the same light were most beneficial to me in terms of strengthening my weakened energies and giving me a renewed understanding of what was hidden from me.

67 On 14 February 1890, Tolstoy wrote in his diary: "Zheltov and his wife, sister and brother-in-law were here today. Most original people. He is very bright and free-spirited. He will have a great influence" (*PSS* 51:18). And a week later he wrote to Dmitrij Aleksandrovich Khilkov: "Among the many people I have come across, I am especially delighted by the Molokans of the Nizhegorod village of Bogorodskoe. They have a thirty-year-old leader named Zheltov. He visited us the other day (though I have known him for some time). He is one of the Molokans who is completely free from dogmatism and superficiality; he is most sincere and genuine, bright and talented" (*PSS* 65:29).

68 Cf. Matth. 5:19: "Whosoever therefore shall break one of these least commandments, and shall teach men so, he shall be called the least in the Kingdom of Heaven: but whosoever shall do and teach them, the same shall be called great in the Kingdom of Heaven."

Already quite a bit of time has passed since I wrote you my letters of 15 October and 23 November [1889],[69] and this has given me considerable time to rethink those concepts I wrote you about. I shall not go into all the details now about the whole range of my thought processes, as I feel that my consciousness is moving, fluctuating, growing. I only know that it is becoming more demanding upon my personal relationship to life, to the clarification of the correlation with life that I must maintain according to the law of Christ. The discrepancy between the life I live and the demand of the law which has permeated the human soul as light, has become a constant reminder of *my own* sin, *my own* weakness, *my own* evil, and this very thing has made me feel compassion for the weaknesses and sins of others whom I used to despise.

It is for me as though a person's individuality has now become the thing that I should love, and the reason I couldn't love someone before, the wickedness which I had been confusing with individuality, this is not the individual but the sin he suffers from, and this alone I allow myself to hate. In order to reach this standpoint, I think that upon meeting a person one must focus only on his good qualities, since everyone has them, no matter how filthy he is, because in these manifestations of the soul God is, because the spark that has a Divine origin may be found under a pile of the most worthless rubbish. This very same spark, by virtue of the fact that it is used therefor according to the law of God, is something I should always look for in a person, and this can happen only when I raise up within myself nothing but that light of life which is in me, that intelligent principle which establishes my relationship to another, according to my expressed opinion that I shall never expect evil from another, but only good — that is, love — and, according to this law, can I deny the same feeling in another person? By the same rule by which I make this demand, another person can make it, and therefore, before expecting another to employ this rule in relation to me, I ought to employ it myself, since what I want to see in another person can only come about when I myself practise what I expect another to practise; only in this way can I bring forth the good qualities of the soul in their lives.

All this, of course, is not new to you, but as someone who is still experiencing it all, I feel the need of sharing my thoughts with you, so that you might express, in words I can understand, whatever you consider not clearly enough defined, and thereby help me in the progression of my understanding.

I know that the issues which are becoming the clearest to me are those that I have not simply thought about but which I have also experienced. This experience lies at the basis of my life as a firm, saving support, which I constantly reach out for when I feel weakness under foot. By experiencing myself the good that I wish to see in another, I gradually gain the true sense of what can be called life. By adopting such a viewpoint on my relationship to life, I at

69 Letters N° 15 and N° 17, respectively.

once delimit the borders of any teaching I do by the desire to enlighten myself first before anyone else, since the only way to bring someone else to the glory of God is by the light of truth expressed in my own activity (Matth. 5:16). If I myself do not observe the rule required by my soul, by which I wish to experience good, rather than evil from another, kindness instead of wickedness, I cannot impose this rule on another in respect to justice for myself if I myself am not expressing this justice, since what I wish to require of another is that law of life which has permeated my soul as light and still burns within me; in this light and in the observance of this law there is that true eternal life whose activity can lead me to the attainment of good.

If I denied God and were in a state of utter negative unbelief, then, even in spite of my complete denial of God, even if I denied Him with my faculty of reason, I could not deny Him with my soul, but I would recognize Him through the revelation that would be taking place in my conscience. I would recognize Him with my soul, my mind. In denying God I would wish for His manifestation, in denying Him I would desire to see Him, since I know that He is that very life that I seek just as a person with his eyes blindfolded looks for a road, knowing that he must go somewhere. And no matter what I did, no matter what I wished, no matter what activity I was engaged in, all this is only fragments of my inner consciousness implanted in me for understanding and attaining good — all this is simply the result of an impetus within me, but reflected in a completely opposite sense: the law was given for me to fulfil in respect to others, but I wanted this fulfilment to come about specifically *in respect to myself.*

The law instructs me, and instead of following the logical conclusion that achieving good for myself means using it for the benefit of others, I only want others not to do me any harm, and so I instruct others without fulfilling the law, thereby working against the natural exchange and circulation of the law in people's lives. I know I need to restore a balance where the law has been violated, but instead of carrying out the law to the full, I pound my fists against the side of the scales, thereby upsetting the balance. And that is what happens when, wishing to restore justice (the balance), I return evil for evil. If that can be called a revenge of justice, then the striking of the side of the scales which upsets the balance can be called a means of restoring the balance, but in so doing this upsets the balance, justice itself, even more.

In order to know the law that makes people's lives happy, I can only, through my own self, come to know God and what He is for me, and I can do that only through my own self. Through knowing myself I discover and learn what is available to me in order to clarify the meaning and the purpose of life. I want people to love me, I want my life to be happy. No one can say that he doesn't want the same. I want people to love me, and in return for loving me I shall also love them that love me. In other words, the result of my love for others is that they will love *me.* By this I am recognizing that, in order to gain people's love, I must first of all show love, since once I express the need of love for people, this means that I recognize this as the means for achieving a manifestation of the power of love. It also means: use this means to gain what you desire.

Please forgive me for going into so much detail and possibly not clearly expressing my thoughts. I have had the opportunity to do a lot of thinking, including about such questions as what is man, and what is his life with all its passions, sins, love, goodness and death. If God is life, then why is there also evil as the death of life? If there is eternity, then why is there also time which is not eternity?

Delving deeper and deeper into the teachings of Christ, you reach the point where you detach yourself from any consciousness of yourself as a person and thereby transfer the weight of your consciousness into another environment, where your personal self is swallowed up in the grandeur of God. The consciousness of life then becomes not what we call time, but that which lives eternally, something which lives, moves and absorbs with its grandeur only that which can be akin to this grandeur.

The flesh and the spirit — Man, the instrument and law of life — constitute by their very nature a life of eternity in time. The life of man, his flesh, is the bridge God has made for us to cross into His kingdom, and has placed intelligence as a beacon at the end of it as a light to point out the way. He who walks toward this beacon without digressing reaches the kingdom of God, and by walking toward the beacon he is fulfilling God's will. He who digresses from this path takes a zigzag course to the right or the left, and either stumbles against a post or falls off the edge of the bridge into the abyss below. Can it then be said that evil and sin are deviations created by God?

Life is governed by laws alone — laws that can only be called eternal, and these laws are revealed to people through their understanding, and through understanding, God Himself is revealed to people in these laws of life, and is revealed in the exact measure we need to put Him into our life.

In closing this letter, I would ask you, dear Lev Nikolaevich, to explain to me the conversation we had on the meaning of marriage. Are we to understand the ideal of celibacy as perfection and as a goal to which we must strive, are we to understand marriage as a falling away from this ideal or must we elevate the sanctity of marriage to the relative degree of the ideal of celibacy, in other words, the two would be comparable in their elevation. I take it that if the ideal of celibacy is seen in the eyes of the people as the goal of perfection, then only when a departure from this striving occurs, only under that condition does the legality and holiness of marriage come into force — that is, an intelligent attitude toward marriage, in cases where there has been a departure from the highest standard to another relative degree of elevation. How do you combine what you have been telling me with the following texts: Matth. 10:4–6 and 10–11, and its correlative Mark 10:6–12 and Mark 12:25?

Do not deny me your brotherly response to these questions, which I shall await. I will not, however, compel you to answer if you do not wish to.

In conclusion I would ask you to convey my sincere gratitude and love to your wife Sofia Andreevna and your daughters Tat'jana and Marija L'vovna, and my wife asks me to convey the same from her.

I embrace you warmly,
your loyal brother, lovingly,
Fëdor Zheltov

1890
March 16

My address:
Fëdor Alekseevich Zheltov
Village of Bogorodskoe,
Nizh. Gub.

P.S. I am sending you, by separate post, two issues on the question of drunkenness.

Nº 20. L. N. TOLSTOY ❧ F. A. ZHELTOV

8 April 1890. Yasnaya Polyana

8 April 1890

I received your good letter, Fëdor Alekseevich.

May God help you go further and further along the narrow path you have chosen, not being concerned about people, nor about danger from them, nor, most important of all, about praise from them.

Your understanding of the question of marriage agrees with my own. Lately I have been involved setting forth the Christian attitude to marriage (as I understand it), and have described it to the best of my ability in the Afterword to *The Kreutzer Sonata,* which I shall try to send you.

Nº 21. F. A. ZHELTOV ❧ L. N. TOLSTOY

12 April 1890. Village of Bogorodskoe.

I thank you, dear brother Lev Nikolaevich, for the letter you sent me. Before I received it I had just finished reading your *Kreutzer Sonata,*[70] and it explained even more clearly to me the Christian attitude to marriage you personally were talking about. I may say that it made a very strong impression on me,

70 The story had not yet been published; in all probability, Zheltov read it in manuscript form.

not only in its inherent literary style (there's nothing more to say about that) but also in respect to the striking truth it reveals. It seems that those words of the Gospel defining the relations between man and woman, which up to now have been expressed in such a narrow, one-sided interpretation, were at once illumined by that broad light which they reflect.

And where do you suppose that interpretation of Matthew 5:28 came from, which flatly states that looking upon a woman to lust after her applies only to some other woman, and not to one's wife? What do you think, if the sin of adultery stems directly from a man's unchristian attitude toward a woman, apart from its other meaning, then the reference to divorce "except on grounds of adultery"[71] might no longer have the sense that all divorce is forbidden except in those cases where the husband and wife acknowledge they are guilty of adultery in the sense indicated above and do not wish to take it any further, if only they can accept this [command]? (Matth. 5:32; 19:9, 11). In sum, if their eyes were opened to their exclusively animal, fleshly attitude to each other, then, having recognized this abnormality, they can consciously decide either to cease from such an attitude or to focus their primary attention on that spiritual union which is based on true Christian love, and not an animal passion called love. I know that you say that the words "except on grounds of adultery," allowing for divorce on these grounds, cannot come under the overall spirit of the Gospel teaching, any more than can justifiable anger. But if the sin of adultery is to be taken in the broader sense, such as explained in *The Kreutzer Sonata,* then this text, as I see it, could be applied to that sense.

It could be judged as not applicable only according to false public opinion, which defines blame for adultery only in such a narrow one-sided sense, which completely rules out any blame in the case of one's wife. I would be most happy if you would respond and confirm this judgement and open my eyes even more. I hope that you will also send me the Afterword you wrote to *The Kreutzer Sonata*, which you mentioned in your letter and promised to send me. It is all the more important because a great many people here have become interested in your story; and they read it not just out of superficial interest — it has generated many different lively discussions and interpretations.

I wanted to write to you about my current difficult mental state, which feels particularly heavy to me on account of the sin which now stands before me, as a result of my living situation; at the root of all this is *money,* or rather, what money represents.[72] I shall leave that until another time, when I feel the urgent need of writing, although I feel this need even now. I sent the letter to Popov on the same day I received yours, and wrote him what you asked me to; he will

71 Translated from the Russian Synodal Bible (Matth. 5:32); the wording in the Authorized Version is: "save for the cause of fornication."

72 The Zheltovs owned leather factories in Bogorodskoe.

probably be writing to you again. If you should find anything interesting in his letters, could you possibly send them to me so that I may become acquainted with the issues he raises?

My wife, my brother-in-law and my sister send their love and respects to you and your family.

I embrace you as a brother and
thank you for the letter.
With sincere affection,
F. Zheltov

12 April 1990
Village of Bogorodskoe
Nizheg. Gub.

Address:
Village of Bogorodskoe
Nizhegor. Gub.

N° 22. L. N. TOLSTOY ❧ F. A. ZHELTOV
29 April 1890. Yasnaya Polyana.

I received your letter, dear Fëdor Alekseevich, and was so glad to see how deeply you have delved into questions of morality and religion and truly understand them.

Yes, I too feel that marriage is not a Christian institution. Christ never married, neither did his disciples, and he never instituted marriage, but told people, some of whom were married and others not, that those who were married should not change their wives through divorce, as was permissible under Mosaic law (Matth. 5:32), and that for those who were not married, it would be better, if possible, if they refrained from marrying (Matth. 19:10–12). He told both these groups they should understand that the primary sin is in looking upon a woman as an object of lust (Matth. 5:28) (naturally this is to be taken as also applying to women's attitudes toward men).

From these postulates the following practical moral conclusions naturally arise:

1) Not to look to see, as is now the case, that every young man and girl necessarily enters into marriage, but rather to ensure that every young man and woman preserves his or her purity in the best possible way, so that nothing may prevent their giving all their energies to the service of God.

2) Not to look upon (as now) the falling of a person, man or woman, into a sexual relationship as a mistake which may be corrected by entering into a sexual relationship (in the form of marriage) with someone else, or even as the forgivable satisfying of a need, or even pleasure, but to look upon the first entry

into a sexual relationship, regardless of who it is or with whom, as an entry into an unbreakable marriage (Matth. 19:4–6), obligating the marriage partners to a specific activity which will serve as an atonement for the sin committed.

3) Not to look upon marriage (as now) as permission to satisfy fleshly lusts, but as sin which requires its atonement. Atonement for sin consists, in the first place, in the liberation of the self, each partner helping the other to free themselves from lust and to attain, insofar as possible, the establishment of a relationship not as between lovers, but as between brother and sister; and secondly, in bringing up any children resulting from the marriage as future servants of God.

The difference between such a view of marriage and the prevailing view is very great: people will still marry and be given in marriage; parents will still see that their children marry and are given in marriage; but the great difference is whether the satisfaction of lust is to be considered exalted, legal and the greatest happiness on earth, or whether it is to be considered a sin. One who follows Christian teachings will marry only when he feels that he cannot do otherwise, and, once married, will not submit to lust, but strive to keep it in subjection (this applies to both men and women); parents concerned about the spiritual well-being of their children will not consider it necessary to marry or give in marriage all their children, but only do so (i.e., give them advice, ease their fall) in the case of those who are not able to maintain their sense of purity, and only when their children cannot live otherwise. Marriage partners will not take pride, as they do now, in a large number of children; on the contrary, they will strive for purity of life, they will be happy that they have only a few children and they can devote all their energies to the upbringing of those children that they have, as well as others' children whom they might serve, if they wish to serve God by bringing up His future servants.

The difference will be the one that exists between people who use food because they cannot do without it — and therefore endeavour to spend as little time, energy and attention as possible on the preparation and consumption of food — and people who make the planning, adaptation, taste-refinement and consumption of food their main interest in life. This was taken to the ultimate stage by the Romans, who adopted vomiting so that they would be able to eat again. It is exactly the same with devices used for the prevention of childbirth.

I wrote on this subject in my Afterword to *The Kreutzer Sonata,* which I shall send you as soon as it is ready. I am very, very happy about that sense of spiritual unity I feel with you; it does not surprise me, since we are drawing from the same source. I embrace you and your family and friends.

Your interpretation of the phrase "except on grounds of adultery" I find true in its spirit, but too artificial, which is also my criticism of several interpretations in *What I believe.* The Spirit is one: the more chaste [people are], the closer [they are] to the teachings of Christ. And this is something that everyone knows and feels with their whole being.

Nº 23. F. A. ZHELTOV ❧ L. N. TOLSTOY

21 May 1890. Village of Bogorodskoe.

Dear brother, Lev Nikolaevich!

I received your letter. Thank you for the response you have given me. Your view on marriage is becoming clearer and clearer to me, especially after receiving your latest letter opening up even wider this issue which you touched upon in *The Kreutzer Sonata*. The whole point is that changing one's view on marriage — in the sense of what Christ says about it — will put people in an entirely different position from current views on it. Public opinion formed under the influence of this view divides carnal relations into those which are permissible — that is, legal, sanctified, treated as a sacrament, and illegal relations. People who fall into the latter by virtue of their inherent human weaknesses are singled out as fallen and despicable people on whom the oppression of contempt fixes a label of shame and puts pressure on them, sometimes inciting them to crime. I know one instance where a girl, under the pressure of society's judgement upon her, decided to kill her child just to hide her shame.

I am surprised how the very same people that have agreed to accept as legal that which would be illegal without the observance of external formalities, have divided one and the same sin into permissible and impermissible — permissible in the sense that, upon performance of conventional rituals, it becomes a sacrament, and if these are not observed, then it is a crime. And so the label placed upon others as one of shame, becomes something sacred and permissible for those who detach themselves from those they consider perverted. The love that many talk about and interpret as something elevated — the love for a woman in the worldly sense — is in fact a cloak with the coarsest animalistic lining, destroying the very [meaning of] the word itself, and is closely linked to the thought of a woman as an object of lust. That higher, non-earthly Christian love, which covers a multitude of sins and which accepts God into itself, cannot be such a pitiful example, manifesting only the motivation of animal passion; the latter is a pitiful shadow of that higher quality which is the embodiment of God.

Even in the love for a woman, true love always manifests the same qualities, and when a person, feeling his or her powerlessness to hold on to the high and perfect ideal of celibacy set before him, fulfils the demands of the flesh, he will then still hold on to that love as a connecting thread to God and His eternal life. In fulfilling the demands of the flesh as a sign of his imperfection, he feels duty-bound to accept that true love into his relationship with the woman he has come together with, as well as with any resulting offspring. Not having reached within himself the fulness of perfection, he is obliged to transmit his spiritual growth to the offspring of his marriage, and this transmission will continue its own forward movement in the same direction. In so progressing, it confirms in people's lives those steps by which a person rises above his animal life to God and passes into His eternal life, becoming one with Him — becoming what God has given him and the only thing He lives by.

I would be most happy if you could write me a letter about this. My spirit rejoices in the unity which I feel with you.

I found Ballou's manuscript most interesting,[73] but the way it is explained suggests that there should be a sequel to it. Has the whole thing been translated? If not, could you not send me the remaining part? Please tell me if I am keeping it too long. I heartily embrace you and your whole family.

With brotherly affection,
F. Zheltov

21 May 1890
Village of Bogorodskoe.

My address:
Fëdor Alekseevich Zheltov
Village of Bogorodskoe
Nizhegor. Gub.

In sincere dedication to L. N. Tolstoy

'Tis not in the world's truthless teaching
That your soul seeks its rest and accord,
Nor to idols of gold is it reaching
For a false and disdainful reward, —

Passions are sheer exaltation,
No vices besmirch its designs,
Its feelings show pure consecration,
Which the Prophet's own glory enshrines.

That glory in life shines reflected
Through the freedom and love of God's law,
The spirit is thus resurrected
From the dust of the Earth's mortal claw!...

F. Zheltov

73 In the summer of 1889, a colleague of the American pastor Adin Ballou, one Rev. Lewis G. Wilson, sent Tolstoy the book *Christian Non-Resistance*. Tolstoy planned to publish a translation of Ballou's book through Posrednik, and commissioned A. P. Barykova to do the translation. He himself wrote the Foreword, which later grew into the treatise *The Kingdom of God is Within You* (1890–93).

N° 24. F. A. ZHELTOV ❧ L. N. TOLSTOY
30 November 1891. Village of Bogorodskoe.

My dear Lev Nikolaevich!

It has been a long time since I wrote to you, and what I wanted to say to you after such a long period I shall put off 'til another time, as I and my thoughts are now occupied with something else. Today we saw Vladimir Vasil'evich Rakhmanov[74] off to Lukojanov Uezd, as he wrote to you. He received your letter with a number of practical hints for organizing soup kitchens for famine relief. Once he has settled in there he will be writing me in detail about the status of food supplies in the uezd, and quite possibly either he or I will be letting you know about this.

The terrible disaster which has overtaken several areas of Russia has caused us to do a lot of serious thinking and to take a hard look around us. What is needed? What are the first steps that need to be taken to relieve the effects of the disaster? And out in the community question after question arises, discussion follows discussion, and one proposal after another comes up, and all these get mixed in together, crowding each other out, and as a result there is a whole new wave of meaningless talk. And time is slipping by unnoticed, and with it the suffering goes on for those who have no food and no means of getting it.

But not everybody is aware of such suffering. Many in the area have enough to eat, and whenever they hear talk of people starving, they reply there is no famine and it's all just idle talk, and they're right: for them there is no famine, they can't possibly have any concept that others don't have enough to eat — they see all this food around them, a lot of it, and they're unwilling to look and see whether it is being blocked by this majority and whether there really is enough for others. They've got accustomed to it and, at the first cry of help they hear from those less fortunate, they bend down and hide their heads, trying to forget it. If they could see the people's sufferings with their own eyes, if these sufferings had a direct impact on people's hearts, then, perhaps, the sparks of love would be lit and glow and, setting each other alight and combining together, would form a real flame. And this is happening and will continue to happen, no matter how little it is noticed.

But in the present situation, when whole masses of people, maybe millions, are going through physical suffering and torment for lack of food — both

74 *V. V. Rakhmanov* (1865–1918) — a doctor, an active farming community member, who wrote articles on raising children and on popular medicine, as well as a collection of reminiscences "L. N. Tolstoj i «tolstovstvo» v kontse vos'midesjatykh i nachale devjanostykh godov" [L. N. Tolstoy and 'Tolstoyism' at the end of the 1880s and the beginning of the 1890s], published in *Minuvshie gody* [Years Gone By] (1908, N° 9:3–32). An acquaintance and correspondent of Tolstoy's, in 1891 Rakhmanov went to the Lukojanov district of Nizhegorod Gubernia to organize relief efforts for the starving peasants there.

young and old, men and women, adults and children are going hungry, — we can't just leave it as is, we have to fan the flame, expand and strengthen it, and use it to throw light on this situation for those who do not see or hear, or who are unwilling to see and hear. Russia is going through a difficult situation right now not only because of lack of food, and to calculate whether there will be food or not before the next harvest is not that important — even if there should in fact be no food at all. There may be enough even when people conclude there won't be any, and there may not be enough even when it is determined that there is a surplus. Consequently it is not important to be concerned about that.

The important question at this moment, which all our thinking, talk and action should be concentrated on, is how to distribute all the existing food, in whatever quantity, as quickly as possible throughout Russia without delay, so there will no longer be pockets of plenty and pockets of scarcity as there are now. There are many pockets of scarcity, and that is because people living where there is plenty of food do not feel the hunger and have no immediate desire to share what they have. But both the hunger and the supply should be shared alike, spread around, and then there will be neither famine nor surplus.

The same thing is happening now to Russia as happened to the people who followed Christ out into the desert to hear his sermon.[75] Some people took provisions along, and others didn't. The time came when those who had not brought food wanted to eat. Their murmurings reached the ears of the disciples, who told Christ. And He performed a miracle. He commanded everyone to sit down in rows and watch what He did, and that everyone should do as He did, and as they did exactly the same as He did, they would see the result. And everyone waited for a miracle. And it happened. He took five loaves, broke them apart and gave them to others who didn't have any, keeping only as much as He needed to eat Himself. And everybody who was given a piece of bread did the same — those who had nothing but were given a lot. And it turned out that everybody ate to the full and there were still twelve boxes of leftovers remaining. And the miracle was that people lovingly shared their own supply of bread with people who didn't have it, everybody ate to the full and was satisfied, there was enough for everyone and still some left over.

But it could have happened that this bread was not enough, it could have happened that the disciples, having counted up the supply and distributed it according to the numbers of people, might have tried to soothe the Master by saying that there was enough food, that there was plenty and there was no cause for concern, and still, in spite of the fact that there was bread, still there would have been many who would have gone hungry without anything to eat. But a '*miracle*' was performed, and that didn't happen, and such a '*miracle*' is needed right now. Open the barns of the rich where food is stored up in the millions, let

75 See Matth. 14:13–21.

this food go to places where there is none, and everyone will eat to the full and be satisfied until the next food comes, and there will be food left over.

What is happening now in places with relatively high yields — where there hasn't been enough food even with a good harvest — [is this]: a peasant who is both needy and tempted by the high price of bread, takes his surplus to market, pockets the money, spends it, and then in a month or two is back at the market, this time not to sell bread, but to *buy* it. Thus the gangrene of hunger spreads further and further across the land, on the one hand feeding the prosperous areas of Russia with its juices, on the other utterly draining these areas and infecting them with that same destitution that is gradually taking hold of the population. And through all this the rich continue to hold on to their food reserves with cold indifference, keeping them under lock and key, like dumb rocks in the midst of a foaming sea, amidst sorrow, despair, tears and all sorts of unbearable human suffering.

And apart from all this there is the appearance of something underway capable of removing the threat of general catastrophe: 'councils,' 'commissions,' 'relief funds' and 'committees' are being set up, and both the *zemstvo* [district council] and the experts are overwhelmed by the whole affair — a multitude of rushed projects, calculations, investigations, correspondence, memos, statements, all resulting in…a lot of formalism and paperwork. But all this smacks of something cold and calculated, superficial and lifeless, and what is needed is not there. There is no spirit of the cause itself, there is no love — that is, there is no *life*. The more people get directly involved in the cause, and the more brightly burns the spirit of love within them and the stronger and friendlier their outreach and the forces they harness in common, the more quickly and easily they will accomplish the task that has as yet not even got off the ground, and the sooner it will be done.

The important thing now is to put this issue before the public as strongly and clearly as possible and to open people's eyes to everything that has been hidden from them and which lies simmering in their conscience — the important thing now is to awaken their dormant consciousness of life: let the dead hear the voice of the Son of God, and they that hear shall live.[76]

We need words, strong words. The time is such that these words must be said without fail — *God demands it.* The rock must be struck so that water may flow out.[77]

And these words must be said by you.

After you wrote your stinging rebuke concerning the *Day of Enlightenment*,[78] after you expressed your opinion on work and thought, on the meaning of celibacy, after you recently published your article *A Frightening Question*,[79]

76 See John 5:25.

77 See Num. 20:11, Ps. 78:20.

78 See Letter N° 11 above.

79 Tolstoy's article on hunger *A Frightening Question* [*Strashnyj vopros*] appeared in the newspaper *Russkie vedomosti* edition of 6 November 1891.

you must definitely let us have your *word* on this — and I think you already feel this, and it is *necessary* and *vital.* It is not necessary to contemplate ahead of time what will come of it; it should in no way be analysed — that would even be sinful. You must do it, say it, and that's it. Whatever can awaken thought will accomplish its purpose, and even if not at the moment, it will still accomplish it. And this already by its very nature *obligates* you to talk about the power and meaning of love as the centre around which everything else revolves as it should.[80]

I shan't go into this issue any further — one could say that people should once and for all give up such a supply system that divides pieces of bread into 'mine' and 'not mine,' and that food supply ought to be a public duty, and then there would be no more starving or surfeited people, which would even be more financially advantageous (just as an example: instead of hundreds of stoves and kitchens there would be only one), and that such things as food-stuffs would never in any way be commodities to be bought or sold — that is, speculation commodities — but on the understanding that all these external things cannot be perceived by external means or brought about by external forces, that this can never come about without the recognition of its internal foundation, and therefore cannot be a commodity or an issue of primary importance — "Seek ye first the kingdom of God and His righteousness, and everything else will be added unto you."[81]

There have always been and always will be reasons why in this current year some will go hungry while others have enough, and this year's poor harvest cannot be the only cause for people going hungry. This year is special only in that it has filled in the gaps whereby those who go hungry in good years are scattered in isolated groups and so remain unnoticed. These have now shown themselves so clearly and fully with all their sufferings against the backdrop of false human life and thrown so much light on this falsity which has taken over human life, that it has become utterly impossible not to speak of them.

One cannot remain silent at such a moment, one cannot help but raise one's voice and utter the words! They are vital, necessary, and long awaited. People will always be reminded of *A Frightening Question* as long as they are far from Christ. And neither America, nor the *zemstvo,* nor the experts nor food reserves can save people from it.

This issue must be exposed for what it really is, along with the fact that everyone is at fault: the capitalists, the hoarders, those who love a life of luxury, the generous eaters, those who live off large salaries, those who go to university so they can sweeten their own pie — yes, even the philanthropists. And whatever is to be said should be said straight — not that generous eating

80 When Zheltov was writing this, Tolstoy had finished his long article *On Hunger* [*O golode*], which was banned in Russia, and was already working on a story, never completed, on the same topic, called "Who's right?" [*Kto prav?*]

81 See Matth. 6:33.

or overeating is a sin, that one must eat in moderation and change one's eating habits, but say out and out that *eating is sin.* There is only one anchor in any question about the concerns of carnal life to which we can attach a line to hold on to and draw ourselves toward Christ, and that is *the Father's perfection.* Everything is in Him and of Him. In Him is the life in the present, without a tomorrow, and this life in the present is therefore eternal because it is not dependent on time.

Forgive me, dear brother, for this letter. You will understand why I wrote it. Listen to the inner voice of your soul, and if it hears the same echoes, then do as I ask. Use your love to cover any deficiencies and unclear thoughts expressed here, and do not fail to write to me. I shall most definitely wait for your reply, otherwise I shall think that you either are annoyed by my letter or do not agree with it.

I embrace you warmly as a brother, and ask you to convey my greetings to your daughters, if they are with you, and your associates.

Sincerely and lovingly,
F. Zheltov

30 November 1891

Address: F. A. Zheltov
Village of Bogorodskoe, Nizheg. Gub.

N° 25. F. A. ZHELTOV ❧ L. N. TOLSTOY
23 July 1892. Village of Bogorodskoe.

Dear Lev Nikolaevich!

I have not written to you for some time, as this year with its forthright demands for the cause has made me look more deeply into my own essence. I have not always had sufficient strength to give practical answers to questions posed by my conscience, let alone, being conscious of my own weakness, to occupy myself with abstract questions of theory and debate. When I was with you, it was impossible for me to tell you what was in my heart — not because I didn't want to, but because I could not.

By today's post I am sending you my manuscript[82] which I was going to send directly either to Chertkov or to some editorial office for publication, but for the sake of the cause I did not do so but decided I should first acquaint you with the contents of the manuscript. If you will take the time to look at it and let me know what you think of it, that is all I would ask of you, though I do

82 A reference to Zheltov's article "Put' literatury — put' zhizni" [The way of literature is the way of life]. Tolstoy sent it to the editor of *Russkoe bogatstvo,* L. E. Obolenskij. The editor returned it to the author for correction. It was never published. (In *PSS* 50:272, it is mistakenly stated that Zheltov sent this article in February 1889.)

not insist upon this absolutely, if for some reason you find it impossible to do it. From the manuscript you will see that it touches mainly upon the mission and meaning of literature, and I treat it not as some independent matter, but as *a result of the true and good life* and the intelligent striving on the path to the eternal ideals of life.

The chief evil which has caused people to stray from this true path is that people have lost their fundamental purpose and have confused their own personality, its interests, the attractions and deceptions of life, with works of literature and art (falsely understood), and thereby serve deceptions and lies instead of good. Such an attitude has made people bestow some kind of legitimacy on words they buy for money, and instead of being a means of communication in love, it has become a means for satisfying lust and a means of distraction from their duties.

In view of all this, what people say about popularly accessible literature, I consider not as just an unavoidable exception to popular ignorance, as do the majority, but as an unconscious perception of the imperfection of that 'refined,' 'artistic' genre of literary fiction read by educated society — here there can be no question of the necessity of having an exclusively popular literature, but only about *worthless* literature as opposed to *good* literature. Both have their recognizable characteristics, undoubtedly based on people's proper attitudes to the true sense of human life, and I should like to elaborate on these in the article I am sending. I don't think it came out very well, as I just said what I was able to, and if what I said represents even the tiniest drop of effort, I think there is room in our general cause even for a drop, like a drop of water against a rock, a waterfall against a granite cliff.

And so I decided to ask your advice: do you think it's worth having this article published in some sort of journal (such as *Nedelja,* or another), and issuing it separately in booklet form through Posrednik for intellectual readers? If your response is positive, could you take care of this manuscript by sending it either directly to an editor or through Chertkov? If you do not approve of what I am doing, then you can either return it to me or send it first to Vladimir Grigor'evich [Chertkov]. If you should send it for publication, do you think you could write a few words in the form of a brief foreword which would sum up, so to speak, the whole substance of its contents? This latter proposal, of course, is entirely at your discretion, and if it is needed at all, then it would be only to benefit the cause itself and to broaden its readership.

I hope that you will write back as to how you have decided to proceed with the article and what you think of it. I await your reply.

I embrace you as a brother,
Lovingly, Fëdor Zheltov

23 July 1892

My address:
Fëdor Alekseevich Zheltov
Village of Bogorodskoe
Nizh. Gub.

Nº 26. F. A. ZHELTOV ❧ L. N. TOLSTOY
4 March 1893. Village of Bogorodskoe.

My dear Lev Nikolaevich!

I just arrived home and read your letter with great joy.[83] My visit to the Kerzhentsy[84] made a rather strong impression on me and my spiritual communion with them gave me unspeakable joy. Their direct approach to the Christian faith, and especially their understanding of the practical significance of that faith, has been achieved through lengthy inner toil and one can only marvel at how they managed to throw off so many layers that weighed down their consciousness and life. In listening to their account of this, I couldn't help thinking of the truth expressed by Christ: "No man cometh unto the Father but *by Me*"[85] and: "No one cometh to Me except his heavenly Father draw him."[86] I am once again convinced that the recognition of the true life is always the inevitable result of that spiritual freedom whereby a person's individuality is drawn into this special state of the human spirit which governs it as the only true law, which, with never a hint of deceit or false reasoning, is the only true indicator of the path it is to follow.

The attainment of such a state is like reaching the centre from where one can see the horizons of life and the paths to the country of light. The more you reflect on this and examine your own life, the more you will be convinced that the human path to the kingdom of God inevitably passes through three stages of spiritual development, similar to those experienced by Christ (1. His life up until He became conscious of His sonship with the Father; 2. His withdrawal into the wilderness, into solitude, for reflection; 3. His service to His Father), such as He expressed in the parable about the lord and his servants, keeping watch during all three watches of the night for the coming of the Lord (Luke 23:35–40; Matth. 24:42–51). Just as changes in human life are possible at these three stages of the ascent of the human spirit, there is also the possibility of great temptations, and that is why one must maintain a cheerful readiness to meet the coming of one's Lord and listen attentively for His return (Luke 12:36, 37). And now these three watches for a living, moving human being are the

83 The whereabouts of Tolstoy's letter of 5 February 1893 are unknown. It was noted by Marija L'vovna Tolstaja (Tolstoy's daughter) in a list of letters sent.
84 A branch of the Old Believers.
85 John 14:6.
86 Cf. John 6:44: "No man can come to me, except the Father which hath sent me draw him..."

three main culminating moments of the path he has covered hitherto and the opening up of a new path.

A person's entrance upon the first watch is his entrance into carnal life through the unconscious union of this life with the son of the Father, whom the Father sent into the world not to condemn the world, but that the world might be saved through Him (John 3:17). This period of a person's life is lived under the inner influence of the demand to know one's true essence, and if one has not overshadowed this demand by the lust of one's body, which lives at the expense of the Son, he comes to this recognition, although the path thereto may pass through a series of doubts and sufferings, along with the toil of winnowing out the chaff from the grain concealed therein.

And then at last the person who has not abandoned his cause is able to hear the coming of his Lord, whom he is to accept as his own true consciousness which has matured in him. The individual rejoices; and as long as he does not forget that his watching is not over, he enters upon the second period; but here too temptation appears: "Yes, it is good to reason about God," "It is man's duty to talk about this," "One must live for the purpose of doing this." The Devil cannot help but not let go of his line of temptation, once he has attached himself to an individual's inner workings. And so he flits by like a barely noticeable shadow and one's inner world begins to gradually change its hue. The individual begins to get carried away with what he has already achieved, not bothering to add to these achievements (Matth. 25:24–30), he begins to dabble in teaching, persuading, changing forms, rebuking some, restoring others and, finally losing sight of his main purpose, he loses his sensitivity, he does not hear the Lord knocking. But the Devil needs this, he needs the person to pause; if it happens, that person is his.

If a person survives these temptations as well, he inevitably undergoes a second change. He examines the purified seed which he sacrificed everything to attain (Matth. 13:45–46). He immerses himself in contemplation and reflection, and at this moment, in order to work out the question of how to proceed further, what to do with this seed, he requires solitude, withdrawal from everything that might distract him; he forgets himself, forgets his flesh (for example, Christ in the wilderness; witness the commandment: Thou shalt love God with all thy heart, and with all thy soul and with all thy *mind*[87]). This period can be passed through in a short time, as with Christ, or a long time. The important thing is that it is passed through. Here one cannot avoid solitude, prayer, the contemplation of God. The coming of the Lord draws near, which is most important in bringing the individual into the glory of the Father (John 4:21; 15:4, 8; 16:7–14).

But the Devil, as a thief, knows the time to break into the house (Matth. 24:43) and again he winds his way like a delicate thread into the inner

87 See Matth. 22:37.

substance of the human spirit, and lurks just like a thief to carry off what is sown (Luke 4:2–12; Matth. 13:19). And again the Devil's thin shadow runs through one's consciousness, darkening clarity of thought. And it keeps on running, penetrating, wandering and snuffing out the little embryos of light, mixing with one's consciousness and putting on a similar external appearance: "Yes, yes, you have now achieved what you desired, now hold on to this gold" (Matth. 25:18, 25, 28), don't lose it and don't spend it. Now you see God; glorify Him, contemplate Him, don't let Him out of your sight (Matth. 7:21; Luke 6:46). Stay on this path, contemplate, contemplate!... (Mark 13:5, 6, 21; John 2:19). And a further instance of distraction occurs in the person who gives in to these temptations: "What further need is there, I have come to know God, I have reached the highest limit, I ought to retreat from it, beat the flesh, contemplate what I have achieved," and the Devil that was cast out returns to the unoccupied place in a different disguise along with many evil spirits (Matth. 12:43–45), and the last temptation is worse than the first: man glorifies God and bows down to the Devil.

These were the same temptations Christ withstood in the wilderness (Luke 4:3–13). One who knows the voice of his Lord and listens to him so he may open the door to him can pass through even these temptations of the second watch (John 10:1–5; 3:8). But this is not the end of temptation, it only changes its appearance, ingratiating itself into the inner state of human consciousness, which it awaits in the third period as well, which inevitably follows as a result of the first two. The third stage of life includes everything achieved by the individual, and reveals to him all the grandeur of the true path.

Here a person should be concerned only about one thing, namely that nothing should delay or hide the demands of intelligence; and in carrying out this demand the Lord himself will assist (John 8:27; Luke 12:37; John 14:21). The person's individuality, having lost its habit of living according to lusts at the expense of the life of the Lord, who gave individual life only that He might dwell therein (John 8:35; 14:10; 15:27; 17:1–2, 21), will be an instrument capable only of magnifying love, since the contemplation and knowledge of God have revealed that this can happen only through communion by this light with other individuals, unified in substance, though separate in actions (1 John 4:12), and since observance of the first commandment of love for God must be expressed through God's relationship to the individual (for it is not we who have loved God, but He us (1 John 4:10), and God sent not His Son[88] into the individual to condemn him, but that he might be saved through Him) — even the individual who has come to know himself and therefore become subject to doing the will of his Father of life.

88 "I do not write 'of one blood' [*odnorodnyj*] or 'only begotten' [*edinorodnyj*], since, as I see it, it makes no difference: if [he is] a Son, that means he is also of one blood with the Father, and if there are no new births, he is the only begotten." — Note by F. A. Zheltov.

From this moment on, man's life is wholly according to the will of God, and the individual as an independent being existing all by itself fades away: it does not speak, it does not create — everything is done by the *"I"* — the son of God, the true substance of man, the son of man. Concern for the flesh and even death itself disappears from view (John 5:24). There are no limits, no rules, no prescriptions here; there is only the one existence with the Father, there is only the kingdom of God; there is only His procession in his own light. But even here, vigilance is the first condition of salvation: the enemy sleeps not and seeks out the path of temptations (Matth. 13:25) and they appear; temptations change their form and penetrate consciousness in thousands of offshoots. These include spiritual pride, one's own opinion of one's self, reliance on one's accomplishments, distinguishing the right hand from the left, searching for meaning wherein to worship God, attacks of fear, etc., and here there is only one thing that is important: to magnify the light and the material for burning (Matth. 25:1–12), so that by that light one can discern the obstacles to progress — it is essential to preserve one's inner purity (Matth. 5:8), since only thus is life achieved and progress accelerated, and for this the *complete rejection of any personal good* is the chief basis for freedom from deception and earthly ties that would hinder our ascent.

The magnification of love is the magnification of progress and the light of eternity must inevitably grow and grow in proportion to this progress, since as we draw nearer to our objective of light, its fulness is increased, and He, as the source of the world's life, this eternal spirit, eternal love, absorbs the individual that merges with Him and, in saving it, brings it into the eternal kingdom of God, into that which is eternal, unshakeable and immovable, that which will live and make alive in immortality…

Of what use here are rules and concerns about the power of external amenities? What additional powers are needed to aid this one eternal power, as if they could strengthen it even further? And where is this power not to be found: it dwells with the weak in spirit and the strong in spirit; it dwells with the person who is striving for self-perfection and with the one who has fallen and made himself filthy in sins; it lives and is doing its work: the power of God works even where there is weakness (2 Cor. 12:9), even where there are no outward signs of its working, where it is revealed only in elusive changes in consciousness. How careful we must be in our relations with people not to employ any but the Divine power, so as not to mix anything of *our own* clumsiness with it (Matth. 13:28–30).

One is involuntarily reminded of Isaiah's marvellous words [quoted by Christ Jesus]: "This is My servant, whom I have chosen, in Whom My soul is well pleased…he *shall not strive, nor cry, neither shall he lift up His voice. A bruised reed shall he not break and smoking flax shall he not quench* until he makes the truth to be known" (Matth. 12:18–20). Now that is the condition of the Christian spirit!... And the path thereto inevitably passes through those three stages mentioned earlier: 1) Knowledge of one's own essence, 2)

Definition of the relationship of this essence to the world and 3) Subjection of the self to this essence through complete subjugation to its will. A person should always have only this positive side as an ideal before his gaze; concerns over external amenities destroy unity of direction and do not allow for integration with the spirit of the Father; they come all by themselves, as the result of overall progress, and hence for the Christian there is no external life — it is only the sign of his inner life.

And if this condition structures even the outward aspects of man's life along the lines of the Divine, this same condition, revealed to people without any naked denials or censure of their lies, deceits or temptations, revealed only in the height of its inner substance, will inevitably all by itself expose the lie more strongly than the naked, albeit justified censure thereof without the light of the true life. Nothing can act more powerfully on man than the demonstration by word and deed of the one and only essence of Christian teaching. There are many turns to take in life, the number of deceptions and temptations is even greater, and to stop before them and shoot arrows at them is useless, when there is a means which will kill them all at once and snatch the ground from underneath their feet.

You see, dear Lev Nikolaevich, how much I have ended up writing to you; please do not be angry at me for tiring you out with my letter. I write what I feel in my heart, and I would have written even more about what interests me, but I fear I would be taking up too much of your time. Tell me what you find essential in this letter; I always get so much from your letters. Sometimes I feel lonely and long to talk with someone, at least in writing. I shall definitely expect your reply.

By the way, let me know how you propose to set up a school among the Molokans — this is something I have been thinking about for a long time, and I think it should be established on Christian principles. I don't know whether I shall actually do anything, but I shall not let go of this thought.

Please accept my sincere love, as well as my love for all your household members and acquaintances.

Sincerely, affectionately yours
F. Zheltov

P.S. In yesterday's post I received an account of the Doukhobor-Molokan tenets of faith. Thank you for sending it. I am happy that finally communication is restored among people seeking the light. I was greatly pleased by the Doukhobor-Molokan answers. Could you give me the address of the society where they are recorded.

4 March 1893
Village of Bogorodskoe.
Nizheg. Gub.

N° 27. F. A. ZHELTOV ❧ L. N. TOLSTOY
25 February 1894. Village of Bogorodskoe.

Dear Lev Nikolaevich!

The bearer of this letter is my acquaintance Aleksandr Aleksandrovich Markov. He wishes to have a word with you and therefore asked me to write this letter of introduction. Please do receive him.

I should like to take this opportunity to assure you of my love.

Yours, F. Zheltov

25 Febr. 94
Village of Bogorodskoe.

N° 28. F. A. ZHELTOV ❧ L. N. TOLSTOY
21 April 1894. Village of Bogorodskoe.

21 Apr. 1894

Dear Lev Nikolaevich!

I recently read over the letter you wrote concerning the upbringing of children.[89]

I too am interested in this question, and I have decided to let you know what I think about the ideas you expressed in the letter. You write that training as it affects children's souls should boil down to a process of *hypnosis,* to the example parents offer in perfecting their own lives and then infecting the children with this example. One cannot disagree that a good, kind example can influence children's souls: the perfection of the individual inevitably sheds rays of light on those around one, but I don't think I can agree that education should depend *wholly* on hypnosis. The example a person sets, after all, his good behaviour, is only the result of his highest inner strivings, and if he did not have this high ideal before him, he could not behave this way. The embodiment in a person of his strivings for the ideal is something he draws not from external examples, but from his inner life, from his consciousness and understanding, possibly when he is not at all thinking about specific behaviour, but only about what his true essence is.

How can it be that a complete inner representation of God as the highest ideal of life, the true concept of the essence of life which is embodied in a person's inner life, is capable of being transmitted to children and people in the individual's environment through behaviour alone? The perfection of eternity is not limited to behaviour, and however many acts of good behaviour there are, however good they are in themselves, none of them in isolation

89 Letter N° 6.

can become the ideal of life for man.[90] They cannot be offered in place of a compass to one starting out on a journey: his compass can be none other than God, and his poles are individuality and eternity. No man hath seen God at any time, it is only the Son Who testifies of Him,[91] and therefore man can only *understand* God, but cannot take in all of Him.

Why not link both these relationships to the raising of children? Why not hope that the inner higher understanding conveyed in words can have a certain degree of influence on children's hearts and souls? I think that along with the progression of the individual the *pure word* will come to birth, and, as the word of God conveyed through the Son, "*shall not pass away*,"[92] but will do its work come what may, including the work of child-raising. "Of the abundance of the heart the mouth speaketh,"[93] and one cannot refuse or ignore [the use of] this tool in the matter of child-raising as well. To rely on "hypnosis" alone is like relying on simply ploughing a field. If hypnosis has its place, it is only in the sense of *ploughing*, and not *sowing*, and the sowing of good seeds is essential to counterbalance the surrounding external life, whose *own* hypnosis is equally as strong, deadening people's consciousness and holding them in a state of sleep.

Hypnosis would have a real significance in the matter of child-raising under one condition, namely its *uninterrupted continuity*, but this cannot be, since we all fall and sin; but even if there could exist such a thing as its uninterrupted continuity, even then such an influence on children would hardly be desirable from the true Christian viewpoint — it would be like someone on the outside holding the reins. God needs not slaves, but Sons — not unconscious performers, but those who *freely* and consciously serve the spirit of truth. What I hear and feel in my heart is much more important for my inner purity than what I imitate — examples: Nicodemus, Peter, the rich young man — all of whom Christ endeavoured to awaken out of hypnosis.

The basis of the purity of a work is not in the purity of the work itself, but in the *purity of consciousness*; moreover, there are no personal works — throughout life a person has but a single task: the *subjugation of his own will to the will of God*. People are not saved from the world's evil by behaviour, but by the *Son* you feel in yourself — not by the number of such acts of behaviour, but by people who know the will of the Father, and whatever becomes [part of] consciousness becomes [part of] life as well. All this is transmitted not just by hypnosis, but also by the *living word*, by arousing the spirit, by refining that which is perceived and that which is experienced — something that fires the heart no less than external hypnosis. One must not stifle the voice of the Son of God within one's self by rejecting its use in child-rearing — only one thing

90 "Acts of behaviour are the turns on God's path" — Note by F. A. Zheltov.

91 See 1 John 4:12; 1:18.

92 See Matth. 24:35.

93 See Luke 6:45.

is necessary, and that is a strict inner relationship to one's self. Exposing and removing the covers of superstition and lies can be done only through the Word, which, in penetrating people's concepts and understanding, illumines their inner darkness. One who has glimpsed the horizon in the momentary glow of lightning (Matth. 24:27) does not need the limited light of a lamp carried by the person ahead of him, who, like himself, is endeavouring to see the horizon.

I would say that children need this inner illumination, no less than our behaviour, to be consonant with the spirit of truth. I hope that you will respond, my dear Lev Nikolaevich, to this letter. I have an inner need for your response, as the matter of relating to children has become for me a matter of the heart and a practical requirement of life.

I embrace you as a brother,
F. Zheltov

Fëdor Alekseevich Zheltov
Village of Bogorodskoe
Nizhegor. Gub.

N° 29. L. N. TOLSTOY ❧ F. A. ZHELTOV
29 April 1894. Moscow.

Moscow, 29 April 1894

Dear Fëdor Alekseevich,

I am in complete agreement with the thoughts you expressed in your letter about the upbringing of children. The word is one of the most natural, widespread and easiest means of conveying thoughts. Unfortunately it is also the most deceptive, and therefore in child-raising, where deception is most dangerous of all — deception is always easily discoverable by children — the best and most effective means which excludes the possibility of (often involuntary) deception has always been and will always be the personal example of the child-raiser's own life. It was in this sense only that I wrote in the letter you mention about the need for an example, or one's own life. The example and one's own life include the word as well. The example teaches how to live and how to speak. The word, however, does not include the example. This was all I meant to say in that letter.

Farewell, I wish you all the best.

Lovingly, Lev Tolstoy

Dear Fëdor Alekseevich,

This letter I wrote as dictated by Lev Nikolaevich, who was at the time having his portrait painted by the artist Jaroshchenko.

Today L. N. left for Yasnaya Polyana.

I do not remember whether I mentioned in my last letter, which I think was rather muddled, that I have sent your story "Kurganikha" to a young publisher I know named Vladimir Dmitrievich Bonch-Bruevich. He is good at getting things through the censors and I hope he will get your story through as well and publish it. He will be writing you about it.

Lovingly, P. B.[94]

N° 30. F. A. ZHELTOV ❧ L. N. TOLSTOY
5 May 1894. Village of Bogorodskoe.

5 May 94

Dear Lev Nikolaevich!

From your letter I gather than in speaking about the influence of an example on children, you meant only that the example must precede the word. This is an unquestionable truth, since only that which has already taken place in a person's inner life and been brought about by his faith and life, only that can become that person's word, and in particular the *pure, living* word and not just the word of an individual, but of God himself. When accompanied by the example, the influence of the word has a stronger effect.

But isn't that a personal position and don't you find that there are general definitions of truth which can be expressed in their totality only through the word? And don't you find that one of the distinguishing features of the spirit is *purity of thought* and that this quality, inherent in every person's nature, still needs purification by way of mutual communication through the word? This is especially [true] in imparting the understanding (to children in particular) that the primary and most important necessity for a person's inner life is the concern for *self-purification* of thought — that is, the development within one's self of a strict, constant and persistent examination of one's inner world, one's progress, one's motives and aspirations and one's relationships to the outside world and one's behaviour. It seems to me that this is what a person's true life in its specific manifestations is based on.

If that is so, then how do you look upon the transmission of general religious truths through talking about them with children in school? I suggest that this should even be done in an environment such as our sectarian group, where we do have religious meetings, but not ones geared to people of such a young age. After all, there are a great many people who have recognized the truth but are still struggling with their weaknesses — why couldn't they spend some time conversing with children by way of moral and religious readings,

94 The text of the letter was dictated by Tolstoy to Pavel Ivanovich Birjukov on the day of his departure for Yasnaya Polyana (28 April).

recounting events from the lives of people who are struggling for truth — after all, that would also catch the listener's attention and play an educational role.

Of course, one of the deficiencies of our children's upbringing is not only the lack of good examples, but also the failure to equip our children with tools for consciously seeking out the path of truth amidst the surrounding darkness. Sometimes children spend so much time surrounded by a stupefying and corrupt society that their sensitivity and clear thinking become dulled and they become cold and insensitive even to good examples. In such a case a good example of an individual set before a person may serve the adult leader as an indispensable means of verification — for himself personally and as a guide to exercising a stronger influence on the child's heart, which, the more weighed down with garbage, the more work needs to be done on it. But that will come about inevitably for both the teacher and the child — one has only to establish a moral link between the two hearts whereby the content of one heart can be poured into the other.

I should like to ask you about such communication with children, whose only purpose is the transmission of general principles of truth. How do you look upon this? Don't you find this to be one of the external teaching activities which is of little benefit to the soul? It seems to me that if, along with striving for one's individual self-perfection (which must of necessity be the basis of every work), people also concentrated their efforts on the task of communicating *exclusively* (in a special sense of the word) with children, then they would be able to make their own beneficial contribution to human life. It seems to me that this is a higher aim than withdrawing from the 'world' and seeking refuge from its sins, contemplating certain things and busying one's self about others, constantly afraid of getting one's self dirty and falling into temptation. Really, I sometimes think that it's not a bad thing to occasionally get dirty and fall, as long as you don't lose sight of that light by which you live — in that case you would start thinking only about your outward purity and lose the beacon which keeps you on the path regardless of any dirt or obstacles you may encounter — and these you cannot avoid going through if you are progressing.

I am still confused by one thing, and that is the question of sexual relations. How and when is one to talk about them with children? Does one need to talk about this with them or not? This is a double-edged question and needs to be considered carefully, and I would appreciate learning your thoughts on this.

For God's sake, please do not fail to write. I can assure you that by writing me you will be offering me moral support and assistance.

Sincerely, affectionately yours,
F. Zheltov

Address: Fëdor Alekseevich Zheltov
Village of Bogorodskoe
Nizhegorod Gub.

N° 31. F. A. ZHELTOV ❧ L. N. TOLSTOY
12 May 1894. Village of Bogorodskoe.

Dear Lev Nikolaevich!

Do not be surprised that I have all at once felt the need of writing you this letter, even before receiving your reply to my last one. Over the past while so many thoughts and experiences have been accumulating within me that, even though I restrained myself from writing you for some time, I could no longer suppress my need to say what I have to say to you — especially after reading your article *The Kingdom of God* [*Tsarstvo Bozhie*]. I do want to talk to you about it and express my thoughts frankly.

I believe that the kingdom of God has an inner treasure of its own, considerably higher than all the treasures of the outside world. To share this treasure with people and give one's all for it, to hold on to it, one must make sense of one's *inner* world, and not the outside world. True, the outside world is simply a reflection of the inner, but this is one more argument in favour of the necessity to look to the inner world for the cause of the damage being done to the outer. All the institutions of evil in the outside world are but a shadow of the inner microscopic workings of the human heart, which is why the evil we see in human laws and institutions has arisen not from the conscious actions of individuals, but from the inner microcosm of the human spirit, from the denigrating of the human individual which is so strongly developed in society itself.

People's actions that go against the law of Christ arise not from some external thing imposing itself on people, but because the person doing such things has not yet begun to live and act according to the higher will, and not because he doesn't want to, but because the inner man — his true essence, his free individuality — is not yet developed in him. It seems to us that this is the result of the outer life and its demands and laws repressing the individual, covering up its light. But it seems this way only because, living according to the outside world, we mistakenly endow it with independent power, forgetting that the outer world *does not exist,* it exists only as the inner world (in its various movements) and that whatever a person can draw upon for his benefit is constantly available to him in his inner world and is always ready to serve him under any conditions and in any situation, according to the demands and requirements placed upon him by his outer world.

All those institutions we see as evil are, in effect, the combined demands of individuals living according to some kind of weakness of spirit. These weaknesses stem from the original excuse for organizing mankind's laws for regulating the life of its society. One cannot blame the people who draw up the tenets of these laws — they are only responding to the demand for it. What we see as complete and generalized had its origins in something that happened before and is still happening, namely a loss of clear thinking on the part of people who make up the society — the consciousness that the full true universal law may be realized in the lives of individuals themselves, regardless of outward circumstances.

Just as there is no evil for God, so *there is no evil — it does not exist — for the Christian.* The Christian does not live in the outer world, but is freeing himself from it. Nobody has authority over him: did Caiaphas or Pilate have authority over Christ?[95] For Christ to exist, was it necessary that there be no Caiaphas or Pilate? Did they further prevent the existence of Christians, Christ's followers? Did Nero or Caligula at any time have authority over Christians, even though they slaughtered them? How did people of faith attain such a complete freedom, a freedom independent of the outer world? Could it have been even more complete if there had been no Roman laws or persecutions or cruel inquisition tortures? All of this had to be, said Christ.[96] This is where Christianity is different from other doctrines — in that it teaches *not the change and destruction of the external world of sin and temptation independent of the believer (Matth. 8:22), but teaches how to relate to this world.* It teaches that this relationship, in accordance with the spirit of righteousness and love as consciously perceived within, is *everything.*

The outer world must burn up and it is burning up through the constant and persistent pouring into it of the fire of the spirit of love and righteousness, above all for the individual, and no external reconstruction of the world, no outward change arising from the change of some institution or another, some law or another, will do what can be done by the unnoticeable, invisible inner workings of individuals, working on the enlightenment of their own consciousness and progressing along the brightened path. This is what distinguishes the nature of this path from others: it is always open and there are always reliable means for moving along it and the outer world has no weapons with which to block it: "come unto me, and drink"[97] — it is only that man deliberately loses his ability to see it. A Christian has only one thing to say to another person as a brother, namely that he examine his own inner world, find out his identity, his joy and goodness, and attain his freedom. The individual's whole thought must be directed toward this goal, because it is the only thing that will expose the whole lie which he must behold. "The Kingdom of God is Within You" and "it is like a pearl of great price, for which a man giveth all that he hath and keepeth it for himself."[98]

So then, open up more forcefully this valuable treasure, show it to people — surely the treasure of this kingdom all by itself is not inaccessible to people's understanding and surely it can draw them to itself, just as they are drawn to their superficial capital with life's superficial charms and treasures? Is not the positive aspect of Christian teaching the exposer of the lie and can it not reveal

95 See John 19:11.
96 See Matth. 24:6.
97 John 7:37.
98 See Matth. 13:45–46.

all the negative aspects of human life? Can the negative aspects of life take form as constant, uniform, external characteristics, so that the identification thereof would forever deliver people from evil, and cannot these be future forms as well with new characteristics, as they have been in the past and present?

All these unthinking mistakes among people cannot be shown for what they are unless they first have revealed to them their *inner* errors and deviations — their false concepts of themselves, of their lives and of the law of the individual. People's errors are not due to the existence of organized violence, organized murder, but to the fact that they have admitted into their consciousness the notion that the good in their lives is an external good and that it can be protected and increased by outward actions and institutions, all interconnected by their misunderstanding of the good in an individual's life and of his obligations and rights.

One cannot regard one's visible, external life, expressed in social institutions and laws, as something separate, self-standing, independent of the individuals subject to this life. Just as capital, wealth, luxury, etc. represent partial aspirations on the part of the public and seem valuable to people only because the public, all crowding in the same direction toward a false centre, have piled up at this centre their various illusory aspirations, making them more noticeable and attractive, so too the institutions of this false human life have been forged from various blows by individuals and hold on to their significance by the same kind of public pressure.

Take the Laplander travelling by dogsled: when his dogs are tired and refuse to go on, he holds before their eyes a piece of fish tied to a long stick; the dogs, upon seeing the lure, rush toward it, run to their last breath, and carry the Laplander forward. So it is with wealth and the institutions which protect it. It is a simple matter, only understanding is lacking: let the public change its centre, set itself different goals, stop trying to press upwards from the lower steps or the back rows, from institutions or the treasures of wealth — all that will crumble like a pyramid of peas when you remove the peas at the bottom. All that we perceive in people's lives as evil is in fact merely smoke from trying to squelch the inner fire of the human spirit, which, once freed, burns clearly and brightly with no soot. So, is the whole crux of the matter in this soot and smoke?..

To sum up: *there is no external evil in the world, there is only inner evil* and therefore a Christian's energies should be directed not at the superficial removal of external appearances of evil which have taken form in the laws and institutions by which society lives, but to *changing one's attitudes to these appearances* and to bringing one's inner state to the point where external life must always lie on a lower plane than a person's inner consciousness and hence no longer represent life for him. The elimination of illegal demands is brought about very simply through the elimination of the illegal demands made by one's own self.

This, dear Lev Nikolaevich, is a brief outline of the thoughts I wanted to share with you after reading your article. I am sure this is not your last word on the subject of the Kingdom of God, you still have stronger words in reserve, which, I believe, you will come out with, since I feel the process which is at work in your heart. The thoughts you express in the "Kingdom of God" article are marvellous, as is the true and faithful progress of your spiritual work, but many people who are weak in their task of enlightening their consciousness, will still find therein things that serve their own negative, perverted interpretation and the cause of hatred — not hatred towards people's essential behaviour and actions, but towards the people themselves who act a certain way. I do not wish to imply that such conclusions can be drawn from the fundamental substance of the article, but from a strict, essential, Christian standpoint, it would have been better to permeate the whole argument more tangibly and prominently with the basis of the Christian view of the subject and set forth in a more conspicuous manner what is meant by the *treasure* of the Kingdom of God. It is essential to keep the reader close to the window through which you see God's world — that's what is needed.

Forgive me for such direct and perhaps immodest words; I write them because I trust in your responsiveness and sensitivity, and that you will offer brotherly assistance if I am mistaken and incorrect in my thinking. In any event, write me what you think of everything set forth in this letter. I shall eagerly await your reply, trusting in advance that you will not fail to keep in touch.

Affectionately,
F. Zheltov

12 May 1894.
Address: Fëdor Alekseevich Zheltov
Village of Bogorodskoe, Nizhegor. Gub.

N° 32. F. A. ZHELTOV ❧ L. N. TOLSTOY
15 May 1894. Village of Bogorodskoe.

15 May 1894.

Lev Nikolaevich!

About a week ago I sent you a registered letter to Tula — did you receive it? I doubt it, as I do not have your current address — I heard that you had left Moscow. I have already sent a second letter through Pavel Ivanovich Birjukov, who will no doubt pass it on to you. Please let me know if you receive these letters. Apart from that, I would most humbly ask you to let me know where I might obtain a copy of your latest examination of the Gospels and your essay *On Life* [*O zhizni*]. These things are of personal interest to me, as I have read excerpts from them and I desire to become acquainted with them. I await your reply,

Lovingly, F. Zheltov

Village of Bogorodskoe, Nizh. Gub.

N° 33. L. N. TOLSTOY ❧ F. A. ZHELTOV
23 May 1894. Yasnaya Polyana.

Fëdor Alekseevich,

I have received your letters and have answered[99] one of them. In another you ask me how to talk to children on the matter of sexual relations. I think that (as I mentioned to you before) this is not a particular problem of child-raising. To bring up a child well, you must live a good life in the eyes of those you are bringing up. And so in the question of sexual relations you must be as pure and righteous as possible. If you consider sexual relations a sin and live a life of chastity, you can and should teach chastity to your children; if you are striving for chastity, but have not attained it, you should explain that to your children. If you are living an unchaste life and cannot and do not wish to live otherwise, you will involuntarily hide that from your children and will not speak to them about it. That is what people do.

L. Tolstoy

The books you mention, I believe you can obtain through Posrednik.

On the reverse:
To: Fëdor Alekseevich Zheltov
Village of Bogorodskoe
Nizhegorod Gub.

N° 34. L. N. TOLSTOY ❧ F. A. ZHELTOV
End of May, after the 23rd, 1894. Yasnaya Polyana.

Fëdor Alekseevich,

I received your third letter and will not hide my displeasure with its contents. Forgive me, but the whole non-Christian structure of our lives, after eighteen hundred years of confessing Christ and after all the sensitive reasonings and sermons about love on the theme of Corinthians,[100] arises from what you are doing in your letter. Love without works is dead. We have so forgotten that, having so weighed down our life with unloving, beastly, devilish institutions that

99 See Letter N° 29.
100 See 1 Cor., Chap. 13.

love is choked in the embryo and there is nowhere for it to manifest itself and it is impossible to manifest it except in giving out a penny with the left hand while grabbing hundreds and thousands of them with our right, or in sentimental love toward *our* family, *our* wife, *our* mothers, fathers and children. And then, just as soon as the demand is heard not to destroy but simply to refuse to co-operate with these institutions which rule out the possibility of expressing love, immediately voices speak up saying that the problem is not in the institutions, but in the love. Just what kind of love can be expressed by the executioner, the soldier, the landowner, the merchant, the corrupt priest, the doctor, the lawyer?

Hence the first manifestation of love in our society inevitably comes into confrontation with institutions — not to start destroying them but to stop participating in them. As to saying, then, that the essence of the whole matter is in love and not in the institutions, it is all very well for people who think that way (like the revolutionaries) to argue that way, but not for me, who, tired of repeating the same thing over and over again, have been struggling against these views, constantly affirming the same thing: Seek the kingdom of God and his righteousness, the Kingdom of God within you, and all these things shall be added unto you.[101]

Moreover, to make a comparison, take two individuals: a non-Christian atheist who in self-sacrifice struggles against those institutions he considers dangerous to people — to his brothers — and a nominal Christian who, like English pastors and many others, reads sermons based on 13 Corinthians, but walks carefully around institutions which are beneficial to him and by which he lives, regardless of their danger to his brothers — of these two, I prefer the former, even though I don't agree with him.

Christ's disciples, just like their Master, seek the kingdom of God and his righteousness and in this search, just like the Master, come up against — inevitably come up against — non-Christian institutions. If they do not come up against them, something is wrong. I have been persecuted and so will you. That is what I think of your letter. May God help you abide in love and truth.

L. Tolstoy

N° 35. F. A. ZHELTOV ❧ L. N. TOLSTOY
23 June 1894. Samara Gubernia.

Stolypino
23 June 94

Dear, kind Lev Nikolaevich!

I am painfully tormented by the thought that you found my last letter displeasing. I wrote it not to contradict you, but simply to say what was on my

101 See Matth. 6:33; Luke 17:21.

mind that I wanted to tell you, but perhaps it was not so clearly expressed. I am in complete agreement with your arguments and am convinced that a Christian's behaviour should serve as the inevitable signs of his faith and love, without which they are dead. If the Christian has the occasion to be confronted by the institutions of evil, then all that he must do is to refrain from participating in them or co-operating with them. I did not lose sight of this in outlining my thoughts in the letter you received.

But there may be two alternatives here: first, a believing Christian, upon encountering demands that go against his conscience, refuses to do what is demanded, and this is bearing witness to the truth; alternatively: someone who understands the evil of the institution's demand destroys the *outward* appearance of the institution, and that is not bearing witness to the truth, but is an evil. I know that the spirit of your words is based on the first alternative, but what the first person does arises not from his acknowledgement of the outward evil of the world, but from the inner renewal of his understanding of life that has already taken place, which automatically shows him the path to follow in all confrontations with life, both expected and unexpected: "Think not what ye are to say, for the spirit itself will tell you what ye must say and do."[102] After all, the root of all evil is in the individual human being and not in an external institution, and therefore everything that is reflected in the visible institution is, in substance, a manifestation of a false and limited inner understanding of life on the part of individuals — this is what I meant to say in my last letter, and I think it needs to be clarified so as to realize what terrible evil holds sway in the world in the trifling deviations of each individual from the truth, from the will of God, and how much true joy and good in life is lost thereby.

I shall write you in more detail after I return home, since right now I am, because of illness, in *Samara Gubernia (Krivoluch'e, Stolypinskie Vody),* where you can write to me until 5 July, if you decide you want to respond to this brief and possibly not especially clear letter. I should be happy to receive a reply, since everything I wrote was aimed at using your words for my inner enlightenment. For God's sake forgive me for expressing myself so sharply and unrestrainedly in my last letter.

I embrace you as a brother,
Yours, F. Zheltov

N° 36. L. N. TOLSTOY ❧ F. A. ZHELTOV
7 or 8 July 1894. Yasnaya Polyana.

Thank you for your humble response to my not-so-humble letter. I ask you to forgive me if you found anything in it displeasing to you. In responding

102 See Matth. 10:19–20.

to you, I was [actually] responding to the many people who wrongly deviate from the demands of Christian teaching. That does not apply to you.

Lovingly, L. T.

On the envelope:
Fëdor Alekseevich Zheltov
Village of Bogorodskoe
Nizhegorod Gub.

N° 37. F. A. ZHELTOV ❧ L. N. TOLSTOY
6 August 1895. Village of Bogorodskoe.

My dear Lev Nikolaevich!

Yesterday I gave A. N. Dunaev a letter from Tiflis [Tbilisi], addressed to you care of me, which Aleksandr Nikiforovich has promised to send you. It concerns what is going on with the Doukhobors in the Caucasus, which you may already know about. If you should require any more concrete details on this matter, the author of this letter can supply them. Write to him if you wish to know more details.

Please accept my sincere greetings and best wishes. Also, please give my regards to Marija L'vovna.

I have a humble request for you, which I would ask you not to refuse me. I am thinking of publishing an anthology whose profits would go to set up a free public library and reading room in our village. Could you possibly provide some sort of brief article or story for this anthology? You would help me a great deal by doing this, since your story placed among the other literary works would significantly facilitate the circulation of the anthology. Please keep this in mind, and even if not right away, please do not fail to respond to my request, and if possible, could you help gather articles from other writers you are acquainted with, which would be a great help to me personally.

Please do not fail, kind Lev Nikolaevich, to write and tell me whether I can count on this.

I embrace you as a brother.
Your truly devoted and loving,
F. Zheltov

Address until 1 Sept.:
Fëdor Alekseevich Zheltov
Shornyj Rjad
Nizhegorodskaja jarmarka

N° 38. L. N. TOLSTOY ❧ F. A. ZHELTOV
19 August 1895. Yasnaya Polyana

Dear Fëdor Alekseevich,

I received the letter about the Doukhobors. Thank you for telling me about it. I cannot offer you anything for the anthology — indeed, I advise against publishing it. All these charitable balls, performances, anthologies, are not good. If somebody wants to help, they will help.

How is your health — both physical and mental? The main thing, God grant, is that the latter is good; then the former will lose its importance.

Give my regards to your mother, your wife and all those who know and remember me.

Lovingly, L. Tolstoy

19 August 1895.

On the envelope:
To: Fëdor Alekseevich Zheltov
Village of Bogorodskoe
Nizhegorod Gubernia

N° 39. F. A. ZHELTOV ❧ L. N. TOLSTOY
19 October 1895. Village of Bogorodskoe.

My dear Lev Nikolaevich!

Forgive me for not responding right away to your August letter. Your acquaintances, as well as my mother and my wife, were most touched that you remembered them and ask me to pass on to you their greetings and their love. They have also asked me to tell you that their fondest recollections, which they will always hold dear, are those associated with their visit to you and your family.

I am equally touched by your heartfelt enquiry as to my health. Yes, for three years now I have been suffering with a bad case of rheumatism, which at first prevented me even from walking. Just this summer I have been feeling comparatively better and it seems that my former pains have gone away. It is true, as you said, that it is not our bodily ailments that are important, but rather that our mental state be strong and healthy. Such a state of mind relieves our earthly, carnal life, its sufferings and deprivations, and what does one's concern for one's bodily health — for eliminating one's sufferings and deprivations — actually represent but an attempt to achieve the impossible? After all, one's whole life is made up of sufferings and deprivations and concern about the flesh is nothing but concern over prolonging a range of sensations which, like links of a chain, form a range of bodily functions. No matter how long they go on, if we could prolong them, we would still not find therein the fulness of life, its satisfaction or completion. Consequently, the sum of our life is not in them, and life cannot be measured by time: one can live a long time, *but have* little, and one can have a short life and have that which longevity in the flesh cannot give.

Physical suffering has its good side too: it aids in the refreshment and concentration of the spirit, something which we need so often, very often. My dear Lev Nikolaevich, how are we to keep ourselves in the Kingdom of Heaven, in that good state of the spirit which results in good will to mankind and peace, when so often in life, in these unjust conditions in which we live, we do not do what we ought to do, but do that which goes against the spirit and love, and we torment ourselves and slip and slide on this path?

It seems there are many such tormenting moments we have to experience, and there is only one thing to be afraid of — the possible dulling of our acuity of spirit which shows our deviation from God's path. What means of support are needed here? There are terrible moments when you imagine spiritual extinction and its consequence — spiritual death. The fleshly destruction of the individual is not as frightening as that which holds on to it for the sake of some higher demands, placed into the carnal being as its law. To be alone with this is both a terrible and a joyful moment. Terrible if there is no consciousness with it, and joyful if one serves and works for this principle, and then and only then can one say with joy, with satisfaction, with a foretaste of complete union and rest: "Father, I have done Thy will and I come to Thee."

I think that all human activity in either its negative or positive form hangs upon only two basic propositions of life: from the fear of being left alone with one's self, fleeing from one's inner concentration, which is deadened by the tormenting and purposeless vanity of external worldly activities by which people are in a hurry to bespatter the clarity and purity of their consciousness, and from the constant and persistent toil they expend on themselves, on the purification of the paths of their inner consciousness, and the frequent inner examinations and conversations with the spirit, the source of life.

Deviations from the middle to one side or another also contribute to a person's good or bad attitude to life. Sensitivity to one's turns and movements and even one's failings is a sign of life in one's soul. For the time being this sensitivity is alive — and benefits man. But it is frightful to imagine this sensitivity dying out — spiritual death, annihilation, complete spiritual annihilation; can anything then be done with the individual and his flesh there in the depths of his spiritual and carnal being?! Perhaps it is reflected in another way even in his carnal being unified by the spirit of life. Perhaps at least part of his bodily death will be something different for him, and his survival will cost him many years of his life? Possibly — no, probably — his spiritual annihilation is not, in substance, the annihilation of the spiritual within himself, but only the development of the forces which run counter to the spirit, which merge into a continuous series of pressures man experiences on the spiritual principle of his life.

It is always useful to talk with our inner self; it is always waiting and ready to reveal something to us. The outer world distracts us from that. This is especially noticeable in children, in how they develop. And we often think about them, how they are distracted by the world, pressured by temptations — how do we keep them from all that? Can we act to limit their freedom where we see that they are imitating others simply because they have not clearly recognized evil? What pain and suffering we experience when we see this, and feel that when it comes to influencing a child's heart there is no one prompting from the sidelines and we are all alone, and we can't yet muster our own courage, we struggle every moment, and sometimes find ourselves taking different measures instead of those which are needed. If we tell them: "Don't do that!," "Don't go there!," because it is wrong and not good and prevent them from doing something outwardly *by prohibition,* when we see evil directly, well, perhaps that is a handy way out, but should we really be making use of it, even in exceptional circumstances? I am asking this in regard to children, who in any case may obey us, though possibly with discontent in their heart. How do you look upon this?

We feel we bear a moral responsibility for our children. If we *demand* obedience, we are not exercising restraint and perhaps acting improperly, but by refraining from physical violence perhaps we are benefiting them. How do we react when they ask us if they can do this or that with a predetermined look and an outward hypnotic charm, and then they may or may not do it, depending on what you say or how you *demand,* and then you see that it is not their inner conviction that is keeping them from doing it — it does not expose the evil at that moment — but rather the *demand: "Don't do it!,"* even though it leads to hidden discontent. Doesn't that amount to moral violence and isn't it a deceptive method?

But perhaps there is a benefit from the demand "Don't do it!" — a person doesn't get accustomed to wrong-doing and his temptation lessens when it becomes less accessible. I'll say frankly that I cannot make up my mind either for or against on this question, but some dark and muddled feeling in my heart is struggling with a reluctance to give up this method, not to let it go when I could use it, and this muddled sense is timidly defending itself, but not in precise terms, and it would be good for me if you would express your opinion on this subject, which I earnestly ask you to do.

As regards your refusal to contribute a manuscript for the anthology, I shall say right now that it grieved me. There is no denying your view on artificial aid, it is quite justified, but I think the project I described is an exception, and therefore, without going into further detail, I trust that you will believe me and share my point of view. If you can find a suitable time to arrange it, please do not refuse — after all, it is all the same to you how your manuscripts get into print — in a journal, an anthology, a newspaper. If you accept, I shall get the project started and contact others; if not, I shall abandon it.

Please cover my deficiencies, along with this letter, with your brotherly love. I am writing to you as someone who will not negatively interpret what has not been clearly and sufficiently expressed.

I embrace you from my heart as a brother,
Lovingly,
F. Zheltov

19 Oct. 1895.

Address: Fëdor Alekseevich Zheltov
Village of Bogorodskoe, Nizhegor. Gub.

Nº 40. F. A. ZHELTOV ❧ L. N. TOLSTOY
27 October 1895. Village of Bogorodskoe.

Dear Lev Nikolaevich!

I recently learnt that you are still at Yasnaya, and just the other day I sent you a letter to Moscow. I hope it will still get to you, but thought I should let you know about it by writing you today. I am sure you will not deny me a response to that letter. I hope to write you again soon. In the meantime please accept my best wishes for peace and the Kingdom of God for your spirit and to assure you of my sincere brotherly love.

I embrace you in the name of Christly love
F. Zheltov

27 Oct. 95.

Nº 41. L. N. TOLSTOY ❧ F. A. ZHELTOV
18 December 1895. Moscow.

18 December 95. Moscow

Dear Fëdor Alekseevich,

I wanted to answer your letter as soon as I received it, as I have some very definite thoughts on the question you raise, but I have been delayed in this up to now, partly by poor health, partly by the bustle of life and duties. I have given a great deal of thought to the upbringing of children. There are issues where one comes to doubtful conclusions, and there are issues where the conclusions one comes to are final, and one does not feel one's self in a position either to change them or add anything to them. Such are the conclusions I have come to in regard to child-raising. They are as follows: Child-rearing is a complex and difficult process only so long as we want to educate our children (or anyone else) without educating ourselves. If we realize that we can train others only through ourselves, by training ourselves, this eliminates the question about child-raising and the one question of life remains: how are we ourselves to live? I am not aware of a single action of educating children that does not involve educating ourselves. How do we feed and clothe children, how do we put them to bed, how do we teach them? Exactly the same way as we do ourselves. If a father or mother dresses, eats and sleeps in moderation, and works and studies, then the children will do the same.

I would offer two rules for child-rearing: Don't just live well yourself, but work on yourself, constantly perfect yourself, and, Don't hide any [part] of your life from your children. It is better for children to know about their parents' weaknesses than for them to feel that their parents have one life to show them and another life they keep hidden from them. All the difficulties in child-rearing arise when parents refuse not only to correct their own faults but to even admit to them, justifying them to themselves, but still do not want to see these faults in their children. This is where all the difficulty lies, and all the struggle with children.

Children are far more morally perspicacious than adults — often without showing it or even realizing it themselves — they see not only their parents faults, but the worst fault of all — their parents' hypocrisy, and consequently lose respect for and interest in their parents' precepts. Parental hypocrisy in child-rearing is a most common occurrence, and children are sensitive and notice it right away, and then turn aside and become perverted. Truth is the first and primary condition for the effectiveness of spiritual influence, and therefore it is the first condition for child-raising. And so as not to be fearful of showing children the whole truth about one's life, one must make one's life good or at least less bad. And thus the upbringing of others is included in the upbringing of one's self, and nothing else is needed.

Lovingly, L. Tolstoy

N° 42. F. A. ZHELTOV ❧ L. N. TOLSTOY

29 December 1895. Village of Bogorodskoe.

29 December 1895

My dear, dear Lev Nikolaevich!

Your letter brought a great deal of comfort to me. It answered the most vital questions of my heart, which, because of the great discrepancy between my outward situation and my inner consciousness, have always caused bitter feelings and pain in my soul. It is with bitterness that I remember the time when our children were at their most innocent age, with their bright childlike hearts and with their pure childlike simplicity and freedom, encouraging the spirit of hope, making me think that I would find the power to keep them in this condition and protect them from the influence of the outside world. But as they grow in age, this sphere of influence over children expands and snatches them unto itself like a monster, pouring its poison into their consciousness, painting their thoughts and feelings in different colours.

The more I realize this, the more pain and suffering I feel, and the more I am tormented by my own powerlessness and helplessness to find any way out. I can only come to the conclusion you speak of, and that is to delve into my own individual position in life, and insofar as it expresses the truth, it will bring benefit to the lives of my children, since the parents' way of life, their behaviour and convictions are inevitably reflected in the children, and when I see even that little bit falling upon the children's hearts, it means that there is no use setting one's self to seek out other methods of raising and protecting the children beyond those which relate to one's own individuality, to its correction and perfection.

That, it seems, should include the whole question about influencing and rearing children, but do we still not have to think about the outward circumstances we live in, with that all-too-common hypocrisy of life which has created a special atmosphere, penetrating right to the marrow in every sphere of human activity, everywhere — in school, in society, in literature, in entertainment, in the theatre — everywhere one feels the breath of that infected atmosphere. Particularly frightening is its special distinguishing feature which we see traces of at every step. Our inevitable encounters with it are not as frightening as the way it slips by intensely and intrusively, as if humanity had already become thoroughly at ease with it and was not aware of the evil but facilitating its expansion.

One must, in this situation, have some concept of the level of the general consciousness to understand how much, how very much is required to uplift it, and how much greater the burden of responsibility on those whose consciousness has been enlightened and who use the tools of upliftment for evil. As regards the public consciousness, both school and literature exercise considerable power, both hold people's consciousness at a certain constant level and direction, and they can be brought out of this hypnotic state only by establishing freedom. But this cannot be done without a special element in their consciousness, and consequently some sort of stimulus is needed to make this element appear. I do think that this situation in society, too, has a not inconsiderable influence on children's consciousness, and there is no way it can be examined independently of family upbringing. If so, then how are we to help bring about the possible freedom of children in this regard? Not to help in this matter would be sinful.

Underlying this, of course, there should also be what you talked about in your letter, but there are many important secondary phenomena which can paralyse one's personal influence and the power of example and render powerless the seedlings of life that have begun sprouting in the soul, feeding other inclinations in children at the soul's expense. One of these which we are accustomed to venerate and bow down to, frightful to say, is literature, namely the special relief image it presents of the make-up of today's society. Its influence is even more pernicious in that a lot of vulgarity and baseness is served up with a bouquet of sensuality in tempting and poeticized images. Whatever thoughts the child may have had, whatever his young soul lived by, what he felt through his purity, starts to waver and decay, chastity and the religiousness of thought are slain and, instead, the imagination becomes filthy, and consciousness, once abased, easily follows other paths to all the worldly temptations which the imagination has close associations with. What do you think about this? I apologize for this letter being so fragmented and uneven — I write in a hurry to take advantage of the opportunity of sending it to you. I bow before you and embrace you with all my heart.

Lovingly, F. Zheltov

N° 43. F. A. ZHELTOV ❧ L. N. TOLSTOY
18 January 1896. Village of Bogorodskoe.

18 Jan. 1896

My dear Lev Nikolaevich!

I am writing to you at a moment of severe emotional turmoil, from which I hope to free myself by talking with you. I am bound by a great many unreasonable conditions of life — a life which now, as my children are growing up, weighs even more heavily on my consciousness: I feel a moral responsibility for them. I think I myself have wandered far onto a false path from which I cannot extricate myself, let alone help the children in their situation. All around is darkness, and in this darkness people are rushing about in different directions, they are living in torment and sufferings and are not aware of their terrible situation, considering life to be the phantasm and deceit of their clouded imagination.

Should I just forget about everything and walk away, as I sometimes think in moments of despair, but would I do any better by walking away, would I be helping myself or others? Everything around me, which I myself am bathing in, all that clouds my reason, so much so that I myself sometimes give in to the deception and follow it, until I turn my thought around.

You who live another life cannot imagine how tangled up we get in our feverish commercial and monetary affairs, how completely they absorb us, overburdening our whole consciousness. Everything around me is permeated to the marrow with the exclusive interests of personal gain and the creating of living conditions which entertain selfishness, pride, fleshly lust, self-conceit and all the capricious demands of idleness and luxury. Each event in life is marked by the same manifestations of self-indulgence and crude self-satisfaction, which irritate the sensibilities of others. If there is anything good in our sectarianism, it is drowning in this sea of common errors and is incapable of leading a life of its own, bringing itself down to the lowest common denominator of its environment. Our children are drawn by the lures and tawdry trinkets scattered about, thinking they will find pleasure in them. We ourselves are confronted in our experience by issues we are not in a position to resolve properly. Only yesterday here there was a marriage between a sectarian girl and an Orthodox Christian, and the church authority has got its hands on her free soul, and subjugated her conscience, which has been confused by illusions.

However unavoidable this phenomenon is, it is still sad, and our children are exposed to these examples and indirectly participate in them — when their friends invite them to a party,[103] they look at the others and want to go; how am I to convince them they shouldn't go? And if they go, my consciousness is tormented by having abandoned them to temptation. What am I to do in such a situation? And there are so many questions like this. I am to blame for the birth of my children, because of my personal inability to completely carry out the law of God within myself. What will happen if I am also the cause of their fall and temptation? Where is the path to the children's souls to protect them from that? We are pressed upon by our environment, it completely stifles my weak individuality, I am swallowed up by it, even though I have inside of me nothing in common with it.

A series of deceptions and annoyances constantly moves before my eyes my whole life long, and draws me in, and so much effort is required to stave off the charms and enticements of this 'beast from the deep,' this image of physicality which darkens the true sense. This is the first crisis point, which is followed by other deviations from the path: "Fall down and worship me"[104] — and I think the significance of that power is expressed more forcefully in our environment than anywhere else. Having been born into this circle, having grown up in it and not being able to get out, I feel an even greater responsibility for the children. One must be more alert, more fearful of an uneven step, so as not to stray even from the ray of light gleaming and shining over the path — not because I want to transmit something to the children, but just so as not to inflict any damage to their soul by a thoughtless act or demand, and then I think, wouldn't it be better to change their environment to make the way to life easier for them?

103 "And these parties are held by church people, as everywhere else, with dancing, music, etc." — Note by F. A. Zheltov.

104 See Matth. 4:9, where the Devil tells Jesus: "All these things will I give Thee, if Thou wilt fall down and worship me."

I have not given my children over to any kind of 'science' — the learned wisdom of this world is foolishness with God[105] — but have I done the right thing? Maybe the other way they would have personally been freer to keep to the true path; perhaps the environment, rather than science, would have had more of a beneficial influence on them both inwardly and outwardly? I am now thinking about this, about the younger children — only in respect to easing their moral and spiritual position. I do not have a good idea of what they would be surrounded with there — that is an environment you are well acquainted with, what will it offer them?

Please believe that this is a very painful question for me to work out, and perhaps it is not clear to me for reasons of my own weakness, and possibly this is not the primary question I should be working out for myself, but what am I to do if I am temporarily bound and not able to go where I wish, where I am led? As I go on suffering with this I think about how I might at least ease the children's situation before they are drawn into life. Sometimes I am confused by the words of the Gospel: "He that hateth not his father, mother, children for My sake (and forsaketh them not?) is not worthy of Me";[106] does that mean we shouldn't care about them, *but only about God,* — the latter includes the former — or does it mean walking away from a situation admitted to be false, giving up everything and breaking ties with one's family?... How do you understand these words? And again I ask: should one forbid children, by prohibition, to do that which is considered wrong, even though they might find the prohibition unpleasant? And how do I maintain my link with them without violating their love and attachment to me, or should I hold on only to the latter, sacrificing their conduct, even though it might be harmful to their souls? Please be so kind, dear Lev Nikolaevich, as to write me and tell me as a brother what you think.

Sincerely, lovingly,
F. Zheltov

Fëdor Alekseevich Zheltov
Village of Bogorodskoe
Nizheg. Gub.

N° 44. F. A. ZHELTOV ❧ L. N. TOLSTOY
7 April 1897. Village of Bogorodskoe.

Dear Lev Nikolaevich!

I would like very much to hear your reaction to my views about Jesus' individuality and about the meaning of his words regarding Christ, the Son

105 See 1 Cor. 3:19.
106 See Matth. 10:37: "He that loveth father or mother more than Me is not worthy of Me: and he that loveth son or daughter more than Me is not worthy of Me."

of God, etc., which I outlined to you in the letter which I sent through A. N. Dunaev. Can all this arise out of Christ's teachings, or does it represent an artificial attaching to His teachings of something that could not stem from them? I think that everything I have said is indeed the basis on which the whole moral aspect of Christ's teachings must rest.

One cannot look upon the moral aspect of His teachings all by itself: it must arise from the quality of the universal inner law which has entered the human race not by the will of man. Can you look at it any other way? To explain Christ's teaching in this fashion, to present the true point of view on Him, means giving the original key to the understanding of the meaning of this teaching, which could well fit in the entry door; but without actually opening the door, one cannot easily walk in to Christ's domain. We are so confused by interpretations on the part of the ecclesiastical world, which has long lost its closeness to Christ and lost the key to His teachings, that we cannot so easily get rid of the half-heathen, half-Jewish concepts imposed upon us and arrive at the practical profession of Christ's teachings.

In the matter of explaining this teaching it is essential to start with the person of Jesus, as the expounder of the *inner* universal Christ; once we have recognized this Christ we can no longer dwell on Jesus and his authority: "*He* said this, therefore it is true." Then the Christ, the Son, will have become [for us] that which lives in man's individuality. By virtue of its universal humanity, its closeness to every person's heart, it can become our support, taking the place of Jesus' personality as the expounder of this truth in our worship. After all, one cannot take Jesus' words "he that believeth in Me shall never die"[107] etc. as relating to His personality: in His teaching Jesus clearly presented the idea of rejecting one's bodily personality for the life of the spirit *in all living things*, and that living power, or understanding, is what He recognizes as that which exists and must exist; the rest is only outward appearance, which cannot constitute actual life.

I recently read about Lao-Tzu. He has a splendid definition of this essence, which can be described by the word *Tao* — this is the same thing Christ speaks about, and in whose name He speaks, and hence in His teachings this *Tao* must be recognized as the point of departure for all our reasonings.

The same thing is expressed in your article *On Life* [*O zhizni*], and this same view, as I see it, must inevitably be merged with the moral teachings of Christ, which can make it fuller and more accessible for an understanding and a more lively and solid acceptance of Him.

I would ask you to write me what you think of this in the name of love and brotherly sharing. I shall most eagerly await your reply, which will be very important for the raising of my spirit, which is so often weak.

107 Cf. John 11:26: "whosoever liveth and believeth in me shall never die."

I have sent Mazaev's second letter (in response to my reply) to Aleksandr Nikiforovich, who will no doubt pass it along to you.[108] The letter is particularly interesting in that it clearly sets forth that deviation I have been talking about in regard to the understanding of Christ.

Lovingly,
F. Zheltov

7 April 1897.

Address: Fëdor Alekseevich Zheltov
Village of Bogorodskoe
Nizhegor. Gub.

N° 45. L. N. TOLSTOY ❧ F. A. ZHELTOV
10 April 1897. Moscow.

Dear Fëdor Alekseevich,

The thoughts you expressed in your letter to Mazaev and to me about the meaning of the Son of God are indeed close to my heart and fully shared by me, as they are the same thoughts which twenty years ago formed the basis of my regeneration, and which I outlined in as much detail as I could in the full translation and harmony of the Gospels, and later in an abbreviated translation, as well as in the book *On Life,* and in everything I have written since then concerning religious questions. What you have expressed — and it is very good that they are the same thoughts — is a great joy to me. If you have expressed them without reading the translation and harmony of the Gospels, then this only proves that these ideas are true and so natural that for the sincere person they arise all by themselves from reading the Gospels. But if (which is more likely) you read the translation and harmony of the Gospels and made these ideas your own without thinking about their source, as often happens, then this is an even greater cause for joy, and confirms even more the truthfulness of such an understanding of the substance of life, since this understanding is none other than the very light of God dwelling in us, which

108 P. A. Mazaev, a wealthy Molokan, lived in the Don region; he published sectarian literature. Zheltov's letter was written after his visit to Tolstoy in Moscow in March 1897. On 8 March, Tolstoy described this visit and their meeting with V. V. Pan'kov, an Old Believer, in a letter to Vladimir Chertkov: "The conversation between the old man and Zheltov was most interesting. The old man tried to persuade Zheltov that if one did not believe in the divinity of Christ, it wasn't right to continue supporting this superstition at their meetings. At this point it came out that a young Molokan by the name of Dubovskoj had broken away, along with several friends, from his community precisely over this point of not recognizing the divinity of Christ. He feels he cannot participate in prayer services which begin with the words: 'In the name of the Father and the Son and the Holy Spirit.' Hence these dissidents are no different from Unitarians. I was greatly impressed and delighted by this" (*PSS* 88: 15).

has recognized itself and detached itself from that animal entity into which it was sent and with which it is associated in this world.

All people must come to this consciousness, and the main — indeed the only — task of our life is to bring ourselves into accord with this consciousness. We can bring ourselves into accord with it in words and in deeds, primarily in the business of life, so that our light may shine before men.[109]

The only good in our lives consists in kindling this light within ourselves, in raising up the son of God within ourselves, and the kindling of this light in the world will cause it to shine for other people as well. Thus it is that the one thing needful, the seeking out of the kingdom of God and His righteousness, fulfills both purposes — the inner and the outer. Thus, helping each other in brotherhood, we shall bring about this "one thing needful"[110] both in word and, more importantly, in deed.

Your outline in the letter is very good; it is evident that you have fully mastered the subject and that the idea is clear to you in all details, and hence I think that it is very useful to circulate such ideas.[111]

My heart is glad for that spiritual unity which I feel with you as a result of this letter of yours.

I greet you and all my friends in brotherhood.

Lovingly, L. Tolstoy

10 April

On the envelope:
Fëdor Alekseevich Zheltov
Village of Bogorodskoe
Nizhegorod Gubernia
Registered

109 See Matth. 5:16.

110 See Luke 10:42.

111 Beginning in 1895, Zheltov participated in the publication of the journal *Dukhovnyj khristianin* [The Spiritual Christian], where he published his religious-philosophical articles. The years 1908–1911 saw the publication of his brochures in St. Petersburg: Follow me [*Sleduj za mnoj*], Two paths (On the letter and the spirit) [*Dva puti (O bukve i dukhe)*], A reasonable service (From correspondence with friends) [*Razumnoe sluzhenie (Iz perepiski s druz'jami)*], What is truth? [*Chto est' istina?*], On the green twig [*O zelënoj palochke*]. The first three as cited are preserved in the library at Yasnaya Polyana.

N° 46. F. A. ZHELTOV ❧ L. N. TOLSTOY
21 April 1897. Village of Bogorodskoe.

21 Apr. 1897

Dear Lev Nikolaevich!

Your letter brought me unspeakable joy and refreshment. I did not actually think that the ideas expressed in my letters would be new to you. From what I had read of your book *On Life,* and your *Brief Synopsis of the Gospel* [*Kratkoe izlozhenie Evangelija*], I could not help but be aware of the general principles in respect to the understanding of the Gospel teaching. For some reason it seemed to me that I had chosen a new point of view and a new approach to illuminating this subject. Perhaps I have not succeeded in expressing what I was thinking, but it is more likely that my consciousness has more fully and clearly appropriated that truth which is hidden in man's soul and spread abroad throughout the world. "The wind bloweth where it listeth, and thou hearest the sound thereof, but canst not tell whence it cometh, and whither it goeth."[112]

It is good if a person can feel Christ as a living force connected with his bodily individuality, and not as an historical personage standing among other human beings and distinguished only by his special relationship to the world. In the former instance a person looks upon everything as his inner, living law which dwells in his individuality not by his own will, whereas in the latter, even accepting that Christ is not God but a person — albeit a person who has given himself over to the will of God and confessed His law which He has expressed to mankind — He will still be looked upon as an *outside* authority. Man's true concept of Christ will come about when he transfers his concept of Him into his inner world and feels Him within himself as a living power independent of his [personal] will. That is not simply a particular understanding of life, it is the *basis* of true understanding, the *power* of this understanding, its source, as was expressed in Christ's conversations with the Samaritan woman and Nicodemus.[113]

After all, the sense of conscience in man's soul is more than a mere external reflection, it is not something dependent on human will and disposition, it is the reflection of that which reigns in the world and which is leading the world to goodness. It makes itself known all on its own. And it is vital to keep one's receptivity to this intangible principle in order, as we are told in the parable of the servants and their lord.[114] The closer a man is to this principle, the more he forgets his own self and the stronger he is in matters of true behaviour. He

112 John 3:8.
113 See the Gospel of John, Chap. 4 and 3, respectively.
114 See Matth. 25:14–29.

has one teacher and one mentor, who is always with him, and in him dwells the whole fulness of life.

I embrace you in brotherhood and thank you for your letter from the bottom of my heart. Your friends send you their greetings. We spent a very joyous Easter holiday in communion and discussions based on your letter. If you feel you have anything to say, I shall be most happy to receive a letter from you.

Lovingly, F. Zheltov

F. A. Zheltov
Village of Bogorodskoe
Nizhegor. Gub.

N° 47. F. A. ZHELTOV ❧ L. N. TOLSTOY
27 December 1900. Village of Bogorodskoe.

Dear Lev Nikolaevich,

Today I had a visit from the peasant Antipin,[115] to whom you showed compassion in his endeavour to bring his complaint to court. He asked me to write to you about his feelings of gratitude to you for the brotherly help you gave him. In so doing I would ask you to accept my deep, heartfelt gratitude as well, as I had hoped that you would set this fellow on the right path and afford him whatever help he needed.

Antipin told me you wished to talk about his case to your acquaintance — Kuzminskij, I think it was — while he was passing through Moscow en route from Kiev. If so, then please do all you can for the sake of this man's peace. I told Antipin that you would not be postponing this matter but taking care of it as you had said, and he will probably come to Moscow again if necessary.

Perhaps you will write me again if there is anything to tell me about this matter.

Sincerely, lovingly,
F. Zheltov

27 December 1900.
Village of Bogorodskoe
Nizhegor. Gub.

115 *A. A. Antipin* (1864–1918) — an Old Believer, a peasant from the village of Vorsma in the Gorbatov district of Nizhegorodsk Province, who was sentenced to exile in the Transcaucasus for his outspoken remarks on the Eucharist. Tolstoy appealed for help to the prominent jurist A. F. Koni, and the Moscow district court commuted his exile to a three-month prison term. At the end of December 1900, Antipin thanked Tolstoy (see *PSS* 72:535). In September 1918, Antipin was executed after being accused of counter-revolutionary activity.

N° 48. F. A. ZHELTOV ❧ L. N. TOLSTOY
27 December 1900. Village of Bogorodskoe.

Dear Lev Nikolaevich,

I have a number of questions I have been wanting to ask you for some time now so as to clarify and put to rest all the thoughts they have given rise to.

I thought I would take the occasion of my letter today to just mention the following points:

Do you think it is necessary to have a closing audible prayer at the end of meetings, such as when sectarians gather on celebration days, for example, for Scriptural readings, discussions or talks about religion, and is it necessary to have a set order for such meetings in the interests of a closer and fuller unity of thought on the core substance of the meeting, or to bring out the true significance of the meeting and man's relationship to God?

How does one avoid the negative aspects of this, which might serve as a temptation for those who are weak in spirit when it comes to ritual, rules and forms?

Christ's words are clear on the subject of prayer. It is evident from his example that his prayer was always in solitude. But we have to deal with customs that have been introduced, albeit not for bad purposes, into our meetings. Our meetings close with the whole congregation joining in a prayerful appeal to God, but might not this be, as a general rule, a hindrance to the life of the spirit?

To me, prayer is just like the threshing or milling of grain into the flour needed to make bread, and as such it can be the personal undertaking of every individual on his own, but for public events it is only the result of this undertaking that is needed, while the actual threshing or milling should be done in one's *own* barn and with one's *own* millstones.

The same, I think, should apply to our meetings, which should be strictly religious and instructive, but without any occasion for a hindrance to the spirit and the introduction of rules. If that be so, then how do we deal with what has been held on to by tradition, and what do we put in its place simply to confirm one's faith and make clear what should be done in the way of God's service *outside* the meetings — not in words of gratitude or petition, but in the actual practical worship of God in spirit and in truth, in the work that is expressed through the will of the Father?

There is a need for this, and I would ask you, dear Lev Nikolaevich, to write me your thoughts on this.

I ask you to accept heartfelt greetings and love from me and my family and to convey our good wishes to your whole family.

Your deeply devoted,
F. Zheltov

27 Dec. 1900

Address:
Fëdor Alekseevich Zheltov
Village of Bogorodskoe
Nizheg. Gub.

N° 49. L. N. TOLSTOY ❧ F. A. ZHELTOV
30 December 1900. Moscow.

I received your letter, Fëdor Alekseevich. I shall do what I can for Antipin. At the moment your friend Khristofor Ivanovich is visiting me. He asks that you pay a visit to his wife and allay her concerns about him.[116]

You have answered your own question.

Prayer cannot be other than in solitude. If meetings are necessary for communion, I would recommend readings and talks, and besides that, on celebratory holidays gathering together the poor of whatever faith, and feeding and serving them yourselves.

Lev Tolstoy

30 Dec.

On the envelope:
To: Fëdor Alekseevich Zheltov
Village of Bogorodskoe
Nizhegorod Gubernia

N° 50. F. A. ZHELTOV ❧ L. N. TOLSTOY
17 September 1909. Village of Bogorodskoe.

In the name of peace and love.

To my deeply respected [Lev Nikolaevich] in the unity of the Spirit in Christ (John 17:21)
Lev Nikolaevich!

My heart is glad at your cheerful state of mind as reported in our papers. It is indeed a joy to feel that the unity of the Spirit of the Father of life is bringing people closer and closer together, and that the time is not far distant when the hymn of heaven — "Glory to God in the highest, and on earth peace, good will toward men"[117] — will resound joyfully in all human hearts.

116 *Khristofor Ivanovich Shalashov* (1860s–1923) — a Molokan sectarian peasant of Nizhegorod Gubernia. In December 1900, he went to Moscow on foot to see Tolstoy and spent several days in Tolstoy's home in Khamovniki. His wife was Domna Vasil'evna Shalashova (d. 1922).
117 Luke 2:14.

This spiritual joy is already now awakening many human hearts to a new and joyous spiritual life and many people are already devoting their labours to the development of those spiritual seeds of life that are to bring to bloom the "fruits of the spirit" in people, so as to give mankind the true bread of life, giving people not a carnal, temporal life but a spiritual, eternal life. Knowing that your efforts are directed to this very aspect of life, we (I speak not only for myself but also on behalf of a number of people who have a similar feeling and awareness) are especially happy to share this joyous feeling with you.

Looking more deeply into life, one sees that in spite of its negative aspects, in spite of the whole carnal vanity of life, this life is being permeated, under the influence of eternal laws, with something new and all-embracing, subjecting everything to itself, and He Who is eternally 'coming' to the truth, Who stands at the end of everything embodied in life, is coming indeed.

Believing in this, one obtains the spiritual revelation which shows how simple the truth is which is hidden in mankind, and how close it is to every one of us. "And it is not in heaven, to bring it down thence, and not on the earth, to extract it therefrom; it is in the mouth and in the heart of every person" (Rom. 10:6–8).[118] And every hour and every minute it is being confirmed in life itself.

Recently, when I happened to be among thousands of people travelling to the Nizhegorod market, amid the commercial bustle and vast darkness ready to swallow up human souls, these words of Christ became very clear to me: "As in the days of Noah: they were eating and drinking, marrying…so shall also the coming of the Son of man be."[119] And: "As lightning lighteneth the darkness, so will be His appearing."[120]

This I saw with my own eyes. Amidst the gloom of commerce, the people who were travelling to pursue their own personal affairs were not satisfied with that, but sought an opportunity to come together spiritually, to use this time not just for earthly profit, but also for spiritual, heavenly gain. And light broke through the surrounding gloom, people came together and served the spirit of life by developing true spiritual concepts and by exchanging ideas; like the infirm at the font of healing waters, they received healing and strength, joy and firmness of faith and spirit.

In close unity with those thirsting for spiritual goodness I had the opportunity to observe how among the various beliefs and outward identifications and convictions, even among people of different nationalities, there began to reign the true spirit of life which was bringing them together, and how closely human thoughts were starting to come together through being uplifted to the mountaintop, the abode of the law of the spirit. Here before me were people

118 See also Deut. 30:11–14.
119 See Matth. 24:37–39.
120 Cf. Luke 17:24.

who called themselves Adventists, Stundists, Baptists, Molokans, Spiritual Evangelists, Free-thinkers, Orthodox Christians, Old Believers, *Subbotniki*,[121] Jews, Muslims, etc. — and all these people in their general spiritual conversation with each other, it seemed, were more closely drawn to each other than ever before, and in observing this, I felt and rejoiced that here was the path of unification, that here was operating the same spirit of truth which unites people into a single whole, which Christ commended to his disciples.

I was especially struck by one young Muslim who began expounding the new spiritual concepts that were now becoming popular in the Muslim world, which so clearly define the beginnings of their road to Christ.

> All faiths (he said) are different lamps which people need amidst the darkness they find themselves in, whereas Christianity in its true meaning is the source of light, and people's eyes are being opened thereby, just as after a night's sleep when the sun rises. The effect of Christianity is the same as the effect of the sun's rays on the earth: it is not something violent, but meek, calm and peaceful; it acts upon everyone with gentleness and tenderness and yet what an enormous life-giving force pours forth from them: everything that lives, breathes and develops, draws its strength only from these rays.
>
> The Koran says: "Cover those that walk with you with the wing of your affection, and if they are not obedient, then say: I am part of what you are doing."
>
> Mohammed said: "My father sinned, and I do not do the same." And he said again after the bloodshed that followed his sermon: "I came not to you in the beginning with a sword, but with words of prophecy, and if you had listened to them, you would not have created that which you now suffer from."

This is the true law of the Koran. That it has been distorted is reflected in other faiths as well.

All faiths, as expressed by the spirit through revelation, lead to that spiritual perfection which is expressed in its high aspirations by Christianity.

I greeted these thoughts with a deep feeling of joy and could not wait to share them with you, dear and respected Lev Nikolaevich.

"If the branches begin to soften, ye know that summer is near; so too if all this begins to come to pass, believe that the Kingdom of Heaven is already nigh, standing at the door."[122]

One feels that the time of change of life is already upon us, mankind is passing to a new stage of life, is putting its foot on the next step of its spiritual development, and there is only one task facing those who truly and

121 *Subbotniki* (Sabbatarians) — a group of 'Spiritual Christians' very close to the Molokans, who held their religious gatherings on Saturday rather than Sunday. The word is derived from the Russian word for 'Sabbath' or 'Saturday.' Bondarev was a Sabbatarian — cf. Part I, Note 6 (page 6) above.

122 See Mark 13:28–29; Luke 21:29–31.

intelligently believe, and that is to work together for the spiritual development of mankind, to bring to bear on this all the forces of the mind and heart, and if one cannot do that, then to do all one can — so as *not to get in the way.*

By this means will come about the spiritual birth of Christ, His embodiment, His second coming into the world.

Further to my conversation with the Muslim, it was interesting to learn of his acquaintance with ancient and modern Arabic literature, from which he quoted several excerpts which are close to your views. Moreover, he recommended becoming acquainted with the teachings of the Muslim Sufi sect, as well as with the works of the Arab writer Al-Imam Ghazzali[123] (a spiritual Sufi) entitled "Ibne" (philosophy) — he is a Spanish Moor.

After that the unrecognized Arab philosopher, the vegetarian Akhmed *Abu al-'Ala' al-Ma'arri*[124] After that his work *Alluzumiyat.* The author's name in Arabic is more precisely pronounced: *Ebul'-Guliæ-l'-maarrija.*[125]

If you have the opportunity to obtain these works, please acquaint yourself with them and give them to others to do the same. If they have not yet been translated into Russian, ask some of the specialists in Oriental languages and literatures to translate them into Russian for general religious use.

If you wish to write to the Muslim who told me all this, his name and address are as follows: *Akhmet Sjunjaev, City of Orenburg.*

From the bottom of my heart I wish you bodily and spiritual health for the benefit of all mankind and for the attainment of even greater joy in the fruits of victory and the triumph of the spirit.

Your truly devoted
F. Zheltov

17 Sept. 1909
Village of Bogorodskoe, Nizhegor. Gub.

Address: Fëdor Alekseevich Zheltov
Village of Bogorodskoe
Nizhegorod Gubernia

123 *Imam Ghazzali* — Muslim philosopher (1058–1111).

124 *Akhmed Abu al-'Ala' al-Ma'arri* — Arabic poet and philosopher (973–1057).

125 Pronunciation indicated on the basis of the Cyrillic transcription.

N° 51. L. N. TOLSTOY ❧ F. A. ZHELTOV
12 October 1909. Yasnaya Polyana.

12 Oct. 1909. Yasnaya Polyana

Dear Fëdor Alekseevich,

I received your letter in good time and, while intending every day to reply to it, have postponed it until today.

Please forgive me. What you say about Sufism is familiar to me. The true understanding of life and the consciousness of man's relationship to the Principle of All and the law of life and human activity arising from that relationship, consisting in love, that is, in the union of one's life with the manifestation of this Principle in all beings and especially in human beings like ourselves, such an understanding of life and the law arising therefrom are common to all religions in their true sense. Also common to all religions are their misinterpretation and darkening by their followers who do not understand their true sense, and their restoration to their true sense that arises out of these misinterpretations. In the Muslim faith this applies to Sufism and other teachings, especially the pure and exalted teaching of Bab's disciple, Baha'ullah.[126] Such are the teachings of the Brahmans, the Buddhists, the Taoists and the Confucians, and, to some extent, those of wise people both ancient and modern, from Socrates to Kant, and others.

As for me, at least, I can truly believe only in that religion (i.e., that explanation of the meaning of life and the rules of behaviour arising therefrom) whose tenets I find in my own heart and consciousness and in all the teachings of the greatest wise people and holy ones of the world.

I received your brochures,[127] and they greatly caught my fancy, especially *Razumnoe sluzhenie.*

Both brochures offer the precious thought and indication that faith without works is dead, and that the kingdom of God, which is within us, is attained through our own power (or effort).

I was glad to receive your letter.

Your loving brother Lev Tolstoy

126 Tolstoy was long acquainted with the teachings of the Babists (from Bab, pseudonym of Sayyid [Mirza] Ali Muhammad, 1819–1850), and back in 1894 had written that "in the books of Bab himself this teaching is lost in the pompous [for us] Oriental verbosity and in interpretations stretched for the purposes of agreement with the Koran" (*PSS* 67:224). The founder of Baha'i was Baha'ullah (Mirza Hosein Ali, 1817–1892). The editor of the journal *Review of Religions*, Mufti Muhammad Sadiga, was asked by Tolstoy: "Are you familiar with the teachings of Baha'ullah...?" (*PSS* 75:16). In the archives there is a manuscript translation of Baha'ullah's work *The Ascent*, sent to Tolstoy in 1909. His *Krug chtenija* [*A Cycle of Readings*] for 14 June includes a Babist saying: "As long as you yourself are a sinner, do not say a word about the sins of others."

127 *Razumnoe sluzhenie* [Reasonable service] and *Dva puti* [Two paths], published in 1909 in St. Petersburg (in the series *Knigi dukhovnykh khristian* [Books by spiritual Christians]).

I am sending you the re-issue of the book *Wise Thoughts For Every Day* [*Na kazhdyj den'*] for the month of June. There will be an issue for each month. As soon as they are printed I shall send them to you.

I hope you enjoy this book.

L. T.

On the envelope:
To: F. A. Zheltov
Village of Bogorodskoe
Nizhegorod Gub.

PART III

The Doukhobors and Pëtr Verigin

Pëtr Verigin

A BRIEF OUTLINE OF THE DOUKHOBORS

On 20 January 1899, Canada witnessed the beginning of its largest mass immigration in its history, as a group of some 7,500 Doukhobors began arriving from the Russian Caucasus[1] and settling, under the auspices of a Canadian government initiative, as collective homesteaders on the Canadian prairies. This was a group that had suffered considerable persecution at the hands of church and state authorities in Russia for their pacifist and other non-orthodox beliefs. An intensified enforcement of the law requiring all citizens to swear an oath of allegiance to Tsar Alexander III and perform compulsory military service had dealt a major blow against the sect. In 1895, the Doukhobors (the name literally means 'spirit-wrestlers') responded by burning all the weapons they possessed in a mass demonstration; this in turn led to increased persecution — including police surveillance, incarceration and physical torture.

The Doukhobors' emigration to Canada was supported both morally and financially by none other than Leo Tolstoy, who saw in their manifest pacifism and simple Christian approach to life a practical embodiment of his own ideals. Tolstoy, in fact, requested his eldest son, Sergej L'vovich, to accompany one of the four boatloads of Doukhobors to Canada, right to their new homestead sites on the prairies. Sergej L'vovich concluded his diary of the trip as follows (Donskov 1998a: 350–51):

> I am happy that I have spent almost six months with them and have come to know them. And not only do I not regret having participated in their emigration, but I am proud to have had at least a small part in bringing it about. It is a pity that these good people have left Russia, but their emigration was unavoidable. Naturally, the first years of their life in Canada will be very difficult, but their future is assured.

The story of the Doukhobors[2] in Russia is largely the story of persecution, exile, suffering and banishment — and the remarkable resilience of the

1 Settlements in the Caucasus were distributed in four regional locations: (a) *Mokrye gory* (Wet Mountains), in the Akhalkalak Uezd of Tiflis Gubernia, in what is now Georgia; (b) *Elizavetpol'* (250 kilometres east of Tiflis, or Tbilisi, in what is now Azerbajdzhan); (c) *Kars* (including the villages of Terpenie, Spasovka and Gorelovka), in what is now Turkey; (d) *Bashkichetskij*, a small settlement in what is now Armenia. A map of the Transcaucasian settlements is given in Donskov 2005: 36; for maps showing their journey to Canada, see 37–38.

2 The term *dukhobortsy* (as noted, 'spirit-wrestlers'), is usually ascribed to Archbishop Ambrosius of Ekaterinoslav, who used it derogatorily in reference to strugglers *against* the Spirit. The sect members adopted the term in its positive sense, of people struggling *for* the Spirit. It should be noted, however, that according to Svetlana Inikova (2000b: 2, Note 6) the term was "first encountered in a report by the Slovenian Archbishop Nikifor to the Synod in March of 1786. In November of the same year the Slovenian eparchy was transformed into the Ekaterinoslav eparchy, headed by Archbishop Ambrosius." Inikova is an ethnographer with the Russian Academy of Sciences' Institute of Ethnology and Anthropology. See her superb article "Spiritual Origins and the Beginnings of Doukhobor History," presented as a keynote address at the Doukhobor

human spirit. It was their rejection of violence and their simple peasant lifestyle that originally brought their plight to the attention of Leo Tolstoy in the early 1890s, who by this time had already written the majority of his principal theoretical works on social and religious questions. The intensive persecution which followed the Doukhobors' Burning of Arms, as it is now known, in the Caucasus in June 1895 was a direct challenge to Tolstoy's whole philosophy of non-violence, his rejection of organized religion and of property and privilege based on social class and elitist authority. This persecution, set against the background of the nationalism and militarism of the times, led Tolstoy to stress all the more the doctrine of non-violent resistance to evil as a fundamental tenet of Christian doctrine.

Tolstoy's eventual intervention in support of the Doukhobors, and their endeavour to escape their persecution by emigrating, represented nothing new. Time and again he had spoken out against the persecution of various religious sects,[3] including the Quakers, Mennonites and other Christian pacifists. In an age of near-universal conscription in Russia and Europe, he had pleaded more than once on behalf of pacifists, but never with such burning interest and fervent action as with the Doukhobors. For one thing, the persecution affected a far greater number of Doukhobors than of other sects in the past (the Molokans or Stundists, for example); also, the intense persecution following the Burning of Arms threatened the very lives of many of the sect's members.

It was the Doukhobors' lifestyle, however, and its closeness to the ideals of Tolstoy's own philosophy, that was no doubt the strongest attraction for the writer. He constantly received reports from his followers (known as Tolstoyans) recounting the Doukhobors' honest toil on the land; their communal sharing; the love of God they cherished within themselves; their absolute rejection of war, killing and violence; and, not least, their willingness to suffer persecution for the sake of truth. In all of this Tolstoy saw the practical embodiment of virtually everything he himself aspired to and promoted in his own works.

Furthermore, Tolstoy the pragmatist was never content to confine his creative output to the purely philosophical plane; he was constantly searching for practical examples to illustrate his theories, especially among the Russian peasantry. Here, in the Doukhobors, he felt he had found his prime example, particularly insofar as this group, more than any other, combined a peasant lifestyle with a strong endeavour to put Christ's teachings to practical, everyday use — in daily living rather than through organized religion — exemplifying an ideal coming together of the spiritual and the practical.

Centenary Conference at the University of Ottawa (Inikova 2000b), and Eli Popoff's companion keynote address: "The Doukhobors: The 'Enigma' and the Reality" (Popoff 2000).

3 *sects* [sectarians] — see Note 1 in the Preface to this volume.

It was during a momentous period of his life — the particularly intense emotional and spiritual crisis which had begun after his completion of *Anna Karenina* in 1877 — that Tolstoy first learnt of the sect. The subsequent impact of the Doukhobors' ideas on his thought at this time is evident in his writings (especially his treatises) of the 1890s — in his advocacy of principles such as *unity of people, the kingdom of God within*, and the advantages of a *simple peasant life* based on manual labour and mutual sharing, removed from the evils of urban corruption. Like the Doukhobors, he too rejected official church orthodoxy and shared their absolute rejection of violence and violent resistance to evil. It was in part this doctrine, found in Tolstoy's writings after his spiritual crisis, that later came to be known as Tolstoyism [*tolstovstvo*].

Even more than Tolstoy himself, his followers, the Tolstoyans, tended to see in the Doukhobors the highest embodiment of the Christian ideals that they themselves had only professed in words. It was the Tolstoyans who were largely instrumental in the decision to choose Canada as the Doukhobors' destination and in arranging for them to be taken there. The two Doukhobor representatives who embarked on an exploratory trip to Canada in the spring of 1898 were accompanied by members of a Tolstoyan community in England. It was the Tolstoyans who conducted negotiations with Canadian government officials concerning the emigration. And, along with Quakers, Russian landowners and Leo Tolstoy himself (through royalties from his novel *Resurrection*), they were among the principal contributors to its financing.

It was also the Tolstoyans (with the encouragement of their mentor) who largely took upon themselves the task of escorting the boatloads of Doukhobors to Canada and seeing to their establishment there. Some of them stayed months, even years, to help the emigrants settle in their new homeland.

As well, many outside Russia championed the Doukhobor cause. First and foremost among these was Vladimir Chertkov, who was then living in exile in England. Others included: John K. Van der Veer in the Netherlands, Eugen Heinrich Schmidt in Germany, Jonas Stadling in Sweden, John Kenworthy in England and James Mavor in Canada,[4] as well as many Quakers (particularly in Britain and America). Through the publication of pleas for help in pamphlets and articles, these individuals and groups drew the sympathy of the Western world to the Doukhobors' plight; a number of them even went to Russia themselves to gain first-hand knowledge of the sect.[5]

4 See Mavor's extensive correspondence regarding resettlement of the Doukhobors in Canada and his continued interest in this group (in Signori 1989). See also Alexeeva 2000 and Mavor n.d.

5 For example, at the end of 1897, the Englishman Arthur St. John, in the company of Tolstoy's close friend (and Moscow Art Theatre actor) Leopol'd Sulerzhitskij, paid a visit to the Doukhobor leaders in the Caucasus, bringing them letters and funds collected by American Quakers. It was these funds that helped more than a thousand Doukhobors settle in Cyprus — a move which proved disastrous. In April 1899 this party relocated to Canada.

The basis of the Doukhobor faith is the belief that the spirit of God resides in every human being and that to violate a human being in any way is to defile the spirit of God within him; hence their pacifism and their firm belief in the equality of all human beings, regardless of their station in life. Since both the Russian state and the Russian Orthodox Church not only tolerated but even condoned warfare, the Doukhobors strongly resisted both conscription and church rituals. In the Doukhobor concept of the Trinity, each of the three 'persons' is associated, respectively, with (a) a spiritual essence, (b) a spatial dimension and (c) a particular channel through which individual assimilation with the Divine is effected: God the Father, with (a) *light*, (b) *height* and (c) *memory*; God the Son, with (a) *life*, (b) *breadth* and (c) *understanding*; and God the Holy Ghost, with (a) *peace*, (b) *depth* and (c) *will*. God, in turn, is defined as "the power of love, the power of life which is the Source of all that exists."

Doukhobors believe in Christ, not as God in the flesh but as the son of God, just as they held themselves and all others to be God's children. With a strong conviction of what is morally right and wrong, they reject nearly all formal aspects of religion — icons, feasts, religious holidays — but still bow to each other as a sign of respecting God within each individual, and still offer guests the traditional Russian symbols of hospitality: bread, salt and water, placed in the centre of the table, symbolizing the basic staples of human existence. They reject the Bible as a written document, although they admit the value of some of its teachings.

The Doukhobors adhere to the belief that heaven and hell are concepts, or states of mind. They reject any mediation (i.e., by a priest) between a person and God, and see no need for a creed,[6] for church sacraments such as baptism, marriage or funeral ceremonies, or, indeed, written records of any kind,[7] including Scripture.

One exception to written records is the so-called *Zhivotnaja kniga dukhobortsev* [Living Book of the Doukhobors], compiled and published in St. Petersburg in 1909[8] by Vladimir Dmitrievich Bonch-Bruevich, who

6 In response to the question as to what the Doukhobors believe or, more specifically, as to what their creed is, sect members are wont to say that they have none — i.e., no formal, codified canon of officially formulated beliefs. In his pioneer work *Christian Martyrdom in Russia: Persecution of the Doukhobors*, published in London (in English translation) in 1900, Vladimir Chertkov begins his section on "Their teachings" by stating: "The chief article in the Doukhobors' profession of faith is the service and worship of God in the spirit and in truth." He then goes on to say: "They know no creed, and only say of themselves that they are of the faith of Jesus."

7 Refusal to keep records of births and deaths, along with their rejection of any source of religious teaching other than their own inner conscience, inevitably brought them into conflict not only with Russian church and government authorities, but also with their Caucasus neighbours and, later, with legislative authorities and a misunderstanding public in Canada.

8 This was a revised and expanded version of Bonch-Bruevich's (1900) *Spisok psalmov, pisem, rasskazov i drugikh rukopisej po issledovaniju uchenija zhizni i pereselenija v Kanadu zakavkazskikh dukhobortsev* [List of psalms, letters, stories and other research manuscripts on the

shared some of Tolstoy's ideas.[9] Comprising the body of Doukhobor psalms and hymns, the book aimed to inspire the right kind of life and, at the same time, emphasize the nature of change in the group's experience over its turbulent history. Indeed, a significant element of the Doukhobor religion is vocal music, with no instrumental accompaniment or written scores, but, as Woodcock and Avakumovic note ([1968] 1977: 21–22):

> ...interpreted as outflowing from the divinely inspired spirit within each of the singers. [...] And the psalms and hymns (containing the major tenets of their religion) that are set to it are the authentic expression of the Doukhobor people, of their beliefs and history, recorded mainly by anonymous folk bands and welded into tradition by the very method of oral transmission that rendered written religious literature unnecessary to a peasant people living in a rural society where literacy was rare.[10]

There have indeed been a number of formulations of Doukhobor beliefs published over the years.[11] One of the most concise was drafted by Doukhobor leader Pëtr Vasil'evich Verigin (1859–1924) in the form of "a Doukhobor psalm"; it is given here in Eli Popoff's English translation (Popoff 1982: 26):

1. The members of the Community revere and love God as the source of all being.
2. They respect the dignity of man both in themselves and in their fellow men.
3. The members of the Community regard everything that exists with love and admiration, and they try to bring up their children in the same tendency.
4. By the word *God* they understand the power of love, the power of life which is the Source of all that exists.
5. Life is systematic progress ahead, and everything strives toward perfection, and through this process strives to unite with its original Source

Transcaucasian Doukhobors' teachings of life and resettlement in Canada], published in Geneva through Chertkov's Svobodnoe Slovo publishing house, soon after his return to Europe from living with the Doukhobors during their first year in Canada (see Woodsworth 1999a: 5).

9 See Bonch-Bruevich 1900. One of many Doukhobor proverbs he recorded reads: *Napishite vo serdtsakh, vozvestite vo ustakh* [Write it in your heart, proclaim it with your mouth].

10 See also Mealing 1995. On the importance of song in Doukhobor life, see Perry 2000.

11 For example, Novitskij's seminal book *The Doukhobors: Their History and Tenets of Faith* (1882); Maude's *A Peculiar People* ([1904] 1970: 12–20, 79–105); Chertkov's *Christian Martyrdom in Russia: Persecution of the Doukhobors* (1900); an outline by an anonymous representative of the Department of Police, published in English translation in Woodsworth 1999a: 26–28; an article in the Russian Orthodox Encyclopædia (see *Polnyj pravoslavnyj bogoslovskij èntsiklopedicheskij slovar'* 1913: 777–79); a summary in the chapter "The People of God" in Woodcock and Avakumovic (1977: 17–34); a summary by Treadgold (1968: 89–91); and by many Doukhobor writers published in *Iskra* (the monthly journal of the Union of Spiritual Communities of Christ) and elsewhere (see Bibliography).

of life, as if from the seeds received to give returns in the form of ripe fruit.

6. In everything that exists in our world we see consecutive stages toward perfection — thus, beginning with a stone, it passes over to plants; then come animals, the fullest development of which is man, regarding him from the point of view of life and in the sense of a conscious being.
7. The members of the Community hold that to destroy or hurt any living thing is blameworthy. In every separate being there is life and hence God, especially in a human being. To deprive a man of life is not permissible under any circumstances whatsoever.
8. In their beliefs, the members of the Community accord full freedom to all living things, and more so to the life of man. Therefore any organization founded on violence they regard as unlawful.
9. The basis of man's existence is the power of thought, or reason. Basic food for his physical existence are air, water, fruits and vegetables.
10. It is recognised that the life of mankind is essentially a communal life based on the moral law, which has as its rule: "What I do not wish for myself, that I must not wish for anyone else."

Certain Doukhobor beliefs, for obvious reasons, aroused suspicion on the part of church and state authorities. On 13 July 1897, Caucasus Governor Prince Grigorij Sergeevich Golitsyn summed up official views on such beliefs and attitudes in a memo to the central Department of Police[12] as follows:

ON THE AUTHORITIES

- There is one tsar, in heaven, there should be no tsar on earth [...]
- Does the emperor have a mark on his body that you call him the anointed one? What extra thing has God given him — an [extra] finger or an eye? Why is he tsar, and not you or I or someone else? [...] We hear that there is an emperor in Russia, but we do not know his name, we are not interested — we do not concern ourselves with that.
- In England, they say, the son of a cobbler is tsar; whoever is chosen by the people is the one who must reign.
- The unblemished tsar is Jesus of Nazareth. Who wanted to kill Christ — wasn't it Herod? Wasn't it the royal governor Pilate that crucified the Saviour? In the same way, they crucify verity and truth, and us. [...]
- Civil servants and the tsar are all brethren, they should be equal; let them all set their hand to the plough, just like everyone else...
- Rulers and robbers, they're all the same, 'craftsmen,' only the latter rob

12 Case N° 1053, Part 1, Sheets 517, 520, 521, listed in Woodsworth 1997 as Document #1897-07-13b. Published (in translation) in Donskov 1995c: 254. A fuller analysis of official reaction to Tolstoy's teachings and Doukhobor beliefs is presented in Chapter 3 of Donskov 2005: 73–108.

at night, while the others (the rulers) attack and rob the people day and night. [...]

ON LAND

- The land is God's, it is created for all equally. Possession is robbery.
- The princes and the landowners have robbed the people, seizing so much land. There should be no partition of land: everyone should have as much land as he needs to feed himself. [...]

ON THE FATHERLAND

- We do not recognize a fatherland on earth, all people are our compatriots. We are 'members of the Christian community of universal brotherhood.'
- We are pilgrims, we are striving [to reach] our heavenly fatherland, and we do not cherish or wish to defend an earthly [fatherland].
- Military service [is something] we absolutely reject, just as before, when it was not accepted by all our Doukhobors, according to the commandment "Thou shalt not kill"...
- Criminals and robbers should be judged by the Lord Himself, not by people who are just as sinful.
- Prisons should not exist. We rejoice with those who are in prison, and grieve over those who put people there. [...]

The rejection of the supreme authority of the tsar (emperor) was a particular sticking-point with the authorities, one the latter were quick to attribute to the harmful influence of the Tolstoyans on the Doukhobors.[13]

During the reign of Catherine the Great (1762–1796), the sect experienced an unobstructed growth in numbers. Partly because of the influence of their teaching upon their neighbours, however, as well as the discord that had arisen within their own ranks, the Doukhobors began to suffer persecution in 1793, when the government ordered the resettlement of those living in the Ekaterinoslav and Khar'kov Gubernias to an area known as Molochnye vody [Milky Waters] in the Melitopol' district of the Tauride Gubernia (now the Crimea).

The persecution was somewhat mitigated with the ascension of Alexander I to the throne in 1801. Known for his tolerance of religious ideas, he showed

13 In a report entitled "On the current situation of the Trans-Caucasus Doukhobors and on the measures taken by the Federal Authorities to eliminate the harmful anti-government movement among the followers of this sect," Golitsyn noted (1897: 517), for example, that "this harmful and dangerous movement is not based on any enactments of governmental authorities provoking the Doukhobors' displeasure, but is deeply rooted in their sectarian views, inculcated in them by the enemies of our political system."

a special fondness for the Doukhobors by offering them generous land grants and additional financial assistance. In 1804, the Doukhobors of Tambov and Voronezh Gubernias were allowed to join their brethren under a similar arrangement. The local authorities were instructed to keep the Doukhobors together and not mix them with the neighbouring populations, to offer them official protection and not oppress them, but, at the same time, to forbid any proselytization on their part. In 1818 the tsar himself paid a visit to the Doukhobor settlements, and left with a favourable impression.

Nicholas I, however, who succeeded Alexander in 1825, saw danger in the Doukhobors' teaching, and ten years later struck a commission to investigate. In the meantime, local authorities had begun to take a noticeably more hostile attitude toward the sect. In 1839, the commission recommended that the Doukhobors be resettled in the Caucasus — specifically to the Akhalkalak and Elizavetpol' regions, where a group of Doukhobors had already been relocated from the Don River area in 1821. The move took four years to complete (from 1841 to 1845). The new area was mountainous (some 1,500 metres in elevation) and required a shift in occupation from grain farming to cattle raising, to which the sect members managed to adapt with remarkable speed.

The Doukhobors worked their new large parcels of land with their customary industriousness and managerial efficiency, and, with modest needs, quickly prospered. Their 'golden period' of prosperity (1864–1886) was presided over by their capable and charismatic leader, Luker'ja Vasil'evna Kalmykova. Enjoying the complete confidence and respect of her followers, Kalmykova was an absolute leader, stern but fair, a mediator in internal conflicts, a solution finder, one who sought to live in peace with the local authorities while at the same time managing to prevent them from encroaching upon the sect's internal and economic life. She succeeded in organizing the internal structure of the community in such a way that, up until her death, it was said that the Doukhobors knew no trouble, terror or financial need. They functioned, in fact, as a virtual 'state within a state.'[14]

Trouble began for the Doukhobors, however, following Kalmykova's death in 1886, when the community divided over the question of her successor. The faction known as the 'Large Party' [*Bol'shaja partija*], led by Pëtr Vasil'evich Verigin, whom Kalmykova had personally groomed for the leadership, triumphed in the end over the so-called 'Smaller Party' [*Malaja partija*]. By 1892, possibly under the influence of Lev Tolstoy, though mainly out of their personal conviction that it was wrong to harm any living being, Verigin and his immediate supporters had become vegetarians, but not all

14 From the early days of their settlement in Molochnye vody in the early nineteenth century, Doukhobor leaders governed from a residential complex known as *Sirotskij dom* [Orphan House] — see Department of Police archival documents in Woodsworth 1999a: 30, 35.

members of the Large Party were willing to take this step. Those who did were known as *postniki* [fasters], while those who resisted were called *mjasniki* [meat-eaters].

In 1887 a new source of trouble arose when compulsory military service was introduced in the Caucasus, and by 1894 all Russian citizens were obliged to take an oath of allegiance to the tsar. Verigin's call to refuse to take the oath[15] was viewed with alarm by the authorities, who had already come to look upon the Doukhobors as a socio-political movement with communist leanings, for which their religious doctrine served mainly as a deceptive veneer. Contributing to the climate of suspicion was the assassination of Alexander II in 1881, after several years of repeated attempts on his life.

Increased proselytizing among the Doukhobors on the part of a number of Tolstoyans only increased official suspicion. These actions, predictably, resulted in further surveillance, beatings and incarceration. Indeed, the closing years of the nineteenth century witnessed the most severe persecution in their history, lasting right up until their emigration to Canada in 1899.[16]

LEO TOLSTOY AND PËTR V. VERIGIN

When the governor of Tobol'sk asked Pëtr Vasil'evich Verigin, then living in exile in Siberia, just "how" he happened to become acquainted with Lev Nikolaevich Tolstoy, the Doukhobor leader replied: "through correspondence." "They were really surprised that people could get to know each other so well through correspondence," remarked Verigin in a letter to Tolstoy (16 August 1898).[17]

While the followers of Pëtr Vasil'evich Verigin[18] were given permission to emigrate to Canada toward the end of 1898, their leader was not allowed to join them until July 1902, when his final term of fourteen years of exile came to an end.

On his way to Canada, Verigin first stopped to see Tolstoy at Yasnaya Polyana, and then for a visit with Vladimir Chertkov in England. Chertkov arranged for Verigin to give a lecture on Doukhobor philosophy in London. His audience was impressed by both his sharp mind and his striking physical appearance.

15 At the same time, Verigin, recently exiled to Siberia, enjoined his followers to abstain from the use of alcohol and tobacco.

16 A detailed account of the Doukhobor emigration to Canada is presented in the diary of Tolstoy's eldest son, Sergej L'vovich Tolstoy, who accompanied one of the boatloads to Canada at his father's request. The diary and pertinent letters are presented in both their original Russian and an English translation in *Sergej Tolstoy and the Doukhobors: A Journey to Canada* (Donskov 1998a).

17 L. D. Gromova, "Two Teachers of Life: A Dialogue" (Gromova 1995: 1).

18 Known as Peter V. Verigin in Canada. To be distinguished from his son, Pëtr Petrovich (Peter P.) Verigin, who succeeded him as Doukhobor leader in Canada. In Russian, the name Pëtr is pronounced *Piotr*.

The months preceding his arrival in Canada in December 1902 were marked by a troublesome incident in the fledgling Doukhobor community in their new homeland, involving the *Svobodniki*, known in English as the Sons of Freedom.[19] Members of this sect, adopting an extreme interpretation of Verigin's call to self-renunciation, had taken it upon themselves to turn their farm animals loose and destroy or give away virtually all their personal possessions. More than a thousand of their number had set off on a pilgrimage to find a place where they could live unencumbered by any external constraints whatsoever.

All attempts by Canadian authorities to resolve the situation proved fruitless. On 15 December 1902, Tolstoyan Ivan Tregubov wrote to a friend: "Perhaps his [P. V. Verigin's] presence among the Doukhobors will help them find themselves more quickly and work out a lifestyle that more closely corresponds to their spiritual make-up."[20]

This prediction turned out to be accurate. A month later, Verigin related to Tolstoy how he diffused the trouble, telling the radicals, as he recounted,[21]

> "Your motives of self-sacrifice for the common good of human life are legitimate and precious ones, but there is no need to let the children go hungry and cold, so for the time being why not remain with all the rest of the brethren and teach them?" Those with families took this explanation too as a revelation from God.

Verigin's arrival in Winnipeg is described in a number of newspaper accounts. The following excerpt from the *Manitoba Free Press* is typical:[22]

> Physically, Verigin is a splendid type of his race. Tall and strongly built, and of erect and graceful carriage, he would attract attention among hundreds of good-looking men.

His followers in Canada, emphasizing what they perceived as his spiritual strength, reprised the title *Gospodnij* (i.e., 'the Godly' or 'belonging to the

19 For some recent, detailed studies of this group, see the series of eight papers by Jim E. Popoff (1987–1988) entitled: "What were the main historical reasons and causes for the rise of the splinter movement known as the Sons of Freedom?"; see also Kolesnikoff 2000 and Inikova 2002. Doukhobors today are divided into three groups: (a) *Independents* (stemming from those who sought accommodation with Canadian government regulations and gradually became independent farmers), (b) *Community Doukhobors* (from those who followed Verigin to British Columbia in 1908 to preserve their communal lifestyle) and (c) the *Sons of Freedom* (an offshoot of the latter, who took the communal way of living to the extreme). The latter two groups are concentrated mainly in British Columbia, while most of the Independents still live in Saskatchewan and Alberta. For more information on each of these factions, see Frantz 1961: 47–52.

20 Woodsworth 1999a: 217–19.

21 See Letter N° 13.

22 *Manitoba Free Press*, 22 December 1902; quoted in Ewashen 2001. For more on Verigin's life and activities in Canada, see Donskov's (2008) article in the *Dictionary of Canadian Biography* 15:1032–36.

Lord,' though often mistranslated as 'the Lordly'), which had originally been granted him by Luker'ja Kalmykova.

As indicated above, the leader's presence among his flock as they adjusted to their new homeland had an overall calming effect on their communal life as a whole. He gave the Doukhobors a new collective name, calling them the Christian Community of Universal Brotherhood (CCUB). He became their spokesman in negotiating questions of his followers' rights and responsibilities vis-à-vis the Canadian government.

The issue of land ownership and registration was a particularly thorny one. The government had originally allowed the Doukhobors the privilege of collective ownership, but in 1905 withdrew this exemption and began demanding registration of homesteads on an individual basis — a procedure which entailed swearing an oath of allegiance to the Crown, thereby obligating sect members to military service if Canada should ever go to war.

Disenchanted with changing official attitudes, in 1905 Verigin sent his lieutenant Ivan Konkin to Siberia to dissuade a party of newly released Doukhobors from emigrating. His advice went unheeded, however, and the new arrivals faced a less-than-friendly welcome in Canada.

The following year, continuing with this protest, he went to Moscow along with several trusted followers to enquire into the feasibility of relocating the Doukhobors en masse back to Russia. Receiving no positive reaction from tsarist officials and, more importantly, no guarantee sect members would be exempted from military service, he was obliged to abandon the idea, and returned to Canada to pursue other options.

In the summer of 1907, Verigin discovered orchard lands in British Columbia which the Doukhobors could purchase communally, with no oath-of-allegiance requirement. The following year a good four-fifths of his flock followed their leader to new settlements in British Columbia's Kootenay region, mainly in the Castlegar and Grand Forks areas. Historian Carl Tracie (2002) speculates that Verigin may have deliberately settled certain Doukhobors in small scattered communities around Castlegar to prevent further fragmentation of the sect, at the same time keeping them isolated as much as possible from the surrounding English Canadian society — a scheme that actually ended up precipitating the dissolution it was intended to prevent.

Indeed, some Doukhobors, contrary to Verigin's advice, had already accommodated themselves to official demands and registered their homesteads, either taking the oath of allegiance or claiming an exemption that had earlier been granted to the Mennonites. These 'Independent' Doukhobors, remaining on the prairies as individual farmers, assimilated more quickly to Canadian ways than did their 'Community' brethren in British Columbia. Verigin himself discouraged any contact with the Independents, and even opposed (unsuccessfully) their exemption from military service during the First World War.

He and his Community followers, however, while finding orchard farming more compatible with their vegetarian philosophy than cattle raising on the prairies, were by no means freed from conflict with officialdom over land, education and the registration of vital statistics. Nevertheless, under his guidance (summed up in his motto *Toil and Peaceful Life*), the British Columbia Doukhobors prospered, while the CCUB expanded into other enterprises, including sawmills and brick factories.

Verigin's dictatorial insistence on enforcing radical moral standards, however, not only provoked conflict with Canadian officials but also caused even some members of his own flock to leave the fold. On the other hand, what steps he did take to compromise with the authorities — permitting public schooling[23] and tax-paying in return for continued exemption from military service, for example — did not sit well with the more radical Sons of Freedom, who resorted to acts of public nudity and arson against the Community Doukhobors' homes, businesses and schools.

In October 1924 the hatred directed against Verigin from both sides led to tragedy, when a bomb exploded in the train carriage he was riding in from Castlegar to Grand Forks. While it was generally viewed as an assassination, the culprit was never found, and Pëtr V. Verigin has continued to live on in Doukhobor memory as something of a martyr to the community's ideal of living a Christian life free of violence and with no requirement to obey any authority other than God.

His exalted stature, even today, among members of an otherwise egalitarian sect may be explained at least in part by the fact that most Doukhobors have considered their leaders to be divinely chosen incarnations of God on Earth. This naturally made Verigin a unique and controversial figure, especially in the Canadian context. He was evidently endowed with a natural ability which fitted him for the role, far surpassing his sectarian brethren both in intellectual capacity and in the development of the philosophical underpinnings of Doukhobor faith, yet at the same time remaining 'one of them' in spirit and community purpose. He embodied the ideal combination of individual prowess and communal bonding, which was only strengthened by his taking on the role of their leader.

His intellectual prowess has been widely noted by both contemporary and more recent commentators — Doukhobor and non-Doukhobor. Woodcock and Avakumovic ([1968] 1977: 185), for example, describe him as "a powerful personality with a mind that was quick, subtle, and capable, even if it was not profound." He wrote a number of sermons and original psalms, which the Doukhobors still hold as a part of their religious creed, along with a series of

23 By 1922 there were so many Doukhobors in the Grand Forks area that a new public school was opened, primarily for sect members' children.

morally instructive dialogues and stories (e.g., "A Fantasy"[24] — a fable condemning drinking, carousing and gambling). Those that are not published are to be found mainly in the archives of Vladimir D. Bonch-Bruevich (a Soviet government official who also collected Doukhobor lore).

It was this capacity for a realistic evaluation of any situation that allowed him, even at a relatively young age, to correctly understand and fully embrace the Doukhobor concept of rejection of violence. The Burning of Arms, in the Caucasus in 1895, had a practical as well as a symbolic significance. One Soviet commentator on the Doukhobors aptly noted that "the class struggle in their midst was taking on an ever sharper focus," and went so far as to condemn Verigin for "physically disarming the Doukhobors."[25] In fact, of course, Verigin made entirely the right choice, albeit a difficult one. He preferred repression against his followers to either a bloody internal quarrel or a prolonged active conflict with authorities, which would be doomed to failure. His spirited correspondence with Tolstoy bears witness to this.

Verigin's special talent became even more noticeable in Canada, where, from the moment of his arrival in 1902, he expended considerable effort in smoothing the Doukhobors' transition to their new homeland, combining the duties of the spiritual leader of a major sectarian community with the extremely fruitful task of managing the community's financial and social development. His capacity for common sense guided him in seeking out compromises with Canadian authorities (examples of which are too numerous to detail here, and rather well known).

It may be pointed out, however, that this common sense also helped Verigin cope with events on an immeasurably broader scale. He was well aware, for example, of what any revolution entailed, and as early as 30 April 1917, when as yet hardly anybody in Canada knew anything about the Bolsheviks, he initiated a letter from the Doukhobors to the short-lived Russian Provisional Government requesting a guarantee that the lives of the tsar and the imperial family would be spared.

No less an important component of Verigin's character was his desire and ability to *learn,* endowing him with a significant breadth of vision, which in turn allowed him to function rather effectively outside the Doukhobor community. He was able to draw from the outside world whatever might be beneficial to the Doukhobors and put it to practical use. This may be seen, for example, in his relationship with Tolstoy and the writer's followers, as well as in the Doukhobors' use of the latest farm machinery.[26] He also had a great

24 Reproduced as part of the Tolstoy-Verigin correspondence in the present volume (following Letter N° 6 below).

25 Klibanov 1965: 111, 113.

26 Because of their collective purchasing power, the Doukhobors were in a much better position than individual homesteaders to afford the newest mechanized equipment available — an

desire for constant inner development and a striving for moral and spiritual self-perfection. In a letter to Tolstoy of 3 May 1909, for example, he writes of his "goal to free myself from the desire for power."

Verigin, of course, was not successful in every undertaking, and not all his failures can be attributed simply to the effect of unfavourable external circumstances. Some of them were due to his own human weaknesses — such as the conflict with his wife and his son. His son, Pëtr Petrovich Verigin, came to Canada twice during his father's lifetime with the intention of settling here, but, failing to find any common language with his father, returned to Russia.

Verigin also had particular difficulty coming to terms with the Society of Independent Doukhobors, formed in 1916. In his attempts to counter their activities he even enlisted the aid of the Canadian authorities, which, of course, went directly against the sect's moral principles.[27]

The observer of today cannot help feeling some discomfort at the way Verigin carried out his duties as leader, using methods that can only be termed authoritarian — a trait early noticed and criticized by Tolstoy. In evaluating this aspect of his career, one must remember that Doukhobor leaders, starting long before Verigin, customarily enjoyed absolute authority, and so one cannot simply fault Verigin for accepting the status quo. At the same time, a Doukhobor leader was also entrusted with setting a moral example for his followers, and it can only be said that Verigin carried out this task significantly better than many of his predecessors.

Some scholars have legitimately questioned Verigin's sincerity. Josh Sanborn has speculated that Verigin called for the Doukhobors' arms burning in 1895 specifically to elicit a favourable reaction from Tolstoy.[28] We have evidence, too, that most of his letters to Tolstoy were meticulously crafted, even copied from preliminary drafts. After all, Verigin benefited significantly from Tolstoy's reputation in support of his cause, just as Tolstoy found in the Doukhobors a practical example of his theories opposing the state (especially state religion) and in favour of non-violent resistance to evil.[29]

It is also worth noting the reaction of the Sons of Freedom to Verigin's attempts to reconcile the practical with the ideal: they concluded that what he said in public (i.e., for the benefit of English-Canadian society) was not what he actually intended for his followers. This confirms the observation that the concept of honesty for the Doukhobors was inextricably linked to their us-versus-them view of the world, in which sincerity in regard to outsiders was

advantage that provoked jealousy on the part of their English-Canadian neighbours (see Woodsworth 1999a: 7).

27 See Woodcock and Avakumovic 1977: 241–42.

28 See Sanborn 1995: 63.

29 At one point, Tolstoy, in a letter to two of his daughters (Tat'jana L'vovna and Marija L'vovna) called the Doukhobors "the people of the twenty-fifth century" (*PSS* 71:497).

not an absolute requirement in a leader. It is quite likely that Verigin himself did not make an exemption in the case of his own followers — witness his above-mentioned "A Fantasy," which he wrote specifically "for the simple people" without regard to their religious sensibilities, and considering manipulation of them an entirely acceptable practice.

Verigin will most probably continue to be remembered as a leader who went a long way toward uniting the two approaches — the practical and the ideal — established, respectively, by the original eighteenth-century Doukhobor leaders: Siluan Kolesnikov and his successor, Ilarion Pobirokhin. Kolesnikov counselled his followers to keep a low profile and not quarrel with the dominant state religion, no matter where they lived, while Pobirokhin, Kolesnikov's idealistic and temperamental successor, paid far less attention to the requirements of objective reality and introduced the first known ideological schism into the sect. It was Verigin's very efforts to balance these two contrary approaches that unwittingly served as the catalyst for the ultimate fragmentation and dissolution of the sect's organizational structure in Canada.

It is important to note that the viewpoint of the modern researcher is only one possible variant of the many perspectives that could be selected in evaluating the life and career of Pëtr Vasil'evich Verigin. It is by no means one which Verigin himself would have been concerned with or have attempted to respond to. In the eyes of his erstwhile Doukhobor followers the man was a prophet, if not a living deity — the embodiment of the 'Spirit,' in fact — and this was the only criterion which bestowed authority in the eyes of many Doukhobors.

An objective analysis of the man would require examining how he came to terms with his unique assigned role in all its many variants — and this would be a major study on its own. It is impossible to evaluate Verigin's career on the basis of one or two instances of success or failure. The discipline of history has still not come up with satisfactory scientific norms for evaluating the lives of those considered prophets by their followers and contemporaries. Further archival study of the Doukhobors and their leaders, however, is one promising step in the right direction.

Tolstoy's exchange of letters with Verigin comprises one of the most noteworthy parts of his overall correspondence on the Doukhobors — a remarkable summary of the philosophies of what appear as two equally powerful intellects, revealing their points of commonality as well as frequently acute differences. It spans nearly fifteen years (November 1895 to May 1910) and while it broaches a broad variety of subjects, it is fundamentally an exchange of thoughts on the meaning of life, man's relationship to God and the purpose of human existence.

The thirty-eight extant letters published here do not represent the full extent of the correspondence. Because of the confiscation of mail by the Department of Police at the time, a good number of letters are missing, especially for the year 1897. Still, what has been published reveals a remarkable and fascinating relationship between two giants — one a nobleman with a worldwide reputation as a stellar novelist, sixty-seven years old at the outset of their correspondence, the other a thirty-six-year-old peasant who had already spent eight years in exile for holding views that bore a striking similarity to Tolstoy's.

The correspondence deals less with the practical questions of emigration than with the ideas germane to Tolstoy and Verigin as thinkers, and hence, while this exchange has already been discussed in a variety of scholarly articles,[30] it may be appropriate at this juncture to elaborate to some degree on the commonalities and differences in the views expressed in the letters.

Of particular interest is the fact that, even though Verigin began the correspondence with a great deal of respect for the writer, and even a feeling of kinship, he was quite confirmed in his own views on life; moreover, he did not hesitate to express them or defend his strongly held convictions. His arguments about the irrelevance of literacy and books in general, for example, are forcefully (albeit one-sidedly) presented.[31] Tolstoy, in turn, despite the discrepancy in such views, as well as the obvious differences in age and professional reputation, was prepared to treat Verigin more or less as an equal.

The letters deal with a broad range of topics. In the first half of the exchange (while the Doukhobor leader was still in Siberian exile in Obdorsk), we find, for example, Verigin's criticism of both secular and ecclesiastical authorities in Russia, whereas his letters written from Canada are characterized more by what seemed to Tolstoy to be an inordinate attention to the material welfare of his flock.

Still, there is no lack of discussion of spiritual matters: man's relationship to God, faith, love of humanity, the meaning of human life (which Verigin in one letter[32] defined as "to keep one's heart from evil"). Another commonality of views is found in the theme of the *unity of people,* which runs like a leitmotif through Verigin's letters, with Tolstoy's responses nodding in approval. In contrast to laws and restrictions imposed by government and church authorities, both Verigin and Tolstoy saw a need for all mankind to live according to the God-consciousness within each individual, united in kindness, love and respect for everything living, regardless of human categorizations.

The chief difference between the two thinkers may be seen in their approaches to the world and humanity's quest for spiritual truth. In contrast

30 See, e.g., Gromova 1995, 2000; Woodsworth 1995; Bumgardner 2001.

31 In this argument, near the beginning of their correspondence, Verigin emphasizes the power of the spoken "living word" which Christ gave his disciples direct orders to spread — as opposed to a written piece that is open to many interpretations, including misinterpretation. He accordingly acknowledges his greater fascination with Tolstoy's life than his writings, and, when it comes to the latter, his preference for Tolstoy's treatises over his fiction.

32 See Letter N° 28 below.

to Verigin's more extreme points of view, Tolstoy seems better able to come to terms with mankind's evident flaws and find a way around them.[33] His letters reveal a greater philosophical and intellectual bent, despite his evident sincerity in his quest for spiritual enlightenment. But he has no hesitation in examining his own (and humanity's) conception of God, acknowledging that it may be all too coloured by a misguided attempt to define a perfect spiritual concept on the basis of imperfect physical human experience.[34] This subjectivity in perceiving God provoked a serious inner struggle in Tolstoy. At the same time, he rejected what he saw as the Doukhobors' tendency to take the perception of God beyond the rational into the realm of the mystical and superstitious.[35]

A close reading of the letters indicates that over the period of their correspondence Tolstoy exerted a significant influence on the Doukhobor leader, even if (initially, at least) Verigin's powerful intellect was unprepared to accept Tolstoy's views when they contradicted his own.[36] Moreover, through Verigin the influence of a number of Tolstoy's ideas was felt throughout the whole Doukhobor movement.[37] Indeed, Tolstoy is held in such high regard by the

33 In his letter to Verigin of 14 October 1896 (Letter N° 3), for example, in discussing the problem of whether the end necessarily justifies the means, Tolstoy rejects the notion that material and spiritual progress are mutually exclusive. Toward the end of the letter he also takes note of the discrepancy between his philosophical ideas and his born-into-nobility lifestyle, claiming he is "surrounded…by all sorts of luxuries which I hate but have not the strength to extricate myself from," and acknowledges the moral support he derives from Verigin's example.

34 See, e.g., Tolstoy's letter of 20 November 1898 (Letter N° 8), where Tolstoy writes: "This misconception of God comes mainly from our inculcated beliefs about the creation of the world, about our knowledge of how the world was created and who created it.… We do not see the frightening absurdity of such a conception only because we are too accustomed to it."

35 See, e.g., Tolstoy's letter of 20 January 1901 (Letter N° 10), in which he urges that "such a superstition…should not be encouraged, as I am sure you fully agree, and that if such a superstition exists, it exists against your will."

36 The gradual 'softening' of Verigin's attitude toward his acceptance of Tolstoy's ideas, along with his resultant character transformation, is extensively examined in Woodsworth 1995. Woodsworth notes, for example, that toward the end of their correspondence the Doukhobor leader "was quite a different person from the Verigin who had first objected to Tolstoy's involvement in book-writing some fifteen years earlier," having undergone "a profound spiritual regeneration over this time, in much the same way as his mentor had done before him," even as he still retained that "strong spark of open and forthright character that had attracted Tolstoy right from the start" (Woodsworth 1995: 250).

37 Noted Doukhobor historian Eli Popoff (author of one of the guest essays in Donskov 2005), however, points out that more of this influence may have actually come through Verigin's son, Pëtr Petrovich Verigin (1881–1939), than through Verigin himself. Pëtr Petrovich, whose adopted surname Chistjakov literally signifies 'the Cleanser,' was invited by the Doukhobors to come to Canada to succeed his father as leader, after the latter's death in a railway explosion. In a personal communication, Popoff (2001) wrote: "One thing that I wished to mention to you about something that has been continually overlooked by researchers on Doukhobor philosophy as it is presently espoused. And that is that although we have on record the correspondence of Peter V. Verigin and Leo Tolstoy, and other historical data pointing to the influence of Tolstoyan philosophy, via Peter V. Verigin, on Doukhobor thought, in my researches and study of the development

Doukhobors that they often refer to him as *Dedushka Tolstoj* (Grandfather Tolstoy).

There was undoubtedly a significant influence in the opposite direction as well.[38] By the time of their first meeting in 1902, when Verigin was on his way to Canada, a fair number of letters had already been exchanged. In addition, Tolstoy had been made aware of the Doukhobor leader's vigorous intellect by a great number of reports forwarded to him by common acquaintances. The fact that Verigin had come from a peasant milieu, a people in whom Tolstoy for so many decades had sought — and, at least partially, found — a meaning of life that could not be destroyed by death, further endeared him to the writer, both on a personal level and as a model for the subsequent portrayal of peasants in his works.[39] Tolstoy's perception of their mutual influence can be summed up in his letter to E. I. Popov of 12–15 March 1896 (*PSS* 69:59–60):

> We need closer communication [with the Doukhobors], whereby we can borrow a good deal from them — in looking at them we can discover our own weaknesses — and they can borrow something from us.

of modern Doukhobor thought I find that Peter P. Verigin-Chistiakov — the son of Peter Lordly, brought in as much if not more Tolstoyan philosophy into modern Doukhobor ideology than did his illustrious father. Whether because he knew of the close contacts his father had with Leo Tolstoy, or whether he did this entirely of his own volition,…it is known that from a very young age Peter Chistiakov made a very thorough study of all of Leo Tolstoy's writings." Note: as indicated earlier, 'Lordly' is a common mistranslation of the Russian *Gospodnij*, which means in fact 'belonging to the Lord.'

38 This aspect of influence is frequently pointed out (and occasionally exaggerated) by Doukhobors today — cf. the section on "Doukhobors' Perceptions of Tolstoy's Ideas" in Donskov 2005: 197–200.

39 This influence is discussed in Donskov 2005: 147–79.

TOLSTOY AND VERIGIN: LETTERS 1895–1910

1. L. N. TOLSTOY ❧ P. V. VERIGIN
21 November 1895. Moscow.

Dear Brother!

Ivan Mikhajlovich Tregubov[40] has sent me your letter to him,[41] and I was very glad to read it, glad to learn of you and to hear your voice, as it were, and understand what you are thinking about, and how you think and what you live by. I see from your letter that you live in a spiritual world and concern yourself with spiritual questions. That is vital for the good of mankind, for only in the spirit is man free, and only through the spirit is God's work done, and only in the spirit does man feel himself at one with God, since "God is spirit."[42]

The thoughts you express in your letter about the superiority of live communication over dead books greatly appealed to me, and I share them. I write books and therefore I know all the harm that they cause; I know how people who are unwilling to accept truth know how not to read or not understand anything that goes against the grain and exposes them, how they reinterpret and distort, how they have reinterpreted the Gospel.

I know all that, yet all the same I think that *in our time* books are unavoidable. I say 'in our time' — in contrast to the gospel times, when there was no printing of books, there were simply no books, and the means of communicating thoughts was purely oral. Back then it was possible to get by without books, because neither did the enemies of truth have books; but now we cannot let just the enemy have this powerful tool to use for deceit and not use it for truth. Not to use books or letters for communicating one's thoughts and to receive thoughts of other people is tantamount to not using the power of your own voice to communicate instantly to many people what you wish to say, or not to use your hearing to understand what another person is saying out loud, but to admit that thoughts can be communicated and received only one on one or through whispering.

Letters and print have simply increased by thousands — by hundreds of thousands — the numbers of people capable of hearing one express one's

40 *Ivan Mikhajlovich Tregubov* (1858–1931) — an Orthodox priest's son who rejected Orthodoxy in favour of Tolstoy's teachings. As an avid Tolstoyan he collected and studied materials on peasant sectarians and publicly defended them in the face of official persecution.

41 Letter from P. V. Verigin to I. M. Tregubov, 5 August 1895, published in Bonch-Bruevich 1901: 14–16. In 1893 Tregubov left the Moscow Seminary to work at the Posrednik publishing house. Thanking Tregubov for the books sent to Obdorsk, Verigin added: "Books help a lot in working things out, but can sometimes be a big hindrance as well. Whereas our own voice of appeal will never deceive you, as long as our desires are sincere, that is, as long as the soul is fully present." Later, Tregubov continued sending Tolstoy letters from Verigin and other Doukhobors.

42 John 4:24.

thoughts, but the relationship between the communicator and the receiver remains the same; just as in oral conversation the listener can delve into and understand what he is hearing, or can let what is being said to him go in one ear and out the other, the same is true with print: just as it is possible for the reader to misinterpret a book he is reading, so can one who listens with his ears; just as one can — as we see — write nonsense or write too much, so is it possible to talk that way. There is a difference, but the difference is sometimes in favour of oral, sometimes written communication.

The advantage of oral communication is that the listener feels the soul of the speaker, but here too is the disadvantage that quite often empty-headed chatterers — lawyers, for example — endowed with the gift of the gab, attract people not by the reasonableness of their words but by their oratorical mastery, which doesn't happen with books; another advantage of oral communication is that the person who doesn't understand can ask for clarification, and yet there is the disadvantage that people who don't understand, often on purpose, can ask unnecessary questions and break the train of thought, which also does not happen with books.

The disadvantages of books are, first, that paper will tolerate anything and you can print all kinds of nonsense, at the cost of enormous efforts on the part of paper and typography workers, which would be impossible in oral communication, since people don't bother listening to nonsense; secondly, the fact that they (books) are multiplying in huge quantities and the good ones are lost in a sea of stupid, meaningless and harmful books.

Nevertheless, the advantages of books are also considerable, consisting mainly in the fact that the circle of one's listeners is expanded by hundreds of thousands compared to people listening to oral communication. And this expansion of the circle of listeners is important not simply because there are a lot of them, but because among the millions of people of various nations and social status who have access to a book, 'kindred spirits' turn up all by themselves; people living tens of thousands of versts[43] from each other, people who don't even know each other, are united into one and live by a single soul and derive spiritual joy and courage from the realization that they are not alone. This is the kind of communion I now have with you and with many, many people of other nations who have never seen me, but who are closer to me than my blood sons and brothers.

But the chief argument in favour of books is the fact that, given a certain degree of development in the outward standard of living, books — and print in general — have become people's means of communication with each other and therefore we cannot afford to neglect this means. So many harmful books have been written and circulated that this harm can be counteracted only by books. You fight fire with fire. Christ said: "What ye hear in the ear, that

43 *verst* = 1.07 km (see note on measurements following the Preface).

preach ye upon the housetops."[44] Well, this preaching upon the housetops is the printed word. The printed word is the very same language, only very far--reaching, and therefore everything said about language applies to the printed word as well: we use language to bless God and to curse people created in God's likeness; and so you can never be careful enough about what you say and hear, just as about what you print and read.

I am writing all this not because I thought that you think differently (I see from your letter that you understand this the same way), but because these thoughts have come to me and I wanted to share them with you. I was especially touched by what you said in your letter to the effect that *"if we preserved what was already given to us from above, we should be perfectly happy. And whatever is necessary and lawful must inevitably be in each one of us, and comes directly from above or from within ourselves."* This is quite right, and that is my concept of man too.

Everyone would undoubtedly know God's truth, know all they needed to know to accomplish what God wants from them in this life, as long as this truth that has been revealed to man is not clouded by false human interpretations. And for that reason to know God's truth man needs first of all to reject all false interpretations and all worldly temptations that would lead him to accept these interpretations, and then the truth alone will remain, the truth which is available to babes, since it is innate to the human soul. The big challenge is in throwing out the lie without throwing out some of the truth with it, as well as, in the process of explaining the truth, to avoid introducing new errors.

I thank you, dear brother, for the greetings you sent me. Write to me in Moscow, if there is nothing stopping you, at the Tolstoy house in Khamovniki Lane. Is there anything I can do for you? You will make me very happy if you give me something to do.

I embrace you as a brother.

Lev Tolstoy

21 November 1895

2. P. V. VERIGIN ❧ L. N. TOLSTOY
1 August 1896. Obdorsk.

I contradict myself.
— P. Verigin

My Kind and Dear Friend Lev Nikolaevich!

I thank you wholeheartedly for the attention expressed in your letter to me of 21 November 1895. — I received it just a few days ago. The simplicity of your

44 Matth. 10:27.

discussion speaks of the clarity and the straightforwardness of your heart, hence: "out of the abundance of the heart the mouth speaketh."[45]

Your arguments about literacy are correct through and through — especially in regard to the present time. — As you yourself say. But I sometimes allow myself — to idealize my thought in general terms, not taking account of time or circumstance. — Forsaking literacy in our day — even for a brief time, i.e., for a moment, would be tantamount to depriving everybody of shoes, or depriving contemporary women of their hats, all decked out with lace and bird feathers. That would unquestionably lead to a state of considerable bewilderment. Just the scandalous image of shoeless and hatless people would be a revolting sight. In spite of the fact that if you look at it seriously, people might still behave lawfully even without entangling their feet in boots and shoes or distorting the natural appearance of the head. I would suppose, as regards the highest cult of emancipated women, that if they didn't wear hats, their brains and thoughts would not suffer in the least.

So too with literacy, it's a kind of 'fashion of the times.' As you yourself argue, literacy is needed as a means of communication for the time. Someone who is literate sees in this manner his own self — even his thoughts, but generally the image is not correct. Being literate is like having fine clothes (though obtained through someone else's labour), but even an illiterate can be a human being, in the larger sense of the word.

I have often had the occasion to witness such scenes — people spending several hours in conversation and instinctively drawing closer together, through the union of the Spirit-thought, and then suddenly parting, cutting off their conversation in the middle of a word, once they find that a third party to the conversation, as it turns out, is completely illiterate. In reply to the question "And which *lycée* did you attend?," the answer is received that he did not attend school at all. — You will completely agree that the judgement of these two (by their own admission) literate people is out and out wrong: if they hadn't found out about the illiteracy, all three would have parted friends.

Just so, a contemporary lady with a hat and veil will not offer her hand to a tanned and bare-headed Tyrolian woman, failing to understand that a hat, or a fancy dress with a ribbon and stars, is only a 'passing fad' which does not enhance the intellect in the least. One can be literate and not understand anything, or *feel* anything, and, vice-versa, be illiterate and yet have a clear comprehension of what is going on around one. Literacy should not be considered a lever for people's mental development, especially their basic spiritual progress. — At the end of this letter I am attaching an excerpt from my diary, about the basic motive-force behind our evolution.

Now I shall answer your specific arguments as to the legitimacy of literacy. — In the first place you say: "How often people do not read and do not want

45 Matth. 12:34.

to comprehend what goes against their habits!" This is because for a patient who has finally given in to a disease, who cannot get up and take his medicine, it isn't enough to supply him with flasks filled with prescribed remedies, or send them to him by post; what is needed is the personal presence of the doctor, his advice, as well as his healthy, cheerful countenance — this is what inspires people. — This is why, as far as I can tell, the more genuine thinkers about truth have gone and helped sick people personally, instead of just offering them medicines.

And Christ did not command his followers to sow the living word just because there was no book-publishing then — there had been publishing for several thousand years before Christ, only in different forms — but because he found the living word a more accurate means of communication, not only because of its simplicity but also the opposite, because of its complexity. One can read and copy what someone else has written, but one can really think and speak only one's own thoughts.

Literacy has caused people to fall into a major blunder: often they take and read the Psalms when they have nothing in common with them, and so it is no wonder that the word is not inculcated in the listeners, "they say and do not."[46] — A writer or reader can be compared to a pharmacist who reads prescriptions and uses them to prepare medicines, one who often does not believe in his own actions but carries out his duties for material gain — for pay. I personally compare the thinker or speaker to the doctor, whose healthy countenance in front of the patient and charming words testify to his faith in the medicine he offers. And what if the patient should challenge the doctor, — as you say: "People who don't understand, often on purpose, can ask unnecessary questions and break the train of thought," which is only natural. But this very criticism will incite the doctor to even more detailed and convincing arguments. — Just like the oral preachers of a proper life did, which would be impossible in the case of books. Just as the pharmacist cannot add one word to the prescription, because he doesn't understand anything. The countenance of the pharmacist who doesn't believe in the medicines only makes the patient feel uneasy; he unconsciously thinks: "Why aren't you completely healthy yourself, if this medicine is so effective?"

When I give out or read humanitarian booklets, people often remark to me: "Why don't you yourself live what you read to us about?" I reply frankly: "I am reading or offering to you what someone else has written." The situation, as you can see, is rather awkward. Asking others to do what you don't believe in yourself. So it is with writing.

To tell the truth, how many writers do we have that write their own ideas? And not just transcribe what has been written for thousands of years?

Just think, is it necessary to write on paper about the danger of murder,

46 Matth. 23:3.

when an inner voice within us calls us to show mercy? — Is it absolutely necessary to write about equality, when the seed of Unity and Brotherhood has been planted in each one of us? — Is it necessary to write in the press about freedom, when the Spirit which lives within us and supports our life is a free entity? There is no need to write about this, the need is to go and live according to what our inner voice tells us. — The voice of justice, not of animality, which we can learn with the help of reason even without being literate.

People who through violent means impose slavery on their fellow brethren do so not because they are illiterate but because they have not been educated spiritually — they are unwilling to submit to the inner call, the voice of conscience. And as far as the usurper is concerned, no book is going to be of any help if he himself has not been made to understand the futility of his despotic inhuman stand. — If there is to be any mediating influence, it will be the example of a living humble person, and not a dead book lying on the despot's desk.

Bear in mind what happened with the Gospel when people copied it on paper instead of the living heartfelt truth, as Christ commanded: "Lo I have written my law in your hearts and will put the word in your mouths, go and preach good will."[47]

Was Christ the only one to say this? — The Spirit dwelling within us is constantly calling us to the law of God, but we are reluctant to trust ourselves to such an elementary simple truth, but think up artificial fetters to encumber our progress toward a free existence. — Tell me, please, would it be reasonable for me to devote whole volumes to the subject of freedom to write, taking no account of the fact that by this very writing I am keeping millions of people in underground mines extracting the wherewithal to realize the goal of literacy? Or as in ancient times to have slaves hew out whole poems on stones (or tablets, as they were called)? In the middle ages they tore skins from animals (parchments) and wrote on them — I consider all that highly unlawful. But without such paraphernalia literacy would not be realizable.

The advantage of literacy is an imaginary one — a misleading one. If you agree that books have been the means by which so much evil has come into human existence, then why must you too bend over backward using books to destroy this evil, citing the not entirely logical saying: *Fight fire with fire*? — If you admit that a dagger is dangerous, why must you try to destroy the dagger by means of another dagger? It is possible to wash away a body of water — a pond for example — by a much stronger stream of water from above, but I submit that it is possible to dry out the place by another means, namely, the gradual lowering of the level of water in the pond, and in time the area will grow over with luxuriant grass.

47 Cf. Jer. 31:33, which, in the Authorized Version, reads: "But this shall be the covenant that I will make with the house of Israel; After those days, saith the Lord, I will put my law in their inward parts, and write it in their hearts; and will be their God, and they shall be my people." For Jesus' commandment "Go and preach," see Mark 16:15.

Christ's saying "What ye hear in the ear, that preach ye upon the housetops"[48] I don't take to mean writing. It must be taken in its literal sense: preach, but preach freely, openly, not being concerned about the circumstances. — For Christ to speak quietly — "in the ear," as he expressed it, meant that he was imparting the teaching of love in a concentrated form, as if in an embryo, and sometimes secret conversation was a necessary measure in the circle of His listeners, at least half of whom were already his followers, until this teaching had gone from one person, i.e., Christ, to many people and had become stronger, so that it could be preached openly, preached "from the housetops," with no fear of being arrested or wiped out by the opponents of truth. Christ was here saying that "when you feel the power of the calling, as well as multiply in numbers, then go and preach openly what you have heard in secret." The most important thing is the example of your life. — I tell you honestly, my esteemed friend, Lev Nikolaevich, out of your whole life, as far as I understand you, it is not your writings, in the form of literary compositions, that appeal to me, but rather your life, your actions, the way you left an artificial life for a natural human one. — If you had simply presented an idealized view of equality/brotherhood with the lowest levels of the populace, as you thought at the time when you were living in Moscow, and hadn't gone into this brotherly people's own milieu, not actually mingled with them in real life, you would not, to tell the truth, have deserved the high authority and reputation you have now. I think this opinion is shared by many who know you. To write the way you have written — well, that could have been done in Moscow, but to live the way you are now living, in the country — in Moscow would be impossible.

You say that "through literacy you can communicate with many, including me." I don't know about other people, but as regards to me, that is not quite correct. I can honestly say that I loved you and knew you even before you wrote to me. — To put it clearly I will say it this way: I love all good people and strive to draw closer to them with all my heart, and somehow it turns out that I share a common life with them, regardless of who they are, where they may be, what their name is, and whether there are a lot of them or not. I believe only in an unlimited number of good people, that is, in the power of good, and if you are good, only then do I sincerely love you. Of course your letter serves as a report or communication of what is already an established fact (according to accepted opinion), but I repeat: for me the greater reality is the Spirit, the power of thought — the power of spiritual love, rather than love of things. — Such communication, as you see, is only possible through true spiritual love, where deception is impossible. If, however, one believes in the power of literacy, the power of paper, it is quite often possible to be deceived.

---

48 Matth. 10:27.

In their press reports about the latest movement in our community in the Caucasus, correspondents are somewhat mistaken when they say the Christians of this community refuse to obey the government, as the main tenet of our convictions is not to disobey but to avoid giving orders to people in any form, especially when it comes to using forcible means. The government knows that we refuse military service, inasmuch as we have simply decided not to violate the rights of any, so to speak, living creature, especially human beings. By refusing to carry out their duties, our elders and community law enforcers have stated that they are not in a position to govern their districts, i.e., people like themselves, not that they would disobey their elders. — In principle, according to our convictions, elders must always be obeyed; it is only that *we must not be elders ourselves.*

I thank you most heartily for your wish to help me with any need. Nothing is needed at the moment. My warmest wishes to you for all blessings from the Lord God. — I am healthy, thank God, in spirit and body. Summer in Obdorsk this year has been very warm and spring came early: even the month of May was warm, which almost never happens here. I am spending the summer doing a little manual work besides. In the spring I began unloading wood from the rafts. Our artel was made up of three people. For tossing the wood out of the water and making fires on the shore they pay 20 kopeks a *sazhen'*.[49] Then we rolled out the logs. This kind of work pays 60–80 kopeks a day.

I have worked alongside a stonemason building stoves; for a simple Russian stove they pay 15–20 roubles, up to 30 roubles for a Dutch stove. — I have gone haying a couple of times, helping widows mow hay.

A small inconvenience is that I am under strict orders not to leave the settlement. Last winter, for example, I went a couple of times to the outskirts of Obdorsk to get wood, and this raised such a fuss that an official came out from Berezov to look into it and collect depositions. Even on such silly questions as "What would Verigin need wood for?" The official lives in the Berezov District, where it gets down to minus forty or fifty; but in spite of all that, there are still people who don't know why people collect wood from the forest.

When I arrived in Obdorsk, I soon found a small hut to rent (it used to be a smithy), remodelled it and began living there. The police authorities wouldn't allow it, they told to me to rent a 'residential' apartment, and made me pay 6 roubles a month instead of $1^1/2$. — I suppose it was just an expression of the high-handed rudeness of the local police, which I am indifferent to.

I was put on official notice that I must under no circumstances leave Obdorsk (meaning the boundary of the populated settlement). I can live with this, since according to my convictions I feed myself from plants; I don't feel it is right to fish. But the region here lives exclusively off the fishing industry. I don't have to leave the settlement to get bread; if only I can get some work,

49 *sazhen'* — a unit of length equivalent to a little more than two metres.

one can earn one's living here in the settlement doing day-labour. — But for an ordinary person such a restriction would be quite intolerable. As I said, the region lives off fish and they won't even let you travel three or four versts to set your nets.

I still hope they will give me a place to live where I can grow my own bread, or do some kind of agricultural work, which I have the talent for. And I am not in the least surprised by such condescension on the part of the government: after all, it will soon be ten years (in 1897) that I have been deprived of real physical activity, which of course has a bad effect on one's moral disposition.

Anyway, being in exile I have learnt a lot of useful things, for example, I have studied almost the whole northern land, in all its aspects. Most importantly, since I have had nothing to do, I have been examining myself, and even though I haven't learnt everything yet, my study is progressing gradually — something it's quite an effort to do when you're involved in organized, unvarying physical labour.

So far people at home have been sending me money, but in my latest letters I have been telling them not to do that. I think it's quite shameful if a physically healthy person like myself can't earn my own living. Especially since the arrests in our community are continuing, which means the family's finances are getting shaky. Lately they've begun imprisoning the women too.

The question of 'non-violent resistance to evil' is completely answered to my mind, for which I offer you, on behalf of the whole community, our sincere and heartfelt gratitude. You, dear brother Lev Nikolaevich, have personally done a great deal for our age. — I completely agree with your opinion — no matter how you look at it, no good deed was done.

Warmest greetings to everyone I know, and I wish you in brotherhood all blessings from God.

Pëtr Verigin

P.S. Write to me, if you would be so kind. — I did not receive from you any letter in the mail.

Yours, Pëtr

1st Aug. '96
Village of Obdorsk.

Diary excerpt

All that is visible to our eyes is the imprint of the Creator, the supreme will. Through visible images, as through a prism, comes the majesty — the will — of the Creator, imprinted in our mind. Like the shadow of a person on a photographic plate. — In other words, we can see God in His creations.

Mind, thought, will — that is the ideal, and all the image-forms seen by our thought — that is the real. When the mind or will comes into contact with the real — that is, with actual matter, harmony obtains: the harmony of reason, of report, and hence of reality as well. Without matter thought would lose itself in space (if it is possible to imagine such a thing), and have no support. — Idealism, or the will, is a bird, while reality, or matter, is a tree. The bird, no matter how easily and quickly it flies in the air, must still alight and rest.

The Divine Will and the human mind are of similar origin, and so we involuntarily pay attention to every form, to every manifestation of matter — that is a Divine secret, a universal law. In considering a prism, we try to penetrate and examine what lies behind it; by the same token we strive to unite with an entity similar to ourselves, or at least to know it. Our brain, as I indicated, is a glass plate, on which are imprinted the shadows of visible objects, and we distinguish clearly the image of what we wish to see.

The more visible images there are, the greater the exhilaration (in us), and the greater our curiosity and inquisitiveness, which also uplifts our soul.

In every object that exists there is the presence of God, since God is life, and what exists also lives. — The Sophists strive in vain to re-create God (in their opinion), calling Him Nature. — Nature is God too.

If our earth should be destroyed because of old age, it cannot be supposed that the existence of God would thereby end as well, since there are still *masses* of worlds in which He will continue to exist. Even if all existing worlds should die, in their place new ones would arise, hence God is eternal.

To believe in God means believing in life. I believe and I live. To truly believe in God — to believe in life — means striving for eternal life. While everything lives and hence everything believes in God, that is, in life, the distinct ideal of the immortality of life belongs to a more rational entity, for example, man. — The desire for eternal life depends entirely on us, on our faith in life, our faith in God. A small example of the meaning of faith, of the desire to live, may be seen in the following: an animal that happens to fall into the water vigorously begins to struggle, thereby expressing faith, the desire to live, and doesn't drown. — The animal is saved by faith in life.

The embryo of faith in life has been planted in us to serve as a proof that we live. — But developing this faith in life, faith in God, as I have said, depends entirely on us, on our desire. If we desire eternal life, to merge with the Divine principle, which Christ calls Father, we shall indeed live — live eternally; if we do not desire this, we shall die; meaning that what we ourselves desire will actually come to pass. — A lack of desire to live leads to destruction, and we lose even that talent which was given to us as an embryo and which we have held fruitlessly without using it.

The thought of faith is a fine-honed arrow of an abstract mental trait. — Like an arrow shot from a bow, or a leaden bullet, it reaches its target as desired by the marksman, so does serious thought concentrated on a known object — an animate one, of course, and will not remain without significance as long as it does not take any kind of distances into account.

It is from this that very often arises, so to speak, extraordinary mutual love. The pair upon meeting almost cry aloud, not to mention the fact that they have been struck with one another spiritually.

Such instances can be explained by the influence of the love exuded by the most delicate fibres of the spirit. — People create for themselves their most adorable ideal and finally begin to deify it, and if this ideal but exists, the spirit of desire, worship or supremacy will find it and cause mutual attraction. — The person — either a man or a woman (sometimes both of the same gender) — unaccountably begins to feel some kind of attraction and finally power taking over. The actual meeting then only complements an already--existing closeness. And if the love or mutual feeling should arise after the usual encounters and getting acquainted, this influence is simplified to the point of clarity.

It follows that age very often is not significant. Young girls may fall in love with old men (I am talking about true love, not about money) because the old man's desire has subjugated this girl many years his younger, or vice-versa. Such an influence is possible only in the case of true spiritual love, not in the play of fantasy.

There is a lot of evidence showing that a horse led out of the stable for the first time will neigh and submit to the approaching rider, while not letting other people get near him, even if they are physically stronger. The horseman's confidence and resolute desire to possess such a horse restrains and overcomes the animal's obstinacy. — Communication with animals helps them draw the animals closer and they begin to love the person communicating with them; here a similar factor is at work, the power of love, of thought or spirit.

If you agree with all this, then you can completely accept the veracity of stories about wilderness-dwellers frequently taming lions and bears.

P. Verigin

Obdorsk
1896

3. L. N. TOLSTOY ☛ P. V. VERIGIN

14 October 1896. Yasnaya Polyana.

Dear Friend,

I received your letter[50] yesterday and hasten to reply. Letters both to you and from you take a long time, and I have not that long to live. There is much that is just and witty in your arguments against books — the comparison with

50 The reference is to Letter N° 2 above.

the pharmacist and the doctor — but they are all groundless, mainly because you compare books with live communication as if books excluded live communication. In fact one does not exclude the other, they help each other. To tell you the truth, your stubborn resistance to books seemed merely a sectarian habit of defending a position once it has been adopted and declared. But this exclusivity does not fit the picture I have drawn of your intellect, especially of your cordiality and sincerity.

God leads people to Himself to do His will in all sorts of ways: both conscious, when people try to do His will, and unconscious, when they are doing what they think is their own will. To do God's will, to establish His kingdom on earth, people must be united among themselves, so that all may be one, as Christ recognized himself as one with the Father.

To reach this kind of unity one must follow first, the inner path — the knowledge and clear expression of truth, as Christ showed us, which unites all people, and secondly, the external path of spreading this message of truth, which is effected in all sorts of various ways: by trade and conquests, by travels on foot and by rail, by telegraph and telephone, and by books, as well as many other means of communication. Some of the latter — conquests, for example — I am obliged to reject, but others, such as books and quick communication devices I have no right to reject, and cannot help using if I do not wish to deny myself a handy tool whereby to serve God.

The same objection you make in regard to books and the railway, about having to go underground for minerals and process them in a blast-furnace, the same could be said about making ploughshares, spades and scythes. And there is nothing wrong with going underground for minerals or working with blast-furnaces, and when I was young, or as any young man today will gladly crawl boldly underground and dig out the ore, just as long as it is not forced upon him and does not continue ten hours a day his whole life long and he is provided with all the comforts people have thought up, as long as everybody works, and not just hired slaves.

Well, let's not talk any more about that, but do believe me that in writing this to you, I am not writing simply because I have written many books and am still writing them — I agree with you that the simplest good life is worth more than the finest books — and not even just because books have made it possible for me to make contact — this autumn, for example — with a Hindu who completely shares our Christian outlook and who sent me an English book written by a compatriot[51] of his, explaining the doctrines of the Brahmans which coincide with the essence of Christ's teachings, as well as to

51 In his diary of 14 September 1896, Tolstoy noted: "During this time there was a letter from the Hindu Tod and a marvellous book on Indian wisdom, *Joga's Philosophy*" (*PSS* 53:106). The book Tod sent was Swami Vivekananda's *Yoga Philosophy: Lectures Delivered in New York, Winter of 1895-6 by Swami Vivekananda on Râja Yoga, or Conquering the Internal Nature* (New York: Longman Green, 1896).

contact some Japanese people who confess and preach pure Christian morality, two of whom came to visit me a few days ago.[52]

This is not what leads me to disagree with you and refuse to reject the printing of books, along with the railway, the telephone, etc., but something else: when I look at an anthill in a meadow, I cannot bring myself to suppose that the ants were mistaken in ploughing up this anthill and doing everything they do in it. Just the same, when I look at everything people have done materially, I cannot suppose that they have done everything by mistake.

As a person (and not an ant) I see deficiencies in the human hill which I cannot help wanting to correct — hence I participate in the general work — but I don't want to destroy the whole hill of human labour, I only want to rearrange whatever has been arranged improperly therein. And there is a great deal that has been improperly arranged in the human hill, which I have written and continue to write about, which I have been and still am concerned about, and try as best I can to change.

What is wrong in our life, first and foremost, is that the means has been established as a goal, while what ought to be a goal — the well-being of one's neighbour — has been established as a means, i.e., that one's well-being — indeed one's very life — is sacrificed for the production of equipment, which is sometimes necessary for everyone, but at other times only to satisfy the whim of a single individual, when human lives are lost for the production of what is needed only by a few, and sometimes even of harmful things, which no one needs. It is wrong that people forget, have forgotten, or do not know that in producing not only something like a mirror, but even the most needed and important objects like a ploughshare or a scythe, there should be no loss either of life or of the happiness of the single most insignificant-looking human being, because the meaning of human life lies only in the well-being of all people. To destroy the life and well-being of any individual for the sake of everyone's well-being is like cutting off an animal's limb for the sake of its well-being.

This is the terrible mistake of our time: not the fact that we have book-printing, railways, etc., but that people consider it permissible to sacrifice the well-being of even a single individual for the achievement of a particular cause, whatever it might be. Once people lose the sense and purpose of what they do (there is only one purpose: the well-being of one's neighbour), once

52 At Yasnaya Polyana at the end of September 1896, Tolstoy received a visit from the Japanese writer and editor of the journal *Kokumin no tomo* [Friend of the People], Tokutomi Sohō, and a colleague from the journal named Fukai. They were recommended to Tolstoy by another Japanese man, Konishi Masutari, who had accepted the Russian Orthodox faith and was studying at the Kiev Seminary. Konishi became acquainted with Tolstoy in 1892 and, upon returning to his homeland, began translating Tolstoy's writings into Japanese. The Japanese seemed to Tolstoy "very enlightened and liberated in their views on people" (*PSS* 69:153). Later, however, Tolstoy befriended Sohō's younger brother, Tokutomi Roka, and fell out with the elder brother because of his nationalistic, militaristic views.

they decide that they can sacrifice the life and well-being of some old man or even an idiot whose life is a burden to everyone, then it is possible to sacrifice someone who is not quite as old or not quite as stupid, and there is nowhere to draw the line, anyone can be sacrificed for a cause. This is wrong, and must be fought against.

People must realize that no matter how useful and important book--printing, railways, ploughs or scythes seem to be, we do not really need them and they can just as well disappear until we learn how to make them without destroying people's lives and happiness. This is the crux of the matter, which people tend to skirt around on one side or the other and get confused.

Some say you want to destroy everything mankind has worked so hard to achieve, you want to take us back to the days of barbarism in the name of some sort of moral law, that moral law is wrong if it is inimical to the state of well-being mankind has achieved through its progress. Others say — and I fear you may be of this opinion, and it is one people ascribe to me — that since all material improvements in life contradict the moral law, all these improvements are in and of themselves false and so must be rejected. To the first group of critics I reply that we don't need to destroy anything, we only need not to forget that mankind's purpose in life is the well-being of all and therefore, if some improvement denies even a single individual's well-being, then that improvement must be thrown out and not introduced again until we find some means of producing and using it without violating even a single individual's well-being. And I think that such an approach to life would eliminate a great many of the useless and harmful products, while ways would be found very soon to produce the useful ones without violating people's well-being.

To the second group of critics I reply that in progressing from the stone age to the bronze age, the iron age, and eventually reaching its present material state, mankind could not possibly have been mistaken, but has been following an immutable law of self-perfection, and that turning back the clock is neither desirable nor possible, any more than is returning to apehood; moreover, man's task at the present time is not dreaming about what people once were and how to make them again that way, but in providing for the well-being of people who are living today. And the well-being of people who are living today requires them not to torture or oppress others, not to deprive them of the fruits of their labours, not to force them to work to produce things they don't need or cannot use, but most importantly, not to consider it possible or legitimate in the name of some cause or material success to destroy the life and well-being of one's neighbour, or, what is the other side of the coin, to violate love.

Once people realize the purpose of mankind is not material progress, that this progress is inevitable growth, and that there is only one purpose — the well-being of *all* people, that this purpose is higher than any material purpose people can set for themselves, then everything will be in its proper place. And it is to this end that people of our time must direct their whole effort.

Whining about the fact that people today can't live without tools, like wild animals, living off fruits, is like me, an old man, whining about the fact that I no longer have teeth or dark hair, or the strength I had in my youth. What I need to do is not to put in teeth or dye my hair or do physical exercise, but rather to try to live the way an old man should, giving priority not to worldly matters but to God's business — that is, to unity and love, to accept worldly matters only insofar that they do not interfere with God's business.

This is what mankind too needs to do at its present time of life. To say that railways, gas, electricity and printing of books are harmful since people's lives are lost because of them is like saying that ploughing and sowing are harmful simply because I didn't get the field ploughed in time, but allowed it to grow over and then sowed without ploughing, i.e., I did first what I should have done later.

I was so glad to read what you write about your life and about how, by applying to it the teachings you confess, you manage to eke out a living for yourself even in the difficult conditions in which you find yourself. There is nothing like this to show how sincere a person really is. I have become rather poor at doing this, surrounded as I am by all sorts of luxuries which I hate but have not the strength to extricate myself from. Hence your example is a support to me, and I keep on trying.

Thank you for sending the excerpt from your diary. In regard to the thoughts you express there, I should like to share with you some of my own ideas along this line. I shall do so at another time.

Farewell for now, and please don't let any bad feeling rise up against me for criticizing the thoughts you expressed, not only in your letter to me but also in the one you wrote to Evgenij Ivanovich.[53] You are very dear to me and I am trying to be as frank with you as possible, in a brotherly way.

Your loving friend, Lev Tolstoy

14 Oct. 1896

4. P. V. VERIGIN ❧ L. N. TOLSTOY
2 September 1897. Obdorsk.

2nd September '97, Village of Obdorsk.

Esteemed Lev Nikolaevich!

The bearer of this letter is a science student at St. Petersburg University, who along with a companion spent the summer searching out flora and fauna along the banks of the River Ob. They were in Obdorsk as well, and

53 Verigin's letter to Tolstoyan Evgenij Ivanovich Popov (1864–1938).

I spent quite a happy time with them. We fell to talking about a lot of things, including you personally. Upon departure the bearer of this letter expressed a sincere desire to see you, and thus I took the opportunity of writing you.

I can't really say anything in particular about myself. By God's grace I live safe and sound. On the 29th of July of this year my official period of exile came to an end. Now they've given [me] another five years. I have now served ten years altogether as follows: I was first sent away for *five* years, after which they added another *three* years, and on being transferred to the Berezov district they tacked on another *two* years, and now another *five*. A game like this is virtually inexplicable.

But I am more disturbed by the frightfully arbitrary treatment of Christians in the Caucasus. You are probably aware that many are being sent to the Yakutsk and Irkutsk regions, and even in the Caucasus itself the [authorities] are dispersing them among the local population, [specifically] selecting places with cruder morals. And typically they are not allowing wives and children to go with their husbands. But I think it is just a question of time before the people settled in the Yakutsk and Irkutsk regions manage to get permission for their wives to come, if [the authorities] are so inclined.

In Moscow, too, it seems, a lot of arrests have been made. For a long time now I have not been getting any letters from Moscow. The last letter I wrote you was on the 10th of March of this year. Another one was addressed to you care of I. M. Tregubov, dated 4th March. Did you receive them?[54]

The most dangerous element in the Christian movement, from the point of view of the established order, is the refusal to kill a human being. As I said, this is the most important, fundamental point both for Christians and the opposing side. I would say it is possible (and essential) to go to all the imperial courts [of the world] and propose that this idea — the idea of humanity and humanitarianism — be enshrined in law — not just as a matter of principle, but so that anyone wishing to live Christianity in any country not be subject to oppression.

As far as drawing up a petition is concerned, let me suggest the following to you, my esteemed Lev Nikolaevich! *You could* write to all Christian communities in America and Europe, who would send some of their members to some place in Europe, and a kind of conference would be held which you could also attend. After working out a plan of action, [a delegation] of no more than two or three Christian people could be selected from all the communities, who would personally visit all the leaders of the established order. I think that such a plan would not be without result.

54 The whereabouts of these letters are unknown. We know that Tolstoy sent one of them in July of 1897 to Paul Boulanger (known in Russian as Pavel Bulanzhe), who was in charge of organizing aid to the Caucasus Doukhobors.

I sincerely wish you, my esteemed Lev Nikolaevich, all blessings from the Lord God. Please give my heartfelt greetings to all my friends. Your brother in Christ,

P. Verigin

5. L. N. TOLSTOY ❧ P. V. VERIGIN
24 June 1898. Yasnaya Polyana.

24 June.

Dear Brother Pëtr Vasil'evich.

All your friends are upset that communication with you has been cut off.

I am sending you this note just to find out if this route is reliable. If this letter reaches you, send me a reply to Moscow care of His Excellency Aleksandr Andreevich Bers,[55] at the Poljakov house on Tverskoj Boulevard. As far as I know, your parents are alive and well. [Ivan] Ivin and Pëtr Mukhortov have gone abroad to see our friends and brothers in England. Nothing has been decided yet about where to emigrate. There have been some good proposals from America.

I shall write you about everything in detail if communication is established.

I send you brotherly greetings. I ask you not to lose heart and remember not only that many, many brothers are thinking about you and love you, but also that God is thinking about us and loves us in the measure that we do His will and help bring about His kingdom in our hearts and in the world.

Your loving brother,

Lev Tolstoy

6. P. V. VERIGIN ❧ L. N. TOLSTOY
16 August 1898. Obdorsk.

16th Aug. '98, Village of Obdorsk.

Esteemed Lev Nikolaevich!

I am taking advantage of a wayfarer to send you this letter with my heartfelt greetings and my wish that you receive all good from God. Thank God I am healthy and safe.

After a period of uninterrupted correspondence I wrote you two or three more letters which the 'censor' has probably not sent on to your address, since I have not received any letters from you either.

So much has accumulated to talk to you about heart to heart that I shall have to restrain myself, otherwise I fear the letter will be a long one.

55 *A. A. Bers* (1845–1924) — brother of Tolstoy's wife, Sofia Andreevna; served in the Moscow Land Bank on Tverskoj Boulevard.

I recently read your account in *Rus'* about the famine.[56] This chronic famine is indeed a sorry state for a people, but even sorrier is the authorities' refusal to give bread to starving people, while taking away their daily bread is openly tolerated, even encouraged by all possible means!

Dispiritedness — or rather, the lack of development of the spirit in the life of a people — is unquestionably the root cause of all a people's ills, but the lowering or raising of a people's spirits largely depends on the material conditions of human life. When you talk of spiritual aid to a people, I presume you mean their total liberation from outside interference by anyone offering 'aid.' Otherwise, wouldn't it mean that Nature, God and life itself were unjust to every living thing, including man, holding man in a state of spiritual backwardness?

It seems to me that what has led to this sorry state of the masses is man's artificial attempt to help his fellow man — especially in respect to his spiritual development. People who have been falsely taught, wanting to protect their fellow man from the cold — not noticing that they themselves are very weak — and gradually covering his body, have piled up such a weight (on top of it) that it only serves to stifle him! This is how all educational accumulations grow in modern life. We must forsake, as much as possible, all artificially developed 'chimeras' — which themselves, as you rightly believe, live off the resources of the people — and give people room to breathe freely, and then the people will strengthen themselves and develop and advance under the influence of the universal evolution of life! All we have to do is not interfere with this movement. Because of our limited strength, we of course cannot really interfere with or stop this evolutionary movement, but we are retarding and disfiguring our own lives.

As an example I would cite the following: it came to people's consciousness a long time ago, as you know, that God is life (Christ's words). But some people, teachers, would have us see God in figures made by craftsmen, figures often sitting on thrones and wearing royal crowns! And this new-fangled teaching, which has held mankind for thousands of years in the chains of ignorance, etc., etc., is called *education.* What people in Russia are thirsting for now is not education but *liberation* in the broad sense of the word, the total liberation of the individual from being watched over by other human beings.

Cannot those who have taken upon themselves the task of educating the masses see and admit the simple fact that all their artificially worked out

56 In his article *Famine or Not?*, which appeared in the newspaper *Rus'* of 2–3 July 1898, Tolstoy wrote: "If by famine is meant not enough to eat, not what people are dying from at the moment but rather what people live off of, but live poorly, dying prematurely, becoming disfigured, degenerating and failing to procreate, then such famine has existed about twenty years already for most of the centre of the black-earth region, and is especially strong this year" (*PSS* 29:221). For running the article, the paper received a warning from the Ministry of Internal Affairs (which could be followed by suspension or closure).

educational plans are a burden of oppression on the already weakened back of the working man?

Last winter the Governor of Tobol'sk was here. He invited me to his quarters and was extremely kind and polite toward me. We talked for over three hours, it was over high tea, and with him were three members of his 'entourage,' who also took part in the conversation. He questioned me with some interest on how I had become acquainted with you. When I replied that I had got to know you simply by correspondence, they were really surprised that people could get to know each other so well through correspondence!

I attach a copy of the petition we sent to the Ministry of Internal Affairs.[57] I wanted to know your opinion, dear Lev Nikolaevich, on the matter of sending the Doukhobors abroad. Personally, I am *almost* positively *against* emigration. You see, the members of our community are in need of self--improvement, and so, wherever we went, we would take our weaknesses with us; and even though an individual can generally live more freely abroad, I don't think the difference would be all that great. People are the same everywhere.

If it comes right down to emigration, then I foresee the following conditions: the government must return all the resettled Doukhobors to their families, and give a two- to three-year grace period for emigration. The community could send three or four trustworthy people to look over the place proposed for us. Then there is also the question as to whether there are places free in America for us, so that the local population would have no objection to our settling there. Finally, we could hire two or three American ships and go at once.

Please write and tell me, dear Lev Nikolaevich, whether you are in touch with any American acquaintances regarding the emigration of the Doukhobor Community. [Write to me care of:]

Aleksej Ivanovich Stepanov
Village of Zaval'naja (suburb)
City of Tobol'sk

Once he has received your letter, he will forward it to me by some traveller. If you have any papers to send me, address them to Stepanov; he is a good friend of mine — and of yours.

The police do not give me any letters at all, and do not send out any of mine. I am allowed to write — as the Governor warned me — to my parents, and my letters should not contain any 'philosophical arguments' (the Governor's

57 The Doukhobors' application for permission to emigrate was originally addressed to the Empress Aleksandra Fëdorovna; she passed it on to the senate, from where it was sent to the commanding officer in the Caucasus, G. S. Golitsyn. Permission was forthcoming only for those who were not in exile or subject to military conscription. Later, Tolstoy wrote to Russian and foreign newspapers, and, on behalf of the Doukhobors, to Tsar Nicholas II. A copy of Verigin's application to the Ministry of Internal Affairs is preserved in the Tolstoy archives.

expression). There is a Russian Orthodox Church mission in Obdorsk, this year two monks have come out to run it — one from St. Petersburg, and they have preached sermons in church over and over again about the Doukhobor community, about its evil, its danger to the State, etc. I warned the monks that if they continued doing so I would be compelled to remind them of certain unjust misrepresentations about our community. One Sunday they allowed me to speak in church. A heated debate ensued, but a lot of the people here accepted my point of view on world issues.

The priests asked about our rejection of icons. I explained that we worship God, to whom everything that exists is subject, not only the earth and everything on it, but everything in the universe too. God is *life* and is present in all that exists, and is equally present to protect man, for example, as the smallest bird or insect, and therefore, I said: God, whom we worship, is immeasurably vast and great, and it is impossible to put Him in any kind of frame, let alone to represent Him pictorially; we can feel God only in our heart and soul, and express His quality of Love to all living things around us.

There were six priests there; one of them spoke with me, but by and by they all started talking; I drew their attention to the noise they were making, and some of the people who were listening agreed with me. The priests got into such a state of excitement that one of them said: Show us your God, or Love! Some of the people even laughed at such a question. I replied: You are repeating the words of the Pharisees which were addressed to Christ; but I am sure you understand what love means, only you aren't willing to confess it, moreover, you are holding the people in darkness for the sake of material advantage.

Before this confrontation the priests had promised to ask questions and hold discussions periodically on Sundays, but this did not happen more than once. The elder priest among them made a trip to talk to the Bishop about the discussion. He recently returned, but what he came back with I have no idea.

Recently someone came to see me on behalf of my relatives. He managed to come into the apartment and was here no more than *five* minutes when the police came and arrested him. Half an hour later they sent him off in a convoy. He didn't have a passport.[58] They don't give out passports to Doukhobors. Last year, too, some people tried to come and visit me, but they never got here. There was another person too, Mikhajlo Androsov, I think he was at your place.[59] I find such trips quite superfluous. But my old mother is extremely

58 *passport* — here referring to an internal identification document required for travel within the Russian empire.

59 Mikhajlo Androsov, along with other Doukhobors, visited Verigin in Obdorsk in 1895. In December 1896 he tried again to see Verigin, but thirty kilometres from Obdorsk he was arrested and sent home in a convoy. On 13 January 1897 he stopped to see Tolstoy on his way through Moscow. In replying to Androsov's story of his life after his return, Tolstoy wrote him in July of the same year: "Give my greetings and love to all the brethren. I have not seen anyone except

concerned and doesn't even trust letters saying I am alive. Even though this person is travelling in a convoy and won't get there quickly, at least he'll tell her he saw me.

I don't receive any mail from those sent to the Yakutsk region, no correspondence is permitted.

In the magazine *Mir Bozhij* [God's World] there was an account of a conference of missionary priests at Kazan'. The question they raised was typical, about taking children away from sect members! Only it turned out after that that there was nowhere to put them! Any discussion of this matter is superfluous![60]

The magazine *Mir Bozhij* [God's World] is available in Obdorsk. I then sent a letter to the editor regarding the conference. I am sending you a copy. It is quite probable that the police did not forward it.[61]

The conference thought your writings extremely dangerous! To tell the truth, you have uncovered a lot of lies lately. The priests are especially angry at you, and with some justification, for you with your "Little Pamphlets" won't let them hide any more in their sheep's clothing, when in fact they are Wolves.

The summer here has been quite warm and relatively long. There are a lot of berries growing here: cloudberries, bilberries, bog whortleberries, *kljazhitsa,* mountain cranberries, there are a few red currants and I have spent almost the whole summer in the field gathering berries. Moreover, I have procured myself a joiner's bench and some tools; I also have a lathe and am working little by little on that. Come winter I thought I would start making boots, even set up a cobbler's shop, since there are no boots here and people are in great need of them. I think the disadvantage of a cobbler's trade is that you have to sit for longer periods than normal, and that is harmful. In general I do not get regular physical exercise; but in any case I prefer work in the open air, for example, this summer I took great delight in mowing and gathering hay. Haying is also quite profitable here; they don't set up hayfields, everyone mows where he wishes. There are not that many haymakers here, since almost everybody goes off fishing for a living.

you, but all of you are closer to me than people I have spent my whole life with, because I see in your lives the manifestation of the God I live by.... More and more brethren who share our spirit are cropping up all over Russia and abroad. I believe that the kingdom of God is drawing closer. Write to me." (*PSS* 70:107)

60 On the Kazan' missionary conference (August 1897), see the Introduction (p. xxviii). Among other steps taken in the struggle with dissident sects, it was decided to petition for a law which would allow children to be taken from their parents and brought up in diocesan orphanages. Shortly thereafter, this measure was applied to the children of the Molokans. After reading an account of the conference in the newspaper *Russkie vedomosti,* Tolstoy noted in his diary: "A disturbing account of a missionary conference in Kazan" (*PSS* 53:150).

61 The whereabouts of both the original sent to the magazine and the copy sent to Tolstoy are unknown.

Last summer there were two students here from St. Petersburg University collecting flora and fauna.

One of them very much wanted to see you, and so I sent a letter with him — did you receive it or not?[62]

Recently some ships passed through Obdorsk, travelling down the river to Ob Province. This is the second time they were carrying bread to exchange for foreign goods, mainly things made of iron. I don't think such trade is particularly profitable. While sending more and more crops away, Russia is going hungry herself; besides, all the soil is becoming depleted because it isn't getting enrichment in the form of crop waste, and so forth. Russians are starting to produce crops more easily, but it's sad that the producers themselves don't get to eat them, trading them instead for various foreign improvements.

Give my sincere greetings to all the Brothers and Sisters in Spirit. I wish you all the best.

Pëtr Verigin

I am sending you "A Fantasy" — an idea that came together last winter. The bishop was here, and I wrote it in honour of his visit. When I met him I presented it to him, but he didn't take it, explaining that he receives all documents through the Consistory. If possible, see if you can make a small pamphlet out of this idea; I think it will be useful for the simple folk!

A Fantasy

This booklet describes how in Russia the Virgin Mary recently appeared to a peasant-fellow.

The peasant returned home later than usual from the forest with his load of wood. His wife asked him why he was so late. As he excitedly unharnessed the horses, he told his wife to call all the people in the village to come at once, and he would recount a miracle. And when the people, both men and women, had gathered, this is what he told them:

"Here I am on my way home, brothers and sisters, carting my load of wood and with the Lord's Prayer running through my mind, and I think to myself: Now when will the Kingdom of God come on earth as it is in heaven?

"'Nightfall was a-comin' on, but I could already see our village not too far away, just over the second brook. And now, my friends, my heart's a-jumpin,' not so much for joy or as if I were afraid. Yeah, here I am tryin' to get ol' Pegasus to get a move on, when all of a sudden, what do I see, just a few *sazhen'* away, but someone — a woman — comin' towards me, an' it looks like Anna Trofimovna Potapova. An' even before I get close I cry out: 'Trofimovna! Where're you off to for the night?' — In the meanwhile Pegasus,

62 See Letter N° 4.

without me noticin' him, has gone off the road and stopped in the soft snow. So now Trofimovna's come up to me, an' she turns to me and says: 'Peace be with you, good man!' An' then I noticed it wasn't Trofimovna, but I couldn't move, somehow a joy too great for words spread right through me. This woman stood there on road on the trodden snow much taller than me, an' I was somehow looking up.

"'I've been wanting to meet you for a long time, my dear fellow,' she began again. 'Listen, remember, go and tell everyone in your village from the smallest to the greatest, tell everyone you meet in your life.

"'You people often turn in prayer to the Lord God, and this is almost pointless, since right after you pray you go and do more wickedness. And still the Lord is [so] merciful that He is patient and waits for the Kingdom of God to be accepted by people, because people in their foolishness do a lot of bad things. Tell everyone that people have now fallen under the influence of three serious vices: vodka, tobacco and card-games. If people do not forsake these vices they will perish, because from these three vices come a whole multitude of sins: poverty, envy, murder, covetousness, and so on.

"'Just think how much you, simple people of God, suffer from vodka and other fermented drinks. You know it's not long now till the Great holiday of the whole Universe, Christmastide, and in the days leading up to it I always come down to earth to comfort the hearts of people who call upon the Lord. But when the day comes to celebrate Christmas, how do people celebrate it? When people call upon the Lord for help in their infirmities, the Lord sends me to the sorrowing and it is good for me to treat the wounds of those who are repentant; but even if a drunkard starts swearing and cursing, mentioning the word *mother*, I must still come to earth and abide in man's world, because they, people, call upon me.'

"I wanted, dear brothers and sisters, to fall upon my face to the earth and ask forgiveness for the whole human race, but the Virgin stopped me by raising her hand and saying: 'Do not do that, but remember most distinctly what I say. When you drink vodka, people's insides gradually decay and it causes harm to the blood — especially when women drink vodka, their children are born already diseased. Besides, when someone squanders his money on vodka, there is not enough to take care of his household, and this leads little by little to resentment in the family, and just think, what kind of a Christian life is that! In fact it would be better for people who drink vodka not to call themselves Christians. After all, Christ was sent by God to proclaim peace and a good life, but when people go and drink vodka there is no room for peace in the family. Tobacco is harmful because smoke infects the blood and makes a person irritable, causing even more quarrels to break out in the family. People who smoke bear children who are diseased, nervous and malicious. Tobacco smoke breathed in by people in their homes, especially by children, is very harmful to the lungs and the brain, and gives rise to frequent headaches. Think again, people, of how much bread is destroyed in vodka distilleries! Truly I tell you that it was Satan who helped man think up vodka distilleries, to drive people deeper into sin. And how much of the best land is ploughed up for tobacco, when something useful could be grown on it.

"'Card-games are bad for mankind because they distract people's minds from thinking about useful things: how the world was created and formed, and what is the best way for people to live — [these are things] they should gather to talk about after [completing] necessary daily chores. Even a country dweller can lose all his property, and again [this gives rise to] unpleasant situations and quarrels in the family.

"'Vodka, tobacco and card-games cause even more harm for rich people. They hold expensive feasts, replete with costly fermented drinks in great quantities, and when the feasts are over, where do they turn to compensate for what has been lost? Like it or not, they have to get it by all sorts of bad and devious ways, since people who drink wine, smoke tobacco and play cards are used to living an idle and luxurious life. And it often happens that rich people lose their whole fortune at cards and the final result is a ruined life and [possibly] even suicide.

"'City people, including civil servants, merchants, priests and all the rich people of this world, who get drunk on vodka, smoke tobacco and play cards, will all meet a most tragic end, because their behaviour is a temptation for the common people; but you, simple country folk, stay away from the cities, because in them is corruption and death for human souls.

"'I say again to you, good man, remember and tell everyone that if people forsake drinking vodka and anything fermented, smoking tobacco and playing cards, they will be saved, and there will reign peace on earth and good will toward men!'

"At these words a bright circle formed around the Virgin and in her arms I saw a child of unspeakable beauty, who said: 'All that my Mother said is verity and truth: I, Christ, confirm this. Go and preach to all who believe in the Spirit of Truth.' Then the bright circle began to get bigger, and the Blessed Virgin and Christ began rising higher and higher until they were hidden in the heavenly clouds..."

7. L. N. TOLSTOY ❧ P. V. VERIGIN
1 November 1898. Yasnaya Polyana.

1 November. Yasnaya Polyana.

Dear Brother Pëtr Vasil'evich.

I was so delighted to receive your letter. The only news I have had about you is the letter you sent with the students. I answered it and sent you another long letter, describing everything that has been happening with the brethren lately. I sent this letter under special circumstances, but I fear that it too did not reach you.[63]

I am now sending you an account of everything that has been done and is being done to date. The ship that is to carry the first migrants (around 2,000 people) is to arrive for them in Batumi on the 4th of December. When the second ship will set sail is still unknown.[64] I was so happy to read in your letter your idea of God in the conversation with the missionaries; but I was especially happy to read your ideas on the resettlement. I share your opinion completely — namely that it is not the place where we live that is important, or the conditions surrounding us, but our inner mental state. Ye shall know the truth and the truth shall make you free[65] — everywhere, no matter where you are.

You write that you are almost against resettlement, and I am too, but living in hardship and exile, you are in a position to tell the suffering people that they should keep on suffering and hold out to the end, whereas I who live in freedom and under all the best conditions find it awkward to tell people who are suffering: keep on suffering, keep holding on. And it is sad that we (Russians) are parting with those who are close to us in spirit (I take comfort in telling myself that our brethren are to be found everywhere), and it is sad, too, that people have not held on to the end and thereby helped other people know the truth, since nothing testifies to the truth more than the sufferings that one must bear for it.

I was very glad to hear about your life and the life of the exiles in Yakutsk. We shall try to have them reunited with their wives.

Your letter to the Minister of Internal Affairs is unlikely to produce any action. But I am almost certain that once all the migrants are settled in Canada, they will release you and the Yakutsk people as well.[66]

I have just received some good news: 300 people scattered around various villages have been given permission to return and are being issued passports.

I doubt your "Fantasy" will ever be published, even though it would be useful. I shall send it to Posrednik.[67]

63 The whereabouts of these letters of Tolstoy's are unknown.

64 The second ship, the *SS Lake Superior*, set sail from Batoum 3 January 1899 (23 December 1898 by the old-style calendar), carrying approximately 2,300 Doukhobors and escorted by Tolstoy's eldest son, Sergej L'vovich Tolstoy. For a full account of the Doukhobor emigration to Canada, see Sergej Tolstoy's diary reproduced (in English translation) in Donskov 1998a: 231–352.

65 See John 8:32.

66 Verigin was able to go to Canada in 1902, the Yakutsk exiles in 1905. See Verigin's letter to Tolstoy from England en route (Letter N° 12) and his letter from Yorkton, Saskatchewan (Letter N° 23).

67 "A Fantasy" was never published by Posrednik. It was published for the first time in its original (along with an English translation) in Donskov 1995a: 34–36 (see pp. 236–238 above).

Don't condemn the account if you find it not that well written. It was compiled by our friend from some English articles (thank God we have a lot of friends).[68] Farewell. I embrace you in brotherhood.

Lev Tolstoy

8. L. N. TOLSTOY ❧ P. V. VERIGIN[69]

20 November 1898 (approx.). Yasnaya Polyana.

Your letter greatly delighted me, dear Brother Pëtr Vasil'evich.[70] I wrote to you at the address you know about, and I am now writing another letter to send with the sisters who are going your way.[71] I'm sending along Khilkov's letter about the situation in Canada,[72] they will tell you about the situation in the Caucasus.

Everything is going well. But what you wrote to us can never be repeated often enough — that it is not the place where we live that is important, but our relation to God and to mankind, whether we believe that life is in the spirit rather than the flesh, and whether we are prepared, remembering this every time we are faced with a choice between our spiritual and corporeal welfare, to sacrifice all our worldly, temporal affairs for the sake of preserving our eternal soul. In all probability I do not have long to live, and there is so much I want to say that seems clear and important to me, yet overlooked by mankind.

Lately I have been preoccupied by the thought that a great many of our troubles come from our misconception of God, and our resulting lack of faith in Him. This misconception of God comes mainly from our inculcated beliefs about the creation of the world, about our knowledge of how the world was created and who created it. From this superstition comes a misconception of a God who, like man, is either resting quietly or setting out to do what he fancies, along with an even greater misconception as to the beginning of the world and of mankind, and therefore about the end of the world and of human life. We do not see the frightening absurdity of such a conception only because we are too accustomed to it.

68 The account was compiled by Aylmer Maude, the English translator of Tolstoy's novel *Resurrection*, who took an active part in the cause of the Doukhobors' resettlement.

69 This letter was published in *PSS* 71:500–02, dated 5(?) December 1898. The date was changed: the letter was sent with Vasilij Pozdnjakov and the Doukhobor wives who were going to see their husbands in Yakutsk, who all visited Tolstoy at Yasnaya Polyana around 20 November. In a letter to his son Sergej, actually dated 5 December 1898, Tolstoy specifically mentioned that "they passed through safely with Pozdnjakov about two weeks ago" (*PSS* 71:499).

70 Tolstoy is responding a second time to Verigin's letter of 16 August 1898 (Letter Nº 6 above).

71 As a precautionary measure, Tolstoy does not mention Pozdnjakov, who was exiled to the Yakutsk area.

72 A letter from Prince Dmitrij Khilkov, written from Montréal, dated 13 November 1898 (25 November, new style), with a detailed description of the future home of the Doukhobors. Khilkov also wrote that Aylmer Maude was planning to go to Ottawa to discuss all the issues with the Canadian Ministry of the Interior.

In actuality, however, for anyone who is not bound by these absurd superstitions, the question of the origin and the end of the world never arises. Such a person sees himself alive in the world in both time and space, he sees neither ahead of him nor behind him an end to either time or space, and having realized this, is concerned only with how to understand the laws of the world, especially the law of his life, as expressed in Christianity — the will of the Father of life. A free and rational person tries only to understand and fulfil in this world the law of his life, which like the world has no beginning or end, to carry out the will of God, that God whom he acknowledges as being behind His laws and whom he cannot formulate any concept of for himself. He knows only that the being who established these laws exists, but he (a rational person) does not attempt to understand this being and his purposes, realizing that he as a limited part cannot comprehend the whole. All he can understand is that the nature of this God of life, manifest in his soul, is love, that is, the triumph of unity over disunity.

In the Judæo-ecclesiastical understanding man has formulated for himself a concept of God, of His attributes, of His activity (creation, redemption, etc.) and does not pay attention to His laws, to His will, which man is called upon to carry out and which is revealed to him in his heart — through reason and love. Yet given a rational, simple understanding of life, without the superstition of a creation, it is clear that man knows only the law of God, His will, and directs all his efforts toward clarifying it (the law) for himself and following it; about God he knows nothing except that He exists and has given man His law to carry out.

At first glance it seems that both the world and mankind began and therefore must end, and death and the end of the world become frightening things; but at a second, rational glance, just as the world never began and will never end, so has our life never begun and will never end, and therefore there can be no end of the world, and death is not something frightening, since it is only a change more acute than all the changes that occur in our temporal life. There are no rewards or punishments, but only what is here already — namely, the fact that the good one does always leads to a common good, while the evil one does leads to a common evil, and good is joyous, whereas evil is tormenting. Good is unity, i.e., love. Evil is disunity, hate.

What do you think about all this?

Embracing you in brotherhood,

L. Tolstoy

9. P. V. VERIGIN ❧ L. N. TOLSTOY[73]
1 February 1899. Obdorsk.

1st Feb. '99. Village of Obdorsk.

My esteemed Lev Nikolaevich, after such a long silence I have been meaning to write you at least a couple of lines. I shall begin right away with the question that is preoccupying my thought at the moment — about the resettlement of the Caucasus Christians to America [*sic*].[74] As far as emigration in general is concerned, I held no prior assumptions, although even back in the homeland some reasoned that if the government still refused to let us live according to our convictions, we would be forced to ask them to let us go abroad. Which in fact has happened.

I have great hopes — once our emigrating brethren are safely across the ocean and settled in their places, they should be able to begin a good life there. Unquestionably a lot of effort will be required to adapt to their new situation. I have to say that over the past ten years the people of our community have been severely shaken in their basic view of the world; they are like a flock of partridges into which several shots are fired, and after some of them fall down dead on the spot, the frightened remainder instinctively all fly off, mostly in different directions. It is possible to collect them together again, but to get the flock back to a normal state requires a certain period of time.

The analogy between people and partridges is flawed only in the fact that *people do not have to lose their self-control,* but this is true only of those with very strong natures; and in a crowd there is always a certain degree of failure. I say this because our brethren in the Caucasus, as a result of going through a *fundamental change in their lives,* moving to a new place, may go against the accepted rule of solidarity. I am not saying our people, having settled in America, should necessarily submit to some kind of *arbitrary regime;* this is my conviction: no matter what may be the communal life of any group of people, first and foremost there must be full freedom of thought for every individual. In communal living people can be united only by their vital material interests, something that requires a sense of community in and of itself.

How I would like to be at this very moment with those who have gone to America! I think some agriculture could be arranged quite properly in the early days. I know that some good people are looking after the resettlement there,

73 Tolstoy did not receive this letter until January 1902 (see Letter N° 11 below). In the archives there is an accompanying note dated 15 November 1901, signed *Chelovek* [A Person] (this was A. I. Stepanov), explaining that Verigin's letter had been all this time going back and forth between Tobol'sk and Obdorsk, waiting for someone who could take it to its destination.

74 It is evident that Verigin is here using *America* in reference to the whole North American continent, rather than the United States of America.

but it is very important to arrange things properly, as their future life depends on it. I would support an agreement whereby villages were constructed as they usually are, i.e., the houses built in rows according to the lie of the land, but even if built by common efforts and using common standards, the little houses would each have room only for a single family. As for space for storing purely communal things like grain, etc., a separate barn should be built for grain. Later, facilities like repair shops, creameries and mills, could be built by each village for their common interest and through their collective efforts. As long as the ground yields fruit, essential agricultural equipment could be purchased on credit from local factories, and even such things as are needed to set up a mill, for example, state-of-the art turbines, etc. This could all be worked out over a period of several years, although getting into debt up to one's ears is not by itself a right thing to do.

The settlements should comprise no more than fifty households each; this is important for convenience in cultivating the fields. The disadvantage of a large village is that the fields are a long ways out. Fifty households must be considered a large settlement when you think of the offspring being multiplied. — But of course then they could move away to new villages.

Teaching literacy to the children, including the girls, must be considered a priority right at the start. The only literacy I consider essential is the *ability to read and write,* without attributing to literacy any positive signification for bringing up children. Ideally, literacy should be taught by the child's father, or an older brother or sister, just like the mending of clothes and shoes, the knitting of stockings, the binding of harrow chains, etc. Only you have to watch out that the child doesn't become a 'professional' cobbler, or a girl become a hosiery-maker, like many people who become 'professors of literacy' but remain perfect ignoramuses in other departments of life, ending up, for the most part, in the position of 'Shchedrin's generals.'[75]

I am in touch with the brethren in Yakutsk. Their life there may not be all that easy, but they write me cheerful letters all the same. They have already tried sowing grain and planting a few choice vegetables, and the results have been satisfactory. Only the tilling of the soil was typical: the first summer they had but one horse to plough with, so they harnessed ten men to the other wooden plough and they ploughed too! I read that in issue N° 51 of *Nedelja,* it was reprinted from some newspaper their Yakutsk reporter had.

I sent them a clipping of that story and asked them to tell me whether they really ploughed the ground harnessed up that way! I don't suppose there's anything special in it, but still it is typical of their determination as regards the land, i.e., to get their 'daily bread' directly from the land, by whatever means necessary.

75 The reference is to the generals of a fictional account by the Russian satirist Mikhail Evgrafovich Saltykov-Shchedrin.

You are probably aware that there are altogether seventy-three of our brethren in Yakutsk. They are settled on the Notora River. Some have had their wives come to be with them. Some serious thought must be given to the plight of the exiles and I have come to the following conclusion: petition the government to let all of us (exiles) go abroad — I already sent a request to the Minister of Internal Affairs, which I asked to be presented to the Emperor for consideration. The only failing of my requests is that they look more like directives rather than the positive requests favoured by the authorities on the whole. In the statement I forwarded to them I indicated that "the government won't lose anything by letting all the resettled Christians of our community go abroad. It will only be ridding itself of people who are a danger to it."

This is my basic belief, namely that all of us exiles should go to our brethren in America (it is worth mentioning here that some of the exile's wives have already gone abroad in the hope that their husbands will win their release by petition); however, if the government positively refuses to let us leave Russia, we should try to adjust to making ourselves at home here, and try as best we can to set up our farming on the right footing. As the experiment has shown, it is possible to grow grain on the Notora; this already gives us some hope for making a living by farming; in that case I shall ask them to transfer me to the brethren at Yakutsk. Three of my blood brothers were settled separately several hundred versts from all the rest, on the river Maja. They were settled separately as the main 'rowdies.'

I only recently received the letter which was written at your place last year by the three Caucasus brethren who were with you, along with your attached note. It turns out they had actually brought it several times to Obdorsk, but couldn't give it to me for fear of the police. During the whole time of my stay here people have been very frightened, and according to one policeman, a person can almost get sent into exile just for one meeting with me, not to mention the possibility of close friendship. The church is especially 'ardent' in warning people against getting close to me. They quite often preach sermons openly mentioning me by name. This is being done by the missionary Church; the one here includes three clergymen, two of them monks. I have pointed out to them several times upon meeting — we have got to know each other through visits — that such an openly hostile attitude goes against even the simplest courtesy, let alone downright politeness. They reply that "current circumstances compel them to act that way" — ?

Last year, or possibly back in '97, in the fall, I got their agreement on my right of reply in the church, in the interests of accuracy in their reports to the people on the nature of our community, — since they are trying to blacken the whole life of our community.[76] Naturally this debate turned out to have a 'scandalous' effect, even today they regret they ever gave me permission to

76 Cf. Letter Nº 6.

speak. Not only had a certain church regulation been broken, but they were placed in a serious and awkward situation vis-à-vis the people — thus the church was packed to overflowing; after I outlined a brief but well-reasoned account of our community's views and our efforts to live as much as possible the Christian way of life, the people looked at the priests' perturbed faces with great astonishment. When I pointed out that the priesthood through their organized ecclesiastical position were only hiding the real truth from the life of the people and consequently the people were being held in bondage, the priests literally revolted. My talk was already drawing to a close, and the debate ended. It was rumoured that the Archbishop of Tobol'sk gave them a severe reprimand for such 'permissiveness.'

In the latest post I received a telegram, saying that my father died on the 15th of January. His death was natural — my father was already well past eighty. His clothing was quite worn out!

A few words about my life at the moment: I occupy a room six *arshins* square;[77] a joiner's bench and a lathe have been set up against one wall; various tools are arranged on the wall itself; by the opposite wall there is a bed and a clothes tree, and beside the bed a table three *arshins* along, with bookshelves at one end. I use this table for eating, taking tea and writing. The room is quite comfy and bright, there are four windows, all facing the north-east sun.

I wish you, Lev Nikolaevich, all good from God, and give my regards to all the people I know; I am healthy, thank God.

P. Verigin

No correspondence is permitted, except with family.

Address: Aleksej Nikitich Chuprov, Obdorsk

10. L. N. TOLSTOY ❧ P. V. VERIGIN
20 January 1901. Moscow.

20 January 1901. Moscow.

Dear Brother Pëtr Vasil'evich.

At Bodjanskij's request I am sending along his letter to you, concerning you as well as the brethren living in Canada.[78] I quite agree with him that if

77 *arshin* — a unit of measurement of length equivalent to seven-tenths of a metre. Note: "six *arshins*" is, no doubt, an allusion to the amount of land needed for one's burial in Tolstoy's story *How Much Land Does A Man Need?* (1886).

78 *Aleksandr Mikhajlovich Bodjanskij* (1842–1916) — a landowner in the Ekaterinoslav and Khar'kov Gubernias who gave up his land to the peasants. In 1892, because of his contacts with the Doukhobors, he was arrested and sent to the Caucasus. Seven years later he emigrated to Canada, where he lived among the Doukhobors, returning to Russia in 1905. The whereabouts

the Doukhobors indeed harbour a personal superstition, ascribing a supernatural significance to your personality, in spite of any advantage which might ensue from such a superstition, such as exercising a beneficial influence on the weaker ones, it should not be encouraged, as I am sure you fully agree, and that if such a superstition exists, it exists against your will.

The only point on which I differ with Bodjanskij is that he would allow an exception in the case of certain individuals' influence. I don't think that's right; I believe that in a Christian society all are equal and that everybody learns from each other: the old from the young, the educated from the uneducated, the clever from the dull-minded, and even the virtuous from the reprobate. Everybody learns from each other, depending on through whom and at what time the spirit of God speaks.

There are no special people: all are sinful and all may be saints. From what I hear from those who have been in Canada, the information he (Bodjanskij) gives about the life of the brethren there is correct, but I think he is too harsh on them and that the spark of religious service to God is not being extinguished in them. If and when it should be dimmed for a while, it will no doubt flare up again with renewed strength. I am sending along to you another letter written to me by Ponomarëv and Potapov, from which you will see what they are concerned about at the moment.[79]

I am very sorry not to have heard any news from you for a long time. I have been writing, but apparently the channels by which I have sent the letters are not reliable. Our friends and I are thinking of you, and I, at least, have not ceased trying to persuade the government to let you and the other exiles leave. I made another attempt just the other day, with a letter on this subject to the Tsar.[80] I have no idea what will come of it. Quite possibly nothing. But I shall try again. Farewell. My best brotherly wishes to you.

Lev Tolstoy

I am enclosing the brothers' letter to you.

of Bodjanskij's letter to Verigin are unknown. Bodjanskij is the author of "The Doukhobors. Collection of stories, letters, documents and articles on religious questions" (Bodjanskij 1907).

79 Ivan Ponomarëv and Vasilij Potapov wrote to Tolstoy from Canada on 31 December 1900 about disagreements with the Canadian government on questions of land ownership and registration of vital statistics. In his reply of 18 January 1901 (*PSS* 73:17–18), Tolstoy considered the first point very important, but thought an agreement with the authorities possible on the registration of births, marriages and deaths.

80 The reference is to Tolstoy's letter to Tsar Nicholas II dated 7 December 1900 (*PSS* 72:514–16), with an appeal to cease religious persecution, along with a request to allow the wives and mothers of those sent to the Yakutsk area to return to Russia.

11. L. N. TOLSTOY ❧ P. V. VERIGIN
17 January 1902. Gaspra.

Dear Brother Pëtr Vasil'evich, I have only now received your letter of February 1899. Some stranger passed it along to me.[81] You probably know from other sources about the life of your brethren and mine in Canada; I shall tell you only briefly that, according to the latest reports, their material needs are being well supplied; not only have they no further need of help, but they are helping others. I only hope they are also prospering spiritually. And I believe they will, in spite of the fact that outwardly many of them seem to have somehow been weakened at present: they have forsaken the communal life and given in to temptation.[82] I think such a departure from the appearance of Christian life will not harm them and will lead them on toward the perfection all living beings strive for and are moving toward. The Christian leaven in them is so strong that, having tasted worldly life, they cannot help but wish to return to the Christian life. And if they return, they will do so consciously, and not simply out of a feeling of gregariousness or submission to authority, as is the case with many of them now.

There is something else I should like to tell you, namely, that I am most unhappy about their refusal to accept personal ownership of land. Such a refusal would be meaningful if they were perfect in everything else. But in the more important things they are departing from the requirements of a Christian life, while here all at once they are wrecking their lives over a formal acknowledgement of land ownership (once they have received the land as personal property, they can always make use of it on a communal basis). The same is true of their refusal to register births and marriages. There will still be questions on which they will have to stand up for their Christian beliefs — or, rather, their Christian life — such as, for example, the question of war, or the courts, and so on — then is the time to stand firm with all their might.

I haven't heard anything about you for a long time. Write to me about yourself, your feelings, thoughts and plans. I am keeping this letter short as I fear it may not reach you, and besides, I have been ill for a long time and I feel I am quickly drawing closer to death, or rather to the transition into another form of life, and I am writing in bed. Perhaps that will serve as an excuse for my poor handwriting.

Embracing you in brotherhood,
Your Brother, Lev Tolstoy

17 Jan. 1902

81 See Letter N° 9, Note 73.

82 Tolstoy wrote about this in February of 1900 in his missive "To the Doukhobors who have emigrated to Canada" (*PSS* 72:305–10).

12. P. V. VERIGIN ❧ L. N. TOLSTOY
15 November 1902. Christchurch.

15th November 1902. England.

Dear Friend Lev Nikolaevich!

Forgive me for not informing you for such a long time on the progress of my trip. I send you my heartfelt greeting, and ask you to pass along my regards to Sofia Andreevna.[83] God give you health and prosperity.[84]

I have been staying for over a week now with the dear Chertkov family.[85] I arrived here on the 5th of the month. On the 20th I plan to leave for America [*sic*]. I have been here rather long; I should have gone straight to see my elderly mother. I was at a meeting in London. I wasn't going to go, but Vladimir Grigor'evich persuaded me that I must show myself to the English community. It still turned out that I presented myself a bit like a Russian 'polar bear,' since I don't understand a word of English. Vladimir Grigor'evich read a rather well-written account he had prepared about the Doukhobors in general and especially about the latest movement,[86] attempting to explain this movement, which grew out of more or less respectable motives, while for the most part it has been rather crudely condemned in the press.

The audience listened attentively, and later I was asked [to explain] the Doukhobor views on several issues. Vladimir Grigor'evich interpreted.

There does not seem to be much practical sense in the new movement, but, God willing, everything will turn out all right.

I shall write you in detail when I get to Canada.

I wish you all good from God. I am in good health.

Pëtr Verigin

83 *Sofia Andreevna* — Tolstoy's wife, Sofia Andreevna Tolstaya.

84 Verigin was in Yasnaya Polyana 30–31 October 1902, on his way from exile to Canada.

85 Vladimir Chertkov was sent abroad in 1897 "for propaganda and illegal interference in sectarian affairs." He lived in England, where he published works by Tolstoy that had been banned in Russia. The Chertkov family was able to return to Russia in the summer of 1907.

86 The reference is to the 'pilgrimage movement' — see Letter N° 13 below.

13. P. V. VERIGIN ❧ L. N. TOLSTOY
12 January 1903. Poterpevshee.

12th Jan. 1903. Village of Poterpevshee.[87]

To Lev Nikolaevich Tolstoy

Forgive me, dear Friend, Lev Nikolaevich, that I have not so far written you a detailed letter about my trip. On the way, of course, I could have written several letters, but I am not a very regular correspondent. Even though I very much wanted to send you a telegram once I had crossed the border, I couldn't, I was afraid I might get left behind by the train, and so I hardly stepped outside the carriage right until we reached London, where Vladimir Grigor'evich Chertkov greeted me with open arms. I spent two weeks with this dear family, hardly noticing the time. Though Anna Konstantinovna[88] is physically ill, she is cheerful and strong in spirit.

Vladimir Grigor'evich went with me to Liverpool and saw me aboard ship. The crossing was quite stormy. All the passengers had to wait four days on the ship in the harbour at Saint John for medical inspection; it turned out there was one person on board with symptoms of smallpox.

Three Doukhobors came to meet me in Saint John along with someone sent by the Minister from Ottawa, who told me that if I had the time free, the Minister would like to see me in Ottawa. I agreed and went to see him. I declined to talk about the matter of the Doukhobor emigration, and advised the Minister that I was still like a guest in Canada. The Minister was very kind to me.

Just three days later I was with the Doukhobors. You can imagine, my dear Lev Nikolaevich, how my soul was overflowing with ecstasy and feelings of joy upon arriving at the first Doukhobor village — that was the village of Blagodarnoe.[89] The second village was the one where my mother is living; I found her extremely cheerful and quite healthy for her years.

I should now like to touch upon a more important question in the Doukhobors' life — their recent 'pilgrimage movement.' The place and time of writing this letter do not allow me to go into detail as to my own opinion on this movement — or rather, on the true significance of what amounts to an accomplished fact. At the bottom of it there are three mixed feelings which prompted some fifteen hundred Doukhobors to leave the place where they were living and set out on the road without any particular direction.

Neither the representatives of the Canadian Government nor the Doukhobor people who have been looking after their liberation from their

87 *Poterpevshee* (pron. *po-ter-PEF-she-yeh*) — lit. 'Enduring' — the name given to one of the Doukhobor settlements in Canada.

88 *Anna Konstantinovna Chertkova* (*née* Diterikhs)— wife of Vladimir Grigor'evich Chertkov. For more on Verigin's stay with the Chertkovs, see Letter N° 12 above.

89 *Blagodarnoe* (pron. *bla-go-DAR-no-yeh*) — lit. 'Grateful.'

sorry plight, beginning in the Caucasus right up to now, have explained accurately or in detail what the political as well as the territorial and economic obligations of the Doukhobors would be should they decide to stay and live in Canada. This state of uncertainty has delayed the acceptance of land, and has led to one opinion among the Doukhobors that the government's conditions are too strict, and so some Doukhobors have decided they should leave the land that was offered to them, saying *Let us go and search of truth,* i.e., in search of a more humane attitude toward the settlers on the Government's part.

Others in this group of three 'feelings' declared that the Canadian climate is too cold and that as vegetarians they would never get used to a climate like this; *let's go and find a milder climate,* they said.

According to a third opinion: "The land is fruitful here, and the climate, even though cold, is still a very healthy one; we shall prosper living here, while out there in the world — in humanity world-wide — there are many poor people, our brothers and sisters; let us go and tell everyone along the way that people must stop smoking tobacco, drinking vodka and quarrelling, put an end to military organizations and the violent oppression of people who are their brethren — people working in the mines, for example, or in other types of community labour." This was the literal explanation given me by those who belonged to the third group of the 'three feelings' — the so-called preachers of Christ's teachings.

My own personal opinion about all those fifteen hundred people, as far as I can tell, is that all these people seem very solid and reasonable members of the community, including the women and girls, many of whom tell me they have decided not to get married but to live and work spiritually for Christ, i.e., for the equalization of human rights in community life.

That is all I know about this movement so far. As a deep-thinking psychologist, Lev Nikolaevich, you will be able to understand this phenomenon that has arisen among the Doukhobors for yourself, in general and in the particular. I shall add my own opinion: I cannot seem to distinguish this movement from the overall question of injustice in life that is vexing mankind.

The whole party was recommended by the government to turn back at Menidos, a hundred and thirty miles [= 210 km] from the Doukhobor settlements. All the Doukhobors behaved very meekly in front of the police and there was no violence. They are now living in their own houses, they have plenty to eat, and since the day I arrived have not accepted government aid.[90]

I might compare this movement to Abraham's actions in bringing his son as an offering to God, and when Abraham took up the knife to slay his son, God's angel stayed his hand — or rather, Abraham himself came to the realization that he did not have to slay his son, and God told him to take his son, go home and live a life of praise to God.[91] I voiced this opinion to almost all

90 See Letter N° 21.

91 See Gen. 22:12–17.

the Doukhobors who were walking, having left their whole way of life behind them, and said: "Your motives of self-sacrifice for the common good of human life are legitimate and precious ones, but there is no need to let the children go hungry and cold, so for the time being why not remain with all the rest of the brethren and teach them?" Those with families took this explanation too as a revelation from God.

I embrace you and pray to God for your family's well-being.

P. Verigin

P.S. There will soon be a meeting to discuss acceptance of land.

14. L. N. TOLSTOY ❧ P. V. VERIGIN[92]
9–13? February 1903. Yasnaya Polyana.

Dear Pëtr Vasil'evich,

I have not replied to you for some time as I have been ill. I am slowly approaching death and am afraid lest the remaining days of my life be poorly spent and yield no benefit to mankind. This is the great advantage of old age and disease, outweighing by a hundredfold the disadvantages of disease and old age.

The account you have given me of the Doukhobors and your explanation of the recent movement seem quite in order. May God help you, dear friend, in that position of responsibility where you exercise considerable influence on people, not to sin against them by giving them wrong direction.

My advice, which I have thought through before God and offer to you in my love for you and the Doukhobor brethren, is to get yourself personally as much out of the way as possible, not taking sides on current issues but encouraging the brethren in only one thing: to act as God desires his children to act, and most importantly, not to violate the love among themselves in the name of this or that understanding of God's will. God's will is the same for all: to love Him and love each other, and in order to be in a position to love Him and love each other, they must deny self and serve one another in everything. The most fearsome evil is the enmity which arises among people out of their differing concepts of man's duties toward God. So I ask you to use all your influence to combat this.

If only those who reject the use of animal labour and those who are content to stay in one place and till the soil would consider love and unity between them an actual possibility, regardless of differences of opinion, if they would only love and help others as well as their own, and put this love above all else, everything would be good, and in one way or another a unity of views would be achieved.

92 Handwritten by Tolstoy's daughter M. L. Obolenskaja. Signed in Tolstoy's own hand.

In a word, the longer I live, and the closer I come to the end, the more obvious it is to me that only one thing is needed: the establishment of God's kingdom, which comes about through people's love for each other. But this love does not come all by itself; we must make an effort to draw it close to us, the same effort by which God's kingdom is revealed.

I think you are aware of all this, and that you feel and act in this spirit, and I am glad of it.

Thank you for writing me; please do write again, and if possible, tell me in detail about how the different Doukhobor settlements are progressing and whether there is harmony among them.

Farewell, and may God grant you and all the Doukhobor brethren the highest possible good in the world — unity and love among yourselves.

Lovingly, Lev Tolstoy

15. L. N. TOLSTOY ❧ P. V. VERIGIN[93]
24 October/6 November [new style] 1903. Yasnaya Polyana.

Dear Pëtr Vasil'evich,

Yesterday I had a visit from old Aleksej Aleksandrovich Fofanov, who was released from the Yakutsk area. As you know, he, Novokshonov and Shcherbakov arrived in the Caucasus, preparing to go to Canada to be re-united with their families. But besides not being granted foreign passports, [another] misfortune has befallen them, which Fofanov himself will write you about: they had all their money stolen from them, so that now they have no means of getting to Canada. I am petitioning for foreign passports to be issued to them, and I hope to be successful in this. But in any case, because of this misfortune, they need money. If the community is willing to give them enough money for their living and their passage, you can send it to me, or to save time you can telegraph me how much you are sending and I shall see the amount gets to these old people.

I was very glad to hear the news that your life and that of your family and our brethren have been progressing and are continuing to get better and better, closer and closer to Christ's precepts.

I am not writing to you with my own hand, as I am not feeling entirely well these days. But my overall health is as it should be for one quickly approaching a change in one's form of life. I shall be happy to hear from you. Farewell, and brotherly greetings.

Lovingly, Lev Tolstoy

6 November 1903.

93 Handwritten by Ju. I. Igumnova, an artist and friend of Tolstoy's daughter Tat'jana Tolstaja. She lived at Yasnaya Polyana for several years, helping take care of correspondence and copying manuscripts. The signature is in Tolstoy's own hand. A note from Aleksej Fofanov was attached.

16. P. V. VERIGIN ☙ L. N. TOLSTOY

1 December 1903. Otradnoe.[94]

Dear Lev Nikolaevich!

My heartfelt thanks for letting me know how you are getting on. May the Lord save you! Please give my best regards to your whole family, with my wishes for all good to you from God.

I received your letter along with the attached note from Alësha Fofanov,[95] and now I am hastening to send you two hundred dollars, which I would ask you to give to the old ones who turned to you for help. Address it to *Vasilij Shcherbakov.*

We are sending this rather small amount for the living expenses of Fofanov, Shcherbakov and Novokshonov, wherever they happen to be staying for the time being. If they are able to come to Canada, we might be able to offer some further help.

How hard you work! Dear, kind Lev Nikolaevich, it seems that wherever we turn you are expending your depleting bodily forces. Happy is the man whose frail body has not yet been forsaken by Soul or Mind and is that much more able to struggle with circumstances around him.

I'm not about to give you [at this time] a whole account of myself and my surroundings since coming to Canada. The main reason is not to overburden your attention.

As for how the Doukhobors are settling in to community life here, I cannot say that things are getting 'better and better' as you suggest, but as far as is humanly possible, especially for a large group of people, to adopt good character traits, the community is coming along well, thank God.

In a brief letter I cannot go into all the pros and cons of the people's community life, except to say that here in Canada the Doukhobors have been faced with a number of good reasons to unite in their community life. There is a great lack of resources and agricultural equipment and under Canadian regulations one can make a fairly good living off the land, but homestead plots are too unequal to [profitably] work the land individually. This summer, though, thanks to collective labour in working the land, the Doukhobors have managed to plough and prepare for spring sowing more than ten thousand acres of land. In addition, since I arrived they have bought about four hundred work horses. They have acquired — as major purchases, very important to them, eight steam threshers: six 18-h.p. machines drawn by horses and two 20-h.p. self-propelled vehicles. The grain and vegetable harvest was fairly good and these eight machines proved extremely efficient in

94 *Otradnoe* (pron. *ot-RAD-no-yeh*) — lit. 'Delightful' — the name of another Doukhobor village in Saskatchewan.

95 *Alësha* (pron. *al-YO-sha*) — diminutive form of the name Aleksej.

the threshing. The six [stationary] threshers have now been set up in various plots of land as mills, they grind the grain and process fibres for cooking oil, while the two vehicles have gone into the forest where they will be set up to saw lumber. In the spring we are planning to manufacture bricks and tiling, using steam power. The Canadians are beginning to be quite amazed: on the one hand there are Doukhobors walking around stark naked, wanting to abandon physical labour altogether, while on the other hand they are acquiring the most up-to-date agricultural equipment and are starting to work in a very business-like fashion so as to protect their equipment from the bankers. Among useful acquisitions I might mention are over a hundred grain scythes, which work very cleanly and quickly. Now each forty-family village has nine pair of work horses, fifteen cows, and a few sheep, and all summer long we have been buying more things. Carts, sleighs, ploughs, harrows, etc. have been bought according to the number of horses. We have also bought some thoroughbred horses and are planning to raise our own acclimatised horses, as they are quite expensive to buy.

We shall be preparing a detailed account of our farming activities over the summer; maybe we shall send you a copy, at least the young people around you might be interested in it.

As to the Yakutsk brethren and their emigration to Canada, if they will permit, I have come up with a plan: to set up a bank account in Yakutsk so that those who are emigrating can draw out money for passage, and another account in Moscow or Batumi, so that travellers who get that far can provide themselves with the means to proceed further. Our whole community has sent notice about this to Yakutsk, also five hundred dollars has been sent to help support — *in that location* — old people like Fofanov, Shcherbakov and Novokshonov, and people who are ill. The community advised them by letter that should a need arise, they could send a request by telegram and we would be sure to send them money, but only if the requests come in the name of all the exiles together. This [past] summer I collected the names of all the people in Siberia and sent them to the English [*sic*] Government, which has promised to intervene with the Russian authorities about releasing them from Yakutsk — we have even set aside some land here for that number of people. But if our brethren in Yakutsk have no patience, if you look at it objectively, it seems nobody is to blame. In the heat of the moment I feel extremely angry even toward such old people as Fofanov and Shcherbakov, whom I have nothing but contempt for. They are looking for they know not what, and consequently misfortune and trouble await these older people, when instead they should quietly eat their daily bread and praise the Lord. Well, never mind! Nothing in this world is ever useless; all that is being done is being done for the better.

I embrace you in thought and wish you again all good from God.

Lovingly,
Peter Verigin

1 Dec. '03
Village of Otradnoe. Yorkton [Saskatchewan].

17. L. N. TOLSTOY ❧ P. V. VERIGIN
2 January 1904. Yasnaya Polyana.

Dear Brother Pëtr Vasil'evich,

I received your letter with the cheques and have sent the money to the old people. I was surprised by your harsh attitude toward them. I don't think they deserve it. They received five hundred roubles from Maude and write that they now have enough money. The question of passports has not yet been resolved, though they are promising to issue them.[96]

I am enclosing Murav'ëv's letter about the Pavlovka villagers who were exiled to labour [camps] with their families.[97] These are deeply religious people, suffering on account of a momentary distraction, who not only have not asked for anything to date, but have even refused the help [that was offered]. Now, it seems, they are in dire need, and I was thinking: if your community agreed to return to Maude the five hundred roubles he sent, I would send this money to the Pavlovka people. I hope that the community of universal brotherhood will not turn this down. Please reply. The news I have of you through Tan[98] and from your kind letter is a delight both to me and to everyone who shares a kindred spirit with your community. You will forgive me if I as an old man take the liberty of giving advice to you and those around you. In all probability you know yourself what I am about to tell you, but it doesn't hurt to repeat an idea if it is a right one. Don't get carried away, dear friend, by the material success of the community. Remember that this success is based on the unity stemming from the religious consciousness which brings everyone together. Thus religious feeling is the basic capital underlying even material well-being, [while the latter] by itself is not only unimportant, but oftentimes destructive, undermining the very source from which it flows. "In this rejoice not, that the spirits are subject unto you; but rather rejoice, because your

96 Tolstoy applied to Grand Prince Nikolaj Mikhajlovich and the head of the civil sector in the Caucasus, Prince Grigorij Golitsyn, with a request to issue foreign-travel passports to Fofanov, Shcherbakov and Novokshonov.

97 In 1901, the peasant sectarians from the village of Pavlovka in Sumy County (Ukraine), under the strong influence of Prince Dmitrij Khilkov, destroyed a local church. A trial took place January–February 1902, where they were represented by lawyer N. K. Murav'ëv (1870–1936). In spite of twelve people testifying in their defence, severe sentences were handed down: four were given prison terms, while forty-five were exiled to hard labour for periods of up to fifteen years.

98 *V. G. Bogoraz-Tan* (1865–1936) — writer, ethnographer, member of the *Narodnaya Volya* [People's Will] party, visited the Doukhobors in Canada in the summer of 1903. His accounts were published in the newspaper *Russkie vedomosti* — it was these Tolstoy was referring to; he did not come to know Tan (Bogoraz's pseudonym) personally until early in 1905.

names are written in heaven."[99] And so I feel that the most important thing is to protect, arouse and support that religious feeling, which is needed not just for one's material well-being but for the genuine happiness of all. So no matter how absurd the movement for animal liberation and Heavenly Life might seem, it is more important than all the steam threshers, scythes, harvesters, etc., just as steam in the engine is more important than all the cars with freight attached to it. If steam senselessly escapes outside, then all one needs to do is to make it work productively. The same goes for the Heavenly Life Party. They have the vital element that brings genuine good to one's self and others, while those who despise their motives and set up marvellous useful machines and see in them the meaning of life have nothing to offer themselves or others but certain destruction. I am sure you know this and feel and act this way, but I wanted to say this to you.

Your loving brother, Lev Tolstoy

2 Jan. 1904

18. P. V. VERIGIN ❧ L. N. TOLSTOY
20 February 1904. Otradnoe.

Village of Otradnoe. — Canada. To Lev Nikolaevich Tolstoy
1904 20th February (n. s.) [from] Pëtr Verigin.

My dear Lev Nikolaevich, forgive me for offending you with my crude comments regarding the old people. It is the fault of an evil that is common to all of us. For all your pains may the Lord send you physical health and peace of mind.

As far as the Pavlovka villagers are concerned, in response to your request for 500 roubles I am sending you three hundred dollars to do with as you please. And as for Maude, if he has sent 500 roubles to the old people, as you say, we shall reimburse him.

With you, my esteemed Lev Nikolaevich, I should like to be even more open than is customary. Which means at the moment I presume the Doukhobors' financial accounts and expenses should be as accurate as possible.

Maude has written me twice now that he has money set aside for loans to the Doukhobors for travel from Yakutsk to Canada. Just how much money there is Maude doesn't say, only that the money is to be used and repaid, but without interest.

On the 28th of this current month of February there is to be a conference with two people attending from each village. I shall raise Maude's proposal among other issues. Since the Doukhobors have accepted a great deal of help

99 See Luke 10:20.

from friends over the last twenty years I don't suppose they will decline this offer. (I am enclosing a brief statement of income and expenses over the past year, which will show that the Doukhobors' financial affairs are not exactly rosy.)

Proper travel arrangements from Yakutsk should be made insofar as possible. For example, there should be at least a small sum of money — an account — available in Yakutsk, a second source in Moscow and a third in England or on the American [*sic*] side. They should select the shortest and cheapest possible route. I came by Moscow, London and Saint John, and found it very convenient. I'm speaking about those who want to emigrate directly from Yakutsk to Canada. This systematic arrangement doesn't apply to those who go [back] to Russia upon being released, these can only be offered some private aid to get by on, as much as people can afford. We are not sending any money now for my sister and brother-and-law. We don't have it.

I am sincerely grateful to you, Lev Nikolaevich, and may the Lord bless you for your warning against getting too strongly carried away by material concerns; I am afraid of that myself, but right now we only wish to have our daily bread, something we really want to earn, since the Doukhobors have a great many children. As it happens, at the moment the Doukhobors are involved in discussions regarding becoming subjects of the English king. The majority do not want to hear about taking out citizenship; they reason that this would violate Christ's basic teaching about the equality of all people. Taking out citizenship would mean observing a formal order: everyone receiving a 160-acre plot of land would have to sign a form pledging an oath of full allegiance to "Edward," to defend his honour and so forth and to live in Canada for ever. If I may express an opinion, apart from violating the principle of equality of all people, I cannot guarantee that I will stay living in Canada for a long period of time, as the climate in the place where the Doukhobors are settled now is rather cold and we have to struggle to sow our grain and to make sure it is not killed by the frost. There are many good reasons for this: almost every year now the grain has had a hard time escaping autumn frosts, since the land has not been tilled properly. The earth should definitely be steam-ploughed for two years running, and wheat sown only in the third year. All that is possible with specialized equipment. (We are considering buying a 25-horsepower steam plough to try out this spring; one that could drive eight ploughs over virgin soil, or ten or eleven over soft soil.) If we fulfil, more or less, all the requirements for dividing the land and sowing the grain and still don't come up with a good yield, then it stands to reason we can't keep on living here forever, and so the question of citizenship I would say is rather premature. We don't know what explanations the English [*sic*] government will accept; that is something only time will tell.

This experiment will take at least three to four years, over which time the Doukhobors, one would assume, will manage to save up at least some money, and if the government should decide to make life miserable for the Doukhobors over some question of citizenship, we shall be willing to agree to it. It will only prove for the umpteenth time that all monarchical governments have outlived their time and are tolerable only as an evil in human life in general.

My love to you, yours ever faithfully,

Peter Verigin

Statement of Expenses and Income for 1903
of the Doukhobor community in Canada

			$	¢
1.	Purchased	35 horses in Winnipeg	6,719	.50
	"	5 colts	3,150	.00
	"	323 horses from Rain & Feirce [?]	25,696	.00
	"	7 horses from Bikyanin and 2 from Plaksin	1,200	.00
	Transport and delivery expenses for all horses, purchase of various items for horse herds and guides:		906	.05
		Total	37,671	.55
	Agricultural equipment			
2.	Purchased	4 horse-drawn steam engines with threshers	9,250	.00
	"	2 self-propelled steam engines with threshers	6,000	.00
	"	2 stationary machine saws	900	.00
	"	Grease for steam engines, [payments] to Inspector and food on journey	142	.24
	Paid for Prince Albert steam engines		2,000	.00
	Supplies for steam engines, engine operators' expenses		1,100	.00
	50 scythes, 32 hay-cutters and 20 000 pounds of threads		10,309	.00
	45 cutters 20 sowers 16 wagons 109 ploughs 234 triple harrows 12 grain-cleaners and 152 sleighs		14,092	.55
			43,793	.79
3.	Purchased	Fabric materials total	29,338	.29
4.	Land accepted from the government and purchased by Pëtr Vasil'evich		36,250	.00
5.	Purchased	wheat, oats and flour	9,720	.20
6.	"	Horse collars and footwear supplies	13,445	.22
7.	"	Winter boots for men and women	4,913	.58
8.	"	Iron, Dishes, implements, etc.	5,901	.11
9.	"	Salt, Kerosene and [?]	2,653	.08
10.	"	Sugar, Tea and lard	2,294	.87
11.	"	Woollens	1,505	.00
12.	"	Soap	1,707	.00
13.	"	Mill equipment and millers' expenses	868	.63
		Total	108,656	.98
		Total for this page	190,122	.32

			$	¢
		[Balance] forward	190,122	.32
14.	Purchased	sheep	1,461	.00
15.	"	Oil and containers for it	1,765	.72
16.	Goods transport by rail		1,530	.75
17.	Money sent to Siberia, Maude and other places		3,086	.00
18.	Railway trips and food on journey		852	.15
19.	Liman School		745	.85
20.	Government Office in Yorkton		303	.60
21.	To Iosif Konstantinovich		300	.00
22.	Vasja Golubov's expenditures on steam engines and threshers		364	.60
23.	Stationery expenses, paper for correspondence and typewriter		284	.35
24.	Paid to Egor Majer (Blacksmith)		255	.00
25.	Given to Archer at different times		157	.50
26.	Loaned to Mifodij		125	.00
27.	Paid for repair of all equipment		142	.00
28.	Sawmill expenses, etc.		155	.00
29.	Ivan Pod.'s expenditures on himself and the workers in Yorkton		41	.46
30.	Fees [?] for wood, bank interest, stable fees, and post-office box in Yorkton		83	.10
	Total		201,775	.40
31.	Petty-cash purchases for all 47 villages		13,769	.52
	Total		215,544	.92
32.	Agricultural income for all 47 villages		152,474	.24
	Outstanding debt		63,070	.68

Payment of debt to be made at the depots in the City of Winnipeg in the autumn of 1904. Without interest.

19. L. N. TOLSTOY ❧ P. V. VERIGIN

3/15 March 1904. Yasnaya Polyana.

I received your letter, dear Pëtr Vasil'evich, with the statement of the community's income and expenses, which I found most interesting, along with a cheque for £61.

Maude didn't wait for the reimbursement of the money he sent to the old people, but sent another 500 roubles for the Pavlovka villagers, which I sent along to them. So your money (£61) remains unused. I shall put it into the bank and await your reply as to what should be done with it. Yesterday I received a letter from Konkin saying that he is waiting for money from you to take him and his daughter to Canada, since he is now released and hopes to emigrate in May.[100] Should I send him the £61? Let me know. So much for business matters.

I quite understand the difficulty and even the impossibility of Christians recognizing the authority of the king and pledging him allegiance. It appears there is no place left on earth where Christians can live without being persecuted. I think this should spur Christians even more to do God's will and live a Christian life, which worldly people are so far removed from. What will come out of this it is impossible to say, but one thing is certain: nothing but good can result from doing God's will, for those who do it as well as for all the people of the world.

I was so glad to hear from you that the material well-being of the community is not keeping you from seeing the need to strive for spiritual perfection, and I hope that this striving for spiritual perfection, which is the sole purpose of each individual, is going on among you without let-up.

Thank you for your good wishes. I am getting along very nicely. I work as much as I can, unfortunately at the easiest task and the one of most doubtful benefit — writing. Right now I am writing about war,[101] about the senselessness of it all, and about how we can be saved from it not by Christ's words, but by practising his teachings, and I am enjoying undeserved happiness, and the love of those good people who are so dear to me.

Farewell. I embrace you in brotherhood and wish you Godspeed in that activity which you never need repent of and constantly draws you nearer to God.

Lovingly, Lev Tolstoy

Write to me about yourself and the brethren at least occasionally.

3 [old style] / 15 [new style] March 1904

20. P. V. VERIGIN ❧ L. N. TOLSTOY
12 April 1904. Otradnoe.

Canada. — Yorkton. Village of Otradnoe. 12 Apr. 1904.

My dear Lev Nikolaevich, I am happy to inform you that we are all alive and well, especially in the Spirit, thank God. Now that spring has come, my mother has begun to recover from a serious winter illness — no doubt like everything in nature. — She sends you and your whole family her warmest regards and her deep gratitude for your attentions to her relatives and everyone else. She

100 Ivan Konkin's letter dated 2 February 1904 is on file in the Tolstoy archives. Tolstoy's reply is in *PSS* 75:58.

101 The reference is to Tolstoy's article *Bethink Yourselves!* [*Odumajtes'!*] concerning the Russo--Japanese war.

asks us to read each of your letters several times to her, and we — Grigorij and I, her children — are happy to do so. You, my esteemed Lev Nikolaevich, are so exceedingly kind and good to me to write so often. I, of course, have a deep appreciation for the Spirit of Peace within you, as do all the Doukhobors; it is just that they cannot so freely express their feelings in words. — I am talking about the true Doukhobors. — No doubt this is an exclusively Christian trait — not to talk a lot. To me even Christ seems to represent more a silent human observer and an exemplary practical life.

Your last letter of 3/15 March has arrived. My heartfelt thanks — and those of all my Doukhobor friends — to you for all you are doing for all the suffering people. Don't send the £61 you have on hand to Konkin just yet. The Doukhobors have sent him two hundred dollars — not for coming to Canada, mind you, but for improving living conditions for him and his sick daughter. Konkin's family may soon be coming to Moscow to see you — I beg you to help them, dear Lev Nikolaevich, to have your friends arrange things for his sick daughter, for example — see if the doctors can't help with this illness.[102] If you still have the £61 on hand, you can spend as much of it as is necessary on this case.

The winter here has been a long one with lots of snow. Now, God be thanked, spring is opening up. All the children in the Doukhobor villages are singing their greeting to spring: "*prishla Vesna k nam molodaya*" [Spring has come to us young and fair]! And really, she is eternally young! How marvellously the world is constructed! How fervently I wish, dear Lev Nikolaevich, that you could be here in the Doukhobor villages and see these 8- to 10-year old children singing their songs of spring — many of them memorized out of good contemporary song-books. I feel such images — these groups of children — would prove a significant reward for your long labours as a fighter for truth.

There are about thirty or forty children in each settlement, some have as many as fifty around ten years of age, of both sexes. I am most excited about the children in our Doukhobor milieu — they are a strong bond between me and the Doukhobors. For example, when the children sing "all our faces look happy," they really do have a little smile on their face at that time. How innocent and carefree the children are in their young souls! They have little use for 'conflicts,' even among the very highest powers in the world.

I embrace you as a son, and in brotherhood.

Lovingly,
Pëtr Verigin

102 Konkin's daughter was mentally ill.

21. P. V. VERIGIN ❧ L. N. TOLSTOY
1 April 1905. Toronto.

1 April 1905. City of Toronto.

Esteemed Lev Nikolaevich!

At the moment I have come along with two Community representatives from our settlements to the cities of southern Canada. We had a small matter to take up with the Canadian Government, whose headquarters is located in Ottawa.

The situation is this: when the Doukhobors settled at Assiniboia and Swan River (the places take their names from rivers), they were told to settle in villages and divide the land up according to their cattle herds, and not by individual homesteads as is customary in Canada. This was granted by the former Minister of Internal Affairs [Clifford] Sifton, who has since retired. But now that the Doukhobors are organized, so to speak, and have begun to till the land that happens to lie close by, leaving most of the homesteads untouched, the government sees this as a violation of official custom and the English-speaking residents have started riding around the fields assigned to us, selecting the good unploughed lands for themselves. They have begun applying to the local department offices to have these homesteads transferred to their name as free homesteads.

The official custom in Canada is that someone who has registered a homestead (160 acres) and lets three years go by without ploughing it forfeits the right to that land. It is indeed a logical system: the land can only be enjoyed by those who work it. Of course, in Canada there are many imperfections and misappropriations of land and greedy hands out only after money. But I am speaking of the so-called Crown lands — which are only given to migrants — every male 18 or over is given a plot free, on a one-time-only basis. It is for this reason that we have come to Ottawa and now the government is once again confirming its promise and is sending notice to the department offices closest to our villages, so that the Doukhobors won't lose their lands to someone else. Still, they consider such a 'privilege' to be a violation of official custom.

The local residents, especially, are beginning to regard the Doukhobors with some degree of envy, since the Doukhobors through their community organization are able to raise their standard of living more quickly and so get ahead of the English. For example, the Doukhobors already have twenty sets of steam threshers (a 'set' consisting of a steam engine and a thresher), up to two hundred scythes, cutters and other state-of-the-art equipment. The wheat is ground at home, they have bought wood-cutting machines, along with ten steam engines for ploughing this summer — last summer we experimented with just one.

Of course all this setting up angers the English speakers in the neighbourhood — they are a self-loving race, and even after twenty years individual homesteaders still can't afford to buy a steam thresher. No wonder, since a steam thresher costs $3,000, and three thousand dollars is not something a person living off wheat or oats can easily come by. The English would love the Doukhobors to break up into small farms and serve out a 'bondage' of individual indebtedness to the banks.

A farmer's life in Canada isn't all that enviable; with the rare exception, farmers each owe five or six hundred or even a thousand dollars; I'm talking about the ordinary have-not immigrants who need to borrow that much at first to get started. And once a person is obliged to fall into a state of indebtedness, this makes his situation extremely difficult, as almost all his income must go to pay interest on the loan. The local 'spider' banks have no hesitation in charging ten or twelve or even twenty percent. And so the Doukhobors with their community organization try not to fall under the 'spiders'' control. The English-speaking farmers who all live on individual homesteads are upset because their own enterprises might fall behind, while the capitalists are upset because they don't get goods or money from the Doukhobors for interest.

The spiritual life of the Doukhobors, dear Lev Nikolaevich, is moving along at its usual pace. After all, these were not highly moral people to begin with and it is impossible to demand they start living an 'angelic' life all at once.

Many find the climate too cold, as they would like to get by without any help at all from cows and work cattle. With this in mind we plan to go this summer and have a look at British Columbia and California; if there is any possibility at all of moving, the ones who want to work with fruit-growing will go.

The Doukhobors are not averse to sending representatives even to Australia; to this end we are in correspondence with a former Doukhobor friend living in Australia. Of course, all of this is not a search for Spiritual Truth but only for a comfortable place to live. But the so-called Sons of Freedom Doukhobors[103] abstract life to the extreme and say that a person living in a cold, harsh climate who exploits animals is that much further from the Truth.

During this trip we went to see a Russian Consul named [Nikolaj Berngardovich] Struve in Montréal, as the Kars Doukhobors were paid for their houses and we had to get the money from him. Struve is a rather likeable fellow. In Toronto we are visiting textile factories to get fabrics and other manufactured goods first-hand for the community. There is a Professor Mavor[104]

103 For more on the Sons of Freedom, see my introduction to "Leo Tolstoy and Pëtr V. Verigin," above (p. 206).

104 James Mavor, a political-science professor, first went to see Tolstoy in 1889. He helped the Doukhobors resettle in Canada; his letters and Tolstoy's replies have been preserved. Tolstoy's son Sergej L'vovich Tolstoj recalled that the proposal to emigrate to Canada originated with Mavor's friend Pëtr Kropotkin: "Mavor started a publicity campaign about the desirability of having the Doukhobors as immigrants, as they were people who had suffered for their faith, hard-working

in Toronto — a good friend of ours; he and I have agreed to go pay you a visit some time, my esteemed Lev Nikolaevich. We are spending a couple of days together. Last night we went to the theatre, where there was playing a comedy-drama, so to speak. You might even be familiar with it: 'Bourgeois' is warned by a Martian not to misuse his position of wealth; in the end the Martian brings on thundering and deprives the earthling of his wealth, turning him into a beggar. The comedy made quite an impression on my companions — Semën Vereshchagin and Semën Rybin; upon returning to the hotel we talked for a long time about the injustices in our life.

Recently I sent a letter to [Aleksej Ivanovich] Stepanov care of you. If you receive it, please pass it on to him.

Give my heartfelt greetings to all our friends. I wish you all blessings from the Lord God.

I'm keeping healthy.

Pëtr Verigin

22. L. N. TOLSTOY ❧ P. V. VERIGIN

28 May 1905. Yasnaya Polyana.

Dearest brother Pëtr Vasil'evich,

I received your kind and interesting letter[105] some time ago now and was so glad both that you remember me and that the financial affairs of your community are coming along well. God grant only that material success does not mean a weakening of spiritual effort and striving for perfection. It often happens that way, just like with a balance: as one goes up, the other goes down. You have to try to raise the level of the fulcrum, but if the balance has to swing one way or another, it is better to let people be materially poor so long as they are enriching themselves spiritually. I think, and I hope, and I wish that this is how it will be with the Doukhobors. The spiritual life in your community is so much aflame that it should not go out, but only keep on flaming.

I am happy that the Yakutsk people have returned. My brotherly greetings to you and all those who know me.

Lev Tolstoy

28 May 1905

and on the whole quite respectable, and he began to lobby the Canadian government to let them into Canada" (see S. L. Tolstoj 1949: 188). Mavor visited Yasnaya Polyana in the summer of 1910, during his travels through China, Japan and Russia.

105 Tolstoy noted, with some sadness, that in a number of his letters Verigin seemed to be overly concerned with the material well-being of the Doukhobors. Hence his urging them to strive more for spiritual goals and less for material ones.

23. P. V. VERIGIN ❧ L. N. TOLSTOY
3 July 1905. Otradnoe.

**Christian Community
of Universal Brotherhood**

The Doukhobors in Canada

3rd July '05. Village of Otradnoe
Yorkton. — Canada.

To Lev Nikolaevich Tolstoy
[from] Pëtr Verigin.

Dear Friend Lev Nikolaevich, I have received your letter and it has been a very big help to me. The word 'Dear' where you are concerned has become simply the kindest word, since you, kind Lev Nikolaevich, are truly a dear person to me. Every one of your words overflows with simplicity and sincerity, and that is something dear to us all, if only people would treat each other more simply and sincerely.

Your fears for the Doukhobors' future in Canada are valid and understandable. But I cannot refuse to accept people's close participation in building material progress — since in many respects the spiritual does not depend upon us, it is something that touches each one individually. — For example, I can give someone a heifer, a horse, a hundred roubles and so on, but I can't give him a soul, and insofar as I am able to observe human life, it strikes me as an impossible task. — There is a special place for that, where the spirit of life and understanding originates. The Spirit "bloweth where it listeth"[106] and where it goes we do not know. Although Christ says: the world knoweth me not, but you know me.[107] Of course, this 'knowledge' should be interpreted as unity of the spirit.

You are aware, dear Lev Nikolaevich, that the Doukhobors came to Canada materially poor and possibly, according to your understanding, therein lies their advantage. Our material insufficiency has probably drawn their hearts closer together and led them to God — since God is manifested in the unity of human hearts.

It seems to me that the whole world was created and exists for good, so why should material wealth — as we deem it — serve us for evil? When someone begins to misuse his wealth or sets the acquisition of wealth as his goal in life, then that is quite a different story. The Doukhobors think a lot about the

106 See John 3:8.
107 See John 14:17.

growth of the soul and it seems to me that they are even doing a lot of work in this direction, and this is their sense of good for the time being, while ahead of them stands the God of mercy — I am saying that we should become more merciful — and this is a person's goal in life.

I must say that the material conditions of our community life are basically in good order, but there is no strong growth yet. Do you think it is easy to get started in a desert place? We had to build more than sixty villages, with housing for each individual family. The climate is too cold to stay in the open air. Even in a desert place each household needs food to eat: what would you have done? — probably not just clasped your hands together and looked up to the sky expecting manna to fall, as the Israelites did.[108] The Doukhobors have a great many children, and I still notice that the children are not yet receiving enough nourishment from their mothers' milk and no wonder, since what the mothers have to eat is meagre indeed.

Would it have been rational for me to walk about the neighbourhoods, comforting the mothers who might lose their children because of malnutrition? As if the spirit which inspires our hearts and the bread which feeds our bodies did not come from the one God and Father?! Unfortunately the people up to now have made a distinction between the spiritual food and the material.

This summer in our community we have ten steam engines doing the ploughing, 25 horsepower each. It is easy for such powerful machines to pull eight ploughs each; that was the way we did it last year experimenting with just one engine. Now we hitch four [ploughs] together along with another machine called a cutter, which trails along behind and breaks up the earth, the way women cut cabbage. Such a tool is extremely useful simply because it reduces the burden on the horses, since [normally] after ploughing you have to go over it two or three more times to break it up, but this cutter is quite a heavy machine. — You probably know: it consists of twenty-inch discs or larger, very sharp, in a row of fourteen or more; with a team of four good horses, if you lower it to full depth it is too hard on the horses. That's where the steam engine has the advantage: you can lower the cutter to full depth right off, and then go over it just one more time cross-wise, and that's enough.

On the 30th of June we got a bank draft from the Yorkton bank to send to Moscow in the name of Aleksandr Nikiforovich Dunaev[109] — ten thousand dollars to bring the Yakutsk brethren over. I asked Aleksandr Nikiforovich to get our Moscow Friends to arrange the tickets to be sent. Konkin too will probably be in Moscow by that time.

I told him that you, Dear Lev Nikolaevich, should not be disturbed [on this matter]; I think such affairs can be looked after by slightly younger people.

108 See Ps. 78:23–24.

109 *Aleksandr Dunaev* (1850–1920) — was a friend of Tolstoy's, who at one time shared his views; he was one of the directors of the Moscow Commercial Bank.

I wish your whole family complete health. And may the Lord send you, Dear Lev Nikolaevich, many more years of a healthy life.

I am keeping healthy myself. Your brother in Christ,

Pëtr Verigin

24. P. V. VERIGIN ❧ L. N. TOLSTOY
24 November 1906. Moscow.

24 November, Moscow.

Esteemed Lev Nikolaevich,

Six of us have come from the Doukhobor society in Canada with the express purpose of seeing you.

Yesterday your son Sergej L'vovich dropped by and told us some people in your house are sick.[110] Please let us know by telegram whether we can come to see you now.

On the trip here we agreed we might take an apartment in the village near your place, get settled in and then see you when it is possible.

With heartfelt respect for you,

Pëtr Verigin

Address:
'Taku' Rooming House
Ostozhenka
Moscow

25. L. N. TOLSTOY ❧ P. V. VERIGIN
30 November 1906. Yasnaya Polyana.

I did not reply to you by telegram, dear Pëtr Vasil'evich, as your letter arrived during the time of my daughter's illness. — I shall be most happy to see you and your friends.[111]

Lev Tolstoy

30 November 1906

110 At Yasnaya Polyana, Tolstoy's daughter Marija L'vovna Obolenskaja was gravely ill. She died 27 November 1906.

111 Verigin and five other Doukhobors (Ivan Faddeevich Makhortov, Pavel Planidin, D. N. Gridchin, Anastasija Golubëva, Marfa Dymovskaja) visited Yasnaya Polyana 6–10 December 1906. The doctor Dushan Makovitskij noted in his diary (1979–81: 2:322–27):

Everyone was very attentive to the Doukhobors. They were most pleasant and interesting… Ivan Faddeevich [Makhortov] brought L. N. [Lev Nikolaevich] a teacup from Canada. L.N. thanked him and said, "When I have a cup, I shall remember." Nastas'ja [Anastasija Golubëva] brought Aleksandra L'vovna [another of Tolstoy's daughters] an Indian needle cushion. Ivan

26. P. V. VERIGIN ❧ L. N. TOLSTOY

10 December 1906. Kozlovka-Zaseka Station.

10th Dec. '06. Zaseka Station.

Deeply esteemed Lev Nikolaevich,

Our whole group, headed by Grandfather Makhortov,[112] is sincerely grateful to you and your whole family for your warm welcome; may the Lord bless you for such hospitality. I did want to see you again today, but was not bold enough to do so. Perhaps we shall see each other again some time, the Lord willing.

Farewell.

Your brother in God,

Pëtr Verigin

27. P. V. VERIGIN ❧ L. N. TOLSTOY

12 January 1907. Sofia, Bulgaria.

12 Jan. (old style) '07. City of Sofia.

Esteemed Lev Nikolaevich,

At the moment we are at the railway terminal waiting for our train to Budapest. After leaving your place we stopped at Khar'kov to see Bodjanskij, and visited Sevastopol' and Yalta.

Bodjanskij recommended we have a look at the Black Sea coast — the western side.

From Sevastopol' we sailed directly to Constantinople and from there by steamship to Burgas.

Not far from Burgas there is some land for sale at 30 roubles per *desjatina.*[113]

If it were necessary, I think we could move a small colony of about 500 people here and set up good orchards.

We are all in good health, thank God, and send our heartfelt greetings to you and your whole family. Our 'Grandfather' is especially lively and keeps us entertained throughout the trip.

Faddeevich, Nastja and Mavrusha [Marfa Dymovskaja] all addressed L. N. using the word *ty* [the familiar form of address]: "*A ty, dedushka...*" [You, Grandpa...]

Ivan Faddeevich had served in the Sevastopol' campaign. In reminiscing about it he asked L. N. where he had been sent there.

L. N. recounted:

"But, thank God, I didn't have to fire even once. There was an order to fire case-shot during an attack, but I wasn't there..."

Pleasant conversations with the Doukhobors; they prayed silently, standing up, both before and after meals. They do that in hotels too, in Chicago for example. And they would sing a psalm (sitting down).

112 Ivan Faddeevich Makhortov was eighty-six years old at the time.

113 *desjatina* — a unit of land equivalent to slightly more than 1 hectare.

Iosif Konstantinovich[114] is with us — he came to help us inspect the location near Burgas, and now wants to go see the sisters in England as well.

Snow has fallen here and the temperature is minus 20°.

We have had to spend an extra three days in Burgas because of snow--covered roads. Now we are hurrying to get through to our friends in Geneva, and then home as quickly as possible. Forgive me for not writing to you sooner.

Pëtr Verigin

28. P. V. VERIGIN ❧ L. N. TOLSTOY
9 March 1907. Otradnoe.

9th March '07. Village of "Otradnoe."
Verigin, Sask.
Canada.

Dear Friend Lev Nikolaevich,

Here we are, thank God, back home safe and sound. Everyone's fine. 'Grandfather' stayed calm and cheerful the whole way home. All my companions have now gone off to their own relations, but they asked me, if I should be writing to you, to be sure to send you their heartfelt greetings and gratitude for your warm hospitality.

The route we chose for the whole trip turned out most successfully, as nowhere in our travels did we meet serious cold spells, and we saw a lot of cities and places. When we passed through Russia in the autumn, winter had not yet set in, and as it approached we were already heading further south and so, returning through central Europe, we managed to avoid severe winter conditions. Throughout the trip I kept jotting down information — at least brief notes — about the life of different ethnic groups, and about the land too, in case we should acquire some land in a warm climate for the brethren of the Doukhobor community. After we left you we went to Khar'kov, Sevastopol', Constantinople, Budapest, Vienna, Geneva and Paris, as well as to see our friends the Chertkovs [in England]. Favourable living conditions are to be found on the west side of the Black Sea in Bulgaria; we could also have plots of land in Switzerland and probably in Italy as well, since the people there do not feel like tilling the ground — the rich classes who own the land are happy to give it away [to be tilled]. There are some free fruit-growing lands near New York. I am talking about these lands in particular because many of the Doukhobors are inclined toward this type of activity. I am planning in the near future to go out

114 *Iosif Konstantinovich Diterikhs* (1868–1932) — brother to Anna Konstantinovna Chertkova (V. G. Chertkov's wife) as well as to Ol'ga Konstantinovna Tolstaja (Andrej L'vovich Tolstoj's wife until 1903). Until 1897 he lived in the Caucasus as 'superintendent of the mountain tribes.' His sympathy for the Doukhobors led to his being exiled from the Caucasus. He took an active part in all their affairs.

and gather information about acquiring lands for fruit-growing on the Pacific coast. I should tell you that we are prepared to resettle in small colonies in different parts of the world. — At least that is how I personally see it.

Upon my return to Canada I was greeted by some big news in the Doukhobor community: all the lands registered in the Doukhobors' name have been declared 'free,' and now they are inviting people who agree to accept British Citizenship and to live and work on the land on an individual basis to register their homesteads afresh. All the rest of the community, including women and children, will only get 15 acres apiece.

Quite a touchy question, isn't it? I wonder what 'devices' the Government will resort to, and how the Doukhobors will react: will they accept Citizenship or prefer to live in an indeterminate situation? Or rather, be in a more determinate position without Citizenship. The Government has cast the die, so to speak; whether it can win or not, only time will tell.

I'm quite satisfied that the Doukhobors have accepted this proposal with quiet equanimity, probably because the majority of them already decided the question of Citizenship about three or four years back — in the negative.

There have been 'whisperings' abroad in the country that such actions by the Government amount to 'dirty tricks.' People have been diligently ploughing and sowing grain, they've been tilling the land in a fairly acceptable manner, and now this land is being taken from them without just cause.

The Doukhobors on the whole are enjoying full health and prosperity.

For me personally the trip was very beneficial. I saw many people who far surpass me in moral perfection, and I have learnt a great deal. Seeing your living example has given me moral support. I am more and more convinced that one's salvation, or the meaning of life, is in this: namely, *to keep one's heart from evil.* This is our highest task — adoption by God the Father.

I have told our brothers and sisters about the hunger in Russia; they will no doubt respond with at least a small contribution of money. We shall leave its disposition up to you.

I wish you, Esteemed Lev Nikolaevich and all your family and friends all blessings from the Lord. I keep healthy,

Pëtr Verigin

29. L. N. TOLSTOY ❧ P. V. VERIGIN*10*

August 1907. Yasnaya Polyana.

Most kind Pëtr Vasil'evich!

I have endeavoured to distribute your community's donation of 10,000 roubles to the famine victims as best I could, in the province of Samara.[115]

115 An imperial Russian province on the middle Volga, southeast of Moscow. During the Soviet period, the city of Samara was known as Kujbyshev.

I was helped in this by my young friends — religious people — Sutkova, Kolesnichenko and Rjabov. They've gone now, and I still have 2,800 roubles left undistributed. Another 800 roubles will probably be given out now in the same Samara province, but that still leaves 2,000, and I would appreciate some guidance from the donors. There is great need everywhere; the money could be given out again in Samara, where the harvest has been extremely poor, or here, where there are many needy unemployed. Please let me know.

I have received word that your community, in spite of being deprived of their land, is coming along well, thanks to their good life of brotherhood,[116] and I am so happy to receive this practical confirmation of the truth that people's well-being depends on them themselves, on their fulfilling or not fulfilling the law of God. I send brotherly greetings to you and all the brethren who remember me.

Lev Tolstoy

10 Aug. 1907

30. P. V. VERIGIN ❧ L. N. TOLSTOY
15 September 1907. Otradnoe.

V. A. POTAPOFF,
Manager

Trading Store of the Doukhobor Society
Dry Goods, Hardware, Groceries, Crockery, Etc.
WHOLESALE AND RETAIL

Verigin, Sask., 15 Sept. (new style) 1907
CAN. NOR. RY.

Esteemed Lev Nikolaevich, I received your letter of 10th Aug. I am most grateful to learn that you are alive and well. My heartfelt greetings to you and all your family and friends.

We are all in good health, thank God.

As regards the money — the donation — I spoke with several of the brethren — they say "They (i.e., you) should do whatever seems best."

I wish you all good. Your brother in Christ,

Pëtr Verigin

116 V. A. Makaseev and Pavel Planidin wrote from Canada in the spring of 1907. Their letters, along with Tolstoy's replies, have been preserved in the Tolstoy archives (see *PSS* 77:109, 111).

31. P. V. VERIGIN ❧ L. N. TOLSTOY
13 June 1908. Otradnoe.

OFFICE OF THE
PETER V. VERIGIN
REPRESENTATIVE
OF THE DOUKHOBOR SOCIETY

VERIGIN, SASK. 13 June 1908
Canada
from Pëtr Verigin

Much esteemed Lev Nikolaevich,

I hasten to inform you that this spring the Doukhobor community purchased some 2,700 acres of land in British Columbia for growing fruit trees. The land is not far from the city of Nelson, at the confluence of two rivers — the Kootenay and the Columbia. The place is characterized by fresh air, clean fresh water and a rather mild climate, where we can grow apples, plums, and a delicious and abundant variety of sweet cherries — right on the banks of the Columbia River, which is one of the most beautiful rivers I have ever seen. The colour of the water, for example, is equal to that of the river in Geneva.

At the moment ninety people are clearing the land for fruit-trees and about 600 young trees were planted in the spring. The move will take place gradually over the next five or six years, since we still have a lot of ploughed land here and harvest time has just arrived.

Next spring we are planning to send out another two or three hundred people to prepare the land for habitation, while our farming activities will gradually decrease in the old place until final termination.

We are living well, thank God. Last year our wheat was killed by the frost, but since the autumn we tried to buy enough for the whole year and for the sowing and now, thank God, we are enjoying good, pure bread. The prospects are good for this summer's harvest and a rather large amount of grain has been sown.

The move to [British] Columbia should mean a rather significant change in our community's farming activities. The basic activity should be the growing of fruits and vegetables, but we also propose to set up a dairy industry through controlled cultivation of hay and vegetables for fodder.

We should also like to acquire a small plot of land in a warmer place for those without livestock.

My warmest greetings to you and your whole family. Your brother in Christ,

Pëtr

32. P. V. VERIGIN ❧ L. N. TOLSTOY
2 February 1909. Brilliant.

OFFICE OF THE
PETER V. VERIGIN
REPRESENTATIVE
OF THE DOUKHOBOR SOCIETY

VERIGIN, SASK. 2nd Feb. 1909

To Lev Nikolaevich Tolstoy
[from] Pëtr Verigin.[1]

Deeply esteemed Lev Nikolaevich, I hasten to inform you of our community's joy. We recently acquired a bit of land in [British] Columbia to experiment with growing fruit-trees. It seems I have already told you about that. But it turns out that the people who have been living there almost a year now are extremely happy with the place. And it is important that a person should be happy with at least something in life. True happiness leads to true prayer on our part to our Heavenly Father.

This is now my fourth visit to [British] Columbia. I was out here on business last summer, but this time I came expressly to see and observe the winter. The climate is remarkably mild and healthful. I have had many conversations with my brothers and sisters here, and they all want me to ask you to come and stay with us, perhaps to live out the remaining of your precious days here in peace. I say this in all sincerity, because I am quite certain that you would be very happy living among the Doukhobors. Especially in the past while the Doukhobors have been drawing closer and closer in their behaviour and understanding to the Kingdom of God on Earth. Maybe you have heard rumours that many of the Doukhobors are falling away from the community life — but this in no way stops the rest — or even the ones departing — from being good Christian people. Recently we adopted the motto: *Keep your heart from evil.* I cannot deny that I was the one who proposed this now (for a long time) fundamental tenet, but it was as if an electric shock-wave had gone through each of the Doukhobors, and each one asked himself the question: What am I to do from now on? Since all the former rituals, even the little ones, are changing, the only thing we have to observe is: *Keep your heart from evil.* I understand this in its simplest everyday sense, namely, use your mind to keep your heart from getting agitated; at the least loss of equanimity — our basic human characteristic: being calm — the blood starts rushing and everyone knows the rest of the story. I think that all the churches in the world might have been founded by mankind to attain this goal — to be at peace for at least a little while. There is no church where anger and violence are accepted as being right. And since the building of temples to pray in has long been abolished by the Doukhobors, we are now faced with an insurmountable barrier: how to get into the Kingdom of God without praying? A sincere investigation of Christ's teachings makes it clear that Christ preached a fundamental commandment: Mercy. Probably not the kind of mercy that consists in going to church once a week and being merciful for an hour or two, then devoting one's self completely to evil intents the rest of the time. The Doukhobors used to do that often. Now there is nothing to be done — even reciting or reading the psalms you were so enthusiastic about in your conversation with Pavel Planidin. (He told me about that.[117]) But if you want to be a Doukhobor, there's only one thing necessary: keep your heart from evil. Wherever a person may be, whether in church or marching behind a plough, the requirement is the same.

I also want to share with you some spiritual joy about myself. I have become kinder of heart. I feel this is the highest degree of joy and virtue man can experience on earth. In your writings you often say that man has not and cannot have a purpose on earth. I think, I feel, that keeping one's self from evil can constitute a purpose and that this purpose is achievable, offering the highest complete human satisfaction, since it draws me toward Divine truth. From what I understand of Christ, it is only through Mercy that he too became one with our common Father. — The creative power is Mercy. — Evil is destructive wherever it appears. By nature man must be good — we can set this as a goal for ourselves, and it will be good and true.

I wish you and your whole family all good from the Lord. Your loving brother in Christ,

P. Verigin

My address is now:
P. Verigin.
Brilliant, B.C.,
Canada.

33. L. N. TOLSTOY ❧ P. V. VERIGIN[118]

18 March 1909. Yasnaya Polyana.

Yasnaya Polyana. 18 March 1909.

I was happy to receive news of you, dear Pëtr Vasil'evich, and good news at that. I have the highest sympathy for your decision to free yourselves from all

117 Pavel Planidin visited Yasnaya Polyana in December 1906 (see Letter Nº 25 above) and once accompanied Tolstoy on his daily walk. Dr. Makovitskij noted in his diary for 9 December: "[…] Planidin marvelled how the old man could walk: he got tired [keeping up] with him."

118 Only an unsigned typewritten copy of this letter has been preserved in the Tolstoy archives. The whereabouts of the signed copy sent to Verigin are unknown.

outward forms of worship, replacing them with works of life. But I think that such a decision, if it is to be a lasting one, must flow from the consciousness of each individual. I am not saying that this is unquestionably right, but it is my opinion based on my personal experience. I have only found that to be lasting which I have attained through my own inner struggles.

Please do keep sending me details about you and your community, about the results of your decision to move, and so forth.

Lovingly, Lev Tolstoy

P.S. Forgive me for not writing sooner, but I have been constantly ill the past while.

34. P. V. VERIGIN ❧ L. N. TOLSTOY
3 May 1909. Brilliant.

OFFICE OF THE
PETER V. VERIGIN
REPRESENTATIVE
OF THE DOUKHOBOR SOCIETY

Brilliant, B.C.

VERIGIN, SASK. 3 May 1909

"Dolina Utesheniya."[119]

The letter I received from you, kind Lev Nikolaevich, was precious to me. It was precious because the few words of your letter expressed the sincerity of your heart. This is indeed the essence of its benefit for others in every respect.

I have noticed many times with myself, when I am writing or conversing from the sincerity of my understanding, only then is it beneficial either for me or for my listener.

I should explain to you that I was the one in our community who proposed exchanging ritualism for contriteness of heart. I can only say and express this for myself, and that's how I put it to all the Doukhobors. The only compulsory rule I make for myself is to keep myself from evil; everything else, even though useful, I may or may not do. But to make myself a better person is for me a must.

All the rest of the people in our community are free to observe their old rules, if they wish.

I myself often attend meetings where they read psalms and sing. But these meetings have now taken on a freer form, rather than a strict one, as before.

119 *Dolina Utesheniya* — lit. 'Valley of Consolation' — the name given by the Doukhobors to their new settlement in British Columbia.

I have now made it a goal to free myself from the desire for power, and that is possible when I free myself from evil.

We have almost finished planting the orchards at our new place. We have planted basic types of trees: apple, plum, sweet-cherry, pear, peach, about fifteen thousand altogether, also lots of small bushes, and 6,000 grape vines.

We've made a good beginning for our first year, thank God.

I am very sorry to hear that you are continuing ill. I really wanted to come and see you once more — even to spend two or three weeks near your home at Yasnaya.

If you should happen to run into her, please give my regards to the elderly lady whose house we roomed at.[120] She was quite annoyed that I paid her so little for the flat. If I come to Yasnaya again, I'll make it up to her.

Greetings to your whole family. With deep respect,

P. Verigin

Brilliant, B.C.,
Canada.

35. P. V. VERIGIN ❧ L. N. TOLSTOY
26 September 1909. Otradnoe.

P. Verigin
Verigin, Sask.
Canada.

26 Sept. '09.
Village of "Otradnoe"

To Lev Nikolaevich Tolstoy
[from] Pëtr Verigin.

Esteemed Lev Nikolaevich, I have been meaning to write you a few lines about things going on in our life.

Today is Sunday: Christ is Risen![121] This year our whole life shows great prosperity, both in our material and Spiritual affairs. People in our community have begun to consciously relate to their situation. It is amazing how God can gradually bring people to the consciousness of Nature around them as well as to the adoption of the eternal laws of spiritual understanding. I have observed this in the Doukhobors and feel it in myself.

Beginning in the Caucasus, it was there they learnt to perform good deeds in terms of physical actions, such as rejection of military service and abstention from wine, smoking and the killing of animals. Those are all good

120 From 6 to 10 December 1906, Verigin, along with five other Doukhobors from Canada, visited Tolstoy at Yasnaya Polyana. See Letter N° 25 above.

121 The Russian word for 'Sunday' [*voskresen'e*] is taken from the word for 'resurrection' [*voskresenie*].

deeds, but they are all concerned with corporeal morality. Now we come to the awareness of the need to strive to perfect our spiritual understanding as well. God has truly done a marvellous job of arranging the universe and putting man into the world to gradually strive for perfection!

We have had an abundant harvest of everything here in Saskatchewan, where we have been growing grain. And our life in B.C. is off to a good start too. We could not ask anything more of the Lord, and we can only offer praise and thanksgiving for the course our life has taken over the past thirty years. Glory to God and thanksgiving to all good people.

I am sending along my letter to our community. This is an example of how I communicate with the Doukhobors, whenever I have something to say to them.

The results of the harvest are in: around 500,000 bushels of oats, a hundred thousand or so of wheat and around a hundred thousand of barley.

We don't sow too much wheat, since the last two years it was killed by the frost and we decided to sow only for our own needs. The oats and barley, except for our own needs — for the year — we sell. Our earnings from this summer are expected to be around 150,000 dollars. — It is too bad that so far we haven't been able to get by without additional earnings. — And now there's the move on top of that. But it is all turning out for the better, thank God!

This summer the wheat has done exceedingly well, but we do not regret having sown so little of it, since per acre oats have proved to be no less profitable than the very best wheat. For example, on an acre of land we can grow twenty-five bushels of wheat [selling] at 70 cents a bushel — $17.50, while oats yields eighty bushels at 28 cents — $20.40 [*sic*], and besides, the oats are a sure crop, while wheat quite often fails in these parts.

The move to B.C. is significant as it means we will require several times less acreage for fruit- and vegetable-growing than here on the prairies. When we did nothing but grow grain and raise cattle we were using more than 300,000 acres, while at the moment, it looks like if we have 15,000 acres in B.C. suitable for fruit- and vegetable-growing it will be more than enough. So we are thinking more about growing fruits and vegetables under the best conditions possible. We have already managed to purchase 7,000 acres of good-quality land, for orchards, vegetable gardens and meadow-lands. Bees do well [out there]. This autumn we already have good, sweet-scented honey — home-made. Only in small quantities. Amazing people, the English: for a thousand miles around we managed to find only twenty beehives, which we bought to get started. The swarming has been good.

I can tell you, esteemed Lev Nikolaevich, that the Doukhobors in their experience of seeking the truth are a unique example meriting serious attention. Suffice it to say that over the past ten years of living in Canada — under rather dreadful conditions, to start with — there haven't been any serious quarrels leading to violence, as happens all the time in Russian villages. Or another remarkable phenomenon: in our forty villages there has not been a single fire. Many houses and barns are roofed over with bog-rushes. I put this down to a more sober life-style and abstinence from tobacco; it often happens that someone will light a cigarette and toss the burning match away just anywhere. And how many kids hide from their elders to have a smoke and set the thatch on fire. In Russia whole villages have burnt down that way. And we are but simple Russian peasants. But the Lord has led us into the light of understanding. Praise be to you too, dear Lev Nikolaevich, for showing people the harm that comes from smoking and vodka.

We are planning on installing an underground system of tubes and taps to provide good irrigation for our orchards in B.C. About 30,000 feet of various sizes of tubing have been delivered for installation this autumn.

If all goes well, in five or six years I imagine some of the Doukhobors ought to be moving back to Russia. With such useful experience they should be quite valuable there.

I embrace you in love and wish you all blessings from the Lord.

Yours, P. Verigin

Christian Community of Universal Brotherhood

The Doukhobors in Canada

24 September 1909
Letter to the Christian Community of Universal Brotherhood
from Pëtr Verigin.

Glory to the Lord.

1. I hasten to inform you, Brothers and Sisters, that I have come here to see how your life is getting on, and all the brothers and sisters living in Dolina Utesheniya have asked me to give you their heartfelt greetings. Life here in Dolina Utesheniya has got off to a good start in all respects, thank the Lord.
2. As you know, on the 20th of this month we held a conference in the village of Otradnoe. The first item on the agenda was an account of the expenses involved in the move to B.C. Secondly it was decided that all the villages should pay off their debts, since we must settle our debts in Winnipeg and other cities. Thirdly, the question was raised about new expenses anticipated in connection with the move, as a result of which it was decided to collect one hundred dollars from each wage-earner in every village.
3. I did propose at the conference that each village should take care of its own grain sales individually, without my participation. However, in

view of the rather low prices offered by the elevator operators — I found out for certain that the Canora elevators are allowing only 23 cents a bushel for oats, and 24 cents in Kamsack — I have decided to recommend that we all ship our oats this fall to Port Arthur[122] [and sell] at their prices. Port Arthur is now offering 35 cents a bushel for N° 2 oats; with freight charges at 6 cents, that gives us 29 cents, and even if there are some extra shipping costs involved, we still get at least 28 cents a bushel, a big difference compared with 23 or 24 cents. All those willing I invite to take their oats to the nearest depot and load the hopper-cars for shipment to Port Arthur. Anyone who can sell for at least 28 cents a bushel here on the spot is free to do so.

Misha Kazakov and Sëma Rybin are in charge of shipping. They are the ones to see about hopper-car assignments.

I invite all the villages closest to our Station to bring their oats to the elevator; the cars will be loaded from there.

4. We have temporarily stopped all purchases of goods; as soon as all the villages have paid off their old debts, I shall ask all villages to come to a conference for consultation and the appointment of new people to look after the purchase and delivery of goods, since Vasja Potapov and Sëma Rybin have asked to be relieved. And I think we shall be able to deliver [new] goods soon and we shall all be clothed and shod through the grace of God. Praise the Lord for good harvests in everything and our earnings this year.
5. I suggest, Brothers and Sisters, that you give your sincere attention to the move. This is not the time to raise extraneous issues, since a lot of expenses will be involved in the move. At the moment everything is going well for us in setting things up in B.C. The little gardens are coming along nicely, and I shall make sure everything is in good order.
6. I would ask the brothers and sisters of the Bogdanovo and Kirilovo villages in the Prince Albert area to hold back any extra wheat they may have to supply our needs in B.C. I suggest they contribute the hundred-dollar levy from this summer's income, and we will pay them for the wheat. It will be fairer that way.
7. We hope to have a large flour-mill in operation shortly, and anyone wanting to grind white flour for themselves may do so. In addition, any village that wishes to can bring at least a hundred bushels of fine wheat to the elevator at the mill, which will be used to grind white flour to take out to B.C.; part of it will be required for community needs. Anyone who wishes can also bring oats for making oatmeal. We plan to make oatmeal for B.C. out of the community harvest oats.

122 *Port Arthur* — a grain port on Lake Superior, which in 1970 amalgamated with the city of Fort William and two smaller townships to form the city of Thunder Bay, Ontario. Canora and Kamsack are small prairie towns on the Canadian National Railway line in central Saskatchewan.

8. I would like to remind you that a carload of various vegetables, beetroot, onions, hops and peas, is being sent to Dolina Utesheniya. They don't need any potatoes, as they have managed to grow their own there, thank the Lord.
9. All those who can should take their oats now to the elevator at the Station, where each village's shipment will be weighed precisely. The other villages should start loading very shortly, as soon as you know where the cars are assigned, so as not to miss the boats at Port Arthur. The oats should be clean, as if you were going to use them yourselves, so that they can fetch a good price.
10. I strongly urge you to pay off all your debts this autumn, since our Office is preparing our accounts for the move to B.C. and replacing the brothers who have been working in our offices up to now.

With my whole heart I praise and thank the Lord for our current life and well-being, and I call upon all of you as brothers and sisters to praise the Lord as well.

Your loving brother in Christ,

Pëtr

36. L. N. TOLSTOY ❧ P. V. VERIGIN
4 October 1909. Yasnaya Polyana.

4th October '09.

I thank you, kind brother Pëtr, for your letter and joyful news of your brethren, especially about the striving for spiritual perfection you wrote about. Whatever good there is in our life is found in the soul, in its drawing nearer to God. Concern over physical things for the most part only detracts from the inner workings of the soul. May God help you and the brethren succeed in the "one thing [that] is needful."[123] Give my love to the brethren, along with my regret that I am physically separated from them and from you. I am sending you several books. I would like them to be approved by the brethren.

Lovingly, Lev Tolstoy

123 See Luke 10:42.

37. P. V. VERIGIN ❧ L. N. TOLSTOY
4 February 1910. Otradnoe.

OFFICE OF THE
PETER V. VERIGIN
REPRESENTATIVE
OF THE DOUKHOBOR SOCIETY
VERIGIN, SASK. 4 Feb. 1910

To Lev Nikolaevich Tolstoy
[from] Pëtr Verigin.

Esteemed Lev Nikolaevich, I received your letter some time ago and am only now getting around to a reply.

I am sending you an account of our community's last conference.

Last summer we had a good harvest of everything. We collected a million bushels of grain all told. Vegetables were also in abundance.

We are having a nice, warm winter.

The community life is coming along well, thank the Lord. I shall soon be going to B.C. for the garden planting.

I wish you and all your family and friends all blessings from the Lord.

Lovingly,

P. Verigin

I am keeping healthy.

38. P. V. VERIGIN ❧ L. N. TOLSTOY
15–17 May 1910. Otradnoe.

Canada
P. Verigin
Verigin, Sask.
Canada.

15 May 1910.
Village of "Otradnoe"

To1 Lev Nikolaevich Tolstoy
[from] Pëtr Verigin.

Ask one of the young people to read this to you.

Esteemed Lev Nikolaevich, even though it's been a long time since I heard from you, I hasten to pen my greetings to you.

You are in need of quiet now, and so the less you have to write the better.

I recently got back from B.C. The garden planting was all finished there before the first of May. Here too in Saskatchewan the sowing is completely done. We are sowing more oats here, as wheat is sometimes killed by the frost. We have sown more than last year.

We are all getting along well, thank the Lord. Lately I have been thinking about the possibility of man's immortality.

Immortality is a definite possibility if man himself desires it. Christ calls this desire *faith.* "If ye have faith as a grain of mustard seed, ye shall say unto this mountain, Remove hence to yonder place; and it shall remove."[124] The same with immortality — if someone desires it — if he believes, it will come to pass. It is an area that is entirely spiritual.

Physical birth marks the beginning of the existence of one's personality. In becoming acquainted with his environment, man can develop within himself spiritual understanding as well. This brings him closer to the consciousness of eternal life. So I'm starting to believe absolutely that if I were able, if I desired, to make the effort to develop within myself an understanding of the value of eternal life and wanted to enter into it, then that, too, would come to pass. It would happen just like with the mountain Christ speaks of in his parable.

My body will be buried in the ground, but my consciousness of and desire for eternal life will remain immortal. And it is only after the death of this body that genuine conscious life begins. We shall not be born again physically, but by the power of the Spirit we shall enter into immortality, and we shall only be regenerated, perfecting ourselves more and more. It is extremely important for man to work out and attain the consciousness of his immortality here, and maintain his faith in immortality within himself, for when man dies physically, this consciousness will not die along with the body but will go on to eternal life. This will in fact be man's resurrection — or rather, the consolidation of his consciousness of eternal life.

Following my physical death and my first spiritual regeneration my faith in immortality will be strengthened a thousandfold; at the moment I have only a mortal awareness of it. Just running this through my mind, I might say that the basis of my life originated here in the body, without my will, while spiritual consciousness is something I must work out of my own free will. If I desire it, I shall indeed enter into immortality — into eternal life. Whereas if I don't want to work it out or decide to leave this question unresolved, I will live only a physical life and will die and nothing will be left of me but fertilizer for the ground.

17th May.

We have got ourselves a small contract to build an embankment along the railway line not far from the villages. And now people are coming together

124 See Matth. 17:20.

from all the villages for this communal work. The plan of action is this: during sowing time all the people and horses were home busy with the sowing. Now that is finished and they are out on contract work. We aim to finish this by the 15th of August and return home for the grain harvest. The [contract] work is 10 to 15 miles from the nearest villages. We should get about sixty thousand dollars altogether for the job. We consider this as household income, as we provide our own meals and tools.

I am on the road with the group, and have taken some paper along to write you this letter.

I would like to again bring up a question which deeply concerns me — the question of man's immortality.

Everything that has appeared cannot be destroyed, but only changed in form — to our observation. For example, luxuriant couch-grass is now thriving where potatoes once grew, and so forth.

There is no way I can believe that I can simply disappear without a trace. If so, I would not be endowed with such a broad range of thought. As Descartes rightly says: "I think, and therefore I am convinced that I exist."[125] Thought within me leads me to believe that I can, through thought — the greatest tool on the human plane of existence — go on to immortality. This thought shows me that the spirit lives outside of time and space. What pleasure it gives me, esteemed Lev Nikolaevich, to remember the times I met with you and we could converse at least briefly. And this memory is re-born within me quite often. Truly I can say: "The Spirit bloweth where it listeth, and whence it cometh, and whither it goeth no man knoweth."[126] In conclusion let me say: Everything depends on man's will, or desire. Our Heavenly Father has given full [freedom of] will to his son, man; as he desires, so he can act; all desires can be fulfilled.

Oh how I wish I could see you now and talk with you face to face!

I wish you all blessings from the Lord. Give my heartfelt greetings to all your family and friends. Lovingly,

P. Verigin

125 A variant of French philosopher René Descartes' (1596–1650) famous saying *Cogito, ergo sum* [I think, therefore I am].

126 See John 3:8. The Greek word *pneuma*, translated as 'wind' in the Authorized Version, is rendered *Dukh* [Spirit] in the Russian Synodal Bible.

PART IV

Lev Nikolaevich Tolstoy
and
Mikhail Petrovich Novikov

Mikhail Petrovich Novikov

LEO TOLSTOY AND MIKHAIL NOVIKOV

One of the more prominent religious dissidents in Russia was a peasant from the village of Borovkovo, in the Laptev district near Moscow, by the name of Mikhail Petrovich Novikov (1871–1939), who frequently met and corresponded with Tolstoy over a period of fourteen years, right up to the latter's death in 1910. The entire correspondence comprises thirty-two letters: twenty-three from Novikov to Tolstoy and nine from Tolstoy to Novikov.

Writing in the 1930s, Novikov described his attraction to the master as follows:[1]

> The most common nickname I was known by in the Laptev district was 'the Tolstoyan.' I honestly don't know to this day what that means. That I was a good friend of Leo Tolstoy's? But is friendship with a great Russian writer something to be ashamed of, let alone punishable by Soviet law? Or perhaps the term *Tolstoyan* in this case suggests some kind of harmful world outlook? I might point out that when I first went to see Leo Tolstoy forty years ago I was drawn to him for the same reasons so many other individuals were, regardless of age, race or social class: I saw in him a great writer and a great seeker of truth for working people. I respected Tolstoy, just as I have great respect and love for Aleksej Maksimovich Gorky, because of his fearless exposure of the criminal life of all the tsarist governors, lords and henchmen, who for centuries oppressed the working people.

Further, I learnt from Tolstoy several rules of living — for example, to live only from one's own labour, to avoid drunkenness, hooliganism and the harming of my health through tobacco, to always stand up for the poor and to always be a useful person in a working society.

His conclusion: "Is it so bad to be a Tolstoyan like that?"

Mikhail Novikov was born in 1871. His family was poor. Both parents were forced to work long hours in the city to make ends meet and had little time to spend home with their son. Even when his father came home from working, such visits were rare, he was nearly always drunk. The young Mikhail reacted to these unpleasant experiences by resolving to abstain from alcohol and be wary of any harmful influences. At sixteen, he himself took a factory job in the city, feeding his extraordinary intellectual curiosity by visits to museums and the theatre whenever he could.

It was in his early twenties, when he was conscripted to military service and assigned as a scribe to a Moscow construction brigade, that he first became acquainted with Tolstoy's writings (including some that had been banned), which he had borrowed from friends, and immediately resolved to meet the writer in person. He relates this first encounter as follows:

> I shan't describe my meetings with Tolstoy in detail, as one may read about them in my memoirs. I shall just say briefly that when I first crossed the threshold

1 Gladkova 1994a [M. P. Novikov: I am to blame for his death]: 161.

into his Khamovniki[2] home, my head was spinning and I felt like a schoolboy caught at the scene of his crime. He met me on the stairs, about to go out for a walk, but on my account returned to his study, where he sat me down on a leather sofa. Out of habit (I was used to showing deference to any figure of authority) I started to address him as 'Your Excellency,' but he at once cut me off, saying that all titles were thought up with the base aims of exercising power over another, gloating and boasting, that they divide people and prevent them from understanding each other, and therefore ought to be abandoned.

He questioned me as to what my job was and where I worked, and said that, on the one hand, he was very glad I came to see him, but on the other, he would always be concerned about me. "Somehow it turns out with all my acquaintances," he said, "that they all end up in prison because of me." I didn't pay any attention to it at the time, but his predictions were accurate and came to pass.

I asked Tolstoy about religion, and he explained to me the significance of the Christian Gospel teachings, mentioning the things that prevent people from living in accord with them. The hindrances are as follows: laws of the state based on violence; laws and regulations established by clerics, as well as laws of the street, custom and fashion. People are so busy with these things that they have neither the time nor the inclination to think about fulfilling their duty to God and their neighbour. But people as God's children in spirit are completely free from all these fetters, decrees and conventions and can live fully in accordance with God, if only they are not afraid of gossip and threats.

He did not give me his banned books, saying that he did not want to land me in prison, and that back in the barracks, even the barracks for soldier-scribes, it would be only a couple of days before they ended up in the hands of the military police, which would be very bad for me.

For the time being he advised me to read over the Gospels in order to better understand what in them was human and what was divine. "You know," he said, "a lot of people come to me to talk about religion, but when you ask whether they have read the Gospels, it turns out that they have read very little of them or haven't read them at all." I then procured for myself a complete Bible, but, no matter how hard I tried, I didn't master it all, since it contains so many improbable stories, repetitions and conjectures. But the reading of the Gospels did leave a very strong impression on my young heart. I wept and rejoiced — it was really the first time I had found and recognized these books for myself. Slowly and gradually the ecclesiastical Christ-God, not quite comprehensible and accessible to mere mortals, became transformed in my consciousness into the great wise man and martyr, who became for me far closer and clearer than the old Christ-God, who had performed so many improbable miracles and then flown off to heaven. I then began to realize that among us Orthodox people there are actually very few real Christians — just about everyone is putting on a pretence and, merely for the sake of external beauty and show, they hide behind Christian signs and names. After that I started feeling weighed down by military service and the deception of the soldier's oath one is supposed to take on the cross and the Gospel, under orders and the compulsion of military laws.

2 A reference to the house in Khamovniki Lane that the Tolstoys used as their Moscow residence from 1882 to 1901.

> And later, when I began to find out from Tolstoy and from comrades that there are such people who refuse to take the oath or to be conscripted, I felt a great love for them and was excited by their spiritual accomplishments, for which they bore great sufferings, ending up in prison and disciplinary battalions.[3]

In 1896, Novikov not only declined to approve but vehemently criticized the construction of an expensive staging facility for the coronation of Nicholas II. At first, he was merely demoted and sent to Warsaw, but this was soon followed by exile to Kazakhstan. The following year he was released into the army reserves and sent back to his native village.[4]

He eventually became active in politics, serving on the special agricultural commission called by the tsar's finance minister, Sergej Witte. But he soon found himself once more under arrest for his outspoken stance on the plight of peasants and the persecution of freethinking individuals, and was freed only through Tolstoy's intervention. (Decades later, his continued activities as a freethinker would land him in considerable trouble with the Soviet authorities.)

Indeed, Tolstoy time and again intervened with authorities to secure his protégé's release or request favourable treatment for Novikov and his family. For example, on 21 October 1910 (shortly before his death), Tolstoy wrote to Dmitrij Nikolaevich Anuchkin, editor of the liberal Moscow newspaper *Russkie vedomosti* (*PSS* 82:201):

> Dear Dmitrij Nikolaevich. My old friend and kindred spirit, a well-respected individual, the peasant Mikhail Novikov, would like to secure a position for his son as a printer's apprentice. If you can do something about it and are willing, I should be very much obliged to you. Mikhail Novikov is not only a very good person, but a talented writer who thinks for himself. I believe his articles may be suitable for *Russkie vedomosti.*[5]

Tolstoy made frequent reference to Novikov in his diary entries and in correspondence with other Russian writers. Here are a few extracts from Tolstoy's diary and from a letter:

- Dear Pavel Aleksandrovich.... Have you seen Mikhail Petrovich? *(Letter to P. A. Bulanzhe, 15–16[?] July 1897)*
- Mikhail Novikov was here. *(Diary, 10 November 1897)*
- Yesterday I took a walk and spoke... in the evening with Novikov. *(Diary, 30 November 1900)*
- Novikov came. *(Diary, 10 October 1902)*

3 Gladkova 1994a: 164–65. For Novikov's reminiscences, see Novikov 1924.

4 For a number of biographical details of Novikov's life I am obliged to A. A. Korolëv and, especially, to Liudmila Viktorovna Gladkova, to whom I express my deep gratitude for her assistance with some of the commentaries.

5 *PSS* 82:201. A similar request was made the same day to Aleksandr Nikolaevich Konshin.

- Wrote letters to Koni and Stasov about Novikov. *(Diary, 2 October 1902)*
- Novikov was here. *(Diary, 28 December 1902)*
- Novikov was here. *(Diary, 4 October 1903)*
- Mikhail Novikov arrived. Had a long talk with him. A seriously clever peasant fellow. *(Diary, 20 October 1910)*

Tolstoy's physician, Dushan Petrovich Makovitskij, for example, took note of the extraordinary attention his employer paid to Novikov's writings (see below). It is quite evident from all this that Tolstoy undoubtedly considered Novikov the equal of two other peasants (V. K. Sjutaev and T. M. Bondarev) from whom, he said, he learnt more than from all writers and academics combined.[6]

Novikov paid frequent visits to Tolstoy during the early 1900s, both in Moscow and at the writer's Yasnaya Polyana estate. His final visit there took place in the autumn of 1910, just a few days before Tolstoy left Yasnaya for the last time. As usual, they talked about the ongoing social and religious issues of the day — the poverty and exploitation suffered by the peasants, further aggravated by rampant moral corruption among all classes of society and its stifling of individuals' attempts to achieve their own inner peace, and, above all, the horrors of war and the imperative to abstain from violence, even in one's attempts to counteract evil.

Novikov's career as a writer on his own began in earnest after 1900, and largely through Tolstoy's encouragement and moral support. Many of his works reflected Tolstoy's own views. These include "Golos krest'janina" [Voice of the peasant] (a treatise which was written in 1900 but did not appear in print until 1904, when Tolstoy helped publish it in England with Chertkov's Svobodnoe Slovo publishing house), and a treatise entitled "Na vojnu! (Zapiski prizyvnogo letom 1904 g.)" [To war! (Notes of a conscript, summer 1904)] published by Svobodnoe Slovo the same year. The first of these made such an impression on Tolstoy that he would frequently read it aloud to Yasnaya Polyana visitors. Upon first receiving a copy from Novikov, in December 1900, he made the following notation in his diary (*PSS* 54:65):

> I got a very strong impression: I recalled things I had forgotten — the life of the ordinary people, their need, their humiliation, and our own culpability. Oh, if only God had ordained me to write everything I feel in this piece!

Tolstoy was equally impressed by Novikov's "To war!". According to Makovitskij's reminiscences (1979–81: 2:21), Tolstoy called it "good," "superb," "strong." He also discussed this work in his own article condemning the Russo-Japanese war, *Bethink Yourselves!* (*PSS* 36:144–45), in which he even

6 See quotation from *What Then Must Be Done?* (1886), cited on p. xxiii above.

included Novikov's letters to him of 24 and 27 April 1904 dealing with the horrors of war.[7]

Novikov's condemnation of the authorities spared neither the landowners nor the official church. A few years later he launched an even more biting attack on the latter in two subsequent publications: *Staraja vera* [The old faith], a major work published by V. D. Bonch-Bruevich in 1908, followed by *Novaja vera* [The new faith] in 1909. His exposés of the wretched conditions of the Russian peasantry and calling those responsible to account were at least partially influenced by the writings of Timofej Bondarev, whose landmark book *Triumph of the land-tiller* had been presented to Novikov by Tolstoy in 1896, in which Bondarev wrote:

> Have mercy upon us, members of the wealthy class! For thousands of years you have ridden us as a wild horse, grinding our whole skin down to the bone. It may seem like only bread that you are eating, but in fact it is our flesh; it may seem as though you are simply drinking wine, but in fact it is our blood.

It is this type of strong plea and protest that is reflected in the following extended passage from Novikov's (1904b) "Voice of the peasant":

> We, *muzhiks,* earnestly do request of those whose hands have grasped or, rather, hold in the balance our free life, to give us back this life, to give it to us as a whole without exception, to place it at our own disposal and not to care for our education, not to treat our diseases with pellets and powders, not to show us 'dark pictures,' not to impose upon us 'faith' in the unseen, the incomprehensible and the miraculous. We shall not suffer for not having all this, nor shall we do worse than at present. We suffer because you take away our goods under the guise of legally sanctioned requisitions. Don't take anything away from us. We suffer because, on account of inequality and misfortune in apportioning out the riches of nature, we are supposed to be your *muzhiks* who clean up after you.
>
> Do not compel us to do this; nurse your own children, prepare your own meals according to your taste, procure for yourselves everything you deem your daily bread, plough your own fields, reap your own hay, feed your own livestock, clean up your own waste, and from this change your life will, all by itself, take on the form of the desired Golden Age even your best people can only dream of. The lies and hypocrisy on which your present life is constructed will fall away from you at once, and you will feel relief from the anxiety, worry, fear and, especially, lies, that now oppress you.
>
> We further suffer from the fact that we do not have everything necessary to meet life's needs, such as all the best lands, forests and even water, which you have seized for yourselves. So turn away from the sin of land ownership, turn away from a ready lifestyle in favoured places. Refuse to demand from others

7 See also Tolstoy's appraisal of Novikov's article in terms of "the folk language it captures" (Gusev 1960 [Chronicle of the life and works of L. N. Tolstoy]: 666), as well as Novikov's (1920) "Razgovor s L. N. Tolstym o japonskoj vojne" [Conversation with L. N. Tolstoy about the Japanese war].

what you have not provided for yourselves, turn away from the privileges of your noble breeding and the titles of 'lord' and 'lady'; let those shameful names retreat into the archives of the past; refuse to be 'lords and masters.' We have one tearful request: do not attack us with weapons, do not deal with us with threats of punishment, do not consider another's labour your own; legalise not land ownership, but the rights of labour to its fruits.

Give us only the opportunity, without fear of your attacks, to engage in our favourite activity of tilling the soil on our own lands. Join us, so that together we can enter as brethren into the joy of life, and do not think or fear that without you we shall run wild or lose our way to God: God is alive in us in spite of your catechisms and sacred stories, and we know it. The good Samaritans do not come from noble breeding!

Do not interfere with God's feeding of His flock. Let Him exercise authority directly over His people and then, most probably, one nation will not lift up sword against another, but will peacefully engage in the struggle with nature, respecting the person and labour of one's neighbour, without being frightened by church wardens, police officers, superintendents, priests, district authorities and the like, who are at present given the 'right' at any time to take away from us what we have earned through fearful labour and effort, and in whose presence we cannot live like human beings, praise God, but can only exist as beasts of burden, carrying in our hearts a constant silent anger and cursing against our oppressors who have imposed this unbearable yoke upon us.[8]

Such views found frequent echoes in the writings of Tolstoy himself, approaching the question of social justice from the opposite side; that is, from within the class assigned to him by his 'noble breeding.' Witness, for example, his concluding statement to his provocative 1905 treatise *Velikij grekh* [A great sin] (*PSS* 36:230):

I should like to think that we, the parasites of Russia, who have been fed and afforded leisure time for intellectual activity thanks to the labours of the ordinary people, will realize our sin and attempt to undo it, regardless of personal profit — in the name of the truth which condemns us.

Another point of agreement with Novikov's views may be found in the same article, when Tolstoy speaks out against the proliferation of "European institutions" attempting to "enlighten the peasantry" (see, e.g., ibid., 220) while actually caring more for their own reputation than the real needs of the peasants. Unlike Novikov, however, Tolstoy still viewed physical labour on the land as a *sine qua non* in the pursuit of moral happiness on earth.[9]

As mentioned earlier, the plight of the peasants is emphasized in a number of Tolstoy's novels and plays — for example, in his 1890 play *The Fruits of*

8 Reproduced in the commentary to Tolstoy's diary entry of 28 November 1900 (*PSS* 54:442–43).
9 In this his views very much coincided with those of the Sabbatarian Timofej Bondarev (cf. the section on Bondarev, above).

Enlightenment, which highlights the question of peasant land ownership, or rather the lack thereof.[10]

In addition to the plight of the peasants, another question permeating Tolstoy's correspondence with Novikov was the horror of war and the compulsory regime of military service, which the latter knew about first-hand from his brief stint in the army.[11] His discussion of this subject with Tolstoy was the basis of Novikov's narrative *To war!*, decrying the immorality of war, its cruel separation of men from their families and workers from their lands, its deleterious effects on the economy, and its destructive influence on the moral integrity of both individuals and communities.

The narrative, especially its touching, poetic manner of expression, made an immediate and lasting impression on Tolstoy, who kept several of Novikov's letters on the same subject close at hand and reread them frequently.[12]

As indicated above, however, the two men did not agree on everything. On more than one occasion Tolstoy tried to persuade Novikov that a person's inner soul was not dependent on external conditions, citing Novikov's own narrative in justification of his views. According to N. N. Gusev, who served for two years as Tolstoy's personal secretary, Tolstoy once remarked to Novikov:

> It's all in you, it's all in you, as Sjutaev said. You as well weren't in any too splendid conditions when you wrote about the reserves [in *To war!*]. Of the thousands of stories, that is one of the best...[13]

Tolstoy was also less than pleased with Novikov's negative views on religion. While he understood Novikov's tenuous status as an educated man in a largely uneducated peasant community, he could not bring himself to accept the latter's almost utter rejection (as set forth in his treatises on 'new' and 'old' faith — *Novaja vera* and *Staraja vera*, respectively) of any kind of religious expression. On one occasion Novikov wrote to Pitirim, the Bishop of Tula and Beljaevsk, with the following requests (cited in Korolëv 1978: 43):

> 1) that the church, as represented by the priests, leave my life and that of my family alone;
> 2) that the children born to me be registered without any prayers or rituals, and only on the basis of my declaration;

10 See the quotation from this play in the section on Bondarev, above (p. 9). The play was written in 1890, but not published until 1891. It should be stressed that the abolition of serfdom in 1861, though technically freeing serfs, did not provide them with any arable land of their own, or a means of living, and so many were left in a state of subjugation to the landowner class.

11 Novikov was discharged for medical reasons (specifically, a hernia). See his letter to Tolstoy of 20 June 1904 (Letter N° 15).

12 Letters written by Novikov on 25 May 1904, 9 and 20 June 1904, and 13 September 1904.

13 Gusev 1973 [Two years with L. N. Tolstoy]: 242.

3) that any marriages my children may enter into be registered without wedding ceremonies and recognized in the legal sense on an equal basis with others;
4) that the land allotted to me and my family not be subject to any taxes by the church.

Tolstoy rejected this kind of reasoning as a mere distraction from more important spiritual concerns. In a letter dated 4 September 1907, he wrote to Novikov in no uncertain terms:

> To bury your children without the services of the clergy, not to fast and not to go to church — that is not faith: you have rejected the superstitions of the old faith, but you have no faith yourself. It is in this, in the fact that you do not believe in a spiritual principle of life and its requirements, that your misfortune lies, and not at all in the lack of land and the unfairness of the economic structure.

It should be noted that Novikov was indeed disenchanted with religion on the whole, not merely with the official church. This may be seen in his evident impatience with many religious sectarians, who, he believed, had simply exchanged one form of ritual for another.

Tolstoy could not help but be disappointed that Novikov, along with many other ordinary Russian people (and even some of his own followers), fell into the trap of misinterpreting one of his most profound treatises on the subject of religion, *The Kingdom of God is Within You*, completed in 1893. This after Novikov had initially declared how much the book had influenced his life.[14]

By 1908, Novikov was writing in *Staraja vera* that Russian peasants on the whole were an irreligious lot, that their faith was by and large based on superstition and heathen rituals and could find little or no compatibility with official church dogma and practices. According to Gusev's records, Tolstoy severely rebuked Novikov on this point when the two met on 10 February 1908. Gusev (1973: 99) transcribes Tolstoy's words as follows:

> "There was one woman in our village," he said, "who lived a very profligate life. Some soldiers were stationed nearby, and she attached herself to them, lay with them and then ran off with them. Her husband caught her and, according to the custom of the time, dealt with her harshly, tying her to a horse's tail. Anyway, one evening I happened to be walking through the village around eleven o'clock at night. It was dark everywhere, but there was a light in her window. What was going on? I stepped up to her window and looked in. Here this same woman

14 On 7 March 1898, Novikov wrote to Tolstoy: "You have given me moral freedom; you have shown me my true self, and while I cannot immediately turn away from my past completely, at least my whole life will not be snuffed out by the internal struggle between two elements of my identity. The struggle serves to perfect us on the path to showing love to everything living and to govern our personal life. The spark that has been lit will not snuff out the consciousness of divine sonship, which refreshes our life and leads to an ever greater regeneration of our inner self."

> was standing on her knees and praying. I walked away, stood for a while, and thought, what was she doing now? I went over, and she was still praying. So I went away again, took a little walk, and well, now, I thought, she's probably finished. So I go over and she's *still* praying. And there's nobody around. She's all alone, and yet there's *somebody* she's talking with.
>
> "You see, the relationship to that *somebody*," concluded Tolstoy, "is what constitutes religion. And in every faith, no matter how crude it may be in our view, that relationship exists."[15]

Even after this, however, Novikov's anti-religious views showed little modification, judging by the publication of *Novaja vera* the following year. Indeed, it is not difficult to see why not only its content but, especially, its crude style of writing would be as distasteful to the general reading public as it was to Tolstoy. The impression of Novikov as a nihilist, which the publication conveys, is partly explained — though hardly mitigated — by a consideration of his awkward circumstances in the community where he lived. Tolstoy, it will be remembered, firmly rejected the notion of external influences on the inner soul, citing again and again Sjutaev's dictum: "It's all in you, it's all in you."

Yet none of these reservations were sufficient to stop Tolstoy from making every effort to have Novikov's manuscripts published in a variety of journals. On the contrary, unlike a number of other peasant writers whom Tolstoy abandoned when divergent views began to surface, Novikov maintained close, friendly relations with the writer right up until the latter's death in 1910. In fact, shortly before his decision to leave Yasnaya Polyana for the last time, Tolstoy wrote to Novikov, asking whether he might stay in his village for a few days.[16]

It should not seem surprising that Tolstoy would seek refuge not with a member of his family or social class, or even with one of his followers, but with a representative of the Russian peasantry who did not even share Tolstoy's ideas on non-violent resistance to evil, yet to whom he felt far closer in spirit than to any of the former.

Novikov's reply to Tolstoy's letter, granting his request but at the same time 'instructively' advising that he reconsider his decision to leave the surroundings of the social class to which he was born and accustomed, reached Tolstoy only on his deathbed, at Astapovo.[17] The circumstance of meeting his end at an isolated railway station, instead of in the company of one of his beloved peasantry, to whom he had devoted so much of his creative and heartfelt energies, may be seen as one more cruel 'irony of fate,' yet also as a bitter confirmation of that seemingly incontrovertible truth that it is difficult, if not

15 One cannot help but agree, at least in part, with Novikov's argument about the 'grey peasant,' so vividly portrayed in Chekhov's *Muzhiki* (1897).

16 See Letter N° 31, dated 24 October 1910.

17 Novikov's letter was read to Tolstoy by Vladimir Chertkov several days before his death (see Chertkov 1911 [On the last days of L. N. Tolstoy]: 16–17).

impossible, to become that which one is not destined to become. This was a 'truth' which had long tormented Tolstoy in his attempt to 'simplify himself' [*oprostit'sja*]. It applies to both the writer and the characters of station that populate his novels.

Throughout the fourteen-year Tolstoy-Novikov correspondence, however, the peasant writer comes across as a complex figure, certainly defying the stereotype of the 'simple peasant' of Tolstoy's ideal. That Novikov earned his own modest niche in the history of Russian epistolary literature there can be no doubt, despite his sometimes superficial reasonings and concomitant prejudicial conclusions.

After Tolstoy's death Novikov continued to maintain contact with the writer's family[18] and to write on social issues, which led to frequent incarcerations. Even in the Soviet era, the fearless peasant did not relax his criticism of the government of the day and its treatment of the Russian peasantry. Witness his daughter Anna Mikhajlovna's 1988 account (as quoted in Gladkova 1994a: 158):

> Even after the October [Revolution], out of a sense of duty, my father constantly sacrificed his time and health for the sake of the common people. He wrote letters to the authorities, including Kalinin and Stalin himself, trying to make them understand the kinds of disasters that were taking over the countryside. But this enormous self-sacrifice of my father's, his deep sense of conviction, was his fatal mistake, as in the eyes of the Bolshevist authorities the peasantry was by no means the true working class.

Novikov's final arrest came in 1937, after which his family saw him no more.

The Tolstoyan legacy embodied in Novikov's continued activities over the quarter-century following the great writer's death gives added weight to the significance of their lengthy correspondence. Not only does it serve as a prime example in elucidating Tolstoy's abiding interest in the fate of the peasantry, their philosophy and its practical applications to daily life, but it shows how the dialogue with peasant sectarians met an ongoing need for Tolstoy to clarify (*ujasnit'*) his own thoughts on various religious and social issues — a role he himself insisted the peasants were in a much better position than the intellectual classes to fulfil. As an *inside* view of the Russian peasantry by a caring peasant, a study of this correspondence, and of Novikov's own legacy for today's generations of students and scholars, is important in gaining a fuller picture of the intricate social relations permeating rural life in turn-of-the-century Russia and, indeed, of the deeper essence of the whole Russian peasantry.

18 Especially interesting here is Novikov's hitherto unpublished correspondence with Tolstoy's eldest son, Sergej L'vovich, and with a number of Tolstoyans.

TOLSTOY AND NOVIKOV: LETTERS 1896–1910

1. M. P. NOVIKOV ❧ L. N. TOLSTOY
13 April 1896. Borovkovo.

Dear Lev Nikolaevich!

I am at fault, very much at fault in your sight! The fact that you entrusted your books to me, which portend the true future life of human beings, means that you were relying upon my experience, but I have not justified your trust in me. Things have happened as they should[19] and just as you warned me.

While on holiday at home, where my brothers[20] and I spent the whole Easter holiday and the following days reading books, including yours, learning and explaining to each other the new Christian teachings, suddenly, on the 6th of April at half-past five in the morning, when we had just started getting up, the 'powers-that-be' came to our door: the Tula Deputy Prosecutor, the District Officer, the District Superintendent and the Tula Police Headquarters Adjutant, accompanied by four policemen and witnesses. They surrounded the house, forbade us to go out or come in, and for three hours prowled about the house, just as your Anis'ja (in *The Power of Darkness*) prowled about her dying husband's house looking for money.

You know better than I do the 'village' with its concepts, therefore I shan't explain in detail the effect these 'princes of this world' had on the village and particularly on our family (our mother and wives), who were unprepared to receive them. I shall only say a word or two about the torture I went through during those three hours, confronting the Power of Darkness face to face, seeing my utter helplessness before it! So many torturing thoughts ran through my head as they were nitpicking their way through belongings that were not their own!

I wasn't afraid for myself, that they might cart me off right away (which the whole village expected, first and foremost the priest). No, I wasn't thinking about that, I was completely overwhelmed by this picture of violence being perpetrated in broad daylight in the sight of everyone. I only thought about how some human beings could barge in on others no different from themselves, toss their things around and mess them up, without them being able to even lift so much as a finger in their presence.

It was during this very time of inner tension that the whole panorama of this eternal violent struggle of some people against others spread itself out

19 On 14 February 1896 the police raided the home of Tolstoy's acquaintance Marija Mikhajlovna Kholevinskaja, a *zemstvo* [district council] doctor in the Krapivensk district. Several of Tolstoy's manuscripts were discovered, along with a letter written by his daughter Tat'jana requesting that some of Tolstoy's banned writings be given to Novikov's brother Ivan. A subsequent search was made of the Novikovs' house in Borovkovo. This led to Novikov's arrest, as described above.

20 Novikov had three adult brothers (nine others had died in childhood): Adrian (1865–1930), Ivan (b. 1868?) and Pavel (d. 1914).

before me for the first time in all its splendour. I thought: this is just a simple search, but how much moral torment there will be for everyone if this is followed by imprisonment, exile, beatings with whips, and the punishment of individuals and whole crowds? Isn't this, in the public perception, that very hell we are threatened with by the priests, for 'sins' and disobedience to the sacred powers here on earth? Before this I suffered over the oppressed people only superficially, vicariously, but now I have become involved myself in this suffering and, as long as I live, no human power will force me to exchange my God of love for a God of evil and violence, nor force me to pray to evil for a better fulfilment of evil.

While I might have said before this that I was happy, I now feel myself at the apex of the happiness people are capable of, not a visible but an inner, heartfelt happiness. Everyone says: "This is God punishing you for ceasing to pray to him and to go to church," but not only do I not feel this punishment, but as one who has lost a rouble as people watched and found a hundred with no onlookers, my joy at this happiness is unspeakable. Perhaps this apparent unhappiness will prepare me for another, even more serious, etc., stage, until I am finally strengthened for open warfare against the Power of Darkness.

My unhappiness at the moment consists only in the fact that I am not able to return Bondarev's manuscript[21] to you, which was taken during the search. I feel frightfully guilty before you, as I have no idea how I am going to compensate you for it. If you are agreeable, I could pay you ten roubles for it. I shall not be satisfied until you have forgiven me or taken the payment. The rest of your books, which were somehow miraculously spared, will be returned to you at the earliest opportunity — when you are at Yasnaya Polyana, my brother[22] will bring them to you there. There was no way I could take them with me; I am being watched.

While I was still at home, on the 5th of April there was a search of my things here too by a police officer and a member of the Civic Court. It's good that they didn't find my notebook with letters. I've now burnt it. The night of the 5th they also conducted a raid on my brother's place in Tula. I mean the brother who lives at the Teplovs' factory and who by this time had already returned from the village to his work. During the search at my place they also took a banned book (Linev's *Ne skazki* [Not fairy tales]),[23] while from my brother Adrian's[24] they took your books *The Kingdom of God*, *What Kind of*

21 The reference is to Bondarev's *Triumph of the land-tiller*. Novikov was undoubtedly influenced to some extent by Bondarev's ideas, despite his calling the latter's work "a Utopian fantasy."

22 *Ivan Petrovich Novikov* — an employee of the Teplovs' factory in Tula, who later worked in the Posrednik publishing house. He was arrested, along with his brother Mikhail, in 1937.

23 *Dmitrij Aleksandrovich Linev* (pseud.: Dalin; 1853–1920), author of sketches and stories of prison life. The book *Ne skazki* [Not fairy tales] appeared in two editions in 1895.

24 *Adrian Petrovich Novikov* (1865–1930). In his youth he worked as a hospital orderly in Tula, then for many years as a valet to Prince Grigorij Petrovich Volkonskij. He wrote "The true story of servant life. A valet's notes," which Tolstoy read along with his other writings. He died in exile

Life Do I Have? and *The Kreutzer Sonata,*[25] which he had brought home from abroad.

Now they are constantly questioning me, gathering testimony, but there is no evidence because there was no crime. Somehow they gathered that I was giving someone copies of secret papers,[26] that I am openly upsetting soldiers by violating my oath, that I supposedly have some kind of connection with suspicious persons — maybe anarchists? They see that I have done nothing, they've just heard that I have been reading your books, but they have no idea what to do with me. They only know that I'm no longer their defender and am a pretty poor aide when it comes to violence.

The major-general questioning me, Buturlin, who says you, Lev Nikolaevich, write "smoothly and colourfully," said a report on me was received from Petersburg, in which my brother is mentioned (the one living in Tula), and the crimes are detailed in point form. I'm not bothered by these harassments and their consequences, but I can't understand just who could have reported on me in Petersburg.

If you need your books and if it is not unsafe to send them by mail directly from the village, please write to me. My address here is: District HQ, Scribe Novikov, and they will be sent to you directly from the village.

Oh, how I would like to see you in person, to apologize in person for the manuscript and look into your kind eyes, give strength to you who have been cursed by 'priests' and the 'princes of this world,' and renew my own spiritual forces. Of course, I feel ridiculous in your eyes when I speak of 'strengthening.' Do not judge me for that.

Your life to me is so precious, and the strength of your will is so precious to many others, that I am greatly afraid lest they have forced you to renounce the teachings of Christ you have affirmed, or rather used some trickery or deception to tell the people of your renunciation of the ideal you have created. What will happen then, I exclaim in fear?! Your life and works shine like the sun over the whole world. What efforts and trickery of the 'princes' will be used after your death to slander you in the eyes of the people and somehow hide your teachings!

at Arkhangel'sk. For more on Adrian Petrovich Novikov, see the commentary to Tolstoy's diary entry of 2 May 1896 in *PSS* 53:447, also *PSS* 58:317–18.

25 These might have been the following editions: *Tsarstvo Bozh'e vnutri vas* [*The Kingdom of God is Within You*] (Berlin: August Diebner, 1894); *V chëm moja vera?* [*What I Believe*] (Geneva: Èlpidin, 2nd ed., 1892); *Krejtserova sonata* [*The Kreutzer Sonata*] (Geneva: Èlpidin, 1890). Tolstoy lent books to Novikov on many occasions. In his diary entry for March 1896 are noted: "(1) *Outline of the Gospels,* (2) *Confession,* (3) *What I believe,* (4) *Sochinenie Bondareva* [Bondarev's composition]. Taken by Novikov." See *PSS* 53:276.

26 As senior scribe of the military headquarters' construction brigade, Novikov had access to secret papers. In fact, in 1895, he brought Tolstoy a secret file on the shooting of workers at the Korzinkin factory in Yaroslavl'. Tolstoy asked him to be careful, and to not bring him any more secret papers. For further details, see Gladkova 1994a: 155–56.

O my dear, kind grandfather, my mentor! Be firm in your convictions right to the end, do not give in to trickery, fear not the threats, don't even think about your life being of no benefit to anyone and everybody hating you. Even if I were the only one who knew and loved you and understood your love for the people, then you could die in peace, knowing that you have been understood by a single individual! And how many people know and understand you! How many people have, either openly or secretly, become your disciples![27] They all love you, and what peace you must have within yourself, surrounded by such love! I weep with tears of joy, and I rejoice with the joy of our God of love!

Let our pastors and crowds of people cry unto their God of evil: "Arise, O God!." But their god will not hold his position for long on water — as an object, he will either float away or drown; there is no place for him to stand on the former secret altar or accept a multitude of bloody human sacrifices. If he is still standing, he has no longer a pedestal to stand on, it has been destroyed by you, and no matter how hard they cry "Arise!," he will still crumble. There may still be many calls for the old god, but you have sown the seed of doubt in many people's hearts as to the possibility of having a god of evil as one's god; let these seeds of doubt result in at least one spurt of growth and then the success of the new Kingdom of the God of love will be secured.

Oh, how good it will be when God will reign anew in human hearts! There will be no more tears heard over people killed in war or taken to prison or sent into exile or victims slain by vicious human perversity. No longer will human blood flow and overflow whole fields, there will be no more fear of someone about to come 'on a search.' The new God will reign not in Petersburg or London or Constantinople, he will reign in the heart of every individual, and in obeying him, the groaning of the people will be silenced, feasts and coronations will cease, nobody will sigh and poison his life on account of his rent not being paid (as you now hear), nobody will rob one another as at present, but they will help each other in secret and avoid taking credit.

27 Novikov was undoubtedly thinking about the Tolstoyans who were inclined to view the Doukhobors and other sectarians as the true embodiment of Christian ideals — the living expression of what they preached. Just as the populists used to look up to and idealize the simple Russian peasant, so too the Tolstoyans considered it their duty to sympathize with (inasmuch as this was possible for people in their social position and educational level) and assist the unjustly persecuted sectarians. Tolstoyans held their greatest task to be the promulgation of the ideas of their esteemed teacher, as well as attracting people to the lifestyle Tolstoy insisted on in his post-crisis writings. These works (e.g., *An Examination of Dogmatic Theology, What I Believe, The Kingdom of God is Within You, What Then Must Be Done?*), permeated with the Tolstoyan doctrine of 'non-resistance to evil by violence' and including a condemnation of authority, the official church, legislation and the prevailing right to private property, naturally aroused mistrust and anger on the part of the powers that be, who had never been known for their tolerance of dissident thinking. However, the Tolstoyans' efforts were crowned with success: the popularity of the writer among the people increased significantly. For more on the Tolstoyans, see the Introduction.

Most importantly, Christ will be resurrected not physically, as they now teach. It won't be the dead Christ that is resurrected but the living Christ, who forbids swearing and killing, deceiving and violating; he will be resurrected not in legendary and historical memory but in the heart of each individual, and everyone will then feel with great force the joy I now feel over the God of love.

Even though people now give brotherly kisses to each other, Christ is still crucified as before. It is not just that he was crucified and died, no, he is being crucified all the time right up to this very hour, ever since his bodily crucifixion, and will continue to be crucified for a very, very long time.

But, I repeat, rejoice, my father, my brother and mentor! Rejoice not because the "fatted calf" awaits us at home, but rejoice in God's light that shines within you. When I know that even one person loves me the way I now love you, then the good of my present life will be overflowing and neither disease, poverty, threats, or anything else will destroy this my non-earthly good, and in that moment I shall not be frightened by my immersion into nirvana (death) itself. Let them judge me, let them send me wherever they wish, but my attackers will never have anything wherewith *to kill* my thought or my new faith. I am not throwing myself headlong, I feel that I am not yet ready for that, but no matter where I am and what they do with me, my God will be with me everywhere and the people that live with me will hear always and everywhere the stories about this new God.[28]

Once more I ask your forgiveness for Bondarev's manuscript and I hope that you will not condemn me for the blunder. When it is possible for me to once more go where I want to, my first trip will be to see you, but for now I am prohibited from travelling and am under surveillance. I would very much like to know when you will be going to Yasnaya Polyana. Please let me know about this by open letter, as well as what I should do about my guilt over the manuscript. They do pass on letters to me. Just write simply, and I'll understand.

Your acquaintance,

Novikov the Scribe

13 April 1896

28 Novikov subsequently wrote about how he left Orthodoxy in his treatises *Staraja vera* [The old faith] and *Novaja vera* [The new faith]. See Tolstoy's letter of recommendation to his close friend, journalist Aleksandr Modestovich Khir'jakov (*PSS* 79:178–99); also, Tolstoy's conversation with Gusev (1960) regarding these treatises.

2. M. P. NOVIKOV ❧ L. N. TOLSTOY
7 March 1898.

Laptevo Station, Moscow-Kursk Railway
Village of Borovkovo, 7 March 1898.

Deeply esteemed Lev Nikolaevich!

I begin with thanking you once more. Reading your work [containing your article] *The Christian Teaching* afforded me great pleasure.[29] The first time I read it, it seemed to contain nothing new; while, as I remember, in reading your other books over the previous two years, I had been quite simply struck [again and again] by the truths they revealed. But in copying and rereading it several times more, on each occasion I discovered in it something new for myself, and the further [I read], the more important these discoveries seemed to me. And it's only now that I realize what a tremendous benefit this teaching will afford anyone who reads it with careful attention and without prejudice in respect to your name. It affords the opportunity for anyone raised in the common traditions of our times to look at themselves through other eyes — to take a good, hard look at their life, their concepts of life — concepts which have been and are now the basis of everything unworthy of a man, desecrating him as a son of God, all that frightening ignorance and the evil resulting therefrom for all people and each one in particular, that has been or is being passed off on the surface for the common good and for both present-life and future-life bliss for each one in particular.

You have given me moral freedom, you have revealed to me my inner self, and even though I can't all at once disassociate myself from my whole past, at least, throughout the rest of my life, the inner struggle between two elements of my selfhood will not be extinguished in its perfecting effect on man on the path of expressing love to all living beings, and regulating man's personal life; neither will the spark of consciousness of [man's] sonship with God, once lit, be snuffed out — it illumines life and gives rise more and more to the birth of man's inner self.

Since January I have stopped eating meat;[30] even in the summertime when I am working harder, I shall try not to eat it. And if I succeed, then I shall be a

29 *The Christian Teaching* — an article by Tolstoy (written 1894–1896). In a letter to Aleksandra Andreevna Tolstaja dated 4 September 1894, Tolstoy described his work on this article as follows: "It is an outline in the briefest and most comprehensible form of my religious confession of faith." Novikov must have read the article in manuscript form, as it was published for the first time in both English and Russian at the end of 1898 by Vladimir Chertkov in Purleigh (Essex), England.

30 This was under the influence of Tolstoy, who had become a vegetarian in 1895 and, later, an especially vigorous opponent of tobacco and alcohol.

true vegetarian, since in the summertime I shall try planting vegetables, so I shall have something to eat instead of meat. I don't know how meat could be a treat for some people; it has never seemed that way to me at least, and if I did eat meat, it was only because everybody eats it; it will not be any great hardship to give it up. The only problem is to find something to replace it with; the thing is that for years we have had at times nothing but bread and grey cabbage, and we don't always have even our own potatoes.

On Epiphany, on 6 January, when the 'holy father with the cross' visited our home, I refused, together with my brother Pavel, to listen to the 'Troparion'[31] or to kiss the 'cross,' and told the 'holy father' that we didn't need this. With each conflict Mother threatens us that she will go to the police and turn us over to the 'authorities' for this. I'm very glad I broke with the church, and would like very much to free the children, too, from the comedy of baptisms and funeral masses at times of birth and death, though for this they will probably start persecuting me in the name of the common good, and for now I am not yet ready [to bear] a cross.

In the village I give out books to those who want to read them; I talk about what I am able to, to the extent that I am beginning to 'have my own disciples'; people in the village say that they — or, rather, we — are "converting them to our faith,"[32] but just what our faith is, I myself have no idea.

Give my regards to Evgenij Ivanovich[33] and Ivan Ivanovich.[34] I am very grateful to him for the books; everybody borrows them from me to read. I have not forgotten his request and I shall try to write something from the country.

Write [and tell me if] I can send you [my] work by parcel post? Up to how many copies? There's no way I can send them to you by hand before the 12th of April.

Mikhail Petrovich Novikov

31 *Troparion* — a brief (one-stanza) hymn in the Eastern Orthodox Church.

32 In Russian: *perevodim v svoju veru.*

33 *Evgenij Ivanovich Popov* (1864–1938) — a follower of Tolstoy.

34 *Ivan Ivanovich Gorbunov-Posadov* (1864–1940) — a close friend and kindred spirit to Tolstoy, who for a long time headed the Posrednik publishing house.

3. M. P. NOVIKOV ➡ L. N. TOLSTOY
7 December 1898.

Village of Borovkovo, Laptevo Station, 7 Dec. 1898.

Dear Lev Nikolaevich!

I am returning your books with gratitude: *Svobodnoe slovo*[35] and *Gde brat tvoj?*[36] Forgive me for keeping them so long, but it means eight people got to read them.

I wanted to copy from them *Istorija pisanij* [History of the Scriptures], it was so interesting for me. But here's what I really want to ask you: *Would it not be possible* through you *to obtain my own copy of* Svobodnoe slovo *and how much would it cost?*

A book like that brings new fire for those that "have ears to hear"[37] in our community.

If possible, tell my brother Pavel the terms, and he will write to me.

Mikhail Novikov

Another matter: *Please help my brother Pavel* find some sort of position.

He was *dismissed for "unreliability"* from Teplov's[38] in Tula, by order of the gendarmerie colonel.

Perhaps you could ask one of our acquaintances to give him a position — [anything] from a caretaker or servant to a minor office clerk.

He wouldn't even mind [working for] Morozova[39] again, given that he left her not just on a whim, but for a 'higher' position.

If you will do me this great favour, [it means] I shall be able to live at home and not go in search of a 'position on the side.'

I feel no shame in asking this of you, since I myself do what I can for others.

Mikhail Novikov

As for me, I'm working in bookbinding. The work doesn't pay much, but then I don't need much.

35 *Svobodnoe slovo* [The Free Word] — a periodical edited by Pavel Ivanovich Birjukov, published by Chertkov in Purleigh (Essex), England, to avoid tsarist censorship. Only two volumes were published (1898–1899).

36 *Gde brat tvoj? Ob otnoshenii russkogo pravitel'stva k ljudjam, ne mogushchim stanovit'sja ubijtsami* [Where is thy brother? About the attitude of the Russian government to conscientious objectors] — a brochure written by Vladimir Grigor'evich Chertkov (published in Purleigh, 1898).

37 Mark 4:23.

38 Vladimir Semënovich Teplov (?–1880) — merchant, owner of a hardware factory in Tula.

39 *Varvara Alekseevna Morozova* (1850–1917) — a Moscow millionairess and philanthropist, an acquaintance of Tolstoy's since the end of the 1880s.

4. M. P. NOVIKOV ❧ L. N. TOLSTOY
27 September 1901.

Laptevo Station, Tsinger Estate, 27 September 1901

Dear Lev Nikolaevich!

Life is, in general, a very difficult piece; in particular, from time to time it gets so complicated that it is very difficult to escape from its nets on one's own without sin: it's hard to tell just where truth ends and evil begins. And one always has the desire at such moments to share [one's feelings] with someone else, to tell them about one's self; one feels like conveying to that other person half of the mental turmoil which one can't cope with on one's own. One wants to observe from the sidelines how other people [cope] in similar situations and somehow manage to survive the same snares of life — to see and learn how these people escape from the webs of life that have ensnared them.

The same with me. You know that I am living in a hut on the estate of I. V. Tsinger;[40] I take knots of wood out of his forest for fuel, and this dependence of my outward material life on a person with legal rights to land, wood, hay — is becoming for me more and more intolerable with each passing day, aggravating the hidden antagonism in our relationship; it shows me ever more clearly that my current existence is built on sand and is becoming increasingly threatened with doom. But over these past three years I have managed to taste the fruits of a freer life — in comparison with communal peasant life — on the basis of an individual plot of land. I have experienced the whole charm of working the land surrounding a dwelling, with the proximity of a hayfield and woods. I have learnt from experience that all the inconveniences of working a plot, as suggested by the opponents of such a regime, simply fall away before long in practice. Most of all, I have experienced [first-hand] the whole charm of 'authority-freedom,' meaning the absence and non-interference in my life of any sort of 'authority,' which always and everywhere poisons the life of each member of a peasant community. And what is important to me and the most important to the children: an aspect of life without priests and without the influence of clerical teachings on the children through all sorts of 'weekend gossips' and those same ugly pious types who [think they] 'can say everything better.'

I would like to continue to live in a situation like that on an individual plot for the rest of my life, earning enough to maintain my family from my work on the land, and bringing them up as a new race of people with my children, trying to be an example in everything at the same time for people I happen to be in contact with. But to live any longer like this on Ivan Vasil'evich Tsinger's

40 *Ivan Vasil'evich Tsinger* — a Tula landlord, son to the famous mathematician and botanist Vasilij Jakovlevich Tsinger.

land is intolerable without abandoning my human dignity, since for that I would have to be a lackey and a day-labourer for Tsinger and from time to time listen to his 'lordly' obscenities and all sorts of insulting remarks. To go off to my father's [and live] on an allotment of land which would entail, among other things, performing church obligations — that would be even worse. What should I do? This is a question demanding an immediate solution, which I am not able to cope with on my own, and for [help in] solving it I am turning to you as an impartial and incorruptible Judge. To give you a better idea of my situation vis-à-vis Tsinger and my relationship to him, let me tell you the following detail about our basic alliance as colonists and colleagues. Tsinger and I agreed to work together and divide everything in half. (The fact that he is unable or unwilling to work I did not know back then and still can't understand even today.) As to labour, that first spring he did some of the work himself or, rather, hired farm hands from the manor house and day-labourers from the village; [however,] more and more of the work fell on my shoulders and those of my family, since during the working period Ivan Vasil'evich would go off to see his friends: the Raevskijs, the Gureviches, and others, while the farm hands and day-labourers he promised didn't show up on the days they were needed. Even though we had made an agreement to supply other working hands in case of need, they [often] didn't show up on time, and their absence made it impossible to get certain tasks done on my own, like carting the sheaves, hay and straw, covering the roof, etc. It drove me to a state of terrible torment — all the more so since the summer was damp, and the buildings we needed for the land-tilling weren't in place yet, and the ones that were there were half-uncovered. And so these past three summers I was obliged not just to work, but to work at a super-human pace, putting up buildings that had been missing and fixing those that were already standing, fencing off what needed fencing, etc. Terrific! That first summer the work somehow managed to get done, and I sold the surplus oats for 42 roubles. This was [our] first income. From this amount I gave Ivan Vasil'evich 18 roubles, secretly thinking that I was paying him not for work, since the work he did was so insignificant that it was not worth the trouble and labour which this entailed, with us feeding him and all, but that I was paying him for the oat seeds which he had taken from the manor house. He hinted about the 3 roubles missing from his half; I hadn't anticipated that and tried to smooth over the conversation, muttering that I could not give him more, as my family needs were a hundred times greater than his.

The second summer, to avoid unpleasantries over the division of income, I decided to keep a daily work record and then divide the income according to the number of days worked. I no longer took account of the quality or quantity of my work vis-à-vis his or that of his hirelings, but simply counted work in terms of time. He agreed to this. But words are words, and deeds are deeds. Our relationship suffered the same trouble as Krylov's "Swan, Pike and

Crawfish."[41] I am used to working and don't know how to make others do my work for me; he, on the other hand, is accustomed to ordering others to do his bidding, and not used to working himself. My plan was clear and simple: apportion the income according to the time worked — if you work for an hour, you get paid for an hour; work for a year and you get paid for a year. His plan, by contrast, was to pay for day labour out of his half of the products sold during all the working days and pocket the remainder. I thought and acted like all rural people who had grown up in poverty, while he tried to think and act like people in 'noble' households are wont to think and act. I wanted to stay away from sin by keeping a record, but it only led to further sin; from this record Ivan Vasil'evich could see that I had had a greater number of working days, which meant I would have the greater income, and, without any further hint of a fifty-fifty division as in the first year, he secretly envied me, and so the third spring — of this year —, to avoid having fewer workdays than I, he suggested he would hire a permanent day-labourer, "and when I feel like stretching my legs, I can do a bit of work myself" — this is how he put it. I refused to work with his day-labourer, since right from the start I had gained experience working with his so-called hired force and decided to work on my own, and since our regular circle of field-work was quite small, I got along with it very well indeed. This summer he was absolutely preoccupied with planting willow trees for basket-weaving, and so we didn't interfere with one another. I worked in the field and vegetable gardens; he kept company with a bunch of women and girls on his plantation. When the girls were leaving work and singing songs, he would follow them on a 'noble steed, just like a knight out of the Middle Ages. My work, which drew upon myself and God, went very well, while his, dependent on his day-labourers, went very poorly and in an untimely fashion, attended by irritation and cursings. Hence this summer our business relationship, too, fell apart. And as soon as Ivan Vasil'evich realized that I was of no further use to him, he began to nag me over all sorts of trifles, probably in the hope that I would leave his estate, especially since he had requested from Petersburg a subsidy of 400 roubles to hire a crafts master and was recruiting pupils to learn basket-weaving, for which he required the hut I was occupying, but was too ashamed to order me directly to leave. Now he's suggesting that I build a hut for myself on his property using his own timber, but this will not save me from his nagging if I refuse to be a bit of a personal lackey and day-labourer for him. In offering me a permanent day-labourer to work with me, he said that I should work and manage the estate while his worker would work in parallel, alongside me. From this I have the impression that Ivan Vasil'evich would like me to act as his foreman and exert pressure on 'his people.'

41 *Swan, Pike and Crawfish* [*Lebed', Shchuka i Rak*] — a fable written in 1814 by Ivan Andreevich Krylov (1769–1844), in which a swan, a pike and a crawfish try unsuccessfully to collaborate on pulling a loaded cart; each creature ends up pulling in a different direction.

And so I ask you: What would you do if you were me, what choice would you make? The poor have only one option: to go begging in Christ's name. I, on the other hand, have a choice, and that is to my misfortune. There are three alternatives: 1) Build a hut out of Ivan Vasil'evich's timber on his land, for which I would be a bit of a personal lackey and day-labourer for him. 2) Go off to an allotment of land at my father's and, [remaining] under his authority even at age 30, carry out all peasant duties and services (including church duties), or 3) Purchase a plot of land with my brother Adrian and build a hut on it far away from the village. That, of course, would be the best, but at the same time the most difficult, given my financial circumstances and the length of time my troubles would last in connection with the purchase and construction on bare ground. So much for government regulations! You live on the land, but have not even a square arshin of land of your own from which you cannot be evicted at any time. And how many millions of families, especially the young ones, lead stagnant lives under even worse circumstances than that! There's lots of places and lands for serfs and serf-owners, but nothing for [real] people. Be whoever you wish, only not a human being, since the 'state' offers no places for human beings. This is the law of Petersburg & C°.

And if only my land were 5–6 *desjatinas*, I would die there; I wouldn't go anywhere and wouldn't torture myself by playing the lackey or trying to ingratiate myself with the owner of that land!

And could you possibly answer another question, over which Ivan Vasil'evich has raised a proper scandal, cursing me in public in a 'lordly' manner, after which my staying 'in his domain' became a great burden to me, and confusing to people whom I happen to come across. Besides, this question has touched a sore spot with me personally, and even though I am coping with it, it is only to my benefit, and I am terribly interested in your opinion as a third party.

It's like this: as I said, this summer I've been working alone, without Ivan Vasil'evich, not interfering with him and his day-labourers on his willow plantation, and not asking his help — even in tasks that are impossible for me to carry out alone.

After the spring sowing every year, during the whole month of May, I work in the gardens, meaning that I always have my vegetables with some left over to sell. The same happened this year: I had extra cucumbers and potatoes. Peasant farmers and women come to me (at different times) and say: "Sell us cucumbers and potatoes (some want one, some the other), only we have no money and to earn it, we must hire ourselves out to the manor house to cut and bind wheat sheaves for them (i.e., they would have to go out and work as day-labourers), and since it is better and more convenient to earn this money from you, we shall be very happy if you'll give us cucumbers and potatoes not for money, but in return for our labour." I agreed, not because it was very profitable for me (it is more profitable to sell for money), but simply because

I didn't want to refuse them, especially since these were more or less poor people, who didn't have any oats sown, and only two or three plots of rye, so that when they ran out of rye, they would usually go the "manor fields" to gather the manor-house crops, where [the owners] would work them terribly hard. And I also thought that since I was the lone [worker] in my family, it would take me too long to do my field harvesting, as my wife,[42] what with the cooking, cleaning, milking, children, calves, etc., had almost no time free to help me in my field work. Well, then, I reasoned with myself, I put so much effort into these vegetables during the month of May, coaxing them out of the ground, and they will repay me this effort during July and August in the form of oats and rye. The way I see it, it is simply an exchange that people can't afford to live without, especially since I am not the keeper of 'dead souls,'[43] but just a poor, overworked [peasant] like them. But Ivan Vasil'evich had a completely different viewpoint on the matter, when the time arrived and these people came to me to repay my effort. Seeing that other people were working on the *desjatina* I myself had sown, Ivan Vasil'evich was furious with me and shamed me in all sorts of ways right in front of these people. He told me I was a liar and just pretending when I said that manor houses were an abnormal phenomenon and undesirable for people's lives in general and that everyone should work for himself. [He said] that I was setting up the same kind of manor house on a smaller scale, making outside people work for me in the field, that it was the height of impudence and idiocy on my part, and so forth. He said that I was gathering his portion of the harvest, through my hired workers, for the sake of profit, that this was the principal method of enriching one's self at the expense of others, that this was the same kind of day-labour that I decried in others, and so forth. In conclusion, he said that it would better for our business arrangement if this day-labour be registered on his side of the record of working days.

And so I ask you: was there sin on my part in the given case as concerning these people? Somehow I cannot find any sin here, but I am afraid to trust myself. Indeed, where do you draw the line between an exchange [of services] and exploitation? I have my own opinions on this subject, of course, but I don't trust them — I want to hear the judgement of a third party.

Oh, how I desire to see you again, at least once, to talk with you about the state of man's transition from one life to the next, which you promised to tell people about on the basis of your personal observations during your former disease! May your 'postponement' of death last for a good long time! Please, Lev Nikolaevich, do answer this letter of mine. If, to my great misfortune, it doesn't turn out that you and I meet again, at least I shall have your reply as a

42 *Makrina Ivanovna Novikova* (from a peasant family in Zvenigorod Uezd) married Mikhail Petrovich Novikov in 1891.

43 A reference to Nikolaj Gogol's classic novel, *Dead Souls* [*Mërtvye dushi*].

precious memory of you for my whole life. I no longer apologize for the silly content of my letter, for who [among us] is not silly?!

M. Novikov

I read Bodjanskij's[44] catechesis, which thoroughly disturbed me and jolted my life off its customary rails.

This catechesis is rather incomprehensible, weak and written in an indecorous style, but, still, it contains some practicable rules for living Christian teachings in life. It makes plain what the life of a Christian, or *human beings* in general, should look like. After reading it, anyone will see their own swinishness and the insignificance of their ideals in comparison with the beauty of the Christian ideal.

I know I did. I saw my own swinishness, and, most importantly, I saw the fetters of life which chain my hands and feet to this swinishness. Human beings thirst for the freedom of spirit and body, they behold the dawn of a new day and are not able to head towards this day of freedom while chained to the habits of the past. How hard [life] must be for human beings such as these.

The lordly intellectuals whose reviews of this catechesis I happened to overhear treat it with unconcealed scorn, and I think this is because they behold in it, as in a mirror, their own lordly swinishness.

I read your reply to the Synod's ruling[45] concerning you and felt at peace for you. Now you can die in peace, since your life's work has come to a perfect summation with this reply. After your death your ill-wishers can no longer (as a result of your reply) obscure the [true] sense of your better philosophical thought.

I desire and pray to God that your life may be extended for a good long time. I await your response.

With heartfelt love, Mikh. Novikov

I wanted to come and see you at Yasnaya, but I heard a rumour that on the advice of your doctors you have left for somewhere in the south[46] (for some

44 *Aleksandr Mikhajlovich Bodjanskij* (1842–1916) — a landowner in both Ekaterinoslav and Khar'kov Gubernias, who renounced his ownership of land in favour of the peasants; he published a newspaper called *Narodnoe slovo* [People's Word]. Tolstoy became acquainted with him in 1892. That same year, Bodjanskij was arrested for his association with sectarians and exiled to the Transcaucasus. Seven years later, he emigrated to Canada, where he lived among the Doukhobors, returning to Russia in 1905.

45 The "Ruling of the Most Holy Synod of 20–22 February 1901, N° 557 with a missive to the faithful sons of the Orthodox Greco-Russian Church concerning Count Lev Tolstoy," published on 24 February 1901 in *Tserkovnye vedomosti*, attested Tolstoy's estrangement from Orthodoxy and called upon him to repent and return to the church fold. In his *Reply to the Synod*, Tolstoy rejected reconciliation with the Orthodox Church.

46 Tolstoy had gone to the Crimea at the insistence of his doctors. From 8 September 1901 to 25 June 1902, he lived with his wife on the estate of Countess Sof'ja Vladimirovna Panina (1871–1957), at Gaspra. See Sofia Andreevna Tolstaya's autobiography *My Life*, (2010: VIII.18).

reason I don't want to believe this rumour — it just doesn't seem right), and here I am writing to you at Yasnaya, in the hope that someone there will no doubt forward my letter to you.

M. N.

5. M. P. NOVIKOV ❧ L. N. TOLSTOY
16 May 1902.

16 May 1902.

Dear Lev Nikolaevich!

I just learnt from the papers that you've taken another turn for the worse (by way of bodily health). I feel sorrow and fright at the prospect of not seeing you again in this life, and that I, like many [others], will miss your spiritual support, which is vitally necessary to people of our time, especially since the struggle between the ruling classes and the people they oppress is being exacerbated everywhere of late. After you [go], who can we look to as an anchor of deliverance, from whom can we hear the word of truth? All the best people in human society either slavishly obey their taskmasters or have been seduced by greed or fear! Violence and falsehood have never appeared in such a scurrilous form as they do today! I should think that if there were at least a third-rate 'tin god' in the world who was not omnipotent — as the priests teach us — but could at least move three arshins of ground, he would probably decide to do this under the feet of those governors who recently had the poor people in southern Russia beaten with birch-rods. But heaven's thunders do not scare those who have built their domains on a deceived conscience… And how hard it is to continue living in these domains for anybody in their general populations who is not and does not want to be a characterless and weak-willed ass!...

Here's what's been going on around here: On 6 December 1901 my third child (a little girl[47]) was born, but I did not take her to be christened, and this was too much for the patience of the priesthood, especially since I had left Tsinger's to live in my own village, whereby I am now committing an offence in the circle of the 'dark *muzhik*.' The Tula 'spiritual' consistory asked for help from the sword-wielding 'Cæsar,' and on the 7th of April of this year I was summoned to the chambers of the head of the local administration Dokudovskij[48] in regard to my defection from Orthodoxy. In the early stages of my incipient freethinking, the priests argued the necessity of the ritual of christening and threatened me with hellish torture and the perishing of my soul if I didn't follow Orthodox rituals; the administration head, on the other hand, — a

47 *Anna Mikhajlovna Novikova* (1901–1992), who later became a professor of folklore.

48 *Nikolaj Petrovich Dokudovskij* (d.1922) — head of the Tula district administration. (The root of the surname, *dokuda*, literally means 'how far?')

realist — threatened me with prison and the prospect of persecution by the authorities. "Russia," he told me, "is alive only by virtue of Orthodoxy, and so you should not take away the number of Orthodox believers in the case of your children. We do not have freedom of conscience, and so we must be obedient to the strongest.... If you obey and christen your children, when it comes to everything else, I shall start helping you and what a peaceful life you will have! Otherwise, if not today, then tomorrow and every day [thereafter] you can expect trouble on every side!... And how happy I shall be if I can convince you rather than the priests!... And I shall report everywhere I should that all is well, that Novikov is christening his children and so everything will be fine.... But if you are contrary, then the Consistory will inform the Procurator, and he will charge you under Article 190 of the Constitution concerning punishments and your case will end in a lengthy prison term, etc., etc." I was given a period of 2–3 weeks to "think it over," and on 5 May I gave the administrative head a negative answer — let them do as they please. (I regret that I don't have the time to make you a copy of my reply to the administrative head.)

This is how I finished my letter: "If (I said) it is not shameful in our day and age to take a person away from four little children and put him in prison just because he does not observe an empty, utterly useless formality, let them do with me as they please. It can never be my will to subject my children to any kind of ritual, in which I see no sense or benefit. If someone finds this painful and difficult, they can do with me and my children as they please, with the help of the police; I shall not offer any resistance."

I have received no reply to this letter and I have no idea what will happen. Of course it is hard for a poor family man to fight against a horde of people and the cunningness of lying Herodians. It makes it even more difficult not to have anyone to talk with directly. I wrote to Ivan Ivanovich Gorbunov[49] and other acquaintances in Moscow, but haven't received a reply from anyone. Anyway, Ivan Vasil'evich Tsinger spoke about this with the former procurator in Tula (a certain Ivan Dmitrievich) and he said that from the point of view of the court there could be no [question of] persecution, and that I could not be charged under Article 190, but that I should be more concerned about administrative arbitrariness on the part of the governor, since Shlippe[50] will do anything to please the priestly crowd, and, moreover, is no stranger to alcohol. And how do I protect myself? Everything I don't do that others do seems to the authorities to be a premeditated protest. Last 'Easter,' for example, the priest carried holy 'icons' through the village, collecting money. I waved them off with my hand so that they would pass me by, [but] how embarrassed they were at passing me by, and at the same time the eyes of the whole village were fixed upon our

49 *Ivan Ivanovich Gorbunov-Posadov* (1864–1940) — Russian and Soviet writer, one of the principals at Tolstoy's Posrednik publishing house. (Cf. Note 33 above.)

50 *Vladimir Karlovich Shlippe* (1834–1923) — governor of Tula Gubernia 1893–1905.

house. Or [another example:] in the middle of May the whole village was 'praying to God' in the meadow, while I was digging up seedbeds and so forth, and my actions were tempting others [to ignore the church], as well as, of course, annoying the authorities. If I had my own piece of land, I would move far away from people's eyes, from the village! But here, if you please, there are various 'Egor'ev Days'[51] when you can't go to the fields; you watch over a priest's calves, if you please, though he would never watch over yours; you work [as a serf] on your master's fields, you provide [the authorities] with wagons and whatever else they require. After all, people around me are happy with my resistance when they speak with me one-on-one, but they themselves are overcome with superstitious fear and dare not actively assist me; even my friends and kindred spirits, will, out of fear, outwardly mouth all sorts of stupidities, so strongly have we been taken in by the authority of Cæsar and the existing order.

I left Tsinger because there was no point in my staying on with him, since he wasn't about to work the land; besides, back home my mother had died, my brother Ivan had detached himself,[52] and my father was left all alone. Observing my mother's funeral with the priests' rituals from the sidelines, I again saw the whole meaninglessness of this spectacle invented by the priesthood to smooth over the burden on the living at the sight of the dead. These rituals only humiliate and dishonour the mystery of death and seriously interfere with one's contemplation of the mystery of being. Farewell, dear Lev Nikolaevich, possibly for ever. Thank you for your truthfulness. Perhaps we shall see each other in another life. My God, how terrible for us is the mystery of life and death! I don't expect a reply. You are weak, although I would love to hear again and again at least another word from you. Farewell. Oh, if only God would grant you to see Yasnaya Polyana and your friends once again! It's springtime — a beautiful time of the year here.

Mikhail Petrovich Novikov

Laptevo Station (Moscow–Kursk Railway), Village of Borovkovo.
24 May 1902.

6. L. N. TOLSTOY ❦ M. P. NOVIKOV
15 July 1902.

Dear Mikhail Petrovich. I was very happy, as always, to receive your good letter,[53] but I haven't answered because I've been ill and weak. I'm writing now just to say I received your letter, I'm delighted with you and I love you. I know

51 *Egor'ev Days* — in medieval times, days when peasants could negotiate for work with various landlords.

52 The term 'detached himself' [*otdelilsja*] meant that he had become an independent homesteader.

53 The reference is probably to Novikov's letter of 16 May 1902 (Letter № 5).

that it is difficult;[54] however, the only path is narrow and difficult, but in the long run it is joyous for the soul.

I greet you as a brother.

Lovingly & sincerely,
L. Tolstoy

15 July 1902

7. L. N. TOLSTOY ❦ M. P. NOVIKOV
17 November 1902.

Your situation,[55] dear Mikhail Petrovich, is of great concern to me. I am doing what I can to alleviate it. When I have any concrete information, I shall pass it along to your family.

54 Tolstoy's remark relates to Novikov's complaints about the hostile attitude toward him on the part of the local authorities and villagers for his departure from the Russian Orthodox faith and scorn for religious rituals. See Novikov's letter to Tolstoy of 16 May 1902 (Letter Nº 5).

55 Tolstoy was referring to Novikov's recent arrest. On orders from Finance Minister Sergej Jul'evich Witte (1849–1915), a special meeting took place in the Tula district on the needs of the agricultural sector. At the meeting Novikov tabled a memo regarding the peasants' lack of land, government corruption, the poor status of local schools and the humiliation of the peasantry, which provoked considerable animosity against him. In a letter to V. V. Stasov of 26 October 1902 (*PSS* 73:312–13), Tolstoy wrote:

"Novikov is a peasant of remarkable intelligence, education and zeal, who has been a close acquaintance of mine for a long time now. He submitted a memo to the Tula committee, which probably had an effect on the Tula conservatives much the same as [Aleksandr Nikolaevich] Radishchev's *Journey* [*from St. Petersburg to Moscow* (1790)] had on [Empress] Ekaterina [Catherine the Great], and so they want to do to him what they did to Radishchev. You cannot help but know where he is, what they are doing and intend to do with him, and couldn't you assist him?

"I am writing about this to Koni. Perhaps you have other channels?"

In his letter to the jurist Anatolij Fëdorovich Koni of the same date, Tolstoy also put in a word for Novikov:

"...It is shameful to live in a nation where such acts can be committed. Could you possibly find out where Novikov is? What have they done, or are doing, with him? And couldn't you offer all possible assistance to this worthy and remarkable person?" (*PSS* 73:311–12).

The next day Tolstoy wrote directly to Witte (*PSS* 73:314):

"Kind sir, Sergej Jul'evich,

"The peasant Mikhail Petrovich Novikov of Tula district has submitted a memo to the agricultural committee about the needs of the peasantry.

"Mikhail Petrovich is an educated man, very intelligent, upright and highly moral. Right after submitting his memo, Novikov was summoned and sent at the behest of the Minister of Internal Affairs to Petersburg, where he probably is now. It is frightening to think that agricultural committees aimed at improving the lot of the peasantry are being used as new instruments of extracting all the best people from the peasant milieu.

"Confident that the use of committees as a trap for the summoning and suppression of the best forces of the peasantry does not meet with your agreement, I am drawing your attention to this circumstance in the hope that you will find it possible to counteract such authoritative actions, and I urge you to help Mikhail Petrovich Novikov, a man who lives by his own labour, a family man, who is frail in health and deserving of respect in the highest degree.

I am writing just a few words, as I am not quite sure that this letter will reach you. If you are able, do write to me about your mental state and about anything I can do to be of use to you and your family.

Lev Tolstoy

17 November 1902

8. M. P. NOVIKOV ❧ L. N. TOLSTOY
2 April 1904.

2 April 1904.

Dear Lev Nikolaevich! Several times now I've had the intention of coming to see you, but, to my great sorrow, have not managed to do so to date. Tied to the family and household, with my daily duties and work, the only time I can find any free time is late at night. It is now spring, and [this past] winter I had to take on bookbinding to earn 10 to 20 kopeks a day to meet current expenses. This constant physical labour (both winter and summer) has been weighing heavily on me ever since my spiritual life has grown out of a limited *muzhik* worldview and taken the path of a universal world life. How much I have now of an unsatisfied thirst for knowledge — [including] the needs of the soul, unexpressed thoughts and contemplation!

I am forced to agree with the opinion of one professor who showed me that until it becomes possible to regulate and equalise the financial status of all people, until then it would be criminal to take the poorer classes out of the shell of their spiritual poverty and squalor, since, in his opinion, it is quite impossible to satisfy people's spiritual needs until their stomachs are full. They say, too, that the life of the soul can be examined independently of external circumstances and the life of the body, and that it is possible to maintain a spiritual balance in all the ups and downs of material-physical life — [but] this is not true: one only has to live the life of a *muzhik* in all its unsightliness to doubt this proposition. Maybe it actually is true, but only in reference to people who in their advanced years have already rejected worldly life and are anxiously awaiting their transition to another existence. To everyone else the enormous ballast of the Earth prevents them from soaring to heavenly heights. Why has this consciousness of life awakened in me — only then to live and suffer, both for my own animal swinishness and for the destitution and spiritual poverty of those around me? It is surprising, but at present [I can say that] no phenomenon of life passes by my spiritual gaze unnoticed: I comprehend

"With complete respect I remain at your service,

Lev Tolstoy"

Witte did not answer this letter.

everything, I feel everything, but this only makes things more difficult; the discrepancy between the spiritual and the animal, which I hadn't noticed earlier, is now something I feel every step of the way. The satisfying of the animal side of life is strongly rebuked and condemned by the consciousness of the spirit; in the meantime one's whole lifetime is wasted on serving these same animalistic needs, since [my] awakened consciousness has caught my animalistic activities completely off-guard, right at the stage when I already have a large family with its difficult and burdensome task of procuring my daily bread and my desire to maintain myself at a certain level of material comforts. Just like the comrades who could not work together in Krylov's fable (the Swan, the Pike and the Crawfish), we are swirling around in some sort of two-faced, androgynous vicious circle. It is now clear to me, from my own experience, why people move so slowly along the path of spiritual and moral self-perfection, and why the man of the Adam story[56] is practically an exact copy of me and, I should think, of almost every human being living today. It has become even clearer and more understandable why people from time immemorial have needed to manacle their own still dreaming consciousness with all sorts of systems and so-called religious doctrines. The bifurcation of the human being into two elements constantly warring with each other, [along with] the suffering and wounds caused by this warfare, as well as the impossibility of satisfying these diverse elements in their respective strivings each for their own happiness, have forced man for ages now to seek salvation in so-called *faith*, that is, in the construction of a certain system which, even though it wouldn't cure wounds, at least would afford weaker beings the possibility of comforting themselves with certain fairy-tales and hopes for a more tolerable existence in another, unknown world, or would explain the interrelation and connection of our duality of body and spirit. From this — and only from this — arose the familiar cultures of so-called religious doctrines, either with a preference for the flesh or with the adoration of the spirit. I have read many, many arguments in defence and justification of these religious doctrines, penned by the brightest luminaries of so-called spiritual literature, and, most importantly, I have not found any degree of sincerity; indeed, all this literature reeks of hypocrisy, sentimentality and deliberate manipulation, while that modern cleric and ecclesiastical authority Ioann Kronshtadtskij[57] smacks, in the first place, of stupidity (also premeditated), secondly of evil, poorly hiding behind a zeal for God. I feel that the desire to judge the church with all its deeds has now left [me] forever. All this ecclesiastical literature has led to frightful exhaustion in me, as well as apathy to the religious question, and imbued me with the kind of repulsion that anyone might feel in regard to

56 See Gen. 2.

57 *Ioann Kronshtadtskij* (secular name: Ioann Il'ich Sergiev; 1828–1908) — prior of the Andreev Cathedral at Kronshtadt, an opponent of Tolstoy's anti-clerical influence. Tremendously popular in his lifetime, he was accorded sainthood by the Russian Orthodox Church in 1971.

a heavy but meaningless burden. I should just go on living my life, and everything else should go on living its own, without any direct connection [to me]. I don't [completely] reject the idea of church, but as for me, I understand the church as a teaching institute, bringing Christian morality into people's everyday lives, as a model for the ease of fulfilling Christian demands in life. By contrast, the church which leads to this goal through dogmas and various superstitious absurdities is incomprehensible and foreign to me, and I think that the chief evil in modern religious teachings lies precisely in its unwillingness to separate the gold from the dross, the pure from the soiled — its unwillingness to understand that the dogmatism, mysticism and superstition [prevalent] in all churches has brought to people nothing but sorrow, crime and constant conflict. Indeed, it could not bring [anything else], since ecclesiastical teachings rest on feet of clay, threatening at any moment to collapse and come crashing down. This is because the Christian Church began its history with the same policies and organization which it inherited from the old, so-called heathen ecclesiastical structure (striving outwardly for splendour and piety, but inwardly for the same old superstition, miracles and confirmation of dogma); it poured new wine into old bottles[58] — and because of these bottles, the wine itself has reeked of old mildew and acidity. At the same time, Christian teachings, as a new discipline of life, needs to have a new foundation, a new form of inward and outward order. What it is doing amounts to covering the real and actual emptiness of life with a prism of illusory promises and hopes for the future, but it cannot wage a decisive war against the sinful filth inherent in man's nature, and it will scarcely include this warfare in its mission. To part forever from this institution, which has been for so long supplying [people,] including me, with dead water instead of living [water], I feel the need to speak my mind, but apart from you, Lev Nikolaevich, I cannot find anyone else whom I can trust with my fears and torments — these arising from my so-called lack of faith in my peasant milieu under our despotic regime and the views on this subject of the prevalent social order, which does not recognize anyone who is faithless — that is, anyone who is not stupid. Such fears shake my long-ago taken decision to live without any connection to the so-called Church. Of course these shakings are not because I doubt my convictions. On the contrary, the area of church politics has become so clear and comprehensible to me, but I can see more and more from my experience how hard it is to live in our environment without observing the religious formalities attached to acts of birth, marriage and death; however, without such observance, the surrounding milieu of 'true Christians' treats you like a monster from another planet. The fact that I myself have to bear all sorts of filth and disdain — this of course does not disturb me very much (such nonsensical stupidity even makes life more comical), but concerning the fate of my

58 See Matth. 9:17.

unchristened children (3 and 5 years old), there's no way I can rest in peace; other children even now refuse to play with them, or it turns out that they accept them to start with, and then chase them off because they are "unchrissened," and even my older children (7 and 9 years) — the ones who are "chrissened" — constantly try to stay away from the younger ones, since as long as they are around [their younger siblings], they, too, are not accepted. Of course, right now they are still naïve and don't feel the insults much, but what will become of them in the future? What will become of them when they are around 10 or 15, when they will understand nothing in the way of faith, but will still at that age be strongly attracted to girlfriends — to people? If they were boys, I would be quite at peace; I've become convinced through my own experience that a man who desires to live an honest life and work industriously loses nothing of life and suffers little from his surroundings, [even] if accused of the most extreme heresy or atheism. But for a woman it is hard, very hard, since her life completely depends on the will of a man as head of the household and husband to his wife (I'm talking about *our* social class). Tell me, Lev Nikolaevich, what am I to do? I am not appealing to your wisdom or scholarliness, but simply to [you as] a simple human being, as one who has no reason not to be absolutely sincere with me; most importantly, I ask you not to instruct me as to what I should do in my given situation, since I cannot guarantee in advance that I shall agree with you. And you, I believe, are not pleased by any [mere] copying of your words or deeds. *I simply want to know what you would do in my place.* As I see it, in my situation there are two more or less satisfactory outcomes: either 1) I shall continue to torment myself over the insults to my children right to their age of maturity, and then allow them complete freedom in their actions, or 2) join them formally now to the ranks of so-called "Orthodox Christians" and also formally drag out my relationship with the institutional church until they reach maturity. I am more inclined to the first course of action and I would like to know which one you would choose, and, in general, how you look at this question. It is impossible to ignore it, since it was an easy matter in my heart to change my views on a matter of faith and find an explanation for everything, but it is not so simple to disengage myself from the formal side of this faith, given our [current] social customs.

Now I shall tell you something about myself. My life is marked with some sort of conflict — though I don't understand with what. As I try to draw closer to the Christian understanding of life in practice and to soften and ennoble myself and my actions in respect to my environment, I fall more and more under the exploitation of this environment, [which makes inordinate demands] on my labour and my time, as well as on my increasing knowledge. Of course, if this exploitation arose from some pressing need [of mine], then everything would be in its proper place, but I have no pressing needs, but there is deceit and insolence, and again, I have no idea how best to escape from this tangle of mutual contradictions. At every step I have to confront situations such as: someone asks for a loan of 3 roubles for three days and still doesn't pay me back even after three years; another uses a loan to buy vodka and starts trading in vodka on the sly; a third asks for a loan of 5 roubles for a week and drinks my hard-earned 5 roubles away, carousing at a funeral feast; a fourth asks me to lend him a sack of rye for a year, pleading that he has nothing to eat, and later it turns out that he has three piglets and he actually squanders his food on them; a fifth tearfully asks for a loan of oats — it is springtime, and he has nothing to sow, but [it turns out that] last autumn he sold his own stock of oats and drank [the proceeds] away at his son's or daughter's wedding; a sixth asks me to write a petition to an appropriate office to overturn a court sentence of some sort of punishment, when he was actually guilty; a seventh also asks me to write to claim a calf or a sheep from his brother which he should have received through the division of inheritance — and so forth. And all of this [for me] is the most vivid reality. Since I am sober, more knowledgeable in legal and juridical matters and more productive in my work, I feel I don't have the right to not share with others or to not help those in need — for this reason many people come to me 'to request,' and so all the time I find I have to drag my feet and cope with the needs of people around me, and again, in addition to such needs — the needs of the beggars who cross my threshold a dozen times a day — not [necessarily] the little, the old, the destitute or the disabled, but simply *muzhiks* like me, only with the difference that I make 10–15 kopeks a day from bookbinding, while these 'poor' make 80–90 kopeks as beggars, or use charity to feed two or three piglets over the winter, whose meat is equal in quality to the priests' own piglets. I don't know, Lev Nikolaevich, how you look at all these things, but, you know, I shall tell you plainly that I have no strength to refuse in these situations, even though I have no love for these people; on the contrary, I offer these people spare change and loans, and write letters and petitions for them with a feeling of annoyance and malice, as I feel that all these people only want to get as much material benefit from me as they can. I work twice as hard as they and in the same difficult circumstances as any *muzhik*, and I have [four] children. And in making such loans to people who ask for them, I cannot help thinking that at the expense of my 15 kopeks I am helping others more easily make a whole rouble. There's something wrong here. Perhaps it is me, or the public — of which there is no let-up — or Christianity, which gives rise to so much idle thinking. I can't even explain to myself what position in society Christians should adopt. It is usually said that a Christian should be on the side of the poor, but if that is true, Christianity for absolutely everyone is unthinkable. Besides, the position of the poor deserves compassion only when this poverty is caused by destitution, [extreme] youth or age. I shall be very happy if you will say something about this; I seem to be lost in a vicious circle in such matters and am unable to find a satisfactory way out. Again I ask: *What would you do in my place?* And here are some new gems of my relationship to the public around me (to write about money and benefits).[59] Last winter, for example, a number of young and not-so-young people attempted to strike up a close acquaintanceship with me. It would usually begin with a request to read a booklet or to tell how to act in some kind of delicate situation. The closer the connection grew, the more often I would hear complaints about poverty and hints at the possibility of [my helping them] clamber out of it. The usual moral rules on industriousness, sobriety and thriftiness, which lie at the basis of my comparative well-being — these they would not accept; evidently they did not believe that I am able to live so nattily under the same circumstances as other *muzhiks*. And since people have long believed in the fairy-tale (from Pan Twardowski[60]), [namely] that we might have sold our soul to the Devil in exchange for 25 roubles a month, these visitors were hoping to gain more benefit from me. But when it turned out that I couldn't simply produce a rouble from my pocket at any moment, they cooled towards me and I lost my former value in their eyes. All that we understand and hold dear under the term *the life of the spirit, or soul,* our people are completely uninterested in, and they will never agree to abandon their former way of life and their faith, which takes so little from them, obligates them to nothing, but promises them so much. Interesting: one elderly *muzhik* was friends with me for quite a long time, and then one time, while drunk, he blurted out: "I am not yet all yours, but if what they say about the 25 roubles a month is true, then tomorrow I will be all yours." And then someone came to me from [a village] 20 versts away and started asking me in confidence where he could come to you and what would be the best time to come and what to say so that you would accept him into your faith and give him money.

9. M. P. NOVIKOV ❧ L. N. TOLSTOY
24 April 1904.[61]

24 April 1904

Dear Lev Nikolaevich, well, today I received a conscription notice calling me to military service; tomorrow I'm supposed to report to the recruitment centre, plain and simple, and after that to go to the Far East under Japanese bullets.[62] I shan't even mention my sorrow and that of my family — you can't

59 These words in parentheses were intended as a self-reminder.

60 *Pan Twardowski* — a well-known Polish folk legend about a sorcerer who 'sold his soul' to the Devil in exchange for riches and special powers.

61 This and a following letter of Novikov's (N° 27) were included by Tolstoy in his 1904 article *Odumajtes'!* [*Bethink Yourselves!*], expressing his condemnation of the Russo-Japanese war.

62 The Russo-Japanese war (1904–1905) was underway at the time over conflicting land claims in Korea and Manchuria (including year-round Russian access to the Pacific Ocean).

help but understand the whole horror of my situation and the horrors of war! For a long time now you've had to endure your fill of [news on] this [subject], and you understand it well. But how I would like to be with you and chat with you! I drafted you a long letter outlining the torments of my soul, but didn't manage to copy it out and [then] I received the conscription notice. What is my wife to do, [especially] with four children, two of whom are so-called unchristened? Will she be able to withstand the clerical clique on her own? I don't expect you, as an old man, to be interested in my family's fate, but you might ask some of your friends to take an excursion and visit my orphaned family, especially since it is less than an hour's walk from Laptevo Station to our Borovkovo. After all, people who live near us are very happy that I am being taken away to war, [evidently] in the hope that I shall not return, but at the same time they shed hypocritical tears and sighs — how shallow and dishonest is that!

I ask you with all my heart that if my wife is not able to bear the tortures of her 'orphanhood' with a brood of kids and decides to go to you for help and advice, that you accept and comfort her. She doesn't know you personally, but she believes in your words, and this means a lot, especially since we have lost our faith in people, so much so that, apart from you, we don't know of anyone who could sincerely relate to other people; everyone has love and well-wishes in their words, but pre-set goals and a personal agenda in their deeds.

I could not counteract the conscription order, but I can say in advance that not one Japanese family will be widowed because of me. Lord, how horrible this all is, how hard and painful to abandon everything you live by and are interested in. How shallow and paltry now seem all the notions and fairy tales about gods and devils, miracles and saints, in the face of the fearful and disastrous horrors of war! They teach that for the sake of some old man God produced a miracle and gave him an undecaying and miracle-producing corpse — where is this God now and why is He so slow at doing new miracles, at putting a stop to this fratricidal bloodshed? Can it be that thousands of innocent victims and orphans are not worth even one miracle? Is it not worth it for God to lift a finger on their behalf? Apparently, He Himself is afraid of modern weaponry and the latest miraculous military technology.

Farewell, Lev Nikolaevich, possibly for ever, eternally. If a Japanese [soldier] doesn't kill [me] — I shall try to visit you. If [he] kills [me], I shall go complain to God about His injustice and cruelty.

Mikhail Petrov[ich] Novikov

My family's address: Laptevo Station, Moscow-Kursk Railway
Village of Borovkovo, Makrina Ivanovna Novikova

10. L. N. TOLSTOY ❧ M. P. NOVIKOV

26 April 1904.

My heartfelt brother Mikhail Petrovich.

I received your letter and cannot to this day read it or think of you without tears [in my eyes].

We shall do everything we can for your family and shall pay a visit to them in a few days. Everything needful will be done on the financial plane and we shall try our best on the spiritual.

Brotherly hugs and kisses. May you receive aid from the God that is expanding Himself more and more within us and blazing in your soul.

Lev Tolstoy
26 April 1904.

11. M. P. NOVIKOV ❧ L. N. TOLSTOY

27 April 1904.

27 April 1904.

My precious Lev Nikolaevich!

Here only a day has passed in my 'active' service, and I've already suffered an eternity of the most despairing torture. From 8 in the morning until 9 in the evening they marched and paraded us around the barracks yard like a herd of animals; the farce of bodily inspection was repeated three times, and anyone who claimed illness was given 10 seconds of attention and declared "fit." When they chased us, some 2,000 hungry people, from the military commander into the barracks, a crowd practically a whole verst long lined the street — a crowd of about 4,000 relatives, mothers, wives with children in their arms, and if you could only hear and see how they clung to their fathers, husbands and sons, pulling on their necks, weeping in desperation! I generally manage to keep my composure and control my emotions, but I wasn't able to hold out and wept tears as well: how cruel that ecclesiastical God must be, Who for the sake of some kindly old man does lots and lots of miracles, but doesn't want to even lift a finger to bring peace and comfort to the hopeless suffering of many millions of people, while God the Son was moved to tears at the sight of people weeping over a single deceased person.[63] And just what is going on here? Where is the measure whereby to take account of all this gratuitous sorrow which is now spread across practically one-third of the globe? As for us, we are [nothing but] cannon fodder, which in the near future people will not hesitate to sacrifice to the God of revenge and terror. Oh, how unbearable it must be for me in this atmosphere, in the paws of

63 Probably a reference to the death of Lazarus (see John 11:35).

a materialistic organization — on the very lowest and most repulsive level, while I myself, i.e., my spiritual life, is wound up almost at the very summit of human thought. A miserable, two-faced, androgynous person cannot abdicate from his spiritual selfhood, giving peace and freedom to the animal [within him]; neither can he do the reverse for the sake of rest and the eternal triumph of the spirit within him!

There are two thousand people around me, but they have less in the way of suffering, as they have an 'animal' peace, an 'animal joy,' nothing sinful or worthy of condemnation in terms of their worldview, while I, on the other hand, am unable by any means to establish my own equilibrium. Oh, how I hate myself for this dualism which prevents me from serving the one Lord and God. I'm surrounded by a crowd of people, but in this crowd I feel like some kind of Cain, to whom the everyday noise of this crowd is so foreign and distant that I cannot forget the melancholy of profound loneliness, which is customary for someone stranded on a desert island. Man is so accustomed to work, plant, sow, raise plants and animals, to be in a circle of family and acquaintances, to live among people, for people — and I have none of that now; there is only such repulsive vermin that frighten me with their odious appearance; there is a huge mountain which the horror of death winds around and through which I still must crawl, being weak and cowardly, for fear of my family being left orphaned. How I envy the Froshel' types,[64] who, without any ties to earthly existence in the form of wife and children, quickly solve the 'Mystery of Life' and abandon forever this tormentress, Earth, stained with blood and tears.

The 10th Corps in the Kazan' and the 17th in the Moscow military districts are being mobilized; after a course in shooting and the appropriate military drills, in mid-May we shall be chased under Japanese bullets and cannon. We've been assigned to the 11th infantry regiment. I'm in the 4th company, 1st platoon.

Precious Lev Nikolaevich, do not forbid me to write to you in these moments which are so terrifying for me.

Mikhail Petrovich Novikov

12. L. N. TOLSTOY ❧ M. P. NOVIKOV
30 April 1904.

I received your second letter,[65] dear Mikhail Petrovich. I sympathize from the bottom of my heart with you and all those unfortunates who have been conscripted along with you to this difficult trial.

Will you be in Tula long? I'd like to come by and say hullo.

64 No further information is known regarding the name *Froshel'*.

65 See Letter N° 11.

There's a lot [I have to tell you that] I don't want to put in a letter. As I wrote you in [my] first letter, you can be sure that you and your family are [my] friends.

Write [to me].

Lovingly,
L. Tolstoy

I didn't like what you wrote about a God Who does miracles but does not stop cruelty among human beings. We needn't bother with the God the Orthodox [Christians] believe in; we have to believe genuinely in a genuine [God].

30 Apr. 1904.

13. M. P. NOVIKOV ❧ L. N. TOLSTOY
25 May 1904.

25 May 1904.

Dear Lev Nikolaevich,

A month has gone by now since I began my 'active service,' but there's no way I can accustom or reconcile myself with this deformed situation, repulsive to anyone who hasn't had the wool pulled over their eyes, and each day, each hour, I am unceasingly tormented by the same torment. What a terrible impression from this whole senseless situation called 'military service'! It is evident that this whole huge throng of young people were compelled against their will to reject [what] their head [was telling them], abandon their usual activities, and engage in silly tricks so unnatural to human beings. Even the so-called officers feel this, and hence, when they spout silly words and silly commands, it sounds very contrived and not at all confident. It feels as though all these intelligent people have given up their will and intelligence in favour of something non-existent, that they've gathered around some kind of emptiness that is [actually] repulsive to them, but they have no sincerity or unifying nucleus; they spout only fragmentary phrases, which demand acceptance as important mysteries of life, but are interpreted by everyone in their own way.

Oh, what coldness, what moral trials the stench of military service brings to man!...

I would give twenty years of my life to "let this cup pass from me"[66] — a cup which I don't have the strength to resist drinking from! The authorities and the papers preach to us, stupid people of the lowest order, about duty to the motherland, heroism and honour, about how some kind of artificial or imaginary Russia awaits our heroic deeds, while the movers and shakers of the highest echelon are motivated by only one thing: corruption, corruption

66 Matth. 26:39.

and corruption, in all levels and ranks. On the 18th of May I submitted a petition to my company commander, who took it to show privately to the appropriate persons. The commander fully agreed that nobody could condone killing people, that this was universally difficult and unnatural for anyone, but — what to do? — in heading into this situation we may weep along with the Tsar, [but] what should we do? — the Japanese attacked us first, not the other way around, etc., etc., but there's no way one can formally submit a petition like this under current circumstances; any thinking person will understand this, etc. This conversation made one thing clear to me: all these [upper] social classes are very far removed from the real causes of war.

As a result of this conversation, on 18 May I was sent back to Tula from artillery drills and transferred to a non-combatant company, where in the distribution of assignments I was attached to the division supply chain; I was given a pair of horses and a four-wheeled wagon, which meant I have now achieved one thing: the possibility of not killing people or running them through with a bayonet. In my judgement, we (that is, the division supply chain) will be intermediaries between the quartermaster's stores and the regimental supply chains, delivering provisions, fodder, bullets, etc. At the moment we are busy feeding our horses rye straw (oats are given out in [containers of] 1 or 2 *garnetzes*[67]), and they are now so well-fed that even if you don't take them to be watered for three whole days, they still won't drink. Poor creatures! People, at least, have the freedom to sell their will, but these [creatures] are completely innocent. So long for the time being, precious Lev Nikolaevich. When we move out, I'll write again. Farewell. My address for now is the non-combatant company of the 11th regiment.

Mikhail Novikov

When I finished writing this letter, I was suddenly informed that I am being sent to the commission on conscription for recertification, which will take place towards the end of May. I have a longstanding hernia, and that gave the regimental doctor an excuse to qualify me for recertification. My hope for a complete resurrection is, of course, weak, but there is still hope, which might turn out successfully with some help from the side. If this hope is fulfilled, then I shall describe in detail everything that I have gone through myself, as well as what have observed in others during this month of 'active service.'

M. N.

67 A *garnetz* is a Russian dry measure equal to 3.28 litres.

14. M. P. NOVIKOV ❧ L. N. TOLSTOY
9 June 1904. Borovkovo.

9 June 1904

Dear Lev Nikolaevich!

I tell you that something joyful for me has happened. I have stayed in Tula, while our regiment set out for Harbin on the 4th and 5th of June.

My personal circumstances turned out this way. On 21 May I was given an appointment for re-examination at the district conscription office, but by a clerical error I was listed as belonging to Company 4, whereas I had already been assigned non-combatant status. Consequently they didn't send me to the office on time, and so my re-examination didn't take place. But since I had already been determined by the regimental doctor as unfit, when the infirm were taken out of the regiment as "not being able to participate in military expeditions" (as the order states), I too was given 'infirm' status and we were assigned to the 11th Personnel Reserve Battalion.

There is nothing definite with us for the time being and nobody knows anything, whether we'll be staying here or where they will send us. The situation at the moment is this. The ones they notice are sent to work at cleaning up the camp, while the bolder ones don't show themselves for days at a time.

We are stationed behind the prison in the camp. On the 4th and 5th I was with my regiment and my comrades, and I can't express in words the eerie and oppressive feeling I got from this frightful picture of 'setting off to war.' Where have all the 'artisans of truth' disappeared to? Why aren't they painting those devastating pictures of people's suffering?

I have never in my life witnessed such unhappy people, bumped out of their normal way of life, as presented by these God-fearing soldiers. A month and a half of training drills, drunkenness and chaos in the barracks has done its work and these people have been transformed, as it were, into a different species which can only shout senseless *hurrahs* until they are hoarse, and sing military songs of courage or, being in the last stages of stupefaction, mumble and curse senselessly left and right.

And their wives, mothers and children — oh, how much they have suffered during this time! Like living corpses, like people sentenced to death, they watched the soldiers' daring, their drunken songs, drunken dances, drunken *hurrahs*. But when they brought in the transport trains, they all literally woke up, and one could hear the children weeping, the wives and mothers howling and wailing, which then gave way to a sobbing on the part of grown-up but helpless and tormented people, which was difficult for onlookers to hear. And this went on for a long time, sometimes dying down, but then rising once more as though from the bowels of the groaning and restless soul of someone deep in despair.

I have heard a lot of crying and weeping at funerals of close friends, but that was not at all the same. There [at the funerals] over all the crying and weeping could be felt a silent, meek resignation to fate, to God, and the crying and weeping itself seemed to have a monotone, almost harmonic character. It was not that way here [at the soldiers' departure]. Here, each one was troubled in the depths of his own soul, notwithstanding the training and trite words of comfort all were aware of, and each one was expressing the torment of his soul through intermittent weeping and groaning.

There [at the funerals] man's restless soul is mentally reaching out to God and wants to find comfort and justification for his sorrow in Him, while here it reaches out to man with the silent question: just what is all this about, just what is going on with us? Each one sees the closest person in his life, the strength and joy of his life, but already feels separated from him for ever, feels the ground slipping away beneath their feet and there is no longer any reason to live or breathe.

The first bell sounds, and everyone seems to be sighing and fidgeting. The soldiers start clambering into the railway carriages which hold forty each, carrying five or ten bags or bundles; the carriages are hot and stuffy, and there's no room for even an apple to fall to the floor. The carriages are surrounded by wives, mothers and children, they start exchanging good-bye kisses, and the crying and weeping drowns out all other noises. No matter how depraved or stupefied the soldiers have become, at this critical moment the human being in them awakens, and the feeling of humanity in them begins to speak. Almost every one of them has a wife holding children out to them who hang around their necks in tears.

It is evident that these 'soldiers' who have come 'out of the people' [*iz ljudjej*] have suddenly taken fright, it is only just now that they have become aware and taken stock of their situation. It is only now that the thought has dawned upon them that they themselves, their wives, children, mothers — indeed, their whole life — have been appraised and sold to someone, and are now heading, before their very eyes, into some wild abyss, being covered over by a fearful emptiness hitherto unknown. A frightening moment!

Here they are carrying right past me a woman who has fainted, and a few minutes later another one. Five minutes later a stretcher goes by carrying a dead or unconscious soldier. There's a lot of noise and talking. People begin explaining, through tears, that this soldier was a widower, that he had recently buried his wife and was left alone with young children, and now, after parting from these children, he had fallen down stiff right in the railway carriage. I still don't know whether he had really died, but I saw him stretched out, all blue with eyes upturned. And what had these five children done in God's sight to merit their whole life being turned upside down from this point on? What had the tens and hundreds of thousands of other children done, the tens and thousands of wives and mothers done to deserve their whole future existence becoming one endless experience of sorrow and torture?

Poor, miserable humanity! Why do you populate the earth, only to water it with your tears and make it resound with groaning and weeping?

The second bell sounds, and a minute later the third. The tension increases to its final stages. Even children three and four years old seem transformed and start speaking in grown-up language. There is one, crying and kissing his father, pleading with him to take him with him, assuring him that he is ready to die with his Papa; another turns his frightened gaze back and forth from father to mother and, as though addressing himself, keeps repeating: *where will we live without Papa, how will we live without Papa?* A third little girl, five or six years old, all in tears, cannot stop kissing a black-bearded soldier who has become so distracted that he stands like a statue and neither hears nor sees what is going on around him.

The whistle blows — long and penetrating — making everyone's heart tremble. The bearded soldier comes to himself again, fearfully holds out his little girl to her mother and cringes, as though he has suffered a blow to his backside, turns away and hides behind others. One can hear shouts of "Farewell, farewell, farewell!" and on top of all this sounds that stupid and senseless word, *Hurrah!* For such a difficult and despairing moment all human wisdom taken together could not have come up with a more stupid or senseless expression.

The train sets off, while the wives, children and mothers go on groaning and sobbing. There is literally no place for them to go and no reason to go. After all, their whole life has gone off with the departing train, and they have lost the ability to engage in any activity. I think it will be a long time before they find the strength to move again, since there ahead of them, where they are supposed to move, something new awaits them, something frightening and revolting, that will torture them their whole lives and take them away from the sunshine and joy of God's world.

Let us say, too, with a broken heart: Farewell, to those poor people who are still sorrowing in cries of *Hurrah!* for a verst[68] or two already, sounding this unnatural cry through the whole city. Farewell, brethren!

As you are dying in pain from wounds and disease, send a farewell greeting to the homeland which has banished you, forgive her and be comforted by the thought that "as a flower of the field, so [man] flourisheth"[69] and that all the human wisdom of all people who are living or have ever lived has discovered nothing except how to send you off to decay in a common pit in fields of a foreign land, under a foreign sky. Farewell, dear brethren![70]

68 *verst* = 1.07 km (see note on measurements following the Preface).

69 Ps. 103:15.

70 As mentioned, Tolstoy valued Novikov's assessment of the horrors of war and, in his own arguments against all manner of war, often resorted to commenting on Novikov's "Na vojnu!" [To war!]. According to Gusev (1960: 542), after rereading this article on 19 January 1906, Tolstoy observed: "How strong this is! I hope I shall be able to write — though I never promise in

Until we meet again very soon, dear Lev Nikolaevich, and thank you for M. A.'s visit to my family.[71]

M. Novikov

15. M. P. NOVIKOV ❧ L. N. TOLSTOY
20 June 1904.

20 June 1904

Dear Lev Nikolaevich, I have good news to tell you about myself: on 11 June we all (apart from the soldiers in 'active service') were sent by the military commander from the reserve battalion to the district military conscription [office] for recertification and for clarification of our suitability (since the physically infirm and those with bodily deficiencies ended up here). And, as rumour has it, for the purpose of testing the honesty of the regimental physician, to see whether he accepted money for leaving completely strong and healthy men in the reserve battalion. Indeed, of the 80 or 90 men sent for recertification, more than half were deemed unworthy and discharged: some outright, some for a year for recuperation, some for transfer to the Home Guard, others to the infirmary for [further] examination. On the presiding officer's first inspection, I, too, was deemed unfit, both because of my chronic hernia and because during my month-and-a-half of 'active service' in the unfamiliar and oppressive barracks atmosphere, I became so terribly weak physically, that I gave the appearance of a rather ill-favoured bloke. On the 14th and 15th we — the 'unfit' — were sent home, and I, to my and my family's joy, also returned home on the 15th. Naturally, I cannot rejoice over my 'liberation,' as day after day the papers report on ever more dozens, hundreds and thousands of victims like me — all the more so since in my field of vision are lonely wives whose soldier-husbands were taken along with me — they went through 'service' along with me and, just like me, experienced suffering

advance — a small Foreword. This will draw attention — deservedly so. I think I shall probably write one." Later, on 31 January 1909, after rereading the narrative once more, Tolstoy noted that it struck him "not only on account of its sincerity, seriousness and depth but mainly on account of its beauty, strength and the imagery of the folk language it captures" (ibid., 666).

Novikov continued to protest actively against the war. After his arrest and imprisonment at Tula for signing a declaration against it, he explicitly stated his position at a court hearing for his fellow petitioners in January 1915: "The enmity of war destroys and oppresses all people, and subjects them to innumerable disasters.... Killing out of anger or revenge is something still comprehensible to me, but killing at a distance, without a direct provocation of irritation, has brought me into such a state that my head has started to spin and my arms to droop from the mere thought of it. And so, when I was conscripted into the [Russo-Japanese] war in 1904, I submitted a declaration of refusal to bear arms — not from any religious motivation but simply that I was physically incapable of this, since killing is something abnormal, and without a specific provocation one should not do it" (cited in Bulgakov 1922 [Bethink yourselves, brethren!]: 34).

71 *M. A.* — identity unknown.

and anxiety, but are already on their way without me to somewhere on the other side of Lake Baikal, drawing closer with each passing day to where people live beyond the bounds of reason and engage in a fearful campaign of mutual annihilation. Our fellow-villagers are especially hateful of me, since they all at once determined that I was freed by "Tolstov"[72], and not the authorities, and that I once more have remained [a yoke] around their necks and that their secret desires to be free of me have not been realized. The first *muzhik* I encountered on approaching the village acidly enquired: "Well, that means, it was Tolstov who rescued you? Anyway, you could have used your mug in service to the faith and the fatherland!" I tried to justify myself to him, saying that "Tolstov" was not identical with the authorities and was not in a position to summon or liberate anyone, but the *muzhik* did not believe me: "All the same," he says, "if he's friends with the Devil, he's even more so with the authorities, and they will act according to his word." And in this and other cases of 'folk wisdom' you're completely helpless, and you part from someone without reconciliation, not having proved anything to him, and he follows you with triumph and malice. But I am still glad, [at least] to some extent, that the authorities themselves rescued me from this fearful and unnatural situation and gave me the opportunity to be once more with my family and be engaged in my favourite kind of work — tilling the ground — which after a month and a half of idle inactivity seems to me especially precious and attractive, and all God's world [seems] especially good and magnificent. True, I feel and have the impression that during this time I was crossing [a river] on a tightrope, holding my breath, at risk of falling somewhere at any moment, and then all at once I came out on the riverbank, where the road is safe and I can breathe freely. Oh, how good life is, and how good is the world around us, if we have the opportunity to do what is interesting and natural to us, and how unbearable and oppressive is this same life and world if we follow the command of someone else's will and are obliged to do what is not interesting and, by our very nature, is foreign and unnatural to us. Now I shall try to commit to paper everything I experienced and noticed during this time of 'active emptiness and idleness.' Pity only that I have arrived home at the most difficult time, when all the demanding field tasks are starting one after another; it will take me a long time to recuperate — I have no strength; we're carting dung around — it's heavy — by the evening I can barely move my feet, not to mention finding time to sit down to read or write letters. Lev Nikolaevich, please convey my gratitude to Ivan Ivanovich Gorbunov for the help he has given my family. I would write to him myself, but I have no idea where he is. Probably somewhere near you at his *dacha*. Pass on to him, too, the content of this letter. At the first opportunity I shall joyfully pay you a visit; perchance I shall see Ivan Ivanovich there,

72 *Tolstov* — an approximation of the peasants' pronunciation of Tolstoy's name.

too, and thank him in person. Lately we had a strong wind, which started to tear open [some of] the roofs here, and the accompanying hail killed the buckwheat and did some damage to the oats. Good-bye for now.

Lovingly yours, Mikhail Novikov

16. M. P. NOVIKOV ❧ L. N. TOLSTOY
13 September 1904.

13 September 1904

Dear Lev Nikolaevich, I am sending you, through my brother Pavel, a manuscript of my observations and partly impressions, recorded during the time I was on 'active service.'[73] I would ask you to read it over, and if it should prove worthy of publication in the pages of *Svobodnoe slovo* [The Free Word], or anywhere else, to send it back to me so that I can make a good copy with a few corrections. I wrote it in spurts, and so it doesn't read all that smoothly [at the moment]. I have no free time to speak of. Besides, I am writing my thoughts about war — that is, so to speak, my personal attitude to it. When I finish, perhaps I shall come and see you myself. There's only one thing I desire with my whole heart — for you to live, and to live a good long time. The manuscript I'm sending you is unfinished; for the ending I thought I might use the letter in which I described for you the send-off of the soldiers from Tula.[74]

My brother Pavel has returned from military duty, and there is absolutely no work for him here, since now we have only three allotments of land left — the community took away two of ours. *I wonder if you would find it possible to give him a letter of recommendation in your name* to some prominent industrialist, like Morozov,[75] or an activist such as P. A. Bulanzhe.[76] My brother has a good service record; as a military scribe, he could serve in any administrative office. Please do us this favour, as otherwise there is absolutely nothing for the two of us to do at home and nothing to live on. And, even though it is hard for one person to earn a living from three allotments of land, for me to find work somewhere else with four children is quite unthinkable. A downright

73 Novikov's article "Na vojnu! (Zapiski prizyvnogo letom 1904 g.)" [To war! (Notes of a conscript from the summer of 1904)] was published in the periodical *Svobodnoe slovo* (1905, N°N° 15–17). Tolstoy gave it a favourable review: "What a good story from Novikov, a reserve soldier, 'To war!' Excellent! How powerful!" (Makovitskij 1979–81: 2:21).

74 See Letters N° 13 and N° 14.

75 *Savva Timofeevich Morozov* (1862–1905) — a classmate of Tolstoy's son Sergej L'vovich at Moscow University. His grandfather, Savva Vasil'evich Morozov (1770–1860), himself born into a peasant family, had been the patriarch of the Morozov industrial dynasty.

76 *Pavel Aleksandrovich Bulanzhe* (also known as Paul Boulanger; 1865–1925) — an Orientalist who espoused Tolstoy's views, and who also helped facilitate the Doukhobors' emigration to Canada. At one time he served in the administration of the Moscow-Kursk railway line.

disaster! The struggle for existence gives one no time to meditate or breathe freely. Such is our life [at the moment].

Lovingly yours,
Mikhail Petrov[ich] Novikov

[Please] send me your article on war,[77] if it is available.

17. L. N. TOLSTOY ❧ M. P. NOVIKOV
End of 1904 — Beginning of 1905.

I have read your manuscript,[78] dear Mikhail Petrovich. Most interesting of all are the dialogues among the soldiers (although the first dialogues sound too bookish), and particularly with the women. If you have time, write. Chertkov, I believe, will publish it. Only try to be as truthful as possible. I know it is difficult to describe the past. You forget, and involuntarily make things up. It's better not to say anything if you've forgotten than to reconstruct something out of one's head and not get it completely accurate. It diminishes one's trust in the rest of the story.

With a friendly handshake,

Lev Tolstoy

18. M. P. NOVIKOV ❧ L. N. TOLSTOY
27 January 1905.

27 January 1905

Dear Lev Nikolaevich! My soul has longed for you and, given my situation as a family man wearied by the struggle for existence without any opportunity to come to see you at any time, I am writing you this letter, but I still hope to tear myself away for a day or so and visit Yasnaya Polyana. I subscribe to a newspaper, and am more or less informed about all current events. It's been exactly a year now since brother first rose up against brother and altogether innocent blood is still being shed, and altogether innocent lives are being lost.[79] It is frightful to think about all the victims, and all the blood shed in the name of a god of revenge just in a single year, about all the crimes and horrors calmly committed by people in the name of arbitrary concepts of faith, Tsar and fatherland. Now all these horrors and crimes are extending into a second year, and God only knows how long they will be strung along and pile up one after the other. Life [itself] is magnificent; everyone wants to live according to

77 A reference to Tolstoy's article *Odumajtes'!* [*Bethink Yourselves!*].
78 The reference is to Novikov's manuscript "To war!," which was published (in Russian) by Chertkov's firm, Svobodnoe Slovo, in England in 1904.
79 A reference to the ongoing Russo-Japanese war (1904–1905).

their own will and thought-patterns, but in place of this [we have] death — a fearful, unnatural death in a foreign country, in a land rotting with the stench of corpses and blood. Again I cannot help going back to the reasoning about the ecclesiastical concept of the subjectivity of the God they worship. Doesn't this war serve to overthrow the existence of their personal God?! Where is He, this personal God of theirs? After all, anyone, [even] an illiterate peasant might think in such times that such a personal God simply doesn't exist, or that He is not so all-powerful as Orthodoxy makes Him out to be. We cannot imagine that God is pleased with these destroyed lives, pleased with the stench of rotting human corpses. Wouldn't these people that have perished have preferred slavery to their premature death — after all, non-resistance to evildoers, in the worst case scenario, leads only to slavery — and so where, in fact, is there any benefit from war?

You cannot imagine, Lev Nikolaevich, how happy my family are that this dark cloud of war affected me only slightly. The wounds from this encounter have already healed over, but they give me no rest in my dreams every night. Every night I dream I am participating in the war one way or another, and every time I feel my limbs stiffening, my heart constricting under the war's heavy pressure and, each time I awake, I experience what amounts to a resurrection from the dead, and I feel no shame whatsoever in delighting in such joy. After all, I might have perished in the war just from the thought that I am not in my right place, and who would benefit from that? Moreover, what would my wife do, along with my unchristened children? After all, it is already hard for the two of us together to endure the hatred, scorn and enmity [shown by] the majority of people around us, while if she were alone, the burden would be altogether too much for her.

Lev Nikolaevich, I have never asked anything of you before. Allow me to appeal to you with a request: since I do not send my children to school, but teach them myself, I always feel the need of having good general history books, of which there are none in my library. I think that a knowledge of our past history should be the basis of any kind of knowledge, especially given our dark peasant milieu, in which I am not able to give any kind of education to my children except primary school, for which I myself am substituting. In order not to leave them in peasant-like ignorance about the Earth and life, I ought to, after the usual introductory children's literature, give them some serious reading, which should be based on general history. I know that these books are expensive, and I shall never be able to buy them myself. And so I appeal to you to help me in this: if you yourself do not have such books on hand, could you advise me who to turn to for help? Besides, I would ask you the favour of leaving me at least one book from your personal library in memory of you, in memory of your kind attitude towards me during the whole time we have known each other. I can assure you that any such book (I would like to have a religious or philosophical work, especially on the history of philosophy or religion) in my family will be so very helpful, much more than if it were simply left to your children, who no longer have need of it, or if it should fall into anyone else's hands. Naturally you understand how difficult it will be to continue my protest against religious superstitions and rituals when your death deprives me of such tremendous moral support. Recent events more and more expose public darkness and more and more arouse in me the desire to fight this darkness to my last breath — in particular to fight against the religious superstition of people around me, who often, in an inebriated state, threaten me with vigilante justice for my godlessness, for departing from and trampling on all the popular traditions and customs, which are forever based on ignorance and gloom.

A month ago I sent Ivan Ivanovich Gorbunov a second manuscript describing my personal attitude towards war. What has become of it, I don't know. I wrote to the paper *Pravo*, but have not yet received a reply. Now I am making a copy of [my] article "Krest'janskie otkliki na sovremennye voprosy" [Peasant reaction to contemporary issues], which I intend to send to the paper *Nasha zhizn'*. I confess to you, dear Lev Nikolaevich, that I am attracted by literary activity. There is too much talk and lies about our peasant life; I feel like crying out and exposing [such]. But I absolutely need to earn 10–15 kopeks a day through bookbinding work to cover ongoing expenses with four children, and such work is not always available. And so all my time is going into this work, and my thoughts and ideas get lost in oblivion among all the new ideas [that come into my head].

Good-bye, dear Lev Nikolaevich.

Lovingly yours,
Mikhail Novikov

19. M. P. NOVIKOV ❧ L. N. TOLSTOY
11 April 1905.

Laptevo Station, Village of Borovkovo. 11 April 1905[80]

Dear Lev Nikolaevich, at the present time people are getting ready to celebrate the crucifixion — they will carve their fatted calves, spend their last farthings on alcoholic poisons, drink all these and eat and be very happy that they seem to believe in God thanks to this gluttony. Oh, how many willingly feast around the name of Christ and how few really desire to learn from His teaching! After all, to live in His light, each one must be able to reason and re-evaluate the phenomena of life within their own mind, but that is so hard and wearisome that it is easier to reject one's own will, thoughts and actions and, like billions

80 At Tolstoy's request, this letter was answered by his personal physician, Dushan Petrovich Makovitskij (1866–1921), on 20 April 1905 (L.N Tolstoy State Museum, M. P. Novikov archive).

of drops in a river, flow along the same well-worn channels traversed by their grandfathers and great-grandfathers. How easy and joyful this all is; the main thing is that everything is permissible and no matter how wild the sin, there is always a cheap means of repentance. They have been given the simple childhood bliss of ignorance and they are very happy with it and cherish it, since they instinctively feel that, should they lose this childhood bliss, they would come up face to face, unarmed, against implacable and severe questions of life, since, like children, they are given no weapons either of knowledge, or [even] of basic understanding. Their cheap childhood bliss is founded on just one thing — on unconditional obedience and absolute faith. What would become of a drop of water that broke off from the flood and wanted to go its own way all alone? It would dry up at once and be lost. And they, these blissfully ignorant 'children,' would also lose their way in the debris of free human wisdom and become dehydrated by its alarming inconsistency. Let them delight in the cheapness of their faith; after all, it does not at all contradict the general desire to have everything on the cheap, at the most moderate prices...

In any case I would ask you, Lev Nikolaevich, to publish my manuscript I left you last time about freedom of faith. Even though Sergej L'vovich[81] told me after having read it, that the Liberal Party is also raising this question, at least in the papers I have not seen one word about taking the birth- and death-records out of the church's jurisdiction, but only an enumeration of relative trifles, which in no way responds to the question of religious freedom or, more accurately, of civil freedom, regardless of what church one belongs to. I would so like to hear what will be said about this in the [current] literature, what excuses they will find regarding this question, which [to me] is clear as daylight. On 3 April I submitted a petition to the authorities, asking that my unchristened children be registered in the district family records, referring to the decree of 12 December forbidding constraints not authorised by the law, as well as to the new criminal code, which no longer recognizes departure from Orthodoxy as a punishable offence.

Interesting [to see] what will become of this! Had I considered my status in the village to be solid, I would not have thought to write such a petition, but I feel that I will soon be compelled by need to get out of the village and I shall be in trouble, once my children are not included in my [internal] passport. How difficult this all is: my soul and its thoughts are tending towards my Father's House, to the Kingdom of Truth, while my body remains under the control of Cæsar. And why was it necessary for God to position us between these two fires? There is so much fruitless torment in this struggle. And the worst thing of all is that neither of the warring forces can ever win, thus dragging out this struggle throughout one's life.

81 *Sergej L'vovich Tolstoy* (1863–1947) — Tolstoy's eldest son, who was also in correspondence with Mikhail Novikov.

You see, Lev Nikolaevich, I recently had a new baby boy,[82] and things turned out just as I told you they would: the priest threatened the midwives not to offer any prayer of purification if one of them should come to help with the birth, and when the labour pains started, one midwife (whom we had always engaged) hid herself in fear when she saw she was about to be summoned to the birth; another declared flat out that she would have been glad to help, but that she feared the priest: "He'll make my life miserable, in that case." So my wife was obliged to endure her labour pains without any kind of help, and though the birth turned out more or less successfully, all this was very, very sad and painful. It was sad to hear the idiotic mumblings of a woman who "would have been glad to help," but "feared the priest" — that is, the very person who, according to the church's idea, should be an example for any kind of help. It is painful to realize at such a critical moment that, just for the sake of a simple and arbitrary dogma and a dead tradition, the Christian Church prevents people from helping each other — thereby contradicting its own self. Tormented in my soul during the birth time, I would have, in the heat of the moment, written a good letter [of complaint] to the Bishop of Tula, but I thought better of it and didn't send it, realizing that nothing [good] would come of it apart from bureaucratic red tape, since the church was not going to relinquish its dead 'letter' just for the sake of me alone. After all, in its essence, the church — that is, the priesthood — has nothing to do with the people it serves and exploits; it is made up of human beings, and human beings inherently care about and protect only their own interests. Hence it is pointless to demand of [the church] what it does not have and what it cannot give.

Farewell for now, dear Lev Nikolaevich. [Please] do not forget my request.

I received from Dushan Petrovich [Makovitskij] the newspaper issue he promised me. Oh yes, and I would also like to ask you whether you could give me the addresses of any sectarians you happen to know, no matter what their beliefs. I read a lot about their lives and their beliefs and I see that they too are involved in various silly external rituals — that is, instead of one cult they embrace another. I should like to enter into correspondence with them and learn what prompts this need of theirs to establish a new cult of worship — and is it actually a need? I think it is merely a desire to show their independence and to distinguish themselves from other factions.

In particular, would you happen to have any acquaintance among the Doukhobors living in Canada?[83]

Yours lovingly,
Mikhail Petrovich Novikov

82 Novikov's son, *Sergej Mikhajlovich Novikov* (1905–1942), perished in battle during the Second World War.

83 Dr. Makovitskij sent Novikov the address of Ivan E. Konkin (brother-in-law to Doukhobor leader Pëtr Verigin), who was corresponding with Tolstoy from Canada.

20. M. P. NOVIKOV ❧ L. N. TOLSTOY

14 November 1905.

14 November 1905

Dear Lev Nikolaevich,

Many times I have promised to visit you, and still have not chosen a time. There's so much I want to talk to you about in the times we are now living through. [People] are now rejoicing in the successes achieved, but in fact very little good has taken place and very much bad. And if the next transfer of power from some people to others demands so much in the way of thievery and murders, this will open many people's eyes, and their eyes will pour forth tears instead of joy. It wasn't that long ago that you were being vilified in the press for your lack of sympathy for the 'liberation' movement.[84] It was painful for me to hear that, for people carried away by the passion of their struggle do not understand you. They don't understand that there is nothing in common between God's eternal truth and the conditional and seeming truth of human beings, and that no matter how attractive the human truth may be, it cannot make people happy — quite the opposite. And here they actually want to substitute the human for the divine and are annoyed that you do not agree with them.

You may congratulate just the peasants in your manifesto of 3 November [1905], but this joy will in fact touch only a very few, as the vast majority of peasants will not improve their lot as a result of the proffered benefits, and these 'free' roubles will still go back to the government through the necks of wine bottles. I hear the *muzhiks* saying [something like]: "Don't worry, Tsar, the money will be yours again!" From this one example it is particularly clear that even the best human truth is of benefit (and even that is doubtful) only to a very few, while all the other truths achieved go completely contrary to the desires of either party. The only thing valuable to me in all this hullabaloo of recent times is the creation of the peasants' alliance,[85] and though

84 In 1904–1906, Tolstoy wrote a series of articles — *Ob obshchestvennom dvizhenii v Rossii* [*On the Social Movement in Russia*], *Edinoe na potrebu* [*The One Thing Needful*], *Velikij grekh* [*The Great Sin*], *Konets veka* [*The End of the Century*], *Obrashchenie k russkim ljudjam. K pravitel'stvu, revoljutsioneram i narodu* [*Appeal to the Russian People: To the Government, the Revolutionaries and the People*] — in which he sharply criticized the violence being perpetrated by both the government and the revolutionaries. In his opinion, all revolutions "are aimed only at exchanging one old form of violence for a new one which merely perpetuates violence and brings the same disasters in its wake.... The fact that the majority of revolutionaries posit a socialist structure as a new foundation for life — a structure that can be achieved only through the most cruel violence and which, if ever achieved, would deprive people of the last remnants of freedom — shows only that these people have absolutely no foundation for life" (*PSS* 36:260).

85 The All-Russian Peasants' Alliance [Vserossijskij krest'janskij sojuz] — a mass political organization of the peasantry, founded in 1905 under the leadership of the Socialist Revolutionaries. The alliance demanded the abolition of private property and the immediate summoning of an executive assembly. It collapsed toward the end of 1906.

most of what they say, as in other alliances, is twaddle, still, this alliance may — through their bloodless and noiseless boycott of landowners and their refusal to carry out government demands in respect to taxes and military service — earn the possibility of owning land which is now in the hands of the wealthy [elite], who make a fortune off it through mooching at a time when millions of peasants have no profitable work to speak of. These ideas of a boycott expressed by the alliance in the course of other loud-spoken words, are especially dear in that they constitute the only means which you have long ago suggested to people and which is the only simple and affordable means [of letting their need be known]. But here they go spouting and shouting: "Success! Freedom!" And yet the people are starving more than ever before and because of the darkness and ignorance they go and commit worse and worse crimes. Without rationalizing for the moment on what has not yet come to pass, I should like to know your opinion: what should we do now with our land allotments? Leave them in private hands as now — that is, in the hands of the one who has most of them on the final day of the buy-out? Or divide them according to the number of souls present [in every participating family]? I think the latter would be fairer. After all, at the moment the land is divided among the peasants quite unevenly — the dimensions of the farming strips are so confusing and strip-farming [in general] has become a corrupt [venture]. Am I, for example, to blame that because of my family situation I have 2/3 of an allotment, while my neighbour who is younger than me [has] 3 allotments? He has a family of four, while I have one of seven. If only the land could be redistributed, then we would fill our bellies or go hungry more or less evenly, and there would be no bad feeling such as [exists now].

Land, land! There is so much land, yet there is still no order [in its distribution], and many millions of people have nothing to put their hand to, nothing to live off of. After all, one pair of working hands could till 4 to 6 *desjatinas* of rye and oats, which would meet their need and still mean some left over for a rainy day. But now it is so bad that every time we get a bad year, there is nothing to fall back on. [People say:] "*Muzhiks* are drunkards." Fine, I agree, but I've never been a drunkard, and yet I've still been affected by poor harvests and malnutrition. Now we've just had a poor harvest, and now there's no money to buy porridge or butter, while just plain cabbage soup and plain potatoes offer little in the way of nutrition. Adults are getting by more or less, but right now it is evident in the children — they look pale and emaciated. The quality of the food is also bad for nursing mothers. But this is not about me: I have not been a drunkard, and I have food, and the children have enough (at least enough bread) that they won't starve. But many have no food at all, not even bread, and they are eating up the local government loans, but there's a long winter ahead. As bad as it is for me, I can comfort myself that many are worse off. And all of this is due to the scarcity of land. You keep thinking about where to get enough land to feed ourselves, but the most important thing is not to see children grown pale from lack of food, and one involuntarily starts to bless and anticipate like manna an agricultural revolution. To go from five children into farm labour and servility is not an attractive prospect — in fact, it's repulsive; and farm labour and servility will not by any means satisfy the need for land on the part of all the indigent and semi-indigent peasants. Hence it will be no surprise if the peasants' age-old injustice, their age-old starvation status and ignorance should explode in the peasants' hatred for and revenge on the wealthy landowners, so fertile and tempting, for this is the soil in the times we are living through at the moment.

I am very grateful to you, Lev Nikolaevich, for the history textbooks you sent me. I would still like to ask you for two books [in particular]: *The History of Religion* by [Ernest] Renan and *The Life of Christ* by [Frederic W.] Farrar. I have heard that they are good [books]. My best to Dushan Petrovich [Makovitskij] and others who know me.

Lovingly yours,
Peasant Mikhail Petrov[ich] Novikov
Village of Borovkovo

21. M. P. NOVIKOV ❧ L. N. TOLSTOY
18 May 1906.

18 May 1906

Dear Lev Nikolaevich,

It is always difficult to write about personal matters — indeed, they are of little interest to anyone but the writer — but I am still writing to you, if only to show the Russian people in their true light. You may remember I was telling you about the partition of our family's [property]. Everything went as it should: my father and brothers allotted me an actual quarter portion. A suitable passageway was found to my estate, adjacent to the land on which my vegetable garden stands. I purposely went to Moscow to track down the widow who owns this estate passageway (estates, as you know, are not an inheritable possession). I bought it from her for 10 roubles, but in addition, I also had to buy an agreement from the community, that after this widow's death they would not force me to demolish the structure, since vacant estates once again become communal property. I gathered people together and asked for a statement of apportionment, as well as their agreement [for me] to occupy the purchased estate, or to give me a new one, as anyone can be given an allotment of communal pasture land in return for a quarter or a half *vedro*[86] of vodka. The answer was quintessentially Russian: "We don' wanna," and if we "wanna," then you pay 50 roubles for a new estate, and if it is the one I just

86 *vedro* (lit. 'bucket') — a unit of liquid measurement equivalent to 10–12 litres.

bought, that will be 17 roubles in cash and a *vedro* of vodka, and you have to serve the vodka yourself.

I could not accept these conditions, both because of my poor financial status and because of their godlessness, since the 'community' was governed by nothing but personal malevolence towards me and the desire to 'squeeze' me, making me beg and humiliate myself. And how they bullied and made fun of me! Finally they saw that I had fallen into their hands, and tried to put one over on me. I declined their conditions, and was not given a *statement of apportionment*, but I was the one obliged to lodge a complaint, but most probably nothing will come of it, as the local 'divine' authorities all advise me to make peace with the inebriated crowd and try to please them. They are not fond of talking about the Tsar's laws, but suggest proceeding according to custom, and everyone knows all too well what sort of customs these are: today it will be a quarter *vedro* from one, tomorrow half a *vedro* from another, and then again a quarter, and so forth, and to please this "kommunity,"[87] aside from the need to buy quarter *vedros* on required occasions, one is obliged to actually participate in their booze parties, otherwise you yourself will be considered a 'smarty-pants' and a '*stalorer*,'[88] and they'll go on squeezing you wherever they can.

In general, the concept of autocracy in the Russian land has been adopted and established not by the despots alone, but also by "kommunities" who practise it themselves on a broad scale. As you can see, Lev Nikolaevich, when it comes to Russian autocracy, it's not just a question of *muzhiks* having no land to work, but also that there's not even an available or accessible plot of land whereon to construct their own hut without all sorts of permissions and drunkenness. Of course, at first glance this may seem like a trifle, but it is from such trifles that [the fabric of] our entire life is woven, and a family man sometimes finds himself at a dead end when he comes up against them.

People in the know now advise me to set myself up on the estate I bought without any quarter *vedros* or community permissions; they assure me that if this widow lives [another] ten years, the decade will cover, by virtue of the time passed, all the community's claims to this estate. They even say that even if this widow should die before ten years is up, the community will still not have the right to demolish any building before it becomes absolutely useless [for anything]. If I could be sure of that, this is what I would do, for there's no way I'll buy quarter *vedros* for the *muzhiks*, and without that they'll never give me their agreement. I was giving them 10 roubles of income, but they still wouldn't listen. And they say that just as a tree will not grow right without watering, how can a hut be allowed to be built without the 'watering' of

87 This represents an equivalent distortion of the Russian word for 'community' used in Novikov's original text.

88 This reflects the spelling used by Novikov, possibly to hint at the local peasant corruption of the word *starover* [Old Believer].

vodka? So much for your celebrated Russian people! The Doukhobors are probably not like these.[89]

Lovingly yours,
Mikhail Novikov

22. M. P. NOVIKOV ❧ L. N. TOLSTOY
5 June 1906.

Village of Borovkovo, 5 June 1906

Dear Lev Nikolaevich,

Fel'ten[90] wrote me from Petersburg that the publication of my booklet *Golos krest'janina* [Voice of the peasant][91] has been delayed because the revolutionary gentleman (whose name I don't know) who was interested in it has somehow disappeared.

Now I am asking Ivan Ivanovich Gorbunov to publish it. If he comes to see you at Yasnaya Polyana, perhaps you could suggest he consider *Golos* for publication. Please do this, Lev Nikolaevich. On the 3rd of June the Christian *muzhiks* gave me a land-distribution document and an agreement to rent an estate which I bought from one of our country widows for 10 roubles. But in doing so they defrauded me like they had never defrauded anyone before — they took 16 roubles, so that just a bare patch of ground cost [me] around 30 roubles. Now I'll build a hut, outfit it with all of life's necessities, I'll be stooping over again to build on that bare patch of ground, and then on the allotment of land I'll proceed with some "intensification," as recommended by our beneficent government in its declarations on the sacredness and inviolability of private land, I'll milk the cow seven times a day, sow crops three times a year, etc. Such a blind government! It is bent on making any humble person into a revolutionary. What are we peasants supposed to do with such a small [parcel of] land? What am I personally, a sober and industrious man, to do on a single allotment? Go work as a day-labourer for some wealthy landowner, on the advice of the government? No — excuse me — I'd rather join the revolutionaries, hoist a red flag and fight for "Land and Liberty"?[92]

89 Evidently, Novikov had a deep interest in and respect for the Doukhobors. See Letters N° 19, above, and N° 25, below.

90 *Nikolaj Evgen'evich Fel'ten* (1884–1940) — an associate of the Obnovlenie (Renewal) publishing house.

91 Novikov's booklet *Golos krest'janina* was published anonymously by Chertkov's Svobodnoe Slovo publishing house in England in 1904. After his first reading of it (in manuscript form), Tolstoy noted in his diary of 28 November 1900: "Yesterday I read Novikov's article and was left with a strong impression — I remembered something I had forgotten: the life of the people — their need and humiliation as well as our own faults" (*PSS* 54:442–43).

92 *Land and Liberty* [*Zemlja i volja*] — a secret Russian revolutionary society in Russia (1861–1864) and later revived as a populist organization (1876–1879).

A week ago I wrote a long letter to our Tula deputies at the Duma, in which I strongly counteracted all those negative arguments against expropriation, as brought forth by our government ministers. I asked them to tell the ministers that, in clinging to the sacredness of the right to property, they are like the silly woman who at the time of a fire clung [tenaciously] to an icon to protect herself from the flames; that they, who are guilty of social devastation and famine, vainly preach to the hungry about the sacredness of the documents (land-sale agreements), specifying that a single person is entitled to 5–10 square versts of land. The people will never understand this kind of "sacredness," since the people measure everything by their heart, and not by stupid legal sciences which, thankfully, they have not yet had the opportunity to become acquainted with. And they do not recognize this law, since in each one is implanted God's greater law — the law of hunger, the law of the will to live — and His law cannot be beaten out of *muzhiks* by any kind of whips or machine-guns.

Once again we have a poor harvest, and there's a drought; the rye is so poor that *muzhiks* have applied for seeding loans. There is nothing to roof the huts with; they need [to purchase] iron rods. Yes, life has thrust me into a difficult situation and is laughing me in the face, whilst long years of work and deficiencies will not succeed in resolving this situation. My best to all my acquaintances.

Lovingly yours,
Peasant Mikhail Novikov

23. M. P. NOVIKOV ❧ L. N. TOLSTOY
29 August 1907.

29 August 1907

Dear Lev Nikolaevich,

For a long time now I have been planning to pay you a visit, but my needs of the past two years have not given me the opportunity to have an extra forty kopeks to spend on coming to see you, and, apart from that, the rainy summer and the related ordeals of *muzhik* labour have not given me three days free to come to you on foot. I would still like to ask your help in one matter: my position as someone with a large family and with the least possible amount of land (I have seven mouths to feed on just one allotment of land) is becoming more and more difficult and awkward year by year. My *barin* [landowner] will not lease me [any more] land, and it is [too] far to go to my neighbour's, and so I have to somehow manage to eke out a living, renting from my own *muzhiks* — one has an allotment, another a bit of a field to seed, but since there are still quite a few people in the village with very little land, in the competition for land you have to keep upping the price to outbid others, or they will outbid you. From this, knowing *muzhiks* in general, you can see what kind of sin results, especially since I, who am at least a little inclined towards the Christian concept of life, am always thereby left behind in any deal; others are always able to grab the best and cheapest before I can. And so the poor harvest these past few years has forced me to experience a great deal of frightful want and sorrow. Eight months we lived without a cow, and the little children, along with the big ones, subsisted on plain potatoes and cabbage soup — and there was not always enough doled out bread on hand.

Now the poor harvest times have passed, but I see that my lot has seen little change for the better, as the land they let us lease is of the poorest quality, and is always practically useless. And my family keeps on growing up, and our needs keep increasing, and there is nothing to grasp hold of. All the more so, since now, after two years of feed and seed loans, we have a lot of food debts, and at difficult moments I have borrowed small sums from kind people. So while the famine may have passed for others, it remains in my case, and there are only two ways out of this awkward situation: either to go to some wealthy people and ask for a yoke to be placed around my neck, or to acquire some land at any cost. For the first alternative my time has expired: my back which is broken from work will not stoop as it should for wealthy people, especially since my comrades in the military service passed the civil service exam and are now Court Councillors[93] and I have no hope of catching up to them, and if I go and earn 7 roubles [a month] at a factory, this is not enough to feed or improve the lot of my family. As a new believer and protestant I cannot and will not exchange my life of labour for an easy, money-oriented life among any wealthy people, who call themselves "princes of this world."[94] My place is here, among people around me who are more unhappy spiritually than I am; it is precisely here that my protest against their religious ignorance and spiritual dullness is required, and therefore, in spite of family difficulties, I definitely do not want to escape from my situation by the first route.

There remains the second: I have to acquire some land, and in this [I am asking] you to help me — not you personally, of course, but through people around you. Our landowner (a capitalist and industrialist) is agreeable to selling our village a part of his land, but he is asking a high price — 140 roubles per *desjatina*, which we cannot [afford to] give him; besides, with the late neighbouring landowner Ivan Vasil'evich Tsinger, even though his land as such is not for sale, his sister recently told me that she would sell me a little of her portion, which I really should take advantage of. Of course, no matter who you buy it from, you still have to buy through the bank, but here's the rub: you still have to come up with a down payment of 10 or 15 per cent of the purchase

93 *Court Councillor* [*Nadvornyj sovetnik*] — the seventh rank of the civil service Table of Ranks (originally established by Tsar Peter the Great in 1722).
94 John 14:30.

price from your own funds, but I haven't any [to spare], and, by golly, nowhere to get them from, and if some one or other is selling land, in spite of being the most destitute in terms of land, I might well be left overboard because of this shortfall. The matter is supposed to be resolved this autumn and I should like to know whether I could hope to find this extra amount through you? For my allotment, 6–8 *desjatinas* would be quite sufficient, and if I assume the cost will be between 100 and 140 roubles, I shall need around a hundred roubles. The sum is not that great and a wealthy person can always come up with it. [Please] answer me, if you can, for which I shall be eternally grateful to you.

There, you see what life is like.... In proudly rejecting earthly bread, Christianity has completed only half the task: it has freed my spirit from awkward dependence on old superstitions and outmoded authorities, as well as from all the general spiritual baggage which I dutifully dragged around with me practically since my infancy, but it left my body in its former slavery to a landowner — or to any wealthy person — and thereby has given rise to a frightful discord and antagonism between what I see as my visible and my "invisible" [existence]. Life has shown me that one cannot be content simply with spiritual freedom, as the early Christians tried to do, since even against physical slavery it is not hands and feet that raise a protest, but the very spirit which neither I nor anyone else has the right to impose by force. And there's no way I can understand how they could be at peace in spiritual freedom and yet remain in economic and even physical slavery, or what kind of compromise they came up with [that allowed them] to silence the protest of the spirit against this slavery? I can no longer imagine that these people were all that different from me.... I want to think that with its proud and beautiful phrase "Man does not live by bread alone," Christianity was only hiding its own weakness in trying to resolve the economic question about bread, since it knew (and could not help but know) those cherished dreams of the best Jewish people and of all mankind about its own (most definitely, its own) fig tree,[95] under which everybody could eat their own bread, not fearing either a *barin* or the *barin's* foreman or the warden, who now and always prowl the fields with a knife to stick at the throat of anyone who cannot get by without [the *barin's*] huge lands, on which grow not one but thousands of fig trees — humanity's cherished ideal. It's possible [Christianity] also knew about the fruitless Utopias of Plato, More,[96] Marx[97] and other do-gooders who each in their own way redrafted the economic life of mankind in the hope of according *everyone their fig-tree of life*, and so, desperate to do at least something on this laborious path of human life, it thrust itself over to the other side and began to create the realm of the spirit, a communist brotherhood in the true

95 See Mic. 4:4.

96 *More* — most probably a reference to English philosopher Sir Thomas More (1478–1535), who published his *Utopia* in 1516.

97 *Karl Marx* (1818–1883) — Prussian-born utopian socialist and philosopher.

spirit, utterly avoiding the reality of life in one's daily bread. But this realm of the spirit soon collapsed and turned out to be the same Utopia which, upon coming face to face with life in the flesh, became merely the domain of the priests of Christianity, and these so easily adapted the teaching of the realm of Spirit to be compatible with their life in the flesh. It is easy to understand how dear and precious this was for them in contrast to the socialist Utopias about the fig tree, which they repudiated and disdained at every juncture. O, how limitless is the expanse of the spirit — there is a place for all and each one in particular; all you have to do is fantasise and fly through the clouds and not think *about your fig tree*.

Yesterday I was walking in from the field behind a cart full of rye, tired, dirty and hungry. My stomach was churning and spilling over, filled with sour *kvass*[98] and plain cabbage soup with milk, swollen with so much innutritious food, but the hard work made me feel hungry. At that point I was overtaken by our *barin* with his wife, in a fancy carriage with a pair of fine, well-fed horses. The couple, too, were well-fed, content, proud of their powerful position. They had gone to Moscow to see a favourite opera on some Doge or Moor of Venice, and were on their way back to their estate; in the meantime, their foreman has been cursing and fibbing from morning 'til night with the *muzhiks* and the day-labourers in order to squeeze out of them more work — to make the extra 500 roubles which the *barin* and his wife urgently needed to travel abroad to take in the warm waters there. It was clear from their smooth, rosy cheeks that they did not feel any hunger or suffer from bloated stomachs, since all their lives they never ate such rubbish as the *muzhiks* have to live on, but ate from dozens of fatted calves and hundreds of full-fed mutton, prepared for them by day-labourers or sold out of necessity by *muzhiks* to settle various rents and accounts with that dog of a foreman.

Here, I thought, the phrase "Man does not live by bread alone" was very apt, since in addition [to bread], they "need" Mozart and Raphael and the French romanticists, and tutors [for their children]. They need a lot, a great lot — thousands of things and objects which the *muzhik* still has no concept of at all. Through their whole satisfied and cheery life they can hide behind this saying and appear to themselves to be justified. The phrase permeates their whole posture and look of pride, since in fact they are not satisfied with bread alone. But as for me, and for all those tired, dirty and sweaty people who now potter about the fields in their pursuit of bread, bread is all we need. Neither the music of Beethoven, nor the statues or paintings of Raphael and Michelangelo, nor the poetry of Dante and Shakespeare, nor the scholarly researches of historians, geologists and mathematicians — none of that means anything to us — none of those academic goodies would satisfy the hunger in our tummies, even if we were acquainted with them. We need only bread,

98 *kvass* — a slightly fermented drink made from rye bread.

nothing but bread, and in our pursuit of it we put pressure on one another and die prematurely from toil without ever attaining the desired fig tree, under which everyone may [sit and] eat their bread without fear. Oh, again and again people will be driven to the barricades by hunger, they'll dam rivers and fix roads with their corpses, since there, ahead of them, they are promised bread — they're lured by bread — but never will they venture to create the Kingdom of God in Spirit, as there is no earthly bread there at all.

Help me get land, get bread, for which all my life I have never yearned so much as now, as it is now quite clear to me that until I acquire some land, I shall never have either free bread or a free spirit, and my large family, who look at me with hungry eyes, will not give me a free moment to tell people any kind of good [news]. During my working days over the summer I note down random thoughts that come to me all by themselves; in the winter I could put them in order and a definite form to share, but now autumn is coming, and winter, and one's need drives one into a kind of subservience to the wealthy. I can get by with so little: 6–7 *desjatinas* would give me free bread, as my work on the land, which is unhampered by the traditional lie of holidays and superstitions, would always bring me substantially greater [profit] than with other *muzhiks*. And it is not [reasonable] in my position to go into servitude in the pursuit of bread, since, as a new believer with "unchristened" children, I cannot count on [finding] happiness or success doing day-labour or going into servitude among the wealthy; the wealthy, in fact, prefer the most orthodox and true believers, ready to stoop to any low or flattery in their servitude to them. [Please] send me some kind of reply to this letter.

Lovingly yours,
Peasant Mikhail Novikov
29 August 1907, Village of Borovkovo.

24. L. N. TOLSTOY ➧ M. P. NOVIKOV[99]

4 September 1907.

Mikhail Petrovich, yesterday I received your letter. It evoked very complex feelings in me. The first feeling was that of annoyance and hostility toward you, a condemnation of you. And since yesterday and through the night I did a lot of thinking and struggling with my feeling and now, today, I have arrived at a state of mind in which I can respond to you calmly and, more importantly, lovingly. That unkind, bad feeling (forgive me) which permeated your letter

99 Reply to Novikov's wide-ranging letter of 29 August 1907 (Letter N° 23), in which Novikov outlined to Tolstoy, rather acrimoniously, the trials and difficulties experienced both by himself and by the peasantry in general. In a subsequent reply to the present letter, dated 26 September 1907 (see Letter N° 25), Novikov strongly disagreed with Tolstoy's contentions, especially in respect to his own envy of the rich and powerful, implying that Tolstoy's class status prevented him from comprehending the peasants' need for some material comfort.

had infected me as well: I wanted to prove to you that you were wrong — to condemn you, but, delving into the motives governing you, I changed my mind or, rather, changed my feelings, and in place of the anger with which your letter infected me, I now feel a sincere, loving compassion toward you and it is in this mood that I now write to you.

The compassion I feel does not arise from the condition of your stomach, which is filled, as you say, with inedible food while well-fed masters pass by you on their well-fed horses and that bastard, their steward, attacks the people. It arises from those terrible, tormenting feelings that all this evokes in you. I feel compassion as well on account of those tormenting feelings of helplessness, and especially on account of that state of mind and the mental revulsion which make these terrible feelings (which can be evoked only by hopeless suffering) possible and even inevitable — feelings of hatred toward brother men out of envy of the material advantages which they happen to enjoy.

These feelings are even more tormenting because the people experiencing them tend to engender more and more in themselves the tormenting feeling of anger, exaggerating the disadvantages of their situation (which it is particularly evident you are doing) and the advantages enjoyed by those provoking such feelings.

The emotional feeling leading you to such a state — the feeling which arouses my compassion for you — is a complete lack of faith in the spiritual (i.e., the true) life, which you keep stating so often in your letter as something you hold dear. Time after time, as though you were content with your discovery, as though mocking it as a "done deal," you keep talking about the fallacy and stupidity of the thought that "man is not satisfied by bread alone."[100] Moreover, it is precisely from your unbelief in this, your unbelief in spiritual life, your unbelief in the necessity for spiritual demands in life, your unbelief in God, that your sufferings and your misfortune arise.

Besides, you write that you have been experiencing some discomfort from being a "new believer." I would say that you are not a new believer, but a non-believer. To bury your children without the services of the clergy, not to fast and not go to church — that is not faith: you have rejected the superstitions of the old faith, but you have no faith yourself. It is in this, as well as in the fact that you do not believe in a spiritual principle of life and its requirements, that your misfortune lies, and not at all in the lack of land and the unfairness of the economic structure.

If you believed in this spiritual principle of life and in the inevitability of its demands, you would not consider, as you do now, the first, inflexible principle of your life to build and support your own individual household on the earth. If you didn't believe in the necessity of such a life, but believed that your life is the manifestation in your limited form in this world of that principle

100 See, e.g., Matth. 4:4.

of all which is beyond time and space, which you recognize in yourself, and that not only the most important but the only life and activity which belongs to you is the striving toward unity with all living things, i.e., love, then you would not be building your life, as you are doing now, according to your own self-constructed and beloved personal programme (though it be a good one), but, carrying out the will of the higher principle, you would trust destiny and circumstances to place you in other conditions of some kind.

Perhaps, fulfilling the higher law of love to all humanity, you would stay in those beloved conditions of yours, perhaps you would be obliged to construct your life quite differently; but no matter how it was constructed, under any conditions you would, no doubt, in fulfilling the higher law of love, act in the best possible manner, and in loving instead of hating people, you would find true good for yourself.

The lack of economic structure of which you complain, fortunately (as is so evident now to everyone), cannot be remedied either by complaints or hatred or violence arising from hate, but only by that same consciousness of spirituality inherent in the fact that *man is not satisfied by bread alone,* which seems so preposterous to you, and by the love that flows from such a consciousness.

So, dear brother Mikhail Petrovich, all this frank talk may be mistaken, but it represents my seriously thought-through opinion about your mental states. From this opinion of mine you yourself may deduce that even if I could (and I cannot, since I don't have money of my own) fulfill your desire, I would not do it, as I would find — and know — many, many people who are in much greater need of financial help than you. I know you: you are a very clever and very proud person, but I think that along with this there dwells in you a great moral force, a religious feeling, and therefore I hope and ask you strongly to think about that.

Just as I have given thoughtful consideration to your letter, I would like you to think about mine and work on any bad feeling which it may evoke in you, and in any case forgive me for possibly insulting you. It is in utter sincerity that I can repeat what I said at the beginning of the letter, that I feel nothing but the greatest feeling of love toward you. Tell me if you feel the same. If you don't, don't answer. I shall know that you are not in agreement with me. I think it is only a matter of time.

Lovingly, Lev Tolstoy

4 September 1907.

25. M. P. NOVIKOV ❧ L. N. TOLSTOY
26 September 1907.

26 September 1907

Dear Lev Nikolaevich, I received your reply. Forgive me if I upset you with my letter. I had no idea it would upset you. I certainly have no desire to upset you even now, inasmuch as I love and respect you as the founder of Russian free thought, from whom I, too, have borrowed the principle of my spiritual freedom. As soon as I had read the first two lines of your letter, I immediately felt guilty over your being upset — mainly because it was too late to correct it. But it gave me all the more pleasure to read and reread the rest of your letter, as I found therein not the slightest shade of reproach towards me, since the whole thing right to the end was not about me at all, describing someone else entirely, in whom, thanks to the spiritual discrepancy between us, I could recognize nothing of myself. That is why your letter evoked in me no unkind feeling towards you, let alone hostility. Granted, there remains some feeling of confusion and lack of clarity: how could you have come to such an opinion of my mental state — [an opinion] which I have been able to explain in no other way except my inability to say to you what I wanted to say in my letter.

It is with longing and pain that I wrote you that letter, and it is with longing that I am still writing you now. Without the slightest exaggeration, I say once more that my situation as someone with little land and a large family is an awkward one, a difficult situation; indeed, a worse one is rarely to be encountered. Some who, like me, have one allotment or half an allotment of land, don't have so many children or they live at factory or workers' [dorms]; others, family types, have managed to fall into servitude to the Volkonskijs, the Golitsyns, the Orlovs[101] and such like and feel quite comfortable. For me, on the other hand, neither of these situations is tenable, and only sin comes from renting land. I leased two allotments from one *muzhik*, while another *muzhik* is reproaching me and threatening to beat me up for "stealing," in his opinion, his land. Now I could rent [some land] from a certain widow, but [if I do,] the previous renter will start to reproach and threaten me, and I don't want to get into a position where someone will be able to accuse me, as your [spiritual] godson, of feeding myself by lying. And I settled on the purchase of land — not because this programme is good, — what good is it when someone buys land through the bank at a market price, and then falls into the clutches of the bank for 50 years — that is, for his whole life? — but because it is the only form of slavery I can reconcile myself to and which in my situation

101 A reference to wealthy landowners in general.

of need I cannot avoid. But since all of this, too, will just end up in dreams and I shall still have to go into personal slavery, which my spirit has absolutely no desire to be reconciled with, I wanted mainly to hear from you an explanation as to how the first Christians explained their situation in personal slavery to wealthy Romans.

You will say that it is possible to live for God and one's neighbour in any situation, but the thing is that in order to remain alive, man is obliged to feed himself, but how to feed one's self — this is not something that can be passed over lightly — if one wants to avoid getting into the position of your *muzhiks*.... In this [situation] alone, it seems, lies the worst mistake of our leading intelligentsia, which cheers in words for the public good, but in practice feeds itself with falsehoods — that is, it does not have a true foundation for its life, though this is precisely where people should start in order to improve their life. This is what I was thinking about when I asked [you] for help in acquiring land. You accused me of envying the wealthy, but is it possible to envy someone in whose position you do not wish to be? God forbid I become a landowner! After all, to do that, I would have to lose what is most precious to me in life: clarity of understanding and the purity of my relationships with people. But to give an illustration of what is around us, what is an eyesore to destitute peasants, does not mean tormenting one's self with malice towards the wealthy. And if I were seriously infected with malice towards them, even temporarily, my consistency in matching deeds with words would prevent me from tormenting myself with pointless malice; indeed, I would probably be able to apply it to these wealthy in a more cruel and practical form. Of course, it is difficult for someone who suffocates from their need and squabbles with the family over every penny to always indulge the wealthy — that is, those responsible for their poverty — but this does not [automatically] mean that this person is harbouring malice towards the wealthy.

As to the fact that I consider it an absolute condition of my life to support my individual household, I see no sin in this, as I don't know how else to act to survive with my family, since past and present history teaches me that people cannot live without setting up a burrow or nest, which is true of every living being, and if the Utopians of the past even dreamt about a Communist structure for the State without individual family households, nothing would come of their dreams. Life has [always] passed by these dreams, just as it is [now] passing by modern socialist Utopias which dream of the communalization of labour and tools of production. True, Doukhobors, the early Christians and the Jesuits in Paraguay have succeeded in putting something similar into practice for a limited time, but all these situations lacked the most important stimulus for life, [namely,] spiritual freedom, which has been surrendered to aggressors or "beloved" authorities. Wherever there is a free human spirit, it would be unthinkable to have such small communes without one's own individual households, since it is natural for man to distinguish himself from other people in both spirit and body, and that is because he *must* live *for himself* and die for himself, as you yourself have put it so deeply and sincerely. Ponder deeply the life of the body — and here, as with the life of the spirit, one's individual personal will appears at every step and cannot help but appear, and to kill it is equally as sinful as killing the freedom of the spirit. Here it is also possible to merely temporary agreements on practical grounds, from which it is absolutely impossible to deduce the principle of commonality of interests, as socialists of different types do coarsely and thoughtlessly.

Dear Lev Nikolaevich, you also accused me of mocking the text of the Christian formula "Man shall not live by bread alone." Believe me, I have touched upon this formula with pain and sorrow; it seems to me sometimes that, in view of how I am eking out a living with my children, squeezing out an extra pound of butter or a fistful of cereal grains, this formula was laughing me in the face, and I doubted I would be able to remain calm in spirit while living in a half-starving body. And I confessed my doubts to you as a dear and trustworthy individual. If I didn't have any belief in the life of the spirit and lived only as a materialist, believe me, I would have nothing to live for at all, I would have no solid ground beneath my feet, as the complete lack of hope of improving my position in any time-frame would rob me every moment of all the charms of materialism. Neither I, nor even a third of all the peasantry — which are either landless or land-deprived — have any hope in fate, nor in any circumstances whatever, since we well realize that unless you can get into the Volkonskijs' front door or to a place where you can steal, we have nothing else to improve our children's food and clothing. As long as we remain in the "beloved" conditions of small landowners, we shall forever have to choose [even] between bread and *kvass* — a choice which (by my count) the land-deprived third of the peasantry are obliged to make today. And so that most bitter word "unbeliever" never touched me at all.

Over the past few years of poor harvests and political struggles and games my soul was plagued by many, many new and penetrating thoughts, new and penetrating emotions, but, thank God, I maintained the same understanding of life I had learnt ten years before, and not only maintained it, but grew stronger, and in my mind I was already considering and analysing various situations in life which give rise to a specific [human] activity. I was told with sincere disapproval that people were perishing, fighting for my freedom, that it was shameful to sit back with my hands folded, but my mind remained faithful to the idea that nothing good ever comes out of fighting, and that no one can fight for my freedom but I myself, and that freedom does not lie in committing crimes or in mentally skipping from niche to niche, chasing after fashionable trends in socialist Utopias, but in reacting critically to any new phenomenon of life and in measuring and evaluating them not by the eloquence of speakers on the right or the left, but by one's own mind and conscience, without linkage to any rigid party affiliation. The term *new believer* I'm using not because I feel it actually applies to me, but that is how I am considered by people around me, who call me to account even over the smallest trifles. I know you understand this, too. People never give nicknames to themselves — this is done by a crowd to anyone who distinguishes himself, even in the slightest, from the "magic circle" of street morality and customs.

Lovingly yours,
Peasant Mikhail Petrov[ich] Novikov

I hope to come and see you in October or November.
26 September 1907

26. M. P. NOVIKOV ❧ L. N. TOLSTOY
11 August 1908. Borovkovo.

Dear Lev Nikolaevich!

I have heard that on your birthday at the end of this month you wanted to go off to stay with one of your acquaintances, to avoid all personal greetings from people, most of whom have no idea as to how to spend either their leisure time or their ill-gotten wealth. I don't know who those fortunate people are — the ones you intend to go and stay with — but I dare say they probably have enough funds and leisure time of their own to go visit you at Yasnaya Polyana whenever they like.

In any case, I might say that our so-called leading liberal intelligentsia is hardly different from any others who feed off the public purse or the commonplace landlords of dead souls who extract rent from peasants even when there's no harvest.

At best, our social elite, like Voltaire, don't believe in God themselves, but consider the outward trappings of faith to be needful to the dark masses, and so, when it comes to this most terrible evil, they turn a blind eye and offer no open resistance to it.

I dare say that your presence in a family of such gentry would have no benefit for them in the moral sense and that after your visit their lives would hum along just as smoothly and easily as before, with their magic tablecloths[102] and flying carpets.

With this in mind, may I be so bold as to ask you, instead, to pay a visit to my family, who would very much like to see you. (Of course my request will not make sense if you do not intend to leave Yasnaya Polyana for some other place.)

102 *magic tablecloths* [*skaterti-samobranki*] — in Russian folk legends, tablecloths that magically supply a meal.

I am certain that your visit will leave a deep impression on the whole future life of my children and will give them good direction and raise their spirits. Dear Lev Nikolaevich, you are most of all needful to the peasants, and not to the gentry who do not need you, only insofar as you can entertain them and satisfy their vain pleasures and egos. I am certain that your moral philosophy of life would do a hundred times more than it has done if it were only as familiar to our own peasants as to the people of the social elite for whom it has so far served as a mere object of theoretical polemics and pleasant discussions, instead of a guidebook for life.

Besides, a visit to me here would cost you practically nothing beyond a rouble for the return trip by rail. Borovkovo is within walking distance of Laptevo Station — no further than from your place to Kozlovka Station. Of course at your age it would not be pleasant to walk alone, even though it is not all that far, but I am certain that someone will be happy to accompany you here from the station. No birthday telegrams will find you here, and you can be completely at ease, free from the fetters and etiquette associated with the ruling classes.

Dear Lev Nikolaevich, we don't have holidays here. Our work and daily tasks afford us no time for quiet breaks. Your presence would mean a holiday for us, since for you we would put aside all our cares and rest like the Hebrew God on the seventh day from all our tasks.

If my request, however, is out of place, I would very kindly ask you not to take offence at it.

Your friendly peasant,
Mikhail Novikov

Laptevo Station, Village of Borovkovo.

27. L. N. TOLSTOY ❧ M. P. NOVIKOV
17–20 August 1908. Yasnaya Polyana.

Yasnaya Polyana, 17 August 1908.

Your request,[103] dear Mikhail Petrovich, could be pleasing to me, if only one could foresee some possibility of it being fulfilled. But I think that, in writing the letter, you knew in advance that this desire of yours and mine will not be carried out. The main topic of my letter to you is the mood which permeates your whole letter and the feeling which weighs heavily upon me. Believe me, not for my sake, but for yours.

I remember that dear, tall and handsome soldier who came to see me in my little room upstairs in a Moscow house — he impressed me with his deep

103 In Novikov's letter of 11 August 1908 (Letter Nº 26).

and sincere questions.[104] At that time you were concerned about questions of your soul and, consequently, questions of humanity as a whole. I am not only afraid, but I see from your letters, that this is not the case now. The main feeling now that permeates almost every word of your letter is a feeling — forgive me — of envy, and the hatred for the wealthier classes that arises from it.

You say, for example that my thoughts — not mine, but eternal, divine thoughts, which are possibly passing through me — cannot have any effect on people of the wealthier class, as though assuming that they are all deprived of that most elemental of human traits — self-perfection. It is hardly possible to find in this corrupted (from my point of view, as you well know) milieu even a single person who would react that way to any whole class of people without allowing any good at all in it — that is, what you are doing in respect to people of the wealthier classes.

As an old man to a younger one, and as one who loves to his beloved friend, I say to you: look about you and think about this, dear Mikhail Petrovich. If the condition of the soul of one who hates even a single brother is terrible, what must be the condition of the soul of one who hates a whole class of people? I shall tell you frankly.

Say I had to choose between two positions. The first would be the one I am now in, i.e., life in corruptive and illegal luxury, even though I have been condemning it, as I still do (something many quite naturally do not believe), or even the life of one who lives in this corrupt and corrupting milieu of the wealthy, who at each step of his life benefits from the labours of abused and oppressed people — and not recognizing this but cheerfully having a good time in conditions to which he is accustomed. The second would be the life of the most hard-working person, eating the bread of his own labours and not only not exploiting the labours of others but sharing his own with others, yet along with this filled with envy and hatred aroused in him by frequent contact with his oppressors. I wouldn't for a moment think of choosing the first.

It is better to be exploited than an exploiter, but this is good when it is done in the name of submission to God's will and love for others. But when it is done apart from submission to God's will, in the name of hatred toward others, restrained only by the impossibility of acting on it, then the situation of the exploited is a thousand times worse. The whole crux of the matter lies not in external conditions, but in one's mental attitude to any type of condition. Most precious of all is an attitude of love *to everyone, to everyone*. This is a state that arises out of love for God. This is exactly what I wish for you.

I know that you with your great intelligence and passionate heart are in a position to understand me, and therefore I have resolved to write this to you. I hope that you will forgive me if I have put anything I have said not softly or

104 Tolstoy first met with Novikov in the winter of 1894 in his Khamovniki Lane house, in Moscow (see Gladkova 1994a: 164–65).

kindly enough. In any case I have been guided only by a feeling of love for you, to whom I remain

a brother who loves you,

Lev Tolstoy

20 August 1908

28. M. P. NOVIKOV ❧ L. N. TOLSTOY
24 October 1908.

24 October 1908, Village of Borovkovo

Dear Lev Nikolaevich, in August I received your reply to my request for you to visit my family, prompted by rumours that you intended to go off somewhere on your birthday in this Jubilee year.[105]

I am accustomed to seeing in you, Lev Nikolaevich, a perfect individual free from any prejudices, superstitions, customs and earthly affinities, and so I was somewhat taken aback and dumbfounded at the place in your letter where you state without any explanation that there is absolutely no possibility of realizing my (and your) desire to visit me and my family. But I am simply mentioning that in passing. The main thing is, I want to justify myself to you, to tell you first-hand about myself, as it is painful and bitter to realize that you have evidently changed your previous good opinion of me without knowing my inner life and its governing principles. I did a lot of thinking while reading over your fine letter, and could not restrain my inner desire to write to you — to justify myself in your eyes.

For two months now it has weighed upon my mind that you are 80 years old and can at any moment leave us for some other life completely unknown to us, taking with you a heavy feeling about me. But it is difficult (as you so well put it) for me, as someone who loves you, to burden you with this feeling in your final days. You can well remember the first time I came to see you in Moscow 14 years ago, but you become annoyed when you compare your loving friend of then and now. You said that back then I was concerned with general questions of humanity, questions of the soul, but that now my soul is full of only envy and hatred for wealthy people.

Dear Lev Nikolaevich, you were mistaken in this. A lot of water has flowed under the bridge during this time, a lot has changed in my views on life, but all this time I have taken no turn for the worse, even though I could have. True, at that time my yearning to understand God as the source of life and light was greater [than it is now], and my soul was more desirous of good, expecting

105 The date of 28 August 1908 would mark Tolstoy's eightieth birthday. While he did everything he could to avoid public attention, Tolstoy remained at Yasnaya Polyana on that day and did his best to keep the adulation to a minimum.

that life ought to be only good, but it hasn't left me; in fact it has remained more solid, more conscious, though it has met with huge obstacles [raised by elements] that are not good in life, which I was ill-informed about back then. As if to say: the heaven of my life back then was very narrow, and I knew but little of good and evil.

Like a poet, I believed that people, including me, suffered only because they saw little of this heaven above them, and they needed only to climb further out of the shell of their everyday life for this heaven to expand, clear up, and for the sunlight of truth to shine brighter and more cheerily. With blurred and indistinct [vision] — only by feel — my guess at the time was that in order to see more of this heaven and the truth of life, one had to be completely free, and all this time I have been striving to be free. I believed that by being free and believing only in good, there was a lot I would be able to do. But as my awareness of the world around me, as well as of myself, expanded, earthly life became more and more oppressive to me, protesting against the abstract yearnings of the spirit. My first priority was to feed myself, and while it was difficult for me as an individual to satisfy all my physical needs from the uneven distribution of the world's goods, it was even more difficult in the caste of the exploited class, where one plough was expected to feed not [just] seven, but [as many as] fourteen mouths. But I took it all stoically and did not make a slave of myself; I did not seek, as did others around me, "positions" with a salary and easy food; all my life I had not depended on satisfaction for success in my pursuit of bread; on the contrary, I cared little for this aspect of life, aiming all my strength at the achievement of greater freedom and the greatest possible heaven, studying to this end human wisdom and knowledge.

Back then I was a youth, taking in everything new simply on faith, and several people confidently told me that I was infatuated with one [thing] just because, in view of my low social status, I didn't know much of anything else.

During this time I studied just about all ideas which had ever had an impact on human life. I studied anarchism, social Utopias, religions of the ancient and modern world, ideas of the latest social reformers and revolutionaries and, in general, everything that had, in its time, ignited the human brain, and, all that said, I never betrayed the foundations of life that I had adopted once and forever, never gave into the tempting of the Devil, in spite of the terrible allurements of power and riches. In the face of critical reason, the study of these Utopias and ideas, which tie salvation and the achievement of happiness in life to the active struggle and external crises and shufflings, showed me their utter unsustainability and only confirmed my previous thought that there is no other life except a life in God's freedom and truth, and no salvation [can be expected] from anywhere apart from this life; in power, riches and glory, [even] more sorrow and unforeseen disasters will all, sooner or later, come crashing down on one's head.

The difference between my previous and current [self] is only that I now no longer have my former faith in the possibility of any quick transformation of either others or myself, as I then believed and as is still believed by all active reformers who have written on their banners the motto "In struggle you shall find your justification."

The difference is that back at that time, like everybody in my [social] circle, I tended towards mysticism from a very young age. I believed in the miraculous and worshipped the authority of Christ, Buddha and Moses as some kind of real messengers of an objectively existing God, and in the previous religious history of mankind I sought something revealed from the mysterious — I sought a miracle. It seemed back then that I would soon achieve something special, that I would ascend to the seventh heaven or move mountains. Now, however, having been made free, I see that all religious teachings — from the lowest (naturalistic) to the highest (philosophical) — are simply products of human thought — either one purer and free, or mystically superstitious, and that the salvation I had sought was not to be and could not be [found] in any one of them. The most important thing is that people be completely free in their choice and confession of *any* of these religions. In other words, back then I believed that religions came from a supreme, external God, while now I know that they come from people, and so there is absolutely no obligation for anyone to choose one over another.

Having been made completely free, at the same time I became very practical, and have been measuring every religious philosophy by experience, and only experience in life has shown me that there is no other, better, life than as [is posited by] Christian philosophy. There is no better guidance for one's actions than the guidance of the Gospels, and not because they, [as some people believe] are derived from Christ, [who is] God, but because, as it has turned out, there is nothing else in this earthly life to do but to try and live according to truth, and because those who live apart from it obtain from life less joy and satisfaction and more of all kinds of fear and suffering. This consciousness and recognition can no longer be taken from me, since it has been attained not by [my] former faith in God but by [my] long experience of life. Now I can say that the best in Christian teachings, by comparison with other "faiths," is that it has shown people the Kingdom of God as being not somewhere in another world, as the priests of the whole world teach, but within man, and that this Kingdom lies not within the power of some external God, but only in our own will and our own actions. So, as you see, my outward religious fervour has gone from me all on its own, without harm, replaced by the experience of life, and my yearning for heaven [has given place to] a yearning for learning about the Earth and earthly matters.

Think about it, dear Lev Nikolaevich: if I am destined to die before you, I would die peacefully, knowing that you remained on the Earth, as one who is capable of being a luminary of life; if the reverse is in store, then you will carry peace and tranquility with you, knowing that at least a drop of Christian light remains in your loving friend.

If I sometimes cannot speak without a shadow of disapproval of people who have been occupying Moses' seat and are devouring the homes not only of widows and orphans but of one-tenth of all mankind and carrying filthiness and falsehood through their own lives into the overall life of the Earth, then how is it, Lev Nikolaevich, that you cannot understand that their filthiness and falsehood are disastrous to the lives of the people of our circle, and they themselves — well-fed, clean and educated — are more frightful [for us] than any fear and more burdensome [for us] than any mountain? Dear Lev Nikolaevich, you spoke rightly of them, you illustrated in pictures their shallowness and shamelessness, but you yourself have never experienced that terrible deprivation which we bear from the heaviness and oppression imposed in many millions [of cases] on our poor and destitute *muzhik* life. If you had experienced this oppression yourself, you would not have condemned me for my [seemingly] unloving attitude [toward them] as expressed in [my] words. Yes, in the words: "Woe unto you, scribes and Pharisees, devouring the houses of widows and orphans"[106] one does not hear of any loving relationship to them, nor in the words: "Go from me to the Devil, the father of your lies and shamelessness."[107] Remember just for a moment the millions and millions of people in our circle who live their lives without the light of their own understanding of [the real] life, as though [they were simply] a support for the luxurious and corrupt life of this powerful and self-satisfied circle of the well-fed chosen ones, and you will understand my attitude to them, understand that there really are people who charge rent even when the land is unfruitful, and then, as a rule, they take money for other people's labour on "their" land, and exploit this labour without any twinge of conscience; these are human beasts, equipped with machine guns and Cossack whips instead of long claws and teeth, and that it is impossible for some *muzhik* to envy them, since he will never agree to take their position of idleness, no matter what the benefits are.

To love one's enemies means to do them no wrong, to not render them evil for evil, and certainly not to give them one's mother as a wet-nurse, or one's wife as a cleaning-lady, or one's labour for the purpose of maintaining their idle luxury and outward lustre, so I can by no means imagine how one could be exploited in the name of God. Having compassion on a brother — [one] accustomed to living as a "*barin*" and ignorant as to how to feed, wash and clothe himself, to fetch water and bake bread — I shall be glad to teach him this; I shall gladly spend time and effort instructing him how to help himself. On the other hand, if he does not desire this, but instead desires to exploit

106 See Matth. 23:14.
107 Cf. John 8:44.

others' labour through land he has seized from the needy — through clipping bond coupons or through "clever" jobs for educated people, there's no way I can support that kind of life — there's nothing I can do here except to condemn such a life both to his face and behind his back and expose it for what it really is. But to willingly support it would be tantamount to offering my body as fodder for lice, as the liberal students in Bulygin's[108] colony did, which his wife told me about. However, I don't think life is about people devouring each other or about us being devoured by lice, but about everyone getting along with each other and, recognizing our brotherhood and the helplessness of any individual acting on his own, about not harming one another and obtaining from Nature what we need to feed ourselves.

Precious Lev Nikolaevich, I understand you very well and love [the fact] that you do not look at people's outward appearance, and that you tell everyone just what you are thinking. This is why I am sure that you understand me, too, and that you do not condemn me.

Lovingly yours, Mikhail Novikov

I hope to see you soon and ask for a small favour in respect to my children.

M. N.

Laptevo Station, Village of Borovkovo.

29. M. P. NOVIKOV ❧ L. N. TOLSTOY
10 April 1909.

10 April 1909

Dear Lev Nikolaevich,

I am sending you for your appraisal the same manuscript I read to you on the 10th of March. Now it has been transcribed and reads easily. Please read it through when you have the time. If it isn't suitable for the Petersburg paper you were telling me about, or anywhere else, then please send it in your name to Bonch-Bruevich;[109] if you request, he will probably not refuse to print it in [the collection] he publishes: *Materialy k istorii i izucheniiu russkago sektanstva i raskola* [Materials on the history and study of Russian sectarianism and the schism].

108 *Mikhail Vasil'evich Bulygin* (1863–1943) — former officer of the Guard, owner of the Khatunka farmstead near Yasnaya Polyana, a Tolstoyan. His wife was *Anna Maksimovna Bulygina* (*née* Ignat'eva; 1862–1909).

109 *Vladimir Dmitrievich Bonch-Bruevich* (1873–1955) — Russian revolutionary, who later served in the Bolshevik government as a personal confidant to Lenin. In 1899 he and his fiancée, *Vera Mikhajlovna Velichkina* (1868–1918), a medical doctor, accompanied the fourth and final boatload of Doukhobors to Canada (see Woodsworth 1999a: 171–92).

Even if just half of what I wrote were printed, I'd be happy [to know] that my work was not in vain. Please do what you can.

Lovingly yours,
Mikhail Novikov

30. L. N. TOLSTOY ❧ M. P. NOVIKOV
8 June 1910.

8 June 1910

I was happy to hear from you. None of us are living the way our conscience tells us we should. All of us have chosen a middle road according to the measure of our spiritual strengths and human weaknesses, more or less along the lines of what we consider to be the truest [path]. But for me to know what the true path is, I have to know in what I am departing from it, and not justify myself, as you seem to be doing in your letter.[110]

Land-tilling is one of the best occupations and is good for the soul. In abandoning it, you would not be acting out of reason, but out of weakness. That's something you should be aware of.

I live a bad life, in wealth, though I [myself] don't own anything, but [I live] with those who live in wealth. Spiritually, thank God, I am making progress. I'm not afraid of death, and I have no regrets.

I sincerely wish you all the best — that is, spiritual perfection. I am sending you [my] books *Wise Thoughts for Every Day* [*Na kazhdyj den'*]. Read them and remember me.

Lev Tolstoy

31. L. N. TOLSTOY ❧ M. P. NOVIKOV
24 October 1910. Yasnaya Polyana.

24 October 1910. Yasnaya Polyana.

Mikhail Petrovich,

In connection with what I was saying to you before you left,[111] I am turning to you once more with the following request: if it should actually come about that I went to you, couldn't you find me, somewhere in your village, even the

110 The whereabouts of this letter are unknown.

111 Tolstoy had had a secret conversation with Novikov several days before the great writer's sudden departure from Yasnaya Polyana. Tolstoy complained about his difficult situation with his family, he spoke of his intention to leave and asked about the possibility of staying with Novikov for a period of time. In his diary of 20 October 1910, Tolstoy notes: "Mikhail Novikov came. Talked a lot with him. A seriously intelligent person" (*PSS* 38:121); on 21 October: "I spent the night thinking about leaving" (ibid., 142); and on 23 October: "I can't stop thinking about Novikov" (ibid., 267).

tiniest hut, as long as it's detached and it's warm, so that I would be imposing on you and your family only for the slightest period of time. Also, if I need to telegraph you, I'll wire you not in my name but in the name of T. Nikolaev.

I shall await your reply, and I extend my hand in friendship.

Lev Tolstoy

Bear in mind that all this must remain known to you alone.

L. T.

32. M. P. NOVIKOV ❧ L. N. TOLSTOY
29 October 1910. Borovkovo.

29 October 1910[112]

Dear Lev Nikolaevich, I received your letter and I am very touched by your closeness to me and your sincerity toward me. I wasn't able to answer right away, as I didn't want to act hastily. I have always been open with you and said what is in my heart, and now I have decided just to tell you what is in my heart regarding the request expressed in your letter, without the thought of pleasing or not pleasing you.

The time when you were supposed to be the one changing the outward conditions of your life (both for the benefit of the cause and by virtue of the consciousness which awakened in you) has passed, and now there is no sense in trying to effect long-term changes. Your life is in decline (in the temporal sense), but it is precious to me and all who are related to you in spirit, and we all want only one thing: that it continue as long as possible. This is possible only in the conditions to which you have been accustomed, in which you have lived your eighty-three [*sic*] years.[113]

No matter how much I desire to see you set at liberty with all the simple people, for the sake of maintaining your life in such an old body — for the contact with you that is so dear to everyone — I cannot wish that seriously. I only want the remainder of your life here not to be constrained by any external conditions for contact with those who love you.

For such time as required for you to visit your friends for a day, a week or two, a month, my hut is very comfortable. It has a bright little room which my whole family will let you use with pleasure, and they will be lovingly at your service, especially since I do not have any very young children who could be noisy at an inopportune moment. The youngest is 5 years old.

112 In the Jubilee Edition (*PSS* 82:211) the date is mistakenly given as 1914. This letter was read to Tolstoy by Vladimir Chertkov, at Astapovo, four days before the writer's death (3 November 1910 by the old-style calendar, or 16 November new style). Tolstoy's departure took place the night of 27 October 1910 (old style).

113 Tolstoy died at age eighty-two.

This is what I think, but if you think otherwise, let it be as you wish, not as I wish, and my little room will then be at your disposal for as long as you want. We are not afraid of your imposing on us, but the other way round. But on this point we shall have constant peace and agreement.

Lovingly,
Mikhail Novikov, peasant

I don't think it is possible for you to live in a separate hut because you are weak. Indeed, peasants really don't have completely detached huts. As a rule we have secondary cold huts, which could be easily adapted for habitation after some renovation, but they would not be separate, but connected by a *seni* [covered passageway]. My neighbour has such a hut of 6 arshins, which he would not refuse to let you use as an apartment. Or else, my ageing aunt next spring will be building for herself the same kind of 6-arshin hut — she is all alone and a very intelligent older woman — she will also be glad to offer you shelter and be at your service.

I went alone to see Konshin[114] in Serpukhov, but he couldn't do anything for my children. At his factory they are in the process of cutting back working hours so that the workers will not be laid off. And when will this unemployment end, this antagonism between the poor and the rich?

My deepest respects to you and to Dushan Petrovich.[115]

Mikhail Novikov

29 October 1910

114 *Aleksandr Nikolaevich Konshin* (1867–1919) — the son of a well-known manufacturer in Serpukhov who had known Tolstoy since 1898 and had offered financial support to the Posrednik publishing house. In 1899 he accompanied the Doukhobors to Canada.
115 *Dushan Petrovich Makovitskij* (1866–1921) — Tolstoy's personal physician.

BIBLIOGRAPHY

Alexeeva (Alekseeva), Galina. 1995. "Literature on the Doukhobors contained in Lev N. Tolstoy's private library in the village of Yasnaya Polyana." *Canadian Ethnic Studies* 27, N° 3: 234–44.

—. 2000. "James Mavor and the Doukhobors." In Donskov, Woodsworth and Gaffield, 149–57.

Alston, Charlotte. 2014a. "A great host of sympathisers: the Doukhobor emigration and its international supporters 1895–1905." *Journal of Modern European History* 12, N° 2 (April 2014): 200–15.

—. 2014b. *Tolstoy and His Disciples. The History of a Radical International Movement.* London: I. B. Tauris & Co.

Avakumovic, Ivan. 1978. "Tolstoy and the Doukhobors." Paper delivered at the Tolstoy Symposium, University of Victoria.

Bank, B. V. 1969. *Izuchenie chitatelej v Rossii (XIX v.).* Moskva. See esp. 132–36.

Bashkirov, V. 1997. "On vstrechalsja s Tolstym." *Bogorodskaja gazeta* (19 June): 3–4.

Bazanov, V. 1973. "Vokrug narodnykh rasskazov L. N. Tolstogo." *Ot fol'klora k narodnoj knige.* Leningrad: Khudozhestvennaja literatura, 297–321.

Bellows, Amanda. 2014. *Serfs and Slaves in the Post-Emancipation Imagination 1861-1915.* Washington, DC: American Councils for International Education.

Belokonskij, I. P. 1905. "Timofej Mikhajlovich Bondarev." In *Na sibirskie temy.* Skt-Peterburg.

Belousov, I. A. 1926. *Literaturnaja Moskva: pisateli iz naroda.* Moskva. See esp. 3–88.

Billington, James. 1966. *The Icon and the Axe: An Interpretive History of Russian Culture.* New York: Knopf. See esp. 174–80.

Blaisdell, Bob. 2000. "Introduction." In *Tolstoy as Teacher: Leo Tolstoy's Writings on Education*, ed. Bob Blaisdell. New York: Teachers & Writers Collaborative.

Bljum, A. V. 1979. "«Posrednik» i ego chitateli." In *Istorija russkogo chitatelja*, kn. 3, 58–72. Moskva.

Bodjanskij, A. M. 1907. *Dukhobortsy. Sbornik rasskazov, pisem, dokumentov i statej po religioznym voprosam.* Khar'kov.

Bolshakoff, Serge. 1950. *Russian Nonconformity.* Philadelphia: Westminster Press.

Bol'shakov L. N. 1978. *Vash drug Lev Tolstoj.* Cheljabinsk: Juzhno-Ural'skoe knizhnoe izdatel'stvo.

Bonch-Bruevich, V. D., ed. 1900. *Spisok psalmov, pisem, razskazov i drugikh rukopisej po issledovaniju uchenija, zhizni i pereselenija v Kanadu zakavkazskikh dukhobortsev, s prilozheniem bibliograficheskago ukazatelja literatury po dukhoborcheskomu voprosu.* Geneva: Ukrainskaja tipografija.

—, ed. 1901. *Pis'ma dukhoborcheskogo rukovoditelja Petra Vasil'evicha Verigina.* Series: Materialy k istorii i izucheniju russkogo sektantstva 1. Christchurch, UK: Svobodnoe Slovo.

—. 1908. *Baptisty, Beguny, Dukhobortsy, L. Tolstoy o skopchestve, Pavlovtsy, Pomortsy, Staroobrjadtsy, Skoptsy, Shtundisty.* Skt-Peterburg.

—. 1922. "Sektantstvo v osvoboditel'nuju èpokhu." *Iz mira sektantov*, 24–35. Moskva: Gos. izdatel'stvo.

—, comp. 1978. *Zhivotnaja kniga dukhobortsev.* Skt-Peterburg, 1909. 2nd ed. Reprint, Winnipeg: Union of Doukhobors of Canada, 1954. Also published in English translation: *Book of life of the Doukhobors.* Saskatoon and Blaine Lake: Doukhobor Societies of Saskatchewan, 1978.

Bondarenko, T. P. 1992. "Russkie pisateli 1800–1917." *Biograficheskij slovar'*. Vol. 2. Moskva: Bol'shaja Rossijskaja Èntsiklopedija. See esp. 263–64.

Bondarev, Timofej (Bondareff, Timothé) and L. N. Tolstoj (Tolstoï). 1890. *Léon Tolstoï et Timothé Bondareff. Le travail.* Traduit du russe par V. Tseytline et A. Pagès. Paris, 1890. English translation (from French): *The suppressed book of the peasant Bondareff. Labour: The divine command. Made known, augmented and edited by Count Lyof Tolstoy.* Trans. Mary Cruger. Toronto, 1890. Excerpts published in *Russkoe delo,* vol. 12–13 (1888).

Bondarev, Timofej. 1906. *Torzhestvo zemledel'tsa, ili trudoljubie i tunejadstvo.* Moskva: Posrednik.

Brock, Peter. 1972. *Pacifism in Europe to 1914.* Princeton, NJ: Princeton University Press. See esp. 442–70.

Bulgakov, V. F. 1922. "Opomnites' ljudi-brat'ja!" *Istorija vozzvanija edinomyshlennikov L. N. Tolstogo protiv mirovoj vojny 1914–18 gg.*, t. 1. Moskva: Zadruga.

—. 2012. *Kak prozhita zhizn': vospominanija poslednego sekretarja L. N. Tolstogo.* Moskva: Kuchkovo pole.

—. 2014. *V spore s Tolstym.* Moskva: Kuchkovo pole.

Bumgardner, April. 2001. "The Doukhobors: History, ideology and the Tolstoy-Verigin relationship." Master's thesis., University of Glasgow.

Butkievich, T. B. and V. M. Skvortsov. 1897. "Tolstovstvo kak sekta." *Missionerskoe Obozrenie*, t. 2, kn. 1, 807–43.

Buyniak, V. O. 1969. "Aylmer Maude on the practical application of the non-resistance doctrine and its implication in establishment of Tolstoyan and Doukhobor colonies." *Canadian Ethnic Studies* 1, N° 2: 87–94.

—. 1978. "Tolstoy and the Doukhobors." *Chelsea Journal* [Saskatoon] 4, N° 3: 151–55.

Camfield, G. P. 1990. "The Pavlovtsy of Khar'kov Province, 1886–1905: Harmless sectarians or dangerous rebels?" *Slavonic & East European Review* 68, N° 4 (1990): 692–717.

Chertkov, V. G. (1897) 1899. *Christian Martyrdom in Russia: Persecution of the Spirit--Wrestlers (or Doukhobortsi) in the Caucasus.* Concluding chapter and letter by L. N. Tolstoy. London: Brotherhood Publishing Co. Reprint, Toronto: G. N. Morang.

—. 1900. *Christian Martyrdom in Russia: Persecution of the Doukhobors.* 2nd ed. Concluding chapter and letter by L. N. Tolstoy; account of the emigration to Cyprus and Canada. London: Free Age Press.

—. 1911. *O poslednikh dnjakh L. N. Tolstogo.* Moskva: Izd. Sytina.

Conovaloff, Andrei. n.d. http://www.molokane.org.

Donskov, Andrew. 1972. *The Changing Image of the Peasant in Nineteenth Century Russian Drama.* Helsinki: Annales Academiæ Scientiarum Fennicæ.

—. 1979. "The peasant in Tolstoy's thought and writings." *Canadian Slavonic Papers* 21, N° 2: 183–96.

—. 1983. "L. N. Tolstoi as an editor of literature by peasant writers." In *Crisis and Commitment: Studies in German and Russian Literature in Honour of J. W. Dyck*, ed. John Whiton, 41–47. Waterloo, ON: University of Waterloo Press.

—. 1988. *Essays on L. N. Tolstoj's Dramatic Art.* Wiesbaden, Germany: Otto Harrassowitz, 1988.

—, ed. 1995a. *L. N. Tolstoj—P. V. Verigin: perepiska.* Skt-Peterburg: Izd. «Dmitrij Bulanin», 1995. Also published together with English translation by John Woodsworth: *Leo Tolstoy—Peter Verigin: Correspondence.* Ottawa: Legas.

—. 1995b. "On the censorship of Tolstoy's early 'Stories for the people': An unpublished *Doklad tsenzora P. E. Astaf'eva.*" *Russian Language Journal* 49, N° 162–64: 223–39.

—. 1995c. "On the Doukhobors: from imperial Russian archival files." *Canadian Ethnic Studies* 27, N° 3: 252–61.

—, ed. 1996a. *L. N. Tolstoj i M. P. Novikov: perepiska.* Munich: Verlag Otto Sagner. See esp. 1–26.

—, ed. 1996b. *L. N. Tolstoj i T. M. Bondarev: perepiska.* Munich: Verlag Otto Sagner. See esp. 1–15.

—. 1996c. "The life of Peter the Publican as edited by L. N. Tolstoy." *Russian Language Journal,* N° 165–167: 241–62.

—. 1996d. "«Zhitie Petra Mytarja» v obrabotke L. N. Tolstogo." *Russkaja rech',* N° 4: 6–9.

—. 1996e. "Sozhzhenie ognestrel'nogo oruzhija (1895 g.) i ego posledstvija." *Novyj zhurnal,* N° 197: 272–87.

—. 1997. "Pis'ma Bondareva k L. N. Tolstomu." *Russkaja literatura,* N° 1 (1997): 163–81.

—, ed. 1998a. *Sergej Tolstoy and the Doukhobors: A journey to Canada.* Comp. Tat'jana Nikiforova. With English translation by John Woodsworth. Ottawa: Slavic Research Group at the University of Ottawa and Moscow: L.N. Tolstoy State Museum.

—. 1998b. "Tolstoj, Tolstoyans and the Doukhobors. From imperial Russian archival files." *Russian Literature* 43:431–44.

—, ed. 2001. *L. N. Tolstoj i F. A. Zheltov: perepiska.* Comp. L. Gladkova. Ottawa: Slavic Research Group at the University of Ottawa, and Moscow: Gos. Muzej L. N. Tolstogo, 1999. English edition (trans. John Woodsworth, ed. Ethel Dunn), published under the title: *A Molokan's Search For Truth: The Correspondence of Leo Tolstoy and Fedor Zheltov.* Berkeley, California: Highgate Road Social Sciences Research Station and Ottawa: Slavic Research Group at the University of Ottawa.

—. 2004. "Leo Tolstoy and Mikhail Novikov: Selected letters." *Tolstoy Studies Journal* 16:55–76.

—. 2005. *Leo Tolstoy and the Canadian Doukhobors.* Ottawa: Carleton University, Centre for Research on Canadian-Russian Relations.

—. 2008. "Peter V. Verigin." In *Dictionary of Canadian Biography.* Vol. 15. Toronto: University of Toronto Press.

—, ed. 2010. *Sofia Andreevna Tolstaya: My Life.* Trans. John Woodsworth and Arkadi Klioutchanski. Ottawa: University of Ottawa Press.

—, ed. 2017. *Tolstoy and Tolstaya: A Portrait of a Life in Letters.* Trans. John Woodsworth, Arkadi Klioutchanski and Liudmila Gladkova. Ottawa: University of Ottawa Press.

Donskov, Andrew, Galina Galagan and Lidija Gromova. 2002. *Edinenie ljudej v tvorchestve L. N. Tolstogo / The Unity of People in Leo Tolstoy's Works.* Ottawa: Slavic Research Group at the University of Ottawa, St. Petersburg: Institut russkoj literatury, and Moscow: Institut mirovoj literatury.

Donskov, Andrew and John Woodsworth, eds. 1996. *Lev Tolstoy and the Concept of Brotherhood.* Proceedings of a conference held at the University of Ottawa, 22–24 February 1996. Ottawa: Legas.

Donskov Andrew, John Woodsworth and Chad Gaffield, eds. 2000. *The Doukhobor Centenary in Canada: A Multi-Disciplinary Perspective on their Unity and Diversity.* Proceedings of a conference held at the University of Ottawa, 22–24 October 1999. Ottawa: Slavic Research Group and the Institute of Canadian Studies at the University of Ottawa, 2000.

Dunn, Ethel. 1967. "Russian sectarianism in new Marxist scholarship." *Slavic Review* 26, N° 1 (March): 128–40.

—. 1976. "American Molokans and Canadian Doukhobors: Economic position and ethnic identity." In *Ethnicity in the Americas*, ed. Frances Henry, 97–114. The Hague: Mouton.

—. 1995. "Spiritual and Economic Renewal among Molokans and Doukhobors." *Canadian Ethnic Studies* 27, N° 3: 164–80.

—. 2001. *A Molokan's Search for Truth: the Correspondence of Leo Tolstoy and Fedor Zheltov.* See Donskov 2001.

Dunn, Stephen P. and Ethel Dunn. 1964. "Religion as an instrument of culture change. The problem of sects in the Soviet Union." *Slavic Review* 23, N° 3: 459–78.

Edwards, Maxim. 2014. "Jewish? No, we're subbotniks." *Jewish Daily Forward*, 13 July.

Ewashen, Larry A. 1996a. "Lev Tolstoy and the Doukhobors." *Iskra* N° 1817: 29–32.

—. 1996b. "Tolstoy and the Doukhobors today." In Donskov and Woodsworth, 225–28.

—. 2001. "The Doukhobor immigration—Leo Tolstoy's project." *Iskra*, N° 1903: 7–10.

—. n.d. http://www.larrysdesk.com.

Fanger, Donald. 1968. "The Peasant in Literature." In *The Peasant in Nineteenth-Century Russia*, ed. Wayne S. Vucinich, 231–62. Stanford, CA: Stanford University Press.

Fersen, Nikolaj. 1979. "Tolstoj i shèkery." *Transactions of the Association of Russian-American Scholars in the USA* 12:162–72.

Fodor, A. 1989. *A Quest for a Non-Violent Russia: The Partnership of Leo Tolstoy and Vladimir Chertkov.* Lanham, MD: University Press of America.

Frantz, Charles E. 1961. "Historical continuities in an immigrant Russian sect: Doukhobor ideology and political organization." *Canadian Slavonic Papers* 5:31–53.

Frierson, Cathy A. 1993. *Peasant Icons: Representation of Rural People in Late Nineteenth-Century Russia.* New York: Oxford University Press.

Galagan, G. Ja. 1981. *Khudozhestvenno-èticheskie iskanija.* Leningrad: Nauka.

Gladkova, L. V. 1994a. "M. P. Novikov: Ja vinovat v ego smerti." *Oktjabr'* 9:155–90.

—. 1994b. "M. P. Novikov. Ukhod L. N. Tolstogo. Stolypinskaja reforma. Pis'mo k I. V. Stalinu." In: *Neizvestnyj Tolstoj. V arkhivakh Rossii i SShA*, ed. I. Borisova, 318–47. Moskva: Tekhna-2.

—. 1994c. "Pis'ma L. N. Tolstogo v kopiroval'nykh knigakh." In *Neizvestnyj Tolstoj. V arkhivakh Rossii i SShA*, ed. I. Borisova, 153–63. Moskva: Tekhna-2.

—. 2000. "Ob istinnom iskusstve (po perepiske L. N. Tolstogo s pisatelem-krest'janinom F. F. Tishchenko)." *Oktjabr'* 9:173–77.

—. 2004. *Mikhail Novikov. Iz perezhitogo.* Moskva: Èntsiklopedija sël i dereven'.

Golitsyn G. S. 1897. "O sovremennom polozhenii Zakavazskogo dukhoborchestva i o prinjatykh Glavnym Nachal'stvom merakh presechenija vrednogo protivo-pravitel'stvennogo dvizhenija sredi posledovatelej ètoj sekty." 13 July. GARF: Delo 1043, L. 513–61. Document #1897-07-13b in Woodsworth 1997. Excerpts published in Donskov 1998b.

Greenwood, John. 1975. *Quaker Encounters: Friends and Relief.* Vol. 1. York, UK: William Sessions Ltd. See esp. 95–148.

Gromova-Opul'skaja (Gromova), L. D. 1995. "Dialog uchitelej zhizni." In *L. N. Tolstoj—P. V. Verigin: perepiska*, ed. Andrew Donskov, 1–10. Skt-Peterburg: Izd. «Dmitrij Bulanin». Also published together with an English translation by John Woodsworth: "Two Teachers of Life: A Dialogue." In *Leo Tolstoy—Peter Verigin: Correspondence*, ed. Andrew Donskov, 1–7. Ottawa: Legas.

—. 1998. *Lev Nikolaevich Tolstoj. Materialy k biografii s 1892 po 1899 god.* Moskva: Rossijskaja Akademija Nauk.

—. 2000. "The idea of 'universal brotherhood' and unity: Lev Tolstoy and Pëtr Verigin." In Donskov, Woodsworth and Gaffield, 158–70.

Gusev, N. N. 1960. *Letopis' zhizni i tvorchestva L. N. Tolstogo.* Moskva.

—. 1970. *Lev Nikolaevich Tolstoj. Materialy 1881–1885 gg.* Moskva: Nauka. See esp. 428–50.

—. 1973. *Dva goda s L. N. Tolstym.* Moskva.

Haugh, Richard S. 1978. "The correspondence between Count Lev Tolstoy and the American Shakers: Introduction and texts." *Transactions of the Association of Russian-American Scholars in the USA* 11:231–40.

Heier, Edmund. 1962. "A note on the Pashkovites and L. N. Tolstoy." *Canadian Slavonic Papers* 5, N° 3: 114–21.

—. 1970. *Religious Schism in the Russian Aristocracy 1860–1900. Radstockism and Pashkovism.* The Hague: Nijhoff.

—. 1971. "Tolstoj and the evangelical revival among Russian aristocracy." *Russian Literature* 1: 28–48.

Holman, Michael J. de K. 1978. "The Purleigh colony: Tolstoyan togetherness in the late 1890s." In *New essays on Tolstoy*, ed. Malcolm Jones, 194–222. Cambridge: Cambridge University Press.

—. 1988. "Translating Tolstoy for the Free Age Press: Vladimir Chertkov and his English manager Arthur Fifield." *Slavonic & East European Review* 66, N° 2: 184–97.

—. 2000. "British Tolstoyans, 'The New Order' and the Doukhobors in the late 1890s: Solidarity in word and deed." In Donskov, Woodsworth and Gaffield, 131–48.

Inikova, Svetlana. 1998. "Problemy ètnokonfessional'nykh grupp dukhobortsev i molokan." In *Faktor ètnokonfessional'noj samobytnosti v post-sovetskom obshchestve*, 99–103. Moskva: Carnegie Center.

—. 2000a. "Rol' «tolstovstva» i tolstovtsev v dvizhenii kavkazskikh dukhobortsev 1890-kh godov." *XXVI Mezhdunarodnye tolstovskie chtenija.* Part 2, 50–63. Tula, Russia.

—. 2000b. "Spiritual origins and the beginnings of Doukhobor history." In Donskov, Woodsworth and Gaffield, 1–21.

—. 2002. "Uchenie L. N. Tolstogo i syny svobody v Kanade." *Religiovedenie*, N° 3.

Institut russkoj literatury (Skt-Peterburg) n.d. G. I. Uspenskij archive, F. 313, op. 3, N° 35.

Institut russkoj literatury (Skt-Peterburg) n.d. S. A. Vengerov archive, F. 377, op. 7, N° 1469.

Ishchuk, G. N. 1958. "L. N. Tolstoj i nachalo «Posrednika»." *Uchenye zapiski Marijskogo ped. instituta*, t. 21, 122–56.

—. 1975. *Problema chitatelja v tvorcheskom soznanii L. N. Tolstogo.* Kalinin. See esp. 70–118.

Iskra. 1943–. Journal of the Union of Spiritual Communities of Christ (Brilliant and Grand Forks, BC).

Ivanov, A. 1886. *O knizhkakh dlja naroda, izdavaemykh firmoju «Posrednik».* Voronezh.

Jasnopoljanskij sbornik. 1968. Tula, Russia.

Kal'nev, M. A., ed. 1911. *Russkie sektanty, kul't i sposoby propagandy.* Odessa.

Khanzen-Lëve, A. A. 1997. "Russkoe sektantstvo i ego otrazhenie v literature russkogo modernizma." In *Russkaja literatura i religija*, ed. R. Grjubel' and V. Odinnokova. Novosibirsk: Nauka.

Klibanov, A. I. 1965. *Istorija religioznogo sektantstva v Rossii, 60-e gody XIX v.–1917 g.* Moskva: Nauka.

—. 1969. *Religioznoe sektantstvo i sovremennost' (sotsiologicheskie i istoricheskie ocherki).* Moskva: Nauka.

—. 1985. *History of Religious Sectarianism in Russia (1860s–1917).* Trans. Ethel Dunn, ed. Stephen P. Dunn. New York: Pergamon Press. See esp. 125–40.

Klioutchanski, Arkadi. 2000. "L'immigration des Doukhobors : une fenêtre sur le Canada en rétrospective." In Donskov, Woodsworth and Gaffield, 171–84.

Kolesnikoff, Nina and James Kolesnikoff. 1978. "Leo Tolstoy and the Doukhobors." In *Canadian Contributions to the VIII International Congress of Slavists (Zagreb-Ljubljana 1978)*, ed. Z. Folejewski et al., 37–44. Ottawa: Canadian Association of Slavists.

Kolesnikoff, James. 2000. "Understanding violent behaviour: the 'Sons of Freedom' case." In Donskov, Woodsworth and Gaffield, 114–28.

Korolëv, A. A. 1978. *Vremën svjazujushchaja nit'.* Tula: Priokskoe knizhnoe izd..

Kosovanov, A. 1958. *Timofej Bondarev i Lev Tolstoj.* Abakan: Khakasskoe knizhnoe izdatel'stvo.

L. N. Tolstoy Archives. Moskva: Gosudarstvennyj muzej L. N. Tolstogo.

Lebedev, V. K. 1968. "Knigoizdatel'stvo «Posrednik» i tsenzura." *Russkaja literatura* 2:163–70.

Lindstrom, Thaïs. 1957. "From chapbooks to classics. The story of the 'Intermediary.'" *American Slavic and East European Review* 16:190–201.

Litvinova, Valentina. 2004. "Torzhestvo zemledel'tsa: Sibirskij krest'janin Timofej Bondarev i graf Lev Tolstoj." *Russkij pereplet,* N° 12. http://www.sibogni.ru/content/torzhestvo-zemledelca.

Makovitskij, D. P. 1979–81. *U Tolstogo, 1904–1910: Jasnopoljanskie zapiski.* Ed. S. A. Makashin. Kn. 1–4. Series: Literaturnoe nasledstvo 90. Moskva: Nauka.

Maude, Aylmer F. (1904) 1970. *A Peculiar People: The Doukhobors.* New York: Funk & Wagnalls, and London: A. Constable, 1905. Reprint, New York: AMS Press.

Mavor, James F. n.d. *The James Mavor Papers.* Ms group 29, Subgroup B. Ottawa: Public Archives of Canada. Also in the University of Toronto Archives: MG 29, C 16.

Mealing, F. Mark 1977. "A study in Doukhobor hymnody and folklife." PhD diss., University of Michigan.

—. 1995. *Doukhobor Life: A Survey of Doukhobor Religion, History and Folklore.* Castlegar: BC: Kootenay Doukhobor Historical Society.

Miljukov, Paul. 1972. "The development of Russian sectarianism." Part 1. In *Religion and the church (Outlines of Russian culture)*, ed. Michael Karpovich, trans. Valentine Ughet and Eleanor Davis. New York: A. S. Barnes.

Minkh, A. N., comp. 1900. *Istoriko-geograficheskij slovar' Saratovskoj gubernii,* vyp. 2: 2. Saratov: Saratov Gubernia Zemstvo Press.

Minokin, M. V. 1962. "L. Tolstoj i krest'janskie pisateli." *Tolstovskij sbornik,* 112–29. Tula, Izd. Tul'skogo pedagogicheskogo universiteta.

—. 1950. "Problema krest'janstva v tvorchestve L.N. Tolstogo (80-90-e gody XIX veka)." Diss. Moscow: Moscow State Pedagogical Institute.

Missionerskoe Obozrenie [Missionary Review / MR]. 1896–1901. St. Petersburg, Russia.

Moon, David. 2001. *The Abolition of Serfdom in Russia, 1762–1907.* Harlow: Longman.

Morozov, V. S. 1917. *Vospominanija o Tolstom uchenika Jasnopoljanskoj shkoly Vasilija Stepanovicha Morozova.* Moskva: Posrednik.

Novikov, M. P. 1904a. "Na vojnu! (Zapiski prizyvnogo letom 1904 g.)." *Svobodnoe slovo* 15–17.

—. 1904b. "Golos krest'janina." *Svobodnoe slovo*, N° 10:1–43.

—. 1908. *Staraja vera. Materialy k istorii staroobrjadchestva i sektantstva*, vyp. 3. Skt-Peterburg.

—. 1909. *Novaja vera.* Gosudarstvennyj muzej L. N. Tolstogo: M. P. Novikov Archive.

—. 1920. "Razgovor s L. N. Tolstym o japonskoj vojne." In V. I. Sreznevskij. *Pamjatniki tvorchestva i zhizni*, vyp. 2. Moskva: Zadruga.

—. 1924. *Iz proshlogo. Moi vospominanija.*

Novitskij, O. 1882. *Dukhobortsy, ikh istorija i verouchenie.* 2nd ed. Kiev.

Otto, R. 1987. *Publishing for the People: The Firm 'Posrednik,' 1885–1905.* New York and London: Garland.

Pchelin, N. 1999. "Puljami—po 77-letnemu Fedoru Zheltovu." *Pravo-zashchita.* http://www.uic.unn.ru/hrnnov/rus/nnshr/paper/list31/list5.htm.

Perry, Shirley. 2000. "The importance of song in Doukhobor life." In Donskov, Woodsworth and Gaffield, 342–56.

Polnyj pravoslavnyj bogoslovskij èntsiklopedicheskij slovar'. 1913. Vol. 1. Moskva: Izd. P. P. Sojkina.

Popoff, Eli A. (Popov, I. A.). 1978. "Vstrecha dukhobortsa s L. N. Tolstym." *Iskra*, N° 1484: 20–28. Reprinted with English translation, "The meeting of a Doukhobor with Lev Nikolaevich Tolstoy," in *Iskra*, N° 1935 (2003): 36–44.

—. 1982. *An Historical Exposition on the Origin and Evolvement of the Basic Tenets of the Doukhobor Life-Conception.* Grand Forks, BC: P. O. P. Press.

—. 2000. "The Doukhobors: The 'enigma' and the reality." In Donskov, Woodsworth and Gaffield, 22–46.

—. 2001. Personal correspondence, 12 March.

Popoff, Jim. 1987–1988. "What were the main historical reasons and causes for the rise of the splinter movement known as the Sons of Freedom?" Series of articles. *Iskra.*

Prokhanov, I. S. 1933. *In the cauldron of Russia 1869–1933.* New York: All-Russia Evangelical Christian Union.

Prugavin, A. S. 1881a. "Alchushchie pravdy." *Russkaja mysl'*, kn. 12.

—. 1881b. "Znachenie sektantstva v russkoj narodnoj zhizni." *Russkaja mysl'*, kn. 1, 301–63. Moskva.

—. 1906. *Religioznye otshchepentsy. Ocherki sovremennago sektantstva.* Moskva: Posrednik.

—.1911a. *O L've Tolstom i o tolstovtsakh.* Izd. 2-e. Moskva. See esp. 35–71.

—. 1911b. "Rol' tolstovstva v dukhoborcheskom dvizhenii (Po otchetam g. ober-prokurora sv. Sinoda)." *O L've Tolstom i o tolstovtsakh.* Izd. 2-e, 201–20. Moskva.

Prutskov, N. I. 1976. "Sibirskaja utopija T. M. Bondareva *Torzhestvo zemledel'tsa.*" *Ocherki literatury i kritiki Sibiri (XVII–XX vv.)*, 132–37. Novosibirsk: Nauka.

PSS (*Polnoe sobranie sochienij*)—*see* L. N. Tolstoj 1928–58.

Pypin, A. N. 1890–1892. *Istorija russkoj ètnografii.* Skt-Peterburg: M. Stasjulevich.

Rancour-Laferriere, Daniel. 2007. *Tolstoy's Quest for God.* New Brunswick, NJ, and London: Transaction Publishers.

Riasanovsky, Nicholas V. 1968. "Afterword: The problem of the peasant." In *The Peasant in Nineteenth-Century Russia*, ed. Wayne S. Vucinich, 263–84. Stanford, CA: Stanford University Press.

Rozanova, Susanna A. 1978. *L. N. Tolstoj—perepiska s russkimi pisateljami.* Moskva, 1962. Reprint, 1978.

Sanborn, Josh (Joshua A.). 1995. "Pacifist politics and peasant politics: Tolstoy and the Doukhobors, 1895–99." *Canadian Ethnic Studies* 27, N° 3: 52–71.
Sanborn, Josh. 2000. "Non-violent protest and the Russian state: The Doukhobors in 1895 and 1937." In Donskov, Woodsworth and Gaffield, 83–102.
Semënov, S. T. 1912. *Vospominanija o L. N. Tolstom*. Moskva.
Shcherbakova, M. I. 2000. "«Brat'ja» (Sektanty I. S. i A. S. Prokhanovy)." In *Mir filologii*, ed. M. I. Shcherbakova and M. A. Mozharova, 320–29. Moskva: Nasledie.
Shesterikov S. 1928. "Zametka Leskova o Sjutaeve." In *Lev Nikolaevich Tolstoj. Jubilejnyj sbornik*, edited by N. N. Gusev, 329–31. Moskva and Leningrad: Gosizdat [Khudozhdestvennoj literatury].
Shokhor-Trotskij, K. 1913. "Sjutaev i Bondarev." *Ezhegodnik Tolstovskogo muzeja*.
Signori, Dolores A., comp. 1989. *Guide to the papers of James Mavor*. Thomas Fisher Rare Book Collection, University of Toronto. Pertinent material in vol. 1 (n.d.), Box 17, File 27, and vol. 3 (1899), Box 1A, File 48.
Silbajoris, Rimvydas. 1996. "The brotherhood and solitude of death in Tolstoy." In Donskov and Woodsworth, 88–101.
Siniavski, André. 1990. "Vassili Sioutaev et les autres rationalistes à la recherche de la vérité." In *Ivan le Simple*, trans. Antonina Roubichon-Stretz, 376–93. Paris: Albin Michel.
Skvortsov, V. M. 1896. *Zapiska o dukhobortsakh na Kavkaze*. GARF: Delo 1053, L. 1–22r. Document #1896-02-a in Woodsworth 1997. Published in Donskov 1998b.
—. 1899. Report to Senior Procurator of the Holy Synod, K. P. Pobedonostsev, 6 February 1899. GARF: Delo 1053, L. 635–36. Document #1899-02-04d in Woodsworth 1997. English translation in Woodsworth 1999a, 112–14.
—. 1900. "Razocharovanija golodajushchikh v Amerike dukhobor i farisejskoe poslanie k nim grafa L. N. Tolstogo." *Missionerskoe Obozrenie*, t. 2, kn. 11 (November): 521–42.
—. 1901. *Dukhobory v Amerike i graf L. N. Tolstoj*. Skt-Peterburg: Izd. Missionerskoe Obozrenie.
—. 1904. "Dukhoborcheskaja sekta." In *Missionerskij Sputnik*, 447–61. Skt-Peterburg: Komarov.
—. 1912. *Dukhobory v Amerike i tolstovtsy*. Skt-Peterburg: Izd. V. M. Skvortsova.
—. n.d. "Dva slova o kanadskikh dukhoborakh." *Missionerskoe Obozrenie*, 703–04.
Smyrniw, Walter. 1996. "Discovering the brotherhood of the destitute: Tolstoy's insight into the causes of urban poverty." In Donskov and Woodsworth, 194–204.
Subbotnik Information Exchange. n.d. http://www.subbotniki.net.
Tarabukina, A. V. 1999. "Lev Tolstoj v massovoj pravoslavnoj literature nachala XX veka." *Pogranichnoe soznanie*, 234–48. Skt-Peterburg: Kanun.
Tarasoff, Koozma J. 1963. "In search of brotherhood: the history of the Doukhobors." Unpublished manuscript. Vancouver.
—. 1982. *Plakun trava: The Doukhobors*. Grand Forks, BC: Mir Publications.
—, ed. 1995. *From Russia with Love: The Doukhobors*. Special issue of *Canadian Ethnic Studies* 27, N° 3.
—, comp. and ed. 1998. *Spirit-wrestlers' voices*. Ottawa: Legas.
—. 2002. *Spirit-Wrestler Voices: Doukhobor Pioneers' Strategies for Living*. Ottawa: Legas.
—. n.d. http://www.spirit-wrestlers.com.
Tarasov, N. P., comp. 1959. *L. N. Tolstoj i krest'jane: iz dokumentov Gosudarstvennogo arkhiva Tul'skoj oblasti*. Tula.

Tishchenko, F. F. 1903. *Kak uchit pisat' graf L. N. Tolstoj*. Moskva.
Tolstaja, S. A. (Tolstaya, Sofia Andreevna). *My Life*. See Donskov 2010.
Tolstoj, L. N. (Tolstoy, Leo). 1886. *Sochinenija grafa L. N. Tolstogo*. Chast' 12. Moskva.
—. 1900. "Pis'mo k pereselivshimsja v Kanadu dukhoboram (15/27 fevralja 1900 g.)." *Svobodnaja mysl'* (Genève), N° 5–6 (May–June 1900): 77–80. Reprinted with French and English translations in Robert Minden, *Separate from the World: Meetings With Doukhobor-Canadians in British Columbia*. Vancouver: National Film Board of Canada, 1979. An English translation was also published in *The Complete Works of Count Tolstoy*, trans. and ed. Leo Wiener, vol. 24, *Letters and Essays; Life; General Index; Bibliography*, 345–52. Boston: Dana Estes & Co.
—. 1905. "Appeal in behalf of the Dukhobors." In *The Complete Works of Count Tolstoy*, trans. and ed. Leo Wiener, vol. 24, *Letters and Essays; Life; General Index; Bibliography*, 338–42. Boston: Dana Estes & Co.
—. 1912–13. *Polnoe sobranie sochinenij*. Ed. and annot. P. I. Birjukov. 20 vols. Moskva: Izd. Sytina, 1912–13. [Distinct from the following two entries]
—. 1913c. *Polnoe sobranie sochinenij v 24 tt*. Ed. and annot. P. I. Birjukov. Moskva: Izd. Sytina, 1913. [Distinct from the preceding and following entries]
—. 1928–58. *Polnoe sobranie sochinenij. Jubilejnoe izdanie* [*PSS*; Jubilee Edition]. 90 vols. Moskva: Goslitizdat. See esp. vols. 68–72.
Tolstoj (Tolstoy), Sergej L'vovich. 1949. *Ocherki bylogo*. Moskva: Izd. Khudozhestvennoj literatury, 1949. See esp. 193–212.
Tolstoy, Alexandra. 1960. "Tolstoy and the Russian peasant." *The Russian Review*, N° 2: 150–156.
Treadgold, Donald W. 1968. "The peasant and religion." In *The Peasant in Nineteenth-Century Russia*, ed. Wayne S. Vucinich, 72–108. Stanford: Stanford University Press.
Unknown author. 1896. "Dukhobory-tolstovtsy i sudebnyj protsess po delu o soprotivlenii vlastjam." *Missionerskoe Obozrenie* [Kiev], kn. 1 (okt. 1896): 296–302.
Unknown author. 1913. "Sjutaev i Bondarev." *Tolstovskij ezhegodnik*. Skt-Peterburg and Moskva: Izd. Tolstovskogo muzeja v Sankt-Peterburge and Tolstovskogo obshchestva v Moskve, 1913: 1–44.
Uspenskij, Gleb I. 1884. "Trudami ruk svoikh." *Russkaja mysl'* 11.
Uspenskij, I. N. 1953. "Lev Tolstoj i russkoe krest'janstvo." *Izvestija Akademii Nauk SSSR (Otdelenie literatury i jazyka)*, t. 12, vyp., 297–314.
Velikanova, Natal'ja and Robert Vittaker [= Whittaker], eds. 2004. *L. N. Tolstoj i SShA. Perepiska*. Moskva: Institut mirovoj literatury Rossijskoj Akademii Nauk.
Verigin, John J. (Ivan Ivanovich), Sr. 1978. "Dukhobortsy pomnjat Tolstogo." *Iskra*, N° 1484 (1978): 50–63.
Wasiolek, Edward. 1978. *Tolstoy's Major Fiction*. Chicago and London: University of Chicago Press.
Woodcock, George and Ivan Avakumovic. (1968) 1977. *The Doukhobors*. Toronto: Oxford University Press. Reprint, Toronto: McClelland and Stewart, and Ottawa: Institute of Canadian Studies.
Woodsworth, John. 1995. "Attitude and character transformation as revealed in the correspondence of Tolstoy and Verigin." *Canadian Ethnic Studies* 27, N° 3: 245–51.
—, comp. 1997. *The Doukhobors 1895–1943*. Series: CRCR Document Series 8. 2nd ed. (rev.). Ottawa: Carleton University, Centre for Research on Canadian-Russian Relations.

—. 1998. "Recent and current studies on the Doukhobors at Ottawa universities." In *Spirit Wrestlers' Voices*, comp. and ed. Koozma J. Tarasoff, 313–26. Ottawa: Legas.

—, comp., trans. and annot. 1999a. *Russian Roots & Canadian Wings: Russian Archival Documents on the Doukhobor Emigration to Canada.* Ottawa: Penumbra Press.

—. 1999b. "Novye perspektivy na istoriju dukhobortsev." *Iskra*, N° 1878 (1999): 13–16. English trans.: "New perspectives on the history of the Doukhbors." *Iskra*, N° 1879: 71–75.

Worobec, Christine. 1991. *Peasant Russia: Family and Community in the Post--Emancipation Period.* Princeton, NJ: Princeton University Press, 1991. See esp. 151–74.

Yokoyama, Olga T. 2010. *Russian Peasant Letters: Life and Times of a 19th-Century Family.* Wiesbaden: Otto Harrassowitz.

Young, Pauline. (1932) 1967. *The Pilgrims of Russian-Town: The Community of Spiritual Christian Jumpers in America.* Chicago: University of Chicago Press. Reprint, New York: Russell & Russell.

Zajdenshnur, È. E., ed. 1939. "Vstrechi s Tolstym. Iz dnevnika A. V. Zhirkevicha." In *L. N. Tolstoj II.* Series: Literaturnoe nasledstvo 37–38: 417–42.

—, ed. 1965. *Tolstoj-redaktor.* Moskva, Kniga, 1965. See esp. 4–77.

LIST OF TOLSTOY TITLES

And the Light Shineth in Darkness [*I svet vo t'me svetit*]
Anna Karenina [*Anna Karenina*]
Bethink Yourselves! [*Odumajtes'!*]
Brief Synopsis of the Gospels [*Kratkoe izlozhenie Evangelija*]
Catechism [*Katekhizis*]
Chicken-Egg-Size Grain [*Zerno s kurinoe jajtso*]
Christian Teaching (*The*) [*Khristianskoe uchenie*]
Confession (*A*) [*Ispoved'*]
Cycle of Readings (*A*) [*Krug chtenija*]
Day of Enlightenment [*Prazdnik prosveshchenija*]
Death of Ivan Il'ich (*The*) [*Smert' Ivana Il'icha*]
Examination of Dogmatic Theology (*An*) [*Issledovanie dogmaticheskogo Bogoslovija*]
Famine or Not? [*Golod ili ne golod?*]
First Distiller (*The*) [*Pervyj vinokur*]
Flowerbed (*The*; Preface) [*Tsvetnik: Predislovie*]
Fruits of Enlightenment (*The*) [*Plody prosveshchenija*]
God Sees the Truth, But Waits [*Bog pravdu vidit da ne skoro skazhet*]
Godson (*The*) [*Krestnik*]
Great Sin (*A*) [*Velikij grekh*]
Haggai [*Aggej*]
How Much Land Does A Man Need? [*Mnogo li cheloveku zemli nuzhno?*]
Kingdom of God is Within You (*The*) [*Tsarstvo Bozhie vnutri vas*]
Kreutzer Sonata (*The*) [*Krejtserova sonata*]
On Life [*O zhizni*]
On T. M. Bondarev. For S. A. Vengerov's Dictionary [*O T. M. Bondareve. Dlja slovarja S. A. Vengerova*]
Outline of the Gospels [*Izlozhenie Evangelija*]
Peter the Publican [*Pëtr Khlebnik*]
Power of Darkness (*The*) [*Vlast' t'my*]
Reply to the Synod [*Otvet Sinodu*]
Resurrection [*Voskresenie*]
Tale of Ivan the Fool (*The*) [*Skazka ob Ivane-durake*]
Three Elders (*The*) [*Tri startsa*]
Two Elders [*Dva starika*]
War and Peace [*Vojna i mir*]
What I Believe [*V chëm moja vera?*]
What Kind of Life Do I Have? [*Kakova moja zhizn'?*]
What Men Live By [*Chem ljudi zhivy*]
What Then Must Be Done? [*Tak chto zhe nam delat'?*]
Where Love Is, There Too Is God [*Gde ljubov', tam i Bog*]
Wise Thoughts for Every Day [*Na kazhdyj den'*]

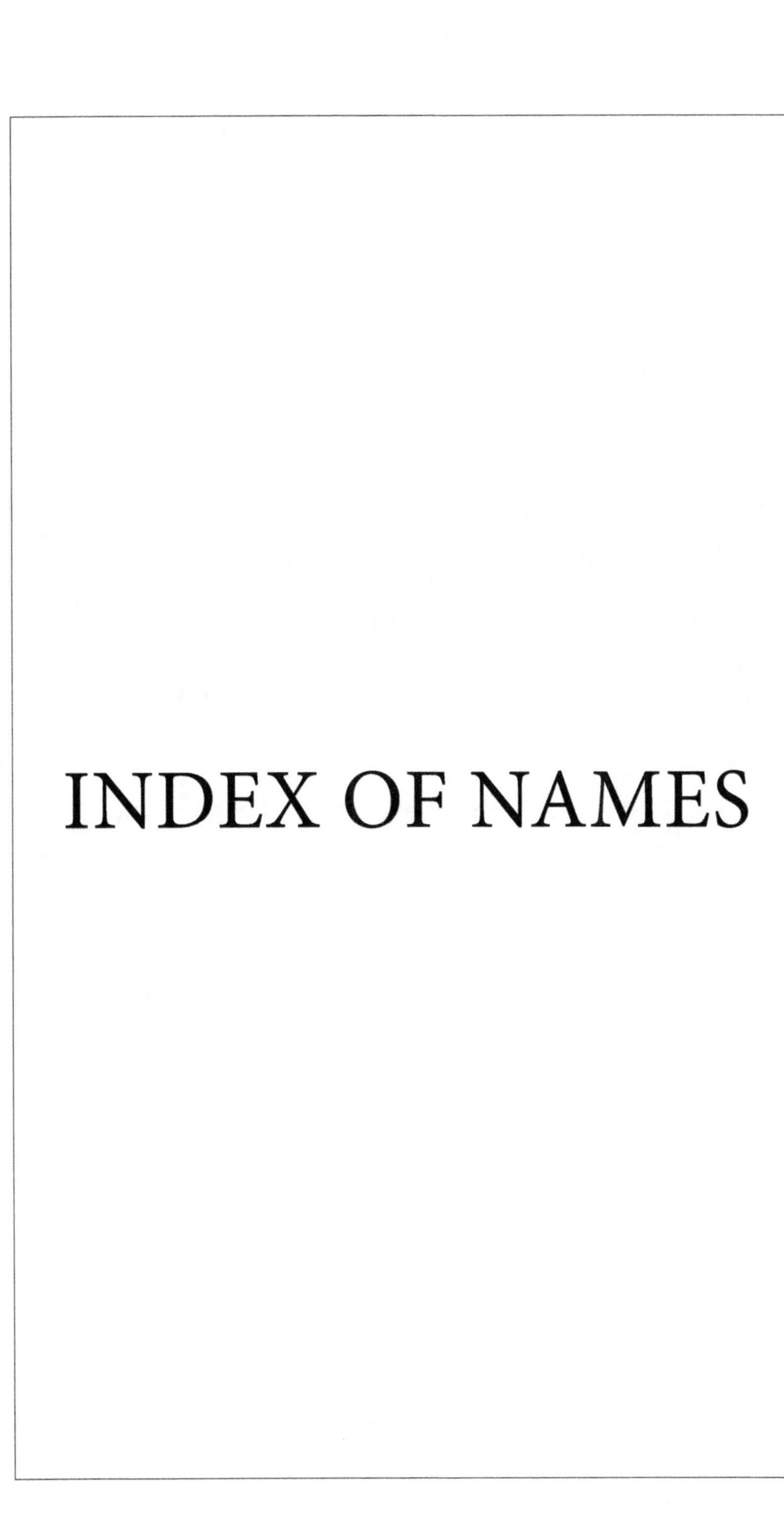

INDEX OF NAMES

INDEX OF NAMES

Collective names are *italicized.*

T

U

V